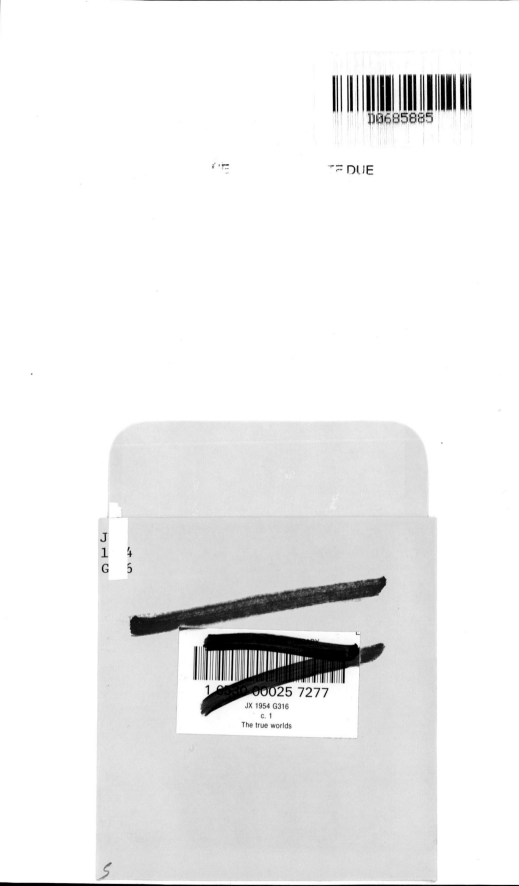

THE TRUE WORLDS

PREFERRED WORLDS FOR THE 1990's

Saul H. Mendlovitz, General Editor

On the Creation of a Just World Order:
Preferred Worlds for the 1990's
edited by Saul H. Mendlovitz

Footsteps into the Future:
Diagnosis of the Present World and a Design for an Alternative
Rajni Kothari

A Study of Future Worlds
Richard A. Falk

A World Federation of Cultures: An African Perspective
Ali A. Mazrui

Revolution of Being: A Latin American View of the Future
Gustavo Logos and Horacio H. Godoy

The True Worlds: A Transnational Perspective
Johan Galtung

A program of the World Order Models Project.
Sponsored by
The Institute for World Order, Inc.
777 United Nations Plaza
New York, N.Y. 10017

THE TRUE WORLDS

A Transnational Perspective

Johan Galtung

THE FREE PRESS
A Division of Macmillan Publishing Co., Inc.
NEW YORK

THE FREE PRESS
A Division of Macmillan Publishing Co., Inc.
866 Third Avenue, New York, N.Y. 10022

Collier Macmillan Canada, Ltd.

Library of Congress Catalog Card Number: 79-7351

Printed in the United States of America

printing number

1 2 3 4 5 6 7 8 9 10

Library of Congress Cataloging in Publication Data

Galtung, Johan
    The true worlds.

    (Preferred worlds for the 1990's)
    Includes index.
    1. International organization. 2. International
relations. I. Title.
JX1954.G316 1979   341.2   79-7351
ISBN 0-02-911060-2

To
Andreas and Harald,
Fredrik and Irene,
with love and gratitude

Und wer von uns verhungert ist
Der fiel in einer Schlacht
Und wer von uns gestorben ist
Der wurde umgebracht.
                    —*Bertolt Brecht*

There were two "Reigns of Terror,"
if we would but remember it and consider it;
the one wrought murder in hot passion,
the other in heartless cold blood;
the one lasted mere months,
the other lasted a thousand years;
the one inflicted death upon a thousand persons,
the other upon a hundred millions;
but our shudders are all for the "horrors"
of the minor terror, the momentary terror,
so to speak.   —*Mark Twain*

CONTENTS

LIST OF FIGURES

LIST OF TABLES

GENERAL INTRODUCTION

I

Scholars and intellectuals, like human beings in other walks of life, need to interpret and come to grips with the crises plaguing the contemporary global political and social system. Indeed their obligation to do so may be a particularly special and important one. They are, or are supposed to be, able to discern trends, detect signals warning us of emerging social problems, think seriously and critically about alternative solutions and possible future worlds, as well as recommend strategies for achieving those solutions and worlds. One would think that this somewhat crucial albeit relatively precious sector of the world's population, more than others, is capable of avoiding too firm an anchor in the particulars of what is. "Reality" may, for a number of reasons, constrain and overwhelm the thinking and imagination of those who have to struggle for daily existence. But surely professional thinkers and analysts have a mandate to look beyond the obvious, the immediate, and to see the possibilities open for reform and improvement.

For reasons that I suspect to be familiar to most of us, social scientists have yet to meet this challenge adequately. There is, initially, the bias in the social sciences against work that explicitly utilizes preferences and values as a way of defining problems to be investigated, and as a standard to be used for what will be considered an adequate solution to the problems. Research that deviates from the confines of a perspective that is viewed by its adherents as empirical and scientific is either dismissed as ideological or as being an exercise in wishful thinking. In this view, description is a proper social science concern, while prescription is not. Second, the same tradition's narrow sense of realism and empiricism operates quite decisively to inhibit futuristic thinking and orientation. If one wants maximum certainty and minimum speculation, concern with what prevails is preferable to what might or will be. If some social scientists manage to get over their reluctance to engage in futuristic thinking, their work generally confines itself to relatively simple extrapolations of current trends. The future then becomes a mere extension of the present, as though humanity has little or no ability to shape the future in preferred directions.

Two additional factors are also to blame for the lack of creative thinking about the contemporary world order system and its major crises—e.g., war, social injustice, widespread poverty, ecological imbalance, and alienation—as well as alternative systems more compatible with a humane and just world order. The crises are global in scope, yet most social scientists who pay attention to them are wedded to an analysis in which the nation–state system informs their definitions and solutions to global problems. At the same time it is becoming increasingly clear that most of the major problems confronting humankind defy national solutions and perspectives, and are generally aggravated, if not directly caused, by the imperatives of national sovereignty.

Finally, creative thinking about the globe, its crises, and future is hindered by an element which is inherent in the nature of social knowledge itself and the extent to which it is culture-bound and geographically circumscribed. Even the most sympathetic and globally-minded scholar can only perceive the world from a particular angle and perspective; his (or her) roots in a particular nation, race, or class help determine and shape the choice of the problems—and the proposed remedies to them—that concern that person. Certain cultural assumptions, values, and concerns may sensitize a person to some problems at the same time they cause the individual to neglect a number of different problems that other people in other places deem important. Or, the same global problem or phenomenon is frequently interpreted in different ways by observers from different cultures. Given the global dimensions of our major world order concerns, these truisms of the sociology of knowledge recommend in favor of transnational and cross-cultural perspectives being brought to bear upon the questions and problems that concern us. In short, it speaks against ethnocentric knowledge and research. While this point has long been well known, there has been much too little social science research carried out in this fashion. The work of other scholars may be available, but collaborative research across cultures and world views is yet to be widely practiced.

II

The True Worlds is one book in the series of volumes entitled *Preferred Worlds for the 1990's* resulting from a transnational research enterprise, the World Order Models Project. Because the World Order Models Project (WOMP) is likely to be the forerunner of many more such transnational and global enterprises, it seems appropriate to say something about its genesis, development, and future.

WOMP was initially conceived in response to pedagogical needs related to the study of the problem of the elimination of war as a human social institution. The individuals involved at the outset of this program brought to it a seriousness one associates with those individuals and groups who, between the eighteenth and nineteenth centuries, advocated and participated in the global movement to abolish slavery, or with those persons in this century who have been participating in the dismemberment of colonialism and imperialism.

To put the matter forthrightly, it was a conscious "political" act, based on a theory of social change which reasoned that most individuals in the globe, including political leadership, were encapsulated in a view of the world in which war, while perhaps unfortunate, was a necessary and permanent ingredient of human society. Thus the decision to enlist the energies of educational structures throughout the globe was partially based on the notion that the seriousness of the idea might be legitimated if the academic community throughout the world were to give it the status of a subject matter of discipline, or at least admit it was the kind of social problem which was amenable to rational analysis. Concomitantly and certainly as important as legitimation, was the possibility of enlisting the talent and skills of the academic community in the research and education necessary for a successful global peace movement.

And so it was in 1966 that we began to examine how to enroll volunteers so that our educational effort would merit serious attention by scholars and educators throughout the globe. WOMP emerged as an answer.

The notion which we began to pursue was that if we were to get outstanding scholars as well as thoughtful individuals throughout the globe to become involved in the problem of war prevention, it would be necessary that they contribute actively in the inquiry. We decided to invite groups of scholars in various parts of the world to direct nationally or regionally based inquiries into the problem of war prevention. We did not proceed very far in our recruitment of individuals for the project when it soon became clear that the subject matter would have to be expanded to include the related problems of economic well being and social justice, if we were to generate a world interest in this inquiry.

There were two reasons advanced for the inclusion of these problem areas. To begin with, there were many persons who argued that it was impossible to deal adequately with war prevention without taking into account poverty and social injustice; that as an empirical matter, these matters were so inextricably interwoven, they should be seen as part of the definition of the problem of war prevention. More importantly, however, it became increasingly clear that while peace, in the sense of the elimination of international violence, might have a very high priority with individuals in the industrialized sector of the globe, economic well being and social justice received a much higher rating in the Third World. When we discussed these three problems, war, poverty, and social injustice, as they persisted in national, regional, and global contexts, and proposed examining them in the light of the next three decades, with particular reference to the countervailing values of peace, economic well being and social justice, virtually all the scholars we approached agreed to participate in the project.

We held the first meeting of the World Order Models Project in New Delhi in February 1968. At that time five research groups had been organized, representing West Germany, Latin America, Japan, India, and North America. Groups representing Africa, the Soviet Union, and some Scandinavian scholars who preferred to present a non-territorial perspective, joined in subsequent years. More recently we benefited from the involvement in the project of a Chinese as well as a Middle Eastern scholar. One meeting was held with a group of economists organized by Jagdish Bhagwati of the Massachusetts Institute of

Technology. This resulted in the first WOMP book, *Economics and World Order: From the 1970's to the 1990's* (Macmillan, 1972). A second book, *Africa and World Affairs* (The Third Press, 1973), edited by Ali Mazrui and Hasu Patel, resulted from a conference organized by the African research group. All together, some nine meetings have been held in various parts of the world: India, Japan, East Africa, Western Europe, United States, and Latin America.

The results of nearly seven years of individual and collaborative work are only partially represented by this and the other WOMP volumes. We set out to create the basic instructional materials needed for a worldwide educational movement whose ultimate thrust would be global reform. No one is more aware than we are today of how many more and different materials still need to be created and disseminated. We set out to do normative social research that was at one and the same time oriented to the future, interdisciplinary, and focused on the design of social change actions, policies, and institutions. No one realizes more than the WOMP research groups how difficult it is to do this task with competence, combined with true imagination and intellectual power.

The project has fundamentally affected the personal and professional commitments of virtually everyone who participated in it. It is fair to say that what started out for almost all the participants as a short term and secondary interest has now become a lifetime scholarly and political vocation. At a meeting of the Directors of the World Order Models Project in Bogotá, Colombia, over the New Year period in 1974, the group decided to collaborate on a series of enterprises which they hope will continue to promote research, education, and a genuinely transnational social movement to realize the world order values of peace, economic well being, social justice, and ecological stability. The first of these ventures will be a transnational journal, *Alternatives,* of which Rajni Kothari will be editor, with a distinguished editorial board of some two dozen scholars throughout the globe.

Second, a number of the individuals associated with WOMP have assumed the responsibility for issuing an annual State of the Globe Message. This Message will attempt to evaluate local, regional, and global trends, rating the extent to which the world order values have been diminished or realized during the preceding year, and to make recommendations as to what ought to be done in the coming years. The State of the Globe Message, issued by a group of transnational scholars independent of any formal structures of authority, should be seen as complementary to the messages which are now coming from such formal sources.

Third, we have embarked upon a modest but significant research program for measuring world order indicators based on our values, which we hope will support the State of the Globe Message and provide alternative ways for social scientists to think about and measure the quality of social life. In addition, there will be a series of transnational seminars for scholars, public figures in all professions, expanded formal educational programming, and the beginning of a mass public education movement on a global basis. All of this programming has already begun in some form and we hope will involve constructive criticism, support, and participation by many people throughout the globe.

III

The world order images and change strategies presented in these WOMP books are strikingly diverse, reflecting the different methods, intellectual styles, and cultural/political backgrounds of their authors. Although we were able to agree on a way of stating world order problems, and establish a framework of value criteria for what we considered to be appropriate solutions, as well as devise a common methodology, it certainly would be premature to attempt to provide a consensus statement for these various manuscripts. There were, however, a set of guidelines which were stated with some precision early in the project; despite repeated critical examination and elaboration they have remained essentially intact. It seems appropriate to summarize these guidelines so that the volumes might be read and evaluated in their proper context.

WOMP was not principally a "utopian" undertaking, despite our refusal to succumb either to a complacent or a doomsday view of reality. Where our thinking is utopian, it advances what we call *relevant utopias,* that is, world order systems that make clear not only alternative worlds but the necessary transition steps to these worlds. In fact, each author was asked to attempt a diagnosis of the contemporary world order system, make prognostic statements based on that diagnosis, state his *preferred future* world order and advance coherent and viable *strategies of transition* that could bring that future into being. A stringent time frame, the 1990's, served to discipline and focus thought and proposals.

While easy to list, this set of steps impose severe demands on our methodological and creative capacity. It is probably fair to say that we discovered more methodological problems than we were able to solve to our satisfaction. Some of these problems are associated with how to do each of the steps, while others arise from trying to link different steps and to integrate the normative, descriptive, and theoretical modes of thought. In the end, most of the WOMP research groups chose to adopt the more traditional analytic interpretive style of research, rather than the more methodologically sophisticated behavioral science approach. The reasons for this choice varied from outright rejection of the presumed conservative biases of strictly data-based methods to pragmatic considerations of limited time and resources. In essence, we decided it was more important at this time to prepare full world order statements involving an integrated treatment of all the steps than it was to do a more rigorous investigation of only one or two of them.

While a full report on the methodological difficulties we faced shall have to await another occasion, it might be useful if I were to outline here the major problem areas and some questions that rose in the course of our investigation. Let me begin, however, by reiterating that we were able to agree that humanity faced four major problems: war, poverty, social injustice, and environmental decay. We saw these as social problems because we had values—peace, economic well being, social justice, and environmental stability—which, no matter how vaguely operationalized, we knew were not being realized in the real world. Our task then was to develop an analytic frame of reference that would provide us intellectual tools for coming to grips with these problems so as to realize world order values.

There was also general agreement that we should go beyond the nation-state system, at least in terms of the traditional categories applied to it, namely the political, military, economic, and ideological dimensions of foreign policy. Instead of asking how states manipulate their foreign policies along these four dimensions, or even, how they might move the present system to a world order value system, there was general agreement that we would have to use a much broader range of potential actors, including world institutions, transnational actors, international organization, functional activities, regional arrangements, the nation-state, subnational movements, local communities, and individuals. Even here, however, each of the groups placed different emphases, diagnostically, prognostically, and preferentially on the roles of this range of actors.

Second, far more effort than I anticipated was put into clarifying the values implied by these problems and into making some ordered value agenda from which operational strategies or policies could be formulated. Among the points to emerge from these efforts are:

1. The crucial importance of developing global social indicators or operational definitions of value goals.

2. The difficulty and necessity of preparing a set of decision rules for dealing with value conflicts.

3. The need for a unified approach to these problem/value areas and for more data and theory on the interrelationships among them.

4. The extent to which one's personal position on the value questions influences every other aspect of the world order research process.

5. The importance of maintaining a tension between some operational notions of "world interest" and the deeply-felt value agenda of one's particular social group and geographic region.

Third, a number of issues not associated with standard empirical research emerged because of our emphasis on constructing preferred worlds. In this connection it should be noted that the term *preferred world* came to have a relatively rigorous meaning. Building on the concept of relevant utopia previously stated, a preferred world is an image of a reformed world stated in fairly precise behavioral detail, including a description of the transition process from the present to the new system. Since it is possible to depict a range of reformed systems and transition paths, a preferred world is the relevant utopia selected by a proponent because it is most likely to realize his or her value goals. Each of these issues that arose in this context requires separate examination, conceptual and methodological advances, and the testing of a variety of integrated research strategies before we will really be able to move systematically through the steps of world order research to preferred world statements that meet rigorous tests of workability and feasibility. To illustrate:

1. What are appropriate criteria for evaluating workability and feasibility and what are the appropriate testing procedures for each?

2. Notions of time and time horizons are critical to both feasibility and workability, yet both are far more complicated than the simple notion of years and decades. Assumptions about time seem to play a critical role in one's optimism or pessimism about the possibility of fundamental change. Also, time, as a key variable, is surprisingly easy to forget or discount when thinking about such things as value and attitude shifts, or reorientations in bureaucratic objectives and procedures.

3. Equally perplexing is the problem of adequately defining the relevant environment and its dynamics within which one's desired changes must take place. The tendency is to define the environment as the nation—state system itself, and to ascribe relatively little destabilizing or fundamental dynamics to it. As noted earlier, this can severely restrict creative thinking about alternative futures and transition processes. But it is not easy to come up with equally detailed and useful alternatives to the nation—state image, so rooted is it in our consciousness. To really examine this question is to open oneself to the most fundamental philosophical and methodological search.

4. On a more mundane level, the presentation of a preferred world in a way that is compelling and persuasive is far more difficult than it might appear. Like good fiction or poetry, utopia writing is an art attempted by many but achieved by few. It involves crucial choices of style and form. For example, how much and what kind of behavioral detail should be used to describe the workings of the preferred world? What are the differences between revolutionary and reformist rhetoric, and, more importantly, what bearing does this answer have on concrete strategies and programs? How much attention is paid to immediate public issues and how are they made to relate to the preferred future, to explicate the method and perspective of the author?

Finally there was a set of issues which arose from my guidelines that each of the groups be as explicit as possible about the kinds of authority structure, about the formal constitutive order of the world community, that would be needed and preferred, both during the transition period, as well as at the end of this century. That is to say, there was a distinct weighting of institutional-constitutional issues and approaches in my original definition of our task.

I emphasized this approach despite the obvious dangers of formalism essentially for three reasons: first, an institutional approach requires a high degree of specificity and precision and focuses attention on procedures as well as principles; second, this approach leads readily to statements in the form of models with all that that implies for comparability across models and manipulation of parts within them; third, as a form of presentation, constitutional-institutional models can be easily, even powerfully, communicated.

In this connection I should like to acknowledge formally my debt to the book *World Peace Through World Law* (Harvard University Press, 1956, 1962, 1966) by Grenville Clark and Louis B. Sohn. My use of this book as an instructional model and as a source of research hypotheses leads me to conclude that many social scientists, as well as lay people, underestimate the extent to which formal constitutional models can lead to clarification of issues, and perhaps even more important, become a mobilizing instrument for social and political action. I remain convinced of the value of this way of thinking about world order, but the extent to which this view has been resisted, revised and ignored by the WOMP groups will be apparent in these volumes. Within this context, it should also be noted that the individual authors resolve the actors-levels-authority process questions differently. Some of the issues that surfaced during our discussions in this context included:

1. The extent to which an institutional or single actor-oriented conception of the world political system is useful either for understanding how the system is operating, how it might be made to change, or how it could or should operate. Such conceptions seemed to some to stultify imaginative thinking about alternatives and to mask important change potentials in the current system.

2. In thinking about transition, some argued for the "primacy of the domestic factor," i.e., fundamental reform in national societies, particularly within the major countries, preceding global social change. Others argued for the primacy of the global agenda and the critical role of transnational functional and political movements and institutions. This debate identified two further issues needing more attention.

3. Which problems require policy making and review at what level of social organization from the individual to the global? How much centralization and decentralization was appropriate in various substantive arenas? What are the relevant criteria for deciding the appropriate level or mix of levels?

4. What are and what might be the linkages between these levels for purposes of analysis, policy making, and practical implementation?

IV

Finally, I wish to state my own view as to the significance of these manuscripts. As I see it, it is necessary to accept seriously not only the rhetoric but the reality of the term "the global village." The fact that the overwhelming majority of humankind understands for the first time in history that human society encompasses the entire globe is a phenomenon equivalent to humankind's understanding that the world is round rather than flat. This knowledge is having an enormously dramatic impact on the images and attitudes we have with regard to the authority structures of the international community, as well as those of our domestic societies. I should like to state here a conclusion, for which I will not fully argue, but which I believe needs to be articulated for an understanding of the significant global political processes that are now taking place.

It is my considered judgment that there is no longer a question of whether or not there will be world government by the year 2000. As I see it, the questions we should be addressing ourselves to are how it will come into being—by cataclysm, drift, rational design—and whether it will be totalitarian, benign, or participatory (the probabilities being in that order).

Since the so-called "age of discovery" (a Eurocentric concept which sorely needs modification in this global community), three major historical processes, or if you will, revolutions, have propelled humankind toward global community, and now toward global governance. These processes are the ideological revolution of egalitarianism, the technological and scientific revolution and the closely allied economic-interdependent revolution. It might be noted in passing that of these three, the egalitarian revolution has been least appreciated in recent times, but in fact may account for much of the disorder, dislocation, and social tensions throughout the globe.

These three processes or revolutions have converged in such a fashion that five problems have emerged and been identified as global in nature. War, poverty, social injustice, ecological instability, and alienation, or the identity crisis, are recognized as having a planetary scope. It is now generally understood by policy elites and observers of world community processes generally that these problems are closely interrelated and that "solutions" in one area affect the other four areas. Furthermore, despite gross inadequacies if not outright failure of the recent global conferences run by the United Nations around the issues of environment, economic order, food and population, it is now obvious that governance processes and structures will become increasingly a focus of international and global politics.

In short, I believe that global community has emerged and global governance is not far behind. To my mind, this book and the other volumes in the *Preferred Worlds for the 1990's* series is a contribution to the serious dialogue about what will be the normative basis and constitutive structure of the global community. We hope these volumes will contribute to creating the social processes needed for a peaceful and just world order.

September 1974   Saul Mendlovitz, Director
                                                                   World Order Models Project

Postscript

This is the final volume in the series *Preferred Worlds for the 1990's.* Since it is certain to enrich the already rather vigorous dialogue in academic and policy circles stimulated by the companion volumes, I should like to clarify one matter that has arisen because of my statement concerning world government in Part IV of the General Introduction to the series.

A number of reviewers and commentators seizing upon this issue have mistakenly attributed my views to the individual authors and more generally to the World Order Models Project. The ideas expressed on this subject are peculiarly my own. They were not an assumption or even a working hypothesis of the series. To be sure, all the individual works reflect a common normative ideology and the view that a just and peaceful world depends on major structural transformation. Most of the authors also explore what kinds of processes and structures are likely to emerge at the global level and do express preferences concerning these matters, as, for example, does Johan Galtung in Chapter 8 of this volume. Notwithstanding this common frame of reference, there is substantial diversity on many issues. This is as it should be. Contrasting perspectives on preferred worlds—perspectives that reflect the real world—are essential to engender meaningful and serious discussion of global transformation.

The events of the past six years lead me to believe that my earlier prognostication on world government is fundamentally correct, although to assign a particular date to growth of governmental functions at a global level may unfortunately have distracted from the underlying point. In any case I believe it is incumbent upon all of us who are attempting to achieve humane governance at all levels of social organization to take into account those processes that are leading in this direction.

This question and other issues related to achieving a just world order will continue to be aired in the ongoing work of the World Order Models Project, particularly through examination of global issues in a Working Paper series, in dialogue through the journal *Alternatives,* and in the research of its working groups on demilitarization and alternative security systems, on emerging global culture and humane civilization, and on science, technology, and economic development. For now, I wish to express my appreciation to all the authors of the World Order Models Project; to Rajni Kothari of New Delhi University and Yoshikazu Sakamoto of Tokyo University, who have joined me as co-directors of the project; to the affiliated institutes in Argentina, Europe, India, Japan, and the United States; and to the individuals and groups throughout the world who have concerned themselves with our work and who are comrades in the common task of contributing to a more just and peaceful world.

January 1980   S.M.

Special Acknowledgment

The Institute for World Order, Inc., would like to thank the Carnegie Endowment for International Peace and the Rockefeller Foundation for the financial support they gave to specific research within the World Order Models Project.

PREFACE

This work has two parts to its title, both of them pretentious.

The title, *The True Worlds,* is intended to convey three ideas. One is simple and has to do with such ideas as adequate description and analysis, prediction and prognosis, with a presentation of the world that can be checked against data and current theories without being found too much wanting.

The second connotation is more important. A "true" world is not a description that is truthful to data, but a real world that is more truthful to its inhabitants, a world wherein being human stands a good· chance. I might have used such terms as "good worlds" or "human worlds," but I have preferred "true," exactly in the sense of being more truthful to human fulfillment, an idea in no need of justification. Thus, my intent is to give both a truthful description of the world and a description of a truthful world. Of one, not the only, truthful world, for there are many, which do not necessarily exclude each other.

Hence the third idea: the plurality of the concept "worlds."

The subtitle is *A Transnational Perspective.* The key word here is "transnational," also intended to carry three complementary meanings. One meaning is simply that this book is not written from the vantage point of any particular country or group of countries. I have attempted to write from a more global perspective, although the reader will probably detect national and regional biases unnoticed by the author.

A second idea is that this book focuses on international organizations and their roles in today's world as well as in a future world. They are referred to as "nonterritorial actors" and are of many kinds. Only some deserve to be called "transnational." When they are seen jointly with the territorial actors, of which the nation states are the most important today, a more complete image of the world can be developed.

The third meaning of "transnational" is the most important one, the sense of giving primacy to the basic unit of all politics, the individual human being who is found across all borders.

One idea permeates this work: no social form is good or bad in itself but only in reference to what it does to people. Society is to serve human needs and self-realization, not social goals abstracted away from man himself, such as "national interest" (i.e., national elite interest), "economic growth," "democracy," "socialism." Such concepts are, at best, means to that end. But if human self-realization is the ultimate goal, then three simple circumstances, rarely heralded by utopian authors, must receive consideration:

Human beings are not similar.
Human beings are not constant.
Human beings are not consistent.

The easy way out is to dream of utopias, assuming human similarity, constancy, and consistency, assuming that human beings are like machine tools, turned out in great numbers in a constant pattern of streamlined design for clearly defined purposes.

Because so much in the very Western culture that during the past generation has produced such phenomena as Stalin, Hitler, and Nixon is built on such assumptions, this book has a certain anti-Western bias. But I am painfully aware that I neither manage nor really want to liberate myself totally from my Western background. Perhaps this book can also be seen as a testimony of the Western world's despair, as experienced by one Western human being. In a sense I am trying, like so many others, to judge the West by some of its own best criteria: equity, diversity, freedom, equality and brotherhood, and absence of violence, to man and to nature. I hope the result to be more than diagnosis and critique (indispensable but very preliminary tools); I hope it to be a framework within which a high number of strategies for very concrete political action can be brought to bear on the common goals of liberation (from inequity and repression) and security (from violence). Above all I have striven to come to grips with the world as a whole in an effort to be holistic as well as Western analytic (although the language herein is very much in the latter tradition). I have thus tried to build conceptual bridges across such gaps as past–present–future; human–national–international levels; problems of poverty and exploitation and problems of war. Too many world models are far too limited. The World Order Models Project (WOMP) forces its authors to attempt such bridge building. How successful we are is for others to judge.

The reader interested in further exploration of some of the themes touched upon in this book may benefit from materials generated by the Goals, Processes and Indicators and Development Project of the Human and Social Development Programme, the United Nations University. Two research programs at the Chair in Conflict and Peace Research, University of Oslo, also coordinated by the present author, are flowing into that project: the World Indicators Program (partly WOMP inspired) and the Trends in Western Civilization Program. Like the present work, there are also efforts to develop more holistic images, to integrate fragmented views.

My gratitude to others in this endeavor is beyond description. Suffice it only to say that the discussions inside the framework of the World Order Models Project under the inspired leadership of Saul H. Mendlovitz have been indispensable. So has the milieu provided by the International Peace Research

Institute in Oslo—in fact so much that this book might also be considered a publication from that institute. I would also like to mention such occasions as the meetings of the Pugwash Conferences, the International Peace Research Association, and the International Peace Academy in Vienna (1970) and Helsinki (1971). Erik Ivås, Margo Öhrn, and Kari-Anne Bryde provided invaluable secretarial assistance at all stages; Per Håkon Christiansen and Knut Hongrö assisted with data; and Beverly Woodward offered penetrating and very helpful substantive editorial criticism. The impact of my wife, Fumiko Nishimura Galtung, is felt in every fiber of the construct underlying this essay on world future.

The book is dedicated to my three sons, Andreas, Harald, and Fredrik, and to my daughter, Irene—with deep compassion for them in the task confronting their generation in trying to change a profoundly false, disturbed, and mishandled world.

Johan Galtung

1. THE REAL WORLD

1.1 A BIRD'S-EYE VIEW

There is a crisis in the world today, now felt even by those of us who enjoy the power and privileges at the top of the world.

There is a crisis of *violence* and threat of violence, which ranges from the U.S. nuclear capability said to equal 615,000 Hiroshima bombs (which killed around 200,000 human beings) to the ever-increasing acts of small-scale terrorism. The whole range from macro to micro violence seems ready, at times, to be unleashed on mankind.

There is a crisis of *misery,* and threat of poverty, in poor countries—where much of the population is still underfed and underclad, lacks adequate shelter, suffers ill health, and has scant or no education—and in rich countries—where major unemployment may soon be manifest by an economy increasingly showing its cracks.

There is a crisis of *repression,* and threat of repression, of all human rights relating to freedom and the opportunity to take part in politics—to participate in governing oneself—not only in the numerous authoritarian and totalitarian countries found in the world but also in the democracies, where repression may any time follow in the wake of the twin crises of violence and misery.

There is a crisis in the *environment,* and a threat of local breakdown of the ecological balance in some places, because of the depletion of nonrenewable resources, the pollution of man and nature alike, and the pressure of an expanding population on a finite environment.

The goals that constitute the nucleus of the present book—an "absence of violence," "economic welfare," "social justice," "human rights," "ecological balance and partnership with nature"—seem rather far from their realization. If they are seriously threatened, then human beings everywhere are seriously threatened. For what are the needs of man if not to stay alive and not be destroyed through violence; to have his fundamental needs satisfied (food, clothes, shelter, health, education) in order to further human growth; to develop in freedom and active social participation; and to live in partnership with the nature of which man is a part, in solidarity with future generations?

What is at the root of these crises?

1

Some people would have us believe that the root crisis is primarily a resource crisis, that our earth is not richly enough endowed to support us all with raw materials and energy. There is much talk about absolute limits in the resources available to man, about limits to growth, even about zero economic growth and "organic" economic growth. But although there are outer limits to the carrying capacity of the biosphere, local and temporary resource scarcities do not mean that we are close to those limits. Rather, the implication should be that resources are maldistributed and mismanaged, taken away from those who need them most and misused to produce unnecessary commodities, including the misuse of precious resources for military purposes. When resources are made available to those who can buy them rather than to those who need them, when production is for demand rather than for need, when waste is built into both production and consumption, and when resources are even underused, it is not surprising that some resource scarcities appear. It is even less surprising that those responsible for the present system prefer to talk about the problem of resource scarcity rather than about the structure of the system.

There are some others who would have us believe that the root crisis is primarily a price crisis, that our world economy cannot stand the pressure of, for instance, a quadrupling of oil prices. It is argued that this increase has created mass unemployment in the rich countries and has hurt their trade and decreased their aid to the poor countries, thereby injuring the economies of the poor countries. Although it is true that poor countries have also based their economies on heavily underpriced oil, the price increase is not at the root of the crisis. Rather, one may argue that the cheap prices have led not only to *underdevelopment* of the countries exporting raw materials and energy (partly by depriving them of resources, partly by denying them all the spin-off effects from processing) but also to the *overdevelopment* of the countries importing raw materials (removing man from nature by creating complex societies based on cheap energy and wasteful production). At any rate, it has become abundantly clear that much of the economic growth in the rich countries is based on the continued willingness of poor countries to be cheated. In fact, much of the welfare distributed through the public sectors in rich countries is based on these inexpensive resources, making it possible to levy taxes on the consumption of such commodities as oil and its derivatives. There is a crisis, not because the prices have increased, but because the economies of so many countries were built on a foundation that was not only shaky but exploitative.

Others would have us believe that what we face primarily is a population crisis, that our planet cannot sustain any longer the pressure from an increasing population making increasing demands. Although there is a limit to the carrying capacity of our planet, that limit is still far away. Only 11 percent of land that can be cultivated has been cultivated, and nobody knows what size population the earth could support if we managed to cultivate the ocean floor instead of mining it for manganese, copper, cobalt, and nickel for arms production. Rather, the problem seems to be that certain economic systems bring the factors of production (raw materials, labor, capital) together in heavily-organized, industrialized centers where productivity is high and ability to consume is also high, creating a periphery where productivity is low and misery impedes participation in the consumer market. The periphery becomes a vast mass of people who are inadequate as both producers and consumers. The fascist reaction to them would be a gas chamber, an atom bomb, or Vietnam-type genocide and ecocide. The semi-fascist reaction would be to see them as the root of the crisis and impose upon them a "family-planning" program to reduce their numbers.

At the root of the crises is not resource scarcity or price increases or population pressure, *but the world structure.* The naive approach to the crises of our world would be to conceive of them as a list of problems, pairing each item with a set of technical solutions. Thus, for the problem of violence, "arms control," of both macro and micro arms, has been tried; for the problem of misery the "transfer of technology, capital, and social structures" known first as "aid," later as "cooperation," and international conferences to "stabilize prices" have been tried. For the problem of repression there is the whole national and international system of legal norms, detection of infractions, adjudication, possibly administration of sanctions. For the twin problems of resource depletion and pollution, recycling constitutes a typical solution; and for the population problem there is, of course, "family planning and birth control."

I do not want to belittle these technical solutions, as there are valid elements in all of them; but they become mystifying, even dangerous, when they are not accompanied by an analysis of the world structure and an even higher dedication to a basic change of structure. Basically, this is politics, and the accompanying analysis is political analysis. An exclusively technical approach, of which we have had much too much, becomes at best a cure of symptoms, a cosmetic applied to the world body. At worst it becomes a source of immense frustration when once more its inadequacy becomes evident, increasing further the danger of extreme violence and sustaining poverty and repression.

All these themes and many more will be developed at some length in this book, accompanied by an effort to create or reshape conceptual tools needed to discuss our world situation. At this point, however, permit me to draw the reader's attention to two points of a different kind, underlying the entire exercise.

First, one thing we know. We know where real happiness lies: in a little boy or girl creeping under the quilts of its parents early in the morning, a bundle of joy and warmth; in the eyes of two in love who know they are going to have each other; in the joy of growing, of creating something; in the joy of being a source of joy and growth for others. All of this is nonviolent, inexpensive, liberating, respectful of nature and future generations. All of it is possible; where it does not work something has gone wrong. Avoidable violence is exercised and must be counteracted.

Second: the Chinese expression for "crisis" (shown below) consists of two characters, one meaning "danger," the other meaning "opportunity." The Chinese have somehow acted upon this highly dialectical conceptualization. Maybe the rest of us also can.

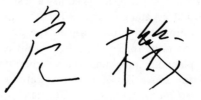

1.2   SOME TRENDS TO CONSIDER

In the preceding section an image of the world was developed based on four crisis dimensions: violence, misery, repression, and environmental deterioration. Newspapers give us the eruption of such dimensions into events. Events are discontinuities—something is that was not before, or something is not that was before. But most of what is is continuous, a trend rather than a jump. The changes from one moment to another, from one day to another, even from one year to another, are small. Sometimes the rate of change is so rapid that one may talk of quasi events; sometimes so slow, negligible, or completely absent that one may talk of constants, of stability. Events are most readily perceived because the jump provides a contrast easily registered. Less easily discerned are the dynamic and static trends—the quasi events and the constants. The factors that remain constant, such as *Homo sapiens* having two legs, are most difficult to register because of the difficulty in thinking them away.

In this section an image of the world will be given based on trends. The reason for choosing trends rather than just one point in time is the need for a dynamic image. It is not enough to know where we are; we must also know in which direction we are moving, although that will not predict where we shall arrive.

The only problem, then, is which dimensions of change to consider. Often the problem is solved by lack of available data. But if we remember that nature is finite and the size of the globe constant (although explored and exploited nature is changing), and that people produce both "goods" (capital goods and consumer goods) and "bads" (means of destruction), then it does not seem unreasonable to make the following tripartite distinction of the basic framework of analysis:

Data relating to the production and use of bads,
Data relating to the production and distribution of goods,
Data relating to the finiteness of nature.

The next step is to decide which data on each point to consider. Above all, the bads include the production and use of capacities for large-scale violence, which in practice means we require data on the military machineries, although many consumer goods could well be included among the bads.

In line with what is said in the preface, the emphasis in choosing among the goods would be on fundamental goods, like food, clothes, shelter, health, and education. One might also consider such abstractions as money, even at such super-abstractions as gross domestic or national products.

The finiteness of nature must be considered because, to make goods and bads, production is needed. Production tends to pollute and deplete, while people multiply. The net result is overpopulation, pollution, and depletion.

Before turning to the data, two objections to this framework should be dealt with. It may be said that this sample of dimensions is biased, loaded to present a dark image of our world. Not all these trends are negative, as will be shown. But even if they were, the sample of dimensions can be defended, not because it is unbiased but because its bias is in the direction of something fundamental: our capacity for destroying ourselves, the extent to which we satisfy the most fundamental human needs, and the danger of running up against the finiteness of nature. In other words, the sampling has been chosen in terms of significance, not in terms of whether the image given will turn out to look negative or positive.

Then it may be objected that no dimensions are given that reflect structure or culture. That is true. Distributions are not the same as structure; they take place within a structure and may serve as an indication of what the structure is. But the answer to the objection is that we are sticking to the level of human beings. Structure and culture are both abstractions, to be judged according to their fruits, not on their own terms, even though such terms exist[1] and will be dealt with at some length in this book.

Let us now look at the production and use of bads, or direct violence, starting with one simple analysis of patterns of belligerence in 1652 primitive societies, taken from an appendix in Quincy Wright's *A Study of War.*[2]

His data are reanalyzed here (see figure 1.1) in an effort to bring out more clearly how the process of civilization is related to the phenomenon of war for economic and political gains (as opposed to defensive war and war as a purely social ritual). A "civilization" index was constructed running from 0 to 6. A society scoring zero is based on hunting and gathering in its simplest form and is a small group (clan) with stratification based on sex and age; a society scoring six is agricultural in its most complex form, with a state organization and a stratification system based on profession or caste. Whereas the former society is nonterritorial with no fixed base, the latter society is territorial with relatively well-defined limits. Thus, the latter society actually corresponds relatively well to a small "traditional society" of the type often analyzed in contemporary village studies, on the assumption that the society is highly isolated from its environment.

In figure 1.1, the percentage of belligerent societies at each level of civilization is plotted. The percentage of societies with a civilization score of zero
engaging in aggressive warfare for economic and political gains is zero, whereas
the percentage of belligerents at the highest civilization level (6) is 95.

As there are many problems with such studies, the reader should be warned
against taking any of these figures too literally. However, the tendency is so
clear, so absolute, that the conclusion seems clear: there is something in
"civilization" that seems to go hand in hand with war. What is this something? It
may be territoriality, it may be vertical division of labor reflected in the
stratification system, it may be economic production patterns, it may be
increasing adjacency, and it may be a combination of these or other factors. But
what matters for our purpose is that "civilization" is still "advancing" in this
respect. Extrapolating from our index, we find that later stages not only lead to
higher levels of civilization but also seem to lead to higher levels of warfare,
which raises the general question of whether humankind is quickly painting itself
into a corner.

To pursue this theme a little further, consider figure 1.2, a chart of war
casualties taken from Sorokin's work on wars.[3] Again, the curves should be
taken as only indicative, but what they indicate is quite clear: an increasing
percentage of Europe's population becoming war victims. The nineteenth century (and to some extent the eighteenth) represents a certain dip on the curve,
which may be related to the balance of power system in Europe at that time.
However, the data for the first quarter of the twentieth century reflected in

Figure 1.1   The relations between belligerence and "civilization"

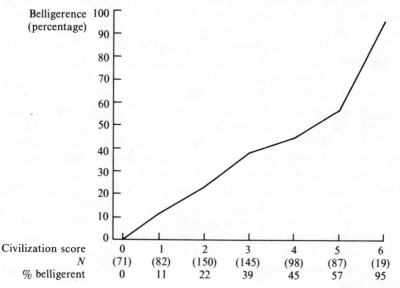

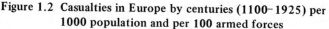

**Figure 1.2 Casualties in Europe by centuries (1100–1925) per
1000 population and per 100 armed forces**

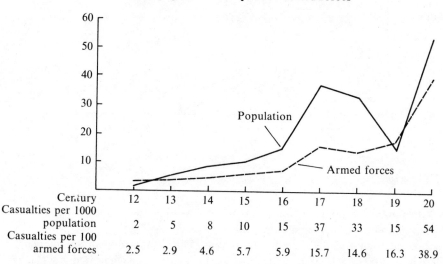

Century	12	13	14	15	16	17	18	19	20
Casualties per 1000 population	2	5	8	10	15	37	33	15	54
Casualties per 100 armed forces	2.5	2.9	4.6	5.7	5.9	15.7	14.6	16.3	38.9

Sorokin's curve has certainly made up for the downward tendency of the
preceding century.

To look more closely at the recent century and a half, a study made by J.
David Singer and Melvin Small is highly informative.[4] I have condensed their
data by reflecting the peaks of their indicator of belligerence, the number of
"nation-months" under war, getting figure 1.3. As can be seen, despite fluctuations, the general trend is as uncomplimentary of our century as Sorokin's data,
and what is even more important, the tendency graphed by Sorokin is shown to
have continued.

For the more recent period this trend is also reflected very clearly in Istvan
Kende's investigation.[5] His indicator of belligerence is a participation index
reflecting the number of participants and the duration. His findings for the
postwar period 1945–69, in which he registered 97 local wars, are shown in
figure 1.4. Although there are problems of interpretation, the trend is so clear as
to withstand attacks that can be launched on data as well as conceptualizations.
It should be noted in this connection that Kende's data clearly show that
whereas Europe shows a decline in belligerence (with Hungary in 1956, Czechoslovakia in 1968, and Cyprus being exceptions), Asia shows an increase, as do
the Middle East, Black Africa, and Latin America. The typical pattern of war in
the postwar period is shifted toward what used to be seen as the world periphery
and is strongly associated with relations between world center and world
periphery. Most of these wars are wars of liberation, with an element of civil war
mixed in. Kende also finds that the most important single contributor by far to
warfare in the postwar period, among countries, is the United States.[6]

Figure 1.3   Peaks in number of nation-months of belligerence, 1815–1965

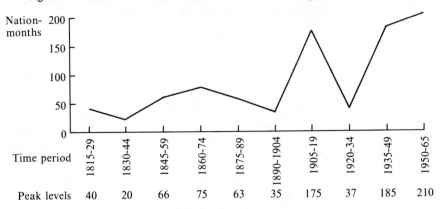

Time period	1815-29	1830-44	1845-59	1860-74	1875-89	1890-1904	1905-19	1920-34	1935-49	1950-65
Peak levels	40	20	66	75	63	35	175	37	185	210

In this connection, it is important to note another trend when it comes to identifying the victims of all this direct violence. In Vietnam, for instance, nature has been added to the list of victims. The composition of the human victims is changing extremely quickly in this century, as indicated by Max Born[7] (see figure 1.5): Only 5 percent of the casualties were civilians in World War I but 84 percent were civilians in the Korean War (and in the Vietnam War possibly more). War becomes total.

A study by Sergiu Verona[8] on the relation between world military expenditures (1949–70) and the yearly number of UN resolutions on disarmament (1946–71) can be used to illustrate the general situation in which we find ourselves right now. The data are indicated in figure 1.6.

I could also have cumulated the world military expenditures on the assumption that what has been invested in the military machinery one year does not all depreciate the next year. In that case the curve for world military expenditures would of course have become much steeper. To keep it within

Figure 1.4   Kende's index of belligerence for the postwar period, 1945–69

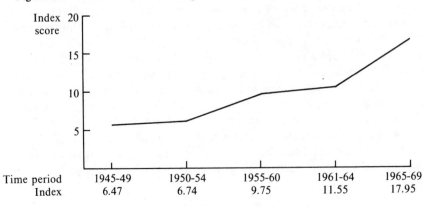

Time period	1945-49	1950-54	1955-60	1961-64	1965-69
Index	6.47	6.74	9.75	11.55	17.95

Figure 1.5   Percentage of civilians among war casualties in this century

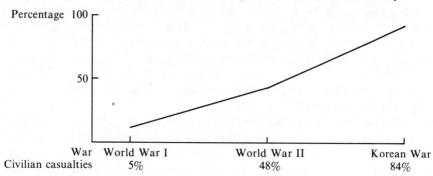

bounds, however, I have preferred to give the data as they appear in the figure. The conclusion is clear, that both disarmament resolutions and arms expenditures accumulate at considerable speed.

The more particular aspects of the military expenditures, including the kinds of weaponry that are being developed, will be treated at some length in chapter 5, although more from a qualitative point of view (the purpose of the weapons) than from a quantitative point of view.

Figure 1.6   World military expenditures in billions of dollars (constant prices) and number of UN resolutions on disarmament (cumulative trend)

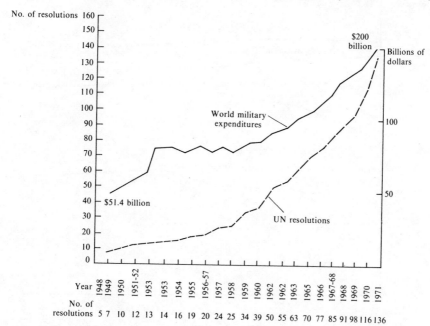

Let us turn then from a focus on "bads" to a focus on some "goods": what is the general world situation, over time, where food, health, and education are concerned? Needless to say, this is a big question, requiring much expertise for any in-depth discussion. Here we will merely cover the basic points.

Let us start with the world nutrition situation and, as is customary, analyze it in terms of calorie[9] and protein[10] intake. Figures 1.7 and 1.8 give some indication of the world situation over time. There are two remarkable features of these two presentations.

First, we see the relative constancy of the situation. True, there is a slight upward turn for Asia, but this apparent trend is tempered by the fact that the absolute level is so low. There are some other irregularities in the curves, but by and large the situation is remarkably stable in spite of the considerable amount of energy that has gone into ameliorating the situation since World War II, particularly in the period known as "Development Decades." More recent data do not show an upward trend.

Second, we see the tremendous difference between continents. For both diagrams this difference is of the magnitude of two to one, a difference hammered into the world social structure and maintained over time, illustrating the contrast between overconsumption and underconsumption. The actual consumption level at the bottom falls dismally short of the potential.

Figure 1.7   Calorie content of food supplies, average per capita per day

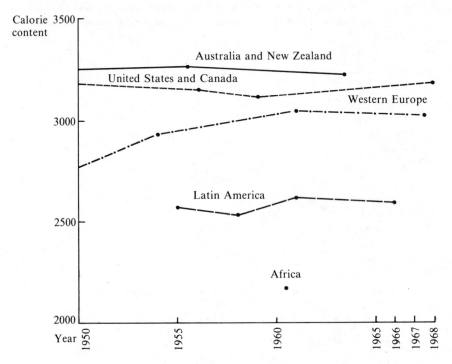

Figure 1.8   Gross protein content of average food supply per capita per day

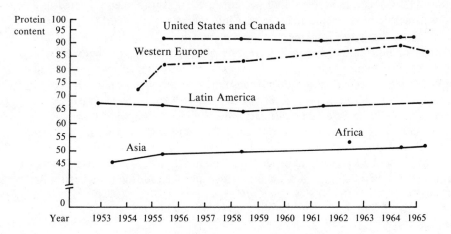

Let us turn from this to the world health situation, making use of one of the most sensitive of all health indicators, the infant mortality rate.[11] The data are as indicated in figure 1.9. The figure shows that in the field of health there has been progress. All curves have a downward slope, and there is a convergence that is not apparent in the curves reflecting food consumption. Nevertheless, in spite of these encouraging signs it still remains a fact that the ratios between the highest and the lowest rates are of the magnitudes 5:1, 3:1, and 2:1. Again, as those who are the most well off give indication of what the potential is, one can only conclude that there is a considerable difference between that and the actual level attained in the greater part of the world.

A UNESCO document[12] on education including some estimates of 1980 gives valuable insight into the world education situation. As can be seen from

Figure 1.9   Infant mortality rates per 1000 live births

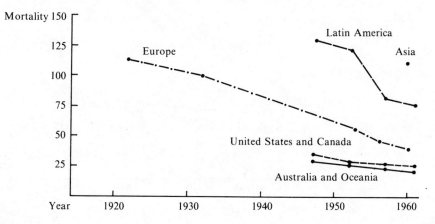

figure 1.10, there is a considerable recent decrease in the adult illiteracy rate, from 44.3 percent in 1950 to 34.2 percent in 1970. This is then reflected in a considerable growth in the number of adult literates in the world. But at the same time, the increase in the adult population is so steep that the absolute number of adult illiterates is also increasing, although slowly. In other words, in spite of the tremendous energy that has gone into literacy campaigns and alphabetization around the world, the absolute number of adult illiterates is still increasing. In addition, there is, of course, the well-known variation between continents. Whereas the adult illiteracy rates (reported by UNESCO in a 1970 document[13]) were 2 percent for men and 5 percent for women in Europe, they were much higher elsewhere: 17 and 18 percent in America, 41 and 61 percent in Asia, 69 and 87 percent in Africa, and 75 and 88 percent in the Arab states. Thus, the gap between high and low is much greater than for food and health. At

Figure 1.10   World adult population and literacy rates

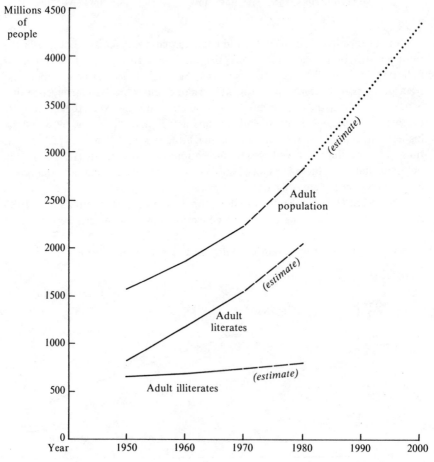

the same time we notice another gap, reflecting the structure of discrimination between men and women.

In figure 1.10 the size of the adult population was indicated. In figure 1.11 there is a corresponding indication of what the total world population curve might look like.[14] As can be seen from the curve, the 4-billion point occurred about one-third of the way into the 1970's and the five-billion point is expected in about 1985. Whereas it took almost forty years to add one billion to the world population of 1920, it will take less than one-third of that time to go from four to five billion. It is hardly probable that the trend will continue at this rate. What *can* be seen in figure 1.11 is the bottom portion of a logistic curve, which always looks like an exponential curve. It is well known that population growth tends to taper off when demographic transition has taken place, i.e., the stepwise transition first from high birth and death rates to high birth and low death rates (due to successful health measures, to some extent reflected in figure 1.9) and then to low birth and death rates.[15] As more and more countries pass through that transition, simple extrapolations from figure 1.11 become misleading.

Now, to try to summarize some of this information. We are still tied to the conventional way of evaluating statistics. For instance, we must speak in terms

Figure 1.11   World total population

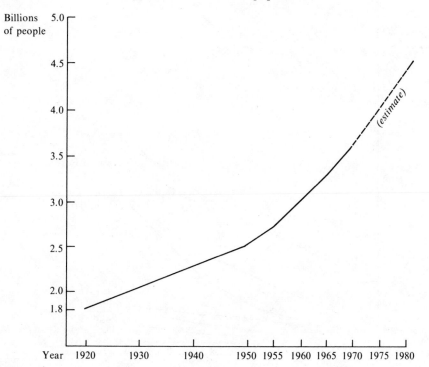

of gross domestic product (GDP) and gross national product (GNP) per capita. Although these indicators say something about the capacity of the production system, they say nothing about the distribution of the products or about the relationship between the products actually produced and any kind of theory of human needs. Production of staple food and production of stereos enter side by side in the equations, which means that what one can learn from such data relative to the perspective of this book is limited.

Nevertheless, let us examine the data for what they are worth, starting with GDP per capita (see figure 1.12).[16] The story told by the data in figure 1.12 is rather well known. North America is way ahead of all other regions, although this would change rather dramatically if recent devaluations of the dollar, not to mention revaluation of certain other currencies, had been taken into account. The various other parts of the world follow in an order we are accustomed to

Figure 1.12   Gross domestic product per capita, in constant 1963 U.S. dollars

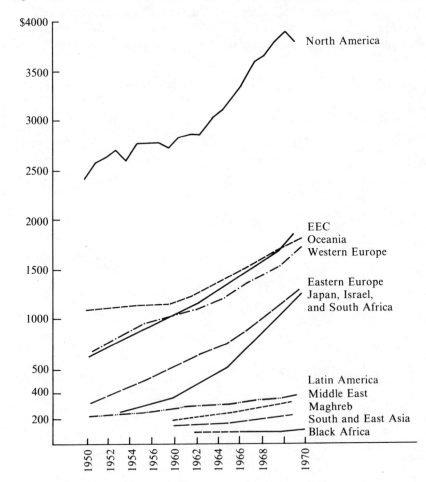

seeing. Further, it is fairly well known that the lower the absolute level, the lower the rate of growth, as is reflected very well in the figure by the almost stable curves at the bottom.

As many countries and regions of the world are "fighting for" a position at the bottom of this figure, that section of the figure is amplified in figure 1.13.

However, all the data presented so far suffer from one consistent weakness: they refer to countries and regions. In other words, they refer basically to abstractions and not sufficiently to situations of individual human beings. On the other hand, the only way of doing that really adequately would be to do what Oscar Lewis did for Mexico in writing the biographies of selected and representative individuals so brilliantly that the totality of their lives stood out as clear testimonies to the inequalities in our world.

It still makes sense to try to go below the country level in presenting data. Imagine that one divides the countries of the world into rich and poor, and the people living in these countries into rich and poor, these being relative terms. For these four groups of people, we may ask how their conditions are changing over time, for instance, since World War II.

It is a telling indictment of the present state of affairs of statistics that we do not have conclusive evidence in this connection. However, figure 1.14 seems to be a relatively accurate account of the situation.[17] The general idea is that in this period after the last world war the rich all over the world, and most people in rich countries, have done rather well, with a solid increase in their level of living. The rich in the two parts of the (capitalist) world have followed suit, for reasons that will be explored in chapter 4. The poor in rich countries have also increased their level of living, but at a respectful distance from the curve for the rich. But for the real masses of the world, the poor in poor countries, there has been, by and large, stagnation or even decline.

To arrive at such conclusions one has to make some cutting points between countries and between people. One such cutting point is given in the percentage distribution of the world population in figure 1.14; clearly, many other cutting

Figure 1.13   Gross domestic product per capita for the poorest countries, in constant 1963 U.S. dollars

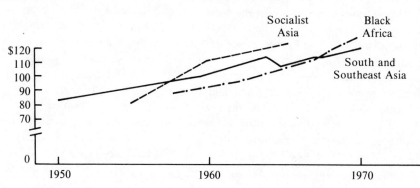

Figure 1.14   The level of living of four groups in the world

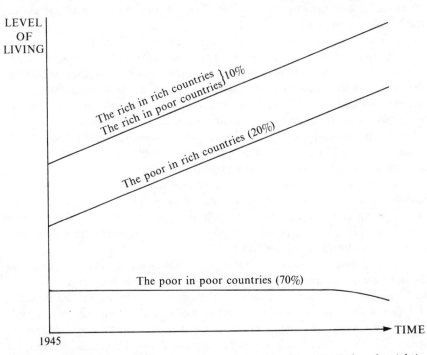

points could be imagined. More particularly, it should be noted that the rich in poor countries constitute a very small fraction of the population of those countries, and consequently an even smaller fraction of the population of the world. When one computes some kind of average between their rapidly increasing standard of living and the stagnation of their masses, one gets the very slight upward bend of, for instance, the gross domestic products for the poor countries in the world as reflected in figures 1.12 and 1.14.

There are many ways of evaluating distributions of this type, but each requires some kind of value perspective or theory perspective. Suffice it to say one thing: the important aspect of the figure from the point of view developed in this section is that the bottom horizontal line by and large falls below the level of the satisfaction of fundamental needs. Hence, there are two different bases on which one can generate political momentum against the present world political and economic system. One is on the basis of misery, because the bottom line falls below the minimum. The other is on the basis of inequality, because the lines are separate and rapidly diverging. There is a gap not only between countries but also between classes within and between countries.

But is the world capable of doing better? Let us say that it is catering quite well to something like one-third of humanity and rather badly to the remaining two-thirds and that this inegalitarian distribution has a very clear geographical and, above all, political address. But can we do better; can we get rid of misery?

Can the world become egalitarian? These are two very different questions, but it seems quite clear that a change in the focus of production toward more fundamental needs and a more egalitarian distribution would create, already today, quite tolerable conditions for humankind. From the point of view of rich people and rich countries this might look like general misery; from the point of view of the masses of the world it might even look like paradise.[18]

But the world is not tackling these problems in this way. What the world is doing is to increase production, and in a way well reflected in the curves of figure 1.12, which leads us to the general problem of the finiteness of the world, the carrying capacity of the planet. Usually this problem is analyzed in terms of demand and supply, and it is then shown how demand curves will cut through supply curves probably even in the near future. As most of these diagrams are well known, I shall not add them to this introductory presentation.

Whereas fundamental needs are relatively absolute, both "demand" and "supply" are highly relative entities. It is dangerous to reason from fixed notions about demand and supply, because demand can be artificially high (e.g., for cheap energy) and supply can be artificially low (e.g., when oil is used to produce gasoline rather than food). There are such things as overstimulation of demand as well as underexploration and underutilization of resources, including human imagination and creativity in general. Whereas one can cut down on demands, one cannot cut down on fundamental needs. But the present world is structured in such a way that it is very often more responsive to demands articulated in the very effective language of money than to needs, ineffectively articulated in the mute protests of the empty stomach, the body exposed to diseases and other hazards of nature, the mind left unfertilized by community and communication.

Nevertheless, it is impressive how short (relative to human history) the duration of some supplies, making reasonable assumptions about the demand, are calculated to be in some regions of the world, as shown in table 1.1.[19]

Adding to this picture of accelerated depletion, comes the equally impressive picture of pollution for which very little data consensus seems to be available. Moreover, such data drive us into the trap of reporting data badly in need of disaggregation. It is equally, perhaps even more, important to know that one single country, the United States, with 6 percent of the world population, is responsible for about 33 percent of the world energy consumption in the form of oil and that the average American is said to pollute twenty, or maybe as much as fifty times more than the average Indian. Data relating to the finiteness of nature have a geographical and indeed a political address, as will be developed at some length in subsequent chapters.

Instead of continuing with such curves let us now try to look for a first approximation in the direction of a synthesis. I have presented no theory at all to explain these phenomena, having only pointed out some trends. Let us imagine for the sake of the argument that the data given are by and large correct. What do they tell about the future?

Table 1.1 Present and estimated future energy use

Region	Population		Per capita energy use		Years to depletion after 2000
	1965	2000	1965	2000	
Africa	313	750	0.3	0.9	300
Asia	1830	3820	0.4	1.5	160
USSR	230	340	3.7	8	1500
Europe	444	585	3.3	8	55
North America	213	310	10	20	300
Latin America	246	685	0.8	2	65
Australia/ New Zealand	17	35	3.5	6	240
Total	3293	6540	1.6	3.3	330

Source: "Population, Resources and the Environment," paper presented at the UN World Population Conference, Bucharest, 19-30 August 1974, table 5, p. 28.

Strictly speaking, nothing; for reasons to be explored later. Human societies, whether at the global or domestic levels, are very special systems, capable of considerable self-transcendence. Not only is absolute prediction difficult; I shall argue that it is meaningless. But *conditional* prediction is not only meaningful but relatively easy and a burning necessity. The simplest way of doing it is to extrapolate from the trends already given, not considering their interrelation. More complex ways exist, such as those based on systems analysis and assumptions about the feedback cycles connecting the variables as are used in the Club of Rome reports. I shall not use them, however, for three reasons: the assumptions are dubious; the results are not necessarily too different from those one gets by using simple extrapolation, one variable at the time; and such exercises often lend themselves to the idea that what has been produced is absolute, not conditional prediction.[20]

The conclusion to be drawn from straightforward extrapolation is simple enough: *humankind is in trouble; we, you and I, are painting ourselves quite quickly into a corner.* Basically, there are at least four reasons for this statement:

The increasing destructiveness of war;
The persistent failure to satisfy fundamental needs, particularly when it comes to nutrition;
The increasing disparity in need satisfaction according to a very definite geographical-political pattern;
The increasing depletion and pollution of nature.

The relative significance of these factors varies around the world as a function of geographical and social position. The danger of a nuclear war, which we have not spelled out, is more of a rich man's problem because nuclear bombs are most likely to fall on rich people's territory, which is most vulnerable. Ordinary bombs fall on poor man's territory. Misery and disparity are also the poor man's problem. The poor share the consequences of depletion and pollution, although they certainly do not contribute equally to the causes. Thus, we are in the same boat in the sense that there are fundamental problems whose effects are experienced everywhere, but the troubles are not the same for the passengers traveling first class, the passengers on tourist class, the crew, and the galley slaves. Up there on first class the passengers are suffering symptoms of overdevelopment. Being overfed and alienated expresses itself in all kinds of aggression, both self-directed (pill consumption, alcoholism, breakdowns, suicide) and other-directed (excessive competitiveness, lack of solidarity, crime, homicide). Down at the bottom, on the other hand, they fight every hour for survival of a most basic kind. The planet Earth may be referred to as one shrinking spaceship, but it is a strangely composed and badly organized ship indeed.

Moreover, one of the saddest aspects of this poor world of ours is the way in which those at the bottom, to a large extent, want to emulate those at the top, just as those at the top start having very serious doubts about the social order and way of life they have brought into being. For some centuries they have been trotting along a road called "economic growth," guided by an idea of progress, hoping to find paradise at the end of the road. Instead they are finding increasing disaster, often of a most unexpected kind, for themselves and for others. What is in a sense even worse, they are rapidly finding themselves running out of program, while those lower down to a large extent are trotting along the same road, with untainted optimism.[21] The same road, leading to the same corner, with basic problems unsolved, new problems added, and a fair chance of increasingly destructive wars on top of it all.

1.3 APPROACHING THE PROBLEM

Let us now start with three simple assertions: (1) what exists can be divided into humankind and nature; (2) human beings, as well as nature, have fundamental needs, the *conditio sine qua non* of their continued existence; and (3) human beings depend on nature for the satisfaction of their needs, but not vice versa. The fundamental needs of nature are not the subject of this book, but some idea of the fundamental needs of humankind is indispensable. These needs are not only fundamental in the sense just defined; they are also fundamental as political goals. Thus, one definition of "socialism" (a definition to which I subscribe) is "a political and economic system that gives top priority to the satisfaction of fundamental needs; starting with those at the bottom."[22] The organization of production for the satisfaction of fundamental needs is also basic, and an analysis of how production is organized nationally and internationally is necessary to this discussion.

Let us then define five such fundamental needs or values, three of them "physical," the other two more "social," and do so more explicitly than was done in the preceding discussion. Longer lists could be imagined.

First, human beings need a certain input-output balance. There must be a physiological input in order for them to function—nutrition, water and air. The energy created and the waste products constitute the output. It is customary to refer to the input generally as "food," particularly in regions where the water supply and the air supply so far have been relatively unproblematic. We shall stick to this usage, although the word "food" conceals the more general input-output idea.

Second, human beings need not only a certain input-output balance, but also a climate balance with nature. Nature's climatic average and range of variation, in terms of temperature, rain, snow, storm, and so on, create problems for unprotected human beings. We shall stick to the common habit of referring to this protection as "clothes and shelter," keeping the more general climate balance perspective in mind. For there are other solutions, for instance, one known to nudists: to seek special habitats where both clothes and shelter can be dispensed with.

Third, regardless of whether input-output balance and climate balance obtain, the human body may exhibit signs of malfunctioning and disease. I shall refer to the corresponding need as "health," leaving aside the tremendous problems in defining this term. Nor do we need to make a distinction here between diseases induced from the outside (by accidents, contagious diseases, and so on) and diseases that can be seen (perhaps) as an expression of general wear and tear.

So far these needs do not refer to human society, only to human beings in a "physical" sense. These needs can be satisfied even where people live as individuals, isolated one from the other. A Robinson Crusoe capable of creating his own energy and climate balance with nature, as well as doing some simple self-doctoring, would have these needs satisfied. But overwhelming evidence suggest that man is a social animal. What makes man unique is interaction with others, actual as well as symbolic.

Hence we find a fourth need, a need for community, in space and in time; a need for togetherness; and also for procreation to preserve the community. Procreation implies sex, but we have not placed sex as such as a fundamental need. There seems to be evidence that many people are, after all, capable of living lives with little or no sexual activity without becoming inhuman. But we all need a community for physical interaction; isolation in early life makes human beings incapable of developing specifically human characteristics.[2 3] In general this need can be satisfied by means of proximity, but for community with people far away some transportation and communication are indispensable. At this point scarcity enters the picture. Transportation and communication become prerequisites for extended community, but that does not make them fundamental goods. The need for community can be satisfied locally—and very, very cheaply.

Fifth, human beings have a need for symbolic interaction, for communication as well as community, for culture. Formulated as a need, the term "education" sounds a bit trite, not quite fundamental enough. Sociologists would talk about "socialization" or "internalization." Nevertheless, we shall view education as a fundamental need, defining it as a process that not only gives access to the culture of .the community but that also permits reflection on that culture, critically and creatively. Whether formal schooling satisfies that need is another question that can only be decided empirically.

With these five needs satisfied, man is capable of forming a society, self-sufficient economically, biologically, and culturally.[24] But the list with these five terms on it—"food," "clothes/shelter," "health," "community," and "education"—looks trivial to all of us to whom the satisfaction of these needs has been as simply gained as the air around us. And yet, after two or three million years of human life on earth, particularly after the last five hundred years of "economic growth," humankind is still in a situation where these needs are far from satisfied for the majority. These extremely fundamental and elementary problems still are (or should be) on the top of the political agenda. Why?

Briefly stated, it is not because we have not worked and produced. But production has somehow been organized the wrong way. At the fundamental level—enough and varied food, clothes and shelter, a reasonable health level, togetherness, and education—these five needs could have been satisfied for us all. The failure to satisfy them is avoidable, which means that there is violence at work.[25] The extremely high level of satisfaction of these needs at the top of the world is empirical proof of the technical possibility of producing the goods; their rapid postrevolutionary fulfillment in socialist countries is proof of the social possibility. Of course, it may be argued that the needs cannot today be satisfied at the rich-country level for the entire world, but at that level they are no longer fundamental needs. Food indulgence, extravagant clothes and luxurious houses, enormous investments to push life expectancy some months or even years further up in the richest countries, and lifelong, even continuous schooling—these are not "fundamental needs."

What went wrong? Many answers will be given to this question in these pages. At this point I merely want to fix attention on how elementary humankind's problems still are when the focus is on *all* of humankind. The problems on the top of the agenda of the people who created the cave paintings around the world are still on top of our agenda today, but in the meantime the agenda has become more crowded. New problems have come up—large-scale violence, repression, and environmental deterioration—that also demand attention. In this sense, I insist, the history of humanity is little to be proud of.

Consider the following highly schematic and idealized image of human history. Imagine, at the beginning, the prehistoric world, with ample space, populated by some small communities of racially and ethnically similar men and women, each community roving around without interfering much with other communities, eking out of nature some food, some clothes, some shelter.[26] Territory was much like the ocean today, with some moving points of occupancy. Admittedly, of the five fundamental needs, people were probably generally short on all, except togetherness. There was enough space: people could afford both isolationism and togetherness and chose the latter. Like people today, they lived in exchange with nature, picking, catching, trapping what they could get, producing and consuming, giving back waste products that might serve as fertilizer, and exchanging oxygen for carbon dioxide with the vegetation around them. The economic cycle in which they participated was a man-nature cycle, as it is today and as it shall always be. But that cycle, unlike today's, possessed three major virtues, at least in some places and in some stages: *ecological balance, even accumulation,* and *limited extension.*[27]

There was ecological balance in the sense that the production process did not interfere with the fundamental needs of human beings or of nature. What was produced was not divided completely equally, but there seemed to be no gross unevenness in the accumulation; that came later. The economic cycle was understandable to the individual who participated in it.[28] The human as well as the nonhuman part of the cycle was comprehensible. Even though people might believe the cycle passed through transcendental powers, they did not believe themselves to be an insignificant part of it. Note the contrast to today's cycles, spanning the world, passing through the mighty and rich as well as the powerless and poor, but with the former as subjects and the latter as objects.

This balanced situation might have continued forever, and it did, in fact, continue until the last ten thousand years or so. Humankind became so clever that it began to sow the seeds of its own destruction. It satisfied fundamental needs to the extent that the population began to grow, albeit slowly at first. The man-nature balance could from then on have been maintained by putting a ceiling on man, or no limit on nature. But man increased and nature did not. Nature was basically finite, constant in size, although nature also reproduced itself. This finiteness in combination with a growing population has had two consequences: ecological imbalances and social interdependencies.

The imbalances have already been mentioned and are well described today.[29] Two terms are frequently used: "depletion" (particularly of nonrenewable nature) and "pollution." Nature is seen as being ruined. Molecules or at least most atoms do not disappear, but they may become irretrievable in the desired forms, at least with current technologies. Even if they are retrievable, the work needed to reconstitute nature might lead to even more depletion and pollution somewhere else. Both nature and man are being polluted by the various waste products from the production process, even approaching a point where the damage can no longer be undone. The health of man and nature is threatened when mechanisms of restoration and reconstitution are impaired.

The interdependencies are equally well known. Just as human beings, except for the occasional Robinson Crusoe, could never simply act but always had to interact with fellow human beings in the community, communities also had to start interacting with each other. They had to take into account the actions of other communities. They were too close to carry on as if they existed in a social vacuum, if only because of nature's finiteness. Some communities settled and became territorial, with fixed territory—one of the most basic events in human history—and the territories became contiguous, separated by more or less "natural" borders. Similar people became nations, contiguous territories became states, and the idea of putting each nation into one state, the nation-state, arose. Parallel to this development, economic cycles expanded, being the core of the interdependencies. The consumers no longer necessarily consumed what they themselves or even their own community had produced. Division of labor became increasingly complex, leading to uneven accumulation within and between communities, with the centers getting more and the peripheries even less even though, or precisely because, they participated in the same production cycle. The result was economic cycles generating ecological imbalance, uneven accumulation, and unlimited extension. I shall later have occasion to refer to the "uneven accumulation" and the "unlimited extension" as types of structural violence, impoverishing and alienating the dominated.

However, direct violence was also part of the scene, community against community, at an accelerating rate by most measures. Clearly, there arose a need to regulate these interdependencies by some means short of war. Communities developed relations with each other. Communities also differentiated internally and used some of the production surplus to maintain a "government," which, together with fixed territory, made them into "states." Governments related to each other; in due time that led to intergovernmental organizations. And "nongovernments" also related to each other and developed (inter)- nongovernmental organizations. Together such organizations constitute what might be called nonterriotrial actors, in addition to the territorially settled communities, the territorial actors. Some of the latter had members of a similar kind, biologically (racially) and culturally (ethnically), who were said to belong to the same nation, and some did not.

I bring up all these matters because we must have some way of cutting into this quagmire of a human condition in which we find ourselves. I have tried to do so as quickly as possible at this stage, sketching a development that takes us from a very simple world to the hypercomplex structure of our existence today.[30] If the nonhuman part of the world, nature, had somehow expanded together with humankind, the world would have been larger but might have retained its simplicity. However, we should have no illusions that such a world would necessarily have solved the problems of the fundamental needs; likewise we should nourish no romanticism concerning primitive society in general. In many of them life was and is brutish, nasty, and short.

But look at what we have today:

Direct violence	*Structural violence*	*Imbalance*
within communities	uneven accumulation	depletion
between communities	unlimited extension	pollution

In addition, we still have not been able to satisfy the fundamental needs of the majority of the world's population!

In today's monetized economies one way of expressing this condition is to say that the majority of the world's population lives in misery and cannot afford food, clothes/shelter, health, and education. They can afford only the togetherness that leads to ever-growing communities tied together in production of various kinds and in relations of structural and direct violence, with considerable loneliness in the midst of masses of people. Let it be said here only that even the most uneven and alienating economic cycle need not dip so deeply into the ocean of misery as is the case today and that the attacks against these cycles would have been muted had the lowest range not been so low but had come higher up on the scale of need-satisfaction.

Where in all this do we find suitable levers, not only for analysis, diagnosis, and prognosis but also for proposals and action? For instance, could we start with "ecological balance?" We put it down as a goal, a major concern, as a constraint on us due to man's expansion and nature's finiteness. But we see ecological imbalance as a consequence rather than as a cause. As a *sine qua non* of humankind's continued existence, ecological balance can be put down as our first world goal, but that does not answer the question of where to look for a cause of environmental deterioration.

Although "fundamental needs" could be reformulated and refined, by and large we shall take it for granted that a fully human life can exist only where these needs are satisfied. Like many of the parameters of nature they do not offer much scope for change.

If neither nature nor humankind as such offers a suitable point of departure for analysis leading to action, it has to be community or society, the stage of man's togetherness. Communities consist of human beings who act and interact, and there are also communities of communities, where communities become actors. In all of them, production goes on, for survival and for accumulation. It ties man, nature, and societies together in increasingly uneven, ever-expanding cycles. Thus societies consist of actors and have a structure. Conceptual tools are therefore needed to say something, for analysis as well as action, about actors as well as about structures. Such an analysis has to relate to structural as well as direct violence; to systems of territorial as well as nonterritorial communities or actors, with their processes of growth, fission, and fusion.

Let me use this conceptual overview to spell out the basic plan of this book.

Chapter 2 develops dimensions of analysis of societies, focusing on actors as well as structures. However, we cannot make use of just any or all analytical dimensions developed by social scientists. They have to be value-dimensions that can be used to analyze the empirical world around us and also to describe a potential world, a preferred world. I shall reject completely viewing these as mutually exclusive frames of reference. The focus is on *world goals*.

Chapter 3 uses these dimensions to give an image of a preferred world as well as a general discussion of its viability and attainability.

Chapter 4 focuses on structural violence, under the heading of the *dominance system*. The dominance system will be seen as world structures that work against the realization of the preferred world; and strategies for their elimination, or at least reduction, will be discussed. Typically, the dominance system is more the problem of the so-called Third World in a broad sense, better understood from the bottom than from the top. As a general system it concerns the whole world, particularly since the "oil crisis" has made it clear how much the overdeveloped part of the world depends on the underdeveloped countries.

Chapter 5 focuses on direct violence, under the heading of the *war system*. The war system will be seen as the machinery for systematic exercise of direct violence between communities; and strategies for its elimination, or at least reduction, will be discussed. Typically, in its nuclear form this is more a problem of the First and Second worlds but as a general system it concerns the whole world, particularly as most wars now occur in the periphery.

Chapter 6 focuses on the *territorial communities,* discussed under the heading of the *territorial system.* Here we probe into the changes necessary for the reduction of structural and direct violence, studying the possibilities of growth, fission, and fusion in that system.

Chapter 7 focuses on the *nonterritorial communities,* discussed under the heading of the *nonterritorial system.* As in chapter 6, the problem to be discussed is what changes are necessary for the reduction of structural and direct violence, considering the possibilities of growth, fission, and fusion in that system.

Chapter 8 focuses on the total world system, discussed under the heading of *world organization.* The problem is how today's world, consisting of both the territorial and the nonterritorial systems, ridden by both structural and direct violence, can be improved so as to permit some moves in the direction of the preferred world of chapter 3.

Chapter 9 turns to what the individual human being can do, discussing this under the heading of *individual activation.* More particularly, since I start with the individual, I also want to end there, believing firmly that it is given to everyone to be the master of his or her own fate, within broad limitation. Hence, the question is what individuals can do, here and now—what I can do—not what should be done by somebody, sometime, somewhere.

The structure of the book is synthetic rather than analytic. I have chosen to start not with concrete situations, except for illustration, but rather with the conceptual building blocks. Gradually I put them together, in the hope of achieving not only an analysis of the present but also visions and strategies for the future. The reader might find some of the road tortuous and want to go straight to more concrete problems, in which case he or she should proceed directly to chapters 4 and 5, 6 and 7, or 8 and 9. But chapters 2 and 3 lay out values and theoretical hypotheses as openly as possible—partly for others to see and react to, partly as an obligation not to neglect the major issues defined by the values.

Before we start with these values, however, some words on the basic philosophy and methodology of this whole enterprise.

1.4   EMPIRICAL AND POTENTIAL REALITY

Nobody could be accused of being irrational if he were to draw the conclusion from the previous discussion that humankind has only a slim chance of survival. And yet, as Kolakowski points out in connection with the expanding Nazi occupation of Europe during World War II: all clouds were dark, yet almost no one believed that it would not end well.[31] Why are we optimistic? Simply because we do not see the empirical reality around us—bad, trending toward worse—as the only reality. We always have a dualistic view of the real world. There is an empirical reality, but there are also potential realities. The relation between the two may or may not be understood dialectically. At a simplistic level these worlds are the world of facts and the world of values, the world that is and the world we want. They are the world of the present and the possible world of the future. My concern is more with the latter, and my basic view is that the potential is always present in the empirical, as its twin brother so to speak, and that neither can be understood without the other.[32]

As this book will be concerned with the future of the world, in the dialectic between the two, the focus will be on potential reality. This is an ambitious and difficult undertaking, and the future of the world cannot be "known" in the same sense this verb is used in empirical social science. The future of any society cannot be predicted, except in general terms or for narrow time intervals. One reason is that it is given to us to reflect on our own existence, and also on our future. We can even reflect on predictions about our own future and at least to some extent base our actions on our reflections. In principle it lies within our capacity to make predictions self-fulfilling or self-denying, depending on how we evaluate the predicted state of affairs. The moment an analysis, particularly a prediction, is made public, it changes the system of which it speaks, simply because it may lead to new types of action based on the new consciousness brought about by the predictions. The conditions for the prediction then no longer obtain.

But this "unreliability" applies only to absolute predictions, not to conditional predictions of the "if, then" type. The conditional prediction may often take the form of a warning: if such and such a tendency continues, then this or that disaster will be the result. The person who predicts is not predicting disaster in an absolute sense. He is not predicting that people will not act on such conditional predictions and, as L.F. Richardson said, "stop, to think." Whether they will in fact "stop, to think" is exceedingly difficult to predict, and even more difficult to predict is what conclusions they might draw from that exercise. But this is not my point.

Human beings and society cannot be regarded as closed systems. Both seem in a peculiar sense to be open systems that draw upon resources that may be immanent yet impossible to perceive and predict in any precise sense. In the Middle Ages nobody could have predicted the exact nature of the phenomena referred to as the Renaissance. In general nobody can, except in very general terms, predict the discontinuities in human history, for then one would in a sense already be there, in the middle or even on the other side of the discontinuity.

If man and society were closed systems, the forms of human life would not have changed so much through history. Each generation would have unfolded itself, but one generation would not differ from the next. Human society would have resembled termite society, the implementation of an immutable imprint to be carried out in the same way from one generation to the next. Human beings are different. We are capable of changing our program, of giving new directions to our lives, individually as well as collectively. We are capable of developing new values, in the form of explicit goals, or implicit interests. We are even capable, to a large extent, of changing the "laws" of our change.[33]

Humankind is self-reflecting and, therefore, makes culture. In the light of a new culture and new images the existing social structure may suddenly appear completely different. Capitalist society has never been the same since Marxism, regardless of how stable and permanent capitalism as an economic and social structure may look. What under liberal theory was regarded as the human society suddenly was seen as a special, even detrimental, yes, even doomed case, soon to be transcended. To see society like this is critical self-reflection, though such self-reflection is neither a necessary nor a sufficient condition for a society to transcend itself.

Social structure does not necessarily respond to a new culture that defines a new structure as preferable to the old. To think so would be to assume ideas and planned change, culture-determined change, as the predominant force in history. Changes may emanate as well from a structure itself, because of its internal contradictions. Such changes may for a long time remain completely unreflected in a culture which then in leaps and bounds may try to adjust to it and deliver the rationale that gives meaning to the new structure. An example is the impact the 1929 world economic crisis had on liberal self-understanding and the changes later introduced in liberal theory, symbolized by the name Keynes and concretized by ever-increasing state control. Doubt was thrown on the capability of the "invisible hand" to obtain and maintain social and economic equilibrium. The hand had to be made visible, even highly visible. The automatically functioning mechanisms of liberal society needed considerable encouragement and support, even in a highly deliberate way. Result: a new society, with central planning in its private capitalist and state capitalism version.[34]

Thus, absolute "prediction" of human society is not merely difficult as a result of lack of information, because our models take too few factors into account and so on; it is also unattainable, because of the self-transcending nature of culture as well as structure. Regardless of which of them changes first, human society is capable of considerable discontinuity with the past. Completely new cultures and structures may be intuited, if not known, and utopias can, of course, be constructed. But to predict that they will of necessity come about, or to predict their exact composition, is to assume not only that we know the laws of transition but also that we know, from the inside, cultures and structures not yet brought into being and discontinuous with our own. Even the most excellent political program should not be confused with a prediction—unless the conditions of absolute social engineering obtain, and they do not.

Hence, this project does not deal with prediction in the absolute sense. It contains some elements of predictions of the conditional type, most of them negative, which say that a given structural trend, if continued, will lead to even more negative consequences than found at present. But my essential tools for probing into the future are prescriptive: the basic tools are not data about our present world but values, combined with theories as to how such values might be better implemented in our shrinking world, our endangered planet, spaceship earth—as various authors have chosen to refer to the human condition today. My enterprise is empirical, but it is also critical and constructivist, with a heavy emphasis on the latter.

This raises two essential questions: how does one decide what values are to be pursued, and how does one arrive at theories of value realization? These are not difficult questions if one assumes that social affairs are governed by eternal, immutable laws, "invariances." One might then do with society what one does with nature: sample it at a given point in time and assume that a sample of man or society today is representative of man and society from eternity to eternity. Under that assumption, theories valid today will also be valid tomorrow. To realize values defined in the existing culture would be a question of steering a known structure toward a known goal, a question of planning.

But what I have said so far indicates that human society is not that simple. To start with the first question, the choice of values: I do not believe that a panel of experts, *in casu* some social scientists, can sit and pontificate about values for humankind. A social science methodology that changes from emphasis on data to emphasis on values may be more open to human concerns and less fatalistic in its determinism and its reification of empirical reality, by its elevation of what happens to be present reality into eternal laws. But it is at the same time fraught with the basic problem of elitism: where do the values come from? Are they extracted from old lists of values, handed down through history, tradition, institutions? Are they some author's own favorite formulations, coming out of his particular life conditions? Are they based on an investigation of public opinion? Are they arrived at by probing into "fundamental human needs"?

I have no answer to offer to these disturbing questions. But it may be that more important than the source of the values is the effort to state them clearly and honestly, for others to see and judge. To be value-explicit, not to be value-free, to be honest, not to be "objective"—meaning data-conforming—that is the short-term goal. The long-term goal would be a society so organized that people in general are more free to formulate their own values.

The question of theories is also problematic. Theories are abstracted from empirical reality and may therefore be more flexible than that reality. Thus, they may lead to an understanding of the potential, not only the empirical. They may define as possible not only what is but also parts of what is not. Like the periodic system in chemistry, a particularly brilliant theory, theories should provide openings for potential realities to be discovered or to be created. Theory should not only account for what is known but also lead to understanding what is unknown. It is in that sense that "there is nothing as practical as a good theory."

The difficulty is that theory operates within a framework set by what is already known. Theories are constructed within a paradigm defined by the variables and units used to describe and explain empirical reality. Such theories may facilitate thinking toward new combinations of known elements, but not to extraparadigmatic insights. In a world of bilateral diplomacy and the United Nations it does not take much thinking to develop the idea of UN embassies around the world by combining these two elements.[35] It takes more to think in terms of a world where foreign relations are also carried out at a nongovernmental level,[36] although that is hardly an extraparadigmatic idea. "Extraparadigmatic" is a matter of degree, for paradigms never exclude each other completely.

Most of what one can hope to do in the present type of futuristic study will therefore be intraparadigmatic, but to varying degrees. This procedure is not restricted to the empirical but is based mainly on empirically known elements that are put together in more or less new ways. Obviously, the more one moves away from the empirically given point of departure, the less reason we have to expect to know how new structures will work. As reality changes, so do the principles used to account for reality, the theories. Correspondingly, as society and human beings change, so do their values and their culture in general. But does not this make any attempt to peer into the future, using values and theories as the basic guides, just as meaningless as a prediction based on data and theories? Or even more so, because both feet are planted in the air, not only one?

The answer seems to be that the significance of an enterprise of this kind should not be measured by the distance from the solid, traditional, empirically based scientific enterprise but by its relevance for a humankind facing an increasingly threatening future. I see that future in terms of my earlier basic conditional prediction of increased violence of either kind. I have chosen to make that formulation less trite by using as my particular definition of violence, "any cause of an avoidable difference between potential and actual human self-realization." In other words, I have chosen to link violence to that basic human value, the highly general and flexible value of self-realization. Moreover, I see the future as increasingly threatening because of the threat of increased violence of various kinds, making people so much less than what they can be.

Methodologically, I am left with no choice. To peer into the future with the methods of empirical science means extrapolation, and prediction based on extrapolation today points to catastrophe. It is completely rational today to predict both nuclear war and worldwide famine. Hence the world situation demands that we do more than extrapolate. Only explicit values and theories about their realization can yield a different perspective. There is no alternative to trying to turn our course in a new direction. More empirical analysis will not do. We know more or less what we need to know about the empirical world. It is potential reality and its realization that we are dismally ignorant of in our excessive empiricism.

Epistemologically, values become as important as data and theories. They abound; many words float around in the air purporting to pick up the basic values toward which the world should move. In a remarkable UN resolution, the General Assembly gives a complete "Declaration on Social Progress and Development," full of human ends and means.[37] The World Order Models Project, of which this publication is a part, speaks of four basic building principles: peace, economic well-being, social justice, and ecological balance.[38] Peace research, of which the present publication is, I hope, an example, has been tied to the minimization of two types of violence, direct (personal) and structural.[39] Growth, freedom, diversity, equality, justice, equity, autonomy, solidarity, participation—there is no scarcity of value concepts.

Nor is there any scarcity of the theoretical concepts that make analysis possible. The big words—"power," "development," "violence," "peace," "nations," "states," "organizations," "structures"—are all at our disposal. We need concepts and theories in order to understand data; but we also need values in order to criticize (or applaud!) the reality the data represent, and we need both values and theoretical concepts in order to construct, if only on paper, blueprints for a viable future.

Thus, we are working with a triangle[40] such as shown in figure 1.15, in order to understand, criticize, construct, and act. With the values a preferred world can be depicted, for we are fully capable of intuiting or conceiving that which is not, even if we do not have knowledge in the empirical sense.

We are free to construct utopias on paper as blueprints, proposals, in any way our imaginations may carry us; and this is not merely an idle pursuit by intellectuals with excess leisure time. Imagination is a scarce commodity, and it

Figure 1.15   Science = Empiricism + Criticism + Constructivism

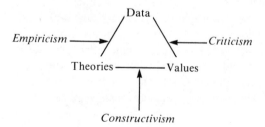

is replenished through use.[41] However, we want utopias that are relevant to our concern—basically, the realization of some of the values mentioned—and also to our time-frame—the end of this century. Out of all the free utopias we can imagine, we would like to pick the relevant utopias, and how may we do that?

Neither data nor values are sufficient; this is where theories come into the game. As theories are inspired by extrapolations from data, they are to some extent tied to the past, but they also permit us to speculate about the future. More precisely, they permit us to speculate about whether a utopia, a potential reality, would be viable, that there would not be built-in contradictions that would make it burst to pieces like a radioactive isotope with a very short half-life. Moreover, theories should also permit us to say something about whether the utopia is attainable or not, from here and now, that is. A utopia may very well be "realistic" in the sense of being viable if attained, but it may not be attainable. The social forces that could be mobilized "here and now" might not suffice to bring us "there," and in time. The utopia people in power positions believed in it or because "belief" was not enough. Deeper social forces might lead development in other directions than would belief.

To illustrate, imagine we are concerned with two values, such as minimum direct violence and maximum social justice. We can combine them in a two-dimensional space and fit in all our notions (see figure 1.16). I have also added the notion of dystopias, the rejected worlds, and included "here and now" among them. No doubt our world can get worse, and a path in that direction is indicated. That might be the path corresponding to no change in program, leaving the present trends toward the worse to continue unchecked.

One important point: I am not among those who believe the future is already embedded in past and present, and essentially predetermined, although qualitatively different. One can easily accept the historical function of views of this kind, of "scientific socialism" as opposed to the utopian tradition, so full of speculative imagination coming out of the minds of the leisure classes. But there is ample ground for a position between a determinism wherein the nature of the society being born is given in advance ("socialist," "postindustrial") and

Figure 1.16   On free and relevant utopias

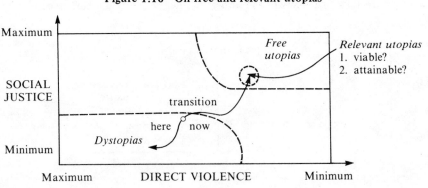

all one can do is to engage in some midwifery, and the view that "anything is possible." Although our minds are both clouded and enlightened by past and present, we are free to conceive of futures within a still much wider spectrum. The fight for freedom—to act, to choose, to think—is precisely the fight to expand this spectrum.

Liberation is the opposite of being a prisoner of the past, whether the prison limits our action potential, our courage to choose, or our ability to conceive of new futures for mankind. Freedom is the insight in sufficiency, not in necessity.[42] Only to the *Knecht* is freedom the insight in necessity, in how to follow the narrow line of the predetermined vision of the future. For the *Herr*, freedom is insight in how to act in a way sufficient to broaden the future cone to include the preferred world, not only the predetermined world (see figure 1.17). In short, although we do not have the total freedom of going anywhere from here, we are not constrained to unilinear necessity.

It is relatively clear what the anatomy of an action strategy has to be. It is located in the interface between culture and structure. Culture has to be used to conceive of and communicate a goal. Structure has its own inclinations: it shows trends and jumps. Some of them have to be checked, and some of them can be used. A strategy does not consist in goal formulation or trend riding alone; it consists in the skilled combination of the two. It is not completely free or completely automatic[43] or constrained, but somewhere in between.

At this point arises a particular question that will run as a basic theme throughout this book: are the values or the goals to be formulated compatible? If they are not, then a preferred future formulated in terms of them is obviously not viable. If it is not viable, one should not waste time exploring it, unless the purpose is social-science fiction for bedtime entertainment.

The general approach that will be taken to the problem of goal compatibility consists of four points.

First, empirical data about the present offer a poor guide to deciding whether goals are compatible or not. Even if it can be demonstrated with perfect adherence to the canons of empirical social science that, say, you cannot have a society that is both rich and egalitarian, I would not be too impressed with that

Figure 1.17   The cone of the future: neither necessity nor sufficiency

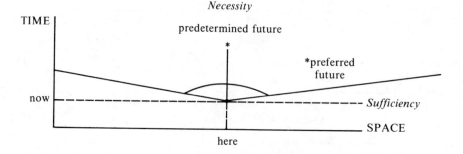

kind of argument. The reason is simple: any social-science "law," any empirical regularity, is only a *ceteris paribus* invariance. As they always presuppose that certain parameters are kept at a constant value, such statements are valid at most as laws about, for instance, U.S. society today.[44]

Second, if a glance at human history does not convince the reader that human society has a strong self-transcending capacity, nothing will convince. If human society has undergone basic social change up till today, chances are it will continue doing so, although that "law" can also be transcended. And it is indeed in our interest to change some of those curves in a very basic way. We have to try to make some goals compatible that so far have appeared to be irreconcilable, for instance, growth and equality.

Third, the general method when it comes to breaking through a so-called invariance in the relation of two variables seems to lie in the alteration of other variables—in changing the parameters, in other words.[45] For that reason the basic method of "preferential modeling" is not based on empirical knowledge, using established invariances, but on intuitions about what might be possible when those invariances are transcended, because of some change in fundamental variables.

Fourth, in this particular book three such changes in basic variables will appear and reappear: a change away from the capitalistic mode of production both domestically and globally, in both its private and state varieties; a change away from bigness and verticality (hierarchical structures) with regard to social organization; and a change away from too strong an emphasis on the territorial mode of organizing human society as opposed to forms of organization not based on ties to land or territory. Needless to say, these conclusions are both problematic and controversial, but I strongly feel that relatively basic changes are needed in a world as poorly handled as ours.

NOTES

References to *Essays* are to Johan Galtung, *Essays in Peace Research,* 5 vols. (Copenhagen: Ejlers, 1975–80) (Atlantic Highlands, N.J.: Humanities Press).

1. Thus, such terms as "democracy" and "socialism," whether they are interpreted as structural arrangements for the distribution of political and economic power or as a set of values and ideas embedded in a cultural system, will not be regarded as self-evident goals in this book. We have to decompose such concepts and come closer to human needs in order to be reasonably sure that we know where to move and in order to escape from the tyranny of overused abstractions.

2. See Galtung, "Belligerence among the Primitives: A Reanalysis of Quincy Wright's Data," *Essays* II, 1. For a critique of this approach, see Hans Hedlund and Åke Norborg, "Theoretical Primitiveness about Primitive Belligerence," *Fredsforskning: Analys och Debatt* (Uppsala University, 1973). The authors ask for an analysis in terms of "the structures behind empirically observable forms and the mechanisms of reproduction and change of

these structures." This is acceptable, but the concept of "civilization" as defined operationally by the index is supposed to play that role. They also maintain that one cannot make a valid distinction between political and economic warfare, which is the reason that these two categories are combined. It should be noted, however, that Quincy Wright himself has stated the thesis the other way, saying that "warlikeness among primitive peoples made for civilization" (in a letter to me, dated 27 October 1966). However that may be, I would agree with the critique that the concept of "civilization" is open to all kinds of discussion and that the modes of production, including possible imperialist spill-overs, are crucial. Nevertheless, I would be surprised if further analysis really succeeded in destroying the relationship shown in figure 1.1.

3. Pitirim A. Sorokin, *Social and Cultural Dynamics* (Boston: Sargent, 1957). *Statistical Handbook* (New York: Wiley, 1972).

5. Istvan Kende, "Twenty-five Years of Local Wars," *Journal of Peace Research* (1971), no. 1, pp. 5‑22; updated in *Journal of Peace Research* (1978), pp. 227‑41. The change in war theater is also very important—away from the rich world into the poor world—as will be analyzed in chapter 5. In addition to Kende, see David Wood, *Conflict in the Twentieth Century* (London: Adelphi Papers, 1968), analyzing 128 cases of war during 1898‑1967 and comparing the period 1898‑1947 with 1948‑1967.

6. Ibid. Kende points out that the United States is the major contributor to belligerence in the period.

7. Max Born, article in *Bulletin of Atomic Scientists* (April 1964). The data from the Indochina wars are still too unclear, but they seem to fit relatively well into this general pattern.

8. Reported in Galtung and Senghaas, eds., *Kann Europa abrästen?* (Munich: Hanser, 1973), p. 33.

9. Data compiled from *UN Report of the World Social Situation, 1963,* tables 1 and 3; *1967,* table 2; *1970,* tables 2 and 3; *UN Statistical Yearbook, 1967,* table 164; *1971,* table 2. Asia is not included, but the trend from about 1955 to 1965 for Asia *minus* Japan and the People's Republic of China shows a slightly upgoing tendency at a level of approximately 1900‑2100 calories.

10. Data sources are the same as those cited in the preceding note. In "Western Europe" are included Hungary, Poland, Romania, and Yugoslavia. Japan is included in Asia for 1949, but later on is excluded. For Africa, data are missing.

11. Data compiled from *UN Statistical Yearbook, 1957,* table 4; *1963,* table 3; *UN Demographic Yearbook, 1962,* table 17; *UNESCO Statistical Yearbook, 1965,* table 1; *UNRISD Compilation of Development Indicators, 1960,* indicator number 1. Data exclude fetal death, and the rates are number of deaths of infants under 1 year of age per 1000 live births. Countries where only cities or only white population is included have been omitted. Asia again does not include Japan or the People's Republic of China, and diachronic data are largely missing.

12. Internal UNESCO Secretariat document.

13. Internal UNESCO Secretariat document.

14. Data compiled from *UN Demographic Yearbook, 1962,* table 3; *UN Statistical Yearbook, 1967; 1968; 1969; 1970; 1971,* all, table 1; *UNESCO*

Statistical Yearbook, 1970, tables 1.1 and 1.2; *UN Report on the World Social Situation, 1963.*

15. There are also very good reasons to believe that this transition will be much quicker for today's nonindustrialized countries than it was for today's industrialized countries, partly because a model exists, partly because family planning is spreading and will increasingly be associated with, for instance, the women's liberation movement and social revolution in general. For an excellent survey, see "People and Population," a special issue of the *New Internationalist,* 15 May 1974, especially the article by Chen Pi-chao on Chinese family planning, "The Largest Nation on Earth"—as this is probably going to be an important pattern in today's underdeveloped countries.

16. Data compiled from many sources, including tables in *Yearbook of National Accounts Statistics, 1969* and *1971.* GDP estimates for 1965 are taken from Hagen and Hawrylyshyn, "Analysis of World Income and Growth, 1955–65," *Economic Development and Cultural Change,* vol. 18, no. 1, pt. II, table 8.

17. The figure is impressionistic and certainly more right than wrong, but it is very difficult to find a good data basis for this kind of figure. The figure was inspired by the excellent paper by Thomas E. Weisskopf, *Capitalism, Underdevelopment and the Future of the Poor Countries,* World Law Fund Occasional Papers (New York, 1972), particularly section 3, "Increasing Inequality." For the idea that the poor in poor countries are stagnating, or at least not increasing, Brazil is often cited as an example. In *Towards a New International Economic Division of Labor?* (Roskilde, 1975), Annerstedt and Gustavsson summarize the literature as follows: "During the 1960's, per capita income in the top one-percent of the population rose by 112 percent, while income for the lower half (50 percent) of the population rose by only 7.5 percent. According to other estimates, the incomes of 80 percent of the population went down, and 15 percent were unchanged, while only 5 percent increased" (p. 25). As to the idea that inequality in rich countries is about constant, data are inconsistent; sometimes the gap is narrowed, sometimes increasing again—very much depending on what kind of measure is used. A discussion for Britain is given by Paul Routledge in "Delving into the Hidden Pockets of Britain's Wealthy," *The Times,* 12 July 1974, which shows that "the share of the rich has fallen substantially since the days of the Depression, from 88 percent to 67 percent for the top 10 percent, but remains high."

18. Data taken from Pestel Mesarovic, *Mankind at a Turning Point* (Reader's Digest Press, 1974). But all these data are highly problematic, to say the least. For example, in a paper presented at the IBRD Executive Meeting, 1974, estimates made by earlier generations are compared to what we know today (Carman, "Comment on *The Limits to Growth,*" p. 18). The volume of oil consumed from 1950 to 1973 was 2½ times the total oil reserve estimated to exist in 1950, and the copper mined from 1931 to 1968 was twice the reserve estimated to exist in 1931. Comparisons of data published in the late 1940's with data published in the late 1960's show dramatic increases in estimates of existing reserves of other minerals as well: estimates of iron ore reserves increased by 1221 percent; of chromite, by 675 percent; of lead, by 115 percent; of bauxite, by 279 percent; of potash, by 2360 percent, and of petroleum, by 507 percent. Of course, such estimates are subject to revision, but these revisions are rather far-reaching, and it is hard to believe that the estimates made in the late 1960's are necessarily more

correct than those made in the late 1940's. On the other hand, they may also be overestimates. Even if that is not the case, the estimates may start converging because of better techniques and better mapping of presently unknown regions. For example, *Dai Dong* quotes Mandel, Spaght, and King Hubbert as reporting that the difference between the 1962 estimate of the world's supply of fossil fuels (coal and lignite, peat, oil, natural gas, shale oil, and tar) and the revised estimate of 1969-70 was "only" 133 percent. On the other hand, this may also merely reflect no major breakthrough in estimation methodology during the period.

19. Data from "Population, Resources and the Environment," paper presented at the UN World Population Conference, Bucharest, 19-30 August 1974, table 5, p. 28.

20. I am, of course, thinking of the debate that followed in the wake of the publication of *The Limits to Growth.* (For my own critique, see *"The Limits to Growth* and Class Politics," *Essays* V, 11.) The weakness of that book can be summarized in one sentence: it does not go into the structural factors causing at least a substantial part of the evils the book focuses on, such as depletion, pollution, and overpopulation, and it is consequently incapable of saying anything about the conditions under which the prediction of a major breakdown sometime in the middle of the twenty-first century will or will not hold true—except for some pious admonitions to a change of values. Essentially the book is an exercise in how to divert attention away from system critique and toward a new scapegoat, resource scarcity.

21. This is a major finding of the study reported in Ornauer, Sicinski, Wiberg, and Galtung, eds., *Images of the World in the Year 2000* (Mouton, 1976). The less developed countries included in this ten-nation study reported an optimistic faith in science and economic growth, a faith considerably shattered according to the opinion data extracted from the samples from the rich countries. See particularly the concluding sections.

22. It should be noted that this definition leaves open what happens when the fundamental needs are satisfied for all, and even equally. And that seems exactly to be the problem of socialism today: at that point, they—with the exception of China—run out of program and fall into patterns of imitation of capitalist countries. For an analysis of Cuba, mainly very positive but also from that angle, see Galtung, "Cuba: Anti-imperialism and Socialist Development," *Essays* V, 7. For an analysis of China, see Galtung and Fumiko Nishimura, *Learning from the Chinese People* (Oslo, 1975). For an analysis of needs beyond the material and fundamental ones, see publications in the World Indicators Program series, University of Oslo.

23. I am thinking of the classical *Homo ferus* literature as reported, for instance, in Kingsley Davis, *Human Society* (New York, 1950). This type of thinking has the advantage that it established "togetherness" as a need, not merely as a value—and from that many statements can be derived that are useful in analyzing, for instance, capitalist modes of production and consumption. Another direction of thinking would lead toward the need for symbolic interaction at the level known to humans as language—all the time assuming that one is talking about human needs, not only psychosomatic needs.

24. One might add two more items to this list of relatively material needs: transportation (of persons and goods) and communication (of symbols carrying meaning) over distances beyond the horizon. I have not done so explicitly at the level of fundamental needs, although I shall bring them in

later. They may be seen as fundamental in a modern industrial society with a nation-state–type organization, but that is only one social formation. Humankind's existence would not be threatened by the disappearance of transportation and communication systems. People can survive very well in small social units more or less like villages, which, after all, have been the dominant form of human habitat throughout history. Doxiades estimates in a study (from the article by M. M. Lacas on Quiroga, in *The Americas*, vol. 14, no. 1, pp. 57–86) that 53.5 percent of the population on earth lives in rural settlements. By now the majority of the world's population seems to live in habitats greater in size than the village. Perhaps more significant than where the majority lives now, however, is Doxiades' breakdown of his total number of human settlements (14.10^6): 4 million single farms and 10 million villages, and then 3 megalopolises, 141 metropolises, 1,460 cities with more than 100,000 inhabitants, and 32,700 towns with more than 5,000 inhabitants. The overwhelming majority of habitats are small, and they have at least had a reasonably high level of self-sufficiency, obviating the need for transportation and communication. Thus, these are clearly needs of a different kind.

25. This conception of violence, very much inspired by Gandhi's life and teachings, is developed in Galtung, "Violence, Peace and Peace Research," *Essays* I, 4, esp. pp. 110ff. It is developed in detail in chapters 2, 3, and 4 in this book, however, because "structural violence," the link between structural analysis and peace research, is here the cornerstone concept.

26. See the analysis given by Robert Redfield in *The Primitive World and Its Transformations* (London: Penguin, 1968), particularly chapter 1, "Human Society before the Urban Revolution." For an effort to synthesize development from that stage on, see "Socio-economic Development: A Bird's-eye View," section 1.2 in Galtung, *Members of Two Worlds* (New York: Columbia University Press, 1971).

27. I have further developed this theme elsewhere: in "Economics and Peace Research: Basic Concepts," mimeo (Oslo, 1976); in *"The Limits to Growth* and Class Politics," *Essays* V, 11; and in "Development from Above and the Blue Revolution: The Indo-Norwegian Project in Kerala," *Essays* V, 12.

28. For a general account of primitive economics, see the excellent chapter "Buddhist Economics," in E. F. Schumacher's celebrated *Small Is Beautiful: Economics as if People Mattered* (London: Blond & Briggs, 1973) (New York: Harper & Row).

29. Most of the literature is American. I am thinking of the works of Barry Commoner, Paul Ehrlich, and Richard A. Falk—not to mention the *Limits to Growth* team (which included one Norwegian, Jorgen Randers, then working at MIT). With the exception of Commoner, this may indicate an American tendency to produce crisis conceptions that are more problem-oriented than structure-oriented; but it certainly also indicates where the problem hit hardest and first, and which country, in spite of all, possesses intellectual cadres most capable of producing responses to crises—in all directions, one might add.

30. I have made two efforts in that direction, one focusing on complexity and the other more on verticality; see "On the Future of the International System," *Essays* IV, 18, and "Structural Pluralism and the Future of Human Society," in *Proceedings of the Second International Future Research Conference, Tokyo* (Kodansha, 1971).

31. See Leszek Kolakowski, "The Opiate of the Demiurge," in *Marxism and Beyond* (London: Paladin, 1971). Kolakowski writes (p. 130): "When Hitler's armies were on their triumphant march across Europe, there was probably not a single Pole who doubted that theirs were temporary successes destined to end very quickly in a resounding defeat. . . . No one had a sound rational basis for this opinion, but it was easily accounted for by a situation in which the monstrosities and horrors of daily life had reached such proportions that no one could imagine them to be a lasting reality, due to go on indefinitely." I agree with this, and with the feeling that a situation may be so absurd, so "monstrous," that it cannot "go on indefinitely"—and add that we live in such a situation today with the amount of structural violence and the machineries of direct violence surrounding us.

32. As an example, take the concept that will play a major role in this book: "vertical division of labor," i.e., an exploitative type of interaction. Empirically this structural element is ubiquitous. Potentially, and also partly empirically, other structural elements exist: "horizontal division of labor" (interdependence, interaction without exploitation) and "self-reliance" (mutual independence). The meaning of "vertical division of labor" changes completely depending on whether it is seen relative to neither, one, or both of these negations. In the first case it looks like a law of nature; in the last case it becomes one of alternative structural arrangements—known in international trade as neocolonialism, cooperation for mutual benefit, and (close to) autarchy.

33. This point is developed in some detail in Galtung, "Science as Invariance-seeking and Invariance-breaking Activity," chapter 3 in *Methodology and Ideology* (Copenhagen: Ejlers, 1977).

34. Obviously, as Academician Sakharov has repeatedly pointed out, a state-run economy permits even higher levels of monopolization, and hence of price fixing, than a private economy. This can, at least for a period, be justified by a concentrated effort to produce for fundamental need-satisfaction.

35. See section 8.4 for an effort to spell out this kind of idea.

36. See section 7.3 for an effort to spell out this kind of idea, up to a certain point at least.

37. This UN declaration has passed remarkably unnoticed, probably because it came before its time. Today it would pass unnoticed for the opposite reason.

38. These are the four world order values as they appear on the letterhead of the Institute for World Order: peace, social justice, economic well-being, and ecological balance. The reader will recognize them from section 1.1 as the negations of the crisis-dimensions indicated. For a rationale, see Richard A. Falk, "Points of Departure," in *A Study of Future Worlds* (New York: Free Press, 1975), esp. pp. 7–31. For my own rationale, see Galtung and Anders Wirak, "Human Needs, Human Rights and the Theory of Development," World Indicators Program (University of Oslo, 1975).

39. See Galtung, "Violence, Peace and Peace Research," *Essays* I, 4.

40. This point is developed in some detail in Galtung, "Empiricism, Criticism, Constructivism: Three Aspects of Scientific Activity," chapter 2 in *Methodology and Ideology* (Copenhagen: Ejlers, 1977).

41. However useful and correct Marx's attacks on utopianism may have been in their time, it is sad to see how generations of intellectuals and others grow up within scientific traditions, liberal/positivist as well as Marxist/dialectical, that deprive them of this dimension of creative and politically extremely

important thinking—unless, that is, the utopian dimension is used as a substitute for solid empirical research and critical understanding of empirical reality. All three are needed, and they do not exclude each other; that is the basic epistemological assumption in the present work.

42. This is, of course, the reversal of famous quotations often attributed to such different thinkers as Spinoza, Leibniz, and Engels.

43. This theme is developed at some length in Galtung, *A Structural Theory of Revolutions* (Rotterdam University Press, 1974), which also appears in *Essays* III, 9.

44. This is the basic idea in Galtung, "Science as Invariance-seeking and Invariance-breaking Activity," chapter 3 in *Methodology and Ideology* (Copenhagen: Ejlers, 1977). The problem is to locate and justify the choice of those variables—which is what this book is about.

45. The reader who wants to go straight to an image of a preferred world is referred to section 3.2. And the reader who wants more on "The Human Prospect" might see the article with that title by Robert L. Heilbroner (*New York Review of Books,* 24 January 1974, pp. 21 ff) and his other well-known writings. Heilbroner's tone is fundamentally pessimistic: "At this final stage of our inquiry, with the full spectacle of the human prospect before us, the spirit quails and the will falters" (ibid., p. 33). His does. That does not mean that everybody has to give in to facile pessimism even when all the trends point in the wrong direction. Much more challenging, important, and, incidentally, difficult is the search for openings, for possibilities of transcending those trends. For another, also brilliant, such exercise in pessimism from the United States, see George Wald, "Why Mankind Faces Its Worst Threat," *Globe and Mail,* 19 August 1974, p. 7. Third World people, when they pontificate, have a tendency to see more openings, as does the late Josue de Castro in an interview published as "The Third World in the Year 2000," *Kayhan International,* 9 April 1969. He thinks, of course, in terms of the possibility of breaking out of the capitalist system. The block in the United States against thinking in such terms, except for marginalized Marxists, has severely impaired the capacity of its intellectuals. Analysis will be in other terms, such as the "environment" (as in, for example, *The Limits to Growth*) or relations between states (as in, for example, Richard Falk's *A Study of Future Worlds*).

2. WORLD GOALS

2.1 TWO PERSPECTIVES ON SOCIETY

There seem to be two basic perspectives[1] for looking at social affairs: *actor-oriented* and *structure-oriented.* As each has its strengths and its weaknesses, I shall try to make use of them both. They should not be identified, respectively, with the liberal view and the Marxist view, for both liberalism and Marxism are complex and evolving philosophies with subdivisions, and both encompass, in nonvulgar versions, both perspectives. But they do so in a highly asymmetric way. It is probably correct to say that, in the dialectics of confrontation between liberalism and Marxism, the former tends more toward the actor-oriented view and the latter more toward the structure-oriented view. The perspectives can, however, be defined in their own right, with liberalism and Marxism, by and large, as special cases.[2]

According to the actor-oriented perspective, societies are the sum total of the actors participating in them. Societies are the human beings that act, the world is the set of countries that act. To act is to have a goal, form a strategy, and pursue it. Action presupposes the freedom to want what one wants, at least within a certain range. Actors are autonomous. According to this perspective, actors possess a certain amount of consciousness (to formulate the goals) and rationality (to conceive of means). In their pursuit of goals they may get into conflict with one another. A basic task of society, hence, is to regulate this conflict so that it becomes a competition (e.g., for shares on the economic, political, cultural, and military markets, leading to free enterprise, parliamentary democracy, cultural pluralism, and military balance of power, respectively).[3] For competition to be meaningful, it has to be free. But free competition produces very different results in open and closed systems or markets, often beneficial as long as the system is open, but disastrous when the system is closed (as in the Prisoners' Dilemma games and the Tragedy of the Commons).[4]

This perspective can now be applied on (at least) two levels: the domestic level, where the actors are persons, and the global level, where the actors are countries. The whole conceptual apparatus as well as the general theories apply in principle to both levels—here and in the rest of the book—with some exceptions.

41

According to the structure-oriented perspective, societies are the structures of interaction between the actors. To use a metaphor from physics: whereas the first view sees only atoms and classifies them, the second view sees the structure of the molecule and disregards the nature of the atoms.[5] I use this metaphor to point again to the obvious: the two views complement rather than contradict each other. The structure-oriented view emphasizes structure because it denies the implicit autonomy assumption of actor-oriented perspective. The actor-oriented perspective is structure-blind, but the structure-oriented perspective is actor-blind.

Thus, from the actor-oriented perspective a society looks like figure 2.1. It consists of actors of various kinds, equipped with distinct personalities, differing in intentions and capabilities, eagerly developing strategies in order to pursue their goals. From the structure-oriented perspective society may look like figure 2.2, wherein the arrows indicate the direction in which net value (in a very broad sense) produced in the structure is accumulating. The circles are positions, and nobody would disagree that society is meaningless unless positions are filled with actors. In the same way no actor exists in a vacuum, and we cannot understand an actor's behavior without knowing something about his position in relation to other actors. Hence, neither view is a complete social philosophy. They are exactly perspectives, differing in fundamental ways, drawing our attention to different aspects of social affairs. They are like two prisms; as such, they direct and determine our thinking and are far from innocent in their effects. Both of them make the human condition transparent in one direction, opaque in others (for there are more than two "directions"). There is no superprism available; but it makes sense to proceed with complementary conceptual tools, in order to shed different light from different angles over the human condition.

More particularly, there are two deeper-lying differences between these perspectives, one relating to the "problem of evil," the other to what may be called "time cosmology."[6]

Figure 2.1 The actor-oriented view of society

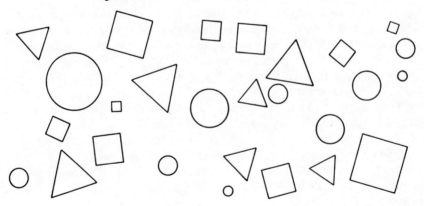

Figure 2.2   **The structure-oriented view of society**

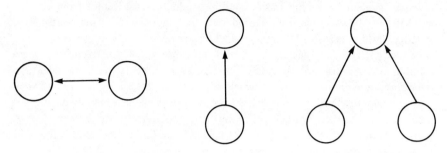

Both perspectives focus on human action and interaction. But whereas the actor-oriented view relates action to the intentions and capabilities of the actors, the structure-oriented view sees action as a function of the position of the actor. This leads to two entirely opposite views when it comes to the problem of evil. According to the first view, evil is caused by evil intentions, particularly when held by the strong and active actor; according to the second view, evil is caused by a bad structure. When an actor contributes to evil, through direct or structural violence, he is *guilty* according to the first view; but according to the second, the structure of his society is *bad*. The remedies vary accordingly: they are also actor-oriented and structure-oriented, respectively.

In the first case there are several possible ways of improving behavior. There is the prophylactic approach of developing in an actor other intentions, of controlling his capabilities—in general, the attempt to lead his activities in the right directions. Then there is the therapeutic view, implemented after the evil act has been committed, of subjecting the evildoer to "punishment" or "treatment." This is done, according to theory, partly to deter him from repeating the act, partly to deter others from similar acts. In domestic affairs these are known as the theories of individual and general prevention of crime, respectively. Translated into international affairs the first view is known as deterrence theory and the second as the domino theory: "If we do not stand up against aggression here, then there will be no limit to aggression in the future."

In the second case there are also many possibilities but they add up to one idea: *change the structure!* Evil, which I here equate with violence, whether of the direct or the structural kind, is traced back to structures, not to actors. The problem of guilt is seen as metaphysical; the institutions of morality and legality, condemning evildoers to hell or prison, or both, are seen as superficial and even detrimental because they draw the attention away from the real causes. The army of priests and lawyers mobilized to define, register, convict, and punish sin and crime are seen as protecting the system because they focus on the actor, not on the structure. Watergate is the veil covering the structure producing Vietnam.

Implicit in what I have said so far about evil is another basic difference that relates to time cosmology. In the actor-oriented view, time is dotted with acts, whether evil, good, or neutral. What happens is discontinuous. The world consists of events, meaning that something suddenly is different from what it was before.[7] In the structure-oriented view the emphasis is on the continuous, and the world consists of "permanents."[8] The structure is about as wrong today as it was yesterday or yesteryear. The significance of this difference for mass communication can hardly be overestimated, as the first view leads to a demand for information about news (that which differs from yesterday), the second view to a demand for "olds."[9] Needless to say, the world press generally favors the first view; it sees the world as a string of events, reports them, and tries to analyze them, to a large extent neglecting the underlying structures. The world press is organized around the actor-oriented perspective and will therefore often carry a liberal message, not by virtue of ideology but by virtue of time perspective.[10]

When it comes to remedies, however, the two views interchange their time philosophy. Neither denies that there is evil. But the actor-oriented view would try to solve this through building an institution (e.g., around morality and legality), in other words, through something continuous, whereas the structure-oriented view demands a discontinuous disruption of the wrong structure, known as the revolution. Underlying this is the basic difference in the approaches to the "problem of good." The actor-oriented perspective assumes that what is good for the subsystem, basically for individuals, is good for the system as a whole; the structure-oriented perspective assumes that what is good for the system is good for the subsystems, and for individuals.[11] There will be ample occasions to discuss the merits of the two approaches, as the distinction between these two perspectives will be a *leitmotif* throughout. Thus, they both have to use social dogma to correct their onesidedness, as in the idea that the system (subsystem) takes care of itself once the subsystem (system) is correct.

Once more, any viable social philosophy would have to combine these perspectives. The problem is the composition of the mixture and how the components should be integrated. I shall make use of both, believing in the significance of intentions and capabilities as well as structures. But there are situations I define as vertical because of the presence of abject exploitation, where I would give primacy to the structure-oriented view, just as there are more horizontal relationships where the actor-oriented view seems most rewarding.[12] In other words, the relative weight accorded to these views for understanding problems of power and development, of violence and peace must vary in time and space, according to the particular characteristics of the situation. There is no simple, general formula.[13]

But the two perspectives generate dimensions that I shall express in the form of goals or values. Needless to say, no such list is anything but a suggestion, but it is explicit, and is chosen as the basis of our analysis.[14] It is also to some extent developed systematically, not just chosen as a shopping list.

2.2   ACTOR-ORIENTED GOALS

In order to develop basic goals we start with the actor-oriented perspective because it has one distinct advantage: the focus is more on the fundamental social unit, on concrete human beings, however naive the conceptions of social structure. I shall try to build on simple words and related concepts, on "to be" and "to have," on "is" and "has," on "are" and "have," on "being" and "having."

Each individual is something and has something; that is our point of departure. The distinction is by no means a sharp one, nor does it have to be in order to be useful. The individual obviously is what he or she already was at birth: e.g., female, black, first-born of middle-class parents. Sociologists refer to such characteristics as ascribed, and to everything the individual adds later on as achieved. But the difficulty with that approach is its poverty (which is also the poverty of sociologism): it only scratches the social surface of the individual. The ascribed side tends to be reduced to highly external characteristics, like the ones mentioned, and the achieved side to highly concrete characteristics, like number of years of schooling, health data, ownership of a radio set, access to public parks and libraries, and so on.

I should like to deepen the "being" side to include more internal characteristics and expand the "having" side to include less material aspects of human life.[15] This does not imply any rejection of the significance of external and material things. In a world where sex, color, class background, and the like still make a mockery of social justice, and material things are both scarce and distributed in such an insane manner that deprivation abounds and the most fundamental needs are left unsatisfied, primacy must still be given to these factors. But individual actors also want to be happy, to be capable of expressing and receiving love, to be rich enough as persons to enrich and be enriched by others—and these are internal characteristics, but hardly given at birth. Simply put, a person is a human body (external) with a self (internal). All individuals have within themselves a potential for expansion if circumstances permit. Sometimes they *are* only if they *have* more, sometimes only if they do not have more. The term "self-expansion" is actually preferable to "self-realization" because the latter may indicate that to each individual there is a given potential to which he may aspire. Any talk to the effect that "humankind only realized 20 percent of its potential"[16] seems meaningless because human potential is both unknown and unknowable. The reservoir for self-expansion seems to be limitless. Expansion of what looks like a maximum potential also seems to be part of self-realization, as when a person starts living, feeling, or thinking in a totally new way.

Terms like "self-individuation" or "self-actuation" are also useful, as they indicate a process whereby a self is developed and a person grows. But the term I shall make most use of is "personal growth." Let it be stated only once more that there is no implicit assumption of Western individualism in these terms.

There is no assumption that in order to grow one has to be dissimilar from others, or to expand. On the contrary, growth could also be a process toward similarity and contraction, a convergence toward the essential. But it is a process, and a willful one at that.

One basic difference between "to be" and "to have" can now be indicated. What an individual, or a nation, *is* does not have to compete with what another person or nation is. If I am male, that does not make anybody else more or less male or female; and my being well educated and healthy does not by itself make you less well educated and healthy. But there is an external, material side to this when I enjoy schooling services and have access to medical facilities; the implication is that economic surplus has been distributed in my direction rather than in the direction of somebody else. Not so for inner personal growth. There are certainly social processes whereby one individual's enrichment is at the expense of somebody else, but it does not have to be that way. It is not necessarily a zero-sum game. The mind needs stimuli—whether a conversation, a look in the eyes, or a gaze at the stars; and stimuli may be unevenly distributed, and competitive, as I shall argue later. But my personal growth does not in itself detract from your possibility of growing.

Personal growth does not have to presuppose any depletion of natural resources, pollution of the environment with the products of waste, or exploitation of others in the process. The human self uses the environment as its "raw material," but only in the form of stimuli that are conveyed, not extracted and depleted, through the senses. The stimuli are processed in the self, which then expands, as any factory (*Homo faber*) does, but there is no need for exploitation or pollution. To become *enriched* as a person is vastly different from becoming *rich*; and that is precisely the difference between being and having, between expansion *of* one's self and accumulation *for* oneself.

Let me then make use of this distinction, simple although certainly not unproblematic, to define five goals that I see as basic. They are all definable in terms of "to be" and "to have" and are within the actor-oriented perspective. They all relate directly or indirectly to individuals that are generally at the domestic level. But they are meaningfully defined also at the global level, for communities or societies.[17]

Two of the goals relate to being (personal growth and freedom), two to having (socioeconomic growth and equality), and the last one to the relation between being and having (social justice).

Let me start with the level of being. The goal is personal growth, which can hardly be expressed more succinctly than Christian Bay, the eminent theoretician of freedom, has done in what he terms "The Most Basic Rights." These are "(1) to stay alive, (2) unmolested, and (3) free to develop according to inner propensities and potentialities; in that order."[18] In my terms, to stay alive is *being* in its most basic sense, and to be "unmolested" is to continue to be, to remain, another way of saying that the fundamental needs are satisfied. And "free to develop according to inner propensities and potentialities" is exactly the personal growth just referred to. In short, the underlying value is basic, primordial existence, as a basis for nonmaterial personal growth. I reject any body-soul dichotomy and see personal growth as including healthy physical existence as a condition for self-realization, self-expansion, or self-actuation. The healthy body is a basis for self-growth. The good society is the society that permits and stimulates personal growth, not a society that has a perfect structure inhabited by shallow automatons. This is the strongest point in the whole actor-oriented perspective: it permits a steady insistence on the qualities of the individual actors. Its weakness is, of course, its failure to capture the structural conditions that have to prevail to permit these qualities to grow and blossom.

Let me try to make this more concrete, if also more narrow, by seeing personal growth as the negation of alienation. Both alienation and personal growth have an internal as well as an external aspect; the relation man-to-himself and the relation man-to-society. Let us focus on the latter, seeing alienation and self-actuation as the two extremes on a dimension of (in)substitutability or (ir)replaceability in a social structure. The more replaceable a human being is, the less he is a *person* in the social context, and the more similar he is to a spare part, a machine tool, or to any other thing or commodity. The less replaceable, the more the person "leaves behind a gap or place that it will be impossible to fill," as it is frequently expressed in obituaries; the more he has become a real person, shaping the position more than the position shapes him, transcending the structure. Correspondingly for countries: what gives them a self, an identity, is precisely their insubstitutability, their irreplaceability. In this there is an assumption that individuation leads to dissimilarity, perhaps a rather Western assumption.

I repeat that this is only one part of the external aspect, the part relating to social structure. But it is an extremely important aspect. In a broad statement we may perhaps say that on the substitutability end of this dimension human beings are made to fit social positions or jobs and countries are made to fit world positions, such as "colonies" or "big powers." On the insubstitutability end they themselves make their position to fit the propensities and potentialities. In ological parlance this is the old contradiction between status and person: the status is a hole in the social structure, a position to be filled; the person is, precisely, a person, unless he is so replaceable that he becomes a thing. Nothing is his or hers; everything is substitutable, something somebody else could have done. Total substitutability means total alienation, from work-product, from others, and ultimately from oneself. Total insubstitutability means liberation from the structure, usually a privilege of the upper strata.[19]

The difference between the actor-oriented and structure-oriented perspectives can now be made more clear. The actor-oriented perspective looks at actors as if they were insubstitutable, totally liberated from structure; the structure-oriented perspective assumes substitutability, subordination to the structure. Hence, through the former prism one captures the upper end of the social scale, the "big" persons and powers; through the latter prism the lower end—and only as parts of a structure. Both are right and both are wrong. In the light of this dimension the actor-oriented view is too utopian and the other too dystopian, if they are to be understood as total social perspectives, encompassing everything and everybody.

Another goal of being, then, is diversity, or high dispersion of being, at least as a potential. I see it almost as a corollary of personal growth: if personal growth is pursued, then diversity follows, except under the very special and undesirable conditions of genetic and social engineering. But I also see diversity as instrumental to personal growth. Diversity means variation, contrast, which in turn is the basis for stimulation. Of course, variation can also be found in the nonhuman environment. But interaction with the human environment, community, is indispensable for personal growth, for the creation of a person (as distinct from a human body) at all. Hence, being both a cause and a consequence of personal growth, diversity is seen as a value in its own right, for the society of persons as well as for the world of nations.

Diversity, variety, or entropy are all closely related to freedom. As we assume "inner propensities and potentialities," in general to be dissimilar, inconstant, and inconsistent,[20] the degree of diversity in a society is a measure of the extent to which there is real freedom in that society. This does not mean that everybody has to make use of the possibilities for diversity, only that they are there as a potential.

But there is a difference between "freedom to" and "freedom." If there are five different conceptions of how primary education should be done in a society, then that is a measure of the degree of political diversity. But if the net result of all that diversity is a compromise in the form of one educational system, the educational system, then there is still no educational diversity, no educational freedom, because the individual is still molded in one form, however democratically arrived at.

In another context I have referred to the difference between cultural and structural pluralism:[21] the freedom to believe and express and the freedom to live in diversity. Obviously, lack of diversity in the structural sense need not be presumed to be the result of dictatorship. As already mentioned, a homogeneous nation-state may also lead to uniformity and combine cultural pluralism with structural singularism under the general formula of parliamentary democracy.

However, no "structural pluralism" or "dispersion into structural types" contributes to diversity unless it is accompanied by freedom of choice, and freedom of choice is only an empty phrase unless there is mobility of persons and of information. For this to happen, in turn, there has to be access, as free as possible, to the means of transportation and communication. I do not count these under the fundamental needs, for survival is not threatened by their absence, but I conceive of them as "almost" fundamental. What counts here, under the general heading of diversity (or "freedom" as one could almost as well have termed it) is the freedom of access to transportation and communication, the means of mobility of the body and of the mind. The general availability of these means is a question of "socioeconomic growth," and equality of access comes under the general heading of "equality," both to be discussed later.

But experience shows that the level of mobility of both kinds can be very high and the access quite egalitarian (e.g., by making them cheap, even free, in such fields as local bus transport and telephone, as is done in Havana). Still, there are barriers making the mobility less than free. Usually these barriers are erected between countries, i.e., at the global level, and take the form of severe restrictions on travel and access to foreign news except for highly selected elites. But they are also found inside countries, restricting travel even to the point of having internal passports and cutting down on the information flow. For each such form of repression of mobility the chances of converting diversity into personal enrichment decreases, and the amount of diversity found between and within countries is rendered useless.

I have mentioned the freedom to receive information. Obviously, the freedom to generate and send information belongs in the same category, usually referred to as the "freedom of expression." In practice this implies access to the means of expression, assembly, print, and radio/TV, almost regardless of the content of the information.

Let us then turn from the level and dispersion of being to the level and dispersion of having, from enrichment to accumulation. Being more material, the discussion is considerably simpler.

At the level of having, the goal is growth, but not of an unlimited kind; that is the difference between being and having. One may think in terms of economic and social growth, and long lists may be prepared of all the valuable commodities human beings should have—such as food, clothes, shelter, medication, schools, transportation, and communication—and what they might have—such as all the amenities of modern urban life. There is a minimum level of production and accumulation below which one cannot go, or anything said about "being" becomes meaningless because there is insufficient "having." But there is also a maximum level of growth, a limit to the process of turning raw materials into processed goods and distributing them, beyond which one also cannot go. The simple reasons have already been indicated. The external world as we know it, nature, is not like our mind; there are outer limits to growth because nature is a closed, finite system.[22] We human beings are already probing its perimeters in some places. We cannot populate, deplete, and pollute forever without irreversibly destroying our ecological basis. Nor can we exploit others and ourselves in the production process and go in for unlimited natural consumption without impairing ourselves, here meaning "our selves"; perhaps also irreversibly. The harm may come not only from the production process but also from the products, from all the things we accumulate—or we may become slaves of them. The day still has just twenty-four hours. If we shall enjoy all that humans have made, from parks and books and theater, to cars and boats and second houses, all the fruits of economic and social growth, what will happen to personal growth? There is a time budget to reckon with: human beings, like nature, have a limited absorption capacity.

Does this mean that we have a choice between "to be" and "to have," that the more we have, the less we are?[23] The problem is often stated in such terms. Consumption is seen as antithetical to contemplation. For Sorokin, this was the choice between an ideational and a sensate culture,[24] a culture based on personal, inner growth and a culture based on controlling nature. One can see the archetypes: on one end a Gandhi and very much "is" and very little "has," enriched and poor; on the other end some impoverished rich person who may remain anonymous, among other reasons because there is so little self to place a name-tag on. Or Koestler's yogi and commissar.[25] But this contradiction is too clear-cut; what Sorokin himself also envisages is an integrated, "idealistic" culture as a third possibility.[26]

The three goals defined so far—"personal growth," "diversity" and "socio-economic growth"—all have their special interpretations within classical liberal-ism, which is not strange because we see the actor-oriented perspective by and large as a generalization of liberal thinking. Under liberalism, personal growth becomes highly individualized, diversity is interpreted as cultural and political rather than structural pluralism, and socioeconomic growth is monetized and operationalized and ends up as per capita gross national product. Individual freedom and production become the pillars of society. The perspective is structure-blind, but emphasizes both being and having. That having may stand in the way of being was always seen as a problem. That having may also stand in the way of having, that there may be limits or ceilings on growth, is a more recent addition to the problem catalog.

Other problems of classical liberalism, however, received more attention, gradually paving the way for the social-democratic interpretation of liberalism. They are the problems of *inequality* and *injustice.* Under classical liberalism both being and having were seen as convertible into more having. What a person accumulated he could invest or pass on to his descendants; he did not have to consume it. External as well as internal being could be converted into having. The white Anglo-Saxon Protestant (WASP) male was accorded advantages that suffered some decline when these external characteristics became less dominant. But "talent," "initiative," "drive"—and later on "intelligence," operationalized into IQ and combined with endurance and conformity to produce examination results—were handsomely rewarded, and still are (leading to the successor of the aristocracy, the "degreeocracy").

In short, this type of society picked out the strong on external and internal being, the positive variants, gambled on them for converting what they had inside themselves into economic and social growth, hoping that some fruits of their endeavor would trickle down to the weak, the negative variants, so that some of the latter (but not too many) might some day pass the borderline and also become strong.[27] The result was socioeconomic growth and also glaring inequality and injustice. Untamed, rampant liberalism had to be tempered with regulatory devices, inspired by two more goals, also easily definable in terms of being and having: *equality* and *justice.* The first has to do with the dispersion of having, the second with the relation between having and being.

The goal of the dispersion of having is equality, or low dispersion on having. This should immediately be differentiated from social justice in the special sense of equality of opportunity, to be dealt with later. Equality as a lasting condition, equality of living, is much more than equality at a certain starting point. Nor should this value necessarily be taken in the mathematically strict sense of zero dispersion, with everybody having the same food, clothes/shelter, education, health, or the same disposable income, and so on. It can also be taken to mean that there should be a lower and an upper limit on having, a more or less narrow nonzero band within which individuals can place themselves. This formulation ties in with the idea of minimum and maximum growth, mentioned before, but not in a simple way. One can place a minimum and a maximum limit on production, yet have glaring disparities in the distribution of the products.

At the minimum end the relation between socioeconomic production and individual consumption is not problematic conceptually. A society may decide on a minimum provision for food, clothes/shelter, education, health, transportation and communication, in short a "living standard," in a minimum sense, as a birthright for any citizen. The goal for production or socioeconomic growth is found by multiplying this fundamental need by the number of persons. But that is not what is done in a market economy where production is demand-oriented rather than need-oriented, under the basic liberal assumption that needs will be converted into demands and that demands express needs.[28] The assumption of individual rationality and the view that social rationality is aggregated individual rationality only reveals the naivete of pure actor-oriented thinking. The social structure makes havoc with this, sending the fruits of labor upward and the bottom strata below satisfaction of fundamental needs.

At the maximum end the situation is even more problematic, for this is the end where decisions are usually made, and those on top have an understandable difficulty fixing a ceiling on their own expansion. Yet, this is a basic question. Does one have equality in an egalitarian country like Sweden when Wallenberg, the top Swedish capitalist, has the resources he commands, however well minimum demands may be satisfied for all Swedes? Many would say no, and they would also gladly see a ceiling (as in Eastern European countries) on the possession of durables (boats, cars, houses) and perhaps also on the consumption of nondurables.[29] This is not to mention a ceiling on the negative side, a limit on the amount of discomfort, focusing on an equal distribution of society's dirty work. And then, why not ask the same question for less tangible "haves"? Is there equality in a country where everybody has passed primary school, many secondary school, some tertiary school, and on top of this some very few have been given the chance of infinite differentiation, depth, and scope through continuous, lifelong, creative work at and beyond their own cultural frontiers?[30]

Is there equality in a country where all are above a high minimum health standard, yet some are super-healthy?

I raise these questions but am in no sense certain of the answer. In a society where stratification is based on what one "has" in terms of money, a program of income equality fixing a not-too-wide band (for instance, 2:1) seems to make sense. But what about a society where social stratification is based on schooling status? Is there no need for equality in that type of society—only a need for a floor, not for a ceiling, not for a limited range of variation? Again, I believe that the abstract way equality has been defined serves exactly my purpose: it raises a question not yet on the political agenda and can force us to question the social role of schooling, as I shall hereafter question the social role of intelligence.[31]

The whole equality approach raises another problem, however, of much more fundamental significance, relating to development strategy. I mentioned that building a society on diversity and growth alone has led to a strategy of investment in the strong combined with the assumption that there will be a "trickling down" to the weak. The strong are motivated to burst through any ceiling, any maximum, if not on personal consumption then at least in total production. In this process they will bring the weak with them, at least part of the way, and at least above a reasonable minimum. Such was, and is, the theory.

If instead we focus on the poor and the satisfaction of their fundamental needs, leaving the rich to their own devices, possibly even imposing a ceiling on them, we get another image of society and a completely different development strategy. The goal now becomes to strengthen the weak, to promote their uplift, first to a minimum, then to an increasing floor, bringing them toward an acceptable level of living. Instead of "investing" in the strong, those of good family, instead of giving loans to the rich and scholarships to the bright so that they may produce and in the process create jobs and opportunities for the less gifted, the focus would be on the weak, the underprivileged.[32]

But this should not be identified with treating the weak as ends rather than means. One can also "invest" in the weak, in the masses rather than the elite, with a view to liberating their creative energy for the benefit of, say, a class, a state, an ideology. A humanist concern and respect for the selves of the weak, the poor, the ultimate or last in society is not guaranteed with a reversed phasing of the development process.[33] One can start with growth, gambling on the strong, and later focus on distribution, according to a more or less strict norm of equality, as done in a welfare state. Or one can start with the weak, with production satisfying their fundamental needs, and then focus on further growth. But as long as there is somebody who "starts with" the weak, the process is only periphery-oriented, it is not periphery-generated.[34] That leads to problems of autonomy, not easily discussed within the actor-oriented perspective, but to be taken up later.

Left to itself, a liberal society will produce growth, perhaps even diversity, but it will not produce equality. Products will accumulate at some places, in some persons, more than elsewhere. Within this frame of thinking, a norm of equality can be fulfilled only through continuous individual redistribution or collective ownership (*res communis*), which changes the problem of equal distribution to one of equal access. For either method a relatively strong central authority is required, as it means taking from the rich and giving to the poor, as in progressive taxation or administration of collective ownership, ultimately leading to a welfare state.

In a sense, Scandinavian social democracy is a strange type of society. First, one makes a society that generates gross inequalities. Economic cycles are made in such a way that benefits accumulate at certain points, and not at others. Centers and peripheries are generated. Second, one says "This is too bad, we must redistribute and share." Obviously, the strong and the rich protest against this idea. They feel that they, not the structure, have produced the heaps of gold accumulating at their feet, and they make an alliance with the middle class for some, not much, redistribution.[35] The poor may demand more and applaud redistribution, not merely because it helps them but also because they enjoy what seems to hit the rich. This process then becomes institutionalized: products continue to accumulate and an enormous technocracy is needed to administer, process, and counterprocess. Redistribution becomes a veil draped over a body of basic inequality, and the solution of that contradiction cannot be provided within the actor-oriented perspective. Redistribution is important, but it is only a liberal answer to the problems of liberalism. It does not really touch the structure generating the inequalities.

Let us then turn to the relation between being and having: the goal here is social justice, which can be defined as little or no correlation at all between being and having. The goal is not that all shall have equally much—that was never the idea behind social justice. The goal is that what one "has" shall not depend on who one "is." Whites and blacks should have the same right to be "free," males and females the same right to be political citizens (e.g., to vote) and economic citizens (e.g., to sign a contract). Homosexuals (beings) should have the same right to sexual and social fulfillment (having) as heterosexuals. Which "is" and which "has" will vary from time to time, from region to region, but the formula of social justice is the same. "Social justice" should, incidentally, be distinguished from "justice" as a legal category, as implementation of human rights, among them "due process of law."[36]

A vast matrix of issues emerges from this program, depending on how many "is" characteristics and how many "has" characteristics are admitted for consideration under the banner of social justice. It can also extend to the collective level: the idea of a people being a nation, and each nation having the right to have a state, independent or within a federation. Or another example: the idea that each state has the right of access to sea, regardless of whether it is landlocked or not.

As a special case of social justice there is the idea of equality of opportunity, which is a justice concept, not an equality concept (in spite of the term).

It certainly does not mean equality of life. What one "is" shall not determine what one "has," this time in the more limited sense of "having access to," not in the sense of what one ends up having. Whites and blacks may perhaps not end up with the same amount of schooling but they shall have had the same educational opportunity, the same access. Men and women may perhaps not end up in equally challenging positions, but they shall have had the same access to the channels that led to them—and so on.

In increasingly education-oriented societies, equality of opportunity becomes more and more identical with equal educational opportunity.[37] Why? Because one basic "is" characteristic had escaped the program of social justice, the "is" characteristic that is counting most at school (despite all pious assurances to the contrary), and that is intelligence. Social philosophers, themselves presumably "intelligent," did not easily arrive at the idea of a low correlation between intelligence and where one ends up in society.

Social justice was directed against the idea that external ("ascribed") characteristics should decide which material and nonmaterial resources one ended up with. Internal characteristics, abilities and talents, should be given free play, unhampered by external constraints. Social justice, thus interpreted, was not intended to tame liberalism but to purify it; to rid it of the "internally weak, externally strong" who concealed their inability under a cover of family background, race, sex, and what not; to promote their "contradiction" to the "internally strong, externally weak."[38] Needless to say, the latter often favored this; they were mainly against a social darwinism that did not favor themselves by giving too much advantage to the already privileged.

Whatever one's philosophy of intelligence, however, it is hard to see why an IQ edge over fellow man (if such a thing exists) should entail privilege forever. If one believes most of it is transmitted through genes, then why should genes, the biological background from the parents, be given a decisive role and the social background of the parents not? Would this not be a relapse to biological determinism, to some type of neo-racism? If one believes differential intelligence to stem from nurture rather than nature, from environment rather than heredity, the matter becomes in a sense even worse. For this would beg the question of what kind of environment, or family, school, groups, work, society at large. If some structures, and particularly some positions in some structures promote higher IQ than others, for instance by being more challenging, why not try to equalize them rather than favor those who happened to get into the right box? Moreover, if the most stimulating structure happens to be in the families that are already high in society, would this not merely lead us back to the point of departure, a society structured by family background, albeit by biological transmission (genes) rather than by social inheritance (of titles, deeds, assets)?

Precisely because of this dilemma I prefer to keep "intelligence" and its correlates and collaterals on the agenda of social justice. If it is not yet on the political agenda, my guess is that it soon will be, and the hippie movement of the 1960s was perhaps the first clear pointer in that direction.

This is as far as the actor-oriented perspective brings us at this level of analysis, playing on being and having, on their growth and distribution and relation. In this perspective, society is an aggregate of individuals, and social goals can be expressed by studying the distribution of certain attributes among these individuals. This view leads to serious problems, of three kinds. First, there is the problem of compatibility. Can one have socioeconomic growth and at the same time personal growth, can one have equality and at the same time socioeconomic growth, and so on? Second, there is the problem of mystification or masking: social justice as a mask for inequality, equality of having as a mask for inequality of a much more basic kind, and so on. Third, there is the problem of analysis: society is a set of individuals, the distributions of being and having are important, and the values mentioned are significant. But society is also much more: it has structure, not only a distribution pattern, and that leads us to examine other values that may be equally, even more important.

2.3 STRUCTURE-ORIENTED GOALS

This is where the second basic perspective on human affairs enters, the structure-oriented view, with its actor-blindness. It does not necessarily deny any of the last four values mentioned: diversity, growth, equality, and social justice (including equality of opportunity), but is much less concerned with what an actor is and has. The view goes more deeply into society by asking one pertinent question: *why* is it that resources, all that an individual or collective actor has, tend to accumulate in such an unequal way? Answer: it is not because of any being-characteristic, although that may also enter into it, nor because a being–having relation has escaped our social justice filter and wrought injustice over the entire structure, but because actors are tied to each other in interaction relations and interaction patterns that in themselves serve to distribute resources in an inegalitarian manner.

Obviously, no social structure could survive if actors did not interact, that is, engage in exchange. A director and a worker are both meaningless in isolation, be they weak or strong in terms of any being and having dimension. It is the exchange relation that gives meaning to their position, an exchange of labor for salary. Exchange, as all agree, may be equal or unequal, and is often, perhaps usually, the latter. But it is not easy to arrive at a definition of equal/unequal exchange. For relations between countries this will be attempted at some length in chapter 4, and for relations between individuals some attempts will be made here (see also the appendix).

In general terms we have a case of equal exchange, or an equitable relation, if the interaction takes place in such a way that the changes in having and being of both actors as a result of the exchange between them can be said to be equal. The significance of emphasizing both having and being should be spelled out, for our definition of equity relates not only to accumulation but also to personal growth (national growth) on both sides. As an example, the director–worker relation may serve. How could that relation become equitable, horizontal? Let me start by rejecting some traditional liberal and Marxist answers.[39]

The liberal "answer" is usually in terms of equalization of many kinds of resources external to the production process itself: equal social security, equal access to health, to schooling, to vacation, even equal salary. Yet even though those things may be equalized, they do not touch the exchange relation in which individuals are engaged *qua* workers and *qua* directors. At best they are made equal *qua* citizens.

There is a next step: the equalization of health hazards and milieu factors, in general the standardization of working conditions from top to bottom in the factory or other work organization. This, however, only equalizes having, not being, in the work situation.

The Marxist answers go deeper, and they may or may not include these liberal thoughts. Generally, the "means of production" are seen as the basic resource, and equalization between director and worker means equalization in the ownership of the means of production, including the right to decide over surplus value. This can take several forms.

Under "macro-socialism," ownership (in the sense of decision making) is equalized by taking it away both from the workers and from the directors, handing it over to the "state" for remote control. In general this seems to stimulate socioeconomic growth and strong state-formation rather than the withering away of the state.

Under "micro-socialism" the opposite course is taken: Ownership is equalized through the introduction of industrial democracy, shared decision making at the local level. Although this is compatible with an ideology of decentralization and transfer of power to the workers, it also leads to problems. Thus, workers get absorbed at the local level and may become less able, through collective, nationwide action, to strike against the government for better conditions.[40] The state is weaker than under macro-socialism, but the workers may still be weaker. Moreover, how do their enterprises relate to each other in the absence of strong, central decision making? If macro-socialism leads to inequality between center and periphery, may it not also be argued that micro-socialism leads to the reintroduction of "free" market mechanisms at the macro level and disparities between enterprises? And will that not lead to macro-centers and macro-peripheries, however perfect the local site of production?

A solution, perhaps, is to be found in some (so far unknown) compromises between micro and macro-socialism. But like the liberal approach, this one still leaves much to be desired. The director is still a director, the worker still a worker, although under micro-socialism their roles may have been brought closer together. So, imagine that the liberal and the two Marxist suggestions have all been carried out; what source of inequality would still remain?

Perhaps the most important one after fundamental needs have been satisfied: the difference in being, in the potential for personal growth. More concretely, I am thinking of the differential amount of challenge inherent in the two jobs. Whereas every telephone call reaching the director contains an element of something new, an uncertainty that has to be reduced and overcome through (often instant) decision making, the worker carries out a routine job with minimum uncertainty. He does not have to stand by an assembly line to have a routine job; Chaplin thwarted our perspective at that point.[41] Most job descriptions in the world for anyone working for fixed salaries or wages (indeed including most white-collar jobs) are prescriptions of routines, regulated by standard operating procedures. To be a proletarian is not only to sell one's labor force, it is also to work without uncertainty and challenge, to pass one's working hours in boring, meaningless activity.[42] For meaning is linked to uncertainty, to choice—and that uncertainty has been reduced by those higher up who have already made the basic decisions. This does not mean that the job cannot be difficult, only that the difficulties are always the same. The job, after some time, becomes boring, *personality-contracting* rather than *personality-expanding,* as a job is for the person who frequently encounters nonroutine situations.

So, what I argue is that there is no equity before there is a better sharing of personality-expanding work, of the right to have work leading to personal growth. Regardless of how many of the having dimensions are equalized, there is still inequity or exploitation as long as this nonmaterial, internal effect is so different on either side of the interaction relation. The basic point is that inequity is built into the relation so that the relation has to be changed, in ways to be discussed. Redistribution will do if equality of having is the goal. If equity is the goal, a change in the structure itself is needed, to get rid of the unequal accumulation of being.

Hence, the first goal to be formulated within the structure-oriented perspective would be *equity:* the equal net benefit on either side of an interaction relation, in having (accumulation) as well as being (personal growth). Equity is seen as a more fundamental goal than equality, and not only because inequity may cause inequality, just as an unequal distribution of resources may lay the basis for a relation of inequity. The *rule of equity* would say that whatever inequality there is in a society shall not come about as a result of the interaction structure itself. The rule does not say that there shall be no inequality. In contrast, it may be argued that the *rule of equality* presupposes a similarity in needs, so much so that it is tantamount to an assumption of uniformity.[43] The rule of equity is a rule against exploitation; it rules out interaction relations that lead to uneven external and internal benefits. Thus, it rules out a broader concept of exploitation than usually found, exploitation not only in the sense of something expropriated from the exploited and appropriated by the exploiter, but also in the sense of what goes on within the actors on either side of the relation. In Marxist thinking, the concepts of surplus value and of alienation point in both these directions, but the Marxist theory of exploitation focuses more on what goes on between than within the actors. Exploitation usually means that something is taken from someone else, not that the numerous spin-off effects generated within each actor are highly unequal.

Equity can be expressed as horizontal division of labor, that what is done on either side of the interaction relation leads by and large to the same net internal and external benefit. Exploitation would be expressed as vertical division of labor, that there are major differences in the total effects on either side. This raises the general problem of how exploitation can be reduced. I have mentioned two ways that do *not* lead to this goal: collective ownership with equal access, including collective ownership of the means of production as a special case, and redistribution. These measures do not go deeply enough into the interaction structure. To go more deeply there seem to be two other methods available at present: work rotation and work reconstruction.

Briefly stated: under work *rotation* the director and the worker change positions, leaving the relation more or less as it was, for instance every other month or every other week. It is done on the assumption that this equalizes the effects over time—not for the positions, but for the persons. Under work *reconstruction* the equalization takes place for the positions: the work done by the director and by the worker is made more similar. Everybody participates in decision making, everybody does all kinds of work, and so on.[44]

Thus, there is no doubt that equity goes deeper than equality as it affects structure and not only distribution. But it is also clearly the more difficult goal to achieve, particularly because our present society is so heavily dominated by exploitative, vertical division of labor, leading to a broad spectrum of professional–client relations, particularly in the form of professionalization. In a more equitable society, inequality would be an expression of diversity. If some want more and some want less, they should not be forced to have less or more than they want. But the distribution should not be an automatic consequence of their interaction, there should be interaction-equality, if not necessarily distribution-equality, to put it that way.

Let us now turn to the second aspect of the interaction relation: here the goal I want to conceptualize is *autonomy*. It differs from personal growth in being a structural characteristic. Autonomy is a relation, personal growth is a quality. One is autonomous relative to somebody or something; one is an enriched person by and for oneself. One is autonomous *of*—but the question is what that means. I conceive of autonomy as a value for the power aspect of an interaction relation, just as equity is a value for the exchange aspect. Hence, what is needed is a discussion of power.

Any interaction relation is a channel in which power may flow, from a sender to a receiver, and inequitable interaction is one way of gaining one type of power-over-others. That does not mean that equity is the only approach to countervailing power. If the relation is equitable, then power components will accumulate about equally on either side of the relation. The net result would be some kind of balance of power—in economic assets, in political, military, cultural and communicational "goods." This is not autonomy, although it is often confused with autonomy.

Autonomy is here seen as power-over-oneself so as to be able to withstand what others might have of power-over-others. I use the distinction between ideological, remunerative and punitive power, depending on whether the influence is based on internal, positive external, or negative external sanctions.[45] Autonomy, then, is the degree of "inoculation" against these forms of power. These forms of power, exerted by means of ideas, carrots and sticks, can work only if the power receiver really receives the pressure, which presupposes a certain degree of submissiveness, dependency, and fear, respectively. Their antidotes are self-respect, self-sufficiency, and fearlessness. These are, then, the three components of autonomy as conceived of here, one for each component of power.

Obviously, these qualities are relational and therefore belong within the structural perspective. No actor, individual or collective, is autonomous in a social vacuum; autonomy is meaningful only relative to a given social context. In this context, "self-respect" can be defined as "confidence in one's own ideas and ability to set one's own goals," "self-sufficiency" as "the possibility of pursuing them with one's own means," and "fearlessness" as "the possibility of persisting despite threats of destruction." Concretely, autonomy is important in a world where the social context and the powerful define goals for others, where goal satisfaction depends on supplies from others, and where destruction at the hands of others is always an open possibility.

The concept is fundamental today. Gandhi talked about doing-oneself, *swadeshi,*[46] Mao Tse-tung about "regeneration through our own efforts," *tzu li keng sheng;*[47] and the Democratic People's Republic of Korea's Kim Il Sung uses the *juche*[48] idea in the same way. All over the world there is much talk about self-reliance. Although there are important nuances in these expressions, they all belong, one way or another, to the autonomy family.

Autonomy does not mean isolation, nor does it mean equity. Autonomy may mean that one can be self-sufficient any moment one wants, not that one *de facto* is self-sufficient in a given moment. The opposite is penetration, meaning that the outside has penetrated into one's self to the extent of creating submissiveness to ideas, dependency on "goods" from the outside, and fear of the outside in terms of "bads."

Equity and autonomy relate to the interaction *relation*. Let us then move on to the problem of interaction *pattern*. A social structure generally links together more than only two actors; suppose now it links together three. It makes a lot of difference whether they are linked together in asymmetric or symmetric patterns, as shown in figure 2.3. On the left-hand side there is clear asymmetry: one of the three actors is central, the other two are peripheral in the pattern. This is the basic structure, which does not disappear if one adds multilateral interaction (where they all meet) or even an organization (the same with more permanency). There is still asymmetry. It can be done away with only by opening the interaction channel between the two peripheries, as on the right-hand side. This is important: it is the difference between a situation wherein subordinates never meet and one wherein they meet, an empire where colonies never interact directly and one where they do, a school in which

Figure 2.3   Two types of interaction patterns

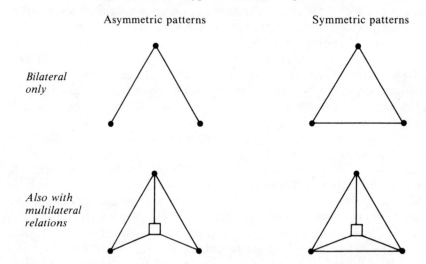

students never interact with each other without teacher presence and one in which they do relate to each other without teacher presence, and so on. Much more concrete illustrations will be given in chapter 4.

Using the four patterns in figure 2.3 one can envisage a transition from the simplest one in the upper left-hand corner through the figure, ending with the saturated, integrated, more complex pattern in the lower right-hand corner (as a result of making the pattern symmetric and adding multilateral interaction). This can also be seen as a transition from a more primitive to a more complex, even advanced interaction pattern. In addition to the focus on complexity there is the problem of verticality: which position, high or low, is likely to be in the center of a pattern?

An indication is given in figure 2.4, where the arrows stand for the direction of exploitation (inequity). The figure illustrates one of the more solid rules of interaction patterns: *The higher in the vertical division of labor, the more central in the interaction pattern.* Thus, there is a horizontal relation at the top, but only one at the bottom where there could be six. Similarly, there is a multilateral relation at the top, and also one at the bottom, but only one, and there is none spanning all three levels.

These reflections give rise to two important values: *solidarity* and *participation.* The opposite of solidarity is *fragmentation,* the situation obtained when two positions are split from each other and tied vertically to the same position: the classical situation of *divide et impera.* The opposite of participation is *marginality,* which is what is obtained when some are integrated in a multilateral relation and others are not, are outside, structurally defined as second class. Solidarity is thus the extent of direct relation at the bottom of a vertical division of labor,[49] and participation the extent of integration into multilateral relations.

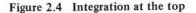

Figure 2.4   Integration at the top

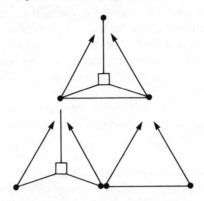

One does not presuppose the other. There can be solidarity, direct interaction at the bottom, without any multilateral participation, and there can be multilateral participation without any solidarity—both cases are illustrated at the bottom of figure 2.4. But in general the marginalized are at the bottom of vertical division of labor, of the extended, exploitative economic cycles, or are even kept outside them, isolated.[50]

Let this suffice. By going into more complex aspects of a social structure one could always develop new goal dimensions, but simplicity would then be lost. Just as the discussion of actor-oriented goals was based on two simple ideas—the being/having and the level/dispersion distinctions—this discussion of the structure-oriented goals has been based on another pair of simple ideas, the relation/pattern and the bilateral/multilateral distinctions. The time has now come to tie all of this together.

2.4   TOWARD A SYNTHESIS: ON POWER AND DEVELOPMENT, ON VIOLENCE AND PEACE

On the one hand I have tried to see social reality in two ways: as a set of actors (which at the level of individual human beings means a set of persons) and as a structure. The persons have bodies and souls, the structures have relations and patterns. Society is neither simply a collection of persons nor simply a structure. But there are more than merely two perceptions, *für mich.* I also conceive of them *an sich,* as two dialectically related aspects. By this overused term I mean that in any concrete situation both aspects are present, and neither can be neglected. The more one aspect is permitted to dominate social reality, the more the neglected aspect will become salient. Concretely, the more a society plays on the actor-oriented perspective to the neglect of structural factors, the more these factors will make themselves felt. By contrast, the more a society makes basic structural changes without any consideration for personal richness and diversity, the more the latter factors will make themselves felt. This is not a question of a pendulum oscillating, for each move brings about a new reality—the pendulum never comes back to the same place. Nor is it a question of stopping the pendulum in the middle, in some kind of eclectic mixture. There is no middle position. Like the mixing of oil and water, eclecticism is only a transitory phase among many. It is a question of transcendence, creating new forms of social existence.

To examine this, let us reconsider the nine values shown in figure 2.5 that, together with *ecological balance,* constitute our ten world goals. The antonyms shown in the figure, most of them already presented in the text, are intended to steer one's thinking in some directions that are developed further in the appendix, where an effort is made to operationalize these value-dimensions.

In accordance with the programmatic statements in chapter 1, the dimensions are seen equally as dimensions for data collection, theory formation, and value-realization. In other words, this is more than a list of values, playing on some famous words from the history of (particularly Western) civilization. It is also an effort to escape from the current schizophrenia in social analysis whereby different families of terms and concepts are drawn upon for those three aspects of scientific activity.

I now want to integrate these dimensions, to get the beginnings of a theory of society. In this section I shall put them together to develop further the concepts of power and development, conflict and peace. I shall also try to show how intimately connected these concepts are and how they are all tied to the value-basis developed.

What is *power?* I have mentioned something about types of power, in connection with the definition of autonomy. Power could be normative, based on persuasion; be remunerative, based on bargaining (*quid pro quo, do ut des*); or be punitive, based on force, single or combined. For power to function—which means for power to affect action, to be the cause of some effect—there

Figure 2.5   A survey of world goals, with antonyms

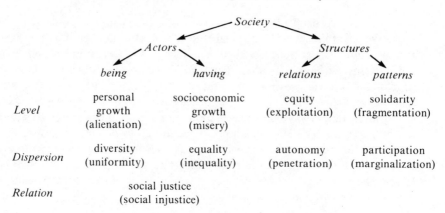

must be a power sender and a power receiver, for power is a relation, not a property or an attribute of somebody or something. Power has to flow to be effective, it has to be a current, not only a potential—and the power receiver has to have some mechanism of reception. As already argued, for persuasion to work, there has to be an element of submissiveness; for bargaining to work, some kind of dependency; and for force to work, an element of fear. That points immediately to two kinds of countervailing power: the *balance approach* and the *autonomy approach.*[51] Under the former, the power receiver has the same *resources* for persuasion, bargaining, and force at his disposal and can turn them the other way. Under the second formula he refuses to receive, by developing autonomy or power-over-himself: self-respect, self-sufficiency, and fearlessness. He inoculates himself against power-over-others from the outside; as he refuses to be a power receiver, power cannot reach him. This is what in Latin America is referred to as *dignidad,* and other places as a sense of identity—different ways of saying "self-respect." This is the basic power ingredient behind the great Asian revolutions of our time, associated with the names of Gandhi and Mao—the poor man's power, Asian power, human power.[52]

But this does not give us a theory of the sources of power, only a theory of how power works if it works. More significantly, it is not a theory that enables me to discuss or present solutions to what I see as the fundamental problem studied in political science: *the problem of power distribution.* For this purpose, power has to be studied at its source and not at the point of impact. This can be done very simply by using the value-dimensions.

More particularly, three types of power need to be distinguished:

1. *Innate power* (being-power)   actor-oriented
2. *Resource power* (having-power)   actor-oriented
3. *Structural power* (position-power)   structure-oriented

A person's being-power may be a commanding personality, a charisma that serves as a basis for ideological influence. Or, it may simply be that one person *is* more muscular or more brainy than another, and is hence more able to use bargaining and force to his advantage. This should be distinguished from a person who *has* a gun and hence commands the type of power said to come out of its barrel; or the person who has many commodities to throw into a bargain. Then, there is structural power. A person may not have any accumulated power resources at all but may simply be located at the top of an exploitation and penetration relation; he can expend the surplus generated continuously to exercise influence. If at the same time he is at the center of a network of bilateral and multilateral interaction relations, he will possess more information and command more information channels than anyone else.

Mutatis mutandis, all this can also be said about countries, although the distinction between being-power and having-power becomes artificial—they may both be referred to as resource power. Structural power for countries will be the major topic of chapter 4, under the heading of dominance and imperialism.

What happens when all these types of power are combined, and particularly when inequity (structural) and inequality (resources) are combined? Imagine a structure in which the positions central in the interaction pattern are also on top of exploitation and penetration relations. Further, imagine that actors high in being-power are also high in having-power, that there is both inequality and social injustice, in other words. And then, to top it all, make those who are high in resource power also high in structural power by putting them in central positions. *Do all that, and we get a not too unrealistic picture of the world.* In the diagrammatic form it looks something like figure 2.6.

Here we have it all: inequality, injustice, exploitation, penetration, fragmentation, marginalization. Why does the social order so easily come out like this? Simply because one type of power is convertible to another: structural power into accumulation of resources, resource power into sufficient command of the structure to get into positions of structural power, and so on. The structure-oriented analyst would usually see structural power (referred to as exploitation) as primary in this process, differentials in resource power as a consequence, and differences in innate power as a propaganda figure, as a rationalization. The actor-oriented analyst would have the opposite view: basic are innate power, strength, and superiority, which then convert into the others, according to the theories of social darwinism.[53]

In short, power or power differential is based on the negation of six of our values: on inequality, injustice, exploitation, penetration, fragmentation and marginalization. For "power" to be "power-over-others" it is not enough that somebody be high in innate power or resource power or both. Somebody else has to be low on them; there has to be inequality in the distribution of resources. Along this power gradient, influence—of the ideological, remunerative and punitive kinds—flows down to the poor periphery at the bottom of it all. No wonder the power elite can be small and the masses numerous, if the difference in power potential can be so tremendous and the gradient so steep.[54]

We can now reap an important theoretical harvest from our explorations so far: *to work for the realization of these six values is to work for a reduction of*

Figure 2.6   The sources of power combined

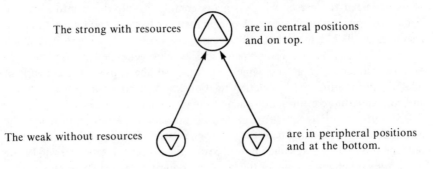

The strong with resources   are in central positions
                                   and on top.

The weak without resources   are in peripheral positions
                                     and at the bottom.

the power differential. By making interaction patterns more symmetric and interaction relations more horizontal, by narrowing the band between high and low, by reducing the correlation between being and having, what one does in fact is to eliminate power differentials. This makes for a power landscape with a very flat gradient except for one factor: realization of the last six values may lead to increased dispersion of being, to increased diversity, in other words, because there is less dominance. Hence, if there is such a thing as innate power it would still have free play.

Let us now define "development," very simply: a society develops to the extent it realizes all (ten) values. Development, consequently, is not the opposite of power but the opposite of unequal power: *development implies reduction of power differentials.* Or, expressed in another way: if the first dimension in figure 2.5 is *personal growth* and the second is *socioeconomic growth,* then the last seven could be called *social growth,* meaning increased diversity plus equalization of power. This is, in my view, a more fortunate way of defining "social growth" than in terms of institution building, not to mention parochial efforts to define "political growth" in terms of proximity to Western-type democracy, whether of the presidential or parliamentary varieties. The definition leaves the concrete institutional form open, as concrete institutions will no doubt have to respond to special conditions that vary with time and space. To what extent specific institutions serve these goals is an empirical question that cannot be answered on theoretical grounds alone; practice and data are needed.

But this does not mean that I see social growth as something leading to a state of *powerlessness.* Would not that be somehow antipolitical, like politics bringing about its own negation? The withering away of power? No, this is not a model of powerlessness, but of some type of *multidimensional power balance,* where several sources of power, not only means of destruction, are more evenly distributed. In a sense this is classical balance-of-power philosophy in an expanded version and shares its strengths and weaknesses. If balance of power in the military sense could be institutionalized and kept either static or dynamic (but at a slow, predictable pace without surprising, qualitative jumps), then some type of freedom from fear (of being dominated) would be the result. This is a big "if." We know that balance of military power tends not to stabilize but to lead to escalating arms races and all of the things that will be discussed in chapter 5. Why should that not also apply to the balance of ideas in the idea market and to the balance of commodities, of "goods," in the economic market?

To this, one may retort that one reason that military balance tends to be unstable is the superficial power analysis underlying it.[55] This analysis equates power with the means of destruction only, in the typical violence-oriented manner of certain Western analysts, and fails to see how other types of power may be extremely unbalanced and extremely effective, operating under the guise of a modicum of military equality. The weaker party in these other types of power may feel tempted to compensate by getting an edge in means of destruction; that leads, in turn, to efforts to catch up militarily, and the result is an arms race. A considerable portion of analytical naiveté is needed to believe that military parity is the same as balance of power.

Nor do I want to add to that naiveté by claiming that my dimensions have captured all there is, although I do claim that they have captured more than typical military analysis manages to capture. How much can only be seen by coming closer to the point where the six values are realized. *The hypothesis would be that at the point where "power-over-others" is somehow neutralized (by reducing inequality, injustice, exploitation and the like), "power-over-one-self" would continue growing.* Thus, instead of conceiving of power in a zero-sum way, such that either *A* has power over *B* or *B* has power over *A,* power should be conceived of as a positive-sum entity. *A* can have increasing power-over-himself, and *B* can have increasing power-over-himself. This is exactly the type of power referred to as autonomy.

I do not assume that "power-over-others" has to decrease to zero for "power-over-oneself" to start growing. The two are interdependent, however. The underdog is the object of somebody else's power; the point of gravity for decisions affecting himself is somewhere outside himself, and even his image of himself is the internalization of the image the power holder has of him. As to the topdog: much of his energy goes into the manipulation of others, by various means, using the power sources at his command. He is also displaced away from himself in his drive for power. Even for him, "power-over-others" may stand in the way of "power-over-oneself."[56] The liberation of the underdog from the domination by the topdog is at the same time the liberation of the topdog from the process of domination.

This brings us back to the problem of innate power. With all other types of power neutralized, innate power remains, which is the reason that this type of political program would not lead to a power-flat society. There will be diverse .personalities, as well as diverse societies, with varying appeal. Their power will be normative, or "moral," as they will not have a resource surplus or structural advantages at their disposal to back it up. Actually, this is not so farfetched as it may sound: it is already largely the case in many places, particularly at the top of the world, in countless meetings and committee rooms and other forms of social encounters where ability to project what is inside a person is what counts. It is true to a considerable degree among Nordic countries, and to some extent among the European Community countries.

Let us now proceed with the concepts of *violence* and *peace.* If development is to build, then violence is to destroy; hence violence is antidevelopment. If peace is the opposite of violence, then peace must have much in common with development. Hence, power (over others) and violence are on one side, and development and peace on the other. But the word-pair "violence"/"peace" brings a different perspective into what has been said so far: the opposite of the opposite does not yield exact identity. These concepts are not redundant, although two concepts may be close to each other.

I define violence as *any avoidable impediment to self-realization.*[57] As the negation of any one of the values implies an impediment of somebody's self-realization, violence is antidevelopment. I have also added the criterion that it should be avoidable. A life expectancy of only thirty years during the neolithic period was not an expression of violence, but the same life expectancy today (whether due to wars, inequality, social injustice, or all of them) would be violence according to our definition. Correspondingly, the case of people dying from earthquakes today would not necessarily warrant an analysis in terms of violence, but the day after tomorrow, if earthquakes become avoidable, such deaths may be seen as violence. If an earthquake, a flood, or a cyclone today kills poor people whose lives could have been saved if the resources of that society had been used to build stronger houses, dams or other protective devices rather than power and status symbols for the strong, then it is man, not nature, that has been violent.

Similarly, if there were reasons to believe that inequality, injustice, exploitation, penetration, fragmentation, and marginalization were something given by nature, something forever beyond the power of man to counteract, then I would not speak of violence.[58] I would go even further. If it could be ascertained that man is by nature "aggressive," that there is an irresistible inner drive, like the hunger drive, that compels him to kill, then only killing above and beyond the demands of the drive would be characterized as violence. If man were irrevocably given to dominance and to aggression, then much of my discussion of violence would be pointless. But there is no convincing proof of either proposition, a point discussed hereafter.

Violence, then, is anything avoidable that impedes personal growth. It may take the form of infliction of "bads," which is what one usually thinks of in connection with violence. But it may equally well take the form of deprivation of goods. Since "personal growth" has been defined as something applying to body as well as to self, to soma and psyche (to avoid the Christian bias of seeing soul as finer than body), "deprival of goods" may mean avoidable denial of what is needed to satisfy the fundamental needs. This is the major theme still, today, of developing countries and of many regions within the so-called developed world. The world is still in that primitive stage of development. But deprival of goods also relates to the inner development, above and beyond the satisfaction of fundamental needs. To deprive people of cultural stimuli or to create societies, however rich, with a division of labor that forces people to stay in the same profession for life are forms of violence.

The major distinction, however, is not between violence as infliction of bads or deprival of goods but between person-to-person violence and structure-to-person violence. They can be referred to as *personal* and *structural* violence, or as direct and indirect violence, respectively. They are violence as conceived of within the actor-oriented and the structure-oriented perspectives, respectively. According to the former, violence is something one actor does to others; according to the latter, violence is built into the structure. Because the exercise of violence and the exercise of power are strongly related, direct violence is based on the use of resource power, structural violence on the use of structural power. Structural violence "just happens" without any specific actor behind it. The slum child, brain-damaged for life because of protein deficiency, who will have a self-realization level far below any reasonably defined potential, is not necessarily the "object" of any evil will of any particular "subject" who has committed the violence. The violence is built into the structure, usually derived from some fundamental inequity that then generates, and is reinforced by, inequality and injustice. It is invariant of actor substitution; like a body, it persists even when all persons (atoms) have been exchanged for new ones.

The distinction between direct and structural violence is not a sharp one. [59] The two may be causally related, and they may be dialectically related. The distinction is important, however, because it extends our perspective on violence, adding to violence-as-action the idea of violence-as-structure. Typically, most thinking about violence has taken place within the actor-oriented perspective, with the focus on violent persons (or countries), not on violent structures, not even on the victims. The cause of violence has been found in a person's evil intentions or in the pathology of his body (or in a country with a violent ideology or a sick social body), not in the structure tying persons or countries together. The Problem of Evil, as mentioned, is seen as a problem of evil actors. What the concept of structural violence does is to focus at least equal attention on the problem of wrong structures. In itself, there is nothing new in focusing on structures; that is as old as the analysis of politics. What is important here is the broader concept of violence; a victim-oriented concept of a violence that generally works slowly and does not presuppose intention. Sometimes it works quickly, though, as in structurally induced traffic accidents; and slow violence can also be intended, as in the case of torture or a siege.

This extended perspective is an almost immediate consequence of adopting the vantage point of the object, the victim, rather than the subject, the perpetrator of violence. From the victim's angle it does not make much difference whether starvation is the result of a military siege or the outcome of injust, unequal, and/or vertical and asymmetric structures. Nor does it make much difference whether one is killed instantaneously by a bullet or slowly by malnutrition. The moment of death remains a moment of extinction, regardless of how healthy or ill one was in the preceding moment. When people have life—i.e., years of living—taken away from them, and this is avoidable, violence is operating, regardless of whether this is the consequence of an actor using innate and resource power or the structural power built into a maldeveloped structure. By using the structure-oriented perspective on violence, the category of structural violence falls like a ripe fruit into our conceptual basket. But what about *peace*?

To fight for peace is to fight against violence, which may be split into two types: the struggle against direct violence, particularly in the form of war—which may be called the quest for security—and the struggle against structural violence, against dominance—which may be called the struggle for liberation. That leads straight to the problem of countervailing violence: do we have to fight "the war to end all wars" (and get security), and do we have to establish the final dominance to end all dominance (and get liberation) as we were told in earlier parts of this century (1914 and 1917, respectively)? This is the big question, and I am not going to adopt any absolutist, dogmatic stand. But let us try to explore it in the light of the ideas brought forward so far, returning to figure 2.6.

The situation depicted in this figure is extreme, and it calls for measures that can bring about basic structural change quickly, which is another way of saying "revolution." Most people would probably agree that rotation of the actors filling the positions is not a revolution because it does not affect the structure. If the rotation takes place among existing topdogs, it is merely a "circulation of elites," even when it happens quickly, in the dramatized and telescoped form referred to as a *coup*. After that the *Knecht* is still a *Knecht*, even if he now has a new *Herr*.

But what if *Knecht and Herr* change positions, establishing a "dictatorship of the proletariat?" Would that not be a revolution? Not according to our definition. In this case there is a new *Herr* and also a new *Knecht*. But the structure is the same, hence there has been no revolution, although what happened may be a means toward a revolution.

What if social justice and equality were obtained, partly by redistribution bringing minima and maxima closer together and partly through collective ownership, at the macro and micro levels? No doubt this is vital, but I would still call such a change an example of "reformism." The basic structure of inequitable relations and fragmenting patterns has not been touched; hence, there has been no revolution. If one is satisfied with the fruits of redistribution and collective ownership, then one may leave it at that. But the arguments against a society that combines exploitation with such measures still seem valid: it is a wasteful society, one that will stifle personal growth and diversity in the quest to compensate for imbalances with new imbalances. I would argue that the search for a less irrational and maldeveloped society has to continue, and that involves basic structural change.

Whether basic structural change should be quick (revolution) or slow (evolution) depends on how extreme the structural violence leading to absolute and relative deprivation is, and on what is more instrumental in bringing about the basic change. The first question is more easily answered than the second, as the first can be answered in terms of data and values, the second only in terms of theory and values. That the structural situation, within and between countries, and particularly in the combination of the two known as imperialism, is extreme enough is hardly to be doubted. But whether a revolution is really instrumental in changing the structure is another matter, to be decided through practice and experience and not through dogma or the sloppy semantics of many "progressive" people or countries who by "revolution" mainly mean a new dominance structure with themselves on top, accompanied by some measures of redistribution, collectivization, and central planning. Moreover, revolution/evolution tends to be a false dilemma because it does not reflect the possibility of having hundreds or thousands of micro revolutions at local levels, in factories, firms, and farms, in families, to gain experience. Recent years have witnessed very many examples of this, and no doubt the trend will continue.

Let me here also point out that the failure to understand structural violence leads to a corresponding failure to discriminate between types of direct violence. More precisely, one should distinguish among four types of direct violence:

1. *Progressive (revolutionary) violence*—violence directed against structural violence, counterviolence. This is *vertical violence from below,* in the interest of no longer being exploited.
2. *Reactionary (counterrevolutionary) violence*—violence directed against progressive violence. This is *vertical violence from above,* in the interest of serving exploitation.
3. *Horizontal violence*—between equals in the sense that neither dominates the other; over some incompatible goals.
4. *Random violence*—violence that is related neither to interests nor to goals.

A general stand against direct violence, implicit in my list of values, should not lead to the type of abstract blindness (found in idealistic pacifism) where no distinction whatsoever is made between the types of direct violence. Thus, the first type clearly differs from the others because it is defensive, and I would agree with Gandhi in preferring progressive violence to apathy, as I interpret him to mean in some of his oft-repeated sayings.[60] And that also applies to direct violence used to fight against efforts to establish structural violence, e.g., through occupation.

The distinction is important because it is connected with the definition of "aggression" and "aggressor." Overemphasizing the actor-oriented view leads to defining the aggressor as "he who throws the first stone," i.e., initiates direct violence. This is a view in the interest of the actor who has been wielding structural violence all along, and who in addition has used his power to penetrate society with a doctrine according to which the underdog who tries to defend himself with direct counterviolence is branded an aggressor. In saying this, no general view against such concepts as "law and order" and "stability" is expressed. It all depends on what kind of structure is kept stable by this law and order, one of dominance or one of equality. Nor is there any stand against the idea that aggression has to do with violence, only that the concept should include "establishing and maintaining structural violence," not only "initiating direct violence." Economic aggression, for instance, can be defined as the systematic application of exploitation, penetration, fragmentation, and marginalization in international economic relations. Thus, it is not an event, it is a structure,[61] and as such it is not readily understood within an actor-oriented world view.

Table 2.1 Relation between the goals and the concepts

CONCEPTS	Personal growth	Socio-economic growth	Diversity	Equality	Justice	Equity	Autonomy	Solidarity	Participation
					GOALS				
Development	Personal growth	Socio-economic growth	←			Social growth			→
Power	Innate power	Resource power	←			Structural power			→
Violence	Direct violence to persons	Direct violence to things	←			Structural violence			→
Peace	Security	Security	←			Liberation			→

A short summary showing the relation between the goals and the concepts of development and power (from international relations in general) and violence and peace (from peace research) might now be appropriate. Table 2.1 shows my complete analysis in condensed form. To the reader who feels this has been in excess of what he is willing to put up with in the way of concepts, I can only say that anyone who tries to say something about our poor world needs at least that much. What I have tried to do is to develop these concepts systematically from fundamental notions and to show ways in which they are related. The *goals* are independent of each other, which does not mean that they are all equally important in any concrete situation. But the four concepts are not independent of each other; they are related through the way in which they combine the values positively (development and peace) and negatively (power and violence).

The nine goals in table 2.1 are custom-made to give substance to the broad notion of "development," implying development of all nine, not only socioeconomic development. The constructivist perspective engendered by the positively formulated values leads one's thinking automatically toward development. Then, power, in the sense of "power-over-others," is seen as antithetical to development as an end—which of course is not the same as saying that it is not needed as a means to achieve development. The goal of development is a society where power takes the form of power-over-oneself, autonomy. Violence is seen as a special type of destructive power, exercised by persons or by the structure, over persons or things (or both), by inflicting "bads" or denying "goods." Peace is seen as the negation of violence, as a society where neither direct nor structural violence is exercised. Obviously, such a society is also a developed society. Thus, "peace" and "development" become two ways of saying the same thing, with different emphasis rather than different conceptualization into, for example, the so-called North–South and East–West conflicts. The oneness of the world should also be reflected conceptually, avoiding a development language for one and peace language for the other. They are two sides of the same coin—a theme to be developed much further in the next three chapters.[62]

NOTES

References to *Essays* are to Johan Galtung, *Essays in Peace Research,* 5 vols. (Copenhagen: Ejlers, 1975–80) (Atlantic Highlands, N.J.: Humanities Press).

1. Of course, there are any number of "basic perspectives"; the conceptual cake can be cut many ways, and not necessarily in only two parts. It should be noted that both perspectives deal with "outer man"—with man in a social setting, and not with inner man, man for himself, or transcendental man— and that in so doing both are relatively Western perspectives. However, they are not necessarily static. Both can be seen as process-oriented, dynamic views, but they are clearly views of the social totality rather than views of man, and as such they are intended. The concept of "being," to be developed in later pages, leads more in the direction of inner man.

2. This definition is developed in some detail in Galtung, "Two Ways of Being Western: Some Similarities between Liberalism and Marxism," Trends in Western Civilization Program (Chair in Conflict and Peace Research, University of Oslo), where the Westernness of these two perspectives is also analyzed in some detail. In the present book that bias is openly admitted, with some efforts in section 9.4 to escape from it. On the other hand, it may be argued that in the present age of Western dominance of the world these are perspectives shared by many and that non-Western perspectives should preferably come from non-Westerners. For an effort to distinguish between Western and Chinese Marxism, for instance, see Galtung and Fumiko Nishimura, *Learning from the Chinese People* (Oslo, 1975), chap. 2.

3. The word "shares" is to be taken in a broad sense. In an ideal liberal society the shares need not be equal; the focus is more on avoidance of monopoly/oligopoly in all four markets and on concrete mechanisms, even institutions, whereby that can be avoided. This includes the right to establish new enterprises, new parties, new ideas and forms of culture, and new foci of power. In the last case, the theory goes more in the direction of equal shares known as balance of power.

4. The idea is simple: given a limited resource and unlimited access to it, it will be depleted, e.g., by sheep grazing on the common. The point is, of course, that acts of individual abstention from resource depletion will only permit others to get more and are thus insufficient as causes of change. The normative approach has to be combined with rewards for abstention and punishment for transgression—some type of institution building, although not necessarily a higher level of organization. A multilateral agreement with no powerful center *may* also serve, although experience (with whaling and with fisheries in general, to mention two international commons) seems to indicate that such agreements do not generate sufficient normative, remunerative, and punitive momentum. Hence an argument for a world central authority to manage Spaceship Earth, a theme to be developed in section 8.1.

5. The "atom-oriented" would see CCl_4 and BF_4 as different, but the "structure-oriented" may not; whereas the former would see all (isomeric) compounds with the formula $C_8 H_{18}$ as similar, the latter certainly would not.

6. But these are only some examples of the theoretical derivatives from this distinction. From this basic division two very different theories of conflict will flow—one a conflict of goals and the other a conflict of values—as developed in Galtung, *Theories of Conflict* (forthcoming).

7. Mathematicians handle events as step-functions of time, which is useful in order to compare them to other types of function. See section 1.2.

8. A typology of variables is given in Galtung, "A Generalized Methodology for the Social Sciences," chapter 9 in *Methodology and Ideology* (Copenhagen: Ejlers, 1977). The "permanent" is the extreme opposite of the event.

9. This is a basic point in Galtung and Ruge, "The Structure of Foreign News," *Essays* IV, 4.

10. One possible answer to that would be to fill newspapers more with "olds," i.e., with articles pointing out more clearly that which does not change. Clearly, a very new style is needed for this, and retraining, for essays and articles usually also focus on change, e.g., trying to see events in the light of other events and of continuous changes. Only in the dialectic tradition is there more ability to see a "permanent" change—or a quantitative change

within a constant structure—as leading to an event. However, the point here would be to report even on the totally unchanging.

11. The first idea (the good subsystem leads to the good system) is typically liberal; the latter (the good system leads to the good subsystems) is typically Marxist. The former justifies the *laissez-faire* state, the latter justifies the opposite. There is certainly room for all kinds of combination here, including some type of phase theory (decentralization to overcome the evils of centralization and vice versa). Again the point is not to fall into the onesidedness of either view.

12. The terms will be defined in chapter 4; for a preliminary definition, see note 32 to chapter 1.

13. Some kind of metatheory is needed to know which perspective to emphasize in a given situation, however. One basic element in a theory of that kind could be built around the question "What is the source of the greatest suffering for the greatest number of people?"—which might call for different perspectives, depending on whether the answer is in terms of violence, poverty, repression, or ecological imbalance. My inclination would be, generally, to search for structural factors—at least if the phenomenon shows some permanence.

14. For an effort to operationalize the goals generated by the two perspectives, see the appendix. These goals also constitute the point of departure for the World Indicators Program. Incidentally, this analysis, in terms of actor-oriented and structure-oriented perspectives, dividing the former in terms of having and being, was written in 1971 while I was visiting professor at the Jawaharlal Nehru University in New Delhi, before the publication of books by Erik Allardt (*At ha. At vara. At Älska*) and by Erich Fromm (*Having and Being*). Both books are excellent, but both are short on structural insights, inasmuch as the first of the two distinctions mentioned is not made.

15. Admittedly, this distinction is somewhat Cartesian. It constitutes, however, one small effort to get out of the problem pointed to in note 1 to this chapter: the focus on outer man only, on what he has and what kind of structure surrounds him. The focus on being and on its dynamic aspect, becoming, leads more toward a search for inner man, to be pursued further in section 9.4.

16. This kind of talk is probably modeled on estimates of reserves of raw materials and the like (see note 18 to chapter 1). In both cases there is the possibility of hidden reserves, and in the human case even the possibility of creating new reserves through transcendence—as when a person is characterized as "completely changed," a "new person." A material culture built around material resources will necessarily be conflict-loaded simply because of the finiteness of the resources; a less material culture built around the capacity for love, for instance, or for joy and instilling joy, would not so easily run into conflict because of sheer scarcity.

17. One major intellectual goal in this book is to work out a unified vocabulary for the two levels in order to avoid the usual schizophrenia of having one set of terms for the domestic level and one for the global level. This, of course, does not mean that the theory for the two levels would be the same, although it makes some sense to see the international system as lagging behind some national systems, from both the liberal and the Marxist points of view.

18. See Christian Bay's article in *Bulletin of Peace Research* (1971), pp. 270–78.

19. And that is how our present structure gives fame and even immortality to elites, precisely because they become insubstitutable.

20. This seems to be very much at the center of the whole debate about utopias, for classical utopias seem to be based on the assumptions of similarity, constancy, and consistency and hence to be rather authoritarian.

21. See Galtung, "Norway in the World Community," *Essays* IV, 8.

22. Which is why *The Limits to Growth* is an excellent title, although the book itself is rather dubious. It presupposes a materialistic perspective on growth; but, then, what else could be expected at MIT?

23. Attributed to Chesterton.

24. This is the basic dichotomy throughout his *Social and Cultural Dynamics* (Boston: Sargent, 1957). See section 1.2.

25. In the title essay of his collection *The Yogi and the Commissar* (New York: Macmillan, 1967).

26. But Sorokin, who also mentions a fourth unintegrated, mixed, eclectic type, seems to underestimate the pluralistic possibility: societies with islands of either kind suspended in a highly tolerant minimal infrastructure in which each island would be relatively "pure" and where people would have a chance of wandering from one to the other as they felt the necessity. The European Renaissance must have offered something in this direction, for a city-state and a monastery are both essentially islands, different only in size.

27. I am indebted to Immanuel Wallerstein for this perspective.

28. See Galtung, "Economics and Peace Research: I. Some Basic Problems," mimeo (Oslo, 1975). There seem to be two solutions: to make people want and demand only what they need, and to produce only what they need. Efforts to do the latter without the former seem to lead to even more consumerism, as can be seen in some parts of Eastern Europe.

29. This idea is built into the World Indicators Program as the idea of a social maximum or ceiling on consumption.

30. The Chinese answer seems to be a relative clear "no," raising the general level of schooling while at the same time cutting down on university education. See Galtung and Nishimura, *Learning from the Chinese People*, chap. 4.

31. This problem is posed in a highly provocative manner by Ivan Illich when he asks, in *Deschooling Society* (New York: Harper & Row, 1971), for a clause of nondiscrimination for unschooled people, meaning people without diplomas, when they apply for jobs. The distinction must be made between schooling and education, and also between medication and health. It is hard, or meaningless, to place any social or individual limit on education and health, but not on schooling and medication—not only because it may create social inequalities but also because too much schooling and too much medication obviously may be harmful to soul and body. The latter point is argued by Illich in *Medical Nemesis* (New York: Pantheon, 1976).

32. Because they need it most. In spite of all the admonitions in the Sermon on the Mount, this is not the practice of Christian societies when banks are giving loans or schools are admitting pupils and students. The strong are favored.

33. For a fine way of arguing reversed phasing, see the article by Egil Fossum in *Journal of Peace Research* (1970), pp. 17–32.

34. An example of what happens when a development project is periphery-

oriented yet not periphery-generated is given in Galtung, "Development from Above and the Blue Revolution: The Indo-Norwegian Project in Kerala," *Essays* V, 12. The point is simply that the surplus gets absorbed in the center unless the periphery keeps the control of the economic cycle.

35. This point is brilliantly argued by Immanuel Wallerstein in many of his writings.

36. For distinctions between human rights and social justice (the latter being a subcase of the former), see Galtung and Anders Wirak, "Human Needs, Human Rights and the Theory of Development," World Indicators Program (University of Oslo, 1975).

37. See Galtung, Beck, and Jaastad, "Educational Growth and Educational Disparity" (Chair in Conflict and Peace Research, University of Oslo, 1974).

38. In a study reported in Bernard Berelson and Gary A. Steiner, *Human Behavior: An Inventory of Scientific Findings* (New York: Harcourt, 1967), the finding is that the upper IQ limit is about the same for all kinds of occupation, but the lower limit is higher the higher the prestige of the occupation. If such findings can be generalized to other countries than the United States, the idea seems to be that there are few "internally weak, externally strong" in the sense just mentioned but many "internally strong, externally weak." The latter category would today be the recruiting basis for peasant, labor, and women leaders. When they get to the top, the vertical, liberal society may be "purified," like a war system brought in balance through the effective operation of arms control measures, as will be argued in section 5.2. But vertical society, as well as the war system, will not only survive but will even be reinforced by being more rational.

39. The reason that they can be rejected together is, of course, that both orientations come out of the economistic, outer-man-oriented thinking that has dominated Western social thought for a long time.

40. The Yugoslav experience, in connection with the virtual elimination of the Praxis group as an effective group of opposition, also shows how manipulable small, self-managed groups are when they cannot rely on the support of nationwide unions. The latter, however, are certainly also corruptible, as the experience from other Eastern European countries clearly shows.

41. I refer, of course, to Chaplin's *Modern Times*. Few movies have been so effective in shaping our thinking, but it focused our attention far too much on industrial production and not on, for instance, schooling or consumption patterns in industrial society.

42. As Schumacher puts it, in *Small Is Beautiful*, if you read about an accident you may be shocked, but if you read one day that a study has shown that most people lead dull, boring lives, you merely think "too bad" and turn to read something else.

43. Is it equality for everybody to have shoes of the same size? That remains a useful question to ask, lest we forget that needs may differ. Difference of needs should not, however, be permitted to serve as an argument in defense of exploitation (e.g., "My need for slaves is enormous!"). It is also interesting to see how the Chinese place their theory of equality much more on the production side (in a broad sense) than on the consumption side. The rule of equity is evident in their conclusion that salary differences are permissible, but the rule of equality is inherent in their belief that problem solving in production should be as widely shared as possible, not the monopoly of a small group of specialists.

44. In a sense this is a bookkeeping-oriented concept, very much a product of having-oriented, trade-oriented society, as opposed to the "in-change"-oriented approach to exploitation that is based more on being, as will be shown in section 4.2.

45. For a discussion of these ideas, see Galtung, "On the Meaning of Nonviolence," *Essays* II, 15.

46. This was absolutely crucial in the theory of the *sarvodaya* villages: the only way to diminish external dependence is to make things yourself, as far as possible. It is interesting to see how Gandhi increasingly appears more and more as a forerunner also in the field of economics.

47. From Mao Tse-tung's speech in August 1945, "Situation and Our Policy after Victory over Japan," quoted from the excellent article by Roland Berger, "Self-reliance, Past and Present," *Eastern Horizon*, vol. IX, no. 3. As Berger points out, the policy of self-reliance was born out of necessity during the years of revolutionary struggle, having "to contend with reactionary merchants who went to any lengths to disrupt the region's finance and commerce. Trade between the Red areas and the outside—economically important—was obviously beset with many difficulties" (p. 8).

48. For one presentation, see the *Pyongyang Times,* 23 September 1973: "In a nutshell, the idea of *juche* means that the masters of the revolution and construction are the masses of the people and that they are also the motive force of the revolution and construction. In other words, it is an idea that one is responsible for one's own destiny and that one has also the capacity for hewing out one's own destiny" (p. 2). It should be noted that to Kim, as also to Mao, the concept is more located in the field of psychology than in the realm of economics; it connotes self-respect, faith in oneself, more than economic autarchy.

49. This is clearly a value-loaded concept. When the *top* comes together, I would see it as fragmentation and marginalization (of the bottom) rather than as solidarity. My defense for conceiving of solidarity as underdog solidarity is obvious: to use the same positive term, "solidarity," in either case is to imply that two types of mobilization, one to reduce verticality and the other to maintain or even increase it, are equivalent. When the social structure is biased, some bias is also needed in our use of words; we would not, for example, speak of a fascist need for "freedom from inferior races." It should also be noted that solidarity as conceived of here is an objective, structural reality, not a subjective attitude. I am in no way belittling the latter, only indicating that the same word cannot carry both meanings without becoming overloaded.

50. There are two meanings of "marginalization"—those that are exploited and those that are kept outside—and the term as I use it has the second meaning. To be kept on the margin may be better than to be exploited because one might more easily become autonomous; on the other hand, one does not have access to any of the resources of the center either. One is *out,* not *in.*

51. This is in power language exactly the same as the distinction between horizontal division of labor and self-reliance as the negation of the vertical division of labor in economic relations. See note 32 to chapter 1.

52. This point is developed at some length in Galtung, *Satyagraha: Gandhi on Conflict* (forthcoming). Both Mao and Gandhi base themselves on profound relational thinking: *power is in the relation,* not in what somebody has. This perspective immediately opens far more possibilities for those who have less,

but it is also a part of deep structure found, for example, in the relational character of the Chinese language. For a similar change in thinking in physics, from Democritos' idea that "in the beginning was the particle" to Heisenberg's relational idea that "in the beginning was symmetry," see Wener Heisenberg, *Der Teil und das Ganze* (Munich: Piper, 1969), p. 371.

53. The strong point in that type of reasoning would be that it is more open for considerations of inner man and could be taken in a soft, Buddhist direction as well as in a hard, more or less fascist direction.

54. After all, that is the experience with most societies. The power elite, usually also the economic elite, is a very small fraction of the total population. All I can say is that most of the explanation for this paradox (namely, "Why don't they rebel immediately?") lies in the difference in structural power rather than in the difference in resource power. It is only when people are no longer mystified by the structure that the resource power has to be used, even as a blunt exercise of force. Unfortunately, our actor-oriented tradition of thinking leads us to see only the latter as tyranny (because there has to be a subject, one or more tyrants). There is little talk of structural tyranny, maintained by no overt display of power at all.

55. No doubt the Indochina wars can also be seen as one big refutation of ridiculous Western thinking about power, focusing on the balance approach and mainly on the military ingredients only, not on the autonomy approach. In order to save the theory, on which so much of the Western war machine is built, there is much talk that "we could have bombed them back to the Stone Age." Apart from the fact that this might not have won the war, given the capacity of the Vietnamese to survive under Stone Age conditions, the point is not simply that "we" did not do it but that "we" were deterred from doing it precisely because of the way "they" fought. If the Vietnamese had acquired atomic arms and had attacked the cities on the U.S. Pacific coast, "we" would have done it. In other words, the decision not to use nuclear arms should not be seen as isolated from the Vietnamese way of fighting, as due only to public opinion and pressure from other countries.

56. This point is currently made very effectively by women's liberation movements and will probably later on in this century be made by children's liberation movements, when children will argue that parents would have more opportunity for their own growth if they focused a little less on shaping their children in their own images.

57. This is the definition used in Galtung, "Violence, Peace and Peace Research," *Essays* I, 4.

58. The key here is the term "avoidable." Considering that the social situation in China in the 1930s and 1940s possibly was even worse than in India, what has taken place must look like a miracle to those in the old generation of today who have experienced the "transition"—a somewhat tame word. The important thing in this connection, however, is that the situation that previously existed must have looked rather much like a law of nature, having been like that for a very long time, although Western and Japanese imperialism brought new qualities to the general misery.

59. If we use a typology based on (1) the presence or absence of a subject who deliberately causes the violence and (2) the discontinuous or continuous nature of the violence, then direct violence would be "presence and discontinuous" and structural violence would be "absence and continuous." But violence can be sudden without any subject, as evidenced by one of the

more important causes of death in modern societies: traffic accidents. A siege would be an example of highly deliberate use of deprivation of the means for satisfaction of fundamental needs. Hence, there are intermediate types. Actually, of the two dimensions just named, the first is the more important, the second the more incidental.

60. Gandhi's preference of violence to cowardice/apathy was a consistent theme throughout his life. See Galtung and Arne Naess, *Gandhis Politiske Etikk* (Oslo: Tanum, 1955), chap. 4.

61. And this makes it difficult to capture the idea in UN resolutions shaped by lawyers, probably the most actor-oriented of all the professionals dealing one way or another with social affairs.

62. Nobody has said this so well as Helder Camara, archbishop of Olinda and Recife. In a paper presented at the meeting of the Scientific Council of the Stockholm International Peace Research Institute, September 1971, he says: "If development is the new name for peace, the underdeveloped world is suffering the results of a real war. . . . Misery is in actual fact producing the tragic effects which are to be expected from the madness of a nuclear or bio-chemical war." On this basis Camara argues that an institution like SIPRI should also concern itself with internal and external colonialism, with the dangers of economism, with the ideological exploitation coming from the capitalist and socialist superpowers, with cultural colonialism (e.g., from tele-satellites), with the exact role of aid, trade policies, multinationals, and marginalization. Camara also makes the distinction between oppression, the reaction of the oppressed, and the efforts to repress that reaction as three stages of violence (p. 4). In this connection I wish to quote another of the great of this century, less known as a social philosopher: Yehudi Menuhin. In the *International Herald Tribune*, 15 October 1971, he gives the following definitions: "*strength*, courage and support, not force and domination; *work*, the pleasure of being of use to oneself and the community; *pleasure*, the satisfaction of work well done; *leisure*, the state of mind and body in which work and pleasure are seen as indivisible; *love*, service of the highest kind; *protection*, that which is offered but never imposed; *discipline*, that which is summoned from inside, never from outside; *progress*, that which is concerned with the widest conception of man's needs, and never at his cost [I would say "development"]; *freedom*, that liberty one does not enjoy at another's expense."

3. THE PREFERRED WORLDS

3.1 GOAL DYNAMICS AND GOAL INTERRELATION

Look at the ten goals presented in the preceding chapter. They are expressed by means of big words; so many of the overused words are there that they come close to constituting some kind of utopian shopping list. As argued in chapter 1, this is not necessarily a shortcoming. But the task is now to come closer to social reality, to the concrete reality in which we live and that we want to help transform. To do so we have to descend from lists of detached goals to views of concrete societies and their interrelation, and we also have to relate this task to real social dynamics, to concrete social processes that take place in the world around us.

Our point of departure is to view social dynamics as goal implementation. Lest this definition sound overly optimistic—very much like the typically Western obsession with "progress"—I hasten to add some words of caution. The goals indicated in the preceding chapter can be seen as expressions of some kind of rolling agenda of world history, and not only of Western civilization. The list contains Western elements, liberal as well as Marxist, and it contains non-Western elements, particularly in the view taken on "personal growth," and the attention given to nature. The statement that social dynamics can be seen as goal implementation therefore says more about the selection of values than about social dynamics.[1] Our thesis is not that the world progresses but that values have life cycles. They gain access to the political agenda, mature, suffer attrition, and recede into oblivion.

Concretely, this means that we can to some extent relate the values to historical processes that can be seen as archetypical. In order to do this the scheme of nine social values (leaving out ecological balance for the time being) will first be simplified to seven by leaving out personal growth and socioeconomic growth. These two stand in a particular relation to what I am going to say. They are both forms of accumulation, internal and external, and can probably be facilitated and impeded by a considerable range of social structures. Thus, such entirely different societies as the American and the Japanese are both accumulating, by and large, the same things, indicating how complicated the relation between social structure and accumulation may be and how much it may depend on the particular period of history and the particular region of geography.[2]

Is there any simple way of getting a concrete and dynamic view of this set of goals? I believe there is—through a kind of image, although it is certainly not unobjectionable. More particularly, this approach relates to history only in a highly simplified and external way, as a rule of thumb, but as such it may be more right than wrong. It is evocative, which may be an advantage. To arrive at this vision however, we have to simplify even further. We start by reducing the goals further down to two, the two that we shall choose to regard as major axes of world history and world structure: diversity and equity.[3] The former is more on the liberal side of the spectrum, the latter more on the Marxist end; both of them are painfully Western.[4] When concretized, however, they can be used to formulate problems that any society will somehow have to come to grips with.

Diversity evokes an image of individualism, of self-realization in the Western individualist sense, of dissimilarity. Equity evokes an image of a structure built according to a certain rule of antiexploitation. They can be seen as perennial themes not only through the history of utopian thought, but also through the history of social action. Diversity is an expression of the quest for freedom, equity is a way of combining the need for interaction with a dream of equality. But in the struggle for both diversity and equity, theory and practice tend to trade off one goal for the other, yielding diversity combined with inequity or equity combined with uniformity. This is the basic contradiction we shall explore further.

Using dichotomies, we get four structures, in the barest outline as shown in figure 3.1. I have referred to these structures as four social models and have suggested some terms, "conservative-liberal-communal-pluralist" or "feudal-capitalist-socialist-communist." Although these words have extremely rich meaning for those who developed them originally, the presentation here is in terms of more basic and naked principles.

Let us try to look inside the cells to find more concrete images. What does it mean to say Model I society, uniformity with inequity? It means a society that is basically vertical, where exploitation is the rule, certainly not the exception. At

Figure 3.1   The four basic social models

	Uniformity	*Diversity*
Inequity	**I** Conservative (feudal)	**II** Liberal (capitalist)
Equity	**III** Communal (socialist)	**IV** Pluralist (communist)

the same time it is also a society in which a fundamental uniformity unites the members of society, spanning the vertical gap from top to bottom, tying them together. This seeming contradiction is made possible through culture: where structure divides, culture may nevertheless unite. It is possible through an ethos of fundamental collective identification, even in highly vertical societies.

Imagine then a move from this society, but a move that changes only one of these dimensions. It can be in the direction of Model II: inequity is retained, but the collectivist ethos is destroyed and an ethos of individualism emerges instead. Individual mobility is added to the structure, so that structure and culture both divide. Or, it may be in the direction of Model III, which is also a consistent society: structure and culture both unite, and horizontal interaction is combined with emphasis on collectivism and similarity.

And then there is Model IV society. As both values are implemented, this is evidently, within our simple frame of reference, the goal, our utopia. There is absence of exploitation, and there is diversity, as a potential, not as a result of coercion. It is pluralist in the sense of being diverse, yet it is egalitarian.

This gives a setting for the discussion: the question is how the other five values can enter this picture. Clearly, in Model I society—the one called "conservative"—these are all negated. As verticality is the rule, there is little solidarity or participation, and social justice and equality would work completely against the whole idea of that society as would autonomy.[5] Thus, the feudal society as here portrayed is antidevelopment (see figure 2.6), which is not the same as saying that it cannot be very high in personal growth, particularly for those at the top, and, as indicated with the case of Japan, high on socioeconomic growth too.

On the other hand, Model IV society, the pluralist or communist society, is seen as total value-implementation, as complete development. It would differ from Model III society in building diversity into the social structure, and it would differ from Model II society in steering clear of exploitation. This would pave the way for autonomy as something over and above equity, because it also opens for equity in vacuum, for the equity of self-reliance, of detachment, even of isolation. But just as in Model III society, once equity has been conquered the assumption would be that a necessary condition for equality and social justice, as well as for participation and solidarity, had also been found.

This means that the real differences with regard to value-implementation are found within Model II society, within liberal society. This is a tautology: it means mainly that these goals came most clearly on the rolling agenda in the liberal era of Western civilization, a period now probably coming to an end. For that reason our perspective on liberal society becomes more differentiated and more lively, which is also an expression of the circumstance that liberalism is today the dominant social form, including its "socialist" variant in Eastern Europe (but not including the People's Communes in present-day China).[6]

Consider figure 3.2, now bringing into play all seven values. In Model I all seven are absent, in Model IV there is full value implementation, and all the others are in between, with five phases of Model II. This is not necessarily

Figure 3.2 A view of social dynamics

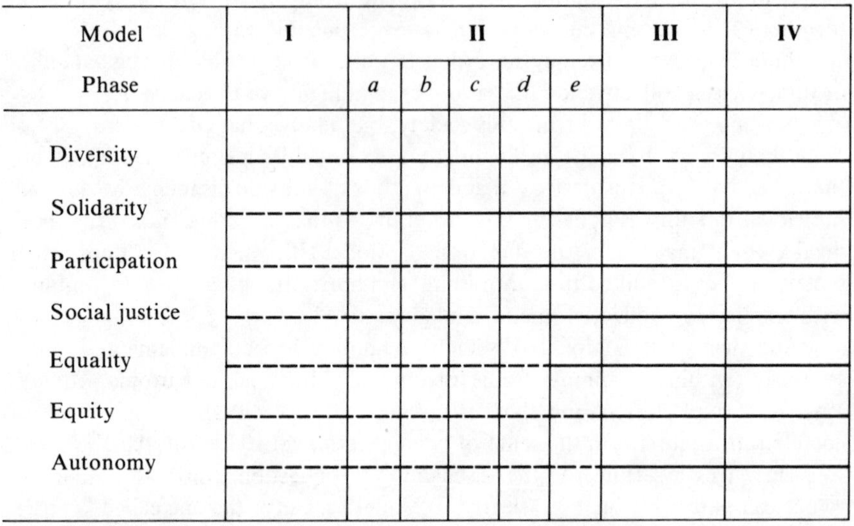

Model	I	II					III	IV
Phase		*a*	*b*	*c*	*d*	*e*		
Diversity								
Solidarity								
Participation								
Social justice								
Equality								
Equity								
Autonomy								

Key: Broken line (–––––) indicates absence, solid line (——) indicates presence; "low" and "high."

historical optimism, because the goals or value dimensions are chosen to reflect current debates and current political processes to enable us to formulate criticism of the real world as well as images of the preferred world and the paths to it.

In this view liberal society goes through five phases. It started around the time of the Renaissance, differing from feudal, medieval society only in its emphasis on diversity, *in casu* individualism. We then assume that the first thing that had to happen for this society to change was that solidarity surfaced as a goal, and was concretized, for instance, in the form of the trade-union organizations of the nineteenth century.[7] This led to a focus on increased participation, for instance, in the form of the right to vote. As a result the doctrine of social justice was launched, which is more or less where liberal society stands today in social democratic, even in "socialist" versions, although "social justice" tends to degenerate to "equality of opportunity." The next phase, now taking shape, would be a phase of equality based on redistribution and equal access to collective goods, currently finding its form in several liberal societies. But the basic characteristic trait of liberal society would remain unaltered: its inequity, particularly as relates to opportunities for personal growth.

These liberal, Model II societies we know. They are all based on a fundamentally vertical structure where positions are filled not by birth, but by some type of sorting of individuals that takes place after birth. In this way they differ fundamentally from the frozen Model I societies. But there is still sorting of individuals for verticality, and the fundamental sorting device, the fundamental classifier, seems to be education. The major function of schooling is not to impart knowledge but to permit "correct" classification. It is interesting to see how well this type of social structure has survived the collectivization of means of production and central planning found in Eastern European socialist societies and in the Soviet Union. In this sense there are also liberal societies with verticality and individualism (and an enforced political uniformity), based on a theory promising too much from some changes in economic structure.[8]

Model III society we also know to some extent: there is this strong, highly evocative image of the People's Communes in China: a high level of equity, but also a very low level of diversity. It is Model IV society that constitutes the big unknown, and as it is the preferred world according to the program indicated by the system of values, it is the one to be spelled out in the next section.

However, before that, there are some remarks to add to what has been said.

First, as there is no implicit belief in historical determinism, there is no assumption whatsoever that social dynamics has to take place in the order I, II, III, IV. There may be some gross indications in this direction, but other trajectories are conceivable (for instance, directly from I to III or directly from II to IV), and there may be reversion to earlier phases (for instance, from IV back to I).

Second, if one wants a global view, at least two levels of social organization have to be discussed, the domestic community of persons and the global community of countries. Because the goals apply to both levels as pointed out, all that has been said can be repeated for the global community. It can be repeated, yes, but with less relevance, for in general the global community lags behind. The global community is much closer to a Model I society, or a Model IIa in its undeniable diversity. Solidarity is weak; participation is weak; social justice is absent; of equality, there is none; of equity one cannot even speak; penetration, fragmentation, and marginalization are rampant throughout. This does not mean that the four models are without any value as models. It means only that there is a basic asynchrony between the levels, although many countries are not further advanced than the global community as a whole.

This is not surprising, if for no other reason than because of the scale involved in the global community, as well as the immobility of the territorial basis of nations. If nations were as mobile as persons, it might well be that the global community would have moved further along the social dynamics axis indicated in figure 3.2. There are, of course, deeper reasons to be examined later. Suffice it here to say that the perspective developed can be applied to both levels.

Third, this is no mechanistic theory of value implementation as either automatic or something that can be planned. As history goes on, values may be implemented, but other values tend to fade out or at least to change character. Thus, in figure 3.1, diversity is not quite the same whether equity is realized or not. And figure 3.2 draws attention to the circumstance that as equity is conquered, diversity tends to be lost, in Model III society. Model IV society solves that problem—on paper. In other words, we are suspended between a sense of realism that tells us to expect very little and a sense of idealism that commands us to hope for very much. Behind that contradiction is one big, glaring fact: history shows that the condition of humankind does change. To say that it can never move in the direction of our ten goals is based on no better data or theory than to say the opposite.

That brings us back to the basic problem of goal interrelation, not to mention goal compatibility, which I have so far only touched upon. I have not said, "Here are ten goals, let us test them for compatibility, starting with all pairs (45), then all triples (120) and so on through the final test of the whole set—altogether 2^{10}-11 testing operations." I have not done so, not because this number is high (1013), making the operation even more boring for the author than for the reader, but for other reasons now to be spelled out.

First, goal implementation should be seen as a historical process, and one image of that was just given. We have already lots of experience with Model I, II, and III societies. What is and was is and was possible. A basic problem posed by my insistence on Model IV societies with both equity and diversity is precisely the question of whether diversity can be added to this list. In the next section I shall indicate one way in which I think it can be added. The key is simple: to make the Model IV society a collection of Model III communities, tied together not only through some central administration but also through a high level of mobility between these communities.

Second, it is felt that we know today that all these social formations are compatible with at least some socioeconomic growth. Japan, the United States, the Soviet Union, and China all produce and accumulate. There is no reason that a Model IV society should not be able to do so also; and if it is on a smaller scale there are many good reasons for that as long as fundamental needs are satisfied. Along such lines, it is felt, lies also the solution to the problems of ecological balance.

Third, more problematic than socioeconomic growth is personal growth. The problem is not so much one of compatibility as one of meaning, for each society tends to define not only personal growth but also human nature in terms compatible with the basic social matrix. In all social formations, we assume, the mature person is to some extent seen as the person who is able to and willing to conform.[9] Since Model IV society is the richest in terms of structural variation, we could argue that it would offer the widest range of opportunity for personal enrichment, including the opportunity to stay, just to be, not to become anything new; even to contract to a point of bliss rather than always to expand.

Fourth, the most problematic is the question of direct violence. Again, I say that no social formation has an absolute monopoly on war or peace. With the reduction of structural violence within and between societies, at least some roots of direct violence are eradicated. Direct violence will not be used for revolution or counterrevolution. However, in a social matrix of equality and equity, direct violence could still be used to establish inequality and inequity. The major bulwark against that, as will be spelled out later, would probably be to tie the societies as well together as possible, in symbiotic and equitable relationships.

Fifth, finally, and more basically, these goals should not be seen as a shopping list from which any subset can be selected at will. Analytically they can be listed, even operationalized, in an atomistic manner. In concrete social reality, however, they come in bundles, in molecules. The social models indicated in this section are examples of such molecules. These molecules must be viewed dialectically: if one adds one goal-atom, the other atoms change. Add diversity to a Model III society and equity takes on another meaning; it is no longer the equity of horizontal division of labor only, but also the equity of possible detachment, of mobility. Add solidarity to a Model I society and the fundamental inequity is already threatened, giving some pointers toward a Model III society wherein solidarity, in turn, would take on a completely different meaning. It would be much less a counterweight in a basically vertical society and much more an expression of what horizontal society is about: cooperative living, on an equal footing.

In all of this, time order is of crucial importance. Many today pay lip service to two goals like "accumulation" and "distribution," but those who first accumulate seem never to really come around to the period when the time is ripe for distribution.[10] Among those who try to distribute first, some are successful, some not, when it comes to accumulation. Thus, in social reality goal implementation is a question of highly concrete processes and strategies, not of superethicism, goal internalization, and abstract construction of structures. But in that process it is one of my basic tenets that a constructive image of a preferred world is *one* important element and something very different from empirical and critical analysis of the real world, however brilliantly done.

3.2 AN IMAGE OF A PREFERRED WORLD

The image I have in mind is a world that is a Model IV global community of Model IV societies (which in turn are a collection of Model III communities). In other words, a world where equity and diversity are the basic rules, a world where exploitation and repression are effectively counteracted—and also a world that would find sufficient two levels of organization, the domestic and the global. My task here is to try to give some life to this schema, to make it not only attractive at the verbal level but also so meaningful that it can be captured by anybody's inner eye. The outer eye, needless to say, will capture the empirical reality we know, rather different from what is here depicted.

Let me first try an intuitive glimpse. I see in my inner eye a piece of world geography, just some kind of geographical Anywhere. The metaphor of the island, so frequent in utopian literature,[11] is not needed. Our society does not presuppose any isolation in space, any more than it presupposes any isolation in time. It has emerged from a historical process, for instance, somewhat like that envisaged in the preceding section. It is not a terminal state, for nothing is; it will generate its own successors.

In this piece of world geography, then, I see many components, all of them self-reliant communities. In one corner there is a Chinese People's Commune, a form of living that seems to have come particularly far in reducing vertical division of labor, or any form of division of labor for that matter. It would exchange experiences with a near kin, the Gandhian *sarvodaya* village, and with the Tanzanian *ujamaa* village—different, but in the same direction. Then there is a Zen monastery, a place of individual and collective meditation, also growing its own food. People of very different faiths come together to meditate and exchange their experiences, living in their separate cells, meeting in the communal refectory and cloister-yard, peripatetically enriching each other, at a low level of material existence and high level of nonmaterial living.

In another corner I see a big city, even a metropolis. It also grows its own food through new technologies, neither exploiting any countryside nor polluting and depleting any nature. The city as we know it is brought under control and has become some sort of People's Commune writ large, with emphasis on diverse urban life, as found in Shinjuku, in Quartier Latin, in Soho. Any institution—factory, university, hospital, prison (if there are to be prisons)—would be run according to the principles of equity, autonomy, solidarity, and participation. All the models of self-management in Yugoslavia, or *les événements de mai* in France, or *autunno caldo*[12] in Italy would have been developed further, gaining through confrontation with practice, enriched through verbal and nonverbal dialogues.

At yet another place there is a *kibbutz,* one of the pioneers among these social forms. And there are rural districts with Nordic, highly individualistic but also highly egalitarian patterns of farming rather than the many vestiges of feudal patterns found in, for instance, Mediterranean village cultures. There are hippie colonies like those found along the Pacific coast some years ago. There are scientific communes and communes for artists. There are hermits, seeking total isolation for the time they need. But above all, there are all kinds of new innovations, for almost all these examples are taken from recent theory and practice. There will be more, gaining in depth and extension.

In each of these communities of subsocieties, then, there is a basic self-reliance. New humans are born and take root in one community, but they learn about others. Economic production takes place, but in a fully participatory manner and essentially for self-consumption and for the satisfaction of fundamental needs. Exchanges also take place, but exploitative exchanges (like foodstuffs and raw materials for processed goods) are ruled out, as slave trade is today, practically speaking, all over the world. Education and cultural production take place, and the emphasis is on generating one's own insight, together, rather than on taking over anybody else's. There is education, not only schooling, as a constant and live dialogue, a horizontal relationship here as elsewhere.

But then one also sees something else. There is dynamism. This is not a folk museum of quaint, interesting social forms populated by the half-committed, forced to stay there forever, or on permanent call to show the commune to inquisitive visitors, dressed up in some local garb.[13] People move, in and out. Some stay at a place for a lifetime, others for a month. They are free to join, free to leave, but to the extent they stay they are committed. Rather than conformity, however, commitment means commitment to participation in the life of the society as an ongoing concern, as a process. Only in this way can the society hope to be not only self-generating and self-sustaining, but also self-transforming, even self-abolishing when the time has come.

On the other hand, nobody is forced to stay beyond his call of commitment. People as well as societies have rhythms: they are not constant, unchanging. There is such a thing as fatigue, at personal as well as social levels. A community that engenders early fatigue in all its members and is incapable of recruiting new members with real commitment is a repressive community. It merits the death that will have accrued to it when the last disenchanted member leaves and it no longer caters to anybody's needs, like an association in a society with free association formation. So people come and they participate; some leave quickly and others say *"J'y suis, j'y reste."* And the total society changes its complexion, ever moving, never resting. At no point would there be any assumption to the effect that the society had arrived at a constant and consistent pattern for basically similar human beings, the axiomatic basis of most utopias. On the contrary, individuals as well as communities and societies are conceived of dialectically, not only as changing but as harboring contradictions, not only as dissimilar but as inducing dissimilarity in each other. No model of the future that does not reflect this basic insight can ever make any claim to viability.

Let me now present fifteen (there could be more!) basic and relatively concrete points concerning what such a Model IV, pluralist, postrevolutionary[14] society might look like. Ten of them refer to the domestic level, five to the global level.

[1] The total society would be *diverse* by providing the individual with a *maximum of internal variation* when it comes to how one might live one's life. No pattern should be seen as deviant so long as it does not make it difficult for others to find a pattern that suits them. Thus, people are today gradually learning to accept that other people have different sex habits and patterns of family and group living, with no partner or with one or more partners of the same or opposite sex, and to understand that this does not decrease the possibility for themselves to realize their own preferred style of life. This is the extension of that principle to the entire community.

[2] The society would be *equitable* by permitting no exploitation of individuals, of subsocieties or communities, or of other societies. In some cases this would be done by cutting down on interaction and emphasizing self-sufficiency and autonomy, in other cases through carefully balanced exchanges, in most cases by combining the two. A new economics, based on a theory and

practice of equitable exchange and not only on comparative advantages, will be an important condition; a regeneration of economics from its present degeneration into "capitalistics," the theory and practice of capitalism, is needed.

[3] Just as the society should offer a maximum of variation among communities (for diversity), it should also facilitate mobility among them (for equity). The world today has variety without mobility (except for the rich), and there are particularly homogeneous nation-states like Norway and Japan that have mobility without diversity. Both of them offer their citizens pretty much the same life from one end of the country to the other. Our task is to realize both goals within one society. Thus, every community may be a Model III society, as are most of the preceding examples. It is the combination of such Model III units, each based on a certain theme and even on a uniform commitment, with mobility between them that could constitute a Model IV, pluralist society.

[4] For mobility to be real and accessible to all it should be free. There is mobility of the body, and there is also the mobility of the mind when it searches and imparts information; the free movement of persons and information can be allowed. But transportation and communication should also be provided freely by the society so that everybody can realize any type of mobility.[15] This seemingly utopian proposal is not stranger than free education; it only emphasizes another aspect of social life. Nobody should be forced to remain in a community not of his or her liking for lack of funds to move. The free means of travel may be uncomfortable and slow, but they should be there, first within communities (as in Havana where telephones are free and buses practically free), then within societies, and ultimately in the world as a whole.

[5] A society of this type would have to offer to its citizens a guarantee of at least minimum subsistence. One alternative would be the opportunity for all to produce their own food. Support could also take the form of a minimum salary to all, free health services, or some other form in accordance with its social function: to guarantee freedom of the individual. This salary would not depend on any work performance but would be an inalienable birthright.[16] No person should be tied to any social relation, e.g., to a work relation, by fear that he would not survive if he did not perform. Nobody should have to sell his labor to survive. Anyone should be free to withdraw from a work relation; anyone should be detachable. In an automated society this would produce few problems, for many types of elementary food, clothing, and shelter production could be automated and, like hydroelectric power, be guaranteed with a minimum of work-hours. Resources for such social reconstruction exist: the world military expenditure of about $450 billion already corresponds to somewhat below $75 per capita for the world population—in other words more than the GNP per capita in many regions of the world. If the world can afford this for military outlays, it can also afford a guaranteed minimum to all human beings—a minimum to which they may add by work performance, up to a maximum dictated by values of equality and ecological balance. By and large this would

not be a rich man's society by our standards, but the days of that type of material richness are probably counted anyhow.

[6] In general, vertical interaction whereby two or more persons interact but in such a way that one is much more enriched than the other would become rare and egalitarian; symmetric interaction would prevail. This would be obtained partly by means of job rotation and partly by means of job reconstruction to make jobs more equal in terms of how challenging, rewarding, and burdensome they are. In a human science of economics the emphasis would be on what production does to the worker, not only on what the worker does to production.[17]

[7] The borderline between work and leisure would tend to disappear. Work and leisure would both be ways of using oneself, of enriching oneself, and the transition from one to the other would be smooth. Some minimum predictability would probably still have to prevail in work relations, but a very great variation in vacation patterns would be stimulated. Some might have six months' vacation and six months' work, others might have half-days of work all year around, and all kinds of in-between mixtures and ratios should be possible. The pluralist element would be to avoid a uniform standard for all enterprises, which would follow the pattern the members decide. There must be opportunity for mobility from an enterprise with one pattern to another enterprise with a pattern that fits one better at that point in life. Automation could also eliminate much of the routine work, leading to more identity between work and creativity, and contributing to the elimination of the borderline between work and leisure, to make work a right more than a duty.

[8] Education would prepare for life in this type of social order, being based much more on horizontal education and self-education. It would probably have to transform dissimilarity, inconstancy, and inconsistency into values to be internalized to some extent. Thus, one idea that has to be given up is the antipluralist idea that there exists somewhere, in thought or in practice, a single social order that is ideal for everybody, forever.[18] He who has that idea tends to become a missionary for the concept, which denies the ever-changing nature of human society, and he becomes a danger to freedom.

But what, then, about the missionaries for pluralism? Do they also become dangerous to those who do not want to live in a pluralist society but want for everybody one social order, namely, the ideal one? In a sense, yes, but the pluralists are also rather tolerant to that kind of people. The pluralist would say that they are free to establish their form of life, free to make propanganda for it, but not free to force it upon others. This position goes much further than many contemporary liberal democratic societies that would only permit others to make propaganda for their social form, not to establish it unless a majority is in favor of it as a general formula for the whole society. Freedom to practice what one believes would have to be given the status of a human right in Model IV society. But those who establish a social form do not have the right to prevent those who want from leaving or entering. If they expand, that is a sign of some type of success, but a pluralist society does not operate on the assumption of a demonstration effect and convergence toward one social form. Nor does a social form become more valid just because more than 50 percent have opted for it.

Correspondingly, pluralist society would feel responsible for future generations. To find one form, canonize it, and raise it to the status of the ideal form, freezing the future into that form, is nothing less than colonization—not the classical colonization in space of other territories, but a new type of colonization in time, of future generations. To be on guard against this type of colonization is both important and difficult, as future generations cannot voice any protest—on, for instance, ecological issues. Consequently, a pluralist society will also to some extent have to serve as a guardian for those generations, trying to preserve a diversity rich enough for them also to have a chance of self-realization.

[9] It goes without saying that education in this type of society would have to be free for anyone at any level at any time. This ideal is already approximated in several societies and its full realization would not be beyond the power of many contemporary Model II societies. However, the very idea of education is a complex and controversial one, certainly much more than a question of tertiary, quaternary, and so on levels of training for jobs in some stratified post–Model II society. There is a limit to how much disparity one can permit in education without engendering new verticalities, at least if jobs are differentiated according to education level.[19] As jobs are supposed to be much more equal (through reconstruction), education would be for insight and enrichment and not merely for status, salary, and power.

[10] Model IV society would, like Model III society, reject the idea that politics is a profession and try to bring politics back to the people. This means direct participation in decision making, but also the freedom not to participate in decision making if one does not want. Enforced participatory democracy is uniformity rather than diversity. As to the problem of how direct democracy can be better reconciled with large-scale societies than at present, multilateral telecommunications may provide some answers.[20]

[11] In global terms, my preferred world consists of many small societies, more of them and smaller than the countries in today's world. They would also differ from each other, but the diversity within is more important than diversity between, because it is more accessible to all. Thus, I would prefer a world of 1500 societies to the present world with around 150, which I would, in turn, prefer to a world with 15 societies. However, the point is not so much the absolute number as the maximum size, "size" referring not only to population and territory but to power in general. I strongly hold that only in smaller societies can the distance between ruler and ruled be small enough to permit self-expression to everybody, and only with smaller societies can large-scale hegemonial tendencies be avoided. Concretely, this would be an argument in favor of breaking up the strongest and biggest of today's countries, not in favor of subdividing the weaker ones.

[12] A world of many small societies presupposes a strong web of nonterritorial organizations. Such a world would have to be tied together; this and the three following points give four such cementing mechanisms. At this point I envisage a very high number of organizations and associations crisscrossing all the many small territorial societies, the organizations also being many and small. Thus, the societies would be tied together by "oceanic circles," although not exactly in Gandhi's sense,[21] putting everybody in community with local neighbors as well as with distant neighbors, only accessible through mobility. Again, this points to the crucial nature of symmetric, accessible, and cheap means of mobility of all kinds, available to the world population and not only to its elites, as in present-day world society. It calls for free mobility, for abolishing all kinds of visa and passport restrictions so that individuals can seek the experience they want where and when they want it.

[13] Citizenship in a society should become more like membership in an association, to be discarded when there is no longer any commitment. That immediately raises problems: how can change of nationality be made easier, with less waiting time, fewer formalities, and the like? The principle of a certain trial period could probably be retained in any association, community, or society.

Could there also be multiple citizenship or no citizenship at all? Why not? Some persons might opt for multiple membership at both the community and the social levels, and they might refuse any citizenship in anything corresponding to today's nation-states. The world would not go under for that reason. Not even community membership should be any absolute condition. The world should also be able to harbor the hermit, the person who prefers solitude for any length of time.

[14] A pluralist world society presupposes symbiotic, equitable interaction as a bulwark against direct violence. The fight for equity and diversity can lead to two types of social orders, to one with highly autonomous, mutually independent individuals, communities, and societies, and to one based on mutual interdependence in a network of horizontal division of labor. One would not be so naive as to assume that even the most equitable Model III or Model IV community or society could not engage in direct violence against others, however much structural violence within and without is ruled out by definition. Only in a symbiotic relationship where hitting the other also means hitting oneself is there the beginning of a structure that would also represent a protection against direct violence.

[15] A pluralist world society presupposes a central world authority for world planning and world execution of essentials. As the equality implied here extends to all, not only to the members of one particular community, there must somewhere be some central authority that can make and enact plans for such matters as world food distribution, world employment, world ecological balance, world water and oxygen budgets and that can administer the riches that belong to all, such as the seabed and oceans, the bio-atmosphere, the cosmos, subterranean deposits, to mention what many would agree on today, and

possibly all of nature if private and national ownership were to be abolished. The reconciliation of this need with the need for decentralization would continue to be problematic.

The list could easily be extended, but let me rather give a more comprehensive image, as I tried in the beginning. Using the broad definitions of peace developed in chapter 2, the goal is clear: *a peacefare world of peacefare societies.* The problem is what a peacefare world and a peacefare society would look like. My suggestion is that it is not enough to talk in terms of the abolition of direct violence within and between societies, for instance, through the control or abolition of the means of such violence. We have to set our sights higher and also think in terms of the abolition of structural violence within and between societies. One way of formulating that is in terms of striving for equity and diversity, against exploitation and repression, at both levels. The assumption then, is that there is a strong relation between the two, that a reduction of structural violence will at least eliminate two forms of direct violence (revolution and counterrevolution) and, as will be argued in chapter 5, probably also reduce the probability of the other two (horizontal and random).

Thus a peacefare society is much more than a society that simply does not engage in aggression or in the preparation for warfare by building up a military machinery and participating in alliances with such machineries. Nonaligned, disarmed societies may still exercise all forms of structural violence within and without, which would not only constitute a threat to peace (in the usual sense that internal or external war may ensue) but would also in itself be unpeace, peacelessness. Moreover, of a real peacefare state one would also demand something active, not only reduction of the means of violence of any kind but also active peacekeeping, peacemaking, and peace-building initiatives.[22]

No country in the world of today would satisfy all these criteria, but of those that rank high Yugoslavia might be mentioned. There is a strong army, but nobody seems to feel threatened by it. Few countries have gone in so consistently for equity (if not equality) inside combined with at least cultural pluralism. Rather than the American melting-pot idea, there are consistent efforts to protect diversity. A future expansion into structural pluralism, pursuing the idea of several roads to socialism in one country, with ample opportunity for mobility, is not inconceivable, for both decentralization and self-management have been carried far. As to foreign policy: Yugoslavia does not exploit anybody (as even small northwest European countries do) and has a long tradition in active peacefare, consistently trying to extend the sphere of nonalignment. Without glorifying the country this is important to note because it puts the visions closer to the empirical reality we know today.[23]

However, the visions go beyond this piece of empirical reality and far into potential reality. The question still remains whether a world without direct and structural violence is a possibility at all. In short, is this preferred world viable?

3.3   IS IT VIABLE?

To ask whether something is viable is to ask whether it has a certain built-in stability. If it is not viable it will disintegrate, like a radioactive element wherein the nucleus of the atom is packed in such a way that it does not persevere. Of course, "stability" and "disintegration" are relative terms. The notion of "half-life" taken from the theory of radioactivity is useful here, although the viability of a social order in human affairs has to be judged relative to social time, not relative to any type of physical time. A social order that survives several human generations is quite stable; but it may also be argued that if it lasts sufficiently long to give a meaningful experience to its members it has already proved itself to be viable—like many hippie communities.

However, more important than considerations of the length of duration would be the mechanism of duration. If a social order is propped up from the outside and will disintegrate the moment the reinforcement is reduced or removed, one would not call it viable. Viability has to be organic, it has to be built-in, generated from the inside, self-supporting. If when given a choice many, even most, of the members would prefer to leave, the society is certainly not viable. There may be short-term transition periods wherein coercive measures limiting mobility are indispensable, but if such measures become a part of the social order, as in the Soviet Union, then certificates of viability should only be issued with the greatest hesitation.

Propping up does not necessarily take negative forms; it may also take such positive forms as the injection of enormous amounts of "technical assistance," investments, loans and grants designed to maintain the system. The rationale behind such measures, although not necessarily openly expressed, would be that their absence would lead to a rapid, even immediate downfall of the regime—again an indication that the system does not have any built-in viability.

With the strong emphasis in the preceding section on capacity for self-reliance—biological (procreation), economic (production) and cultural—this kind of artificial life would certainly not be built into the program. We know from world history that even very small communities, down to the size of one family, or one person, for that matter, have been viable,[24] and because what is is possible, the existential proof is there. But that does not absolve us from delving into more general problems of whether violence would nevertheless be rampant, both in its direct, personal form and in its indirect, structural form. Because in recent years the old debate about instincts of aggression (leading to direct violence) and instincts of dominance (leading to structural violence) and instincts of dominance (leading to structural violence) has been reawakened, I shall use this frame of reference in discussing these problems.

It is perfectly well known that man is capable of both direct and structural violence; the question is whether this is built indelibly into his biological constitution and can be referred to as an inborn, innate, or inherited trait. This is

not the place to go into any detailed discussion of the many difficult epistemological, theoretical, and empirical questions in this connection. The following
gives a pattern of argumentation in outline, without pretensions as to the details.

Essentially we are again dealing with the Problem of Evil. There are two
evils, direct and structural violence, and the basic problem posed is whether the
factors conditioning them are modifiable or not. If they are not modifiable, the
striving for world order less replete with direct and structural violence than the
present would seem a futile exercise, a display of the vanity of human beings
believing themselves to be gods. If they are modifiable, then the exercise should
be directed toward their modification, and whether it is futile or not becomes an
empirical question, not a question answered in the negative *a priori*.

Figure 3.3 is a little sketch of some possible ways of viewing the phenomenon of violence. The first model sees violence as built into the human species;
according to the next two models, the human species has a potential for
violence, but it is enacted only under certain structural or ecological conditions;
and according to the last two models the root of the violence is found in the
structure itself, which then works on actors to create "violence in general," a
feedback cycle between structural and direct violence. Actually, the last model is
equipped with two feedback loops, indicating that structure and ecology
together may release certain potentials in actors that lead to a vicious feedback
cycle between structural and direct violence.

The most simplistic model is the first one, according to which violence is
indelibly embedded in the human actor. An example might be Freud's *thanatos*-
instinct theory, according to which all human beings have built into them also
some type of striving toward death, unmodifiable by external conditions.

Figure 3.3   Five models of conditions of violence

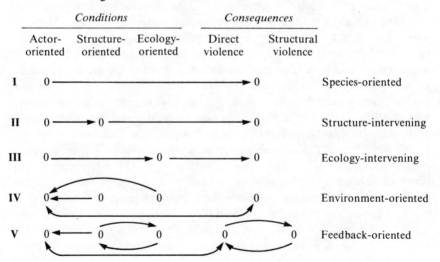

One would predict *a priori* that theories of this kind would emerge in cultures like the Western one, with heavily actor-oriented cosmologies. The concrete mechanism postulated on a scale from biological to psychological is of less interest in this connection than the general structure of the theory. Thus, whether the aggression instinct can be related to needs or not, which would indicate that individual human beings would oscillate from tension build-up, via aggressive acts, to tension release, and then to increasing tension again as time elapses, is not of major significance. This so-called hydraulic model (or toilet-flushing model, in less venerable terms)[25] is just one particular case of this first model.

But there is one thing that all such models have in common and that also seems to be the one major factor on which they can be proved to be false: they lead one to expect universal, ubiquitous and even relatively standardized forms of aggressive behavior—including behavior to establish dominance. Man is continuously at work to satisfy needs for food; shelter, including clothing; and community, including sex. Patterns, even institutions, built around these drives are found in all societies. There may be gross variations in time (history) and space (geography), but there is no variation in the circumstance that there is pursuit of food and the other needs. But this variation is exactly what we find in connection with aggression—even enormous variation in time and space where the incidence of aggression itself is concerned.

Actually, all we need is reference to the data presented in chapter 1 to illustrate this. Thus, how could the immense variation found in figure 1.1 be possible if man were equipped with a universal, stereotyped instinct of aggression that would urge him on to aggressive acts? As with other drives there might be variation, but not variations of that magnitude, particularly not variations that seem so easily explained as those emerging from figure 1.1 and similar data. Just to mention one simple illustration of variations in space rather than in time: in 1972, 601 murders were committed in Detroit, the U.S. "murder capital." If Detroit had had the Norwegian murder rate, the number would have been 3 or 4. It is hard to see how this difference can be explained in terms of any species-oriented model.[26]

The next two models are intended to cope with this problem and thereby modify this image of human beings. What they purport to say is more or less the following. We are inherently aggressive, but our aggressiveness has to be triggered by certain structural or ecological conditions. Thus, there are conditions that would facilitate its release, such as overcrowding or another's penetration into one's own territory. There are conditions that would impede the release of aggression, such as a hierarchical structural order. According to these kinds of theory, advanced by researchers like Lorenz,[27] Storr,[28] and Ardrey,[29] the optimal habitat for man would be territorially well-defined, uncrowded units; within each unit there would be hierarchical structures capable of keeping man on a tight leash. In this connection it is also pointed out that man does not possess the inhibition factor against intraspecies aggression found in other comparable species, consisting of the capacity to send and receive signals of submission that stop fights short of killing, or serve as the fight's equivalent.[30]

There are several comments to make with regard to this type of thinking. First, it should be noted that there is a tremendous difference between these two models and the first one. In all three, man somehow has an urge to be aggressive, according to the first model this urge is expressed everywhere, presumably implying that if no adequate expression is found for this urge, then the species itself would be fundamentally threatened. In the next two models the urge is seen as mediated through structures and ecologies, which means that the significance of extra-species variation is recognized. But that means that although the urge may be universal, its release into action may no longer be universal, which is already a good step in the direction of environmental reasoning. This is certainly not the same reasoning that underlies the next two models, but it is compatible with existing data about the tremendous variations in time and space when it comes to incidence of aggression and dominance.

Second, the moment structural and ecological variations are brought in, the theories become testable. Is it in fact true that hierarchical structures are more peaceful than egalitarian structures, within as well as without? Is it in fact true that the human species reacts as certain animals are said to react when there occurs penetration of a territorial border (of any shape) encircling themselves? Moreover, is it really true that overcrowding leads to aggressiveness?

The data by no means support such theories, although they may be said to give no clear indication in the opposite direction either. If one should rely on data of the type presented in figure 1.1 the conclusions would be in the opposite direction, for the least belligerent societies are precisely those with no fixed territorial boundary and with no hierarchical structure at all, with very simple social configurations. Actually, it rather looks as if the crystallization of the human species inside well-defined territorial units with centralized hierarchical structures has been a correlate, if not necessarily a condition or a cause, of tremendous increases in belligerence. And when it comes to overcrowding: it may very well be that at a certain stage in a crowding process aggression may result, but it also looks as if in later stages a certain type of withdrawal and apathy, which may or may not be interpreted as self-directed aggression, ensues.[31]

These and similar considerations have at least made the present author regard theories of the kind mentioned as a rationalization, of status quo with its division of the world into centralized, hierarchical nation-states with programs to stave off too many immigrants and too many babies. The action consequences that would follow from such theories all fall on the conservative end of the political spectrum, which makes it small wonder that these books have been acclaimed by military and other status-quo–oriented groups in status-quo–oriented countries.

Turning then to the third group of theories, there is again an important difference to note. Thus, human beings are no longer seen as programmed for aggression, the release of which may or may not be inhibited and facilitated by structural and ecological factors. We are seen as essentially benevolent, perfectly capable of living in a nonaggressive, nondomineering manner, but under certain structural and/or ecological conditions we may become violent, even extremely violent. Clearly, there is another conception of human nature at work here. Instead of certain structures and ecologies putting brakes on or aggravating an essentially malevolent nature, the perspective would be that certain structures and ecologies destroy an essentially benevolent nature. Another question is what those structures are, and here the stage is certainly set for scientific controversy between the ethologists and peace researchers. For instance: there seems to be considerable correspondence between the structures recommended by Lorenz and others and the structures rejected in this book. More precisely, a structure exhibiting the four characteristics of structural violence defined in chapter 2 (exploitation, penetration, fragmentation, and marginalization) does not seem too far from what ethologists might recommend, but is seen here not only as leading to direct violence and to direct counterviolence but also as a form of structural violence. As to the ecological question, I believe that the correlations between violence and habitat are not that strong. A more fruitful point of view might be to look at how the interaction between structure-oriented and ecology-oriented factors works on human beings to produce a dialectic between direct and structural violence. But that would lead to complex formulas, much beyond the current level of debate.

More precisely, there may be something in the structure of human society, whenever and wherever it is found, that produces effects on human beings that in their consequences are violent, taking the shape of aggression and domination. Would this not be the same as the first model? No, for the idea is that there would still be a state of affairs under which the people would not be violent: when living in isolation or in very small numbers, as hermits or as small scattered groups, roaming around like a nomadic clan or tribe.[32] The moment we go beyond that, erecting more complex structures, we may not bite into the fruit of the Tree of Knowledge but rather build something that takes hold of us and places us well out of reach of any peaceful paradise.

There is much to support this kind of view, and it has to some extent been reflected in the preceding section. Equity, mobility, and nonterritoriality have been emphasized. But that is not the same as a return to prehistorical, nomadic conditions; rather, it is the search for the contemporary functional equivalents of some of those conditions. To fight against structural violence today does not mean to return to conditions before these forms of structural violence were brought into being, but to learn from these conditions. The basic idea is to try to stem and even turn the trend toward increasing bigness and increasingly steep gradients between centers and peripheries in an increasingly uniform world.

3.4   IS IT ATTAINABLE?

To ask whether something is attainable is to ask whether strategies exist, or can easily be imagined, that with a reasonable probability would lead to the desired goal if people engaged in them. One may also ask whether society by itself would tend in that direction, and the answer here seems clearly to be no. Extrapolations from the type of trends given in chapter 1 generally point in a quite different direction.

One may then say, correctly, that extrapolation is a naive model, that trends produce countertrends because forces meet with counterforces. But to posit that such counterforces necessarily should point in the direction of what is defined here as the preferred world would be more wishful than thinking. One might then see those counterforces as more real than any preferred world, any goal, and say that the direction to which these forces lead us constitute the goal, or the range of goals. But that leads us back to the discussion in section 1.4: at about the point my presentation becomes distinctly non-Marxist. I believe that society possesses no *Naturgesetzlichkeit,* that there is no way of foretelling what the counterforces will be or how they will act, that we are guaranteed neither bliss nor catastrophe, neither Paradise nor Inferno. People live in a double world of empirical and potential reality, and it is given to human beings to develop consciousness of goals as well as of existing reality with its instabilities and trends and to engage in concerted action, based on this consciousness. This thought will be developed further in chapter 9; suffice it here to repeat that the concept of strategy I have in mind combines emphasizing some trends with deliberate goal-directed action.

The reader will see from the organization of this book that the last section of each subsequent chapter is devoted to the question of strategy. Hence, what I am trying to do in this section is to present my thoughts about strategy in general terms, since the level of discussion of goal formulation has so far been relatively general. Later discussions will become much more specific.

One way of approaching strategy, which in a sense summarizes much of the contents of this book, is given in figure 3.4. This map of strategies should be conceived of in a dynamic fashion. If we start in the upper left-hand corner, the general problem is how to get out of a situation of dependence or dominance. Five components are mentioned, giving as a conclusion a state of independence, obtained through violent or nonviolent methods. The five components are about the same in either case, although there would be much more emphasis on consciousness formation when the revolution is nonviolent. A detailed discussion of nonviolent revolution (NVR) as a process is given in section 4.3.

In the bottom left-hand corner the corresponding associative strategy is indicated. Two equals are now brought together, on the basis of an equitable relationship. However, the basic assumption is that for this *re*coupling to take place a *de*coupling has been the indispensable condition: a situation of equity cannot emerge gradually, continuously, from a structure of dependence and

Figure 3.4   A map of peace strategies

Fighting for peace = *Fighting* against violence

Two *types* of violence: STRUCTURAL (exploitation, penetration, fragmentation, marginalization)
DIRECT (tearing, piercing, crushing, burning, exploding, etc.)

Two *ways* of fighting: DISSOCIATIVE (keeping parties apart, demolishing false structures)
ASSOCIATIVE (bringing parties together, building true structures)

Fighting against STRUCTURAL VIOLENCE	Fighting against DIRECT VIOLENCE
1. Consciousness formation **2. Organization building** **3. Confrontation** **4. Fight against dominance**	

D I S S O C I A T I V E

	Actor- oriented	*Structure- oriented*
Slow	mobility, indirect democracy	people stop one activity; people start another
Quick	banishment, seclusion, killing	noncooperation, civil disobedience, decoupling

	Distance	*Impediments*
Geographical	oceans, deserts	mountains, rivers
Social	prejudice, stereotypes	military, nonmilitary
Artificial	use of technology, use of third parties	

5. Self-reliance

A S S O C I A T I V E

1. Recoupling, on the basis of **equity**

2. Entropy, interaction at all levels, in all directions, not only at the elite level

3. Symbiosis (making the parties interdependent)

4. Broad scope of interdependence (many spheres, widening agendas)

5. Large domain (more than two parties, but not too many)

6. Superstructure for planning, for problem and conflict articulation and resolution dominance. Horizontality is more easily built from a zero relationship of complete self-reliance than from a vertical relationship, for there is not only exploitation but also penetration to counteract. In addition, fragmentation must be counteracted, and the principle of entropy, interaction in all directions, not only involving elite levels, is seen as the guiding principle here.

In the lower right-hand corner the two strategies just discussed are continued, for equity and entropy alone do not constitute sufficient guarantee against direct violence. For direct violence to be counteracted, according to this theory, the basic defense in our age consists in association.[33] But the association has to be relatively tight, it has to be so symbiotic that both parties feel that to hit the other is to hit themselves. In other words, there has to be true interdependence. Further, there has to be a relatively broad scope of the interaction, involving, for example, not only trade but also political, cultural, and social events, not to mention highly personal matters. Further, if there are only two parties the system will too easily polarize when a conflict appears. The domain should be more extensive, but perhaps not so much that a split into two opposed alliances is likely. Examples would be the European community or the Nordic countries, consisting of between five and nine participating countries, able to manage multilaterally most conflicts that arise.

Then there is the need for a superstructure; some kind of central authority for problem and conflict articulation and resolution. In the present book this will be dealt with particularly in chapter 8, under the heading of "world central authority." In this general presentation the idea of the superstructure is that some kind of nonexploitative center is needed, some kind of reference point capable of dealing with problems the parties cannot resolve by themselves.

Finally, in the upper right-hand corner are listed most of the strategies of classical peace thinking, which characteristically enough is limited to the concern with direct violence and dissociative strategies. The strategies are rather trivial, being based on geographical, social, and artificial distance and impediment. Most famous is the military form of "social impediment," the idea of being strong enough not only to punish the transgressor but also to make him so afraid of the punishment that he curbs his evil intentions. Ultimately, this crystallizes into balance-of-power strategies with their well-known consequences, such as arms races, military–industrial complexes, and the like, as discussed at length in chapter 5, where I argue heavily against such approaches and raise the general problem of how the world can get out of the distortion it is subjected to at present because of centuries of reliance on this approach to peace. In that picture, a nonmilitary defense stands out as one item, as one possibility among many (discussed in chapter 5) and world police forces as another (discussed in chapter 8).

Summarizing this map of strategies one might perhaps say that it is an effort to synthesize thinking on structural and direct violence not only conceptually (that was to some extent done in chapter 2) but strategically. The two are intimately linked together, as direct violence is often used to establish structural violence, and structural violence leads to direct violence, whether of the revolutionary or counterrevolutionary variety.[34] A peace theory that deals with only one of these four cells, as classical peace theory has been doing and as Marxist peace theory also to some extent does, is probably more dangerous than no peace theory at all, and much of the concern of the present book is precisely with the types of structure that are currently rationalized by reference to that type of truncated peace thinking.

Is a better world attainable? Yes. Simply because these strategies are known (under different names), they have been tried, and they have often led to good goals. There is nothing mysterious or esoteric about them. People are not asked to convert, undergo psychotherapy, or meditate; they are asked to understand, organize, and act in manners that are perfectly rational and reasonable. One condition is deeper understanding of the systems of dominance and war, of structural and direct violence, which is the subject of the next two chapters.

NOTES

References to *Essays* are to Johan Galtung, *Essays in Peace Research,* 5 vols. (Copenhagen: Ejlers, 1975-80) (Atlantic Highlands, N.J.: Humanities Press).

1. Because the values have, to a large extent, come out of a tradition that is a reflection of Western history, they can be used to say something about that history, as is attempted in figure 3.1. That is only one model, certainly not unrelated to the Marxist perspective, but it is spelled out in terms that I think are richer because they are not so limited to economic relations.

2. Of course, one basic factor that the United States and Japan have had in common and that explains how so much accumulation could take place across basic differences in social structure is capitalist imperialism, practiced in various ways by both of them from the turn of the century. In the terms of this section, the two societies may have a dominant Model II and Model I configuration, respectively, domestically; but they are both practicing Model I on the global level. For more on this, see Galtung, "Japan and Future World Politics," *Essays* V, 6.

3. These are the cornerstones in Galtung, "Structural Pluralism and the Future of Human Society," in *Proceedings of the Second International Future Research Conference, Tokyo* (Kodansha, 1971). I have developed the theme further in such articles as "Social Structure, Religious Structure, and the Fight for Peace," *Essays* I, 17; "Perspectives on Development: Past, Present, Future," *Essays* III, 9; and "Social Structure and Science Structure," chapter 1 in *Methodology and Ideology* (Copenhagen: Ejlers, 1977). I mention this because the two variables seem relatively fruitful in providing a simple explanatory basis for a relatively wide variety of phenomena.

4. Diversity, when interpreted as "individualism" will tend to run against Buddhist values: "The most serious form of *dhitti* [heresy, "wrong view"] according to Buddhist tradition is to assert the reality and permanence of the individual human ego . . . ," quoted from S. G. F. Brandon, *A Dictionary of Comparative Religion* (London, 1971). And as to equity, there seems to be a long Asian tradition of equity in the sense of autonomy (the hermit, the

nomadic tribe, the isolated community), but not in the sense of equitable, horizontal relations. That is probably more of a Marxist heritage that the Chinese have interpreted more broadly.

5. The uniformity is inclusive, collectivist; everybody is *in*; he who is not in is not a part of society. The comparison could be with a monastic order or an army: even the most solitary monk is abiding by rules applying to all members of the order; there is no sense in a soldier operating alone, according to Model I logic.

6. The extent to which the People's Communes constitute examples of Model III societies—and that is to a considerable degree—is analyzed in some detail in Galtung and Fumiko Nishimura, *Learning from the Chinese People* (Oslo, 1975), particularly in chapter 3 on the cultural revolution. It should be noted, however, that there are considerable differences among the communes as well as considerable mobility between them—although not permanent resettlement—indicating some moves toward a Model IV type of society.

7. Now, in retrospect, we can see more clearly that this was a very limited move, leading to phase *b* of Model II society in figure 3.2. But at that time it was a move shaking the entire order, based, as it was, on the fragmentation of those who sold their labor.

8. This theme is developed, to some extent, in the first sections of Galtung, "European Security and Cooperation: A Sceptical Contribution," *Essays* V, 2.

9. It may be objected that this is not the case today. In the writings of R.D. Laing, for instance, it is repeatedly emphasized that the conformist to a sick society is himself sick, and Jessie Bernard makes a similar point about women who say they are "happy" in their present state of subjugation. Increasingly, the mature person is seen as the nonconformist. This, however, in my view is only a sign that the present social configuration is about to break down, that we are living through a period of transition from Model II toward Model III and/or Model IV societies that will develop their own criteria of what constitutes a mature person.

10. This is also one of the challenges of the Chinese pattern of development: *start with those most in need*, which also should be a Christian pattern of action.

11. Best known from St. Thomas More, of course.

12. The *autunno caldo* ("hot fall") in Italy (1969) produced a number of new approaches to workers' demands, particularly for more interesting work.

13. Like Disneyland. However, although it is easy to be intellectually arrogant toward such ventures, they may have considerable pedagogical and curiosity-raising impact. What is missing is usually some way in which visitors can participate, not only watch and listen—but that applies to most museums. museums.

14. This is spelled out in some detail in Galtung, *Future Societies* (forthcoming); see also Galtung, "Structural Pluralism and the Future of Human Society." The word "postrevolutionary" is chosen on purpose to contradict Daniel Bell's (and others') concept of postindustrical society, connoting no major change in the vertical order, only a decrease in the secondary sector and an increase in the tertiary sector, toward a more automated, information-based society. However, the term "pluralist" or even "humanist" is preferable. It is more positive and less deterministic, for it does not presuppose a revolution in the violent sense.

15. That does not mean mobility at any speed, however. As pointed out by Ivan Illich in *Energy and Equity,* the higher the speed, the more elitism in travel. Rather, one might be thinking in terms of free or inexpensive collective transportation on land and on sea, first within cities, then between cities— and first within countries, then between. The first phase is already realized in Havana.

16. It could also be in kind, providing for food, clothing, shelter, health, and education, but money gives more freedom of personal budgeting.

17. And that is the basic point in Galtung, "Economics and Peace Research: I. Some Basic Problems," mimeo (Oslo, 1975).

18. The nonhistoricity of the future seems to be a fundamental part of Western thinking, shared by liberal and Marxist patterns of thought. See Galtung, "Two Ways of Being Western: Some Similarities between Liberalism and Marxism," Trends in Western Civilization Program (Chair in Conflict and Peace Research, University of Oslo).

19. With decreasing labor intensity, less and less of the person will be in the product. The differentiation will be between those who make highly labor-intensive blueprints (production plans, social and technical innovations) and those who implement those blueprints. The more of the person is in it, the more education (as distinct from schooling) is needed. Hence, the key to a society less stratified by level of schooling would be much higher labor intensity, which means less productivity, but also products that can last longer and contain more love and meaning.

20. See Galtung, "Mass Communication and Future Society," a chapter in *Future Societies* (forthcoming).

21. Gandhi's famous phrase suggests the common anarchist belief that if the basic units (here the villages) are all right, then the rest will take care of itself, through "oceanic circles" of solidarity and cooperation. It is hard to share this faith; at least nobody so far has found a formula that guarantees that small units will remain nonaggressive. At most, we can trust that when they make wars they will tend to make small ones.

22. This point is explored in some detail in Galtung, "Three Approaches to Peace: Peace-keeping, Peace-making, and Peace-building," *Essays* II, 11.

23. But the conditions for continued development of Yugoslavia are probably better understood by members of the left opposition, such as Mihailo Markovic in his insistence on the need for continued creation of a social culture, including socialist political ideology—which in turn presupposes much more freedom of expression and impression than the present regime is willing to grant.

24. See, for instance, Robert Redfield, *The Primitive World and Its Transformations* (London: Penguin, 1968). The level was probably lower on material needs, but was it lower on the need for love, creativity, meaning of life, togetherness?

25. For a good description and overview of several such models, see Roy L. Prosterman, *Surviving to 3000: An Introduction to Lethal Conflict* (Belmont, Calif.: Duxbury, 1972), esp. pp. 119–34.

26. Of course, one may say that at the latent level the propensity is the same, but some conditions trigger the potential and some do not. That brings us immediately to the next models in line, and to the basic conclusion, "OK, the problem then is to know the conditions that do not serve to release the potential."

27. Konrad Lorenz, *On Aggression* (New York: Harcourt, 1963). Against Lorenz there is a very important German literature, such as Herbert Selg, ed., *Zur Aggression verdammt? Psychologische Ansätz einer Friedensforschung* (Stuttgart: Kohlhammer, 1971); Hanns-Dietrich Dann, *Aggression und Leistung* (Stuttgart: Klett, 1972); Schmidt-Mummeney and H. D. Schmidt, *Aggressives Verhalten* (Munich: Juventa, 1972); and Lepenies/Nolte, *Kritik der Anthropologie* (Munich: Hanser, 1972). Their argumentation is partly that what Lorenz writes and states is simply not true, partly that it has served as some kind of excuse for aggressive aspects of the contemporary world, national and international.

28. Anthony Storr, *Human Aggression* (New York: Atheneum, 1968).

29. Robert Ardrey, *The Territorial Imperative* (London: Collins, 1966). For an excellent critique of Ardrey, see Alexander Alland Jr., *The Human Imperative* (New York: Columbia University Press, 1975). Alland makes the same point as made in the text: that if aggression were innate, humans everywhere would behave aggressively, and in a standardized, predictable manner. He points out that there are societies with very low levels of violence and others that are very violent, and that the variations seem to be culturally determined in a way that is "a far cry from the rather automatic and highly patterned aggressive responses which occur in lower animals." As examples he mentions the Semai of Malaya (nonaggressive) and the Abron of the Ivory Coast. Aggressiveness in the latter seems to stem from reactions of the first born when siblings are also paid attention to, and the severe punishment inflicted upon them when they vent their jealousies.

30. This, of course, raises the problem of whether "species" may mean something different for man. In-group killing is more rare, and the in-group has better developed means of communication, generally speaking. Even in small, isolated communities there is probably an in-group around most people within which killing is highly unlikely. We know very little about the reasons—which leaves us free to ask the question "Are there some unknown mechanisms behind the in-group taboos against killing that, if they were better known, might be extended to all of mankind?"

31. A number of findings in this direction were reported by the Japanese sociologist Hidetoshi Kato to the Quality of Life conference organized by the IG Metall, Oberhausen, April 1972. The proceedings of this conference are published as *Qualität des Lebens*, 10 vols. (1972).

32. Prosterman, in *Surviving to 3000*, attacks "prehistoric man: the myth of savagery" (pp. 135–45) and goes on to examine the idea of "lethal conflict in primitive societies" (pp. 146–66). I am not competent to judge the evidence in this connection, but I would like to make one point here. According to the fundamental creed of Western society, in the Idea of Progress both prehistoric man and primitive man *have* to be violent, even belligerent, or else increasing violence and warfare would have to be defined as progress. Since such mental configurations probably steer research and thinking more than almost anything else (certainly more than data), Prosterman's exposure of these ideas and myths attains a certain *a priori* credibility.

33. This idea is developed in some detail in Galtung, *Co-operation in Europe* (Oslo: Universitetsforlaget, 1970), pt. I. For another version of the same basic idea, see Galtung, "Europe: Bipolar, Bicentric or Co-operative?" *Essays* V, 1.

34. See the typology of violence given in section 2.4.

4. THE DOMINANCE SYSTEM

4.1 ON THE FORMS OF STRUCTURAL VIOLENCE

The theory of dominance that is sketched here takes the particular form of a theory of imperialism. Whether expressed as dominance or imperialism, structural violence is vividly at work, as in many cases direct violence also is. But imperialism is a special category under the general heading of dominance. Imperialism, as here conceived of, presupposes that there are two collectivities, usually societies, not just one. A teacher may dominate a class, a father a family, the ruling class may dominate a society, but in these cases the word "imperialism" would be improper. Imperialism is at a higher level of social complexity; it is a type of relationship whereby one society (or collectivity in more general terms) can dominate another. Often these two societies may be found within the same political borders, in which case one may talk about internal imperialism.

We assume that structural violence is tremendously significant because of its two major forms of expression discussed at some length in chapters 2 and 3: *repression* (or uniformity; as the opposite of diversity, pluralism, freedom) and *exploitation* (as the opposite of equity). In extreme cases structural violence may be so repressive that it virtually leads to the psychological death of the people exposed to it, or so exploitative that it leads to their physical death by keeping them well below the limit of fundamental need satisfaction.

It is well known that in the social science literature in general, and more particularly in the Marxist literature, a highly impressive tradition exists that purports to come to grips with the phenomenon of imperialism. One might therefore ask why we do not simply stick to this tradition, why we do not accept that as a sufficient basis for exploring the phenomena we are interested in.

By and large, there are five reasons why it has been felt that there is a need for some new thinking in the field of theorizing about imperialism. Although what is presented here is not presumed to be the successful answer to the problems raised, the problems demand attention and must be answered somehow.[1]

First, there is the age-old problem about the primacy of economics. In the presentation to be given in the following section no such primacy will be assumed, nor is any doctrine against the primacy raised; there is a preference for an agnostic position. It is strongly felt that imperialism is a general structure that may be filled with very concrete economic, political, military, social, cultural, and communicative content—singly or in any combination. It may well be that at the present juncture in world history, in looking at international relations at large, an economic point of view would be the most fruitful in explaining what is going on. However, it is felt that there is a need for a broader theory of imperialism that also can come to grips with other phenomena, some of them contemporary, some of them from the past, some of them to come in a possibly very near future.[2]

Let us look at three examples from contemporary international relations that, I feel, are not easily handled in terms of a theory of imperialism that presupposes the primacy of the economic factors.

The first example would be relations between the two major socialist powers, the Soviet Union and the People's Republic of China. It is well known that the Chinese have accused the Soviet Union of "social imperialism." In my own view the term chosen by the Chinese is a very precise and significant one and is therefore included in the list of six just given. The Chinese do not by this term mean economic exploitation. On the contrary, trade statistics between the Soviet Union and China for the 1950s seem to indicate that the Chinese were given increasingly better access to the Soviet Union for their processed goods and were not merely made use of in the traditional pattern of colonial economic relations, with raw materials from China going to the Soviet Union and processed goods in the other direction.[3] Nor is the accusation raised by the Chinese against the Soviet Union formulated in such terms.

On the contrary, what they claim is that the Soviet Union tried to push on them a particular social configuration, more particularly, a Model II society based on professionalism, with an educational sorting of people into categories with power to some extent proportionate to the level of education, professionalization, and position in various bureaucracies, particularly those of the party.[4] It is the export of a social structure, and the effort to imprint this upon what in the early 1950's must have been a relatively receptive Chinese social body that has been so much resented by the Chinese. Whether this is done out of economic motivation or not, for possible future economic profit or not, is in a sense irrelevant because it is considered sufficiently wrong and evil in its own right. Moreover, is there any reason to assume that a big power would not be willing to forgo economics gains, short-term as well as long-term, if it were able to reproduce its own social configuration elsewhere, thereby creating the type of homology between states so useful for any type of domination?[5]

The second example would relate to the present relations between East and West in the traditional Cold War sense, meaning by "East" the Soviet Union and Eastern Europe and by "West" the United States and Western Europe. Clearly, what Russia did in 1917 and the Eastern European countries in the years subsequent to World War II with the participation of the Red Army can be understood only in the context of a theory of imperialism. It was a clear, and to a large extent successful, effort to get out of the economic grips of Western economic penetration. It was intended as an effort to become master in one's own house and to build an economy with the purpose of satisfying fundamental needs of the population at large, not only of catering to demands articulated in the money language of those who can participate in a market.

However, one significant component of imperialism seems somehow to escape the attention of those who have been building socialist societies in Eastern Europe: the more fundamental goals. Any observer will be struck by the extent to which the goals of the production systems in Eastern Europe are remarkably similar to those of the West. Consumers' goods are very much the same as in the West and goals of industrial production are the same; this situation is accentuated when programs are formulated in terms of "catching up" and "surpassing" similar production dimensions in the West.

In short, the general cultural matrix within which the meaning of society, of life, as defined, seems to be still dominated by the West. More particularly, whenever a new and important development takes place in the definition of goals in the West it is reflected, sooner rather than later, in the goal-setting patterns of the countries in the East.[6] Needless to say, this is impossible without a high level of cultural penetration, without an orientation of, for instance, Eastern European universities toward Western universities, an admiration for the Western capacities, and a corresponding lack of faith in the strength and vitality of their own contribution. Instead of finding socialist solutions to, for instance, the problem of transportation, the tendency seems to be to import capitalist solutions (individualized car transport), however much they are controlled by machineries that are referred to as socialist (although the category of "state monopoly capitalism" might be more appropriate[7]).

This cannot be easily explained by reference to economic penetration alone. Few countries have been so effective in shielding themselves off from economic control from the outside as the Eastern European countries in the postwar period, yet the cultural penetration is a remarkable factor in the contemporary scene, which seems to be greatly facilitated through the present pattern of exchange referred to as "East–West trade": raw materials go from East to West in exchange for technology from West to East.[8] That no technology is culturally neutral requires no elaboration.

The third example would refer to Japan and the theory of why Japan did not really succeed as an imperialistic power.[9] The point is not that her expansion since the Meiji, particularly since her defeat of czarist Russia in the 1904–1905 war, led to a head-on collision with Western powers and ultimately to Japan's capitulation on 15 August 1945. The point is rather that, both when Japan was successful before that defeat and in the present postwar period with the Japanese economic empire expanding at tremendous rates, her success was and is still very limited. In an effort to cut through a complex reality in one simple formula let us just say: Japanese economic imperialism has been unaccompanied by a corresponding cultural imperialism. Japan has had no message that has captured people's minds, penetrated them, defined their general outlook on the world, and made them look to Tokyo as the source of goal setting and the ultimate meaning of life. There is no book, either black or red, emanating from the Japanese economic center, only material goods.

Thus it is that in Japanese cars the agents of Japanese economic imperialism in Southeast Asia will drive their sons and daughters to international schools propagating American, English, and French culture, not Japanese; that on Japanese-made radios, tape recorders, and phonographs American and Western European music and other forms of culture will be broadcast; and that in Japanese refrigerators there will be an ample supply of Western and local foods and not even an indication of Japanese food habits. This means, in turn, that Japanese goods are substitutable. The moment they no longer are the best at the best prices they will be turned down, as opposed to the goods from some other centers in the world that will be adhered to also because of their cultural connotations, because the recipients have lived there parts of their lives, studied and done business, and so on.

In short, it is strongly felt that a theory of imperialism as a special case of the theory of dominance has to be broadly based and not include dogmas to the effect that there is one and only one type that is primary. But this is not to deny the paramount importance of relations where the ownership of means of production is at the same time the ownership of means of subsistence, a question of life and death for those who sell their labor. Any analysis of, say, U.S.–Latin America relations, European Community–Black Africa relations, and also to a large extent Japan–Southeast Asia relations will have to reflect this. My only plea here is for a more general theory that also can handle other relations that may be important in other periods, and today in other regions. To state it bluntly: there is probably a high correlation between Soviet, and in general socialist Europe's, failure to understand what went wrong in the relation to China and what today is very quickly going wrong in their relation to Western Europe, and their dogmatic faith in the primacy of economics in shaping imperialistic relations. There seems to have been a general faith stimulated by dogma to the effect that if only economic relations do not take the forms of private monopoly capitalism, particularly in its imperialistic form as described by Lenin, then there will be no problem of domination, by definition.[10]

Let us then move on to the second reason for this approach to imperialism: the need for a more general analysis of exploitation. The basic point has already been presented in chapter 2 and will be amplified in the subsequent section: exploitation cannot be comprehended only by analyzing the interaction or exchange between two parties, it also has to be seen in terms of the intra-action and the *in*-change taking place within them, as a result of the interaction. Moreover, it should not be interpreted only in terms of bilateral relations between exploiter and exploited, whether defined as individuals, as classes, or as countries, but as economic cycles and other types of networks, as patterns of relations wherein after some time the total system proves to be much more beneficial for some components of the network than for others. The actor-oriented type of analysis would then focus on differential characteristics, on the extent to which those who have benefited most can be said to be more talented, more industrious, more endowed with the protestant ethic, and so on. The structure-oriented antidote to this will be given later, with its focus on relations and patterns.

The third reason for a new approach lies in the shortcoming of any analysis that defines global conflicts in connection with imperialism in terms of two classes or groupings only. One cannot in the long run insist that world capitalism induces a bipartite division between those who buy and those who sell their labor, when there is such an overwhelming evidence on the contemporary world scene to the effect that there are only two categories that look relatively unambiguous: the powerful in the rich countries and the powerless in the poor countries. The less powerful in the rich countries seem increasingly to become what Lenin himself referred to as a labor aristocracy, and the rich in the poor countries, exemplified by the local bourgeoisie, also constitute an ambivalent group. The total conflict formation, hence, should be conceived of in terms of four classes or groups rather than in terms of two, and analytic schemes that purport to reflect the empirical reality of today should be flexible enough to accommodate some of the many variations found in the conflict constellations. The Indochina wars, for instance, can be seen as wars between two parties: the conscious masses of Indochina on the one hand, pitted against an unholy triple alliance of the rich in rich countries (first Japan, then France, then the United States), the less powerful in the rich countries (often sons of workers and farmers, first from Japan, then from France, then from the United States), and the local bridgehead indicated by one word: "Saigon."

A fourth reason for a new approach lies in the circumstance that the world society of today is so complex that any analysis that uses only countries as building blocks is doomed to fail. On the one hand it is too comprehensive, it gives an image of a country as a class-divided billiard ball, not sufficiently reflecting other internal differentiations. Where the latter are concerned one word is sufficient to indicate the problem: "Pakistan," belonging in quotation marks exactly because it was a myth. But there are many such myths around, to be explored further in section 6.2, where in addition to class, race and other ethnic factors are considered.

On the other hand the image of the world as divided into countries does not reflect nonterritorial entities, such as some of the international organizations. Between them there may also be imperialistic relationships, with strong similarities to the relations found between countries. This may not be a major point in contemporary analysis, but it is important enough to have an influence on the strategy of theory construction in this field. Theories should be formulated in such a way that it is possible also to accommodate thinking about relationships between organizations, not only relationships between the classical polities, the countries, particularly in the form of the nation-states.

Finally, there is the fifth reason, growing out of the general theoretical scheme presented in the preceding chapter with its emphasis on exploitation and repression. Theories of imperialism have so far mainly been used to explain how basic inequities and inequalities are generated. They have been used to explain how inequalities that are sometimes extremely lethal for those at the bottom are maintained, even reinforced. It is felt, however, that this is too narrow a scope for a theory of imperialism. Not only inequality, but also repression can often be traced to imperialistic relationships. There is a strong center somewhere from which patterns emerge—thought patterns and cosmologies as well as social patterns and structures. Through mechanisms to be discussed later, particularly through penetration—bridgehead building—repression may take the form of imposition of a structure.

The People's Commune in the People's Republic of China has often been used in these pages as an example of how inequities may be transcended through the reduction, even abolition, of not only vertical but also horizontal division of labor, and they are possibly unequalled in the world of today when it comes to nonexploitative relationships.

Yet, the problem still remains of whether China is not also an example of internal structural imperialism, with a center in Peking from which certain configurations emanate, with bridgehead building into the smallest com- mune, with groups dispersing a cultural message and building social structures with a level of uniformity so high that it must be referred to as repressive. Suspicions to this effect arise when one is confronted with the remarkable uniformity not only among, but also within the People's Communes, a unifor- mity hardly to be explained in terms of uniformity as an ethos alone. Because it is hard to get data from China about such matters, this will remain a speculation. But it also remains a guiding light for theory formation: theories should be constructed in such a way that they can cope with phenomena of this kind. Exploitation, inequity, is not the only problem with which the world is con- fronted; repression is also basic, although possibly affecting a higher level on a scale of human needs. It goes without saying that it is the Soviet imposition of its particular social structure that is our major example, not a hypothesis about China.

What we need is a theory encompassing all these phenomena. In my experience, theories of imperialism are the only ones that come to grips with such a range of phenomena and at the same time connect the world, make us see the world as something structured and related, not merely as a set of billiard-ball countries. The questions become "What are the *mechanisms* of imperialism, what are the *types* of imperialism, its concrete manifestations or apparitions; and what are the *phases* imperialism, as a historical phenomenon, is going through?" Those are the themes of the next section.

4.2 AN ANALYSIS OF IMPERIALISM

4.2.1 THE MECHANISMS OF IMPERIALISM

Imperialism is a structure; it is not a collection of wicked people, although it may make ample use of such people. It can be understood only within the structure-oriented perspective; the actor-oriented perspective will always fail to capture the essence of imperialism. More explicitly, imperialism makes use of all the four dimensions of structural analysis presented in chapter 2 and combines them in a particularly effective way. These four dimensions were presented positively in earlier discussion, as values or goals. Here they will be dealt with negatively, as antigoals, as mechanisms of imperialism. They are exploitation (also called vertical division of labor, inequity), penetration, fragmentation, and marginalization. We shall examine them in that order, starting with the *raison d'être* of imperialism, exploitation, which means that we shall start with the interaction relation between countries.

The basic point about interaction is, of course, that people and countries produce different goods that complement each other, and then engage in exchange. Some nations produce oil, other nations produce tractors, and they then carry out an exchange according to the principles of comparative advantages. Imagine that our two-nation system has a prehistory of no interaction at all, and then starts this type of interaction. Obviously, both will be changed by it; more particularly, a gap between them is likely to open and widen if the interaction is cumulatively asymmetric[11] in terms of what the two parties get out of it.

To study whether an interaction is symmetric or asymmetric, on equal or unequal terms, I insist again that two factors arising from the interaction have to be examined:[12]

1. The effects of the exchange between the actors–inter-actor effects,
2. The effects generated inside the actor– intra-actor effects.

In economic relations the first point is most commonly analyzed, not only by liberal but also by Marxist economists. The inter-actor flow can be observed as flows of raw material and processed goods, of capital, and financial goods and services in either direction and can literally be measured at the main points of entry, the customs houses and the national banks, unless they take the form of internal transfer in multinational corporations. The flow both ways can be compared in various ways. Most important is the comparison in terms of who benefits most, but for this purpose intra-actor effects also have to be taken into consideration. It is certainly meaningful and important to talk in terms of unequal exchange or asymmetric interaction but not quite unproblematic what its precise meaning should be beyond simply wage differentials.

In order to explore this, the interaction budget indicated in table 4.1 may be useful. In this table the usual exchange pattern between a "developed" country, *A,* and a "developing" country *B,* wherein manufactured goods are exchanged for raw materials, is indicated. Whether exchange takes place in a barter economy or a money economy is not essential in a study of exchange between completely unprocessed goods like crude oil and highly processed goods like tractors. There are negative intra-actor effects that accrue to both parties, indicated by the terms "pollution" for *A* and "depletion" for *B.* (Of course, there may also be depletion in *A* and pollution in *B.*) One basic point is that these negative spin-off effects are not taken systematically into account, but more important are the positive spin-off effects for *A* that will be a cornerstone in the present analysis. To see this more clearly it may be helpful to think in terms of three stages or types of exploitation, partly reflecting historical processes in chronological order and partly reflecting types of thinking about exploitation.

In the first stage of exploitation, *A* simply engages in looting and takes away the raw materials without offering anything in return. If he steals from pure nature there is no human interaction involved, but we assume that he also forces "natives" to work for him and do the extraction work. It is like the slaveowner who lives on the work produced by slaves, which is quantitatively not too different from the landowner who has land-workers working for him six out of seven days a week (in terms of the proportion of the food he has produced that actually is consumed by him and his family).

In the second stage, *A* starts offering something "in return." Oil, pitch, land is "bought" for a couple of beads; it is no longer simply taken away without asking any questions about ownership. The price paid is ridiculous. However, as power relations in the international system change, bringing the power level of the weaker party up from zero to some low positive value, *A* has to contribute more, for instance, pay increasingly more for oil, leading up for example to the present situation with OPEC countries and other raw material producers. The question is now whether there is a cut-off point after which the exchange becomes equal, and what the criterion for that cut-off point would be. Is it the

Table 4.1 An interaction budget

	A ("developed")		*B* ("developing")	
	Inter-actor effects	Intra-actor effects	Inter-actor effects	Intra-actor effects
Positive (in)	Raw materials	Spin-offs	Manufactured goods	Little or nothing
Negative (out)	Manufactured goods	Pollution, Exploitation	Raw materials	Depletion, Exploitation

absence of subjective dissatisfaction—when B says that he is now content? "Objective" market values? The number of person-hours that have gone into the production on either side? What then about raw materials that have not been worked at all?

There are difficulties with all these conceptions. But instead of delving further into this, let us direct our attention to the shared failure of all these attempts to look at intra-actor effects. Does the interaction process as such have enriching or impoverishing effects inside the actor, or does it just lead to a standstill? This type of question leads us to an examination of the third stage of exploitation, where there may be some balance in the value flow between the actors, but there are still great differences in the effect the interaction has within them.

As an example let us use countries exchanging oil for tractors. This exchange involves different levels of processing, where we define "processing" as an activity imposing culture on nature. In the case of crude oil the product is (almost) pure nature; but in the case of tractors it would be wrong to say that it is a case of pure culture, pure form (like mathematics or music). A transistor radio or an integrated circuit would be better examples because nature has been brought down to a minimum. The tractor is still too much iron and rubber to be a pure case, although linkages to other industries are considerable.

The major point now is the gap in processing level between oil and tractors and the differential effect this gap will have on the two countries. In one country the oil deposit may be at the waterfront, and all that is needed is a derrick and some simple mooring facilities to pump the oil straight into a ship—e.g., a Norwegian tanker—that can bring the oil to the country where it will provide energy to run, among other things, the tractor factories. In the other country the effects may be extremely far-reaching because of the complexity of the product and the connectedness of the society.

There may be ring effects in all directions, and table 4.2 is an effort to show some types of spin-off effects. A number of comments are appropriate in connection with this list which, needless to say, is very tentative indeed.

First, the effects are rather deep-reaching if this is at all a correct image of the situation, and the picture is hardly exaggerated. It is possible to set up international interaction in such a way that the positive intra-actor effects are practically nil in the raw-material–delivering nation and extremely far-reaching in the processing nation. This is not in any sense strange either: if processing is the imprint of culture on nature, the effects should be far-reaching indeed and strongly related to development itself.

Second, these effects reinforce each other. In the nine effects listed in table 4.2 there are economic, political, military, social, cultural, and communicative aspects, mixed together. Thus, the country that in the international division of labor has the task of providing the most refined processed products—like Japan with its emphasis on integrated circuits, transistors, and miniaturization (or Eastern Europe's Japan: the DDR, with similar emphasis)—will obviously have to

Table 4.2 Intra-actor effects of interactions across gaps in processing levels

Dimension	Effect on Center country	Effect on Periphery country	Analyzed by
1. Subsidiary economic effects	New *means of production* developed	Nothing developed, just a hole in the ground	Economists
2. Political position in world structure	Central position reinforced	Periphery position reinforced	International relationists
3. Military benefits	*Means of destruction* can easily be produced	No benefits, wars cannot be fought by means of raw materials	
4. Communication benefits	*Means of communication* easily developed	No benefits, transportation not by means of raw materials	Communication specialists
5. Knowledge and research	Much needed for higher levels of processing	Nothing needed, extraction based on being, not on becoming	Scientists, Technicians
6. Specialist needed	Specialists in *making*, scientists, engineers	Specialists in *having*, lawyers	Sociologists of knowledge
7. Skill and education	Much needed to carry out processing	Little change needed beyond a hole in the ground	Education specialists
8. Social structure	Change needed for ability to convert into mobility	Little change needed, extraction based on ownership, not on ability	Sociologists
9. Psychological effects	A basic psychology of self-help and autonomy	A basic psychology of dependence	Psychologists

engage in research. Research needs an infrastructure, a wide cultural basis in universities, and it has obvious spill-over effects in the social, political, and military domains. And so on: the list may be examined and all kinds of obvious types of cross-fertilization be explored, forward and backward linkages.

Third, in the example chosen and also in the formulations in the table, we have actually referred to a very special type of gap in processing level: the case when one of the countries concerned delivers raw materials. But the general point here is the gap, which would also exist if one country delivers semifinished products and the other finished products. There may be as much of a gap in trade relations based on exchange between textiles and transistors as one based on exchange between oil and tractors. However, I have looked in vain for a theory of economic trade where this gap is meaningfully operationalized so that not only a theory but also a practice of equal exchange could be based on it. In fact, the degree of processing, which is the basic variable behind the spin-off effect, seems absent from most thinking about international exchange.[13]

What is involved, and this is observation number four, is not merely a question of analyzing differences in processing level in terms of what happens inside the factory or the extraction plant. It has to be seen in its social totality. A glance at the right-hand column of table 4.2 immediately gives us some clues as to why this has not been done: academic research has been so divided that nowhere in a traditional university set-up would one come to grips with the totality of the effects of an interaction process. Not even in the most sophisticated inter-, cross-, or trans-disciplinary research institute has that type of research been carried so far that a meaningful operationalization has been offered. Yet this is indispensable for a new program of trade on equal terms to be formulated: *trade, or interaction in general, is symmetric, or on equal terms, if and only if the total inter- and intra-actor effects that accrue to the parties are equal.*

But, and this is observation number five, why has the idea of comparing the effects of interaction only at the points of exit and entry been so successful? Probably basically because it has always been natural and in the interest of those on top of *A* and *B* to view the world in this way, not necessarily consciously to reinforce their position but basically because interaction looks more like interaction only to the center. They sit at the top and do not see so clearly what happens or does not happen below them. What was formerly nature is through the "beneficial interaction" with another country converted into money, which in turn can be converted into many things. Very little effort was needed in *B*, which was precisely what made the exchange so disadvantageous, as became clear only after some time. The disastrous theory of "comparative advantages" served as a rationale, and countries like Japan and Switzerland even managed to convert the absence of raw materials into a blessing for the economy. It was not in their interest to develop another economic theory.[14]

Some implications of the general principle of viewing intra-actor effects in addition to inter-actor effects can now be spelled out.

One is obvious: asymmetry cannot be rectified only by stabilizing or increasing the prices for raw materials. Of course, prices exist that could, on the surface, compensate for the gap in intra-actor effects, converting money into a corresponding development of subsidiary industries: the education industry, the knowledge industry, and so on. Much of this is what raw-material–producing countries can do with the money they earn. But this is not the same. It is one thing to be forced into a certain pattern of intra-actor development in order to be able to participate in the inter-actor interaction, quite another to be free to make the decision without having to do it, without being forced by the entire social machinery. Thus, it is hard to see how the psychology of autonomy can be bought for money.

The second implication is also obvious but should still be put as a question to economists. Imagine that country A gives country B a loan, L to be repaid after n years at an interest rate of p per annum. There is only one condition in addition to the conditions of the loan: that the money be used to produce goods at a high level of processing in A. Each order will then have deep repercussions in A, along the nine dimensions indicated, in addition to the direct effect of the order itself. The value of these effects is certainly not easily calculated, but in addition A also gets back from B, if B has not gone bankrupt through this process in the meantime, $L(1 + p)^n$ after n years. If procurement is in terms of capital goods rather than consumer goods there will also have been intra-actor effects in B. In all likelihood the intra-actor effects of the deal in A are more far-reaching, however, for two reasons: the effects of the interaction process enter A at a higher level of processing than B, and A has already a socioeco-nomic–political structure enabling it to absorb and convert and redirect such effects for maximum beneficial impact.

Imagine now that n is high and p is low; the loan is said to be "on generous terms." The question is whether this generosity is not deceptive, whether it would not even have paid A to give L for eternity, at no interest, i.e., as a grant. Or even better: it might even have paid for A to persuade B to take on L with negative interest, i.e., to pay B for accepting the loan, because of all the intra-actor effects.[15] The situation may be likened to that of a man who pays some people a certain sum on the condition that they use the money to pay him for a lecture on, say, imperialism. By having to produce, by having obligations to fulfill, the'man is forced to create and thereby expand and consequently to enrich himself.

In short, I see vertical interaction as the major source of the inequality of this world, whether it takes the form of looting, of cheating, or of highly differential spin-off effects due to processing gaps. But I can also imagine a fourth phase of exploitation, where the modern King Midas becomes a victim of his own greed and turns his environment into muck rather than gold, by polluting it so strongly and so thoroughly that the negative spin-off effects from processing may outstrip all the positive effects. This may, in fact, place the less-developed countries in a more favorable position: the lower the gross national product, the lower the gross national pollution. Pollution is only one reason why developed countries should be seen as overdeveloped; there are many others.

But this phase is still for the (near?) future. At present what we observe is an inequality among the world's nations of a magnitude that can be explained only in terms of the cumulative effect of strong structural phenomena over time, like the phenomena described here under the heading of imperialism. This is not to deny that other factors may also be important, even decisive, by no analysis can be valid without studying the problem of development in a context of vertical interaction.

In fact, the two letters A and B are too symmetric to represent this vertical reality, so from now on we change to C and P, standing for "Center" and

"Periphery" (countries), respectively. As this vertical division of labor is also found inside countries, the same process takes place there, generating domestic centers and peripheries: Thus four groups or classes are created: the center in the Center, the periphery in the Center, the center in the Periphery, and the periphery in the Periphery, symbolized by *cC, pC, cP,* and *pP.*

So much for the first mechanism of imperialism, exploitation. Let us proceed to the second one, penetration. One way of defining it would be as the opposite of autonomy, which in chapter 2 is split into three components: self-respect, self-sufficiency, and fearlessness. Penetration, hence, would be the opposite of this: a combination of submissiveness, dependence, and fear. However, those are only words, not mechanisms.

As to mechanism, I shall use one particular meaningful word: "bridgehead." The basic idea in penetration is that the Center country somehow penetrates "under the skin" of the Periphery country by establishing a bridgehead there. And this bridgehead, the center in the Periphery, will then play a crucial role in the whole structure of imperialism.

More particularly, there are two basic elements in the bridgehead mechanism, two pillars so to speak, that should be spelled out.

First, we have *the harmony between the center in the Center and the center in the Periphery*. In order to function, the bridgehead has to be kept at a highly acceptable level of living. The two centers have to be like communicating vessels, and the center in the Center has at all times to be willing to concede to their bridgehead most of what they want to enjoy themselves. In fact, in the world of today some of the richest people are found in the centers of the poor countries, and they can be used, if they see the harmony link with the other center up in the north as a guarantee of their own continued existence. But it also applies to political assets such as the right of local autonomy. So many of the so-called independence wars, particularly in the western hemisphere—north and south— were certainly not fought for the masses but for the local elites to get the political autonomy needed to do for themselves what so far had been done from London, Lisbon, and Madrid. In all probability Britain could have retained her colonies on the eastern seaboard of North America for a much longer period had she been willing to grant to the local elites more political rights, and the same might have applied further south one and two generations later. For the concept of "freedom" harbored by those bridgehead people seems to be a concept of equality with the people for whom they constitute the bridgehead. They are maybe willing to suffer declines, but only if compatible declines are suffered in the center of the Center.

In other words, a strong coupling is the essence of this relation, as in a very harmoniously structured couple: they go up together and down together, sharing good and bad days. Later, I shall have occasion to point out that no institution is so well organized for this purpose as an international organization in general, and a multinational corporation in particular. No other organization can so well equalize the conditions of the elites and make all of them share the fate of the organization.

Second, we have *the inegalitarian distribution of inequality*. If I should point to one empirical regularity that seems to be more crucial than any other in underpinning imperialism, it must be this one.[16] For what is hidden behind this formula is not only inequality between center and periphery in any country of the world, a fact that is well known and comprehensible in terms of vertical division of labor. What is more important is that even this inequality is distributed in an inegalitarian manner between Center and Periphery countries. There is a gap between rich and poor in both, but that gap is an abyss in a Periphery country.

Thus, the businessman or the scientist from a Center country who travels to visit his colleagues in a Periphery country will from the moment he steps off the plane be able to enjoy conditions very much like what he knows at home. The conversations at the cocktail parties, the whole style of life will be confusingly similar. But some steps away, the steep gradient of Periphery society can be experienced in the slums, in the bush, in the vast poor nothingness.

If one now connects these two pillars of the bridgehead, one arrives at one very simple and well-known fact. Since the average level of living is much lower in a Periphery country its center has to be small, and it is; the small elites and the vast masses are well separated. If it were not, then there would not be in the Periphery countries the availability of what the Center is looking for: cheap labor, combined with an elite than can serve as a market for consumer goods. As a matter of fact, as economic history moves on it will be in the interest of the Center country to change the composition of the Periphery country, having less need for cheap labor and more for consumers, the so-called middle classes. But this has so far happened only in some countries relatively close to their metropolitan centers, such as Mexico, Tunis, and Hong Kong. The general situation is that the Periphery elite has very much to lose if it should be reduced to the level of the masses, that both these elites and the masses and the center in the Center know that, and know that it is in elite interest to try to maintain present conditions.

It is important to note how false it is to conceive of local elites only as a traditional bourgeoisie in the capitalist sense, a collection of businessmen representing metropolitan firms and their adjuncts. Political elites trained in the metropolitan country, not to mention intellectual elites whose souls remain in the metropolitan university at which they got their degrees, could just as well be included. They may be no less privatistic in their interest for "intellectual tourism," free travel to world conferences for instance, than the local businessman is when he sees a chance to serve at the world headquarters of the corporation he is representing.

Let us now return to the terms with which we started, giving meaning to the concept of penetration. The submissiveness in this process lies in the total internalization of Center ideology, including its linguistic expression in the mother-country language. Concretely this means that when negotiations take place between Center and Periphery the former may have the best representatives among the delegates from the latter. It facilitates negotiations in the interest of the Center tremendously when her interests are represented well at both sides of the table.[17] Incidentally, one very clear expression of this principle is found in the field of social sciences where the intellectual penetration of the Periphery by the Center is particularly pronounced, in Latin America, in Africa, and in Asia. That it is in the Center's interest to have that particular branch of economics that could best be referred to as "capitalistics"—the branch of the total science of economics dealing with various forms of capitalism as if that were the only economic arrangement possible—widely diffused is obvious. That the Periphery countries should embrace it so eagerly is often less obvious, but the signs of resistance are now more and more frequent. This is important, for one particular consequence of liberal economics is the faith in the doctrine of "comparative advantages," which will always serve as a justification for vertical division of labor.[18]

The meaning of dependence is equally clear in view of these mechanisms. Dependence simply means that a need is generated that can be satisfied only from the Center. But this is not the need of the masses but the need of the elites, and the needs of the country are identified with those needs. As these needs become articulated, so do the corresponding investments, whether they take place under the formula of development assistance or not, and the Periphery country is then hooked on the spiral of capitalistic production with escalating demands for spare parts that can only be supplied from the Center, new models also only available from the Center when the old product generations fade away, and so on. It becomes much like drug addiction, and if the supplies are cut off chances are very high that this will only introduce a process of weaning for a few among the elites; the others will end up sooner or later in the Center countries where the old supplies are abundant and no weaning is necessary. In other words, they will become economic refugees, like most of the many Cubans currently living in the United States. Or, they may become some kind of ideological, political, intellectual refugee like the hard-liners from Hungary and Czechoslovakia who found their refuge in their particular mother country, the Soviet Union.[19]

Thus, the theory of penetration is more than simply a question of investment.[20] It is based on a skillful play on the combination of harmony of interest between the centers and their peripheries. Thus, the model of imperialism is no longer as on the left-hand side of figure 4.1 but as on the right-hand side.

We then turn to the third mechanism of imperialism: fragmentation. This mechanism also splits into two different parts, one of them international, the other one a special combination of international and intranational, as illustrated in figure 4.2. On the left-hand side of the figure is an illustration of the old *divide et impera* idea; a Center country that is able to exploit one Periphery country is probably also able to exploit others. Needless to say, this depends in part on how successful the penetration is, but the basic mechanism of fragmentation works in this way: whatever interaction there is is vertical, between

Figure 4.1   Exploitation and penetration

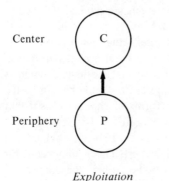
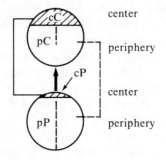

Exploitation
"Billiard-ball" model

Penetration
Center-Periphery model

Key: Solid line (——) indicates harmony, broken line (- - -) indicates disharmony.

Periphery and Center; and there is very little or no interaction at all between the Periphery countries. How does one obtain this?

There are some classical methods, and they all belong—strangely, it may seem, but actually quite rationally—to the classical dogmas of peace theory, as pointed out in chapter 3. The basic mechanism is separation, which can be geographical or social. In the geographical case the metropolitan country may make use of simple distance between the Peripheries, as seen very clearly in the maps of colonial empires, particularly when one takes into consideration who were in command of the means of transportation and communication. One could also make use of impediments such as mountain chains, deserts, and other

Figure 4.2   Exploitation and fragmentation

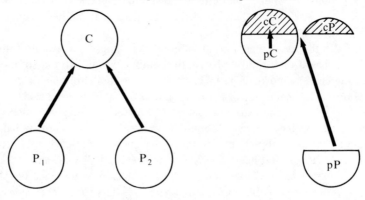

International model

Intranational model

whims of nature. The same applies to the social approach, in terms of "social distance," as when the Periphery countries have nothing but scorn and contempt for each other, and "impediments" by partly making use of existing conflicts between them, partly engineering some conflicts to fragment them properly.[21] When such techniques of imperialism have also survived in what today are very classical theories of peace this tells something about the compatibility between the two and whose interests a classical peace theory served.

The mechanism illustrated on the right-hand side of the figure is a direct consequence of what has already been said in connection with the theory of penetration. The two peripheries do not at all enter symmetrically in the picture. They are kept apart by considerable gaps in level of living, not to mention the geographical and social distance between them. Of all the bilateral combinations these would be the least likely allies, contrary to the theory that imperialism is essentially a question of the internationalization of capital creating an international bourgeoisie exploiting the proletariat everywhere. For this is not only a question of geographical and social distance, but also a question of simple and clear interest. As indicated in figure 4.1, there is also a relation of disharmony between the two peripheries, to the extent that the center of the Center is willing to share with its periphery the fruits of exploitation. This means that any such sharing measure, taking the form of political democracy or an economic welfare state, are important contributions to a structure of imperialism, making the masses in the Center countries the allies of their elites in case of a confrontation. Locally, inside the Center countries they may very much want to displace their bosses, but they may also fear that if this happens the successors would in no way be so successful in establishing and maintaining imperialistic relations with other and often very distant countries as the present elites.

Thus, there is small wonder that anticapitalist revolutions have taken place only in Periphery countries, starting with the Russian Revolution. Only in these countries will one find a periphery that is unambivalent and at the same time a center that may have grievances because the rule of harmony of interest has not been respected. In the Center countries the masses will be tormented by the ambivalence just mentioned and be more likely than not to join their elites in imperialistic wars. Post–World War II history must be disillusioning to those who believe in a world proletariat solidarity, witnessing how French workers were fighting in Indochina and Algeria, Dutch workers in Indonesia, British workers around the world, American hardhats in Indochina and elsewhere, and so on.

Thus, imperialism is supported by a double structure of fragmentation, between countries and within countries. On the other hand, it should be mentioned that the contacts between the exploited will remain low or negligible only so long as means of transportation and communication are completely beyond their command. The moment they have such means, signs of solidarity may flow from one to the other and constitute the first threads in a complex loom of solidarity.

Let us then turn to the fourth and last mechanism of imperialism, marginalization.[22] Under this formula something else takes place: a transition from separate imperialism to joint imperialism, as indicated in figure 4.3. In the left-hand side of this figure we have three Center countries, two of them exploiting one Periphery country each, the third one evidently being rich and well "developed" but not in charge of any particular Periphery country. On the right-hand side of the figure the three Center countries have joined together in an organization like, for instance, the European Community, all of them jointly exploiting the two Periphery countries that may or may not have a loose organization in common.

The point about marginalization, now, is that it drives a wedge between Center and Periphery countries, defining the former as first class and the latter as second class, like, for instance the "Associated States" in the structure the European Community is trying to erect.[23] Thus, marginalization is definitely not the same as fragmentation, with which it may or may not be combined. It is a way of constituting an inner and outer circle in the world, leaving no doubt as to where the point of gravity for important decisions concerning the whole world is located—to the point of isolating the Periphery.[24]

There is one important point to be made in this connection: the lonely Center country to the left on the left-hand side of the figure. It appears as nonimperialistic under the formula of separate imperialism, but under the second formula it is part of an inner circle, of a structure that jointly is exploitative of the outer circle, the second-class countries. Obviously, a perspective like that may add more realism to the understanding of, for instance, small northwestern European countries.[25]

That concludes our review of the mechanisms, simply using the building blocks already presented as world goals in chapter 2. There are four structural

Figure 4.3   Exploitation and marginalization

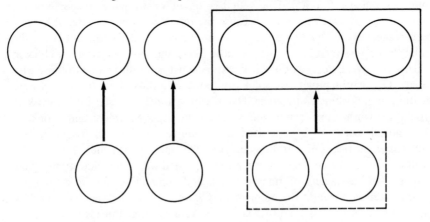

Separate imperialism   Joint imperialism

building blocks, and accordingly this is a structural theory of imperialism. Concretely, it is not a theory that presupposes bad intentions, or bad will, for its establishment or perpetuation. When confronted it definitely requires such actor-oriented elements if it is to be maintained, and that of course is the whole point about confrontation: to make the structure bare to all participants.[26]

In this theory of imperialism, exploitation is, of course, the fundamental element. The other three can be seen as supporting factors, not all of them necessary. I am inclined to say that for an exploitative relation between countries to be imperialistic an element of penetration is a condition, a point to be explored later in this section. An act of robbery on some foreign coast resulting in shiploads of tusks, gold, and slaves does not constitute imperialism, although it may be said to be exploitative. I would rather think of it simply as robbery. Imperialism involves a far more sophisticated structure and has to be understood from this perspective in order to be combatted.

Let us now return to our desiderata in the preceding section to see to what extent our building blocks have yielded what we wanted: an image of imperialism rich enough to capture a wide variety of phenomena, yet specific enough not to be a tautology.

When it comes to the first point, the need for a theory of imperialism that is not only economic in its orientation, it is clear that this requirement is satisfied, since the concept of "vertical division of labor" by far transcends the idea of economic exchange. This will be developed much further in table 4.3.

Second, a more comprehensive definition of exploitation has been supplied not only in the preceding paragraphs but also in chapter 2. The basic key is a more total approach including not only exchange but also in-change.

The third point about conflict formation has been emphasized very much in treating penetration and fragmentation. According to the present model one is dealing with a four-class world rather than one divided into two classes, although alliances may take place. However, when it reduces to two classes it is very likely to be the periphery in the Periphery against all the others combined rather than the classical Marxist model of "bourgeoisie vs. proletariat."

The fourth point about the complexity of the world society of today is also implicitly taken care of. There is no doubt that this theory can be used to relate building blocks other than countries, for instance, organizations. The United Nations may be seen as having a bridgehead inside the specialized agencies, and they in turn very often have bridgeheads inside nongovernmental organizations, constituting a chain of center–center communication channels. More important, the whole model of imperialism stated here can be repeated with no particular change inside countries, the so-called *colonización interna,* to be dealt with in detail in chapters 5 and 6.

And finally, because it is as much political as economic, the theory can be used to study repression as well as enforced exploitation—the Soviet and U.S. specialties, respectively, to use contemporary examples. In either case, bridgeheads are needed under postcolonial conditions to set up patterns of submissiveness, dependence and fear; fragmentation can be made use of, and so can marginalization. This means that imperialism as a structure can serve to constitute both types of structural violence, against equity as well as against diversity, within as well as between countries. It constitutes in and by itself a Model I international structure and will tend to reproduce that structure inside the Periphery countries, leaving the Center more free to engage in experiments in the other social forms.[27] In short, the effects of imperialism are as in figure 4.4, another way of saying that *imperialism is antidevelopment,* however much "economic growth" may accompany it. In fact, imperialism permits Center countries to grow and theoretically even to become increasingly egalitarian because the Periphery needed for capitalistic growth is located outside themselves. But these Periphery countries have no outside peripheries unless they also engage in imperialism, as they sometimes do. If not, then their peripheries are doomed to stagnation, unless they break out of the structure.

A basic question to ask, then, is "How big can the center become, under capitalism?" The Center countries might proudly point at their statistics and say, "look, the poor fringe in our society is less than 10 percent, even less than 5 percent, in some cases even less than 1 percent. This proves that it is possible to provide an adequate level of living, practically speaking, to everybody!" But if there is anything the present theory of imperialism purports to say, then it is precisely that this is a false statement. Capitalism, in its private and state varieties, is based on a mobility of production factors—raw materials, labor, and capital. This is bound to generate centers and peripheries, depending on whether production factors show a net inflow or outflow. In its imperialistic stage this process becomes internationalized, in the way indicated here. That permits the center to grow in the Center country, under the assumption that it does not grow too much in the Periphery country. For that reason country-based statistics are false; statistics on level of living should increasingly be calculated on the basis of vertical blocs or, less politely, empires.

And let me here venture a guess, a conjecture: that capitalism presupposes that the center does not comprise more than from one-fifth to one-third of the total population involved, because it is based on division of labor and a relatively

Figure 4.4   The effects of imperialism on social forms

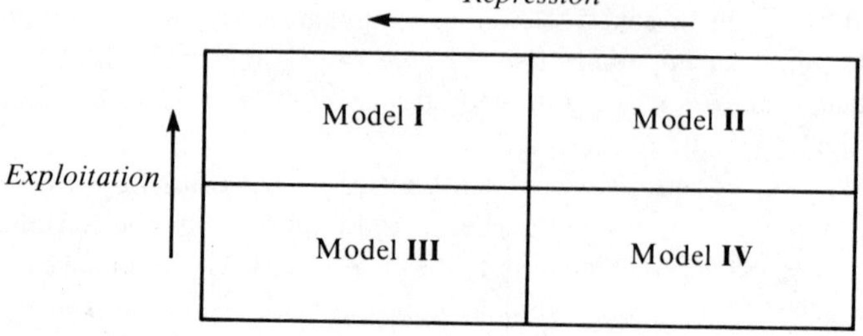

Repression

Model I	Model II
Model III	Model IV

Exploitation

steep center-periphery gradient. To expand the center further the country has to engage in imperialism to have an external periphery to fall back upon. Concretely, in an empire of, say, half a billion people, one hundred million or maybe close to two hundred million people may have a relatively good level of living; the rest will live under considerably worse conditions.

For the United States and for Western Europe that does not constitute too much of a problem, for with these figures most of their populations are already included in the good life except for the bottom 10 to 30 percent. For the peripheries in Latin America and Africa the situation is just the opposite. For the masses in India this would mean, if India is a relatively closed economic system operating under mildly controlled capitalism, that adequate living conditions would be extended to 100 million, perhaps somewhat more, and that the rest will be condemned to poverty. Unless, that is, India engages in imperialism along her perimeter and beyond.[28]

It is reflections such as these, and I am aware of no convincing evidence against these propositions, that lead to the conclusion that imperialism has to be eliminated. It is possible that capitalism may survive in a Center country where it has already taken root and not lead to too abject conditions of exploitation if center and periphery have a long tradition in sharing the fruits of imperialism and, one may add, of their own hard work. Under such conditions the destruction of economic imperialism may not necessarily lead to the destruction of capitalism at home; the center may simply generate more and new peripheries. The destruction of political-military imperialism will not necessarily lead to the demolition of highly repressive political and military structures inside a Center country; on the contrary, they may be strengthened.

But those are problems of the Center countries, important in their own right, but even more important is what these countries do to other countries within their dominance system. This system is so paralyzing, so alienating, that any serious development has to start with its demolition. That is a *necessary* condition, though certainly not a sufficient one; to assert the latter would be to manifest a facile optimism and faith in the automaticity of the historical process. For imperialism is an even more ramified and entrenched phenomenon than so far described.

4.2.2 THE TYPES OF IMPERIALISM

I shall now make this analysis more concrete by distinguishing between six types or aspects of imperialism, according to the type of exchange, i.e., the content of the division of labor, between Center and Periphery nations: (1) economic, (2) political, (3) military, (4) communicative, (5) cultural, (6) social.

The order of presentation is rather random; I have no theory that one is more basic than the others or precedes the others. Rather, this is like a pentagon or a Soviet star; in that imperialism can start from any corner. They should all be examined regarding the extent to which they generate interaction patterns that utilize the four mechanisms of imperialism so as to constitute imperialism. It may well be that in certain regions in space and time one type, e.g., the economic, is the cause of all the others, but our concern here is with a more general theory.

The basic mechanism is vertical interaction, across a gap in processing level. In other words, what is exchanged between the two collectivities is not only not the same things (which would have been stupid) but things of a quite different kind, the difference being in terms of where the most complex, challenging, and stimulating operations take place. One tentative list, generalizing what has been said above about economic interaction, might look like that in table 4.3. The order of presentation parallels that of table 4.2, but in that table cultural imperialism was spelled out in more detail as spin-off effects from economic imperialism. In fact, economic imperialism is used to exemplify both definition and mechanisms. Let us now look more at the other types of vertical interaction.

I have discussed the economic type at some length, so let us proceed to the others. The political type is clear: the very concept of a "mother" country, the Center country, serves as an indication of how in such cases the decision-making center is dislocated away from the country itself and toward the Center. These decisions may then affect economic, military, social, and cultural patterns. Important here is the division of labor involved: some countries produce decisions, others supply obedience. The decisions may be made upon application, as in "bilateral technical assistance" or in consultation, or they may simply emerge by virtue of the model–imitator relation. Nothing serves that distinction quite so well as the typical Western unilinear concepts of "progress," "development," and "modernization," according to which Center countries possess some superior kind of structure and culture for others to imitate (as long as the Center's central

Table 4.3 The six types of imperialism

	Periphery country provides	Center country provides
Economic	raw materials, markets, raw labor	processing, means of production, capital, know-how
Political	obedience, imitators	decisions, models
Military	discipline, traditional hardware	protection, means of destruction
Communicative	events, passengers, goods	news, means of communication and transportation
Cultural	learning, validation– dependence	teaching, means of creation– autonomy
Social	reinforcement through isomorphism	model social structure

position is not seriously challenged) and which gives a special aura of legitimacy to any idea emanating from the Center. Thus, structures and decisions developed in the "motherland of liberalism" or in the "fatherland of socialism" serve as models by virtue of their place of origin, not by virtue of their content.

The military implications or parallels are also rather obvious. It cannot be emphasized enough that the economic division of labor is also one that ensures that the Center countries in an economic sense also become the Center countries in a military sense: only they have the industrial capacity to develop the technological hardware—and are also often the only ones with the social structure compatible with a modern army. He who produces tractors can easily produce tanks, for *Tank-Kommunismus* as well as *Tank-Kapitalismus,* but he who delivers the oil can hardly defend himself by throwing it in the face of the aggressors. He has to depend on the tank producer, either for protection or for acquisition (on terms dictated by the Center). And just as there is a division of labor with the Center producing manufactured goods on the basis of raw materials extracted in the Periphery, there is also a division of labor with the Center processing the obedience provided by the Periphery into decisions that can be implemented. Moreover, there is also a division of labor with the Center providing the military hardware (and often also the officers or at least the instructors in "counterinsurgency") and the Periphery the discipline and the soldiers needed—not to mention the apprentices of "military advisors" from the Center. By overpricing the military hardware, the Center can also recover money lost when the price for raw materials goes up, especially if the center in the Periphery really feels threatened.

In the analysis of communication imperialism, the emphasis is usually on the interaction structure: excellent connections between Center and Center, not too bad between Center and its Periphery, bad between Center and somebody else's Periphery, not to mention between Periphery and any other Periphery. That this largely holds for most world communication and transportation patterns has been amply demonstrated. But perhaps more important is the vertical nature of the division of labor in the field of communication/ transportation. It is trivial that a high level of industrial capacity is necessary to develop the latest in transportation and communication technology. The preceding generation of means of communication/transportation can always be sold, sometimes secondhand, to the Periphery as part of the general vertical trade/aid structure, alongside the means of production (economic sector), the means of destruction (military sector), and the means of creation (cultural sector). The Center's planes and ships are faster, more direct, look more reliable, attract more passengers, more goods. And when the Periphery finally catches up, the Center will have moved on, for instance into the field of communications satellites.[29]

One special version of this principle is a combination of culture and communication exchange, news communication. We all know that the major agencies are in the hands of the Center countries, relying on Center-dominated, feudal networks of communication. What is not so well analyzed is how Center news takes up a much larger proportion of Periphery news media than vice versa,[30] just as trade with the Center is a larger proportion of Periphery total trade than vice versa. In other words, the pattern of partner concentration as something found more in the Periphery than in the Center is very pronounced. The Periphery nations do not write or read much about each other, especially not across bloc borders, and they read more about "their" Center than about other Centers because the press is written and read by the center in the Periphery who want to know more about that most "relevant" part of the world—for them.

Another aspect of verticle division of labor in the news business should also be pointed out. Just as the Periphery produces raw material that the Center turns into processed goods, the Periphery also produces events, but the Center decides which ones are converted into news. This is done by training journalists to see events with Center eyes and by setting up a chain of communication that filters and processes events so that they fit the general pattern.

The latter concept brings us straight into cultural imperialism, a subtype of which is scientific imperialism .[31] The division of labor between teachers and learners is clear: it is not the division of labor as such (found in most situations of transmission of knowledge) that constitutes imperialism, but the location of the teachers, and of the learners, in a broader setting. If the Center always provides the teachers and the definition of what is worthy of being taught (from the gospels of Christianity to the gospels of Technology and Science), and the Periphery always provides the learners, then there is a pattern of imperialism. The satellite nation in the Periphery will also know that nothing flatters and pleases the Center quite so much as asking the Center to teach, as seeing the Center as a model, and that the Periphery can get much in return from a humble, culture-seeking strategy. Similarly, it will get little but aggression if it starts teaching the Center anything, as did Czechoslovakia, which started lecturing the Soviet Union on socialism. For in accepting cultural transmission the Periphery also, implicitly, validates for the Center the culture developed in the center, whether that center is intra- or inter-national. This serves to reinforce the Center as a center, for it will then continue to develop culture along with transmitting it, thus creating lasting demand for the latest innovations. Theories, like cars and fashions, have their life cycles, and whether the obsolescence is planned or not, there will always be a time lag in a structure with a pronounced difference between center and periphery. Thus, the tram workers in Rio de Janeiro may carry banners supporting Auguste Comte one hundred years after the center of the Center forgot who he was.

In science we find a particular version of vertical division of labor, very similar to economic division of labor: the pattern of scientific teams from the Center who go to Periphery nations to collect data (raw material) in the form of deposits, sediments, flora, fauna, archeological findings, attitudes, opinions, behavioral patterns, and so on for data processing, data analysis, and theory formation (like industrial processing in general). This takes place in the Center universities (factories), in order to send the finished product, a journal, a book (manufactured goods) back for consumption in the center of the Periphery, first having created a demand for it through demonstration effect, training in the Center country, and some degree of low-level participation in the data-collection team. This parallel is not a joke, it is a structure.[32] If in addition the precise nature of the research is to provide the Center with information that can be used economically, politically, and militarily to maintain an imperialist structure, the cultural aspect of imperialism becomes even more clear. If to this we add the brain drain (and body drain) whereby "raw" brains (students) and "raw" bodies (unskilled workers) are moved from the Periphery to the Center and "processed" (trained) with ample benefits to the Center, the picture becomes complete.

4.2.3 THE PHASES OF IMPERIALISM

I have mentioned repeatedly that imperialism is one way in which one country may dominate another. Moreover, it is a way that provides a relatively stable pattern: the countries involved are linked to each other in a pattern that may last for some time because of the stabilizing factors built in through the four protective mechanisms of fragmentation and marginalization.

A criterion of imperialism is that the center in the Center establishes a bridgehead in the Periphery nation and, more particularly, in the center of the Periphery nation. Obviously, this bridgehead does not come about just like that: there is a phase preceding it. The precise nature of that preceding phase can best be seen by distinguishing between three phases of imperialism in history, depending on what type of concrete method the center in the Center has used to establish the harmony of interest between itself and the center in the Periphery. This is indicated in table 4.4. In all three cases, the Center nation has a hold over the center of the Periphery nation. But the precise nature of this grip differs and should be understood relative to the changes in means of transportation and communication. No analysis of imperialism, with distinctions between colonialism, neocolonialism, and "neo-neocolonialism," is possible without a reference to these means that perhaps are as basic as the means of production in producing social formations.

Table 4.4 Three phases of imperialism in history

Phase	Period	Form	Term
I	Past	*Occupation*, cP' physically consists of migrant cC people who engage in *occupation*	Colonialism
II	Present	*Organization*, cC interacts with cP via the medium of international *organizations*	Neocolonialism
III	Future	*Communication*, cC interacts with cP via international *communication*	Neo-neocolonialism

Throughout the overwhelming part of human history, transportation (of human beings, of goods) did not proceed at a higher speed than that provided by pony expresses and quick sailing ships; and communication (of signals, of meaning) not at higher speed than that provided by fires and smoke signals that could be spotted from one hilltop to another. Detailed control over another country could only be exercised by physically transplanting one's own center and grafting it onto the top of the foreign body—in other words, by colonialism in its various forms, best known in the form of "white settlers." According to this vision, colonialism was not a discovery of the Europeans subsequent to the Great Discoveries: it could just as well be used to describe great parts of the Roman Empire, which, by means of textbooks and the traditions of history writing, so successfully has dominated our image of empire building, probably also of political development.[33]

Obviously, the quicker the means of transportation could become, the less necessary this pattern of permanent settlement. The break in the historical pattern came when the steam engine was not only put into factories to provide a new means of production (leading to conditions that prompted Marx to write *Das Kapital*) but also into a vessel (by Fulton) and a locomotive (by Stephenson). In other words, a new means of transportation gave Europeans a decisive edge over peoples in other regions, and colonialism was enabled to become more firmly entrenched. Control could be accurate and quick.

But then decolonialization came, partly because of the weakening of cC after World War II, partly because of the strengthening of $cP,$ which might not challenge what cC did but certainly wanted to do it themselves. Neocolonialism followed; and in this present phase of imperialism, control is not of the direct, concrete type found in the past. It is mediated through the means of transportation (and, of course, also communication), linking the two centers to each other. The control is less concrete: it is not a physical presence, but a link; and this link takes the shape of an international organization. The international organization has a certain permanence, often with physical headquarters and a general secretary in the mother country. But above all it is a medium in which influence can flow, with both centers joining as members and finding each other. Their harmony of interest can be translated into complete equality within the international organization, and vice versa. The organization does not serve as a bridge between the centers; it is the bridge.

These organizations are well known for all types of imperialism. For the economic type, the private or governmental multinational (or transnational) corporations (BINGOs) may serve as examples; for the political type many of the international governmental organizations (IGOs); for the military type the various systems of military alliances and treaties and organizations (MIGOs?); and for communication the shipping and air companies (COMGOs?), not to mention the international press agencies, offer ample illustration; for cultural imperialism, some of the international nongovernmental organizations (INGOs) may serve as conveyor mechanisms; and for social imperialism a combination of the others. But this is of course not to say that international organizations will necessarily serve such purposes. According to the theory developed here, the extent to which they do is an empirical question, depending on the degree of division of labor inside the organization and the extent to which penetration, fragmentation, and marginalization are built into the structure. A further analysis of this will be given in chapter 7.

Next, the third phase. If we now proceed even further along the same line of decreasingly concrete (but increasingly effective?) ties between the two centers, we can envisage a phase where some international organizations will not only fall into disrepute but dissolve. What will come in their place? Instant communication, whereby parties who want to communicate with each other set up ad hoc communication networks (telesatellites, for example) that form and dissolve in rapid succession, changing scope and domain, highly adjustable to external circumstance, guided by enormous data banks and idea banks that permit participants to find their "opposite numbers" without having them frozen together in a more permanent institutional network that develops its own rigidities.[34]

In other words, I envisage a future where very many international organizations will be threatened in two ways. First, they will be exposed to increasing criticism as to their function as a tie between two centers, communicating and coordinating far above the masses in either country, which will in itself lead to a certain disintegration. Second, however, the result will not be that the centers, if they are free to do so, will cease to coordinate their action, only that they will do so by other means. Instead of attending ad hoc or annual conventions, or in other ways instructing a general secretary and his staff, their leaders simply pick up their viewophone and have a long-distance multilateral conference organized, where the small group of participants can all see and talk to each other in an informal way.

To penetrate more deeply into the role of the international organization as an instrument of imperialistic dominance, let us now distinguish five phases in the development of an international organization. As an example we take one economic organization, International Business Machines (IBM), and one political organization referred to in general terms as the International Communist Movement (ICM)—at present not organized formally as an international. The phases are indicated in table 4.5. Needless to say, these two are taken as illustrations of economic and political imperialism, as this is not a study of IBM and ICM respectively.

In the beginning, the organization exists only within national boundaries. Then comes a second phase when it sends representatives, at that stage usually called "agents," abroad. This is a critical stage: it is a question of gaining a foothold in another country, and usually subversive from below. If the other country is completely new to this economic or political pattern, the "agents" often have to come from the "mother country" or the "fatherland" upon the invitation of dissatisfied individuals who find their own mobility within the

Table 4.5 Phases in the development of international organizations

	International Business Machines (IBM)	International Communist Movement (ICM)
Phase 1: National only	in one country only ("mother country")	in one country only ("fatherland")
Phase 2: National goes abroad	*subsidiary*, or branch office, established by "agents"	*subversive* organization, established by "agents"
Phase 3: Multinational, asymmetric	other national companies started, with "mother country" company dominating	other national parties established, with "fatherland" party dominating
Phase 4: Multinational, symmetric	total network becomes symmetric	total network becomes symmetric
Phase 5: Global, or transnational organization	national identities dissolve	national identities dissolve

system blocked and who think that the present system does not satisfy the needs of the population. But this phase is not imperialist, for the center in the mother country has not established any bridgehead in the center of the offspring country, yet. Rather, I am thinking in terms of a little industrial nucleus in a feudal country and a small communist cell in a capitalist country.

The agents may be highly instrumental of social change. They may set into motion patterns in economic life that may reduce significantly the power of feudal landlords and introduce capitalist patterns of production; or they may set into motion patterns in political life that may reduce equally significantly the power of industrialists and introduce socialist patterns of production. Both activities are subversive of the social order but not imperialist and are, consequently, examples of other ways in which one nation may exercise influence over another.

But in phase 3 this development has gone a significant step further. The agents have now been successful, so to speak: national companies/parties have been established. Elites have emerged in the Periphery countries strongly identified with and well harmonized with the Center elites. The whole setting is highly asymmetric; what we have identified as mechanisms and types of imperialism are now discernible.

There is division of labor. The "daughter" company in the Periphery country is particularly concerned with making raw materials available and with securing markets for the mother company in the Center country. If it enters into processing, then it is often with a technology already bypassed by "development" in the Center country or only leading to semifinished products. Correspondingly, the company/party in the mother country makes more decisions and the parties in the Periphery provide obedience and secure markets for the implementation of orders. Thus, in both cases the implicit assumption is always that the top leadership of the international organization shall be the top leadership of the company/party in the Center country. Headquarters are located there and not elsewhere. This location is not by rotation or random choice.

In fact, the general interaction structure is clearly fragmented. There is interaction along the spokes, from the Periphery to the Center hub, but not along the rim, from one Periphery country to another. There may be multilateral meetings, but they are usually very heavily dominated by the Center, which takes it for granted that it will be in the interest of the Periphery to emulate the Center. And this structure then spans across all six types of interaction, one way or the other—in ways that are usually fairly obvious.[35]

I have pointed to what seem to be basic similarities between the two international organizations, IBM and ICM. Precisely because they are similar, they can do much to impede each other's activities. This similarity is not strange: they both reflect the state of affairs in a world that consists of countries of highly unequal power and level of development along various axes and too small for many of these countries to stay within their bonds, so they spill over with their economic goals and their gospels, and patterns are established that are imperialist in nature.[36] For phase 3 is clearly the imperialist phase; and because so many international organizations are in this third phase, they at present stand out as vehicles of imperialistic center-center cooperation.

This is the present state of most international organizations. Most are extensions of patterns developed first in one country, and on assumptions that may have been valid in that country. They are usually the implementation in our days of the old missionary command "Go ye all forth and make all peoples my disciples" (Matthew 28: 19). This applies not only to economic and political organizations but to the other three types as well. Typical examples are the ways in which cultural patterns are disseminated. In its most clear form, they are even handled by official or semiofficial institutions more or less attached to the diplomatic network (such as USIS, British Council, Alliance Française, Goethe Institut, and the various cultural activities of the Soviet and Chinese embassies in many countries). But international organizations are also used for this purpose by Center nations who firmly believe that their patterns are good for everybody else because they are good for themselves.

However, the Periphery does not necessarily rest content with this state of affairs. There will be a dynamism leading to changes toward phase 4, so far only brought about in very few organizations (among them IBM, but not ICM—a minor reason for the Sino-Soviet conflict). It will probably have its roots in the division of labor and the second-class stamp given to the Periphery in general through marginalization, and to heads of Periphery companies and parties in particular. Why should there be any written or unwritten law that IBM and ICM heads are located in he United States and the Soviet Union, respectively—why not in France and China? Why not break up the division of labor completely, distributing the research contracts and the strategic planning evenly; why not rotate the headquarters; why not build up interaction along the rim and build down the interaction along the spokes so that the hub slowly fades out and the resulting organization is truly symmetric? This is where the Norwegian IBM president and the Rumanian ICM general secretary have, in a sense, common interests. I predict that this movement will soon start in all major international organizations following some of the very useful models set by the United Nations and its specialized agencies. It should be noted, however, that it is not too difficult to obtain equality in an international organization wherein only the elites participate, as they already to a large extent harmonize with each other.

But this is not the final stage of development; nothing is. The multinational, symmetric form will always be artificial for at least two reasons: the countries are not symmetric in and by themselves, as some contribute more than others; and they form artificial pockets relative to many of the concerns of the organizations. Any multinational organization, however symmetric, is also a way of reinforcing and perpetuating the nation-state, as will be elaborated in chapter 7. If nation-states are fading out in significance, much like municipalities in many parts of the world, multinational organizations will also fade out because they are built over a pattern that is becoming less and less salient. What will come in its place? The answer will probably be what has here been called a hypothetical phase 5—the global or world organization, to be spelled out in chapters 7 and 8.

4.2.4 FROM SPIN-OFF TO SPILL-OVER: CONVERTIBILITY OF IMPERIALISM

I have now presented an analysis of imperialism based on four mechanisms, six types, and three phases. As is usually done in any presentation of imperialism, economic imperialism was used for the purpose of illustration. However, I have tried to carry the analysis further: for economic imperialism, exploitation was not only defined in terms of unequal exchange because *A* gives less to *B* than he gets from *B*, but also in terms of differential intra-actor, or spin-off effects. Moreover, it is quite clear from tables 4.2 and 4.3 that these spin-off effects are located in other areas in which imperialism can also be defined. Vertical economic interaction has political spin-offs, military spin-offs, communication spin-offs, social and cultural spin-offs; and vice versa.

In that connection I shall now make a distinction between spin-off effects and spill-over effects. When a country exchanges tractors for oil, it develops a tractor-producing capacity. One possible spin-off effect is a tank-producing capacity, which becomes a spill-over effect the moment that capacity is converted into military imperialism, for instance in the form of *Tank-Kommunismus* or *Tank-Kapitalismus.* Of course, this does not become military imperialism unless exercised in cooperation with the ruling elite in the Periphery nation. If it is exercised against that elite, it is a simple invasion, as distinct from the *intervention* that is the typical product of cC-cP cooperation.

A glance at tables 4.2 and 4.3 indicates that the road from spin-off to spill-over is a short one, provided there are cooperating elites available both in the Center and in the Periphery countries. It is not necessary for the same person in Center and Periphery to be on top of the economic, political, military, communication, social, and cultural organizations. Many would cover two or three such positions; few would command four or five or six. But if the elites defined through these types of exchange are coordinated into generalized upper classes based on a rich network of kinship, friendship, and association (not to mention effective cooperation), then the basis is laid for an extremely solid type of generalized imperialism. In the extreme case there would be rank concordance in both Center and Periphery, which means that there would not even be some little disequilibrium present in either case to give some leverage for a revolutionary movement. All groups would have learned, in fact been forced, to play generalized roles as dominant and dependent, respectively.

But for this rank concordance[37] to take place, gains made from one type of imperialism must be readily convertible into the other types. Spin-off effect must become spill-over effect—that is the whole point I try to make.

Concluding this theory of imperialism, let me now try to concretize it by bringing in world geography, the world map depicting the territorial system into which we people are divided. In figure 4.5 the reader will find an effort to bring out the salient features of world political geography, in line with the theoretical orientation of this book. The reader does not need to point out two immediate weaknesses in that exercise, that the map is territorial and presents states and regions as billiard balls and that the real world is more complicated than indicated in the figure and my comments. I know this, but nevertheless hope that the map, as a rule of thumb, is more right than it is wrong.

The reader will find the countries and regions of the world divided according to two double dichotomies. One is simple and geographical: the east–west axis and the north–south axis, which orders them more or less as in a real map. Japan, Southeast Asia, and Oceania–Australia–New Zealand occur twice in the map for two simple reasons. They are at the same time east of east and west of west. Moreover, I want to avoid the standard Eurocentric way of looking at the world, according to which the world is split along the middle of the Pacific so that the possibility of emerging Pacific transactions or even a Pacific region is systematically disregarded.

The second double dichotomy is more complex and political: rich versus poor, combined with autonomous versus not autonomous; the first reflecting the actor-oriented approach to development, the second the structure-oriented. There are four rich and autonomous parts: the United States, the European Community, the Soviet Union, and Japan, capable of setting their own goals and pursuing them. This also applies to the fifth big power, China, which, however, is

Figure 4.5 A political map of the world

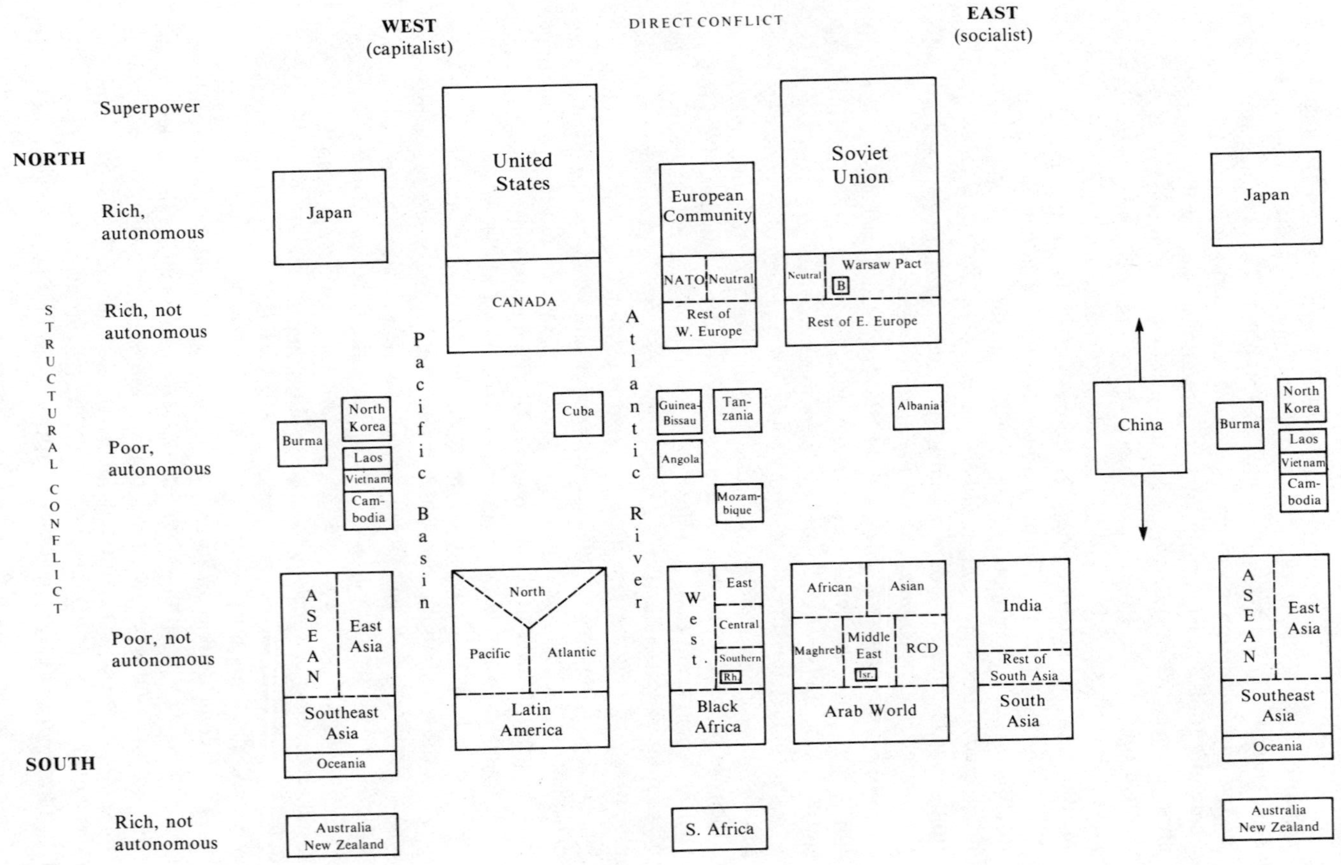

located in a belt of poor and autonomous countries around the world, some of them in close contact with China.

Then we have the rich but not autonomous: Canada, Western Europe, Eastern Europe, and the "white" Commonwealth countries in the southern hemisphere. Actually, the label "S. Africa" refers to the white enclave of that part of the world, temporarily serving as an occupant power.

And then there is the rest: the poor, not autonomous part of the world, encompassing about half of mankind. Southeast Asia is divided into the ASEAN (Association of Southeast Asian countries) region and the rest (meaning Kampuchea, Laos, Vietnam, Taiwan, and South Korea—the last two more properly referred to as belonging to East Asia). Latin America is divided into a Caribbean part (which also has some Anglo-American members), a Pacific region, and an Atlantic region. This is a relatively fruitful division both in ecological and historical terms.[38] Correspondingly, Black Africa or "Africa south of the Sahara," can be subdivided geographically; and the southern part of that division would then not refer to the white enclaves. The Arab world is a more complicated entity; the term partly refers to Arab in the ethnic sense and partly to Islamic countries (with the exception of ASEAN Islamic countries). A special category here are the RCD (Regional Cooperation for Development) countries: Turkey, Iran, and Pakistan. Bangladesh, however, would probably best be classified as part of South Asia because it seems to be a part of the Indian perimeter, in a way Pakistan is definitely not. (Afghanistan falls between the two.) The reader should also note that I have put into the map three "islands" that have played a disproportionate role in crystallizing contemporary conflict: West Berlin, Rhodesia, and Israel.

This map can now be used to discuss the extension and shape of the direct East-West conflict and the structural North-South conflict. The basic point, however, is that the map permits some reasoning about possible new regions of cooperation, even integration, as a response to the two types of conflict indicated. Moreover, the map can serve as a warning against the traditional way of organizing "area studies," cutting up vertical regions so that patterns of imperialism are systematically disregarded.[39] According to this "map" there are vertical and horizontal regions that are relatively well defined and do not respect the conventional geographical division of the world into continents. But more about this in chapter 6. Let us turn to the question of what to do about imperialism.

4.3 FROM VIOLENT TOWARD NONVIOLENT REVOLUTION

To fight dominance is to fight against exploitation and repression and for autonomy and liberation. I shall start out by making no assumptions as to whether this fight will have to be violent or nonviolent, as I do not think it has to be either. This is one more false dichotomy: it can be both or neither.[40]

Moreover, the social logic of the two is similar, which is not strange, as the point of departure is the same situation of dominance, or dependence, and the goal is the same state of autonomy, or independence. But I am interested in exploring the scope for a nonviolent fight against structural violence, because this fight will go on and on and because the weaponry at the disposal of mankind today makes it more desirable than ever that alternatives to violence be explored. Some type of nonmilitary offensive is needed, as the old formula of nonmilitary defense is no longer sufficient.

Imperialism is not only evil, it is obstinate and must be fought. But how? Nonmilitary defense (see chapter 5) is an effort to prevent the establishment of dominance; nonviolent revolution is an effort to fight against established dominance. The former may be status-quo maintaining, the latter not. NVR is a fight to change a social structure away from exploitation and repression. The fight against the particular persons who maintain a structure of dominance, often because they think they benefit more from it than from its alternative, can at most be a part of this struggle.

I shall distinguish between five phases of a successful liberation fight.[41] To what extent such a fight should be called a revolution depends on two factors in connection with the fourth phase: the extent to which there is really structural change (not only rotation of personnel in an old structure) and the speed with which it happens. The five phases are the same as given in the first cell of the general map of strategies in figure 3.4.

1. Consciousness formation
2. Organization building
3. Confrontation
4. Fight against dominance
5. Self-reliance

These phases appear and reappear, and phase 5 often gives rise to a new phase 1, if "self-reliance" is interpreted as "self-government," with rulers and subjects that may become new victims of new types of structural violence. However, they are not chronological phases; a revolution can start anywhere among the five. Each revolution will add new insights, or it is not a revolution but only a predictable social pattern that can be institutionalized like any other.

If one reads through the five phases with a single individual in mind they read like an autobiography: gradual awakening, organization of a personality, confrontation with the parental generation, break-away during puberty, self-reliance. This is an institutionalized pattern in many societies, and for that reason not a revolution but just an institution. What has made it look more revolutionary recently is that it has become collectivized, with generations of university and high school students and to some extent young workers running through these phases *together*. When that wave hits younger and younger adolescents until collective uprisal coincides with individual puberty it might become a considerable social force. But today maturation during puberty is still, by and large, fragmented and individualized, which makes every young person lonely with what they think are problems peculiar to them and not to the structure.

But even though each real revolution will have a pattern of its own, the five phases may still be recognizable. Moreover, as signposts for development that will continue to take place in our dominated world in the decades to come, they may be significant. It should be remembered that the point of departure is all the time the four-class model of the world, with the periphery of the Periphery (and of the Center) fragmented and divided against itself, exploited and deprived of the means of developing a consciousness of its own situation. It should also be remembered that in the worst cases the periphery of the Periphery will have to fight against the unholy triple alliance of the other three classes, the center in both Center and Periphery and the periphery in the Center.

The first phase, consciousness formation, is closely related to self-respect. Basically, it involves awareness of the forces shaping one's own condition.[42] A "force" is something that can be different; it can be reduced, altered, canceled, superseded. It is not something to be accepted as unchangeable. Hence, consciousness formation is insight in changeability, a demystification of any myth that holds that matters cannot be changed. Consciousness is more than a reflection of human affairs, it is a prelude to changing them. There is no guarantee that increased consciousness will lead to efforts to bring about changes in the direction of the goals here posited. Hitler also had considerable awareness of social forces, more than most persons. It is the consciousness of those who are exploited and their awareness as to how the situation may be changed that concern us. Through their consciousness formation the interests of the dominated become conscious goals, with strategies for their attainment.

The obvious means of raising consciousness are education and propaganda, but much more important is practice. Precisely for that reason the five phases should not be seen as consecutive in the sense that one of them has to be run through completely before the next can be attempted. Nor are they concurrent in the sense that one should work on all fronts simultaneously. Rather, they are recurrent and in a complex time pattern; one probably runs through all phases within any one phase. There is nothing like a confrontation for really learning the social forces of a society, so confrontation leads to added consciousness formation, which may have organizational spill-overs for still other confrontations, and so on.

The second phase is organization building. If consciousness formation is something that ultimately has to take place inside the individual, then organization building takes place between individuals. We could actually just as well reverse the terms and say that the individual becomes organized through understanding and that the group or class becomes conscious through mutual awareness expressed in a structure. In terms of our general goals, consciousness formation is a part of autonomy and organization building is solidarity, which means that realization of these two goals is seen as prerequisite to a fight against the other aspects of penetration and exploitation itself. Together the two can be expressed in one word: "mobilization," integrating apathetic masses into a conscious actor capable of bringing pressure on the structure of dominance. To exercise power-over-others the weak have to start by building up power-over-themselves.[43]

This can be achieved with or without structural violence built into the resistance organization. In the first case there will be centralization, sharp and vertical division of labor, with fragmentation and marginality, as in a classical army organization. Socially privileged individuals, like intellectuals, may even occupy privileged positions. In the second case there will be decentralization, less division of labor, and direct participation in decisions. In practice this means that the latter will take the form of relatively small groups, like guerrillas, commandos, and small nonviolent direct-action groups. They may of course cooperate for mass action by aligning their activities. But heavy repression that may come from above, with capture, torture, and similar tactics, is likely to favor the second model for the organization of the periphery: either fragmentation (each man knows at most two others, the minimum needed to connect the structure organizationally) or decentralization (many small and disconnected groups with only general awareness of each other in the common struggle) become indispensable means of self-defense. The second solution is also preferable if the organization is in itself to be a model of the structure one wants to obtain after the struggle, a model for the participants to learn in and for observers to learn from. The structure of revolutionary struggle largely predetermines the outcome. It has to be goal-revealing;[44] from the very beginning it should implement goals.

The third phase is the confrontation, a generic term covering a multitude of phenomena. By "confrontation" I mean the situation where the chips are all down, the social forces are pitted against each other, and it at least seems clear that one, or both, of the parties has to yield. In other words, the latent conflict between dominator and dominated has now been made manifest because the dominated party has converted its interests into goals through consciousness formation and its activities into strategies for obtaining those goals through organization building.

Before a confrontation comes there will be an exploratory phase, a mutual sounding out. The newly awakened periphery will formulate demands, make propaganda for them, and demonstrate for them. If all demands are accepted the process is terminated, and the conclusion can be one out of three: that there is no real structure of dominance, that consciousness is still insufficiently developed to formulate the essential demands, or, very possibly, that the people on top of the dominance structure are extremely flexible in their strategy of self-defense and know when to give in. We shall assume that this is not the case, that at least one demand seen as essential is not agreed to. It has become clear that the two parties have incompatible goals, that there is a goal conflict.

Moreover, we shall assume that this conflict requires solution now, that the dominated group does not opt for protraction of the conflict.[45]

The choice of demand is crucial.[45] It should satisfy two conditions. First, it should be "reasonable" not only to the dominated groups, but also to third parties. It should even be constructive in the sense of building up something, as when Dolci in Sicily launched his *sciopero alla rovescia* ("strike in reverse"), starting to build a needed piece of road that the authorities had not authorized, or the occupation of abused or unused resources, such as unused land or empty houses, the boycott in reverse. In other words, if the demand is granted something would be done that could serve as a clear signal of what the dominated party wants to construct, such as land distribution. And if it is not granted, this would be an equally clear signal of what kind of system the dominant party wants to maintain.

The second condition is that the issue should be so chosen as to make the dominant group overextend itself. It is assumed all the time that the dominator not only is superior in coercive hardware, but also is willing to use it, even if not necessarily on the scale of a Stalin, a Hitler, successive U.S. presidents in Vietnam, or a Yahya Khan in Bangladesh. It is assumed that the dominator cannot be beaten in open battle, man against man, arms against arms. He can be overcome only by means of superior "software" (consciousness, organization) on the other side, by pitting the weak man's power-over-himself against the strong man's power-over-others.

In the real confrontation, then, there is an element of dilemma, even coercion. The dominant group is presented with two alternatives: either to give in to the demand or to use force. The dominated must have made it clear that if there is no significant acceptance of their demand, then they will go ahead, which means that the demand has to be made on such an issue that there is something the dominated group can do (occupying land, sailing with medical supplies to North Vietnam), or at least attempt to do. When brutal power then clamps down on them, the true nature of the repressive structure is revealed for everybody to see. But this is much more than an educational experience for the two groups and for third parties. The reference at this point is very often made to jujitsu, which seems appropriate. In the confrontation the dominant group is sooner or later lured into an exaggerated use of violence that will demoralize it. One example is the U.S. experience in Vietnam: an overdosage of naked, brutal power that in the longer run debilitated the dominant, perhaps even more than the dominated.[46]

The confrontation should be structure-revealing to an even greater degree than consciousness formation can manage.[47] Consciousness formation translates interests into goals, and it maps strategies; it makes participants see what they should request from a society and what they should no longer be willing to accept. Confrontation brings this process further. It brings out into the open not only goal structures but also power structures. More particularly, it makes clear to all when and where structural violence is converted into direct violence for its own protection.

Confrontation is to the social theorist/practitioner what an experiment under extraordinary conditions is to the scientist/engineer. To study materials or compounds, extreme pressure, stress and stretch, heat, and bombardment with nuclear particles or rays of various kinds are employed so that properties hidden under "normal" circumstances (i.e., such as one atmosphere of pressure and 15°C, "normal" being a highly anthropocentric term) are revealed. It is like exposing people to stress (e.g., in concentration camps)—the properties revealed under pressure become raw material for self-insight and insight by others.

The defenders of the system will say that these properties are not revealed by the extraordinary circumstances but created by them. Further, they will say that there is a power base on which each society rests, that this is no great discovery, only a rediscovery by those who are fortunate enough to live in societies where this power base is not in the open for everybody to notice in the form of manifest repression. The answer is not to deny that there is a power base for each society but to ask under what circumstances in a particular society will direct violence be applied. When somebody smashes a shop window? When students try to look into the secret files of research contracts? When sharing of power is demanded? Perhaps in all cases—but when most strongly?

The fourth phase is the fight against dominance. For the sake of perspective, I shall develop a more comprehensive theory than is actually needed when the emphasis is on nonviolence and revolution, precisely to evaluate better the alternatives facing groups struggling for liberation. This is of major significance lest a revolutionary process stop with the third phase, return to the first and second again, and get stuck in repeating that cycle—as student revolutions to a large extent have done. Each student generation builds up its own consciousness and organization, has a confrontation or two, and then leaves the university behind, very much as it was before.

Let us have a look at the categorization of approaches to social change in general shown in figure 4.6. Our basic distinction appears again in this typology. A social change process for more independence can be directed against the powerholders as persons, against the power structure, or against both. In concrete practice a strategy will have to be in terms of both/and rather than either/or. For the whole idea of nonviolence is to work on persons, but in order to change structures.

Another distinction is the age-old one in terms of slow versus quick processes, evolution versus revolution. These terms are difficult to pin down with more precision, and they may also be misleading. For that reason I have added a third word-pair, "continuous/discontinuous." What passes for a revolution may in fact not bring about basic social change any more quickly than an evolutionary process does, but it works by marking a historical watershed in time. It may very well be that the only concrete thing to happen during the revolution is that one person escapes and another takes his office after a popular

Figure 4.6 A typology of social change processes

	Actor-oriented	*Structure-oriented*
Continuous; *slow processes* (evolution)	attitude change, social mobility	people stop one activity; people gradually adopt new policies
Discontinuous; *quick processes* (revolution)	ousting old elites through banishment, seclusion, killing bring in new elites to former center from former periphery	emptying old structures through noncooperation and civil disobedience creating new structures, occupying old institutions, building new ones

uprising. And, still, life may never be quite the same in that society. The psychological change inside its members may be much deeper than external changes. Even a small discontinuity is magnified through the lenses of personal experience. A much more thorough social change process brought about by politicians and bureaucrats may be so continuous that adjustment is too easy. There is no feeling of any new departure, a new deal, a new stock taking; it is not perceived as a real change.

This is no effort to reduce a revolution to a question of the psychology of perception of time structure. Quickness and discontinuity are indispensable ingredients in an effort to overcome a reactionary society before the power-holders get too much of a chance to entrench themselves. An evolutionary process does not carry with it the same psychological spin-off effects as a revolution may.

In person-oriented, individualizing social science it is, of course, evolutionary person-oriented change that has been most closely studied, particularly in sociology and political science. These are the processes through which societies undergo some change. Attitudes change, although very slowly. In fact there are strong indications that attitudes developed during adolescence as a response to the basic problems at that time stick. These attitudes are then carried through life, becoming increasingly relevant as the person acquires more power and decreasingly valid as the objective situation changes.

In evolutionary change there is some rotation of personnel in power positions through such institutionalized processes as occupational mobility, replacement upon retirement, elections into some positions of legislative power and selection, and appointment into executive power. The assumption in this (Model II) society is that each person is a carrier of certain values and will try to implement them *ex officio*; for that reason a change of personnel is also a change of values to be implemented. This notion is then supplemented by the even more questionable idea that other persons in power are flexible enough to change their values, for instance as a reflection of political pressure, and engage in social change without any rotation.

This process is at best excruciatingly slow, adapted to stable societies and to the dominant rather than to the dominated. It is not only slow because there is little mobility of persons or of values inside persons but also because these processes are not aligned with each other. Radicalism in the government may be canceled by conservatism at the top of the institutions of that society, or vice versa. Hence a major function of a revolution: it is like a magnet that aligns and coordinates all these changes and amplifies the social force brought to bear upon society, simply by inserting people whose values point in the same direction in all positions of significance, at the same time. The critique of this model of change is equally obvious: the leaders may pull in the same direction all right, until the whole society collapses because of insufficient attention to the significance of details and begins to pull in other directions. But there is a counterargument: that some societies need to be pulled down before they can be recreated.

For this quick substitution to take place, violence is usually deemed necessary. How else, why indeed, should the holders of power leave "voluntarily"? The answer is partly that in general, perhaps, they do not—but also that securing change may not be a question of ousting the person, but of changing his will. Here again confrontation enters as the major ingredient in the whole strategy for revolution. What confrontation can obtain is not that the powerholder give up his power but that he start doubting its (and his own) legitimacy. Confrontation is revelation to first, second, and third parties. A landowner in a feudal society may love his property, his absentee landownership, the fact that the peon works six days a week for the landowner and only one day for himself. But there is a world of difference between the landowner who feels he has a right to all this and the one who starts doubting that right—for instance, because it has been made clear to him what it means to the downtrodden, to the peons, or because his confreres in other places throw away their privileges or have them taken away. He may cling to them, he may fight tenaciously, but he no longer has that extra strength derived from thinking he is right in what he does.[48] He is demoralized, particularly if he feels there is an alternative and that the alternative works, that he is not only an exploiter but worse still, superfluous.

The direct violence techniques of banishing, secluding, or even killing off the powerholders are not our concern here. We would like to know much more about the stages in the process that can make an illegitimate powerholder leave his position without the application of violence. Under the general banner of "nonviolence" impressive insight about this has been developed, and it may be formulated in proposition form. It seems reasonable to assume that patterns of confrontation can be found that may open the eyes of the powerholder to his wrongs so effectively that he prefers to leave. The difficulty is that the decision is usually not his alone; he is also a part of a structure, the top of the power structure. He also has a family and friends and others who may depend on him, rightly or wrongly. Even if he is demoralized he may think that his colleagues, those who share his position, are not; and he may feel bound by ties of solidarity. There are many reasons apart from lust for power or greediness for the fruits of exploitation that may prevent him from yielding. For instance, he may simply believe in the system. Hence it is on this network that the liberating forces will often have to work, making signs of demoralization at any point visible to others.

Let us then turn to the much more important structure-oriented approaches, because the emphasis is on changing what people do, not the names of the people in certain positions—without in any way denying that the latter may be a condition for bringing about the former. Perhaps it should also be pointed out that there is no attempt to reify a "structure." No social structure has any concrete meaning unless there are people acting in the prescribed manner in the prescribed positions. No structure exists in and by itself. New structures come into being because people—new people or the old people—start doing new things, start dealing with each other in a new way. The point is only that for this to happen the concerted and deliberate action of many people, and usually people in several positions, are needed. A teacher or a pupil alone cannot change the education structure of a school; many teachers and many pupils have to change their behavior. If their action is on a large scale and aligned, *gleichgeschaltet,* then a revolution has taken place.

I assume that one of the most important forms of social change is also the one least noticed by theoreticians because it is so obvious: structures change simply because people stop doing something and do something else instead. They may gradually stop dueling and resort to verbal dueling by proxies, their lawyers, instead.[49] They may gradually stop going to church and start active participation in all kinds of secular associations. They may withdraw from military service, from military research institutes and military production and start more peace-related activities or international service like the Peace Corps;[50] they may stop applying for the foreign service of their national government and opt for some type of international, or rather transnational, organization; they may stop going into business and prefer science, culture, or the arts. The mechanisms are usually simple. As some dysfunctional consequences of the old pattern become a shared concern (e.g., premarital abstinence), it becomes legitimate to talk openly about it. At that point the old pattern is no longer sacred, and there is a search for alternatives.

The notion of an alternative is in itself the real breakthrough; in the light of the alternative the existing institution also becomes an alternative to be evaluated, not an apodictic truth. The rest is often a question of courage: who is the first to opt for the new? From the anti-elite this may spread to the elite, and from there to the counterelite or vice versa.

These are complex psychocultural and sociopolitical processes that stretch out in time, and perhaps, given the inertia of persons and societies, the processes may become more genuine if they develop at "natural" speed. We probably have too little feeling for social time. We know something about the biopsychological processes connected with the maturation of a person, but very little about the time needed for a social process to mature. What we do know is that the type of thinking just presented is often used by status-quo-oriented forces to justify any postponement or any change "with all deliberate speed" only, permitting almost unlimited continuation of glaring, blatant inequalities, injustices, and inequities. Nonetheless, this may in fact be the most frequent way of bringing about change, some kind of silent revolution—silent because it is gradualist and increm-entalist, revolution because it really touches the structure, not only the position holders.

That brings us to the fourth and final type, the one usually associated with the words "nonviolent revolution." In a sense it is nothing but the type just described, but in quick and coordinated motion. Instead of people gradually stopping one kind of activity, emptying one kind of status, they do it all at once. The process is characterized by a speed commensurate with the speed of person-directed revolution, and it is two-sided—not only disengagement from one type of activity but also the start of an alternative that points toward new social forms. It is civil disobedience and noncooperation combined with positive action, simultaneously.

Theoretically, this approach has a purity and a direct relevance to the revolutionary task of changing structures that the traditional person-directed approach seems to be missing. Thus, argumentation in favor of this approach does not necessarily have to be based on the ethical pros and cons of violent versus nonviolent revolution, but on what constitutes a revolution. Take Eastern Europe: the argument may not be against revolutions, but that they were not revolutionary enough. The structure of the factory by and large remained the same below the managerial level, despite important changes at the top level. One reason is that the workers were never given the chance to fight for another structure, under the theory that with the conquest of changes at the top the revolution lower down will be an almost automatic consequence.

The strategy of noncooperation and civil disobedience involves any level, any structure where dominated people join together and refuse to do what they are supposed to do. Statuses are emptied; structures are killed. It is a generalization of the strike as it is known all over the world in its negative aspect, and it may or may not include a positive aspect. To formulate any general rule here seems, at best, difficult, at worst even meaningless. The positive aspect is what is referred to as "to start doing something else," as when students boycott lectures and initiate their own seminars, leave universities and start their own, go on strike against exams and develop their own procedures. Under what conditions the birth of something new can run parallel to the death of something old instead of coming after it can hardly be foretold. It seems to depend on the revolutionary process itself.

This is not the place to go into any detail about these basic strategies, as my purpose here was to place them in perspective. More detailed examples will be given later. Besides, most authors in the field give very detailed descriptions and prescriptions.[51] The only point to be made is the position of this phase between the confrontation and the self-reliance phases. Confrontation focuses the struggle on one issue. It should be narrow in order to be effective as a learning process for first, second, and third parties. Civil disobedience/noncooperation/positive action broadens this, with the confrontation giving the motivation for nonparticipation in the old structure.

The fifth phase, then, is self-reliance. The struggles led by such twentieth-century giants as Gandhi and Mao[52] are telling illustrations of how important it is to initiate self-reliance during the struggle rather than afterward. Broadly speaking, self-reliance means to build up new structures with one's own means without dependence on outsiders, much as boycotted nations or besieged cities have had to do. Autonomy grows through practice.

In a sense "self-reliance" is merely another word for "autonomy," which I have already spelled out in terms of self-respect, self-sufficiency, and fearlessness. These are all constituents of a new social reality, a reality that has to be constructed, with all its cultural and structural aspects. Concretely, there is a blend of attitude and behavior in this, of mind and action; and I doubt very much that anything useful can be said about autonomy at this general level. In the next section on strategies, however, the level of concreteness can be increased, and many of the strategies relate directly to this phase in the struggle.

What, then, is the conclusion? Probably only that if a nonviolent revolution succeeds, then success can be seen in terms of these five components. But it may also be that such components can become institutionalized in such a way that when the first rungs on the ladder have been conquered the rest tends to follow. Large parts of the world have internalized the symbolism of the majority vote and institutionalized it in parliamentary and presidential democracies. The nonviolent revolution, or the civilian offensive, might acquire similar symbolic status. If it did it would give increased power to the small unit and, hence, stimulate decentralization, equity, and diversity—precisely the values here considered basic. For NVR would counteract any kind of dominance, from the dominance that receives its legitimation from the majority vote to dominance by the ultimate unit, the individual. Seen in that perspective the five phases above become more than a recipe for nonviolent revolution: they become the heart and soul of politics itself.

4.4   STRATEGIES OF DEVELOPMENT

Let us retrace our steps for a moment. In chapter 1 the four major problems were identified as they appear in newspapers and everyday conversation, simply as the problems of violence, poverty, repression, and environmental deterioration. They can also be formulated positively, as in the World Order Models Project, as peace, economic well-being, social justice, and ecological balance. Today more and more people seem to stress how these pointers into the future somehow belong together: there is the idea of "peace with justice" or of "ecodevelopment," combining them into pairs. Here the idea is that none of them makes much sense without the other. Development is to move forward on all four.

In chapter 2 this value basis was expanded, in line with the simple thesis put forward from the very beginning: that the basic problem of our world is structural, or political as many would say. Exploitation, penetration, fragmentation, and marginalization were added to the *problématique,* not only as an expansion of the problem catalogue, but in order to provide tools for a causal analysis. In chapter 3 these tools were used to formulate some visions of an alternative world; in the present chapter they have been used to develop a theory of imperialism. The theory is structural; it sees the two major forms of imperialism today (capitalist and social) not as a series of deliberate actions by dominance-oriented people, but as a structure, as a pattern of billions of acts, almost all of them routine, spun around the four themes of exploitation, penetration, fragmentation, and marginalization.

These structures are strong. They have a great absorption capacity and can distort, even pervert, many well-intended measures. So the basic thesis as to strategies of development would be that technical solutions are likely to be either irrelevant or—in the worst case—even counterproductive, partly by mystifying and masking the problem, partly by strengthening the structures of dominance. Fundamental structural change is indispensable, in order to create a world in which some of these more technical solutions would be meaningful, meaning both destroying old and building new structures.

The standard package of technical solutions to the four problem areas above looks something like the list in table 4.6. By and large this list constitutes the major elements in the standard Western package. The criticism of these elements is also fairly standard today, but it was not some years ago.

Violence. The approaches do not solve the underlying conflict but deal with symptoms of that conflict, the violence itself. In fact, the approaches may even freeze a status quo not worth keeping.

Table 4.6 Sociotechnical approaches to global problems

Problem area	Technical approach
Violence	arms control, peacekeeping forces, legal approaches to terrorism
Misery	technical assistance, "green revolution," international agencies
Repression	human rights conventions, reporting machineries
Population	birth control, family planning
Depletion	recycling, use of renewable resources
Pollution	clean production, cleaning-up industries

Misery. Since the approaches do not attack the underlying economic structure, the benefits are likely to accrue to those who need them least. The decision-making power will still be on top of the dominance structure, and that structure is likely to be reinforced because of new dependencies on technologies introduced through technical assistance.

Repression. As for violence, repression (e.g., in the form of torture) is usually generated by a structure of dominance (as an effort to maintain that structure) and like the arms race will only find new outlets if effectively stopped at one point.

Population. The relation between poverty and population is a complicated one that depends essentially on whether the economy is labor intensive or capital/research intensive. In the former case a big population may be a condition for development; in the latter case productivity in the center is so high that the periphery becomes unable to compete but also unable to consume the products since the price has to reflect all the research and development that went into producing them. (The "green revolution" is an example.) If large segments of the population do not enter the economy, either as producers or as consumers, but function only as labor reserves, the fascist conclusion would be to send an atom bomb in their direction. The semifascist, also demopolitical solution would be to limit their numbers through family planning. The human solution would be to change the structure, particularly the economic structure, to suit human needs.

Depletion and Pollution. These approaches are expensive and make the products even less accessible for the masses of the world, at the same time as they create new dependencies on antidepletion and antipollution technologies. As such they are likely to reinforce the dominance structure, bringing in transnational corporations with world-encompassing economic cycles, specializing in undoing some of the evils perpetrated on humankind by the other corporations, but structurally identical with them. Like intergovernmental agencies, they tend to reproduce world structures, even to reinforce them.

That the people at the top of the world dominance system try to solve world problems with such technical approaches is only to be expected, because they would tend to pick from a spectrum of political options those that do not challenge the structure from which they benefit. That in doing so they would by and large have the cooperation of what above has been called the center in the Periphery is not strange either; that is what penetration is all about. It is also to be expected that such technical approaches will be continued until the system runs itself into some real crisis. It would be strange if the center in the Center should start learning from their mistakes, see the structure they try to maintain as responsible rather than "problems," and undergo a basic change in strategy. For the scheme in table 4.7 is probably as good a guide to the world *probléma-*

tique as any. By and large I assume, in line with preceding chapters, that the relation is about as follows.

>   *Violence.* As will be spelled out in some detail in chapter 5, most wars since World War II have been vertical; they have been wars of liberation and repression. Most of them have been generated by capitalist imperialism in its colonial and neocolonial forms; but social imperialism is also of considerable importance, being the dominance formation within which the Sino-Soviet conflict should be understood.
>
>   *Misery.* The political geography of poverty is simple: it coincides with the periphery of the capitalist system, mainly in the Periphery countries, but also in the Center countries, including the United States. By and large, extreme poverty has been abolished in socialist countries, including the Soviet Union, and of the developing countries it is only the socialist four (North Korea, North Vietnam, China, and Cuba) that seem to have been able—in a surprisingly short time—to satisfy the fundamental needs of the masses of their population.[53]
>
>   *Repression.* Again the political geography is relatively simple: the periphery of the capitalist system and all over the Soviet-dominated system— making it very ubiquitous. It is only in the capitalist Center (the United States, Western Europe, Japan) that repression, as commonly conceived of, is relatively low, at present, but even there such forms as racism and sexism are well developed.
>
>   *Population.* The problem is essentially generated by the structure of the capitalist economy, but may also appear in socialist economies as productivity increases.
>
>   *Depletion and Pollution.* This seems to be a more evenly shared problem and more related to industrialism in general.

In distributing causal connections on capitalist and social imperialism alike I am by no means engaging in the objectivistic game of symmetry: "A plague on both your houses!" Rather, there is little doubt in my mind that the key source of world problems today is capitalist imperialism, and for at least four reasons. As table 4.7 is intended to reflect, capitalism is related to *more* problems, socialism (even Soviet socialism) being much more rational when it comes to

Table 4.7   Relations between world problems and world dominance structures

	Capitalist imperialism	Social imperialism
Violence	x	x
Misery	x	
Repression	x	x
Population	x	
Depletion/Pollution	x	x

problems of poverty and population. Second, it is related to more *fundamental* problems as it has proven so incapable of satisfying fundamental needs for the masses in its vast periphery. Third, it affects *more people,* simply because it is more extended.[54] And finally, it is *more deeply rooted,* having a history of five hundred years (after the Great Discoveries) or at least two hundred years (after the Industrial Revolution).[55] Social imperialism is a newcomer on the scene, having a history of only sixty years (after the creation of the Soviet Union with a strong Moscow ascendancy) or at most thirty years (after the satellization of Eastern Europe). In fact, it may today be argued that social imperialism is to some extent integrated into the world capitalist system; the opposite may not even be argued.[56]

In short, something has to be done about capitalist imperialism, something basic. As it is being done, every day, every month, and every year, what is now listed beyond is less a catalog of prescriptions than a catalog of predictions about crucial policy areas that will be activated in the years to come. Admittedly, however, it is difficult to draw a strict line between prescription and prediction because of the tendency to predict what one hopes will happen and to hope for what one predicts will happen anyhow. So let me rather stick to the terminology just introduced and talk about these as "policy areas," leaving the question of whether they are essentially predictions or essentially prescriptions for others to decide (particularly as they are obviously either).

To change a structure means partly to destroy an existing one, partly to help create a new structure. The remainder of this chapter is devoted to key strategies in this connection; I would claim that they were not picked at random but flow easily and logically from the entire theory of dominance developed in this chapter. They fall into four parts: changes in Center–Periphery relations; changes inside the Periphery countries, changes inside Center countries, and changes in the global system.

4.4.1 CHANGES IN CENTER–PERIPHERY RELATIONS

What already is taking place is a certain change *from the old economic order to what is referred to as the new economic order.*[57] This is a progressive change because it may lay the basis for the next step to be developed. It would imply such measures as better terms of trade, brought about through producers' cartels for raw materials (the key example being the OPEC's quadrupling of oil prices); the right to control natural resources (e.g., through nationalization) and Periphery control over more of the economic cycle (e.g., shipping and insurance and some of the financial elements) to ensure that more of the surplus generated accrues to the Periphery; and increased trade and cooperation among Periphery countries. These are important structural changes brought about by concerted Third World action; they are not technical "solutions." As they do not go far enough, they are likely to cause disappointment relatively soon. Thus, improved terms of trade will only touch the top of the exploitation iceberg; the basically vertical division of labor will remain, as will the dependency of the Periphery on the Center. Further, there is no guarantee that better Third World control over their own resources means that they will be used to satisfy fundamental needs of the masses; they could also be used to satisfy far from fundamental needs of the local elites and for national prestige projects, including militarization of the society. Periphery control over more of the economic cycle may only imply that the masses will be exploited by their own rather than by the capitalist Center and its local bridgeheads, such as daughter companies. This is also true when a more horizontal division of labor, with increased export of industrial products form the Periphery to the Center and the Periphery to the Periphery, is added to the facts of world trade (not only to the programs and not only in the form of transfers within transnational corporations). Counterpenetration, e.g., Periphery investment of petrodollars in the Center, is a strategy; but it has the limitation of preserving, perhaps even strengthening, the capitalist system as a whole.

Hence, consistent moves should be made into the next phase, *from the new (or not so new) economic order to self-reliance.* In this phase the Periphery would gain total control over its own economic activity and would decouple itself from Center-dominated economic cycles. It would not rest content with ownership over natural resources but would also process them, in the Periphery— and for consumption predominantly in the Periphery. This would immediately raise the question of in what direction raw materials should be processed. In the first part of this phase the answer would probably be conventional: in the old direction. Oil would be processed into gasoline; what would be new would be the idea that the Center would have to buy the processed product (and have it shipped on Periphery-owned ships) so as to keep not only the better part of the profits but also more of the spin-offs in the Periphery. In the second part of this phase, however, it is expected that strong movements will be generated to direct the processing more toward the needs of the masses. In Cuba[58] for instance, this meant concretely the processing of sugar cane into pharmaceutical, house-building material and the like—not only using it as a cash crop to earn foreign currency to buy consumers' goods (for elites) and some capital goods, with the technological dependency that implied. Similarly, oil can possibly be processed in the direction of fundamental need satisfaction, e.g., through conversion into protein.[59]

Self-reliance implies reliance on one's own resources. It does not mean autarchy for it does not exclude trade. But the idea would be always to try to produce a product locally rather than getting it through buying and selling, through trade. The reason is not only that the latter maintains an exploitative division of labor and creates dependencies, but also that it is wasteful. It does not force the local population to ask some very fruitful questions: how can we produce that product using some other raw materials that we have rather than what is customarily used; how can we produce it developing some new technologies through our own work rather than importing foreign technology; is it absolutely certain that we need that product, or could it be that some other product that we are able to produce can be a very satisfactory substitute (such as very cheap bicycles or scooters combined with abundant collective transportation instead of private cars)? These are the questions asked in times of war and times of economic boycott, and they tend to generate autonomy and creativity.[60] In fact, economic sanctions are probably among the best instruments in the world if the goal is autonomous development.[61]

Self-reliance means that one really makes use of one's own resources, often leading to unexpected solutions, not that one only makes use of one's own resources. In some of the most poorly endowed countries these resources will be insufficient; goegraphy is mercilessly asymmetric in its distribution of natural resources (although it is to a large extent people who define what is a natural resource and what is not). There is scope for trade, but with two important observations. First, to avoid dependencies this phase will probably witness *a general decline in vertical trade* and *a general increase in horizontal trade*. It is between countries roughly speaking at the same level of industrial development (here simply defined as capacity for processing) that the doctrine of comparative advantages makes sense; for countries at highly uneven levels, the doctrine only masks the exploitation that stems from differential spin-off benefits.[62] To pull together with other countries at the same level can be referred to as *collective self-reliance;* it is already emerging as increased interaction and institution building in regions of the Third World, and it will sooner or later be Eastern Europe's answer to Soviet hegemony.[63] What remains is only that these regions increasingly decouple themselves from their dependency on the United States, the European Community, and Japan. As that happens the world will witness a gradual change in trade composition: a decrease in North–South trade, an increase in South–South trade, and probably also an increase in North–North trade. This may be accompanied by a general decrease in world trade (which recently has grown at such astounding rates as 7 to 10 percent per year), which generally should be welcomed since trade very often implies low reliance on own resources, hence waste. Needless to say, traders and countries specializing in trade (such as the European Community, which handles about 40 percent of world trade) will view this issue differently.[64]

The second observation on the relation between self-reliance and trade concerns internal trade. The logic of self-reliance, as the Chinese have so convincingly shown, applies equally well inside a country, because the structure of imperialism applies equally well between central and peripheral districts as between central and peripheral countries and regions. Nowhere is this so clearly expressed as in the Arusha declaration,[65] which is important because it constitutes a link between the ideology of self-reliance and the ideology of fundamental needs satisfaction. It is assumed that if people have control over their own economic situation then they will use productive forces first to satisfy basic needs, maybe at a low level, and then to proceed to higher needs. Admittedly, there is an assumption of enlightened self-interest here—for instance, that people know what is best for their health—and that assumption is sometimes doubtful. But what is not even to be doubted is that the center of a country, under the doctrine of national self-reliance, may continue, even strengthen exploitation and repression at home, as was done by the three major prewar fascist regimes. Hence, in order for self-reliance to spread inside the country, certain assumptions about the inside of the Periphery have to be made (for more on self-reliance, see section 9.2).

4.2.2 CHANGES INSIDE PERIPHERY COUNTRIES

There are problems inside the Periphery countries beyond the structure of their relations to Center countries. Basically, there is not only the problem of Periphery countries relying more on themselves but also the problem of ensuring that the fruits of self-reliance accrue to the masses. A good example here is the mental and economic trap of overemphasizing mineral resources, particularly ores. In what direction is iron ore, or other ores, processed? Directly they do not serve fundamental needs; they figure neither in diets, nor in clothes or shelter in any significant manner (except for the urban population), very little in health, and very little in education. They are important indirecly, converted into capital goods for the production of food, clothes, and shelter—but not in the quantities currently exploited. Much of it goes to the production of unnecessary goods, very much of it even to the production of military hardware, the means of destruction. To a large extent the focus on minerals is a part of the vertical trade heritage that reappears in the focus on the nodules on the ocean floor, more likely to be converted into military hardware for the control of the masses of the Periphery than into goods that will lead to direct satisfaction of their basic needs.

Thus, the first and basic strategy inside a Periphery country would be *production for fundamental needs first,* and from the bottom up, starting with those who rank lowest on their satisfaction. In fact, this should be the new definition of development: not some measure of average production or consumption, but the level of need satisfaction for, say, the lowest 20, 33, or 40 percent. Concretely, this means that groups with this kind of orientation as their political priority have to come into power, and there is little doubt that in most cases this can happen only through some kind of revolutionary process. In the preceding section an image of nonviolent revolution has been given so as to break at least the almost logical connection that seems to exist in many people's mind between "revolution" and "violence." But there are many scenarios as to how this type of change can take place, and one of the more important ones in recent years would be that the power machinery itself—the military—turns against its old masters and makes the satisfaction of the needs of the masses its top priority. A change of that kind would be objectively progressive, as it seems to have been in Peru and Portugal, even if it is not necessarily born out of a progressive ideology or sufficiently long-lasting.

A second point would be *to decentralize Periphery society,* usually heavily centralized precisely because that was the only way colonial and neocolonial regimes could run it. Frequently, the capital was built around a harbor, with communication and transportation radiating inward in the country and outward toward the metropolis. This leads to a politics of Chinese boxes, of district and village autonomy and self-reliance, just as for the Periphery country itself. It also presupposes horizontal cooperation between villages at the same level, particularly at the bottom, with obvious consequences for the road network that should connect periphery villages rather than leading only from the capital to the district capital and from there to the village in a feudal fashion. Some type of local, direct democracy has to be developed to release dormant sources of creativity and development, which would probably have to be accompanied by some kind of *knowledge reform,* similar to a land reform, whereby knowledge is distributed more evenly in the society. This is more than a question of dissemination of knowledge through general education, adult education, and popularization. As with land reform, it is a question of a more even distribution of the means of producing knowledge, which probably would imply less reliance on the universities and high schools in the centers and more reliance on locally generated knowledge, building on traditional knowledge. Needless to say, the Cultural Revolution in China is the great example here, and it is hard to see how autonomy can be generated in the Periphery, not to mention in the periphery of the Periphery, without similar measures.

A third and basic point in this connection is *to find some way of dealing with local parasitic elites.* A Periphery country will never be able to overcome poverty if something like 25 percent of the population not only decides over 75 percent of the social surplus but also consumes it. These are the economically privileged groups, and one way of dealing with them is, experience seems to show, to deprive them of economic privilege. Under programs of austerity, for instance as a result of economic sanctions, they tend to emigrate to the Center country, even at the risk of entering that country at the bottom, in the periphery.[66] Another way of dealing with them, actually more Chinese and Eastern European than the Soviet and Cuban method hinted at above, is to let them keep some of their privileges but give them new jobs, e.g., as state bureaucrats rather than as private capitalists. They would no longer be capable of making profit, but they might become loyal supporters of a new regime precisely because the structural change was directed against the nature of their previous job rather than against their personal level of living. The problem may still be, however, whether a Periphery country would be capable of maintaining an elite of that kind, and whether the elite may not simply turn into a "new class."

A fourth point is the need for a much stronger *political mobilization* in the Periphery. The masses work against tremendous odds, exposed to all means of repression, being highly manipulable, at subsistence-level living. A major tactic in that situation would be to prepare oneself, gain experience, and make use of the opportune moment. The structure will always produce crises because of the many contradictions built into it. Those are the moments to be utilized as when the ·OPEC countries made use of the October 1973 war to launch their embargoes and price increases. There will be many such situations in the future; the wise tactic would be not to expose oneself unnecessarily to repression as long as the structure is strong, but make use of its contradictions in the moments of weakness.

Finally, and in a sense underlying all of this, would be *a higher level of consciousness* in the Periphery about how the present structure works, about alternative structures and about strategies for destroying structures of dominance and building structures that serve human needs better. This can only develop at the Periphery's own creation. The point that importing Marxism as an antidote to liberal thinking and capitalist organization only substitutes one type of Western dependence for another should not be pressed too far, but it is important. Much of the Chinese autonomy today derives from their ability to create their own Marxism,[67] so to speak, emphasizing much more strongly the idea of trusting the people (in addition to serving the people). Consequently much of the consciousness formation in the Periphery will take the form of rejection of Center-generated thinking, and "leftists" from the centers of capitalist and social imperialism would be wise to understand that they may also be objects of rejection. Westerners, left and right, usually share the assumption that they have the key to Periphery future—an accusation that also may be raised against the present author.[68]

4.4.3 CHANGES INSIDE CENTER COUNTRIES

The basic changes that have to take place in Center countries would not, in my mind, necessarily have to be so deep as to warrant the use of the word "revolutionary."[69] On the contrary, they may actually be seen as relatively modest, for if revolution were really needed in all the Center countries the prospects would be bleak indeed. More particularly, what is needed can possibly be put into two broad categories: weaning the Center of its dependence on the Periphery and making the Center keep its hands off the Periphery. Thus, what is seen here as fundamental is not that the Center countries should fulfill their promises to give 1 percent as technical assistance, or any percentage for that matter, for if a system works badly at 0.3 percent it is hardly to be expected that it will work much better at 1 percent. What is needed is not that the Center should give anything, but that it should stop robbing and interfering. For example, the United States got professionals through brain drain with a discounted educational value of $3.8 billion in 1971 alone, the value of technical assistance to the Periphery that year being $3.7 billion.[70] The problems cannot be solved with money; they have to be solved through structural change.

First, just as the Periphery countries have to raise everybody above a certain floor or minimum level when it comes to food, clothes, and shelter, the Center countries have *to start thinking and acting in terms of ceiling or maximum levels.* Given the limitations of nature, it is no longer acceptable that, for instance, the 6 percent of the world's population living in the United States should consume 33 percent of the world's oil, partly because it taxes world resources too much, partly because it leads to an inequality gap that is much too easily translated into a power differential that is used, for instance, to intervene militarily. Moves toward more proportionate consumption will have to be taken. At this point it is important to note that this reasoning is increasingly accepted when the Center overconsumes resources taken from the Periphery. Tomorrow we may, however, go one step further in our thinking and define certain resources as belonging to humankind as a whole, no matter where they are located.

The second basic strategy inside a Center country would be *to prepare for self-reliance,* which will have to come about if for no other reason than the increased self-reliance in the Periphery. Concretely, this means to decrease the dependence on raw materials from the Periphery for the simple reason that they may very soon not be available, or be available only at prices the Center will not be willing, or even able, to pay. This is partly a question of getting raw materials from elsewhere, including new sources of energy, but it is also a question of developing new styles of living in general and which consume fewer nonrenewable sources of energy in particular.

The best way of using all the money set aside for technical assistance may well be for this purpose: to prepare the Center for times to come by a restructuring of the productive capacity rather than to reinforce Periphery dependence on the Center through continued "aid."[71] But much of this is also a question of change of mentality, of building on the yearning for simpler life styles clearly expressed in many Center countries in recent years. It may be objected, though, that this protest is essentially an urban, intellectual youth phenomenon, which may be true. However, such life styles may soon become a necessity as the crisis deepens. Wise statesmanship, hence, would be to prepare the population through early warnings and by building on such currents in Center culture.

A third and equally basic point would be *to find some way of dealing with the Center instruments of direct and structural violence in the Periphery.* Quite concretely, this means finding some way of controlling the Center machineries ready for subversion and military intervention,[72] and the major Center instruments for capitalist imperialism, the transnational corporations. These themes will be developed more in chapters 5 and 7; suffice it here to mention some key tactics. Thus, the danger of U.S., Western European and/or Japanese intervention to retain privilege is considerable. To expose all such plans, to have people inside the intelligence agencies and military forces ready to reveal them, to try to train soldiers to make a sharp distinction between military self-defense and intervention in Periphery countries when the latter somehow try to create better structural conditions for themselves—all this is basic. But stronger means would also be needed, such as denying the military research capacity by stigmatizing scientists working for such purposes, by denying them vital supplies, and so on. And the same applies to transnational corporations: they should be exposed. Not only should they be made more accountable, but the worst of them, in terms of the structural damage they cause, should be boycotted as places of work. As for the military, their "secrets" should be published, particularly patents in the field of fundamental needs, such as pharmaceutical patents. In short, the key contribution the Center can make to Periphery development is negative, to stop intervening in any way, rather than anything positive—*in our present world.*

A fourth point would be the same as for Periphery society: a certain *decentralization* of Center societies. The motivation would be the same: only in smaller, more autonomous units can human beings be big enough to count; in oversized, centralized countries they become too small.[73] But there is also an additional motivation seen very clearly in, for instance, the Indochina wars: for a poor peasant in that part of the world it would have been a great advantage if the United States had consisted of fifty disunited states, incapable of producing, say, a B-52. Somehow the Center countries have to disarm not only militarily but also structurally, and one way of doing that would be through decentralization—a theme to be developed more fully in chapter 6.

Fifth, just as for the Periphery, there is a need for new *consciousness formation.* It is in the process, and has been for several years, at least since 1968, when the U.S. war in Indochina made it more clear to people what the true nature of Western liberal democracy was like. It may be argued, and probably correctly, that had the United States been as effective in Indochina as the Soviet Union in Czechoslovakia (or the United States in the comparable case, the Dominican Republic), then there would have been no such awakening—that disenchantment, even criticism, was born out of defeat and would have been but the hobby of some cranks had the United States "won" in Indochina. But an awakening there was. More important than discussing its causal origin and its moral character would be a discussion of its depth and scope. Thus, the critique had a tendency to be actor-oriented ("a tragic mistake," "an unfortunate decision") rather than tied to structural analysis of the more lasting characteristics—an analysis that should come easily because the war was about the same even though it passed through the hands of about five different presidents. Also, the Watergate exercise in actor-oriented analysis, leading to the sacrificial demise of a president, also served effectively to block a structural analysis when it was most needed. The Christian approach to "sin," sacrifice rather than any structural change, was used in an effort to wipe the slate clean with some presidential blood. Finally, not so many people became that conscious of what happened. After all, all of us in the Center, periphery and center alike, somehow share the spoils of our imperialistic structures.

The question is how consciousness raising can continue. Here is one simple proposal. *It might help political consciousness if everybody who sells a product has to declare the price composition.* That means simply stating in writing on the product what percentage of the price the customer pays goes to Periphery countries (to workers, to owners of means of production, to middlemen), what percentage to Center countries (to wholesalers, to retailers, to the government in all kinds of taxes), what percentage to middlemen (shippers, insurers), and how much of that ends up where. After all, we are used to having the most weird chemical analyses presented to us on the bottles in which we buy our mineral water. If chemists can do that, economists should be capable of doing similar analyses—or else we need other types of economists. Thus, it is reported that only 11 percent of the price paid for a banana goes to the producer country[74] (and out of that only a minor fraction, one would assume, to workers). We have a right to know such things. Of course, such knowledge does not unambiguously translate into any action (no knowledge ever does), particularly since the greater proportion might be the part taken by one's own government in various types of taxes. But it could clear the air.

Most important, however, would be demystifying, sharp analyses revealing in detail how the present structure works, with the explicit purpose of demoralizing the Center, and particularly the center in the Center. After all, there is, as pointed out, a difference between an exploiter with a good conscience and one with a bad conscience—and it is in the world interest to increase the proportion of the latter.

Finally, there is the need for a much stronger *political mobilization* in the Center. Again, it is not a question of mobilizing public opinion to "give" more technical assistance; it is a question of mobilizing people of all kinds to help change structures—and as a very minimum to prevent the Center from using its repertory of direct and structural violence. This is not going to be easy in the years to come. In general, it is not very likely that the Center will turn in time toward more self-reliance. When the Periphery proceeds via the new international economic order toward more self-reliance, the changes will hit the Center increasingly, and the more so the less prepared it is. The first to lose their jobs, as is already seen very clearly, will be the workers, starting with "guest workers" and the unskilled. But these are also the first to be used as soldiers, in a military machinery that will expand partly because its expansion is used as a neo-Keynesian device, partly because the contradiction in the imperialist conflict formation is sharpening. This may create very dangerous situations, for workers would be tremendously useful allies with radical youth, students, and others.

4.4.4 CHANGES IN THE GLOBAL SYSTEM

The world is not only Center and Periphery and their relations; there is also a global superstructure. Most of this will be discussed in chapters 7 and 8, but in a section dealing with "strategies of development" at least three key points should be made.

First, we need *new concepts of technical assistance.* Nothing of what has been said above should be interpreted to mean a total stop to the transfer of capital and know-how from the Center to the Periphery. Nor is there any reason to regard these transfers as gifts. They could be seen as reparations, and not only for damage done in the past, but as some step toward compensation for the continuous damage built into the structure.[75] This type of reasoning, however, is mainly interesting as a way of getting rid of feelings of gratitude. It does not give any answer to three crucial questions: what is the best setting for technical assistance, what should be the content, and how can one diminish the asymmetry between donors and recipients?

As to the setting; the arguments in favor of using UN institutions seem by and large to outweigh the contra-arguments in terms of excessive bureaucracy and slowness. It is not only that UN assistance is somewhat less open to manipulation in favor of strong national (U.S., Soviet, Japanese aid) or regional (EC or Nordic aid) interests, but also that the United Nations in principle can draw on know-how from the whole world. Multilateralism, however, should not stop at the level of the UN (Specialized Agency) Headquarters but be carried into the field. It could take some of the form the Cubans practice so well when they invite experts in the same field from several countries,[76] presenting them not with a Cuban counterpart but a "countercommittee," drawing on their (often contradictory) advice but implementing it themselves. Somehow it is important to get away from the idea that one expert, one country, one region, or the whole world, for that matter, has the sole solution—and to face the contradictory nature of any social situation in an open dialogue from which, ultimately, all will learn.

As to the content, underlying everything said is the idea of increased self-reliance in smaller units. Phrased in different language: the idea of intermediate economic cycles, which is an extension of the concept of intermediate technology.[77] Probably these concepts, full of promise as they are, are now forced to carry too much of the answer to the development *problématique,* but they are nevertheless pointers to a new future. Here are some of the elements:

> The idea of using local resources as much as possible, trading only in relatively small cycles—cutting down (but not to zero) on the macro cycles that span the whole world and expanding the micro cycles that operate only within a small village,
>
> The idea of production without waste, of a shift toward renewable sources of raw materials and energy in order to counter depletion and pollution,
>
> The ideas of nonalienating work and nonexploitative work relations, partly through more labor-intensive and creativity-intensive production, partly through labor-saving devises and automation;[78] in short, technologies and economic cycles that do not generate exploitative structures, respect

the limits of nature, and at the same time respect the human nature of human beings.

As to the asymmetry, one should search for the type of technical assistance needed in all countries, and the content just mentioned, the intermediate technology and the socioeconomic structure that goes with it, would constitute a good example. Take the field of health: the Center countries have much to learn from the socialist developing countries, such as Cuba and China, when it comes to middle-level health manpower, e.g., the barefoot doctor. But the Periphery has much to learn from Center countries when it comes to intermediate technology in the field of informal education—study circles, adult education of various types and so on. To the extent that the world does/should move toward a higher level of local self-reliance, these will be the new technologies, and their implementation will be the new idea of development—and relative to that, all countries underdeveloped and overdeveloped alike are "less developed countries." So, I am not suggesting a new UN agency for intermediate technology, but that the concept should permeate all existing agencies.

Second, *globalization of the world's commons.* Essentially this is the old list: internationalize (e.g., by establishing some type of UN jurisdiction) everything not under national jurisdiction (certain unclaimed regions of the world, the oceans, the ocean floor and what is below, the air space above the oceans, outer space and celestial bodies) and use it partly to levy taxes on the users (e.g., ships, airplanes, telecommunication) partly to explore and exploit, to process and market. There are some important caveats, though, partly hinted at before, partly to be explored in later chapters. Thus, the UN agencies still mirror the dominance structure of the world, although less so than they used to do. Hence an international seabed regime will easily become like the World Bank, a reflection of certain interests and certain ways of organizing answers to the world's problems.[79] Moreover, there is no built-in guarantee that more resources in the hands of Periphery governments or global agencies would benefit those most in need of these resources. Often their representatives would not fit into any international framework, either in terms of form or in terms of the content of their presentations. This is one of the key reasons that I would place more emphasis, in general, on local self-reliance than on global institutions: only the former harbor some promise of giving people a say over their own affairs; the latter should mainly help in providing a setting in which self-reliance could unfold itself.

Third, *globalization of world production for fundamental needs.* Later I shall have occasion to discuss globalization of transnational corporations; here I shall focus only on production for fundamental needs. The point can be made in one sentence: food (and water), clothes, housing materials, and products needed for health and education, as well as for transportation and communication should not be treated as commodities. They should not be for buying and selling; they should be seen as birthrights of everybody, like the right to be free, not a slave. These products, like paper for textbooks to be used in schools, should not be seen as something that can be given or withdrawn as the suppliers wish; their availability should be built into the productive system. Above a certain minimum they may be treated as commodities, like the luxury restaurants available in China. But satisfaction of fundamental needs should be hedged around as jealously as the right not to be a slave. Given the global nature of these problems today, the best guarantor of these birthrights would probably be some global institutions, capable of global budgeting, allocation, even rationing—always giving priority to the most needy and not using availability and withdrawal for political pressure. It will take time to institutionalize something like this, as it should also be solidly built into our concepts of human rights, but it will have to come in one form or the other.

Let us then return to the problem areas again, to arrive at some judgment as to the relevance of these approaches.

Violence

I am here in a somewhat ambivalent position. On the one hand there is hardly much doubt that most of the large-scale violence we have in the world today is related to the structure of dominance, as wars of liberation and repression. But from this follows that many of the strategies mentioned are likely to increase the amount of direct violence, in a sense converting structural violence into the direct variety. By many this will be used as an argument not to proceed: the Third World should not liberate itself for fear of U.S.-EC-Japanese counterattacks, nor should Eastern Europe for fear of violent Soviet reprisal. The answer is that the situation is already violent, although the violence is of the structural variety, and that the conclusion must be as much as possible to use the methods of nonviolent revolution and watchdog strategies inside Center countries to impede their use of counterrevolutionary violence. Even so, it is hardly to be expected that the curve of violence since 1945 is in for a sharp drop. Rather, it is likely to continue rising. The responsibility for that, however, will in most cases have to rest with the Center countries.

Misery

Here I am less ambivalent: the strategies indicated will in all likelihood lead to considerable decrease in misery and even quickly. The socialist countries give evidence in that direction, particularly China. But structural change is only the necessary condition providing the setting within which new technologies can be put to work. Thus,

> *In the field of food:* Relatively small cycles using natural fertilizer instead of depleting and polluting with artificial fertilizer and human waste; three-dimensional agriculture (e.g., by cultivating the seabed with highly extended plants kept vertical through water buoyancy and tied to a buoy at the surface, to be harvested at several levels of altitude); all kinds of multi-cropping cycles set up (e.g., combining rice paddies with fish

ponds)—doing all this labor/creativity-intensively rather than capital/research-intensively.

In the field of shelter: much more use of industrial waste for housing material, more use of age-old housing traditions (improving adobe houses rather than replacing them).

In the field of health: developing further traditional medicine, introduction of health technicians in all countries, use of herbs, but above all a return to societies that produce fewer patients (and clients) through stress, alienation and pollution.

In the field of education: much more use of the highly innovative techniques developed by the Cubans and the Chinese of horizontal learning, learning together, deprofessionalizing to a large extent the teaching profession.

In the field of communication/transportation: the development of cheap methods, e.g., by developing further sailing ships, collective ground transportation based on renewable forms of energy.

The possibilities are many once the structure is changed.[80]

Repression

There is no illusion that repression would disappear through such measures as I have indicated, but in a world where neocolonialism as well as colonialism belongs to the past there would at least not be the repression that stems from that particular international structure, for instance in the form of torture.[81] There might be intranational repression, for instance to maintain some international hegemony—the cities over the villages, the capital over the rest, the local center over the local periphery. It is also with a view to this that local self-reliance has been stressed so much, in the Center as well as in the Periphery.

But what about social imperialism? It has been, particularly in the Stalinist period, one of the more repressive systems in world history. It also illustrates one basic point: there are needs beyond the fundamental needs. There is the need for freedom to express oneself and to be impressed, through communication and travel; the need for work that permits creative self-expression, not merely jobs; and the need for politics—for some kind of process that permits free consciousness formation, mobilization, confrontation, fight, and at least some limited type of transcendence. All these needs have been left highly unsatisfied in the Moscow-dominated system, through censorship, limited travel (even within the country), and elite monopolization of politics, which then degenerates to fierce struggle between factions and interest groups at the top.[82]

Such a system cannot last. It generates periphery apathy and consumerism, but also periphery protest that will take nationalistic, religious, and highly political forms. Sooner or later the system will develop cracks; one of the elite groups may join the people—even the army—against the *apparat*, for instance. In such moments it is very important that the repressed have relatively clear answers to the basic problem of Soviet-type socialism: *after satisfaction of fundamental needs, what?* If no socialist answers are given to this question, the danger might be that the system would develop into some type of nationalism with religious undercurrents, as expressed, for instance, by Solzhenitsyn, also capable of mass repression.[83]

Then there are all the other types of repression in the world not captured by the formulations "capitalist and social imperialism." More particularly, I am thinking of racism, sexism and—to coin an expression—ageism (the suppression of the young and the old by the middle-aged). These are highly ubiquitous phenomena, and although capitalist imperialism has made use of them in creating a system ruled by white, middle-aged males it does not follow that these repressive structures will disappear with capitalism. And yet "development" should not be permitted to be conceived of as transfer of power from one group of middle-aged males to another. The general norm of "social justice" would direct our attention toward societies with participation more equally shared at all levels between sex and age groups, in the family, at school, at work, in public life. It would include, just to mention what might look like a very small item, making public transportation in such a way that it does not exclude very young and very old people (simply because they are not able to enter). And yet, development cannot possibly mean equal participation of the colored, the female, the very young, and the very old in, say, CIA and KGB; in an exploitative multinational corporation making senseless products; or in a repressive university system, however much "social justice" would make us move in that direction. It is very much to be hoped that the energy created by the revolutions of women and youth (to be followed, one hopes, by the revolution of the old for the right to participate, not be marginalized in old-age homes) will make us move toward more horizontal societies, not merely toward a more egalitarian distribution of the right to exploit others. In so saying, I—myself a white, middle-aged male—am painfully aware that such changes will hurt (being a male noncapitalist it is considerably easier to act against capitalism than against male dominance), but I am also full of hope that other groups could infuse society with other styles of living—less vertical, individualistic, and competitive.

Population

Will the measures indicated contribute to the solution of the "population problem"? The answer depends on how one defines the problem. If it is taken as axiomatic that the solution consists in reducing the world population (or at least preventing it from increasing much more) then the answer is clearly no. But I have criticized this assumption by pointing to the obvious: in a highly capital- and research-intensive economy with very high productivity in the center, the periphery will be increasingly unable to participate, either as producer or as consumer; in a labor-intensive economy their labor would be converted into products at least for their own reproduction, possibly also for a surplus when combined with intermediate technologies. Since this is the gist of what is suggested above—self-reliance, intermediate cycles, lower productivity—there is a built-in solution to the population problem: another economic system, more similar to what is found in China. But the very reference to that country brings out the point that this can at most be one factor in the total picture, for the Chinese themselves practice family planning, even quite rigorously.

Family planning should, in my view, be practiced, but not as a way of relieving the pressure on our resources, and only if the population becomes much bigger. The success of the socialist countries in satisfying fundamental needs gives strong evidence to the contention that poor countries are able to support quite adequately even a growing population once some basic structural change has taken place. But there are at least three other, very good, reasons for limiting the population:

If parents, particularly the mothers[84] (given our conventional division of labor) are to live more fully, realize themselves more completely, there is a limit to how many children they should have.

If human society is to continue to be innovative, to create new forms, we need space; we cannot overcrowd the whole planet, even if we could feed the population adequately.

Sooner or later the outer limits will be reached. It is obvious that we cannot go on multiplying forever, even though we are still far from those limits today (except, possibly, in South Asia).

We should, however, be careful in formulating norms. Obviously, the simplest one would be that from two people should come, on the average, two people. This may be too little for underpopulated regions that might introduce labor-intensive economies (Africa? Latin America?). The norm might make sense in the Center countries, though, but the basic point would be to avoid any norm that singles out any specific group, e.g., the poor in the poor countries, as the group that should limit their number. That this is *demopolitics* can be most clearly seen by arguing the opposite way, by asking some pointed questions. Who has participated in most wars since 1945? Who are on top of most of the institutions that constitute capitalist imperialism? Who are on top of the structure where most of today's repression can be found? Who are responsible for most of the depletion and pollution in the world? Who are the 6 percent consuming 33 percent of the world's annual oil output? An institute in New York staffed with Latin American, African, and Asian demographers exploring how Americans can overcome prejudices against drastic reduction of their numbers might be resisted in the United States. Resistance against U.S. institutes of the same kind (e.g., in New Delhi) was what exploded in the face of the Western delegations to the UN Bucharest conference on population problems in 1974.

In short, my argument is not against family planning but against its use as an instrument in the interest of capitalist economics (and to protect those at the top of it by reducing the numbers of those at the bottom); in short, *demopolitics*.

Depletion and Pollution

When it comes to this type of pressure on the environment the package has a definite structural change that, I claim, contains much of the solution: the intermediate economic cycle. The insanity of depleting our resources and polluting nature and all of us is clear enough—in principle. In practice it is not very clear when the economic cycle is so world-encompassing that decisions are made in one corner, depletion in another, pollution in the third, and consumption in the fourth corner of the world. The temptation will be to locate depletion and pollution where there is little or no resistance, either because there are no people or because they are weak. As we know today, that works only for a limited time: people, or nature, or both hit back. Contrast this with the way farming has been done for ages: a very limited economic cycle with the farmer perfectly well knowing that if he depletes or pollutes his soil he will not survive for long. He can himself see, feel, smell the consequences of ecological imbalance, and generate his own countermeasures, more or less effectively. But we do not have to go back to family farming to generate this social force: all that is needed would be cycles short enough to generate the necessary social forces against depletion and pollution within a workable self-reliant unit—say of the magnitude of $10^{3\text{-}5}$.

Again, this structural change would only be a necessary, not a sufficient condition (and the optimists would say it is not even necessary, that we can plan on a global scale so that these twin evils are avoided—which may be true, but only at the expense of a very powerful world bureaucracy). There is also the scope for new technologies, or for the improvement of traditional types of recycling. The way the Chinese are practicing their slogan of "production without waste" is highly inspiring and would put them very high on the list of technical assistance experts in the field once the structural conditions have been made available.

4.4.5 SUMMARY OF STRATEGIES

For reference, here is a list of the strategies just presented in each of the four main categories:

Changes in Center–Periphery relations
>   From old economic order to new economic order: better terms of trade; more control over production
>   From new economic order to self-reliance: processing at home; decline in vertical trade; collective self-reliance, also local self-reliance; cooperation among Periphery countries

Changes inside Periphery countries
>   Production for fundamental needs; concepts of social minimum, floor
>   Decentralization, for local self-reliance
>   Nonviolent revolutionary approach to parasitic elites

Political mobilization
Consciousness formation

Changes inside Center countries
New life styles; less consumption; concepts of social maximum, ceiling
Preparation for self-reliance
Control of Center-generated direct and structural violence
Decentralization, for local self-reliance
Consciousness formation
Political mobilization

Changes in the global system
New concepts of technical assistance; multilateral, intermediate technology
Globalization of the world's commons
Globalization of world production for fundamental needs

NOTES

References to *Essays* are to Johan Galtung, *Essays in Peace Research,* 5 vols. (Copenhagen: Ejlers, 1975–80) (Atlantic Highlands, N.J.: Humanities Press).

1. These five points arise out of countless discussions I have had in connection with the article "A Structural Theory of Imperialism," *Essays* IV, 13, originally published in *Journal of Peace Research* (1971), pp. 81–117. (Much of that article is included in section 4.2, but much is new, and the notes are all new.) Consequently, reference to *social imperialism* has been added. Also, there was a need to point out more clearly how the present approach differs from a Marxist–Leninist perspective on imperialism, which is the purpose of section 4.1. The most brilliant Marxist analysis of world capitalism is no doubt by Samir Amin, in his *Accumulation on a World Scale: A Critique of the Theory of Underdevelopment* (New York: Monthly Review Press, 1974) and *Unequal Development: An Essay on the Social Formations of Peripheral Capitalism* (New York: Monthly Review Press, 1976). For a good introduction, see "Review Essay: Dependency in the World Economy," *American Journal of Sociology* (1978), pp. 728–39, by Alan Sica. For Amin introducing Amin, see "Growth Is Not Development," *Development Forum* (April 1973). For a good discussion of U.S. imperialism, see "A Debate" between Miller, Bennett, and Alapatt of the New York University Center for International Studies on the one hand and Harry Magdoff on the other in *Social Policy* (September/October 1970), pp. 13–29. For recent development, Kreye et al., *Die Neue Internationale Arbeitsteilung* (Hanburg: Rororo, 1978) is indispensable.

2. In concrete cases, though, it may very well be that a purely economistic approach will be most valid. But it is difficult to find good examples. Were the "loss" of China in 1949, the "loss" of Indochina in 1975, the "loss" of Chile only losses of markets? Was it not also that these were political satellites, military support areas, cultural and communicative receivers of messages and knowledge, raw societies on which the structure of the master country could be imprinted? And correspondingly, for the Soviet Union in

Eastern Europe, would the "loss" of Czechoslovakia merely be a loss of a pupil in the making of socialism, an adolescent revolt where the son suddenly starts teaching the father? Or, could there also be some very concrete economic interests involved—for instance, a supply of manufactures against raw materials at bad terms of trade for the Czechs? By and large we may use the paradigm of economic imperialism in order to understand U.S.–Latin America relations and social imperialism to understand Soviet Union–Eastern Europe relations, but we must always remain open to the ways in which the various types of imperialism tend to combine.

3. See Galtung, "Social Imperialism and Sub-Imperialism: Continuities in the Structural Theory of Imperialism," *World Development* (1976), pp. 153–66.

4. This is described in some detail in Galtung and Fumiko Nishimura, *Learning from the Chinese People* (Oslo, 1975), in chapter 3 on the cultural revolution and chapter 6 on China's foreign policy.

5. There is hardly any reason to put a question mark, for this is the very essence of missionary zeal. But how many civilizations, regions, countries, groups, people are missionary? One tentative hypothesis, explored in detail in the Trends in Western Civilization Program at the University of Oslo, Chair in Conflict and Peace Research, is that this bent is characteristic of Western civilization and, underlying it, Christianity and to some extent Islam. Missionarism, then, has to be distinguished from subjugation of other peoples merely to tax them or rob them in some other ways. Missionarism implies conversion of minds and changes of societies.

6. I am thinking of all kinds of fads, from rock-and-roll and blue jeans to public opinion studies in social sciences; they have a tendency to arrive and become rooted in Eastern Europe at just about the time they are left behind in Western Europe. For a view emphasizing equality between the two Europes, however, in a historical perspective, see Bosl et al., *Eastern and Western Europe in the Middle Ages* (London: Thames & Hudson, 1970), perhaps particularly G. Barraclough's introduction, "Towards a New Concept of European History."

7. On this point Academician Sakharov is rather explicit, having on many occasions stated how he agrees about the dangers of monopolistic capitalism, particularly when there is one monopoly for the whole field of production: the state.

8. This is analyzed in some detail in Galtung, "European Security and Cooperation: A Sceptical Contribution," *Essays* V, 2, first published in *Journal of Peace Research* (1975), pp. 165–78.

9. This is analyzed in some detail in Galtung, "Japan and Future World Politics," *Essays* V, 6, first published in *Journal of Peace Research* (1973), pp. 355–86.

10. See the article referred to in note 8.

11. This is Gunnar Myrdal's excellent idea of cumulative causation, or of positive feedback as a better paradigm for social processes than negative feedback, implying that the rich will get richer and the poor will get poorer.

12. Maybe this can serve as a concrete example of what the trite words in the definition are about, from a pamphlet issued by the Manchester Chamber of Commerce, as quoted in Parker Thomas Moon, *Imperialism and World Politics* (New York: Macmillan, 1927), p. 66. It is from a speech that Henry Stanley delivered to a gathering of the Manchester Chamber of Commerce,

chiefly cotton merchants. He was assuming that "civilization" would teach the naked natives of the Congo to wear decent cotton clothes, at least on Sunday, and he estimated that one Sunday dress for each native would mean "320,000,000 yards of Manchester cotton cloth" (cheers from the audience); and in time, when the natives had learned the importance of covering their nakedness on weekdays as well as on Sunday, the amount of cloth required would amount to 26,000,000 pounds sterling per year. "There are forty millions of people beyond the gateway of the Congo, and the cotton spinners of Manchester are waiting to clothe them. Birmingham foundries are glowing with the red metal that will presently be made into ironwork for them and the trinkets that shall adorn those dusky bosoms, and the ministers of Christ are zealous to bring them, the poor benighted heathen, into the Christian fold." I am indebted to K.W. Grundy for this reference.

13. Some reflections on this will be found in the appendix, section A.3, under the heading "Equity." For an important use of the concept, see Bela Belassa, *The Structure of Protection,* UNCTAD, TD/B/C.2/36, where Belassa shows very nicely how tariffs relate to degree of processing. He uses four levels of processing showing that the tariffs increase from 4.6 to 22.1 percent of the export value. He also notes that 71.2 percent of the exports from under-developed countries are at level 1 of processing, only 2.1 percent at level 4. But still missing is a way of relating degree of processing to positive and negative externalities (spin-offs).

14. This is clearly contrary to the theory of free trade, as was pointed out by Friedrich List in the 1840s: "England therefore *prohibited* the articles competing with those of her own *factories,* the silk and cotton goods of the East. This prohibition was absolute and under severe penalties, she would not consume a thread from India. . . . Did England, in so doing, act unwisely? Undoubtedly, according to Adam Smith and J. B. Say, and their theory of values. . . . We hold a different theory, which we call *the theory of productive power;* a theory which the English ministers obeyed, without fully comprehending, when they determined upon their industrial policy: to buy raw materials, and sell manufactured products. . . . Their policy has been attended with the most splendid success. . . . Her own production is now from fifty to a hundred times greater than her former commerce in the manufactured articles of India. What would have been her condition had she purchased for these last hundred years the cheap goods of India?" I am indebted to A.G. Frank for this reference. And Frank, one of the leading specialists on imperialism, in his *Latin America: Underdevelopment or Revolution* (New York: Monthly Review Press, 1969), pp. 158–59, has this to add about the Japanese case: "Japan is the crucial example among the capitalist economies, as the Soviet Union is among the socialist, of a country which, in order to achieve the take-off into economic development in a world of already industrialized and imperialist countries, began by isolating itself substantially from foreign trade and totally from foreign investment and control. Neither country found it necessary, let it be noted, to permit such foreign investment to take advantage of the technology of the industrially more advanced countries. Only *after* they had forged an economic structure and their own control of it, which permitted them to take advantage of . . . other countries, did [they] enter into such relations."

15. And this is in fact what happens, but there is no direct negative interest: there is a grant, and the fringe benefits to those who travel on a good per diem basis to negotiate about the grant.

16. In fact, the correlation between the Gini index for income inequality ("disparity") and GNP per capita is -0.90; with the percentage working in nonprimary sectors of the economy it is -1.00; and with the trade composition index (a measure of the extent to which a country follows the rule List attributes to the British—see note 14—"to buy raw materials, and sell manufactured products") it is -0.83. In other words, the higher the level of economic development as measured by these three different indicators, the lower the level of inequality, as measured by the Gini index.

17. I am indebted to Helge Hveem for this felicitous formulation. However, as the leaders of the Third World countries decreasingly have their educational background in former colonial countries and their roots in the preliberation atmosphere of submissiveness, this may become decreasingly true.

18. This is perhaps the doctrine that has done most harm to the economies of the Third World countries, precisely because it looks so rational and can be presented mathematically in such a convincing manner. Everything is correct, except that the range of variables included is too narrow. What I have called spin-off effects, and what the economists tend to refer to as "externalities," are not included. They are rejected as noneconomic variables, which is where it all goes wrong. The matter is evidently too important to be left to economists alone. For an article that is a heavy attack on "the conventional comparative advantage or gains-from-trade analysis of the textbooks which incorrectly assumed the independence of the partners," see Richard D. Wolff, "Modern Imperialism: The View from the Metropolis," *American Economic Review* (May 1970), pp. 225–30 (the quote is from page 229).

19. Rakośi from Hungary, for instance, stayed in Siberia for a long time.

20. "Penetration" should be kept as a rich concept with many connotations. In general it is tantamount to gaining a foothold, or a bridgehead, as it is called in the text. One of the best methods would be to make use of the existing rulers, administering a combination of reward and punishment to make them work for the Center country. One of the best rewards would be to promise them protection, precisely the meaning of the British law and order: existing elites, together with the new settler elites, are protected in return for certain services for the mother country.

21. This is where the British are supposed to be the masters, "divide and conquer," "split and rule." Thus, it would be in their interest according to this principle to draw colonial borders in a way opposite to the way nations were sorted into single-nation states in Europe, creating colonies as multinational as possible, particularly with nations in conflict with each other, so that the British could use these conflicts to establish themselves as "objective" third parties, earning a certain amount of gratitude from all. The legacy of this tradition, deliberate or not, is found in Africa today, clustering around former Rhodesia, creating considerable difficulty for the new states and some backing for right-wing nostalgia for the days of *pax britannica* or *pax gallica*.

22. This term is particularly used in Latin American analyses.

23. See Galtung, *The European Community: A Superpower in the Making* (London: Allen & Unwin, 1973), chap. 6, and Galtung, "The Lomé Convention and Neo-capitalism," *Africa Today* (1976). Lomé II does not look much different.

24. Other examples would be the OECD, the Security Council, and the International Energy Agency.

25. Thus, although a country like Norway is outside the European community (because of the referendum of September 1972, certainly not because of establishment and governmental policy), Norway is nevertheless a part of the general system of Western economic imperialism; see Galtung, "Norway in the World Community," *Essays* IV, 8.

26. This is spelled out in section 4.3.

27. The dependency in the Periphery, as Theotonio Dos Santos points out in his famous article "The Structure of Dependence," *American Economic Review* (May 1970), pp. 231–36, is "a situation in which the economy of certain countries is conditioned by the development and expansion of another economy to which the former is subjected." Substituting "social structure" for "economy" gives a definition of social imperialism (see the article referred to in note 3). Thus, the United States is much more free to permit limited experiments than are the satellite countries—as is the Soviet Union, although they do not make use of that possibility. Dos Santos, however, limits his analysis to the Western hemisphere, as do almost all Latin American social scientists, thereby avoiding any analysis of the Eastern European experience. They have good reasons for focusing on their own situation: "The ratio of remitted capital to new flow is around 2.7 for the period 1946–47; that is, for each dollar that enters $2.70 leaves. In the 1960s this ratio roughly doubled, and in some years was considerably higher" (p. 234).

28. I am thinking, of course, not only of the incorporation of Sikkim and Bhutan and the domination of Nepal, but also of a possible expansion through economic domination into Burma, Sri Lanka, Bangladesh, Pakistan, and Afghanistan, thereby constituting an external periphery that would permit by imperialist means an increase in the standards of living of some of the Indian masses. However, there is a problem here: the European centers were small relative to their empires; an Indian center would not be. Besides, China would not permit this kind of expansion because it might interfere with Chinese designs, however much they declare that it is their policy not to seek hegemony.

29. Herbert Schiller was a pioneer in the field of studies of communication satellites from the point of view of imperialism theory and practice. See his study *The Mind Managers* (Boston: Beacon Press, 1973), especially the last chapter, "Information Technology as a Democratizing Force?"

30. Wilbur Schramm was a pioneer in this field with his studies for UNESCO.

31. For one effort to analyze this, see Galtung, "After Camelot" and "Science Assistance and Neo-colonialism: Some Ethical Problems," chapters 6 and 7 in *Papers on Methodology* (Copenhagen: Ejlers, 1979).

32. I am indebted to J. Graciarena for this parallel and have made use of it in an article that explores this general issue using more of the theory of imperialism, "Is Peaceful Research Possible? On the Methodology of Peace Research," *Essays* I, 12.

33. Thus, it is surprising that Gollwitzer in his excellent *Europe in the Age of Imperialism* (London: Thames & Hudson, 1969) does not make any reference to this rather important predecessor.

34. The more the development proceeds in this direction, the more crucial will the control of communication be, for there will be fewer alternatives to

electronic communication—fewer personal encounters, less letter writing, and so on, relative to all the forms of telecommunication.

35. And at this point IBM is not the best example. ITT in Chile is more obvious.

36. The socioeconomic system has outgrown the geopolitical borders, and there is no built-in brake on the expansionism; on the contrary, it is stimulated by the greed for economic and political profit (see note 5). On the other hand, the spill-over could also lead to symmetric, equitable forms of interaction, when each spills over into the other with comparable goods and gospels.

37. Rank concordance is the generalization and rank equilibrium to more than two rank dimensions; rank discordance is the generalization of rank disequilibrium to mixed profiles (high–high–low–high–low, for instance) involving more than two dimensions. One point in this connection is the idea that disequilibrium and discordance are among the ingredients out of which instability and even revolutions are made; see Galtung, "A Structural Theory of Aggression," *Essays* III, 4, and further elaboration in "A Structural Theory of Revolutions," *Essays* III, 8. For an analysis of the underlying concepts, see Galtung, "International Relations and International Conflicts: A Sociological Approach," *Essays* IV, 9.

38. It must always be remembered that ships came long before railways and that mountains often separated peoples more effectively than the seas. It is true for the biggest inland sea or ocean in the world, the Mediterranean, and toward the end of this century the whole Mediterranean area may constitute a very clear region, contiguous, socialist/communist in the socioeconomic systems, no longer separated with the colonial powers to the north and the colonies to the south. In retrospect the OPEC action for higher oil prices in the fall of 1973 will probably stand out as the turning point for the Mediterranean region, but the process will be both slow and complicated. Another such region, incidentally, might be constituted by the Mexican Gulf-Caribbean area, and may one day even evolve a formula whereby the southern states of the United States would become members. Still another region of that type is Southeast Asia, possibly extending to include Japan when Japan eventually becomes less imperialist (after one more war?)

39. Typically, "area studies" are a reflection of the way the world is divided in foreign offices. "Latin America" is an area because it is an object of foreign policy in a broad sense to the United States. Similarly Black Africa is an area, gradually being replaced by ACP (about fifty African, Caribbean, and Pacific countries that are signatories to the Lomé convention). Much better units of analysis would be the vertical regions in figure 4.5—the United States *with* Latin America, the European Community *with* Black Africa (or ACP) and so on. Of course, if the purpose is only to study *differences* between regions, the type of subdivision into ten regions used, for instance, by Pestel Mesarovic in *Mankind at a Turning Point* (Readers' Digest Press, 1974) may be used. That leads to very primitive analyses, however, unless the *relations* between regions are taken fully into account—and they are predominantly vertical.

40. It can be both: there may be violence in some phases, regions, and segments of the population, and nonviolence in others. It can be neither: both violence and nonviolence are deliberate strategies, not just random bursts of action. Nor is "passive resistance"—e.g., of the type some of the Norwegian population engaged in during World War II—the same as nonviolence, for reasons that will be evident from the text.

41. This is very similar to the five phases in George Lakey's excellent analysis, *Strategy for a Living Revolution* (New York: Grossman, 1973), but they were arrived at independently here, in connection with my work on *Theories of Conflict* (forthcoming), from a more theoretical rationale.

42. This includes both external forces from the social and nonsocial environments and the internal forces of one's own mind and body.

43. This follows directly from the power theory developed in section 2.3.

44. This was a basic point in Gandhi's way of organizing his campaign and is brought out very clearly in Arne Naess, *Gandhi and Group Conflict* (Oslo: Universitetsforlaget, 1974).

45. Here Lakey's analysis is particularly stimulating, giving much detail about the practice of confrontation—probably the best analysis in the field. For the most comprehensive analysis of nonviolence, however, see Gene Sharp, *The Politics of Nonviolent Action* (Boston: Sargent, 1973).

46. It may be objected that fascists do not mind that. Such an argument gives one reason why the U.S. society in its genocidal and highly alienated warfare against the Indochinese peoples should not be characterized as fascist but, perhaps, as "structurally fascist." The structure produces fascist actions like extermination of peoples, without necessarily also producing fascist ideology. This is made possible through technification of warfare by running a war like a business corporation, in which everybody performs jobs "just like any other job."

47. For another contribution to the theory of confrontations, see Daniel Cohn-Bendit on the 1968 student revolt in France.

48. I am indebted to Eduardo Hamuy, the Chilean sociologist, for this observation, as the only positive thing one might perhaps say about the ill-fated Alianza para el Progreso: it served to communicate certain new norms and values about landownership rather than doing anything of importance about it.

49. See Galtung, "Institutionalized Conflict Resolution: A Theoretical Paradigm," *Essays* III, 15; and Sivert Langholm, "Violent Conflict Resolution and the Loser's Reaction," *Journal of Peace Research* (1965), pp. 324–47.

50. This is typical of the German situation, where about 10 percent of the cohort refuse to do military service (but about half of those with completed *Gymnasium*)—and the conscientious objectors even serve abroad, for example, at peace research institutes.

51. The best discussions are those by Gene Sharp (see note 45) and in Adam Roberts' anthology *The Strategy of Civilian Defense* (London: Faber & Faber, 1967).

52. I am currently making an effort to compare the strategies of the two against a background of the structural and cultural reality in which they were fighting. One obvious similarity is their power theory: autonomy-oriented rather than balance-oriented in a narrow sense (see section 2.3).

53. The time period was longer for China than for the others, perhaps even twenty-five or at least twenty years after the revolution. For the others it was more of a question of five to ten years, it seems. Cuba, of course, was relatively rich.

54. Social imperialism hardly affects more than 350 million people, as dominators and dominated, unless one adds China's 900 million as indirectly affected because it keeps them in a constant state of preparedness. But as

much of this preparedness seems to be of China's own making, it is hard to accept it as a consequence of social imperialism only. When it comes to capitalist imperialism, however, the three vertical blocs headed by the United States, the European Community, and Japan amount to around half a billion, with some overlaps (add South Asia to this, and it also comes out about right in terms of the world's population).

55. Gollwitzer, for instance (see note 33), uses the industrial revolution as a take-off point for his study; I would prefer to use the Great Discoveries and see the Portuguese rather than the British as the forerunners because I do not tie imperialism so closely to capitalist economics.

56. See the article referred to in note 3.

57. I am referring to the Sixth and Seventh Special Sessions of the United Nations General Assembly and to the Charter of Economic Rights and Duties of States. For an analysis, see Galtung, "Self-reliance and Global Interdependence: Some Reflections on the New International Economic Order," *Papers* (Chair in Conflict and Peace Research, University of Oslo, 1976) (Ottawa: CIDA, 1978).

58. See Galtung, "Cuba: Anti-imperialism and Socialist Development," *Essays* V, 7.

59. So far, however, there seem to be some health hazards connected with this kind of protein according to experience in Japan.

60. This is very well analyzed by Paul Baran in *The Political Economy of Growth* (New York: Monthly Review Press, 1968), chap. 2, "The Concept of the Economic Surplus," which focuses particularly on the potential surplus.

61. See Galtung, "On the Effects of International Economic Sanctions: The Case of Rhodesia," *Essays* V, 4.

62. Ricardo's classical example was wine and textiles, where the spin-offs probably are of the same order of magnitude, not like those between wine and computers and textiles and color TVs.

63. It could also be the Soviet Union's answer to a trade pattern relative to Eastern Europe that puts them in the role of the supplier of raw materials. In case of a breakdown in economic relations, the countries of Eastern Europe would have to pool together their considerable but hardly sufficient raw materials and energy resources, which might force them into a pattern of creativity that might have a positive effect on their socialism.

64. Thus, it might be argued that UNCTAD should be renamed UNCTOD, the UN Conference on Trade *or* Development.

65. The key passage from the Arusha declaration makes the self-reliance of the higher unit dependent on the self-reliance of the lower unit (the village on the block, the block on the family, the family on the individual, etc.). One could also reason the other way, however: it is very difficult for the lower unit to remain self-reliant when the higher units become dependent; it is a contagious phenomenon that only the very strong (monks and nuns, *kibbutzim* inhabitants) will be able to resist.

66. Since they are of the Center's creation, it may be argued that it is the duty of the Center to receive them, thus letting off considerable amounts of steam.

67. See Galtung and Nishimura, *Learning from the Chinese People,* chaps. 2 and 3.

68. And there are many in my situation—a kind of center in the Periphery in the reverse, with identification, solidarity, one's soul in the Third World (partly by having lived there for some time, no doubt mainly under center in the Periphery conditions), yet with the body tied to one's roots in the Center countries. Increasingly our role will consist in being a bridgehead in reverse, and probably very sensitive to how the Third World reacts to us when self-reliance becomes a real force.

69. This term I take to have two connotations: it refers to a structural transformation away from exploitation/penetration/fragmentation/marginalization— in other words, a reduction of structural violence, domestically and/or globally—*and* over a relatively short period. It does not connote violence unless one is so positivistically inclined as to deny the possibility of transcending the link between revolution (in the sense just defined) and violence in the past. Of course, section 4.3 was intended to indicate some of the instruments of this transcendence.

70. I am indebted to Suvendra Patel for this information.

71. This idea has been put forward by J. Pronk in the Dutch program for development aid; see *Netherlands Development Policy 1974* and "Development Is Growth Plus Structural Change," in *Informatie*, 25 October 1973.

72. The Cocoyoc declaration states unequivocally the link between development and subversion/intervention: "There is an international power structure that will resist moves in this direction [toward self-reliance]. Its methods are well known: the purposive maintenance of the built-in bias of the existing international market mechanisms, other forms of economic manipulation, withdrawing or withholding credits, embargoes, economic sanctions, subversive use of intelligence agencies, repression including torture, counter-insurgency operations, even full-scale intervention. To those contemplating the use of such methods we say: 'Hands off. Leave countries to find their own road to a fuller life for their citizens.' To those who are the sometimes unwilling tools of such designs—scholars, businessmen, police, soldiers and many others—we would say: 'Refuse to be used for purposes of denying another nation the right to develop itself.' To the natural and social scientists, who help design the instruments of oppression, we would say: 'The world needs your talents for constructive purposes, to develop new technologies that benefit man and do not harm the environment.' "

73. By far the best book on this seems to be Leopold Kohr's *The Breakdown of Nations* (London: Routledge & Kegan Paul, 1957).

74. From an UNCTAD study conducted by Frédéric Clairmonte.

75. District policy inside counties may be seen in the same light.

76. My own experience as an "expert" at the Universidad de la Habana stems from August 1972, and the pattern used was clearly based on the following principles: have the experts for a short period, not all year long; have a fairly clear, specific idea of the field of expertise; have several experts with different backgrounds in the same field, even when they give contradictory advice; have a good reception system of people also from different fields.

77. For the importance of arguing in terms of cycles and not only in terms of technology, see Galtung, "Development from Above and the Blue Revolution: The Indo-Norwegian Project in Kerala," *Essays* V, 12; a short version of this article appeared in the FAO magazine *Ceres*, no. 42.

78. These are not two different scenarios, one based on high labor intensity and

the other on automation, but two modes of organizing the economy that we somehow should try to combine. One can use treadmills to produce some energy, but it hardly ennobles man; hence automation may be asked for in that field. One may also produce textiles through automation, but only at the expense of depriving people of a type of work that may be highly nonalienating. For an effort to analyze this dilemma, see Galtung, "Alternative Life Styles in Rich Countries," *Papers* (Chair in Conflict and Peace Research, University of Oslo); also published in *What Now?* (Uppsala, 1975) and in *Development Dialogue* (1976).

79. See Galtung, "Human Needs, National Interest and World Politics: The Law of the Sea Conference," *Essays* V, 13.

80. But the danger here is that we would be too mesmerized by the concrete technologies and forgetful of the purpose of the whole thing, which is not merely to deplete and pollute less but to develop technologies that are compatible with the social structure we want, domestically and globally.

81. Thus, torture has been a part of an international structure of subimperialism, with Brazilians partly trained in U.S. institutions torturing in Chile, Czech police officers partly trained in the Soviet Union introducing secret police methods in Cuba, and so on.

82. This is analyzed in considerable detail in G. Skilling and F. Griffiths, *Interest Groups in Soviet Politics* (Princeton University Press, 1971).

83. For an analysis of what Solzhenitsyn stands for politically, see the interesting article by Paul Avrich, "Solzhenitsyn's Political Philosophy," *Interrogations* (1974), pp. 103–15, pointing out how he resists the idea of Westernization in any form, from Peter the Great onward, nostalgic for the old Russian *mir*.

84. Once this idea is fully realized, it will constitute a tremendous political force in favor of family planning, all over the world—few children in order to permit the self-realization of the parents, particularly the mothers, rather than many children as cheap labor in precapitalist economic settings (the farm, the family shop) and as a source of security during old age. A condition is an alternative source of that security, though—maybe something like the Chinese People's Commune. In general, the relation between men and women is very similar to the relation between Center and Periphery discussed in this article: women delivering raw material for reproduction, the Periphery raw material for production. But then these two relations both come out of a deeper lying structure in, at least, Western society.

5. THE WAR SYSTEM

5.1 ON THE USE OF DIRECT VIOLENCE

The war system comprises all the machineries for organized, collective use of *direct violence,* or *means of destruction,* with both "software" (people, social organization, armed forces) and "hardware" (arms) components. There are many ways of approaching this system analytically: one may study *what* it is, to understand its *structure* better[1]; one may study *how* it is used, to understand its *function* better[2]; one may study the structures and functions of two subsidiary systems (classes, ethnic groups, countries, alliances, regions) pitted against each other, to arrive at some conclusions about the *balance of power* for deterrence or victory between them;[3] and one may study the *dynamics* of the total system, to see how structures and functions and balances of power may change over time in what is termed the *arms race*[4] or the *military race.*

However, I shall take a different point of departure: a study of *where* the war system might be put to use. Just what are the "tensions," the conflicts that may stimulate arms races and eventually become war theaters? This question can be answered only in terms of a model of the world. The answer given by the analyst who canvasses all the information about "trouble spots" around the world according to news bulletins is based on a naive and actor-oriented model of the world: that the cue to future use of direct violence is direct violence in the past.[5] The more sophisticated analyst would study all such empirical cases, the events, to understand what was there before even the slightest sign of "trouble" in the sense of direct violence; he would search for common denominators and then look for similar structural combinations elsewhere. Such a procedure would almost certainly lead him to formulations in terms of *structural violence,* i.e., of dominance. Direct violence is so often used to maintain or destroy dominance that this point can hardly escape any analyst, but he must avoid the naive formula that direct violence is used only to establish, maintain, and destroy dominance relations.[6]

Once more one is back to our fundamental distinctions in ways of thinking about social affairs. According to the actor-oriented perspective, direct violence is initiated by actors, both groups and nations. According to the structure-oriented perspective, direct violence is a companion of structures pregnant with structural violence. The first view leads to the classical *strategic analysis* of the intentions and capabilities of actors; the second view to *structural analysis* for conditions of revolution and counterrevolution, within and between nations, with particular emphasis on *mobilization*. Since I believe that the two views do not exclude each other, but rather supplement each other in a most valuable way, I shall turn to the question of where the war system might be employed. In this chapter the analysis will not be carried out in anything like concrete geographical terms (that will to some extent be done in chapter 6), but in more general structural terms, making full use of the analysis in the preceding chapter.

Let us take as our point of departure a simple world consisting of four countries, two in the Center and two in the Periphery, organized in two systems of dominance, as shown in figure 5.1. The arrows connecting Center and Periphery nations in the same empire stand for dominance relations, and all the lines with rings at the ends and with numbers indicate some possibilities for the application of two war systems. The diagram is not complete, as more lines could be imagined, but the most important ones have been included.

The following list shows twelve types of war systems, twelve types falling into five groups of possible theaters.

Figure 5.1   Where can the war system be employed?

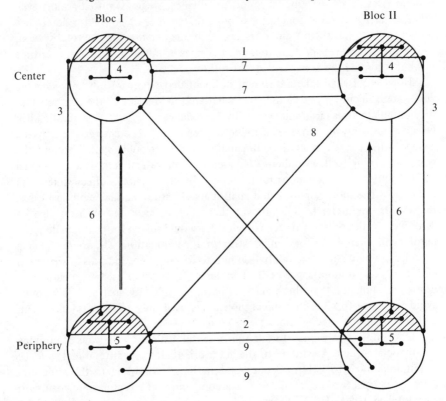

External Wars (intercountry)
 1. *Center–Center warfare*
 2. *Periphery–Periphery warfare*
 3. *Center–Periphery warfare*
Internal Wars (intracountry)
 4. *intra-Center warfare*
 5. *intra-Periphery warfare*
Imperialistic Wars (intrabloc)
 6. *Center participating in intra-Periphery warfare*
Subversive Wars (interbloc)
 7. *Center participating in intra-Center warfare*
 8. *Center participating in intra-Periphery warfare*
 9. *Periphery participating in intra-Periphery warfare*
Internationalized Class Wars (more complex)
 10. *periphery in Periphery and Center joint warfare* (intrabloc)
 11. *periphery in Center joint warfare* (interbloc)
 12. *periphery in Periphery joint warfare* (interbloc)

The first group consists of the *external wars,* with countries seen as billiard balls, at war against each other (types 1, 2, and 3). There may be wars between Center countries, wars between Periphery countries, and wars between countries in the Center and countries in the Periphery. As to the last, I have included only war situations within empires, not wars against somebody else's Periphery, which are unlikely as long as the Center nations are at odds with each other and also with their own Periphery nations. After all, why attack the potential enemy of your enemy—he may be your best friend! Thus, the United States attacked North Vietnam in an effort to keep as much of Vietnam as possible, not as a prelude to a fight against the entire Soviet system (of which it was not obvious that North Vietnam was a part).

The basic idea in this type of war is that wars generally take place between equals. If the two parties are highly unequal in capability, one will prevail over the other and domination will be the result, perhaps with no war at all, as when many non-Western peoples were colonized. But the Indochina wars of France and the United States show clearly that capability must not be interpreted narrowly as hardware alone. The will to fight and the capacity to organize may be much more important. For that reason I speak of the military race, not only of the superficial phenomenon known as the arms race.

Let us simplify figure 5.1 to bring out a point about these three types of external wars. Figure 5.2 shows the five phases in the decline of empires and the spread of external wars.

Phase I. The two Center countries are building up their empires by attacking and dominating Periphery countries. As there are a limited number of countries to be dominated, the Center countries are at odds with each other.[7]

Figure 5.2 The decline of empires and the spread of external wars

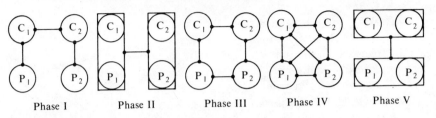

Phase I   Phase II   Phase III   Phase IV   Phase V

Phase II. The empires have been firmly established as vertical blocs, e.g., as military alliances, pitted against each other.[8]

Phase III. The empires, or vertical alliances, have loosened up. As the Center nations no longer monopolize the use of violence, two new theaters of war are opened up, one inside the former empires and alliances and one between Periphery nations.[9]

Phase IV. Subversive "diagonal wars" have also become possible; the whole relation of simple bloc domination is about to disappear.[10]

Phase V. Periphery countries, as well as Center countries, have found each other and have become so integrated that wars within Center and within Periphery are no longer possible.

We are then back to the point of departure, only that this time both Center and Periphery are bigger and new Centers and Peripheries may be challenging them.[11] In other words, a cycle from the establishment and consolidation of vertical blocs with empires at (horizontal) war with each other to an international class (vertical) war between horizontal blocs of nations.

I see Phases III, IV, and V as typical of the situation today. There is dominance combined with spheres of interest, but at the same time there is decolonization, meaning the acquisition of some type of political independence by most countries. *One aspect of political independence is the right to acquire one's own means of destruction and to fight one's own wars rather than to participate in the wars of others (as in Phase II).* International democratization of access to means of destruction and the right to wage wars widens considerably the range of war theaters. At the same time, there is also a consolidation of macro Centers (the European Community, the U.S.-Soviet system).[12]

In general, one would predict Periphery–Periphery wars to come first when imperialist structures loosen up, since wars are generally between equals.[13] Center–Periphery wars (not to be confused with wars of liberation from dominance, which have a much more complex structure as "billiard-ball" wars will come later, when the Periphery is strong enough and has acquired and accumulated enough experience from Periphery–Periphery wars.[14] The imperial system was a vertical peace-keeping system; its disappearance had and will continue to have obvious impacts on the war system. The question of alternative peacekeeping systems will be looked into in section 8.3.

Thus, this classical approach to wars gives us three types of external wars: Center-Center, Periphery-Periphery, and Center-Periphery. They all presuppose a very high level of homogeneity within countries, a national cause, or at least an unquestioning acceptance of center decisions. But these are only three out of at least twelve types of wars.

The second group consists of the internal wars (types 4 and 5 in table 5.1): inside Center nations and inside Periphery nations. Again, I would see internal dominance, internal colonization, as a major basis for internal wars, but not the only one. At present, I would predict particularly frequent internal wars in Periphery nations that have been exposed to imperialism. For according to the theory of the preceding chapter, there is less inequality in Center nations, hence less motivation to launch an internal war. Moreover, after independence the new center in the Periphery very often simply fills the holes left behind when the colonists leave, keeping the old structure and making it possible to draw on the same ideologies and the same emotions as in colonial times. Bangladesh is a good example.[15]

I have spelled out how internal dominance divides a country in a center and a periphery. Quite often, however, there are two additional factors that will increase the likelihood of internal war considerably. If it is only a question of dominance, then a war between center and periphery is clearly a class war. But if the center-periphery distinction is correlated with *racial* and *ethnic* factors, then it usually becomes much more polarized and intensive, as in Biafra or Ulster.[16] And, if these two are correlated with *geographical location* so that the center belongs to one racial or ethnic group living in one area, and the periphery to another living in another area, then the stage is set not only for internal war but for secessionist warfare (see section 6.2).[17]

The third group is made up of the imperialistic wars (type 6). The Center country participates in intra-Periphery warfare in such a way as to establish or maintain dominance (France and the United States in Indochina; the Soviet Union in Hungary, or the United States in the Dominican Republic). When they are fought to maintain dominance, they are euphemistically referred to as "counterinsurgency." Since they are the opposite of subversive wars, the next category, we may coin a new term and refer to them as "superversive" wars, serving the precise purpose of dominance. In general the periphery in the Periphery (PRG) will be pitted against an alliance with three partners: the center in the Periphery (Ky-Van Thieu), the periphery in the Center (U.S. "hardhats"), and the center in the Center (Pentagon). Needless to say, there may also be other actors, and there may be very many spectators, for in general the periphery in the Periphery would not be able to make it against such a formidable triple alliance. For if imperialism is enacted in a professional rather than an amateurish way, then the Center nation will not be split along class lines over the issue. The periphery in the Center will join enthusiastically, not only because of vested interests in sharing the spoils of exploitation but also out of racial or ethnic arrogance, to participate in the *mission civilisatrice,* accepting its definition as a national cause. Incidentally, participation may also take the form of ousting one exploitative center in the Periphery in order later to install another that can be used as a bridgehead for Center imperialism (the Spanish-American wars in the Western Hemisphere as well as in the Philippines).[18]

The fourth group is the *anti-imperialistic or subversive wars* (types 7, 8, and 9). These wars are both interbloc and intraclass. They are "diagonal" wars, with horizontal and vertical components. A country in one bloc participates in what goes on inside countries in the other bloc. I have distinguished three types. First, there is Center participation in intra-Center warfare on the other side, which would be like Soviet support to the Black Panthers and U.S. support to Ukrainian nationalists. Type 7 is extremely dangerous because, being close to what would take place in warfare of type 1, it could easily be a cause or a consequence of type 1 warfare, with all the unleashed weaponry that implies.

Much more frequent would be Center meddling in intra-Periphery warfare on the other side. This type is important. In the preceding chapter it was pointed out that for the periphery of the Periphery in one empire the center of the Center of the other empire might be the only ally sufficiently motivated and capable of being of help in an emergency. But help from the center in the Periphery of a competing empire may also be of value; it may have less capacity but compensate for that by being closer (as the PRG being helped by North Vietnam and China and the Soviet Union, although one probably should be careful in seeing Hanoi as dominated by either at that stage). As in the case of imperialistic wars, we assume that in the anti-imperialistic wars the whole nation participates, not only the center. This assumption may not always be equally valid, however, for the gains to the periphery of the Center in an anti-imperialistic war are less substantial, less tied to simple interests than the gains that may accrue to them in an imperialistic war. On the other hand, anti-imperialism is often only a way of establishing one's own imperialism.[19]

Fifth, there are the *internationalized class wars* (types 10, 11, and 12). Two peripheries may join together to fight the centers, who would then also quickly join together. These might be the two peripheries inside an empire, the two peripheries of the Center countries, or the two peripheries in the Periphery countries. In principle, the periphery in the Center and the periphery in the Periphery of the same empire should join since they are exploited by the same center alliance; this is a basic Marxist assumption. In practice, however, due to the inegalitarian distribution of inequality (see section 4.2) it is highly unlikely that the U.S. and the Latin American proletariats will form an alliance in the near future. There is also the classical example of World War I: instead of the French and German working classes joining forces to fight their class enemies, the capitalists (which would have been type 11), one got a very traditional international war of type 1. But in Latin America something like type 12 is emerging because of the relative ease with which peripheries in these Periphery countries can join and because of the similarity of their positions. Castro's and Che Guevara's slogans and activities found an institutional expression in the famous Tricontinental (OSPAAAL),[20] an alliance of liberation movements, coordinating, crystallizing, *and above all internationalizing* intra-Periphery warfare against domination, domestic as well as foreign (type 12).

At this point we can draw three tentative conclusions basic to our reasoning about the war system:

First, most types of war theaters (in fact 10 out of 12) on this list are tied to the system of dominance one way or another. If they are wars, they are vertical wars or at least have vertical components. There are only two clear examples of horizontal wars: between Center countries and between Periphery countries (although there may also be horizontal internal wars). *Any theory of wars, weaponry used, arms races, disarmament, or security based on horizontal assumptions that the two belligerents are equally autonomous is naive indeed.* Relations obtaining between the United States and the Soviet Union are exceptions, not the rule, and even there the dominance perspective will have to enter any serious analysis.

Second, although it makes a lot of sense to talk about an East-West conflict (type 1), to talk about North-South conflict is only confusing. Usually it is some type of wishful thinking. There is a vertical dimension in the world, but it cuts through and across countries and blocs in very intricate ways. The expression "North-South conflict" can of course be taken to mean any mixture of all types of wars except the first two, but then the classification is diluted by combining diverse types. Moreover, that classification also tends to blur the difference between West and East. There are many similarities, but the Soviet sphere of hegemony in Eastern Europe pales in comparison to similar efforts made by the United States, if not those of the EC countries and Japan. If the world conflict situation is to be defined by using the compass, then it would probably be more correct to say that *it is North-West against the rest of the world,* the developed capitalist world (DC) against the socialist countries (SC) and the underdeveloped capitalist countries (UC).[21]

But any such formula is also too crude and too naive as an analytical view, since it blurs the intranational class nature of dominance relations. *Dominance does not serve to define international wars but to internationalize intranational wars.* In a possible future where today's dominance relations have been abolished, the countries in the South may, perhaps, one day gang up together against the nations in the North in a classical war of conquest. But today their centers are too tied to the North to make this type of simple confrontation meaningful.

Third, all these twelve types of war possibilities are very real, and will serve to crystallize conflict, arms sales, "trouble," and international politics in general. There are those who in the usual Euro-centric tradition see only the East-West conflict (type 1) as "real" and the rest as "local" derivatives of the East-West conflict. That type of thinking only betrays ignorance and parochialism.[22] In fact, people will probably feel much more motivated to die in a vertical war of types 3 through 12 than in the traditional horizontal wars of the first two categories.[23] People fighting for liberation may not have as sophisticated arms, but they will demand them, and if they do not get them, they will make them. Dominated countries and peoples will not accept any idea to the effect that they have less right to fight than others, that they are irresponsible, that their wars are significant only because they may escalate into the "real" war, a war of type 1: a cynical and white-man-centered perspective.[24] The only alternative they can see to war is an end to domination, increasingly so as political consciousness becomes increasingly widespread and as arms of all types, big and small, conventional and nuclear, proliferate.[25]

Against this background we now turn to the dynamic aspect of the machineries of war: the military races.

5.2   AN ANALYSIS OF MILITARY RACES

The traditional way of writing about this phenomenon, the accumulation of the instruments of destruction, deplores its increasing prevalance and muses on alternative uses for the funds spent this way.[26] We shall not take this approach. In general terms it has been repeatedly proven that a great deal of money is spent and that the present capability for destruction is more than sufficient to put an end to life on our planet many times over.[27] We know this.

But in more precise terms the whole matter is uncertain, for there is no reason to rely on the figures for capital and manpower input into the military machineries and their potential destructive power output. The various yearbooks and balances may be the best-educated guesses available, but their information cannot be corroborated. As such figures have not proved at all accurate in the past, there is no reason that they should suddenly prove accurate today.[28] There are too many good reasons for governments to inflate and deflate inputs and outputs, so many that I am tempted to say that the figures publicly available are probably inaccurate in most cases. There are hidden inputs and outputs. Moreover, in a complex society there will never be a clear borderline between the military sector and the rest of society. The economics of modern societies are not only economies of scale, they are also economies of interconnectedness.

There is also in the traditional approach a tendency to explain military races in terms of the inability to stabilize a balance-of-power relation. This tautology is too narrow as a perspective for understanding the general phenomenon. In our terminology, this perspective refers to a horizontal arms race between parties that are essentially equals, not only in capability, but also in social structure, facing each other in a horizontal conflict, much like the East-West conflict. In this situation "balance" is, at least, a meaningful concept, but efforts to explain military races in general in this way overemphasize the kinds of phenomena that can be perceived and understood by means of the actor-oriented perspective. They fail to capture the relation between structural and direct violence, except by some attempts to see the leaders of the oppressed as "agents" and "agitators" and to consider revolts against structural violence as only a projection of the "real" conflict, a type 1 conflict like the horizontal East–West conflict. Hence, military races have to be broken down by types of war to be understood, since the reason for one type of military race is not necessarily useful in understanding the other types.

Finally, most people are now becoming aware of the non-war functions of such races, that they serve more than the twin purposes of deterrence and military victory if war occurs.[29] But these non-war functions are highly ramified and have to be understood in a general perspective in order to account for the impressive growth of the military sector. I say "military" because these races are military races, not merely arms races; they embrace software as well as hardware components of the war machines.

Thus, we have to consider war functions as well as non-war functions of the races, and among the former we have at least to distinguish between the races that are tied to horizontal conflicts and those that are tied to vertical conflicts. To this we now turn.

5.2.1 MILITARY RACES AND THEIR WAR FUNCTIONS

Horizontal Military Races

In the Kennedy era it was fashionable to say that the old tripartition of military forces in terms of land, sea, and air was as dead as the corresponding distinction in the science of zoology. A more scientific distinction, it was claimed, would be that among the capacities to fight *nuclear war, conventional war, and guerrilla war*—the latter euphemistically but not incorrectly referred to as counterinsurgency. That term clearly indicated its true character as reactionary, counterrevolutionary warfare.[30]

We accept this new tripartite distinction since it can be easily related to the distinction among wars of type 1, wars of type 2, and the rest. Which natural elements are chosen for the fighting is a question of tactics, not strategy. *For strategy one has to know what kind of war one is engaged in,* not whether land, sea, or air dominates.[31]

Let us start our analysis with the logic of the horizontal races, corresponding to horizontal conflicts of types 1 and 2, although it is too well known really to be elaborated here. These races have received most of the attention of the theorists, but we shall try to see them in conjunction with some thinking about vertical races.

Essentially, a horizontal race corresponds to a well-known market mechanism: "If we don't do it, the other side will do it, and then they will gain an edge over us." This way of thinking can be compared to a similar argument against stopping the slave trade: "If we stop, the trade will still go on, and the other side will make profit that could have been ours."[32] The argument is perfectly rational and holds for any unilateral withdrawal from any competitive market, however obnoxious the market may be in its consequences and however closed the total reservoir of inputs into the market may be. It seems to hold equally well for positive and negative markets, that is, for markets (like the slave trade) yielding gains for participants as well as for markets (like the arms races) threatening punishment for the party that reduces or withdraws its participation. In short, it holds for markets of profit as well as for markets of fear. Planning is carried out under the assumption of the worst possible behavior on the part of the other side.[33] Game theory is called in to rationalize behavior under this assumption.

As pointed out in section 1.3, free competition for market share may be highly stimulating, but it may also be self-defeating in its general consequences. If the reservoirs from which the market inputs are taken are limited (and which external reservoirs are not?), then free competition leads to depletion. Whaling constitutes one example; fish of various kinds may follow suit. In the military races the reservoirs are national budgets and the spending is usually held to be at the expense of the consumer[34] or of socioeconomic growth[35] in general, but this may not be altogether true since a military race may generate and stimulate growth up to a point.[36] At any rate, free competition may lead to depletion here as elsewhere and to pollution with waste products. There are in fact those who would argue that military production is in itself pollution, a littering of nature and society.[37] And then, even fear may be depleted.

However, in connection with the market of means of destruction it is not so much the closure, the finite nature of the reservoir of inputs, as the nature of the outputs that is a cause of major worry (to understate the matter). This has to do with the relationship between what is good for the subsystem (the individual, the firm, the nation) and the system (the society, local or global). If all participants in an economic market get richer, then the society becomes richer, at least up to a certain point, before public poverty starts cancelling the private affluence.[38] But if all participants in the security market get more "security," meaning more means of destruction at their disposal, the total security seems to decrease quite quickly, rather than increase.[39] At any rate, total security, in the sense of improbability of a war, is not proportionate to the total (or to the average) of the means of destruction available to the parties. The relation is much more complex, not completely understood, and perhaps not completely understandable.[40]

What we do know is that the military race goes on, that there is growth in the potential available for destruction.[41] The growth rate need not also be increasing; that would be an accelerating arms race. Nor are budget figures, or even lists of hardware, even if they were completely reliable, a valid way of measuring these changes. An *increasing* budget may be a response to increasing prices in the acquisition and maintenance of the means of destruction (not necessarily the same as inflation); a *decreasing* budget may conceivably be the result of increased productivity, of initial investment in production capacity that is paying off, yielding steep decreases in unit costs, and so on. *Military races have to be measured in terms of destructive capacity achieved, not in terms of budgets.* It is in order to evaluate this that spies need a military background, not training as economists.

At this point it might be fruitful to distinguish between two types of arms races, the quantitative and the qualitative,[42] depending on whether more is produced within the same weapons system or new weapons systems are launched.

The logic behind qualitative races is similar to the logic behind production cycles in industrial, particularly capitalist, societies in general. There is research and production capacity to be used; hence the need for planned obsolescence, for looking several stages ahead, withdrawing one product when the next product is entering the market (is being "deployed," in military parlance), the next in line is being "developed," and the still next in line is being "researched."

Diagrammatically, the process may look something like that shown in table 5.1.

There is nothing Machiavellian about planned obsolescence; it is simply good capitalist practice and perfectly rational within its frame of reference. At any given time the existing research capacity is used, and at any time the existing production capacity is used. There is no idle machinery anywhere, no unemployment, no layoffs, and so on. For example, in year 5 system I can be sold to the Third World, system II to allies, system III be reserved for oneself, system IV be used for threats, and system V remain as a reserve system in search of justification.[43]

This structurally induced pattern, with cycles from research to withdrawal, becomes shorter and shorter, from ten to fifteen years down to five to ten years and below. The shortening is reinforced by the very simple market-of-fear mechanism, "If we do not do research on new systems, then the other side will, and then they will gain an edge over us." The result is a "transition from quantity to quality" in the total arms race; a constant quest for qualitatively new systems after a quantitative race (more of the old system) has gone on for some time. Thus, fear and profit cooperate well, and which comes first is by and large a chicken-and-egg problem.

Table 5.1 Production cycles compatible with qualitative arms races

	Year 1	Year 2	Year 3	Year 4	Year 5
Weapons system I	Research	Development	Production	Marketing Deployment	Withdrawal
Weapons system II		Research	Development	Production	Marketing Deployment
Weapons system III			Research	Development	Production
Weapons system IV				Research	Development
Weapons system V					Research

The atomic, bacteriological, and chemical warfare systems were clearly qualitative jumps away from quantitative, conventional arms races, as were the vertical races connected with guerrilla and counterinsurgency warfare to be discussed later. These are clearly "extraparadigmatic" developments, not only in terms of new technology but also because a new way of thinking is needed for their research, development, and deployment. The old paradigms could not conceive of mass murder on this scale. There was a switch from a balance of power to a balance of terror.[44]

An interesting arms race phenomenon located between the two extremes of the clearly quantitative and the clearly qualitative varieties might be termed the "negation of the negation" approach, to use once more our dialectic formulations. Imagine that a weapons system W exists (see figure 5.3). The first response on the side without W would be to develop W also, and to improve on it. Both sides interpret "balance" as meaning balance in one's own favor. Why? Partly to be on the safe side lest the estimates of the capacity of the other side should be too low, partly to be on guard against sudden technological breakthroughs on the other side, and indeed to have some excess capacity in case deterrence does not work.[45] The result is a classical arms race.

Figure 5.3   The "negation of the negation" approach to arms races

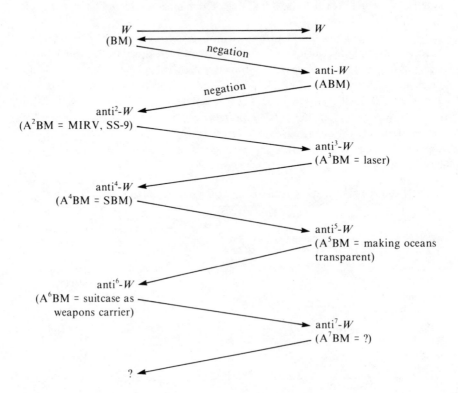

But then one of the sides, in an effort to outsmart the other and possibly for other non-war reasons, chooses a new approach. It develops a new system, anti-*W*, which instead of copying the effects of *W* negates them. To take an example: if *W* is the ballistic missile (BM), then anti-*W* is the anti-BM, usually called ABM, used to negate BM. In the old days one talked about offensive and defensive weapons; the former were thought of as aggressive, the latter as innocent. Today they both enter the total strategic balance equation, adding to or subtracting from the power of destruction, *both being equally relevant when the total is to be estimated.* To develop a new defensive system may be to change the balance as much or more than would a new offensive capacity. This point, often overlooked, applies not only to active defense, but also to such means of passive defense as civil defense shelters, the hardening of missile sites, the tunnels under Peking, and so on. But what has been done once can be done again; the negation can be negated. An anti-BM invites the anti^2-BM, which would then clearly be a MIRV or an SS-9, since the time between separation and impact is too short for the ABM to sort out trajectories, eliminate decoys, and the like.[46] This will then lead to an anti-MIRV (i.e., an anti^3-BM), e.g., some type of laser belt in order to melt or otherwise incapacitate all incoming hardware before impact.[47] The obvious anti^4-BM would be to bring the warheads close to the target by some more suitable means than the costly and cumbersome ICBM rockets. A system of SBM's launched from submarines close to the enemy coast would be one example.[48] But the obvious anti^5-BM, making the oceans transparent, will possibly outdate this approach relatively soon.[49] A suitable response, therefore, would be a suitcase, placed in a locker at some central railway, air, bus station, with a long-distance, electromagnetic ignition.[50] The obvious (or not so obvious?) anti^7-BM against this device I leave to the reader to find. No more lockers? International control of suitcase production? Obligatory shelter life for all?

What new factors have nuclear arms brought into this dismal picture? Actually, surprisingly few, because people's thinking and the institutional framework are about the same. Obviously, nuclear arms have made military technology potentially more efficient, i.e., capable of bearing more destructive output per unit of input, which has had an important reinforcing effect on arms races. Destruction may be so great that not only population and "value" in general may be wiped out, but also an opponent's means of destruction, "force." As a first strike may wipe out *X* percent of one's own retaliatory force, one has to see to it, the reasoning goes, that regardless of the strength of the first strike the remaining (100-*X*) percent will still be sufficient to deal the enemy an unacceptable blow in the retaliatory second strike. Only under that condition will he be deterred from launching the first strike. The situation becomes precarious the moment he has reason to believe that he can launch a first strike so effective that (100-*X*) percent will be insufficient to deal an unacceptable return blow.

How high is *X*? That is the whole point: nobody knows, nor is it knowable. It can be fixed at any level by a politician, strategist or hand-picked theorist.[51]

If one sets it at 90 percent, one obviously has to produce ten times as much as one needs for an "unacceptable" retaliation; if one sets it at 99 percent, one needs one hundred times as much, and so on. However, we cannot estimate the superpower estimate of X from the magnitude of their overkill capacity (even if that were known), for that capacity may also have come about as a result of other factors, for instance, a calculation of what is "unacceptable" to the other side. All we can say is that no better theory than the first strike–second strike concept has ever been produced for justifying the present quantitative arms race: this concept constitutes something qualitatively new in the history of arms races.[52] One always had to reckon with planes being destroyed before takeoff, warships being destroyed at anchor and so on, but never with an X of the magnitude that may enter the calculus of nuclear war. Although this reasoning is completely "rational," it is valid only at the subsystem level: therein lies its irrationality. Globally speaking, for humankind as a whole, it is, of course, far beyond any ordinary madness.[53]

Thus, any weapons system W can lead to its parallel development on the other side and also to its negation. Just as quantitative development invites further quantitative development, a qualitative negation invites qualitative negation. The former leads to quantitative races, the latter to a semiqualitative race ("semi" because each negation is, in a sense, a prisoner of the preceding one). There is not the complete freedom to make a totally new departure. The new weaponry is not completely extraparadigmatic as a weapons system, yet it is something new.

The basic point I wish to make is that the arms race is an open-ended agenda, both in the sense that each sheet is open-ended and in the sense that there is no end to the number of sheets in the agenda. Once a weapons system has been put into production, there will be many convincing arguments from the point of view of this type of logic in favor of overproduction, oversaturating one's own defense system, and so on. But any weapons system also leads, dialectically, to the research, development, production, and deployment of an antisystem, or at least to the suspicion that this is what the other side is doing; that the other side will tamper with the balance equation not only by production up to or above parity of the same weapons system, but even by producing an antisystem. Hence, the stage is set for continued production of the original system (for the opponent might also choose to fight with that one) and for production of the antisystem, and the anti^2-system, and so on. Thus, under Eisenhower there was a bomber gap, under Kennedy a missile gap, and under Nixon an ABM gap. What will be next, a laser gap?[54]

It should be no cause for surprise if in this process one or both of those who are able to join in this strange death race will ultimately try to change the whole arms race to its own favor by making the basic qualitative jump, an extraparadigmatic transition not dictated by the logic of the original system, that is to say, by the introduction of a system so formidable that it would dwarf all others in existence. Absolute power would accrue to its possessor. Gas in World War I and nuclear arms in World War II are examples; no Hitler was needed for that type of arms.[55] And there is no scarcity of candidates on the list of new weapons systems that currently may be developed:[56]

> *Much more effective guerrillas,* equipped with B (biological) and C (chemical) weapons targeted on individuals or small groups;
>
> *Much cheaper nuclear weapons* through new separation methods that would make them both easy to produce and to hide so that they could be used by participants in all types of war;
>
> *Laser death-ray technology.*
>
> *Three-dimensional, deep-ocean warfare,* combined with hovercraft, submarine, and ocean floor bases;
>
> *Holes in the ozone layer,* lethal burns due to ultraviolet rays, destruction of crops;
>
> *LSD-related drugs* to induce temporary madness with soldiers throwing arms away and going on a "trip" instead;
>
> *Robot warfare* with walking bombs and self-administering, to some extent self-repairing, war machines;
>
> *Artificial droughts* produced by removing moisture from clouds through seeding before they arrive;
>
> *Artificial tsunamis* (tidal waves) produced by tipping icebergs and mountains already in unstable equilibrium into the sea;
>
> *Artificial earthquakes* produced by triggering an unstable equilibrium in the earth's crust.

How far these systems have come in their development only very few people know.[57] But many of them represent clearly new departures for human creativity in destruction. Still, they are not very sophisticated since they are so clearly people- and property-oriented. More up-to-date weaponry would aim at the brains, at the control centers, of the other side, like demagnetizing all the tapes in their computers![58]

Thus, the horizontal arms race has its simple logic, dictated by the fear that the other side may gain the upper hand. When both sides act according to that logic the result is obvious: quantitative, semiquantitative, and qualitative races. However, the objection runs, a race is not the same as a war; it may go on and on without being converted into a war, as the Cold War has shown. But, has the Cold War really shown that? Or is it rather that this arms race is only in part related to the East–West conflict and that the world is a small planet where races and wars of one kind and one place will never be completely unrelated to races and wars elsewhere? To explore this, let us look at the logic of the vertical races, in which there is (characteristically) much less of a research tradition.

Vertical Military Races

If we look at the vertical components of all the wars of types 3 through 12, we find a preexisting situation of structural or frozen violence. Aggression has already taken place for a long time, but we have gotten used to it and it has become a "social law." Very often it has been brought about exogenously by some direct violence from the past; it also has often come about through internal exploitation and differentiation, creating, endogenously, a center and a periphery. In either case there will be a vested interest in maintaining the status quo. Moreover, the center (or the Center, not to mention the center in the Center) *will have a monopoly on arms, or at least on decisive arms, according to the logic of the vertical bloc, the empire.* One cannot talk about an arms race in any conventional sense. One party, the dominating group, has almost all the hardware; the other party, the dominated, has little, in terms of destructive capacity.

But the dominated have something else. They have interests, basic human interests, that can be converted into goals as they acquire increasing political consciousness. They have masses, often very numerous, that can be converted into politically effective actors through organization.[59] Once these masses have become politically conscious, organized, and mobilized they can also become militarily effective through smuggling in arms or making them clandestinely and gradually liberate territory through guerrilla tactics. Needless to say, much of their strength will lie in their ability to demonstrate that they can provide an alternative to the structural violence against which they struggle, by practicing what they preach in the liberated territories, and by organizing the fight in such a way that the fight itself is a negation of structural violence.[60] Undeniably, guerrillas are violent in the direct sense. But by the way in which they are organized, in small, decentralized units based on "participation" with "equality," "justice," "equity," and "solidarity" present, they are also examples of what they stand for. Whether they are able to avoid structural violence after victory is another matter.[61]

This brief and oversimplified analysis serves to bring out a simple point concerning vertical arms races: a liberation movement goes through three stages, and the repressive response of the dominant group will be adjusted to each stage, as follows:

Stage 1: Consciousness formation, mobilization, organization. In this stage the repressive emphasis will be on reinforcing the control of the structure and on suppression of any effort to increase political awareness about the structure or the ability to mobilize and to organize. Torture enters here, partly to extract information, partly to depoliticize by spreading fear.[62]

Stage 2: Guerrilla warfare. In this stage there is open fighting, but conventional weapons are of little use, for the guerrillas do not come out in the open, pitched for battle. The repressive emphasis will be on spotting and hitting small units, on quick transportation and communication, on micro-warfare, on automated detection based on electronic sensors with semiautomated response, e.g., carpet bombing, and so on.[63]

Stage 3: Horizontal warfare. In this stage territory is already liberated and the two actors are pitted against each other in a more traditional way. One may be weaker in arms but compensate for that in terms of motivation, ingenuity, and number. The emphasis will now be on running a more regular macro-war (but not the mega-war of type 1 warfare or the higher rungs on Kahn's infamous ladder).[64]

The dominant group will try to do its utmost to prevent the liberation movement from progressing from nothing at all to stage 1, from stage 1 to stage 2, and from stage 2 to stage 3. It is not self-evident that they will try to do so, since stage 3 with its all-out fighting may have some advantages for the dominant group: *let them come out in the open and we shall get them!* But the oppressors are not operating in a vacuum; there is a world of third parties around them, and any transition to higher stages will increase the visibility of repression and throw increased doubts on the legitimacy of center rule. The traditional military will try to stay "clean," leaving stage 2 to the paramilitary and stage 1 to the secret services. Nobody should be fooled by this tactical division of labor.

There is nothing special about stage 3 from the point of view of arms and arms race analyses, because horizontal analysis applies, but this is not true for stages 1 and 2. *Anything the dominant group makes use of to maintain structural violence becomes a means of direct violence, even if it looks nonlethal.* A footstep detector, based on microseismology, an infrared body-heat detector, or a urine sniffer are methods that may be employed against organization and mobilization and that consequently may be means of reactionary violence.[65] The incredible repertory of spying gadgets that have been developed may be used to prevent consciousness formation, and hence they may be instruments of violence. Telecommunication and supervisory devices to detect any "underground activity" attain immediate political significance in this perspective, as do infrared photography and television devices placed in planes or in orbiting and stationary satellites likewise. Even the public opinion poll and talented sociography of an area can become important instruments of suppression, as was so clearly understood, for example, by the U.S. Army in connection with Project Camelot.[66]

That there is a special communication–transportation technology as well for fighting in a vertical micro-war is well known. Helicopter and VTOL will play an important role. Emphasis will often be on speed to prevent buildup rather than on mass delivery. But all depends, of course, on the geography. The United States had to send marines to the Dominican Republic; the Soviet Union can send T55 tanks into Eastern Europe for reasons of geographical adjacency. Herbicides and biocides in general, defoliants (not so much to make the jungle transparent as to drive out peasants who can provide the guerrilla "fish" with their "water"), antipersonnel bombs, napalm—all these are of particular significance in vertical wars.

If one now had reliable data on inputs and outputs in the military production machineries, on the personnel as well as the hardware side, it might be interesting to split the arms race into horizontal and vertical components as to both absolute levels and growth rates. My guess would be that the absolute expenditure may be in the order nuclear to conventional to counterinsurgency, whereas the growth rate may be in the opposite order.[67] That ordering would be in complete harmony with the general transfer of the theater-of-war point of gravity from Center-Center to various types of vertical and Periphery-Periphery war theaters that I have hypothesized on the basis of changes in the world political structure (figure 5.2). Moreover, I would not assume the military centers in the world to be poorly equipped with analytical insight. Those who analyze the military may be poorly equipped, in this regard military men themselves have a keen sense of where military capability may be needed in the future, and plan accordingly. They have their rationality.

Again, it should be pointed out that as a race the vertical arms race has a completely different structure from the horizontal race. It is basically a unilateral arms race, for on the oppressed side the first stages are more political. *It is not a military-military race, but a military-political race.* But that does not make it less dynamic as an arms race; it is only that the mechanisms are different, so that it is an arms race in the making. Instead of "We have to develop this weapons system lest they change the *military* status quo" it is "We have to develop this weapons system lest they change the *political* status quo." In this sense the vertical race is broader in scope and even more stifling in its effects. The horizontal race is at least somewhat more limited to the military sector, giving somehow the same right and obligations to either side, and is therefore less status quo preserving. This gives the horizontal race more political legitimacy, making the (waning) East-West conflict serve as a pretext for developing capabilities that can be used in a North-South context.

Finally, just as there is no sharp dividing line between a quantitative and a qualitative arms race there is no sharp dividing line between a horizontal and a vertical race either. *What has been developed for one can be used for the other.* I have already indicated that I do not accept any arbitrary division of armed forces into military, national guard or militia and police units with the latter two exempted from the war system.[68] Such distinctions are only rationalizations of the use of direct violence and of the doctrine justifying the intrastate monopoly on violence on grounds of "internal security." The total system is interconnected, a change at one level has some effect at another, and so on. All kinds of races go on, and these *arms are being developed because somebody in power thinks they may be used, for deterrence and/or for fighting, not because of anybody's miscalculation, irrationality, semantic confusion, or anything like that.* There are at least twelve war theaters waiting for the arms to be used. And it does not look as if they are waiting in vain; 450 billion odd dollars per year is probably a low estimate of what the military power centers have at their disposal.

5.2.2 MILITARY RACES AND THEIR NON-WAR FUNCTIONS

Any social structure has other functions than the intended ones, although what is intended is often difficult to know and not very important either.[69] Objective consequences are what count. Military races should certainly not be seen only in the light of their military functions, deterrence and fighting, whether in a horizontal or in a vertical context. Other factors sustain an arms race and make it grow: it has an internal dynamic, *Eigendynamik,* not only an action–reaction cycle between two opposed forces. What are these factors, and who are the people or the power groups that articulate them? If they are many and important then it is an illusion to believe that military races are intersystem problems only; they have also intrasystem origins.

Table 5.2 gives one possible list of such sustaining factors, along with the groups that might articulate them. Some of the factors in table 5.2 merit comment because they may, in fact, be much more significant than the "arms races as a response to real or imagined tension" dealt with earlier.

Table 5.2 Non-war functions sustaining arms races

Sustaining factors	Articulated by
1. *Political warfare*: military power as a symbol of political power, of prestige, as something that has to be on par with other aspects of power, prestige races.[70]	anyone, including common citizens, also political leaders, nationalists
2. *Economic warfare*: arms races as a way of forcing a certain economic structure on the other side, at the expense of consumer and capital goods.[71]	more subtle political designs
3. *Arms trade*: profitable trade on an arms market expanding with the democratization of the right to fight wars, with the increase in buying power and with the general transition from wars of type 1 to all other types.[72]	private and state capitalists alike, important for trade balance and political balance
4. *Arms races as a stimulus to the economy*: spin-off effects to all other sectors in the economy because the military sector is dynamic and connected with so many other sectors.[73]	anyone, including common citizens and investors
5. *Military as a reservoir society*, ready to take over when "they are called upon." This may take two very different forms: soldiers substituting for workers in a strike, or the military *coup d'etat* — at the bottom or at the top of society, respectively.[74]	usually very status-quo-oriented circles, in any kind of regime, but the military can also be used in a progressive way
6. *Military as an emergency relief organization*, particularly in connection with natural catastrophes. In this case it is manpower and capacity for transportation and reconstruction that are called for, as well as effective organization.[75]	anyone, especially common citizens

(continued on next page)

Table 5.2   *(continued)*

Sustaining factors	Articulated by
7. *Arms races in order to use idle production capacity* – for reasons of profit, power, and/or prestige. The role of the *military-industrial* complex.[76]	industrialists for profit and power; workers for fear of unemployment, local communities
8. *Arms races in order to use excess research capacity* – for reasons of grants, power, and/or prestige. The role of the *military-academic* complex.[77]	scientists and technicians, particularly those with no alternative employment
9. *Arms races out of sheer bureaucratic inertia*, there today because they were there yesterday. The role of the *military-bureaucratic* complex, and Parkinson's law.[78]	bureaucrats and politicians afraid of new practices
10. *Arms races as a response to vested interests.* The role of the *military-military complex*.[79]	the military themselves with obvious interests in expansion

The use of military capacity for nonmilitary political power should not be underestimated. Take the "threat of the use of force" component away, and there is still very much left. Merely to possess some military capacity satisfying certain minimum requirements already defines a nation as a state; to possess even more places it is still higher on an international ranking scale. In the world there are some vague notions about just what military capacity corresponds appropriately to a state of a certain size and a GNP, and a state living up to those expectations is somehow completing a configuration. Thus, Japan (partly because of Article 9 in her constitution) is so far an underachiever militarily speaking, and efforts to equilibrate constitute a major source of motivation.[80] To display power is to display a symbol of prestige, to participate in an arms race is also to participate in a prestige race. Soviet nuclear missiles in Cuba would put the Soviet Union equal to the United States on two counts: in terms of justice—"If you have your nuclear missiles in Turkey, we have just as much right to have ours in Cuba"—and in terms of domain—"If you can become a global (as opposed to regional) power by spreading your military capacity all over, we also can do so."[81] Neither function is, strictly speaking, a military function—nor is the Argentinian–Brazilian aircraft-carrier race.

The use of arms races as mechanisms of economic warfare should not be minimized either. By its logic a horizontal arms race forces upon the other side an expenditure of roughly the same magnitude in absolute terms, but if the two GNP's are different (that of the United States, for example, being much above that of the Soviet Union), then the economic impact will also differ. A halt to the arms race would release economic potentials that could be converted into a higher standard of living for the citizens of a country, the more so the lower the point of departure. Hence, taking the lead in an arms race becomes one more form of structural violence.

As the arms trade is a well-known phenomenon today,[82] I want to point out a less-noticed factor. The question of military alignment enters here at both the sender end and the receiver end of the arms channel. A nonaligned arms producer can more easily sell to both sides in a conflict, and he almost has to sell to both sides to prove his "objectivity." He can also, with some reason, argue that to buy from him is also to buy a certain freedom from dependence on the aligned producers, particularly the superpowers. A buyer who wants to remain "nonaligned" in the usual sense of "equidistant" would otherwise have to play the game by buying from both sides, which may often mean buying incompatible weapons systems, again leading to overspending as the price for balance. Conclusion: one more stimulus to arms production in nonaligned and aligned countries alike.[83]

Points 4, 5, and 6 in table 5.2 all have to do with usually domestic functions (although the latter could also involve international relief), and points 7, 8, 9, and 10 relate to functions inside the military complex itself. This complex has many ramifications, penetrating into industry, into academia, and into bureaucracy. As there have been many explorations of them recently, I feel there may be a need to rediscover the military–military complex. The fact is that the military machinery, as operated in our century, is an ongoing concern, continuously in need of inputs and continuously capable of producing outputs to defend itself against demilitarization.[84]

If arms could be manufactured more the way one makes a dam, the scaffolding could be torn down after the military capability had been produced and leave no excess production capacity unambiguously designed to produce destructive power. After all, this was the way basic military instruments like castles were made in the past: an *ad hoc* input of capital and manpower, and the castle was there, not a factory crying to produce more castles. An ongoing productive concern, based on factory methods and mass production, needs new input all the time, hence the need for sustained or even increased budgets. It continually produces more output, hence the need to find new ways of using the output. Under the doctrine of the need for an overkill capacity, stockpiling that leads to a quantitative race can go on for some time. Then there are planned obsolescence and the introduction of new systems, which lead to a qualitative race. And there is the deepening of the system from production for horizontal conflicts to production for vertical conflicts. Finally, there is the expansion of the whole system through the arms trade. All together these protect the system for producing means of destruction fairly well, with long-term plans and budgets that serve as shock absorbers against sudden conflict resolution that might threaten its growth.[85]

In short, the present war system is self-reinforcing and among the most ugly creations of humankind. It is symptomatic of the whole global and domestic system based on competition and domination and is at the same time cause and effect (but mainly effect) of this system. The arms races, in fact, serve so many important functions for this type of society that if they did not exist, something similar would have to be invented in their place—as the saying, taken from structural-functional analysis, goes.[86]

But I do not accept that argument, which presupposes, with the usual conservative bias of traditional functionalism,[87] that the "functions" will somehow always be there, that only the structures can vary. This attitude gives a very limited leeway for social change: the basic purposes are accepted, and only some of the methods are varied. But look at the list in table 5.2. Do we really accept that states shall compete with each other to be Number 1, Number 2, in GNP, and the like? If we do, we can argue that they should switch to socioeconomic growth and competition instead of military growth and "balance," but that still means that *we would accept competition as the basis of international relations.* For this reason, I am very skeptical of the idea of substituting a space race for the arms race. It is a lesser evil, but it maintains the competitive structure for world domination.[88]

Or, take points 3 and 4, or 7 and 8, on the list. They all add up to the same prescription: *stimulate the nation's economy.* Is it obvious that this is so important? The arms-producing countries are generally very rich countries anyhow. Similarly with points 2, 5, 9, and 10: I would rather do without them, not only as structures but also as functions. On the other hand, I have little quarrel with function 6, emergency relief, but we do not need an entire military organization to carry out such valuable services.

Hence, in the search for ways and means to halt the arms races we should not be overimpressed with the "functions" of the races. We should not let the war system twist our thinking into ignoring the competitive dominance system to which it is so inextricably linked; we should not let a distorted world steer our thinking. We would much rather think in terms of nations cooperating for the betterment of the lot of humankind. It may be argued that such considerations are for the distant future. As the functionalist program of searching for substitutes for the arms races when it comes to their non-war functions may nevertheless be most practical for the near future, the search for alternative competitive games should go on. We shall return to this later.

But there is another approach to military races, the "arms control and disarmament" approach, to which we now turn.

5.2.3 MILITARY RACES: CONTROL AND REDUCTION

Concern about arms races leads to calls for the control or institutionalization of arms races as well as of the use of arms, and even for their reduction and abolition (disarmament). The latter proposals are usually limited to specific weapons and/or to specific geographical areas (like the concept of Latin America as a nuclear-free zone). Conferences are convened, and from time to time it even looks as if relevant decisions are not only made but even implemented in this field, such as the Partial Test Ban Treaty (PTB)[89] and the Non-Proliferation Treaty (NPT),[90] the Strategic Arms Limitation Talks (SALT)[91] and Mutual and Balanced Force Reduction (MBFR).[92] But it is also known that the arms race proceeds and at times even progresses.[93] Let us try to look more deeply into these matters.

I have described the arms race as a negative race into which countries enter for fear of the consequences of nonparticipation. Arms races differ from their companion phenomenon, the highly lucrative arms market, from which a country expects the positive benefits of participation. In terms of our theory, what could induce states to opt out of this kind of race? Let us consider this problem in terms of the three compliance mechanisms mentioned in section 2.4: punitive, remunerative, and ideological power. These mechanisms do not exclude each other, but in this area they are all problematic, to say the least.

Thus, it is painfully obvious with regard to punitive mechanisms that our world does not have any supra-actor, no world government that can simply close the whole market, as a police force would clamp down on trade in narcotics, illicit gambling, forced prostitution, or the like. A superpower or a big power could perhaps do so for a part of the world, but that would mean a return to a vertical system, a type from which the world, for other reasons, is moving away. Nor does the police parallel convince: it is generally much easier to cheat than to detect.

As for remuneration, there is no scarcity of plans to lure the parties into more wholesome pursuits. I have mentioned some of them above. For the arms race substitute the GNP race; for military might as a symbol, substitute production and productivity; and if there is a need for mass participation and identification there is always the sports arena as a stage, isomorphic to the battlefield, not to mention to cosmic sports arena, the space race! Countries can challenge each other as boxers do for the heavyweight championship, and arrive at ranking lists if that is the purpose. What is diplomacy but the continuation of war by other means? So why not reverse the cycle and convert war into competitive diplomacy rather than diplomacy into war?[94]

The answer is that these are only some of the reasons we have arms races. Countries engage in arms races because they have reasons for their fear, and unless something is done about horizontal and vertical conflict they will not be bribed away from involvement. *There is no functional equivalent for a war system when it comes to fighting a war.* A world government might force the parties away from the war market, but they will not be lured away.

Nor will they be persuaded out of inner convictions, i.e., for normative reasons, when the basic element in inner conviction is fear, translated into suspicion not only of the other side but ultimately also of oneself. Each party doubts its own ability to stay outside a war market. Unilateralism inevitably appears as tantamount to nonparticipation in the market, leaving multilateralism as the only possibility—but one with very weak motivation, since there would only be mutual promise to sustain nonparticipation. The belief that states will simply throw away their war machineries is unsupported by facts as well as by theory. What they *might* do is to throw away parts of this machinery (which parts will be explored later) and put some constraints on the use of the rest, taking measures of relatively marginal significance.

Disarmament does not seem to be the road to peace, but peace may be the road to disarmament. In general, it seems rather unlikely that disarmament can be obtained by dealing with the arms system, or the entire war system, as if it were isolated from the rest of society. *But if basic conflicts are resolved and parties are tied together in new associative relationships, disarmament, or at least distargeting, may come about as a consequence of that.*

However, a distinction should be made here between governmental and nongovernmental approaches to the control of arms races. Since governments not only have the monopoly on ultimate power inside states but also a *de facto* monopoly on interstate relations, it may look as if this entire field can only be handled by governments. But there are strong reasons to say that precisely for these reasons governments are the least fit to deal with such serious matters. Here we shall indicate why; in section 5.4 some alternative approaches will be outlined.

Why so little can be expected from governments in this particular field can be expressed in three simple propositions:

Proposition 1: Governments will be willing to control only horizontal, not vertical, arms races.

Proposition 2: Governments will be willing to control only quantitative, not qualitative, arms races.

Proposition 3: Generally, governments will enter into agreements concerning control of horizontal or quantitative races only if

    (*a*) the weapons system is at the end of its life cycle, and sales are not good either;

    (*b*) the qualitative arms race can continue;

    (*c*) there are some possibilities of cheating on even the very limited agreements achieved.

The reasons for these propositions are easily spelled out.

Why should governments ever come together to stop vertical arms races? Under the entire doctrine of monopoly over the means of violence in internal affairs these races are legitimate. Often they are directed not against other governments but against their own people. Hence, the people against whom military force is designed to be used (minorities, dominated groups, secessionists) would be interested counterparts, not other governments, but they are usually not present at the negotiations. Moreover, governments as such have a common interest in not bringing this matter up for discussion. They may discuss horizontal arms races because they are interstate or interbloc without ever touching the intrastate and intrabloc vertical arms races. They may want to limit the means of nuclear and conventional warfare, but when it comes to counterinsurgency they may be more interested in exchanging information to get some new ideas. "How do you handle your demonstrators?"

Next, why should governments stop qualitative arms races? These concern potentials for the future. To expect them to arrive at an agreement about something not yet manufactured, not even yet invented, is difficult enough, but to agree to something which both parties could clothe in extreme secrecy—including keeping secret the fact that they may be doing nothing—is to expect too much. Pious declarations about "limiting research," or something like that, would be the most one could expect. As long as more penetrating approaches to the problem are not enacted, all the reasons for engaging in arms races will still be there. Hence, the maximum one can expect would be to control or bring to an end a quantitative race, particularly one that has come through the research and development stages that made thousands of expensively trained researchers relevant. The danger is that they will then develop the rationale for a new weapons system to remain relevant.

But why then do states go to any arms control conferences at all? There may be many reasons for this. Pressure from "world public opinion," inside and outside each country, is one. The desire to make political gains in the arms control and disarmament market by trying to expose the other fellow is another. Disarmament negotiations as a way of exchanging information, mutual espionage, not the least on all kinds of collateral issues, is a third. A desire to reduce costs is still another, which has to be done on a basis of mutual understanding lest it be misinterpreted as a giving in. The hope to create a better political atmosphere for better economic deals also enters into consideration.

However, there is another set of reasons that are located somewhat deeper in these war machineries and that in my opinion are much more important. I have defined arms control in terms of institutionalization, rather than reduction. In short: *all these conferences can be seen as ways of perfecting the balance-of-power mechanisms rather than as means for the reduction of the war machineries.* By exchanging information, testing each other, and agreeing on ways of removing some of the dangers in the system (such as misinterpretation of the other side, "errors" in the hardware or software, escalation of minor incidents), the balance-of-power mechanisms are purified to operate better.

Even if some systems are seriously curtailed, even abolished, the total war system can still expand and the disarmament conferences yield a setting wherein some of the conditions for relatively safe expansion can be explored. In this sense they are armament rather than disarmament conferences.[95] But this function should not be discounted easily. Even when the war system expands, the balance of power may work in such a way as to yield mutual deterrence and hence no war. Whether, in the long run, war is avoided because of or in spite of the deterrence system is another issue. This appears not to be a lasting solution, partly because of the instabilities in the system, and partly because of the spread of the war machineries generated to other arenas.

Thus, the Partial Test Ban Treaty (PTB) was, in my interpretation, signed only because there was, literally speaking, a hole in it: the permission to continue underground testing.[96] This testing has been carried out for at least two reasons: to test and develop more advanced systems, such as ABM and MIRV, and to make enough cavities in the ground to be able to continue testing even after a comprehensive test ban treaty (CTB) is signed, making it very difficult to pick up seismic signals.[97]   Similarly, the Non-Proliferation Treaty (NPT) will hardly be signed and ratified around the world before new methods for the separation of weapons-grade material, cheap enough and small enough to hide, have been developed, enabling the many states that want to enter the nuclear arms market to do so. From the gas diffusion plant via the centrifuge[98] to the modern laser[99] and chemical[100] methods, there is an unmistakeable trend that will facilitate this development. But that does not mean that CTB and NPT may not serve to institutionalize the race, or that the conferences may not be useful as a process of mutual education and information so as to increase predictability and prevent discontinuous escalation. SALT 1 (and SALT 2, the Vienna 1979 accords) is still worse; it is even an armament agreement.[101]

In short, what I am saying is that this entire approach is limited to horizontal, quantitative races; as such it is not very effective because of cheating and the suspicion of cheating. Most significantly: arms control agreements will generally stimulate qualitative races precisely because they symbolize so clearly that the old weapons system has come to an end. The choice may actually be between an ineffective arms control agreement on the one hand and a qualitative race on the other: the more one tries to fill the loopholes, the more stimulus there will be to develop a new system. This dilemma is certainly not unknown to the politicians in the field, and they will probably maneuver together toward some sort of gentleman's agreement of a more tacit nature, favoring the first alternative because of their shared fear of a qualitative race (as terribly expensive, not well institutionalized so that there are too many unknowns in the equation, and so on). In that way, a compromise will be found between disarmament and armament, basically in favor of the latter,[102] but with less of a qualitative race than there could have been had the quantitative race been completely curbed.

So much to expect from governments. The basic mistake seems to have been that the entire arms control approach has been left to the articulators of fear, prestige, and power; to the people who would most easily yield to any argument against control of the arms race. The question therefore is whether the whole vicious circle might not be attacked at some other point; but in light of the list of sustaining factors, this does not look too promising. Just consider one example from history: the naive idea that the nationalization of arms manufacture and trade for the sake of eliminating private arms profiteers would somehow improve the situation. What has happened is simply that the nation-state has taken their place, adding to the traditional international competition for power a new competition for profit and adding to the arsenal of Keynesian mechanisms the role of arms production in order to curb unemployment and control class tensions.

This is where our present civilization has brought us. The picture could have been painted in still darker colors without deviating from the empirical reality of a growing war system that too frequently is activated. So, where is the potential alternate reality? What can be done about our predicament? What is the alternative? Where are the "constructive proposals"?

We must avoid the perennial fallacy of the peace movements, the notion that if X does not produce peace, then for sure non-X will bring it about. If armament does not help, then disarmament will do the job; if governments cannot bring about disarmament, then nongovernment organizations will be able to do so. No such simple-minded thinking is acceptable.

Rather, I stand by the basic idea of the preceding section that there are reasons, fundamental conflicts, underlying the whole war system. If one is against direct violence, *the correct approach is to do something about these conflicts*; if that fails, then some nonviolent way of fighting has to be found. For the case of vertical conflict a means has been indicated in section 4.3: nonviolent revolution. The corresponding indication for the case of horizontal conflict— nonmilitary defense—will be given in the following pages, not as a panacea but as an approach that will work under certain conditions and that may be improved upon in the future.

These are alternatives to the war system, strategies to get around the war system. But the war system, the militarization of the entire society, also has to be attacked directly, not only circumvented by nonviolent methods very few would believe in today. Such necessary strategies of demilitarization will be taken up in the final section of this chapter, 5.4.

5.3   FROM MILITARY TOWARD NONMILITARY DEFENSE

This section contains an argumentation and concrete proposals for non-military defense (NMD) as an institution that could, to some extent, be introduced in lieu of military defense—in somewhat the same way as court procedures and the due process of law in general were introduced in lieu of duels and other means of settling disputes.[103] I am not suggesting that military defense should be abolished overnight in one or all countries of the world and nonmilitary defense introduced in its place. What is argued is some gradualist procedure that does not view the two types of defense as altogether mutually exclusive.

There are many reasons for this gradualism. I would like to state some of them at the very outset:

[1] Most people in most countries today, however skeptical they might be about military defense, would probably be even more skeptical about nonmilitary defense. Consequently, any sudden introduction of nonmilitary defense would have to be enforced upon masses of people, which would be incompatible with basic rules of democracy. Since a basic element in nonmilitary defense (in addition to abstention from direct violence) is the choice of means compatible with the end, such a procedure would be unacceptable.

[2] Nonmilitary defense can be enacted only by people who to some extent believe in it. Creative NMD can only come out of an inner conviction, like

creative military defense. Nonbelievers in military defense are forced, every day and all around the world, to contribute to that institution; nonbelievers in nonmilitary defense cannot be forced to contribute to NMD. At most, they can be persuaded not to sabotage it. More believers have to be more constructive.

[3] In a country that goes in for NMD in the same one-sided manner in which almost all countries in the world today go in for military defense, there would be the basic problem of what to do with those who refuse to participate in NMD and who want to pursue a military course of action in case of attack. They might become "conscientious objectors" who would have to appeal and apply for recognition of their right to be recognized as participants in military forces. If that right is not recognized, they would probably, from the best motivation, fight for their right to fight; and the denial of their right to act according to their choice of appropriate form of defense might lead to a civil war that would weaken a society even more in case of an attack.

[4] Since NMD is a social form of defense that defends social institutions, as distinct from territorial military defense,[104] it is also a form that asks much of the social structure in terms of equity and solidarity. Not all societies would be ready for this form of defense. But the more societies develop in the sense defined in this book the more ready they would be. In this process, NMD might even serve as a stimulus and incentive.[105] I should also mention that some of the mechanisms on which NMD is based would probably be less effective if NMD were combined with military defense. This point will be more clear after the basic strategies of NMD have been spelled out. First, it may be worthwhile to look into the conditions that seem to *favor* the introduction of NMD elements in many societies around the world today.

First, four basic conditions for classical dissociative peace policies (see section 3.4) seem to be weakened every day, at least in the developed part of the world. Geographical distances and impediments shrink and wane. The structural conditions behind sustained prejudice and nationalism (social distance) are decreasingly valid in a world with as much moving around and as much mutual exposure as exists in the world today. But the machinery for punishment in case of transgression—the war system—becomes increasingly dangerous to use. What peacekeeping and technology can do to counteract this is very limited.[106] On the other hand, the conditions are increasingly propitious for associative peace policies, and it is exactly within the framework of associative peace policies that NMD becomes most relevant. If groups live in a separation protected by both geographical and social factors, then the use of extreme means of direct violence becomes much easier because of the low levels of human empathy and sympathy. Other groups can much more easily be portrayed as nonhuman, and whatever nonmilitary action such groups engage in will fail to communicate. In a more associative world this no longer holds true: there will be transnational ties through which empathy and sympathy can flow, there will be that mutual infiltration into each other's social systems which is a *sine qua non* for nonmilitary defense to become operative, and there will be a much higher level of mutual insight into capability and intentions.

Second, with every passing day new experiences are gained in the general field of nonviolence and direct action. Here is not the place to spell it out in detail,[107] but it can safely be said that this social phenomenon is in a phase of rapid growth. Just as the institution of military defense seems doomed because it has become so counterproductive, so nonmilitary defense, although still in its infancy, seems to have a promising future. For humankind to develop it is an unavoidable necessity, a job that calls for its executors. The social need is obvious, since in a more associative world, even a disarmed world, there will still occur acts of transgression, of aggression.

Nonmilitary defense should be kept distinct from the much more subtle doctrine of nonviolence and from one particular expression in action of this doctrine, namely *satyagraha*.[108] NMD does not make metaphysical assumptions; it is more geared to the Western mind, more "technocratic," and modeled more along the same logic as military defense. As mentioned, NMD is a social defense, as opposed to the traditional military defense, which is territorial. Where the latter is based on the idea of protecting territory in the sense of keeping out enemies, the former is based on the idea of protecting values and social structures, whether the antagonist is physically inside one's own territory or not.

The third basic reason that nonmilitary defense will become increasingly relevant is that it seems to be the type of defense that corresponds well to a world in which increasing emphasis is placed on nonterritorial actors. The magic of territory is waning somewhat; to defend values, styles of life, and structures is becoming more meaningful than to defend geography.[109] For that reason, nonmilitary defense might more properly be labeled social defense.

There is another form of defense, which lies between NMD and military defense as commonly conceived of: guerrilla warfare. This type of defense is social, but it is also violent. What then about the other logical possibility: nonviolent territorial defense? I am inclined to say that it is an impossibility, or at least an impracticable form, given the insights we have today. An enemy who wants parts of one's territory, just as territory, and who has no interest in the social structure or the physical property that may exist there, can probably not be stopped by means of NMD as it is envisaged here. He who wants submarine bases along an unpopulated and uninhabitable coast can of course be faced with demonstrators who try to block his access, but it would be easy to deal with such action. More promising would be the possibility of some type of physical tripwire that would trigger explosions or some other process that would make the territory unexploitable. The answer may have to be to make territorial occupation less important by focusing on values and structures.

If we assume that "defense" means "defense of autonomy," there are two broad classes in which defense becomes relevant, whether that defense is military or nonmilitary: *occupation defense and exploitation defense.* Exploitation may be merely an occupation that has lasted for a long time (colonialism) or something that has emerged by internal differentiation (class societies). In terms of our basic distinction between forms of violence, occupation defense is defense against direct violence; exploitation defense is defense against structural violence. In their military forms these kinds of struggles are usually referred to as defense and revolution respectively; in their nonviolent forms they can be referred to as NMD or NVR (nonviolent revolution). The latter two are entirely different: NMD assumes that the social order is found worth defending, the opposite of the assumption underlying NVR. "Nonviolence" today thus covers a spectrum of strategies, from revolution against vertical structures to defense in more horizontal conflict. The spectrum is rich,[110] and will grow richer.

After all this introduction, let us now look at twelve fundamental strategies for NMD, which may be organized in three groups with four strategies in each:

I. Antagonist-oriented defense strategies
    A. "Attack should not pay"
        1. Self-inflicted sabotage
        2. Noncooperation and civil disobedience
    B. "Incapacitation of the antagonist"
        3. Creating empathy
           (a) Positive interaction before attack
           (b) Cooperation with the person; noncooperation with the status
        4. Creating sympathy through suffering
II. Defense strategies aimed at protecting oneself
        5. Efficient communication inside one's own group
        6. Effectively hiding selected people and objects
        7. Decreased vulnerability of the population
        8. Communication and enaction of one's own values
III. Defense strategies aimed at deterring the antagonist
        9. Organization of NMD prepared in peacetime
        10. Communication of preparedness through maneuvers
        11. Communication of commitment to NMD
        12. High level of satisfaction in one's own group.

From the outset I should emphasize that these strategies must be combined, as each one is far more meaningful combined with the others. Also, the parallel with military strategic thinking should be pointed out. Just as with military defense, the primary idea is to deter the antagonist so that he does not attack at all; if that fails, the idea is to see to it that his "attack should not pay" and to "incapacitate him."[111] Throughout this process one should also protect oneself, by measures very similar to civil defense.

5.3.1 ANTAGONIST-ORIENTED DEFENSE STRATEGIES

"Attack should not pay"

[1] *Self-inflicted sabotage.* If the antagonist is after anything of value, then that value should be denied him as far as possible, not necessarily by a scorched-earth strategy but rather as people protect their cars against theft. Who

would install a mechanism in his car that would make it explode when a thief tried to force an entry? From the point of view of nonviolence, one would certainly not be inclined to kill the thief in the explosion, although it may be argued that one would have the right to blow up one's own car if the thief had been warned. But this type of defense would still run contrary to another basic element of NMD: that defense should mirror the goals of the fight, which evidently would not include a general destruction of all physical property.[112] Hence, the car owner would rather take that least action that would cause the most difficulty to his antagonist, the would-be thief. In the case of a car he can remove the key, although few cars are constructed in such a way that there are no other ways to make them run. Fortunately, cars have other crucial parts besides keys that can also be removed, but they would also be replaceable. However, if they were as unique as a key, the thief would face a more difficult situation.

The basic point in what has been said can be stated in a positive way: if some physical construction exists that has no unique minimum part that causes maximum uselessness when removed, then it should be subject to reconstruction.[113] Defense thus consists exactly in making one's property conform to the ideas and ideals of this elementary but fundamental part of social defense. Technology must give due consideration to social defense, rather than assuming that defense will take place along the borders of a territorially defined unit.

[2] *Noncooperation and civil disobedience.* These elements of resistance are well known today. The basic idea is refusal to participate in a structure dominated by the antagonist, whether the antagonist comes from the outside or is an internal exploiter. It amounts to some type of decoupling from the antagonist. One refuses interaction with him because that interaction is seen as illegitimate. This type of noncooperation, combined with passive and active disobedience, can permeate an entire social structure from top to bottom, from one end to another, so that no part of it is any longer subservient to the goals of an illegitimate antagonist. Actually, this part of NMD is very similar to NVR.[114]

"Incapacitation of the antagonist"

[3] *Creating empathy.* Experience shows that one cannot generally rely upon human beings to be sufficiently equipped with innate empathy not to strike a killing blow, even in the form of torture, to their fellow human beings.[115] Empathy has to be created out of the experience of social interaction. In the theory of NMD, this requires two things:

(a) Positive interaction before attack;
(b) Cooperation with the person, noncooperation with the status.

The first of these involves some type of goodwill investment in times of peace. Only through positive and nonexploitative activity in all directions, toward both potential friends and potential antagonists, can there be established the types of ties and contacts through which genuine human feelings of cooperation and even love may flow. Obviously, this process presupposes a basic infrastructure of associative rather than dissociative peace policies. Concretely, the best examples I know of are probably found in connection with emergency relief, which has the strange consequence that social and natural catastrophes become raw materials out of which future peace and cooperation may be processed. The problem is that such events play into the hands of the rich with sufficient resources to engage in relief and hence may also reinforce dominance structures.[116]

To cooperate with an antagonist as a person[117] but not to cooperate with him *ex officio* is a distinction not easily made. Is giving water to a thirsty enemy soldier to comfort him as a person or to help the enemy occupying one's land? Obviously, it may be both. Even to show him a friendly smile might strengthen his morale, as is so often pointed out when norms against fraternization are established. But from the point of view of NMD, the borderline between antagonist *qua* person and antagonist *qua* antagonist is not so difficult to draw. The moment the antagonist tries to force one to do what one would otherwise not do, noncooperation must start. As long as what one does is to try to behave toward other human beings as one wants interhuman relations to be, one is on the right track from the point of view of NMD. Many actions of friendliness ruled out by military defense would be included in an NMD approach, which could lead to accusations of treason as well as to severe internal doubts. In practice this probably is one of the most difficult strategies to implement.

[4] *Creating sympathy through suffering.* One difficult aspect of doing this, whose role should not be exaggerated, is to make it evident to the antagonist that one is suffering at his hands. One may convey to the antagonist an image of what the situation was like before his occupation or exploitation started and then communicate to him as effectively as possible what the difference is. Combined with the strategies of friendliness this should make it more difficult psychologically for the antagonist to engage in any measure of extreme terror or to seek to bend to his own purpose a society that is not his.

5.3.2 DEFENSE STRATEGIES AIMED AT PROTECTING ONESELF

[5] *Efficient communication inside one's own group.* This cannot be emphasized enough. Because a basic means of domination is fragmentation or disintegration of society at the bottom, and because most societies have fundamentally nondemocratic social structures, all an antagonist has to do is to conquer the social center. The rest is then often fragmented enough to be unable to rally together and unify the resistance. Hence, an effective resistance calls both for decentralization and for effective integration at all levels, for local autonomy as well as coordination. Of course, communication also has a technical aspect, but having electromagnetic devices, popular walkie-talkie systems, or even smoke signals, if that is the level of technology in the society, is less important than the social structure involved. What is required is a structure that

is fundamentally democratic where communication is concerned. In other words, a social structure of solidarity and participation in itself provides a strategy of social defense, because messages can so easily be disseminated.[118]

[6] *Effectively hiding selected people and objects.* In this version of non-military defense, secrecy plays an important role. There is no assumption here that human beings in the industrialized societies we know today would have such a strength that some of them, like *satyagrahis* of the Gandhi type, would be able to conquer and tame an antagonist. Rather, it is to be feared that an antagonist with free access to the individuals whom he identifies as leaders and to their physical means of struggle (e.g., devices of communication) would not abstain from arresting and confiscating. Nor does it seem realistic to assume that such tactics on the side of the antagonist would not be relatively effective in the long run or even the short run. Hence, hiding places become essential. If hiding places do not exist, then the architect has to make houses serve this need, the urban planner has to make cities do so, and everybody has to make nature do so.

[7] *Decreased vulnerability of the population.* Since it is to be expected that an antagonist will engage in repressive policies, the population has to be protected as much as possible. An antagonist may try to deprive the population of food, or strategies of noncooperation and civil disobedience may themselves lead to a severe reduction in the living standards of a population. The answer to this problem may be to hide effectively miniaturized food reservoirs,[119] with a maximum density of highly nutritional elements. But however this might work, one should probably not fool oneself into believing that a population cannot ultimately be forced into submission by various terror techniques (decimation, random selection of victims for torture or execution, mass deportation). Hence, the real defense against this tactic is not the passive one of protecting the population by making it less vulnerable but the active defense of incapacitating the antagonist by making him phychologically unable to engage in such extreme deeds, as through strategies 3 and 4.

[8] *Communication and enaction of one's own values.* The concrete struggle, the actions with which one fights in NMD, should not only be compatible with one's ultimate objective, whether that be to preserve an existing structure, as in the case of occupation defense, or to build a new structure, as in the case of exploitation defense. These actions should also be chosen in such a way that they are directly goal-revealing[120] and the strategies themselves will communicate something to the other side. For example, in exploitation defense, occupying an institution run by the adversary (e.g., a factory or a university) in order to destroy it would not be goal-revealing. To occupy it in order to show how it should be run, a boycott in reverse, might be.[121] In this point NMD would be more similar to guerrilla warfare than to conventional military warfare. A basic point in a guerrilla fight is the ability to realize immediately, rather than postponing till after victory, such basic goals as land reform, education, and, very significantly, fundamental democratization of the fighting unit itself. This illustrates also the many-sidedness of the communication process in this kind of

struggle: it is directed not only toward the adversary, but also inward, toward one's own group, and in addition toward third parties.

5.3.3 DEFENSE STRATEGIES AIMED AT DETERRING THE ANTAGONIST

[9] *Organization of NMD prepared in peacetime.* The experience of Czechoslovakia seems to show two things clearly: it is possible to gain substantial short-term victories through improvization, but this alone is not sufficient.[122] Whether any amount of careful preparation before the 1968 invasion occurred would have been sufficient is another matter; I do not claim infallibility for this method (but it is also true that there are no infallible methods).

Peacetime preparation has the disadvantage that it may have a provocative component. Other countries or groups will ask "Just whom are you preparing yourselves against?" But the provocation effect should be slight, since it is inconceivable that the type of defense just outlined could be used to transgress into the territory of other groups. It essentially presupposes that a relation of dominance has already been established and constitutes a defense against that relation.

Concretely, the organization of defense could revolve around three kinds of axes: territorial, organizational, and associational.[123] A modern society has a territorial base, but it is organized for production and other purposes into organizations (which tend to have a vertical character) and associations (which tend to be more horizontal). Each farm, each factory, and each firm could work out its plan for defense; the same would apply to each association, whether it is professional, hobby-oriented, or value-oriented (goals or interests). Each group should ask the basic question "What can we do in case of occupation?"

These various plans could then be coordinated locally and nationally to more territorially based NMD preparations. Great emphasis should be placed on decentralization for at least three reasons: the defense should not be vulnerable to an attack against the center of society; the defense should be compatible with a truly democratic structure, which must reflect elements of decentralization; and the defense should be able to draw upon enthusiasm and creativity at any point in society.

[10] *Communication of preparedness through maneuvers.* There must be some type of rehearsal for NMD just as for military defense; there must be some practice of maneuvers. The basic, most fundamental type of maneuver would be nonviolent direct action in peacetime against any kind of illegitimate domination. But other types could also be used: workshops, mock exercises, simulation, large-scale maneuvers as for civil defense today, and so on.

A basic objective, in addition to the obvious training effects, would be the communication of preparedness. Just as with military defense, NMD would have to see to it that the level of secrecy is sufficient to protect plans at the level of operative concreteness, but the preparations must be visible enough to communicate preparedness. Military—or possibly nonmilitary—attachés should be invited

to inspect the maneuvers, provided one is sufficiently convinced that communication of capability would be the result.

[11] *Communication of commitment to NMD.* Capability is not enough;
intention crystallized into commitment is also essential for deterrence—in NMD
as in military defense. There are several ways in which this commitment can be
operationalized and institutionalized. One is through a set of "tripwire" mechanisms so that various stages of the plans will be set into action automatically
upon adversary transgression. A photoelectric cell might trigger explosions so as
to make an airport inoperative, for example. At the same time there will be a
need for a flexible response that would decrease the level of automaticity so that
although commitment is high, there would always be options or degrees of
enactment available. Nevertheless, the commitment should be so automatic that
two fundamental alternatives are ruled out: military defense as the only strategy
to be applied, on the one hand, and total submission, on the other. For even if
NMD should not be effective in the sense of protecting one's own group against
domination, it will nonetheless be effective as a way of communicating to
everybody inside one's own group, to the adversary, and to third parties the will
to resist and the attachment to one's own values. In fact, this is perhaps the most
important consequence of the type of NMD engaged in by the Czechs and
Slovaks: a means of communicating exactly this perspective in all three directions, with lasting effectiveness—the dominant regime is still seen as illegitimate.

[12] *High level of satisfaction in one's own group.* The basic objective here
is to avoid really substantial collaboration between the occupier or exploiter on
the one hand and the dissidents in one's own group on the other. The strategy
would have to be that one's society should not have basic discontinuities in its
social structure that make for systematic differences between first-class, second-
class, and third-class citizens. The best preparation for nonmilitary defense and
the best way of deterring an antagonist is found in basically democratic policies
that aim at horizontal, egalitarian societies.[124]

Looking back on these twelve points, we see that they do not represent a
demand for a new utopia or anything of that kind. Points 5, 6, and 7 above are
not too different from what civil defense would be doing within a framework of
total defense that includes a dominant military component. But there is the
important difference that NMD presupposes a basically democratic structure and
uses democracy as a way of fighting, a way presumably not incompatible with
predominant value systems in many societies in the world. It may be incompatible with demands for continued power from certain power elites, but those
demands have decreasing legitimacy after the breakthrough of new thinking at
the end of the 1960's, anyhow. Moreover, the whole basic paradigm, divided
into three classes of strategies, is in itself so similar to the paradigm on which
military defense is based that the type of thinking should be easily comprehended.

One important argument against this type of defense is that it favors some
types of societies over others. Where military defense favors the rich, centralized

society with a technical–economic capability that can be converted into military hardware, nonmilitary defense favors a democratic society, since structural peace and democratization in general have become means of defense. Decentralization, for instance, becomes a major key to invulnerability. It also favors a society with a high level of ability to organize and to improvise. Moreover, strategies 9–12 can be applied only for occupation defense, not for exploitation defense, as the antagonist is already firmly settled. Therefore, like military defense, NMD works much better as defense against occupation than against exploitation, and it must be supplemented with NVR. But the other eight strategies should all be applicable even under situations of extreme exploitation. The basic strength of NMD would then become apparent. Just as military preparedness will stimulate technical–economic development, centralization, and vertical societies, so preparation for nonmilitary defense will stimulate autonomy, precisely as self-respect, self-sufficiency, and fearlessness, and the growth of fundamentally democratic, egalitarian societies. A formal democracy in a vertical society is a way of making people accept dominance and injustice—and consequently also a way of preparing them for occupation and exploitation in any form. It is a way of weakening the social defense of a society. To strengthen a society is to strengthen its social defense and vice versa; this concept is the basic key to nonmilitary defense.

For this reason, I am here arguing not in favor of disarmament but rather in favor of *transarmament.* To disarm is to make a society defenseless; to transarm is to change from one type of defense to another. I do not claim that nonmilitary defense can be used in all possible situations but that what military defense was to an essentially dissociative structure of territorial actors, nonmilitary defense can become to an essentially associative structure with more nonterritorial actors. Since I believe this is the structure that the world is moving toward, steps in the direction of this type of transarmament could be taken now.

Thus, I end up advocating neither the abolition of all kinds of defense institutions nor the immediate abolition of military defense. I simply do not believe that all direct violence can be traced back to structural violence and that a world with no built-in structural violence would also be a world without any direct violence. There are two simple reasons: direct violence is of course used to establish structural violence, but direct violence is also used simply to fight— presumably for "inner reasons" as one might put it—and not in order to establish any kind of exploitation. The "inner reasons" may find their roots in social structure or in personality structure (hardly in human biology). To believe that the causes of national belligerence are found only in the international or social structure would be dogmatism.[125]

Transarmament is a process, not a sudden change from one day to the next. What I plead for is the gradual dismantling of the increasingly absurd military machine and gradual implementation of nonmilitary defense, possibly supplied with an element of guerrilla methods. Military defense with the war technology of today involves a willingness to sacrifice a considerable part of the population on either side in order to protect territory and social institutions; nonmilitary defense is quite willing to sacrifice territory in order to protect institutions, but with a minimum of sacrifice of human lives on either side. This transarmament process will take time, given social inertia and resistance. It has to come, but it will not come about by itself. NMD is far more than merely another way of fighting the same defense battles. It is also a branch on the big tree of nonviolence, which implies a new way of conceiving of power in particular and society in general.[126]

5.4 STRATEGIES OF DEMILITARIZATION

Let us return to the problem of how the war system can be fought directly, and let us refer to that fight as *demilitarization,* not disarmament. It is my feeling that the need for new thinking in this field is so desperate that "unrealistic" is a much less killing comment than "old hat." After twenty-five years of blatant failure in curbing the arms race, the burden of proof rests more on those who insist on the old models than on those who argue in favor of new strategies of demilitarization.[127]

The strategies come in two groups, depending on whether they point to actions primarily to be taken in the relations between states or in the relations within states.[128] The dividing line is not a very sharp one, however. Moreover, other proposals or strategies are certainly conceivable; I have simply limited my list to what I see as the least unpromising ones. The strategies are grouped as follows:

Intersystem approaches
1. Mutual force reduction (MFR)
2. Exchange of observers and information on the movement of alliances
3. Control systems
4. Zoning
5. Broader participation in disarmament conferences
6. Nongovernmental disarmament conferences
7. An international storehouse of disarmament ideas

Intrasystem approaches
1. Reducing the hardware
2. Reducing the software
3. Reducing the budgets
4. Publication of military secrets
5. Nonmilitary defense
6. More public debate on disarmament
7. Turning warfare states into peacefare states

5.4.1 INTERSYSTEM APPROACHES

Mutual Force Reduction (MFR)

Few formulas should elicit as much initial skepticism as this new acronym for what many have tried to do. But as opposed to the McCloy–Zorin doctrine, there is now less mention of the two types of control (control of what is destroyed or removed as opposed to control of what remains) than ten years ago.[129] That may be a sign of growing insight into how counterproductive premature insistence on control may be.[130]

I doubt very much that there is much to be gained under the MFR formula alone. There will be some insistence on balance, and for that there has to be a baseline, a commonly agreed-upon estimate of the military capability on either side. But is any side really interested in having the other side know its capability? Will the other side ever believe that it knows? Why suddenly assume that in the 1970's governments, for some reason, will become honest about their military capabilities? What would make them refrain from cheating sufficiently to keep the edge they believe to be significant?

Yet they may proceed without a precise and generally agreed baseline, just trying to get rid of some of the military machinery. If "balance" is interpreted this way, assuming that the parties are more or less equal and only trying to cut off the top of the capabilities, MFR may be more meaningful. In other words, one might proceed on the basis of exact pairing, a dollar for a dollar, a man for a man, a fighter-bomber for a fighter-bomber. One might also develop more complex formulas, taking geographical asymmetries into consideration. In the past, this approach has not proven very fruitful—there simply has been no reduction—but there may be more leeway in the system now. Particularly, there may be some possibility for withdrawal of foreign troops on a balanced basis, if "balance" includes reference to geographical parameters.[131]

Three special components in any MFR deal should be singled out for attention, since they appear frequently in public debates and may represent important pitfalls. They are manpower reduction, budget reduction, and research reduction.

Manpower reduction might be the obvious answer to the increasing unpopularity of military service in many countries, expressing itself in increased resistance of an ideological or material nature. Manpower reduction may for that reason also be a disarmament issue popular in public opinion, since its impact is highly visible and well dispersed among the families from which the forces are drawn as well as in the districts where they are stationed. But few measures can be so deceptive. If disarmament is to mean anything it must mean a reduction of destructive capability, not merely the reduction of one destructive component that can be compensated for elsewhere. Since most organizations in modern societies are accustomed to structural rationalization, to transitions from labor-intensive to capital-intensive and then to research-intensive production patterns, the military would hardly be an exception. It is to be expected that a software cut would be accompanied by a hardware increase. Where there is little or no hardware, a 50 percent software cut would mean business; with much effectively automated hardware, even a 75 percent manpower cut might in fact mean increased destructive capacity.

If manpower reduction would encourage more capital-intensive military machines, budget reduction would encourage more research intensivity. A cut in the budget would mean a tremendous stimulus to the imagination and general inventiveness of the top planners who suddenly would have to obtain the same or more destructive capability for less money. One way of circumventing this would be to put a ceiling on research capacity. Any discussion of MFR that does not include research capability should not be taken quite seriously. An MFR agreement that would set a ceiling on military research capacity, or even institute some control mechanism, at the same time that it institutes manpower reduction and budget cuts might begin to look serious.

The situation bears considerable similarity to the arms-trade problem. It is relatively obvious that curbs on arms trade (or other forms of transfer) would stimulate local production, e.g., in Periphery countries, and that curbs on the transfer of arms technology would stimulate local innovation. It is equally obvious that such propositions can be used by those who deliver arms and technology as a rationale for their activity. But the conclusion to be drawn is certainly not that curbs on the transfer of arms and arms technology should be given up as futile. The conclusion is that such measures must be accompanied by other measures such as curbs on domestic production and innovation. In other words, the total system has to be considered, for it is like a system of communicating vessels: if you press down at one point, it goes up somewhere else. Whereas a limited approach may stimulate increases elsewhere, the total approach may be impossible to carry out. Conclusion: other approaches may be better.[132] And the best approach in this connection would be alliance-reduction as a form of force reduction: a spread of the nonalignment movement inside the two blocs.

Exchange of Observers and Information on the Movement of Alliances

These are now conventional issues that have been on the agenda for a long time, in various forms.[133] One Soviet leader once suggested that since there were many spies in the world who in fact derived their pay from both blocs because they were employed by both, it would be much more rational to agree on a joint salary and exchange information more directly. The exchange of observers can be seen as an institutionalization of espionage, though possibly less effective, that would hardly do away with espionage. It might demystify some aspects of the military machine, and it is also likely to lead to an even greater degree of homogenization between the military machines because of the increased flow of legitimately obtained information.

One idea here might be using third parties as observers in addition to the exchange of partisan observers, so that the world community as a whole is also brought in. The third party could then take the form of UN-appointed observers, also from non-European countries. There is the great risk, however, that the observers might learn too much about military machines not yet developed in their own countries or regions of origin, and that this might serve as a stimulus for increased armament.

Similar comments can be applied to information on the movement of alliances. By pressing really hard on these points, expanding the traditional roles of military attachés, one may get to know more. But one may also create a new situation where there is more to know, so that the proportion of known to knowable actually decreases. Spy satellites can conceivably be internationalized and staffed by third parties who relay their findings to the world. Or satellites can come in pairs, or there can be dually manned satellites that relay their findings to both parties. In any case the result may be the same: a stimulation of inventiveness that creates more unobserved movement, i.e., more to know.

In an effort to avoid such pitfalls on the road toward at least some disarmament, let us therefore take a fresh look at the control issue.

Control Systems

In the whole history of disarmament the legal paradigm has been the dominant model.[134] The idea has been that one has to arrive at binding rules defining an arms level or a disarmament process and that there has to be a control machinery. The latter would, roughly speaking, have these components: a detection machinery to register reports of infractions, a verification process, an adjudication process, and finally some system of sanctions. Experience seems to speak against this paradigm: the more control, the more motivation to cheat. If in addition there are sanctions, parties will simply withdraw from the system or be challenged into very high levels of ingenuity.

On the other hand, from the failure of strict control to lead to disarmament it does not follow that no control at all leads to disarmament, either. The control dimension may actually be less relevant, or (the position I take here) there may be some optimum point of "soft" control—enough to constitute an incentive to stick to the agreement and abstain from cheating, yet not enough to stimulate the development of new weapons systems.

But who is to carry out the control if neither party is willing to assume that the other side can be trusted? Moreover, what can be done if neither side wants to permit the other side to come close enough to carry out effective inspection? There are two answers, two by-and-large untapped resources: the population on either side[135] and third parties.

The population on either side can only be expected to be a part of the control system at home and report possible infractions to some international control organ if (1) it is told to do so explicitly by its own government, not only by the other side, (2) it is given access to report channels, (3) it has some guarantees against retributions from its own government, and (4) the government is willing to see the population as an ally against possible infractors (ambitious military circles and the like). None of these conditions should be ruled out as utopian.

Not only the right but the duty of any population to report infractions of an arms control or disarmament agreement in its own country should be worked into any treaty in a standard clause. The government should pledge itself to make the treaty known all over the country, including this clause, with some suggestions as to what kind of infractions to expect, and to encourage the citizens to cooperate with the government against others who might engage in some act of circumvention.

Report channels pose a technical problem. Some kind of citizens' hot line might be imagined, some kind of international telephone number that could not be blocked locally or be abused for other subversive purposes either. This would require a combination of international and national participation in supervision. A system of well-dispersed offices belonging to an international control commission might be useful, but the problem is, of course, to guarantee citizens against intimidation from their own government, which obviously would be spying on citizens spying on itself.

Protection against retribution is more difficult, but not if the first and second points are taken care of. Anonymity of telephone calls would also encourage pranksters. Intimidation of citizens reporting infractions would at least signal to the surrounding world that a government has something to hide, but an honest government might be made to appear dishonest by systematic blackmail from its own citizens. It might then respond with voice detection techniques and the like.[136]

If any disarmament effort is to be taken seriously we have to get away from the old idea that military machinery is a normal part of government, with both military and government far above the general populace. We have to make some, however small, moves in the direction of creating a government-people (not to mention people-people) shared interest, if not alliance, in curbing excesses in the military machinery. Ultimately, we even have to internationalize this shared concern, in a cooperation between intergovernmental, internongovernmental, and transnational organizations.[137]

With regard to third parties I am thinking of some sort of nonaligned corps linked to the United Nations, similar to a UN peacekeeping force. One of its essential duties would be to *not* report whatever it might find of a dubious character inside one of the parties to the other side, to avoid the use of alleged reports to stimulate military escalation. It might report to some kind of security commission established by the United Nations.[138] Needless to say, it would be spied upon by both parties, for which reason only persons of exceptional integrity could be used, willing to submit to rigorous briefing and debriefing procedures.

The corps might also be stationed in certain special zones. If these are border zones, it might even constitute a *cordon sanitaire* between two opposed parties, and this concept might be extended to include naval and air force units.

The latter would in part have the function of preventing the parties from creating risks when they test each other's warning systems, and it would symbolize effectively the duty and the right of the rest of the world to be concerned with such problems.

Zoning

Zoning is also merely a *component* in a disarmament plan, not a complete plan. It should be discussed from two angles:

Its domain, the extension of the geographical area involved and its location; and

Its scope, the extent of the disarmament, itself a dual problem of what kind of military capability and what degree of limitation (freezing, thinning, emptying).

These two dimensions involve the whole problem of disarmament, which concerns precisely to what degree what kind of military capability shall be done away with. So what is gained, if anything, by bringing in the concept of zoning?

First, the zoning concept provides some flexibility, because there is one more variable to throw into a bargain, the geographical extension and location involved. Second, there are zones in the world that are or have been empty of some or all kinds of military capabilities. There has been the hope that if empty zones could be institutionalized as empty (e.g., by establishing nuclear-free zones in outer space, in the Antarctic, or in Latin America), then there might be a spread effect. The theory of the spread effect may or may not be valid under

Figure 5.4   The two dimensions of zoning

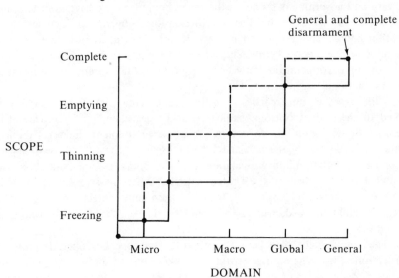

certain conditions; the problem is that we do not seem to know those conditions. However, *to freeze what is already empty is nonarmament, not disarmament.*

Experience does not seem to warrant much optimism when it comes to a spread effect from the freezing of empty zones. But from the freezing of non-empty zones some process of escalating disarmament might be expected. Thus, consider figure 5.4. In the lower left-hand corner is the present situation; in the upper right-hand corner the ideal image, "general and complete disarmament," involving maximum domain and maximum scope, where the whole world has been emptied of all military capability. The figure can be used to illustrate one more way of producing non-results at disarmament conferences, in addition to freezing empty zones: insisting on general and complete disarmament, even though it obviously cannot come about by a jump from the real (corner) to the ideal (corner).[139] There has to be a *process*; there has to be some image of a path; and there have to be concrete first steps.

The major purpose of figure 5.4 is to indicate two such paths, two modes of thinking. Both have as a point of departure something very modest: a small territory and the freezing of one component, a component already there. Then comes the escalation hoped for: it may start in either direction, by expanding the territory involved, or by proceeding with new military components; *no attempt should be made to do both at the same time.*[140] The best will only be the enemy of the good.

Further, one should not move ahead "before some experience is gained," a diplomatic way of saying "before forces and interests in favor of rearmament have grown accustomed to the change." Whether one should move along the domain axis by adding territory or along the scope axis by reducing military capability depends on which is easier in the concrete situation.

To get such a process started is more important than the precise point at which it gets started. The Balkans (as suggested by Romania), the Nordic countries (as suggested by Finland), and/or some modified version of the old Rapacki–Gomulka zone in Central Europe (e.g., without Poland) as nuclear-free zones might be excellent. *Real denuclearization* (including research capacity) of Latin America and Africa might be other examples. But in fact nothing of this kind has happened. Perhaps the zones are too big, and one should think smaller. It may also be that the zones should be defined by other than state borders, e.g., by borders that would facilitate some type of control pattern.[141] The Baltic Sea with its littoral as well as the Black Sea with its littoral might perhaps constitute nuclear-free and submarine-free zones. So might Berlin, and from Berlin some pattern of concentric expansion, as suggested by Jules Moch many times,[142] might be envisaged. What is happening today with the military machineries in such neutral countries as Austria, Finland, and Sweden also provides examples of country zones in which there are moves toward freezing (the military budget in Sweden)[143] and toward thinning out (the software component in Austria).[144]

Zoning could also be given a more direct content, as can be illustrated with some European examples. There are six pairs of countries where East and West in the traditional European sense border on each other: Norway with the Soviet Union, the two Germanys, FRG with Czechoslovakia, Bulgaria with Greece, Bulgaria with Turkey, and Turkey with the Soviet Union. If some border areas on both sides could become armament-free zones of however limited extension, starting perhaps with the shortest borders (Norway-Soviet Union and Bulgaria-Turkey), this might be helpful, though not if it leads to compensatory armament elsewhere.

Morever, such border zones might be given a positive content in at least two ways:

First, in the zones there could be placed some institutions of cooperation, like summer camps, joint educational institutions of a more permanent kind, even some intergovernmental organization for cooperation (such as a canal, rail, or road authority) as distinct from intergovernmental organizations for control.

Second, the zones could house international control forces of one kind or another. Elsewhere I have argued strongly for the inclusion of non-Europeans and neutral Europeans in such forces.[145] This would offer an excellent opportunity to globalize the concern for disarmament.

In short, there are advantages to zoning that go beyond general MFR concepts; there are things the parties can do by themselves and things they have to do together. As a variable, zoning proposals can be thrown into an MFR bargain to give more to play with. Zoning arrangements are visible and concrete, unlike the SALT type of agreement, which affects very few people directly. And they can be given a positive content: the zone may not only become a zone of negative peace (disarmament) but also a zone for positive peace (cooperation).

Broader Participation in Disarmament Conferences

In principle the United Nations is a standing disarmament conference, but this has proved to be one more example of the best being the enemy of the good. In practice, the superpowers have had a decisive influence in the field of disarmament, but an intermediate level between superpowers and the UN membership emerged in the 1960's: the Conference of the Committee on Disarmament (CCD). Participation of non-European states and recent colonies is a significant gain, even if it has been at the expense of basic decisions being moved out of the CCD and back to the superpower level.[146] The question is what to do about this.

Reasoning in terms of scope and domain can also be utilized in this case. It may look as if the greater the domain (the more nations participating), the lesser the scope (the fewer the issues that are discussed, with even fewer and less central ones being decided upon). However, the problem is not only one of decision making but also one of *articulation of issues.* When the superpowers meet to discuss issues they all decide which are the issues meaningful to them, and they may not be the most meaningful to others.

Thus, a strong case can be made that despite many dissimilarities there is very much in common between the U.S. 1965 intervention in the Dominican Republic and the Soviet 1968 intervention in Czechoslovakia.[147] The super-powers have this issue in common, although two separate pieces of behavior are involved and there is no shared concern between them. To articulate common but unshared issues, one would need a conference where the Dominican Republic and Czechoslovakia were not only represented but represented precisely by the social forces that were the targets of the interventions.

Two important expansions of these issues must be articulated at disarmament conferences, both concerned with efforts to bring in the *vertical* dimension of disarmament.

The vertical dimension concerns the kinds of arms and the kind of attacks a *strong power* may make on the weak within its own sphere of influence and the kind of arms and the kind of attacks a strong *government* may make on the weak people within its own territory. The problem raised is nothing less than to organize disarmament conferences to bring about

An articulation of the problems of *states* threatened by *strong-power* intervention, and

An articulation of the problems of *people* threatened by *governmental power* abuse.

The problems here are tremendous, and many of them are obvious. If a state is in danger of being intervened with, it will probably not even dare articulate that fear; and if a "people"—a minority or a district with some tradition of separatism—feels threatened by new arms developed or acquired by the central government, it will hardly be permitted any conference participation and will also have considerable difficulty articulating its fear. Others will have to represent it, but usually these others will be the big powers in the other camp, generally more than eager to point to sources of dissent within and between countries that oppose them. The result of this form of articulation is often a reinforcement of the conflict between the big powers in question and a transformation of the vertical problem of disarmament back into the traditional horizontal form. The vertical problem is lost sight of, while those are strengthened who want to see the world as a stage for only the big powers.

Something new must be done, and here are two suggestions.

The first is that there be *a special governmental conference on disarmament for small powers only*—partly to look into issues involving themselves only, and mainly to look into issues involving the relations to the big powers. Since the overwhelming majority of these interventions have taken place in the capitalist world[148] and have taken the form of big capitalist powers intervening in small capitalist states (or small states on the way to becoming socialist), such a conference would not have to be balanced in the conventional East-West sense.

The second is that there be *a special nongovernmental conference of oppressed minorities or majorities on the disarmament of governments.* The focus here would be on *the type of armament governments use against their own peoples,* such as all kinds of eavesdropping devices, spying machinery, and counterinsurgency hardware and software: in short, the equipment for micro-war. The objective would not necessarily be to abolish all armaments; it might well be agreed that governments have a right, perhaps even an obligation, to keep a minimum of this equipment. Rather, the idea would be to discuss criteria for armament reduction, upper limits, documentation on use and abuse, searchlights on research and development, and so on.

Thus, I would strongly support the idea of a *world disarmament conference.* However, that conference should be seen in a wider perspective than as just an expansion of the Conference on the Committee on Disarmament. In fact, if horizontal expansion were the only dimension, a special session of the UN General Assembly, as in 1978, might be sufficient. *What is needed, however, is a world disarmament conference that adds the vertical dimension.* The vertical dimension among nations can be taken account of at the governmental level, but the vertical dimension inside nations presupposes participation of nongovern-mental units, even of antigovernments or countergovernments. If this does not take place within the conventional setting provided by intergovernmental meet-ings, as it hardly will, all that is proved is the inadequacy of this setting and the need for alternative or at least complementary settings in order at least to *articulate* the true problems of disarmament.[149]

Nongovernmental Disarmament Conferences

Disarmament is indeed a public concern, but this is not reflected in disarma-ment conferences. SALT 1 and 2 are typical examples of covenants that were not openly arrived at, and there are serious doubts as to whether they are open covenants in any sense (i.e., there may be secret protocols). Disarmament conferences are conducted according to the old model of secret diplomacy, yet with an eye to the political impact on the public, particularly in election years. The usual rationalizations are made ample use of: the issues are too difficult for the public to understand; the negotiations are too sensitive, too delicate; the negotiators have to have free hands.

Elitism in this case can be attacked on the basis of its failure to deliver the promised goods. Hence the call for active and public involvement of *counter-elites* (elites with views differing from their governments) and *antielites* (the masses, the peoples, public opinion). The question is how to achieve this.

The model best known so far is the model of counterelites and antielites exercising pressure on their respective governments. A counterelite can do this secretly by walking in the corridors of power, establishing itself covertly as a lobby or openly by organizing as a party or a pressure group and by publishing alternative plans, military secrets, and so on. Antielites can collect signatures, make demonstrations, occupy offices, and destroy some components (such as draft cards)—with or without the help of the counterelites. All this activity, however, has one thing in common: the target of the pressure is the national government in its executive, legislative, or military branches. The process is intranational.

The countermodel proposed here would imply not so much a change of methods as the addition to the target of the intergovernmental level. The new target immediately splits into two, for intergovernmental organizations can be *institutionalized* organizations (like the Disarmament Section of the United Nations, or the CCD for that matter) or *ad hoc* conferences (like SALT). By and large it is the former that to some extent have been approached by international nongovernmental organizations; the latter have too often been left to themselves. Their plea for peace and quiet, even secrecy, has been respected.

It is high time for the public at large to start exercising pressure on these intergovernmental organizations, institutionalized or *ad hoc,* at a truly transnational level. By that I mean to suggest a *parallel conference* or a set of parallel manifestations—though not necessarily an anticonference or a demonstration aiming at disrupting any work. The parallel conference should take place at the same place and at the same time as the governmental conference, be informal, rich in articulation, prodding and insistent, a way of airing issues and bringing them to the attention of the public as well as the governmental delegates, as happened at the UN Environmental Conference in Stockholm in June 1972. An important aspect would be demystification of the intergovernmental conferences by demonstrating that technical expertise as well as political will are not monopolized by governmentals and by setting a pattern for constructive proposal making as well as basic criticism.

Of course, on occasion what the intergovernmental conference deserves is what the world needs: a genuine transnational demonstration, a confrontation of the governmental with the nongovernmental, of elites with antielites and counterelites. Needless to say, this may be met by the use (possibly also the abuse) of police, by encapsulation of the governmental conference, by cries of anarchy, and so on—the usual reactions when elite monopolies are challenged in a basic manner. But these occasions would, one hopes, be extreme cases.

An International Storehouse of Disarmament Ideas

It is vital to have good documentation of the current state of affairs in the field of armament, disarmament, and arms control, as is done, for instance, by the Stockholm International Peace Research Institute (SIPRI).[151] But it is a major fallacy of empiricism (or positivism) to believe that by some kind of automatic mental alchemy, solutions can be found to a problem.[152] It is not even obvious that the motivation to solve a problem increases with the quantity and quality of documentation on it. On the contrary, some may be led to believe that the problem is unsolvable, others that it is not that frightening, still others that enough is already being done. Documentation is not enough.

What is needed, besides excellent descriptions of the current state of affairs, are predictions of what will happen if the system is left unchecked, and some theory as to why the world is as it is. Simply stated, two things: (1) some vision of *the goal,* a "disarmed world," a "world without the bomb"—but in detail, with specifications—and (2) a vision of *how to get there,* with some very concrete ideas as to the first steps. An ultimate goal without any indication of the first steps becomes empty utopianism; first steps without a vision of the long-term goal and tactics without strategy become bureaucratic pragmatism, even ritualism.[153]

It is customary to say that there is no scarcity of ideas, that what is lacking is the requisite "political will." This is a highly misleading statement that can only serve those in whose interest it is to defend themselves against new ideas and perspectives. It would be more correct to say that there is no scarcity of ideas within the narrow band considered "realistic," that narrow band compatible with strong-power, particularly superpower, interests. Nor is there any scarcity of ideas within the broad spectrum considered "idealistic" or "utopian," and some might feel that most of the ideas expressed here fall into that category. What is missing are ideas in the middle range, ideas not yet on the political agenda but likely to come there (often through unconventional means) relatively soon. A storehouse might be one way of channeling new ideas in the direction of the political agenda.[154]

Of some importance in this connection is also all the excellent work that has been carried out to assess the magnitude of the burden of the arms race on the world economy and to develop some images of alternative uses of these resources. The significance of the work on the economic and social consequences of armament and of disarmament lies in invoking images so attractive that they may become *real forces when coupled to the interests of groups and countries.*

Images of a goal can be developed into a strategy by creating a vested interest in the goal. Thus, a world may be envisaged where resources released by disarmament are all channeled in favor of poor countries and poor districts—not with a view toward developing their trade with richer and richer districts, but with a view toward making them self-reliant and self-sufficient. Such images have already led to a certain pressure from poor countries for disarmament.[155] Imagine that the poor regions of countries very rich in armaments were also brought into the picture and that some, however small, transfer of resources (brought about by freezing at least some parts of the military budget) was initiated now—rather than on some abstract day in the future when suddenly the locks will be opened. This move would surely lead to an accelerating pressure created by vested interests not only between but also within countries, which is precisely the pressure we need. The richer the storehouse of goals, the richer the possibilities for creating concrete forces, provided they are well publicized, because the military use of all these resources looks so utterly wasteful.

5.4.2 INTRASYSTEM APPROACHES

Reducing the Hardware

To produce military hardware one needs raw materials, capital, and work. Work, the most human factor, can be divided into two parts: *scientists* to develop qualitatively new weapons systems and *workers* to produce larger quantities of already developed weapons systems. In addition there are people hiring them and making them work, through ideological commitment, reward, or punishment. Let us assume that these people, who presumably also are well represented at disarmament conferences, are immune to being changed, but that scientists and workers are not.[156] The question is "What would one have to do to make scientists and workers withdraw from contributing to the military machinery?"

Traditionally, *scientists* have been available at the call (and the pay) of government to do what it wanted, including develop weapons. If not all scientists have participated, there have always been some who have. The situation bears some similarity to that involving the slave merchants who also professed to work for the benefit of the national or local economy, in addition to their own. What will make scientists abstain from this activity? One might think in terms of three different strategies here, namely the three strategies that are used to make scientists work.

> *As to ideology:* a new generation of scientists is now growing up, mainly in the West, with an ideology that is much *more critical,* and also *more transnational.* The proportion willing to serve defense research establishments is probably decreasing (although the absolute number may well increase).[157] A scientific oath, *some kind of Hippocratic oath for all scientists,* might be useful.[158]

> *As to reward:* competitive salaries outside the defense industry, or a premium for scientists who publicly leave the defense industry might be very useful.

> *As to punishment:* public exposure of scientists working for the defense industry,[159] expulsion from scientific unions, and withdrawal of academic honors, including Nobel prizes,[160] might all be considered.

Traditionally, *workers* have been regarded as vulnerable because they must earn their living somehow. If this were the entire truth there would never have been trade unions and political fights, often with tremendous achievements. But why do workers in general not fight against producing for the military?[161] For the simple reason that they are not motivated for this fight. The defense industry pays; and defense industry aimed at the production of hardware to be used against workers in other parts of the world, particularly in the neocolonies, certainly does not pay any worse than any other defense industry. If this is to change, workers have to change; they have to see more clearly the impact of what they are doing and throw away such rationalizations as just mentioned.

To argue that it is impossible to expect strikes of workers against the defense industry, based not on salaries or working conditions or participation demands but simply on the nature of the production itself is, in a sense, to argue that anything workers could do in this connection is impossible. This insult to workers enjoys a curious popularity among many intellectuals on the left.[162] That those on the right also engage in such thinking is not surprising, since so much of their ideology is based on the notion of the worker as inferior.

A higher level of consciousness among workers would be one precondition to their going on strike against the production and transportation of at least some types of weaponry—for instance, that used against other workers, in other countries or in their own. A reward and punishment system of the type indicated for scientists might also have some function. However, at this point there is one basic difference between workers and scientists: the availability of fewer workers may just lead to more automation in the production process, whereas the availability of few or no scientists may stop the qualitative arms race. It may be argued that *some* scientists will always be available, but whether they belong to the elite class or to the intellectual riffraff among scientists is very important. The possibility of a sustained arms race may depend on precisely this distinction; only the elite class has the capability to maintain it.

Reducing the Software

To make military hardware work, people are needed, including officers and soldiers. In addition people higher up hire officers and soldiers and make them work. Once more let us assume that the others are immune to basic change, whereas officers and soldiers are not. The question is "what would one have to do to give officers and soldiers a more detached view of the military machinery, seeing it less as a career and more as a very special activity that easily lends itself to excesses of the type the world has witnessed in the Dominican Republic and Czechoslovakia, Vietnam, and Chile?"

Officers are persons who have chosen a military career. This career should be made less attractive, even to the point of being discredited, at least in countries that show persistent tendencies to engage in repressive military activity. In countries that once headed colonial empires, like Britain and France, this is probably already happening. In general there are two strategies that may be less contradictory than they seem: isolation, even to the point of ostracism (as when the ROTC was thrown out of the Ivy League colleges), and a higher level of critical awareness. However, as officers, unlike most scientists and workers in military production or soldiers, have chosen their military career, it is not to be expected that these strategies will yield much in terms of reduced software capacity.

In regard to soldiers, I am thinking of volunteer soldiers and most professionals, but leaving aside the truly committed professional who is more similar to an officer. What makes a soldier shoot to kill? He may be motivated through indoctrination, for which reason war propaganda instilling hatred for other groups and nations and for the members of other classes should be outlawed. Cinema glorification of violence such as occurs in most capitalist countries falls into the same category. A higher level of consciousness would make it possible for everybody to be able to discriminate between wars, particularly between wars between equals and wars that are vertical and interventionist.

Soldiers also kill because they are rewarded when they do so and punished (as deserters, as disobedient) if they do not. A world campaign against mercenaries, with the promotion of a higher awareness among people that regards that kind of money as the same as, say, money obtained by selling slaves, would be useful. Correspondingly, with regard to punishment: the right of the military to have their own judiciary and even to exercise capital punishment cannot be tolerated. The abolition of the whole system of military courts would be useful in this connection. If military machines cannot function except by a combination of the carrot and the stick, even using big money for big killing and a big stick for failure to kill, there are major weaknesses in the military machinery.

In this connection the "modern" social-scientific approach to the problem of how to make soldiers shoot to kill should also be exposed. Research seems to indicate that soldiers are more effective when they work in teams, with big weapons requiring teamwork and together with friends, so that revenge will be added to their motivation.[163] The lonely soldier with a rifle, an isolated individual among strangers, is ineffective. My point here is that soldiers as people should know that they are being manipulated, that social science has been let loose on them to make them "better soldiers," so that they can mobilize their defenses against this manipulation.[164]

Conscientious objection to military service must also be mentioned in this connection, although today it stands as only one among very many strategies. Whether those who have the "critical awareness" mentioned should leave the military or "work from the inside" is a problem of "both/and" rather than of "either/or." Thus, some will leave and some will make antiwar propaganda on the inside, hand back medals given them in a dirty war, and so on. The danger of this approach, however, is that it may degenerate into empty trade unionism aiming at better conditions for the soldiers rather than at disabling the military machine itself.[165] The result may be a stronger military machinery rather than any weakening from the inside. What is advocated here is not absolute pacifism but a critical attitude that would make it impossible for any leadership to expect obedience to *any* order whatsoever. What is argued is the imperative necessity of developing military personnel at least capable of making a distinction between wars of aggression and wars of defense and between wars for or against repression. Once that distinction is made, one would also expect them to develop sufficient integrity to obey or disobey, accordingly. It is the unquestioning hierarchical obedience, the residue of a feudal social order, that has to disappear.[166]

To conclude: the military machinery has reached proportions of such magnitude that it constitutes a major danger in the world. Like the Inquisition it has become a self-reinforcing, self-generating machinery; and like the Inquisition it will not last forever.[167] It is urgent that this machinery should not be permitted to be seen as a regular part of the total society, as a normal institution among others, like education, health, or science. The least that can be done would be to emphasize its special character, how much of a deviation it represents from a sane society, and to submit it to ordinary review and control processes.

Reducing the Budgets

I have mentioned before that budgets might be included in the intersystem approach under both the MFR and the zoning approaches. However, since the budget is essentially under national control, a discussion of these possibilities also belongs here.

All the many ways of approaching the problem of the military budget are complicated by the circumstance that the military budget is hard to isolate. Like hardware production it can consist of all kinds of civilian components—for instance, police and "internal security" forces—put together for a military purpose in a way known to only a very few. With increased critical awareness in society, this practice may become more widely recognized than it is today, but let us assume that it is for the time being meaningful to talk about a " 'military' budget."

A first task must be to *freeze the budget,* which must be done *in absolute terms,* not in relative terms. To peg the budget on a percentage of GNP, national income, or central government expenditure has nothing to do with freezing, unless the country has zero economic growth and/or a stagnant public sector. Such countries are rare, and particularly rare among the big countries whose military budgets matter most in this connection. Of course, there is the problem of salary adjustments and inflation, but then the formula for freezing the budget should be based explicitly on such factors and not on a general assumption that the military budget has the same right to expand as the economy as a whole or the public sector.[168]

The second task is to look more closely at the *composition of the budget,* and most particularly at the allocation for research and development. If R-and-D are not subject to cuts but are regarded as sacrosanct, or even permitted to expand, then even with a budget that otherwise is shrinking little or nothing is gained. What looks like a gain may even be a loss to the cause of disarmament, as has been pointed out several times.

The third task is to think and act in terms of *cuts in the budget.* Some of this may be negotiated internationally as part of a MFR. Much, perhaps most, action of this kind will have to be done inside the countries concerned, and not necessarily in institutionalized forms. Thus, one can make the military budget a major issue and organize against decision makers who do not go in for cuts. Or, one can take recourse to such methods as tax withdrawal or refusal to pay taxes in the amount of the percentage corresponding to the military sector. The latter is difficult in capitalist countries with pay-as-you-earn taxation, and in socialist countries because of the very low level of direct taxation.[169] In both systems, heavy punishment would be the likely result, since such decisions are seen as the prerogative of the decision makers. If military taxes are the focus, an element of military adjudication might also enter.

Publication of Military Secrets

The concept of "spy" has so far been reserved for a person who, often through great danger to self, gets military secrets from one side and hands them over to the other—with or without handsome material rewards to himself. This type of spy is inseparable from the whole war system. He is needed both in order to estimate the destructive power on the other side, as well as to locate its vulnerable spots, and in order to fight against the spies from the other side.

This type should be contrasted with a new, transnational type of "spy" whose proliferation one might hope for: the "spy" who gets military secrets and publishes them *to the world at large,* to humanity. He does it for no material reward, although his job would be so useful that he might also be paid for it from some transnational fund, if that could be made available. The basic point, however, is the third source of loyalty: neither "our side" nor "the other side," but humanity. It would imply a new polarity: not between "us" and "them," but between the military machineries on the one hand and people on the other, the polarity often referred to here.

This spy's task would be to expose the military machine, much as Daniel Ellsberg did for the Pentagon when he published the Pentagon Papers or as the group in England that some years ago exposed the secret hiding place (in case of war) of the central government.[170] Again, the point would be not necessarily to publish everything, but to publish the secrets about the excesses of the war system. What constitutes an excess has to be discussed thoroughly, and the whole society should participate in this discussion. Since the military appears as a society within society, somewhat exceptional methods have to be utilized to stop it from growing further in the cancerous way we have seen during recent years. One of these methods is precisely to make use of one of the idiosyncrasies of the military machine, its dependence on secrecy.

How will the military establishment react? Probably by repression and by rebuilding and reshaping in an effort to stave off the effects of publicity. This course, however, may be so cumbersome and so expensive and also so dangerous that military leaders may prefer to come to some kind of terms with the Ellsbergs of the world, which might give the population at large some leverage for bargaining with the military establishments, since loyalty is no longer automatic.[171]

Nonmilitary Defense
The significance of nonmilitary defense methods today lies in the new perspective on disarmament mentioned at the end of section 5.3: *transarmament.* "Disarmament" has always carried with it the connotation of something rendered defenseless. The idea behind "transarmament" is to switch, however gradually, to other kinds of defense.[172]

It is unnecessary to open here the theoretical debate on whether forms of nonmilitary defense can be developed that under all circumstance can stave off attackers. From recent and past history, it is quite easy to pick pairs (A,B) where it is quite clear that *no* nonmilitary defense so far known and developed could for a particular B offer a protection against a particular A. But it is also quite easy to carry out this mental exercise for the case of military defense.[173] The basic point is not to fight battles of the past but to develop new forms of defense, synchronized with changes within and between countries that are less threatening to one's opponents and less devastating when put into action.

Thus, a *first* step along this line, and one not usually included in the list considered by pacifists, would be to scan the entire military system for components unnecessarily offensive in the sense that they can justifiably be said by the other side to constitute a threat. The military should then be challenged to redesign systems to appear less offensive.[174] A good example here would be "distargeting" of rockets, particularly of rockets targeted on neighbors (where border confrontations may play a role). There is a world of difference between a rocket stowed away in a storehouse and a rocket targeted and ready to go.[175]

A *second* step would be to develop some components of nonmilitary defense that are understandable and acceptable also to the military mind. One good example would be to design systems of self-inflicted sabotage in case of enemy occupation based on the question "What is the minimum damage (or removal) necessary to make a factory, a ministry, or a university maximally useless to an occupant?" Another example would be to develop emergency communication systems for the civilian population in case of enemy occupation.

A *third* step would be to introduce elements that would involve the civilian population more directly, such as detailed discussions among citizens about how best to organize civil disobedience and noncooperation with an unwanted foreign army. This step would have to be coordinated with the preceding one to be meaningful.

A *fourth* step would be to establish some kind of division of labor between military and nonmilitary defense, the so-called MIX. One formula would be that nonmilitary defense takes over when military defense has capitulated. Another formula would be that military defense is used in the least populous areas (where destruction is more tolerable), nonmilitary defense (which obviously depends in one way or another on people-to-people, even person-to-person contact) in built-up areas. From the warfare of recent years military methods have been developed and become known of such kind that the population might prefer almost anything to their unrestrained application. A military–civilian dialogue about the *limits to defense* might therefore be called for.[176] It is long overdue.

A *fifth* step would be to internationalize even the nonmilitary defense. One great advantage of this type of defense is that it will hardly appear threatening. In discussions with the other side this hypothesis may be tested. It is possible that the other side will feel nonmilitary defense to be more ideological and hence more attitudinally aggressive than military defense. If this is the case, one must discuss what to do about it. To the extent it is generally agreed upon that nonmilitary defense is nonaggressive, much international cooperation could be imagined. For instance, ideas might be exchanged about how to organize it. No country that harbors no aggressive intent would be opposed to giving others ideas about how to organize a defense that cannot be used offensively across borders. A country does not necessarily make its own nonmilitary defense more vulnerable in doing so, for it does not have to reveal details, only general principles. In addition, why could not NMD also be based on international alliances—on the idea that an attack on one of us is an attack on all of us? In practice this would mean an extension of the current practice of demonstrations outside big-power embassies when those powers misbehave—so the seeds are already there.

In short, this dimension should now also be brought via some constructive debate onto the political agenda. It will not satisfy absolute militarists, or absolute pacifists, or absolute revolutionaries, but it may be of great significance to the rest of us, not as a panacea but as one contribution to demilitarization.

More Public Debate on Disarmament

The significance of how people think about armament and disarmament can hardly be overestimated. How people arrive at a conclusion may be more important than the conclusion itself, because it says something about future conclusions. The framework or paradigm of thinking steers thinking. Paradigms are fundamental, and it takes special training to become aware of one's own intellectual framework. Efforts to bring one's assumptions to the surface are usually resisted because they are so intimately linked to basic interests and because of the fear that the total intellectual edifice will fall like a set of dominoes once the assumptions are challenged.

In the field of development theory and development practice a change of paradigm is relatively frequent; in the field of disarmament it is not. Thus, even in strong capitalist countries there are many people who see the difference between "development from above" and "development from below": development that starts by giving credits to the rich and scholarships to the gifted so that they can become even richer and even more gifted, assuming that they will enrich and enlighten others through the spill-over from their work, and development that starts with satisfying the fundamental needs of those who have least. When it comes to "development from below" there is also a basic difference between development initiated from below, and from above. In all three, some physical results may look more or less the same—a house or a hospital bed—but the processes that brought them into being are entirely different.

Similarly with disarmament. Whether various parties see the arms race as primarily produced by the action-reaction effect or by internal dynamics, or by both, they may still come to the same conclusions when it comes to, say, budget control. But the strategies chosen to obtain such a goal, and to maintain it under stress, will differ according to the paradigm used. For that reason it is essential that there be a debate not only on disarmament but also on how to think about disarmament. This debate should be carried into all societies, and elites should be challenged to state not only their disarmament conclusions (if any) but their demilitarization perspective. The goal is not to conduct an intellectual exercise but to obtain a breakthrough in thinking in this deadly important field. The old intersystem paradigm has to be enriched with the intrasystem one; we cannot afford to continue thinking in the old frameworks forever.

The field of disarmament now shows the typical symptoms of a paradigm coming to the end of its usefulness. Increasingly more elaborated studies are produced, using as a point of departure "strategic thinking"—which here means the intersystem paradigm applied to arms control and disarmament issues.[177] Irrelevance and futility may even seem correlated with the degree of elaboration, simply because a certain number of experts have been produced whose task it is to solve puzzles within the old way of thinking.[178] Extremely intricate control systems may be worked out without any analysis of the effects of control, or of whether the real enemy of disarmament is only on the other side or also within oneself. Mutually agreed-upon ceilings on some military components may be instituted, with little regard to expansion in other components, for instance of weaponry that may be used against internal "enemies" of the regime, etc.

Elites have generally had a tendency to entertain too narrow views of these matters, which should now be challenged. The public has been misled. They have not been told how and why a qualitative arms race tends to follow a quantitative one, or how a vertical arms race may accompany a horizontal one. At the same time, the public hardly believes what its elites tell it, though when one is told only one thing, there is little else to believe in. SALT, for instance, is hardly believed in by many, perhaps not even by the elite circles who produced it in accordance with their extremely narrow (which does not mean uncomplicated) model of arms races and how to control them. In this field there is a great task ahead of us. We need a thorough discussion of strategic doctrine, the doctrine of deterrence, a general enrichment of the disarmament debate, and a retraining, and often replacement, of governmental delegates, negotiators, politicians, journalists, and peace researchers who are incapable of introducing changes in the paradigms that guide their thinking.

Turning Warfare States into Peacefare States

In a sense all the topics mentioned in this section have been specific variations on the theme of turning warfare states into peacefare states. But something more general can also be stated.

If each group in society went through a process of thorough self-criticism to find out how it benefits from the war system and how it sustains the war system, this might be far more than an idle intellectual exercise. A government does not usually invite the opposition to do such a thing, and certainly a country does not invite its foreign opponents to do it. But groups within countries may do so, and they may coordinate their research efforts to present a *transnationally produced image of the forces sustaining the military machines.*

One such force is obvious: fear of internal dissent escalating into some type of revolt. The *actio-reactio* paradigm is useful as a rationalization to maintain large forces that can be used against those *inside* the country who challenge the status quo in a basic manner. Usually these are groups that are exploited and/or that are ethnically or racially different and/or that live in separate regions of the country. Since there are very many such groups around the world[179] there is an almost limitless reservoir of problems to draw upon. Since no state would like to say that it maintains an army in order to put down internal revolts and secessionist movements, external threats have to be invoked in rough proportion to the internal problems.

The conclusion is obvious: for societies to be less threatening to others they also have to become less threatening to their own citizens. Less trivial is the corollary, that outsiders are entitled, indeed have a duty, to be concerned about the internal conflicts of a given society. Such conflicts are found all over the world, across all kinds of conflict borders between countries, which means that they should appear on the agendas of intergovernmental conferences and organizations and be discussed openly, in part also as a way of preventing internal conflict from generating threatening military postures. Thus, the whole world has a right to know and discuss unemployment in the United States and minorities in the Soviet Union, lest they may spill over into international war.

Another important factor is found in well-known economic forces underlying arms production. Particularly important is the way in which the production system generates weapons even when there is no conceivable military need for them, simply because the production system has to produce and the decision-making system has to decide. A laboratory capacity made idle because it has already done the research needed for a new weapons system may be a source of threat to the scientists working there if they risk losing their jobs and to the administrator concerned about output and efficiency. The idle laboratory constitutes a production vacuum waiting to be filled with orders.[180]

Several strategies could be used to reduce the strength of this factor.

First, giving much lower priority to military purposes. A scientist boycott of military laboratory facilities (and their proliferating civilian counterparts) so that as few as possible are affected by "slacks" in the production process—and hence that much less motivated to generate new orders—would be highly useful.

Second, when laboratories are set up to fill a research need for the military, this need should be very precisely defined. It should be limited in time; and included in the contract should be plans for dismantling the laboratory after it has done its job and plans for the reentry into civilian life of all the parts, software and hardware. Everything should be done to avoid a situation whereby an empty military laboratory facility exists after the job has been done.[181]

Yet other factors are the privileges and broad social and political roles given to the military in many countries. As long as top military personnel in militarized countries have exceptionally good salaries and privileges (such as fringe benefits, service cars, excellent education opportunities, and special recreation facilities) it is scarcely reasonable to expect them to go in for a reduction. A society cannot at the same time try to persuade people *into* the military and phase the military *out of* society. It is difficult to recruit people into an institution about to be abolished. Some hypocrisy is needed, either about the recruitment or about the abolition. *Modern society has chosen the former; it should now be forced more in the direction of the latter.* More particularly, there should be less participation of the military in political life since this makes a society seem very threatening to the outside. Delegations to disarmament conferences, for instance, have too many military advisors, and the role accorded to top military in decisions leads to anxieties among those who seriously hope for measures to curb effectively the military machinery.

5.4.3 CONCLUSION

I am arguing that demilitarization be taken seriously. As it is carried on today, there is hardly any difference between armament and disarmament. Both are handled, by and large, by the same people, a military–civilian complex—perhaps more military in its composition when pure armament is on the agenda and a little less so when so-called disarmament is. The military, like anything else, is divided into sectors, and they cannot all grow at the same time. Besides, sectors wax and wane according to doctrine and technology, sometimes also according to objective external circumstances. This is perfectly normal and applies to all social institutions in a changing society; such are the rhythms of any institution. What is peculiar about the military institution is only that when a sector grows the process is called armament and when it does not it is called disarmament. The former term is correct; the latter is a far too dramatic term for perfectly normal pulsations in any institution, like the breathing exercise of a dinosaur.[182]

It is now high time that something be done about this institution, something beyond putting semantic labels on its pulsations. Otherwise, it may very well some day kill us all. Basically, as I have argued repeatedly, it is a question of doing something about the underlying conflict formations. But failing that, the measures discussed here may yet have some value, and it is in that spirit they are offered.

NOTES

References to *Essays* are to Johan Galtung, *Essays in Peace Research*, 5 vols. (Copenhagen: Ejlers, 1975–80) (Atlantic Highlands, N.J.: Humanities Press).

1. This would be what military analysts would be engaged in and is, of course, a highly technical subject.
2. One would imagine that this would be the task of the military historian and that it can only be done with reference to empirical data—in other words, with reference to the past.
3. This is the type of analysis carried out by, for instance, the International Institute of Strategic Studies, with its annual publication on the military balance.
4. This is the typical study carried out by, for instance, the Stockholm International Peace Research Institute, in its yearbooks.
5. The general idea would be that the world is in a sense divided into two parts: the unstable and the stable. There is insufficient understanding of how stability can blur the vision, of how years, generations of stability may lead to a certain qualitative change and eruption of violence.

6. This would be the typical leftist fallacy, based on the highly optimistic perception of man as being entirely conditioned by external structures when it comes to his exercise of violence.

7. One could think of the history of Western European colonial empires or the history of U.S.–Soviet relations after World War II.

8. In this phase there is a more complete integration of the two vertical blocs. Thus, as Tarsis Kabwegyere has pointed out, England was able to make even Uganda fight for her during World War II; and there is no doubt that during the Cold War NATO and WTO members would define what retrospectively would look like a fight for the interests of the United States and the Soviet Union as a fight in their own interest.

9. Thus, in the Cold War system contradictions between Center and Periphery countries became evident: Czechoslovakia pitted against the Soviet Union, the Mediterranean countries increasingly against the United States. What we have yet to see, however, is detachable conflict behavior at the periphery level—between, for instance, Greece and Bulgaria—without involving the total system.

10. The pattern becomes more and more disorderly: the Center on one side penetrates economically into the Periphery on the other side; the Center on the other side penetrates ideologically (through the Communist Party system) into the Periphery on the first side.

11. I am thinking here of the pattern of condominium to some extent established by the United States and the Soviet Union together, exercising considerable influence over all of their client nations—to some extent together. Another and perhaps better example would be the European Community relative to the fifty or so client countries emerging in the ACP system (Africa, Caribbean, Pacific), almost all of them former colonies of what were once highly competitive colonial powers.

12. This would take what was mentioned above even further, in the direction of some type of system by which a few powers (the United States, the European Community, the Soviet Union, Japan, China) would dominate the rest of the world. The general pattern is the same: there is some kind of liberation struggle from the Centers, after which the semiliberated Peripheries suddenly wake up to see that their former masters have joined together instead of disintegrated. Dialectically it is of course to be expected that if Periphery countries constitute economic, political, and/or military trade unions or blocs then the Center countries will do the same. Thus, in his famous speech in Kansas City, Missouri, on 6 July 1971, Richard Nixon said: "So, in sum, what do we see? What we see as we look ahead five, ten, and perhaps fifteen years, we see five great economic superpowers: the United States, Western Europe, the Soviet Union, Mainland China, and, of course, Japan. . . . These are the five that will determine the economic future, and because economic power will be the key to other kinds of power, the future of the world in other ways in this last third of this century."

13. This is very close to a tautology: for wars to last for some time and be registered as wars there has to be a certain equality in destructive capability. Periphery countries are increasingly developing this, and it is to be expected that we shall have more wars of the Algeria–Morocco, India–Pakistan, Honduras–El Salvador, and Vietnam–Kampuchea type, not to mention the Middle Eastern wars, in the near future. This theme is

developed in the important article by Istvan Kende, "Wars of Ten Years (1967–1976)," *Journal of Peace Research* (1978), pp. 227–41. Kende notes that "in the last two years the time-curve of Third World 'foreign' participation rose to a level higher than the time-curve not only of the colonists but of all the Western countries together. This again indicates that the newly-independent developing countries have acquired a new role in international politics" (p. 236).

14. At this stage one would imagine the possibility of confrontations between Latin America as a whole and the United States, between Africa as a whole and Western Europe, between Southeast Asia as a whole and Japan. The possibility of such wars being fought some time in the future with nuclear arms is far from negligible—as long as the Center countries of today do not clearly enough understand that their time is up, that it is no longer possible to insist on the privileges of past centuries.

15. East Pakistan was, of course, a part of the British Empire. When the British left, Punjabis moved into the holes left behind by the British. The result was a highly exploitative structure; it looked quiet and stable to the naive, but the result is well known. Two of the best analysts of this structure are K. P. Misra and Jorge d'Oliveira e Souza.

16. The present tendency to see conflicts mainly in terms of structures of dominance (also the basic tendency in the present book) often leads to an underestimation of the importance of *dissimilarity*, for instance racial, religious, and linguistic, as a basic factor behind conflict formations. Or, formulated more positively: it looks as if similarity in race, religion, language (or culture in general) may be a more solid factor of integration than the absence of exploitation, equity. One reason may be precisely that the former is a positive element and the latter is the absence of a negative factor.

17. The hypothesis is that this type of warfare will be increasingly significant as the second millennium after Christ comes to an end, even so much so that it could overshadow international warfare. The reason, formulated in one sentence: It is the natural reaction of a very complex human geography against the predominant political trend of the last centuries, the building of nation-states.

18. I am thinking of the way in which the United States created two centers for the expansion of not only economic but also highly political and military imperialism: one in the Caribbean and Central America, particularly in Cuba and Panama, and another in Southeast Asia using the Philippines as the bridgehead. Seen in retrospect it would probably have been highly advantageous for those countries not to have been "liberated" from the Spanish so that later on they would only have had a weak Spain to contend with, not the militarily strongest power in the world.

19. It would be interesting to find out how often imperialism is established under the pretext of "protecting" the satellite from somebody else's imperialism. See, for instance, the preceding note.

20. The Organization for Solidarity with the Peoples in Asia, Africa and Latin America, with its important journal *Tricontinental,* has a unique structure. It is not intergovernmental, nor is it inter-nongovernmental; it is inter-antigovernmental in tying together revolutionary movements pitted against capitalist imperialism all over the world.

21. I am indebted to J. Pajestka, of the Planning Commission in Warsaw, for this particular symbolism.

22. This type of parochialism seems to be equally shared between NATO and WTO powers, but also to be substantially eroded by the rise of the People's Republic of China.

23. The reason would simply be that vertical wars are reflections of what has been a stable, almost permanent state of affairs for a long time with only two rather fundamental changes: there have been increasing consciousness and increasing mobilization. Thus, people are prepared to sacrifice through years, even generations, of desire for liberation. A horizontal war comes more of a sudden, and although willingness to sacrifice may build up quickly, the ideological basis will be less comprehensive.

24. A typical example of this is the perspective so often encountered in connection with discussions of the Middle East: that the real problem in the Middle East is escalation into a world war. Of course, the real problem in the Middle East is that one group of people (Jews) have occupied the territory of another group of people (Palestinians), partly through economic power, partly with the ambivalent protection of the British, partly through the political power of the majority of the United Nations after World War II, and above all through military means.

25. The nonproliferation treaty (NPT) should be seen in this perspective: in a world of equality and equity small and poor countries might accept the idea that nuclear arms should be the monopoly of big and rich countries. But when at the same time size and economic strength are correlated with domination it looks different, for which reason the NPT is doomed to be a failure unless something is done with the structure of domination in the world.

26. Although Alva Myrdal makes use of this rhetoric in a highly persuasive way, I tend to see it as a waste of time. The underlying hypothesis is that the military race is somehow a misunderstanding and could come to an end through moral restraint. My assumption is that military races are related to conflict formations and can only come to an end when something is done to these conflict formations.

27. Senator Stuart Symington told the UN General Assembly on 21 October 1974 that the U.S. nuclear stockpile is equal to 615,385 atomic bombs of the type dropped on Hiroshima in 1945. It is also claimed that the United States has 7,000 nuclear bombs deployed in Europe and 3,000 in Asia, making a total of 10,000, to which one could add the estimate for the Soviet Union (2600), for China (200), for Britain (192), and France (86)—making a total of about 13,000 bombs. If the non-U.S. bombs are of the same average strength, it should make a total of 800,000 Hiroshima bombs, and the one Hiroshima bomb we know killed 200,000 people. Given the same "efficiency," the nuclear stockpile should be sufficient to kill 160 billion people, or forty times the world population.

28. It would be rather strange if the information should be accurate—since the data produced by spies, who are not necessarily the most reliable sources in the field, are also kept secret. In fact, we do not even know whether we are operating with underestimates or overestimates in the many yearbooks published in the field.

29. At this point a strong warning should be issued against an exaggerated

emphasis on the *Eigendynamik* approach to the theory of arms races. From the idea that such races are not necessarily only reactions to external stimuli, the perceived threats from the outside, it does not follow that they are only reactions to internal stimuli, for instance capitalistic or bureaucratic expansionism. There is ample space for both—and thinking in this field, rather than one single factor perspective substituted for another.

30. If any single person at the top level of executive political power should be singled out as responsible for this trend it would have to be John F. Kennedy—as pointed out by David Halberstam in *The Best and the Brightest.*

31. And in order to note that some kind of typology similar to the one developed in table 5.1 is indispensable.

32. There is a story of two slave dealers from Liverpool, uncle and nephew, and the conversation runs about as follows: "Uncle, I really do not like the trade we are engaging in. You know, we separate husband and wife, and mother and children; we mistreat them; many die on the way. . . ." "My dear nephew, I agree with you. But on the other hand slaves have to be sold and they have to be bought—and if we do not do it somebody else will do it." Needless to say the nephew did not dispute the basic premise of that conclusion; as little as do the arms dealers of today. The similarity with the mafia bosses in *The Godfather* is obvious.

33. This is of course to a large extent the result of projection: if one is oneself planning, or at least contemplating, "the worst possible behavior," then one would have to assume that the other party is willing to behave equally badly against oneself—otherwise one's own self-image would suffer irreparably.

34. By playing on this argument one hopes to stimulate the material interest of the masses in the countries devoting a high proportion of their GNP to arms races.

35. By means of this argument one hopes to stimulate the material interests of the developing countries who could make use of some of the resources used in the military races for their own development. But just as for the preceding argument the underlying assumption is that the military race somehow is based on a misunderstanding and is not inextricably linked to highly concrete conflict formations. Of course, there can be cuts, and there can be transarmaments into less capital-exhausting sectors; but in general it is a misunderstanding to believe that all these resources are up for grabs.

36. If one believes in Keynesian mechanisms, then the military sector, being a public sector, is obviously a possible instrument. However, it depends on the extent to which the military sector proliferates into the total economy, and the interconnections are probably much more widespread in a country like the United States—where so much of the civilian economy is somehow involved—than in the more compartmentalized economy of the Soviet Union. This might also serve to indicate that the U.S. economy would have more to lose from a disarmament than the Soviet economy—a point that would argue strongly in favor of the Soviet way of organizing the economy at this point. To this should be added the obvious idea that although the military race may serve as a stimulus locally, because of the

many spin-off effects, from a *global* point of view, adding all the national economies together, it is of course a tremendous waste of resources.

37. The argument would be that the military sector not only depletes raw materials, capital, and labor but also pollutes in the way all industrial production pollutes, not to mention through military warfare itself, as has been so amply demonstrated in the case of the Indochina wars.

38. The case in mind is not only the United States but also Japan; the idea, of course, stems from Galbraith. It should be pointed out that the converse is not the case: private poverty does not guarantee public affluence!

39. I am indebted to Alva Myrdal for this formulation.

40. What I am thinking of is that as the means of destruction increase in quality and quantity the system undergoes dramatic changes that we do not even understand. In all probability we still have not understood what it means to us to have nuclear arms in such quantities available; maybe it will only be understood by future generations.

41. This is actually true, even if there is no arms race going on, as long as there is economic growth and population growth; both of them constitute potentials available for destruction.

42. This distinction is due to Samuel Huntington.

43. On the one hand there are political and military strategists deducing needs for weapon systems; on the other hand there are researchers developing such weapon systems inducing from the systems the type of strategies to be pursued. Which trend is more important (they are no doubt dialectically related) is difficult to tell; it would probably have to do with the differential allocation of talent to the political/military versus the research sectors.

44. One new element was probably that this brought into power a new type of people: the defense intellectual, highly equipped with abstract thinking, with a language partially couched in mathematical terms that protected him from ever understanding the implications of what he was doing, leaving him totally cold to human suffering. Research-intensive weapons are accompanied by abstraction-intensive, a-human brains.

45. The important point here is that whereas there is a norm governing "balance" in the mechanical sense, there is no norm, only an everlasting discussion, as to what would constitute sufficient "excess capacity."

46. This is *a fortiori* true with the development of MIRV.

47. As a nonphysicist I remember the reaction by Pugwash physicists when I predicted this development in 1969: it was "impossible." But budget appropriations went very quickly in that direction. Thus, articles on laser technology in this connection appeared in the *International Herald Tribune*, 11 February 1972; the *New York Times*, 25 May 1972 ("Smart Bombs Used by U.S. Are Guided by Laser or TV"); the *New Scientist*, 13 July 1972 ("Laser for War," by R. Barkan); and *Time* magazine, 4 September 1972 ("Now, the Death Ray?")—to mention only some examples. See also the note in *Frankfurter Rundschau*, 2 July 1971, that Soviet scientists could not participate in the Lindau Nobel physics prize meeting, speculating that they were engaged in laser research.

48. SBM: Seaborne Ballistic Missiles.

49. It is very difficult to tell how far this has come, but it is probably one of

the factors underlying the difficulties in connection with the Law of the Sea conferences. There are certain military installations the superpowers would prefer others not to see, not even to know about.

50. This is, of course, technically completely possible. But it is nevertheless extraparadigmatic for the time being since so much of the thinking about nuclear war is tied to the idea that it has to be fought with missiles. For this reason one often reads about the Chinese as being "behind" because they are supposed not yet to have the missiles even though they have the bombs. The similarity to the idea that a German attack against France had to be across the German–French border and consequently run against the Maginot Line is obvious. Thus, it is quite possible that the heavy missiles will never be used; they will be circumvented, by-passed.

51. This is generally a very interesting feature of strategic theories: they look precise except for a couple of parameters that are absolutely basic to the system and for which there is no theory at all. This leaves the minister of defense more or less free in his plea for increased budgets.

52. Of course there is nothing new in the idea of "excess capacity"; what is new is probably the quasi-intellectualization, leaving a big gap that serves as a rationale for unlimited military expansion of destructive power.

53. This kind of madness can be understood only in the light of modern science: it requires a very high level of abstractionism—detachment from reality and particularly from humanity, from concrete human beings. Nobody with a deep attachment to fellow humans could devote his or her creative capacity in such directions. For one very useful survey of such weapons, see Erik Prokosh, *The Simple Art of Murder: Anti-Personnel Weapons and Their Developers* (NARMIC, 1972). Prokosh also contributed to the important work by SIPRI, *Anti-Personnel Weapons* (London: Taylor & Francis, 1978), written by Malvern Lumsden.

54. Or, something else, depending on where the zigzag pattern in figure 5.3 has led us at that point.

55. As it now stands Hitler serves as an excuse for the development of even post-Hitlerian measures. Perhaps this is the ultimate influence that man had: not the evil he wrought upon others, but Hitler as a point of reference, as someone who expanded our vision of what is possible so much that action one might otherwise abstain from suddenly looked reasonable, because it was presented as sub-Hitlerian.

56. This list, taken from Nigel Calder, is by now somewhat dated, but still serves as a good illustration.

57. What we do know is the development of the electronic battlefield.

58. I am indebted to Per Håkon Christiansen for this idea. If God wanted a way of proving not only his existence but also a fundamentally benevolent attitude to man, a good sign would be the demagnetization of all the tapes in military possession around the world—defining "military" broadly rather than narrowly.

59. There is hardly any better example of this today than the whole history of the Arab nation, and the subhistory of that Arab subnation, the Palestinians. For each day, it seems, political consciousness and effective organization are on the increase. When one adds to that the economic means that today can be used to support consciousness and organization the result, even relatively short term, in that part of the world is obvious.

60. This method constitutes a very good example of how similar Mao Tse-tung and M. K. Gandhi were in their ways of fighting.

61. Cuba and Algeria would be important examples here, as would also China—but the latter has had a "cultural revolution" that has served to counteract the reemergence of structural violence. As for the former it is still too early to tell.

62. Torture, not to mention the threat of torture, constitute the major instruments against consciousness formation, mobilization, and organization. Because they do this they should be counted as a part of the total military machinery. One should no longer think of military races without immediately including what happens in the basements under the prisons, the paramilitary, the various types of secret police organizations—for this is the most important part of the vertical warfare in its early stage.

63. See some of the references in note 65.

64. Unfortunately, the type of thinking reflected in publications from the ISS and SIPRI are still dominated by this type of warfare, although SIPRI publications are quickly changing in political perspective.

65. Most famous here is *Igloo White,* the whole family of electronic battle-field techniques; see, for instance, John L. Frisbee, "Igloo White," *Air Force Magazine* (June 1971), pp. 48ff., and *Investigation into Electronic Battlefield Program* (Washington: Government Printing Office, 1971). For Britain, see *The New Technology of Repression: Lessons from Ireland* (London: British Society for Responsibility in Science, 1974), reviewed by Jonathan Rosenhead in *New Scientist,* 16 May 1974. He mentions such methods as water cannons, CS, CR, rubber bullets, sound curdlers, and sensory deprivation interrogation. For Germany, see *Der Spiegel,* 2 July 1973, p. 16, indicating a budget of DM 17 million for antiriot equipment for Nordrhein–Westphalen alone.

66. For an analysis of this project, see Galtung, "Scientific Assistance and Neo-Colonialism," chapter 7 in *Papers on Methodology* (Copenhagen: Ejlers, 1979).

67. This is rather difficult to prove, though, since data are unreliable and certainly not organized that way; too many different agencies are involved!

68. This, then, is a typical example of choosing conflict formations, possible war theaters, rather than the structure and function of the war systems themselves as point of departure for analyses.

69. This is one of the basic differences between an actor-oriented and a structure-oriented perspective: the former asks for intentions in addition to capabilities, the latter is more concerned with how the total structure actually works.

70. The classical example of the prestige race is the race between Argentina and Brazil as to heavy battleships and aircraft carriers. But the Indian nuclear development can also be seen in this perspective: "Why do people pay attention to China now? Because she has the bomb. When will they start paying attention to India? When she has the bomb" (Indian defense intellectual at a seminar on international relations, Jawaharlal Nehru University, March 1971).

71. This is today a commonplace observation in connection with the U.S.–Soviet race.

72. The SIPRI analyses of arms trade are very important sources for further development of such hypotheses.

73. The famous *Report from the Iron Mountain*—hoax or not—lists the basic arguments in this connection.

74. In recent years close to 50 of the 150 or so countries in the world have had military regimes. This probably means that the military profession has now taken over from the legal profession as an avenue leading ultimately to political power.

75. This is the only positive function in the list—and is, of course, used as a figleaf function. Thus, Maxwell Taylor suggested that U.S. troops could be brought into Vietnam under the guise of flood relief operations.

76. It should be pointed out that this complex cannot be seen only in terms of profitmaking for capitalists. It should also be seen as a way of securing employment for labor, interesting jobs for researchers, taxes of various kinds for the government, and so on.

77. This is a crucial point: not only monopoly capitalism, big business, but also monopoly scientism, big academia, have a tendency to expand in all directions for the sake of expansion. Without the military sector the current overproduction of intellectuals, relative to what society can meaningfully absorb with the present structure of work, would make itself even more strongly felt.

78. David Halloway's article in *Journal of Peace Research* (1974, no. 4) is directed toward this point. If one accepts the idea of vested interest in preserving, possibly also expanding, rank and power, then it is hard to believe that arms manufacturers in a state capitalist economy would gladly see their own sector significantly reduced.

79. As any complex organization, the military will always have some internal disequilibria, between manpower, money available, and equipment. To obtain equilibrium between these "production factors" they will tend to adjust upward. The net result is growth, hence a military race—and the two sides to the race will have very similar interests in some kind of expansion.

80. See the analysis in Galtung, "Japan and Future World Politics," *Essays* V, 6, first published in *Journal of Peace Research* (1973), pp. 355-85.

81. The Soviet Union did not succeed in September 1972 but may succeed now, using naval power rather than nuclear bases—in other words, the old British strategy.

82. As a matter of fact, I would even say that it is *too* well known, that it is overanalyzed rather than underanalyzed and that it thus detracts attention from the much more important analysis of its relation to conflict formations.

83. I have in mind here Sweden and Switzerland as arms producers and India as arms consumer.

84. Any analysis of demilitarization becomes incomplete unless one tries to gain some insight into how the proponents of the system will try to defend themselves against such attacks. This is rather obvious: no profession, no sector of society, would fail to react with counteroffensives when large segments of domestic and global society start talking about their abolition, gradually or quickly.

85. Thus, attempts to introduce long-term growth planning in the military sector should be fought, precisely because they tend to freeze the growth pattern and make the system less flexible, less able to contract if a new situation (meaning a situation where conflicts have been resolved or are in the process of being resolved) should arise.

86. See Galtung, "Functional Analysis in a New Key," chapter 5 in *Methodology and Ideology* (Copenhagen: Ejlers, 1977), particularly the analysis of the difference among conservative, liberal, and radical functionalism. Characteristic of liberal functionalism is the idea of accepting the functions but providing for much flexibility and variation when it comes to structures. If one structure has one unfortunate consequence, then the answer is to find another without that consequence, not to question the entire set of functions (which would be more characteristic of radical functionalism).

87. This conservative bias is the typical outcome of developing an analytical instrument having in mind relatively stable societies, or societies believed to be relatively stable.

88. Here, of course, it does not help that the two superpowers want to join and cooperate in the space race, organizing themselves into a joint venture for world domination.

89. This, of course, was already implemented in 1963. Its limitation was very clear; it permitted underground testing, and consequently even served to legitimize such testing.

90. The limitation of this approach was and is equally clear: it permits existing possession and production, which at the time of the treaty was limited to the five big powers—thus legitimizing their power status in the world.

91. The limitation of SALT 1 was very clear: it permitted an expansion in the number of warheads, thus legitimizing the search for new types of multiple-targeted missiles and also for stronger warheads. The limitation of SALT 2 is probably the inability to give equal weight to the negation approach. With parity in the sum of ICBMs, SLBMs, ALCMs (bombers with cruise missiles), land- and sea-based single-warhead missles (including some MIRVs), and bombers without cruise missiles, further innovation in the field of antiweapons will upset the balance completely.

92. The limitation of this approach seems, at the time of writing, to be more quantitative: it is a question of reductions in the order of magnitude of 5 to 10 percent—which seems disproportionately low relative to the reduction in tension in Europe, certainly considerably more than 5 or 10 percent. See Galtung, "European Security and Cooperation: A Skeptical Contribution," *Essays* V, 2, first published in *Journal of Peace Research* (1975), pp. 165-78.

93. One wonders, however, whether this type of information any longer makes the slightest impact on people—since its news value is about as high as reports about rain in Ireland, or murder in Detroit, or military coups in Latin America.

94. I am indebted to Professor Levy of Louvain University for the expression that "diplomacy is the continuation of war with other means."

95. And the most dramatic example so far is SALT 1, where it is even explicitly permitted (Articles 4 and 7 of these soon-to-be-forgotten docu-

ments make use of the term "may") to change the content of the warheads in accordance with technological development. The Vladivostok accords of late 1974 were even more incredible in this regard, permitting both the United States and the Soviet Union to replace first-generation missiles with missiles with multiple warheads, giving to the Soviet Union an estimated 6,700 warheads instead of its previous 1,400 and to the United States 11,000 large MIRV warheads rather than 5,000 smaller ones. Most important, "Mr. Ford . . . proclaimed at his news conference not only a 'right' ,but an 'obligation' to increase the American strategic offensive missile and bomber forces to the new permitted levels of 2,400 delivery vehicles, of which 1,320 may be missiles equipped with MIRV multiple warheads" (*New York Times* editorials, 5 and 19 December 1974). In other words, an obligation to *arm*.

96. For an analysis of this, see the excellent series by I. F. Stone in the *New York Review of Books,* 9 April, 23 April, 7 May 1970: "A Century of Futility," "Theatre of Delusion," and "The Test Ban Comedy." In the last article (p. 7) Stone points out how testing went up after the partial test ban treaty: there were 98 U.S. tests in the eighteen years from 1947 until 5 August 1963 and 210 tests in the seven years from 1963 to 1970. This is how ABM and MIRV were developed. But then PTB, as well as NPT, were primarily intended to keep China out.

97. In Pugwash circles dampening factors in the order of magnitude of above 99 percent in the seismic signals after suitable cavities had been made were quoted—in private communication—as early as 1967.

98. This is the method used in the Anglo-Dutch-German consortium in the Netherlands, and hence of potential use for the European Community. See Galtung, *The European Community: A Super-Power in the Making* (London: Allen & Unwin, 1973), chap. 8.

99. This is the method that seems to be favored in Japan.

100. Such methods have been developed in Japan and in South Africa, and definitely also many other places. The point is not so much their geographical distribution as the naiveté underlying the refusal to understand that there will be generations of technologies in the nuclear field (as in other fields) as long as this type of research continues. Nevertheless, for a long time politicians were talking as if the costs of building a gas diffusion plant constituted an effective barrier against nuclear proliferation!

101. Thus, it should be compared to the naval agreements before the war where the directions of future armament were also clearly indicated; only that instead of packing the ships more densely the superpowers are now packing the missiles more densely.

102. The general formula here seems to be transarmament; neither armament nor disarmament, but armament in another direction.

103. For discussion of duels as ways of solving conflicts, see Sivert Langholm, "Violent Conflict Resolution and the Loser's Reaction: A Case Study from 1574," *Journal of Peace Research* (1965), pp. 324‑47. For a more general theory in this connection, see Galtung, "Institutionalized Conflict Resolution," *Essays* III, 14, first published in *Journal of Peace Research* (1965), pp. 348‑97.

104. The distinction between social and territorial military defense is developed in Galtung, "Two Concepts of Defence," *Essays* II, 13, first published in 1964.

105. This is a general argument in this section: the more the world in general and societies in particular move in certain directions defined in this book as positive (that is, toward realization of the goals set forth in chapter 2), the more will the type of defense compatible with these values be possible.

106. This theme is developed in some detail in section 8.3.

107. Important work has been done in this field by such authors as Adam Roberts, Bengt Höglund, A. Mack, and A. Boserup, not to mention the leading author in the field, Gene Sharp. See also the classic in the field, Krishnalal Sridharani, *War without Violence* (Bombay: Bharatiya Vidya Ghavan, 1962).

108. This doctrine, Gandhi's doctrine, presupposes very much in terms of direct contact between the antagonists and in terms of one's willingness to suffer, and it is based on considerable optimism when it comes to the possibility of suffering to "stir sluggish consciences."

109. This point was made in the Norwegian debate in the late 1940's by Professor Arne Naess. It is of course more true for older Western countries, particularly for the smaller ones, than for "developing" countries. Thus, if the spectrum of "nonviolence" consisted only of NMD, it could be seen as a doctrine of the right; if it consisted only of NRV, as a doctrine of the left. Including both, nonviolence transcends in a certain sense that rather worn-out distinction.

111. This parallel with military strategic thinking is of course no coincidence; the presentation is made on purpose in such a way that the similarities become apparent. This, incidentally, also extends to alliance formation. "Attack against one of us will be considered attack against us all" could also apply to countries basing themselves more on nonmilitary defense. Of course, the major battle would have to be in the country attacked; the others would be restricted to diplomatic and economic boycott, possibly coordinated by a UN agency for NMD!

112. When it comes to physical property, there is probably considerable disagreement among the adherents of nonviolence. We view the destruction of physical property as very much less important than taking human lives, but it is important to contemplate that when intellectuals have this attitude it is usually because they are thinking of economic property, windowpanes in shops, luxury items, and such means of repression as military files of conscripts and police records. The attitude of intellectuals may change if one instead thinks in terms of destruction of books, scientific data, museums, and cultural relics of different kinds.

113. Points such as these are developed in some detail in Galtung, "On the Strategy of Non-military Defence: Analysis and Recommendations." *Essays* II, 15.

114. The reader will find it developed in section 4.3 and also in section 3.4—in connection with the general chart of strategies.

115. From this, however, does not follow that human beings will always under all circumstances do such things unless impeded from doing so, as indicated in section 3.3.

116. This theme is very well developed in Theresa Hayter, *Aid as Imperialism* (Penguin, 1972). At this point Gandhi was a great master, in distinguishing between the antagonism and the antagonist. The Chinese, too, are proficient: a sharp distinction is drawn between the contradictions in

capitalist society and the necessity of destroying that society on the one hand but, on the other, of utilizing the capitalist as a person (who can enter socialist society on a fixed salary, using his capacities).

117. Gandhi's distinction (see the preceding note) presupposes at least some kind of communication with the antagonist, some way of making clear to him that he is seen as a potential friend and even ally in the fight against the antagonism. For a discussion, see Galtung and Arne Naess, *Gandhis Politiske Etikk* (Oslo: Tanum, 1955).

118. Once more, I would like to point out how nonmilitary defense differs from military defense in this regard. In order to make nonmilitary defense as efficient as possible, society has to become maximally democratic, and one has to play up to the best in people. In order to make military defense effective, much more autocratic, even fascist structures are called for. Both of them, however, call on heroism and sacrifice.

119. This is of course already done by the military, for instance, as emergency food reservoirs for shipwrecked and airwrecked people.

120. I am indebted to Professor Arne Naess for this felicitous term. Again it should be pointed out how much Gandhi was a master in designing his campaigns so that the goals were very clearly communicated.

121. This is offensive civil disobedience as opposed to the defensive civil disobedience known as noncooperation. In either case there is a concept of institutions as never belonging to any "owner." At most, those at the top of institutions where others work, or live, hold these institutions in trust. If they fail to live up to their obligations, it is not only the right but also the duty of the others to empty the institution, possibly to occupy it and redesign it in the direction it should be run. The best examples of the latter are, of course, occupation of unused or misused land and empty houses by the landless and houseless.

122. This was done in Prague immediately after the Soviet intervention, and the impression gained was that the only preparation on which the Czechs could draw was made by the military in case of nuclear attack. Emergency plans for that situation (it was, of course, imagined that the attack would come from the West!) included detailed plans and facilities for mass communication, and they were made use of.

123. For the use of these terms, see Galtung, "A Structural Theory of Integration," *Essays* IV, 11, first published in *Journal of Peace Research* (1968), pp. 375–95.

124. Again the same point: the positive feedback between the effectiveness of nonviolence and the democratization of the society.

125. Of course, in social theory and practice, things are always complicated. Take Hitler's excess: some of it was rooted in international and social structure, but there have been other countries in similar situations without the same consequences, fortunately. In all cases of aggression there will be a mixture of these factors; the dogmatic stands on either side would be to insist that aggression is either structural or innate.

126. And essentially this is the theory of power given in section 2.4, based on self-respect, self-sufficiency, and fearlessness.

127. Those who argue in favor of the old strategies, unfortunately, are found not only in ministries of foreign affairs and defense but also very often in the peace movement. The latter sometimes differs from the former only

in insisting that one should move along those roads more quickly, not in questioning the roads or approaches. The dilemma of peace research is that peace researchers often become alienated from either when presenting what they conceive of as new insights.

128. The same distinction is made use of in section 4.4.

129. For an analysis of this, see Galtung, "Two Approaches to Disarmament: The Legalist and the Structuralist," *Essays* II, 3, first published in *Journal of Peace Research* (1967), pp. 161–95, esp. p. 169.

130. By and large, it may probably be stated as a relatively well established proposition that efforts to control disarmament and arms control processes have been given up.

131. And the geographical parameters are problematic. The United States insists that it is advantageous for the Soviet Union to be close to a possible battlefield in central Europe; the Soviet Union insists that it is advantageous for the United States to be so far away! Of course, they are both right; it all depends on what kind of war and what phase of the war.

132. It is also characteristic that the MFR negotiations seem to be relatively stalemated.

133. Particularly at the Conference on European Security and Cooperation.

134. For a discussion, see Galtung, "Two Approaches to Disarmament: The Legalist and the Structuralist," *Essays* II, 3.

135. This possibility, using the population as a control agent, is discussed in some detail (and with largely negative conclusions) in Galtung, "Popular Inspection of Disarmament Processes: The Reaction of a Norwegian Population Sample," *Essays* II, 8.

136. This, of course, is the major point around which Solzhenitsyn's brilliant *First Circle* is built.

137. A truly representative (along the lines suggested in section 8.1) world disarmament conference, possibly even on a biannual or triannual basis, might be helpful here.

138. See section 6.3 for more details.

139. Even with the best of political will this would be impossible. It has to be recognized that military machineries, where both hardware and software are concerned, are built into modern societies in such an intricate and interwoven way that a considerable inertia is created—some of it no doubt deliberately.

140. For if experience is to be one guide, and it should to some extent be, all the reflections in section 1.4 notwithstanding, to try both at the same time seems like a good example of letting the best be the enemy of the good.

141. This is, of course, the perennial argument in connection with the effort to establish Israel as a state in the midst of Arab territory. It is hard to see that the argument can have that much validity with the use of airplanes for war purposes being already more than half a century old. It is not easy: the Indian Ocean is also at present far from being a "zone of peace." See the report to the General Assembly, *Declaration of the Indian Ocean as a Zone of Peace* (A/AC.159/1/Rev. 1).

142. At Pugwash conferences and in other settings. Maybe it should be pointed out once more that the basic idea in this connection—and a successful one!—was the whole concept of nonalighment as spearheaded by Tito,

Nehru, and Nasser—as it means precisely withdrawal from a field of military engagement. There is, however, nothing to prevent the nonligned from becoming their own alliance, for instance against a NATO–WTO combination.

143. This would also include moves toward more people-intensive, less capital-intensive armies—based more on local and less on general national defense.

144. The best, of course, would be to make the army less capital-intensive and people-intensive at the same time, which brings us back to the argument in note 140.

145. See sections 6.3 and 8.3.

146. Here the superpowers may, incidentally, make a wrong calculation, thinking that they will preserve the major breakthroughs in the negotiations for themselves. They may one day discover that the SALT system of negotiated deals is regarded by the world as very much inferior to other outcomes of the total negotiation exercise.

147. See Galtung, "Big Powers and the World Feudal Structure," *Essays* IV, 10.

148. Of course, the interventions within the socialist world have been given more publicity, on the average, and are more readily integrated into the Western conceptual framework than the others. This, however, is not to belittle the significance both of the permanent interventions (by having the Red Army stationed on one's soil) and of the more intermittent ones in the CMEA system during the last twenty-five years or so. For general observations on socialist war participation, see Istvan Kende, "Wars of Ten Years (1967–1976)," *Journal of Peace Research* (1978), pp. 227–41, esp. p. 236.

149. This is elaborated further in section 8.1, where the major task of the world central authority is seen as a provider of adequate fora for articulation—solutions having ultimately to be more local.

150. The most famous so far was the system of nongovernmental conferences organized in connection with the human environment conference in Stockholm in June 1972.

151. That series of yearbooks should be seen in terms of the excellent contribution they offer to make the world somewhat more transparent rather than in terms of the obvious that they do not tell the whole story, being weak both on theory and on structural violence.

152. This faith seems to be very deeply rooted in people of the Fabian Society variety, who somehow believe in the rationality of man and in the power of intellectuals while ignoring the significance of consciousness in a deeper sense of mobilization, of dreams and utopias, not to mention of *power*.

153. And that ritualism is highly compatible not only with losing sight of the goal but actually with working in a manner that is counterproductive to the goal of disarmament.

154. But it may also be one way of burying them effectively, having as an excuse that one knows where they are buried.

155. No doubt this was an important factor in the 1960's: the idea that the world economy as a whole, and that of developing countries in particular, could benefit from disarmament in a significant manner. One important argument against this faith can be obtained by comparing what goes into the satisfaction of basic material needs on the one hand and what goes

into the satisfaction of the demands by military people on the other. The latter tend to demand capital, research, the products of industrial sophistication, whereas the satisfaction of basic needs actually requires very little capital, research, and metal/mineral-based industrial products.

156. As president of the Norwegian branch of the War Resisters' International (Folkereisning Mot Krig), I had occasion to observe how easily one local chapter combined their pacifist attitude with their work in a Norwegian factory mainly concerned with producing barrels for heavy artillery: "We must make our living on something." Examples from scientist/researchers who combine their ideological conviction with work for organizations that contribute actively to just the opposite of what they profess, using the rationalization that "I do this to gain experience," are countless.

157. One should not be too mesmerized by the figures of researchers working for such establishments. It is the willingness to join any kind of anti-human project in the name of national defense that counts.

158. This theme is taken up in a more general context in section 8.4.

159. This was done quite successfully by university groups in connection with the participation of U.S. scientists in the Vietnam wars. Thus, the members of the Jason Division, a technical advisory organ of the Pentagon doing research on chemical and bacteriological warfare, military applications of lasers, counterinsurgency, and electronic battlefield techniques, were blacklisted by the Collectif Intersyndical Universitaire d'Orsay under the slogan "Do not let the war professors speak of 'pure' physics until they have denounced their participation in Jason and condemned publicly the American war crimes." Actions were also taken by members of the American Physical Society against the war involvement; see, for instance, the *New York Times,* 1 May 1969.

160. The difficulty here is, of course, the high level of homogeneity and fraternal protectionism in academic communities. Those who bestow such awards on people are usually not very different from those who get them, and for that reason they are not too likely to differ very much in values.

161. There are exceptions, such as the famous case of the Lukacs air industries in Britain where the workers asked for advice as to how the industries could be restructured with a view to producing more acceptable products. And there are other examples to the contrary. The *International Herald Tribune,* 16–17 January 1971, carried a short article, "Italian Workers Refuse to Make Arms for NATO," reporting that "850 workers of an Italian factory that has supplied arms to the North Atlantic Treaty Organization warned their employer today that they will make no more weapons of any kind." Their resolution reads: "The problem of peace and disarmament concerns workers too, and since peace is the supreme interest, we warn our company against accepting orders for material aimed at armed violence, of which we do not want to become accomplices."

162. The idea also serves to protect intellectuals from realizing how different the value profiles of the "masses" often are from what they postulate. The consequence of that, however, is not to stop postulating certain values, but not to entertain illusions as to the level of support that will be automatically forthcoming from the people in general.

163. This is one of the major outcomes of the social science contribution to the U.S. war effort in World War II, as related in *The American Soldier:* a utilization of the finest human values and emotions, to protect and also to

avenge one's friends, to increase the "productivity" in wars. No doubt it works.

164. A major point in Galtung, "Science as Invariance-seeking and Invariance-breaking Activity," chapter 3 in *Methodology and Ideology* (Copenhagen: Ejlers, 1977).

165. Is it any victory over the military system to obtain permission to grow one's hair to the length of one's choice or to be able to claim overtime pay for exercising (ultimately also for fighting) after regular working hours, with double overtime for weekends and nights? It is difficult to say—maybe more experience is needed to see how this turns out—but, intuitively, one is doubtful; it seems best to be rather skeptical.

166. One reason why the feudal analogy is a good one is precisely that the feudal unit was so well protected against penetration from the outside, constituting a closed system with its own jurisdiction.

167. The Inquisition must have appeared as an almost eternally valid institution in its time, however, having as its rationale such an obviously legitimate task as that of fighting evil, not unlike the military, and sharing with the latter the consent, even blessing, of most of the establishment.

168. On the other hand, if taken seriously, such rules might be useful from the point of view of demilitarization in times of economic contraction, particularly in times of depression.

169. In an economy based on a higher level of local self-reliance the population would have more power simply because it could survive without depending on centrally produced goods with taxation built into the price structure.

170. This was an anarchist group, the Spies for Peace. Communist groups would probably have some hesitation since their argument with a centralized structure is only that they do not control it, not that it is centralized. For an account, see "The Spies for Peace Story," *Anarchy* 29 (1963), pp. 197–228.

171. The major function of the Vietnam War was perhaps precisely this: some kind of mystique was broken—for a long time, one might hope. The Western democracies could no longer be seen as necessarily fighting for worthy causes.

172. I am indebted to Bengt Höglund and Theodor Ebert for this felicitous expression.

173. Most countries, perhaps all, would be unable to stand up nonviolently against Nazi Germany, just as most countries would not be able to stand up militarily against the United States or the Soviet Union. Fortunately, most combinations of potential war antagonists are less fatal; and it is particularly important that Hitler's Germany not be permitted to dominate our thinking too much, since it was, we hope, an extreme case in Western history.

174. One of the founders of peace research in Europe, Professor B. V. A. Röling of Groningen University, is engaged in this type of research.

175. One positive development in recent disarmament thinking and practice is precisely a move in this direction, asking not for destruction of what has been difficult and costly to produce but for making it less threatening.

176. One good topic to be discussed: about what proportion of the population would the military be ready to sacrifice before any kind of capitulation?

A significant step forward will be made the moment such problems can be discussed openly and are no longer surrounded by massive taboo protection.

177. This is not strange, given the social position and the value profiles of those who usually carry out such studies. They are so tied to the establishment that a more detached view of their own societies, including the possibility of applying intrasystem perspectives, is not only unlikely but almost impossible. If something is wrong, reasons are found either in the antagonist or in the world system, for which they feel they have less of a responsibility.

178. Kuhn's famous work, *The Structure of Scientific Revolution* (Chicago: University of Chicago Press, 1970), is entirely relevant here.

179. See section 6.2.

180. It would be hard on a director of such a laboratory to ask him not to look for orders. For that reason, such laboratories must either be dismantled or given new functions. As an example, consider that then U.S. Deputy Defense Secretary David Packard once wanted to "enable major contractors to keep most of their skilled designers and engineers together rather than breaking up experienced teams when they lost out on a contract to another concern, only to have to gather a new team when starting to compete a year or two later on a major program." The method: "the Soviet practice of keeping several designing teams working all the time on new aircraft, missiles and other weapons" (*International Herald Tribune,* 13 August 1973).

181. There are several formulas here, but only those that do not involve destruction or dismissal should be taken seriously. Thus, a laboratory might be a component in a bigger research system immediately capable of giving it other and nonmilitary tasks.

182. The dinosaur, however, like the Inquisition, ultimately disappeared from the face of the earth.

6. THE TERRITORIAL SYSTEM

6.1 GROWTH IN THE TERRITORIAL SYSTEM

We now return to the problem formulated in section 1.3: the future of the territorial system. We shall first look at the possibility of *growth* in the system, then at the possibility of *fission,* and finally at the possibility of *fusion*; all the time guided by the perspectives of liberation from dominance and security against war.

One significant aspect about the territorial system today is that it is coming up against limits. At the end of the fifteenth century one would not have spoken in such terms: the possibilities of growth—of the expansion of old actors and the creation of new actors—were tremendous because the territory available was constantly expanding with the Great Discoveries.[1] Today, humankind will have to go outside the globe we inhabit to have a similar experience. This forces upon us an analysis at a higher level, adding an interglobal system to the international system we have today. But the Apollo and Soyuz moon landings so far have only demonstrated very clearly how *dependent* a moon colony would be on Mother Earth even for such elementary life-ingredients as oxygen and water. A Moon Colony viable enough to launch a "Moon Tea Party" seems rather unlikely; its oxygen supply might be cut off, although there are claims that both oxygen and water may be produced from lunar soil.[2]

This, however, does not mean that the possibilities of growth are zero. More precisely, there are three ways in which new territorial actors may come into being on this earth without affecting those that exist.

First, there are still close to seventy territories (most of them with fewer than one million inhabitants, according to a UNITAR report[3]) that are not states (national actors) because they are nonself-governing territories,[4] trust territories,[5] states in association,[6] disputed parts of federations,[7] overseas territories integrated with metropolitan states,[8] and the like. Many of these are in the category of prospective mini-states,[9] and it is important to have a clear conception of them, of to what extent they should enjoy full UN membership, and so on. However, it is not felt that their impact will be of really major significance in the world of today, except perhaps in some regions such as southern Africa (where independent Angola and independent Mozambique became significant factors in changes in the balance of power[10]) and, perhaps, in Oceania.[11]

Second, there is the possibility of inhabiting and developing into an actor territory that is either unclaimed or has such a low level of claims on it that it almost does not count among the existing territorial actors. I am thinking of certain isolated islands in the polar areas, the Antarctic territory, Greenland and Spitsbergen, and so on.[12] There are also some desert territories around the world, some of them even referred to as "neutral" territory.[13] It is well known that any move to lay claim on them would be met with heavy reaction from some territorial actor, and this could in itself change them into real actors. Since the areas in question are (almost completely) dormant, undeveloped and unpopulated, one can meaningfully talk in terms of the birth of new territorial actors. New technologies for water supply and cultivation may actuate this dormant possibility because of the pressures from overpopulation.[14]

Third, there is the possibility of going outside traditional land territory, invading outer space, air space, and the oceans by establishing permanent space platforms, floating cities, and underwater colonies,[15] and there is the possibility of reclaiming land. Because of the expensive technology needed, the latter possibility would probably merely lead to expansion of already existing, over-populated, rich countries like the Netherlands and Japan[16] rather than to the formation of new ones. But the other possibilities might, like space platforms, not be contiguous with existing countries and could lead to interesting constellations if they were established by nonterritorial actors and not simply controlled by some rich state. Such control would, of course, add to the power potential of that state, e.g., by controlling water, air, and space transport, and to new patterns of colonization of ocean and space rather than ground. It might also set us back many centuries in terms of the possibilities of free travel and place a barrier of ownership between us all and the remaining free nature, air, and water.[17] But there is also the possibility that this development could lead to new actors, which might even experiment with new forms of social life and contribute to peace through a strengthening of the nonterritorial system outside the control of the territorial system.[18] Thus, so far every nonterritorial organization has had to put its physical headquarters down on *land* territory belonging to a territorial actor, with Vatican City as a partial exception.[19] A location in the other two elements might decrease the dependence on states, and underline the nonterritorial character of these organizations.

However, it is difficult to see that such measures, singly or even combined, would affect the territorial system or the world system in general in any really significant way in the near future. The world system has a high capacity for coopting what is new, particularly if it comes from the periphery. Even a UN headquarters located on an ocean or a space platform, which would presuppose that some fundamentally new technology were invented, would be an important symbol rather than a qualitatively new reality. Much more is to be expected from the next two possibilities: fission and fusion. *For the territorial system has basically reached its limits; it is through internal change, not through expansion that qualitative changes are likely to come about.*

6.2   FISSION IN THE TERRITORIAL SYSTEM

I shall start by discussing fission, in the sense of disintegration of already existing countries, drawing on the theory of dominance developed in chapter 4. Actually, the dominance relation is often more complete inside a country than between countries, partly because there has been more time to establish it, but mainly because control is better since communication and transportation are both easier. Contiguity facilitates dominance, but also the fight against it, which is one reason why internal wars so often look more cruel than external wars.[20]

However, a relation of dominance, counteracting equity and diversity inside a country, is not enough to yield a basis for understanding secessionist tendencies—in other words, fission. Dominance in the sense I conceive of it, based on exploitation, penetration, and more integration on the top than at the bottom, is found in all societies I know of, in one form or another. It may lead to class war, to revolution, but such a war is a struggle for control over one country, not a secessionist effort to split a country into two or more parts.

A relation of dominance seems to be a necessary rather than a sufficient condition for a secessionist struggle. In addition to this structural factor there seem to be territorial and nonterritorial components at work as well, i.e., *geographical segregation* and *racial and/or ethnic differences.* Often the dominators live close together in one part of the country and the dominated in another; the dominated belong to one racial and/or ethnical group (depending on whether they share biological and/or cultural characteristics[21]), the dominated to another. The territorial segregation may indicate the possible future borders of new *states,* the nonterritorial characteristics may define the difference between two *nations.*[22]

In short, I am basing a theory of secession on three factors:

1. A *relation of dominance,* establishing dominator and dominated;
2. A *high correlation* between the dominator-dominated dimension and geographical location;
3. A *high correlation* between the dominator-dominated dimension and some racial and/or ethnical dimension.

In simple terms, there are an upper class and a lower class that belong to different racial or ethnic groups and live in different parts of the country. These conditions obtain in many parts of the world, in the order of magnitude of 10^3 rather than the order of magnitude of the present number of states, which is only 10^2. Hence, the possibilities of fission seem extremely numerous.[23] The conditions define a situation of latent secessionism rather than manifest struggle, which is found in a far more limited number of cases.[24] But dominance is found all over the world and is often correlated with location, particularly in the important urban–rural relationship, and very often due to a prehistory of colonialism (not necessarily white) with racial–ethnic differences.[25]

To understand this phenomenon better let us look at the obvious counter-strategies against secessionist tendencies. The amateur strategy would be cruel repression of all the symptoms of manifestation, from killing freedom of expression and symbols of nationalism to killing people.[26] The professional strategy would be to eliminate one of the three factors.

First, there might be the attempt to build a state without any relations of dominance. Whether under socialism or capitalism this has proved difficult unless the units are very small, which would in itself point toward fission.[27]

The second possibility would be to spread the dominant group in a thin or thick layer all over the nation so that there is little or no correlation of status with residence, only with race–ethnicity. This is the solution attempted in such different countries as the United States, most Latin American countries that are racially mixed, Ethiopia, the Soviet Union, and so on.[28] In the British tradition it can even be combined with some kind of parliamentarism, depriving the dominated of the right to vote if the layer is too thin (Rhodesia)[29] or drawing borders so that a dominant majority is guaranteed (Ulster).[30] However, it is very difficult to make the correlation with territory disappear completely. Usually there will be pockets with high concentrations of the privileged and high concentrations of the underprivileged, in the poor districts of cities and in the countryside. When we speak of high correlation with location what we really mean is low entropy, a sorting of the groups, in two parts of the country.[31] But the parallel with relations between countries is important here: cities may exploit villages in exactly the same way as Center countries exploit Periphery countries: *colonización interna.*[32]

Then there is a third possibility, that of reducing the correlation between position in the dominance system and race or ethnicity. This is done all over the world: it is referred to as desegregation, is an important aspect of social justice, and takes the form of some type of proportionate representation in government, in the police forces, in top military circles, and the like.[33] This may or may not be combined with an effort to eradicate every kind of residential segregation whether it is between districts, inside districts but between towns, or even inside towns.

All these strategies are being tried in various forms in many parts of the world today. Europeans have a tendency to see Africa as a region split by "tribalism" (the word for nationalism outside European nations), quoting such figures as the existence of 6,000 tribes in total, 120 of them in Tanzania alone.[34] The tendency is to forget the time and the blood it has taken to sort nations in Europe and that the degree of sorting today found in that peninsula of the Asian continent is still very far from perfect—nations are still split, states are still multinational.

I am thinking, of course, of such European phenomena as the movements in the United Kingdom (Northern Ireland, Scotland, Wales), in Spain (Cataluna, Galicia, Pais Valenciane, Euzkadi), in France (Bretagne, Alsace, Corse and Occitanie), in Switzerland (Jura), in Italy (Tirol), in Belgium (the Flemish, the Walloons), and the Lapps. And outside Europe: Canada (Quebec), Sudan (the South), Ethiopia (Eritrea), Chad (various groups), Nigeria (Biafra), Pakistan (Bangladesh), Sri Lanka (the Tamils), India (the Nagas, etc.), New Zealand (the Maoris)—to mention just a few.[35] These examples, incidentally, also show that it is not necessarily the dominated group that wishes to secede. It may also be a dominant but small group that feels disinclined any longer to subsidize the rest, like Biafra (and Sào Paulo in the 1930's).[36]

Other examples would involve more nations, such as Kurdistan (Syria, Iraq, Iran, Turkey, the Soviet Union) or a possible future Lapponia (Norway, Sweden, Finland). The latter sounds highly implausible because of the low level of political consciousness among the Lapps, but that may change.[37] It is well known that Africa is full of such examples, and a relatively good picture of the potentials in this direction can be obtained by placing a transparent *tribal* map on top of a *political* map of Africa to record systematically the almost complete lack of coincidence between borders.[38] The same applies to many parts of Asia, such as India;[39] but much less to Latin America.[40]

It is hardly farfetched to assume that the relative peace and quiet at the moment observed in the three major powers of the world, the United States,[41] the Soviet Union,[42] and China,[43] or in various territories in Western[44] and Eastern Europe,[45] is relatively artificial and that some time later in the 1980's we may hear much more from secessionist initiatives. As the conditions are present, the conflict exists in latent form—and in the Soviet Union also at the manifest level. One used to think that where the European scene is concerned a final peace treaty for Europe might even serve to stimulate intransigent independence movements,[46] since thirty years' absence of such a treaty left a certain flexibility that might have given some hope to some potential leaders of such movements. But I would like to add that the arguments in favor of the final act of Helsinki recognizing the present borders seemed more significant.

The question is how one should regard such movements from the political and from the theoretical points of view. Evidently, from the point of view of what can be referred to as naive theory, according to which there has been a by-and-large uninterrupted expansion toward ever-larger regions with important world centers as foci of crystallization, this secessionist tendency is retrogressive, a step backward to something that was left behind years ago.

However, as is so often pointed out by the leaders of secessionist movements, this perspective, often expressed in terms of the lofty ideals of world peace, is typically a perspective held in the predominant power centers of the world. In the old Center of the world the crystallization into ethnically relatively homogeneous nation-states has to some extent taken place, and since the Center of the world has solved its problems there is a tendency to believe that these problems have been solved also for the world as a whole.[47] To paraphrase Marx: *the leading problems are the problems of the leading nations.* The Periphery, and also the periphery of the Center, will say "Why do we have less right to align ethnical and national borders than those old nations had one decade, one century, or one millennium ago?" It is difficult to deny the validity of that argument, as when elements in the Black Power movement in the United States talk seriously about secession from white United States or if the Central Asian republics in the Soviet Union should start a serious confrontation with Moscow.[48]

To take another line of argument: from the point of view of *world diversity* it is also hard to accept the naive supposition that secessionism will necessarily be disastrous. Rather, it will permit a much larger variety of cultural forms and social structures for humankind as a whole and hence enrich human existence. Disintegration of existing states can be seen not only as an instrument of more equity (less exploitation) but also as an instrument of more diversity and as a way of decreasing the distance between the ruler and the ruled.

Let us therefore look at the theory of disintegration,[49] since integration, under Western assumptions of progress, and growth = progress,[50] has been seen as the *normal* process. We find that there is no such theory. There are theories of integration as a process, but disintegration is seen as a crisis rather than a process that may even be desirable.

One point of departure here would be the theory and practice of federalism,[51] based on a list of social functions, some of which should be taken care of by the central political authority. Such lists indeed exist, but the classical list is hardly satisfactory. The classical formula seems by and large to be that *foreign policy, military policy,* and *financial policy* (central banking, rates of exchange relative to foreign currencies, major lines in economic policy), *external trade,* and *communications* (post, telephone, and telegraph) should be in the hands of the *central* authority; and other matters (among them education) could be decided at a more *local* level (republic or state in a federation; department, province, or prefecture or even a municipality in a country). Economic policy, at both the production and the consumption ends of the continuum,[52] is often also held to be a matter that can be decided over at the local level, particularly within a nonmonopolistic free enterprise system or within a decentralized economy in general.

Now, imagine that we turn this list upside down. In other words, conceive of foreign policy and military policy as something to be decided by local units and regard education and economic policy as subject to more extended control. Take the case of the United Kingdom, for example: Scotland, Wales, and Ulster as well as the "United Kingdom," or actually England, would be represented in the United Nations by delegations instructed by foreign ministries located in these territories (provided Ulster would not choose to affiliate with Ireland). Would that be any more of a threat to peace than recent events in Ulster?[53]

It should be noted in this connection that the classical pattern, where foreign policy is the monopoly of the central level of political organization, is a pattern that emerged at a period in history when there were, practically speaking, no international organizations, in other words no international forum where national identity could also find a means of expression. With the very rapid growth of international interaction and organization, internal disagreements as to what is proper foreign policy also increase in importance, since foreign policy now matters more, and to more people, than ever before. If spokesmen in delegations to such organizations speak with one voice, then the higher the relevance of foreign policy and the higher the level of political consciousness, the less likely that this voice is representative of a consensus. It may be objected that this has always been the case in bilateral diplomatic relations among nations, which may well be true; my point is only that this is accentuated by the emergence of international organizations and big powers, even superpowers. One solution is to have pluralistic delegations, representing either (as in the Council of Europe or the European Community) political parties or representing districts, paving the way for transnational and subnational voting. The latter means that districts in a certain sense become international actors, but why not? The Soviet Union has already shown the way with the participation of the Byelorussian and Ukrainian republics, although it might have been more significant as a pointer toward the future if the UN behavior of Moscow, Minsk, and Kiev had shown some variation.[54] The European mini-states may possibly be more useful models, also because of their size.[55]

Leaving military and educational matters aside, one could easily imagine as a counterpoint to this, without necessarily endorsing the idea, that patterns of relatively centralized economic cooperation might be continued. In other words, a "functional secession" along the lines indicated here would not necessarily presuppose a mutual rupture of economic ties that have grown strong and organic during centuries. Under the heading of financial policy it may very well be that distribution keys for surplus value of various kinds might be considerably changed, and there might also be cases where there would be no basic disagreement on these matters. As secession may purely and simply be an expression of a desire for identity, the important question is *"how is national identity best expressed today?"* My tentative hypothesis is that it is increasingly expressed at the international level as an international actor, *inter alia* in international organizations, and that this is the type of formula under which disintegration might be highly workable.

What we now have to consider from the point of view of peace theory are the advantages and disadvantages of big versus small units and of few versus many units in the international system. There are few problems that the social sciences have been so inattentive to as the theory of the optimal size of societies.[56] Whereas *economic growth* in the conventional capitalist sense (private or state) may be a problem of *scale* (one retarding factor in many poor countries possibly being that they are too small for local *industry* of any magnitude to develop because the local market is too small), it looks as if the problem of peace may be more easily solved with *many small* actors than with a few big actors.[57]

Thus, we are faced with two models of world future development:

Model A	Model B
1. Integration, leading to a few big regions or superstates.	1. Disintegration, secession, leading to many small states.
2. Global institutions weak relative to most powerful (super) state.	2. Global institutions strong relative to most powerful state.

I feel the arguments favor model B. I also feel that important trends are on the side of the latter, as witnessed by the current trend toward aggressive minority self-expression: there are more signs toward disintegration than toward integration in the world today. However, our political thinking, our theories, our concepts, our actions favor model A because it has been taken for granted. This situation should be rectified by imaginative research and action to find new formulas, both to release creative forces pent up in deadly struggles against intranational domination and for the sake of international peace in general.

But all of this thinking nevertheless presupposes some degree of validity to the old Herder concept of the *nation-state*,[58] the idea that a state (a territorial unit) should be the home of only one nation (a nonterritorial unit), sometimes adding the more radical idea that it should be the *only* home of that nation. Carried to its extreme consequence the nation-state idea leads to continued fission and secession, as long as there are more nations than there are states. But that entire approach can now be criticized on at least two grounds, for the road advocated here is different, stressing dominance more than ethnicity.

First, the nation-state program is viable only for nations that are at least to some extent geographically separated inside the same country. If the entropy of the mixture [59] is too high, a separation of the two nations into states will tend to be an extremely painful process.

Second, we must consider whether the territorial separation of different nations is necessarily a good idea at all in a shrinking world, even if the two states are tied together in an associative, egalitarian relationship. The arguments given for *many* territorial actors are not necessarily arguments in favor of ethnically *pure* actors. It may well be that the struggle for *singularist* states (states where one nation is clearly dominant numerically and culturally[60]—if not necessarily dominant in the sense of being exploitative) will have to continue for some time. But the state ideal should rather be a *pluralist* state, combining pluralism with the negation of all three criteria.[61] In other words, there is the danger that the pursuit of the old nation-state idea and ideal may be an escape, however painful, from the much more difficult task of creating nonexploitative social structures. A dominant group might prefer to see its territory reduced to a mini-state rather than give in to demands for basic structural change and to the need for coexistence on an equal footing.

In a pluralist state there would be no first-class and second-class citizenship. This does not mean there would be equality, but it does imply social justice.[62] Any singularist state, by definition, denies social justice by spelling out racial and/or ethnic criteria for first-class membership, or simply by having a concept of first-class membership. A pluralist state would be more like a value-oriented association (a party, a hobby group), whereas the singularist state would be more like an interest-oriented association (a trade union, a professional organization). In the former one may join regardless of who one *is*; the latter is only for people of the same kind, the same training, and the like.

Thus, I see two great battles in the future within this general perspective of intrastate relations: the battles for new and more graded forms of secession that take separate international participation more seriously *and* the battle for more pluralist states. The two battles not only do not exclude each other but probably even presuppose each other. They are both based on the idea of a higher level of mixture of different nations, avoiding complete separation in mutually isolated nation-states. Which form to prefer depends very much on the concrete circumstances. The right of a nation to have a state is a part of social justice at the global level, but the right to exclude others from that state is contrary to ideas of social justice. There is hardly any neat, simple formula that can guide us here, but both alternatives can be spelled out further, which will be done to some extent in the final chapters.

6.3   FUSION IN THE TERRITORIAL SYSTEM

I now turn to the second important process in the territorial system: the tendency toward various types of integration. I shall discuss this process in a concrete way, with reference to concrete states and concrete prospective actors, not to general principles, and I shall make use of the map discussed in section 4.2, despite my comments about its imperfections and limitations. Its major imperfection is shared by all political maps: countries are treated like billiard balls, as if they were homogeneous. But this territorial perspective also yields some insight, to be complemented in chapters 7 and 8.

By "fusion" or "integration" I mean the process whereby two or more actors are able to act as one, or at least "speak with one voice," in some, not necessarily all, contexts. Partly this is a problem of internal coordination, partly of external recognition of the political unification.[63]

Since there are a couple of such processes going on in the world today, we need a simple typology of fusion processes, for which two classifications will serve.

On one hand, we need the usual distinction between integration at the *subregional, regional,* and *global* levels. By "global" I mean (near) universal. "Regional" is conventionally defined, in terms of the traditional continents found in geography textbooks and in terms of the regions bordering the major oceans (the Pacific, Atlantic, Mediterranean, and Indian oceans). I shall refer to them as continental and oceanic littoral regions, respectively. "Subregional," then, simply refers to any unification process below this level.

On the other hand, we also need the much more important distinction between *vertical* and *horizontal* integration. In vertical integration Center and Periphery states are brought together, whereas horizontal integration obviously can be of two types: integration of Center states and integration of Periphery states. Integration processes have to be built around interaction processes and are strongly colored by them, as argued before. If the fundamental underlying interaction process is vertical, in other words an inequitable relation, then the fusion that takes place is vertical, regardless of how much equality is built into the machinery of the intergovernmental organization that runs the fusion.

All together this leads to the six models of territorial fusion shown in figure 6.1. They are all, to varying degrees, visible in the world today, and it is not meaningful to ask which is good or which is bad. They can all be discussed from the points of view of dominance and war, of liberation and security theory, but since the processes are dialectically related (one of them is often meaningless unless one or more of the other processes is also present), conclusions will be neither simple nor very clear-cut.

6.3.1 MODEL I: SIX VERTICAL BLOCS

It is unnecessary to spend much time on this system, as it has already been described in detail in chapter 4. It is the imperialist system, though I note that imperialism, like other social phenomena, should be discussed in terms of the *type* of imperialism as well as the *degree* of imperialism.[64] The chart gives an image of what that model might lead to, including the idea of *imperialism via intermediary* that also is rich, but not autonomous.[65]

In figure 6.2 the world is seen in terms of six empires: one Japanese, one American (which is regional), one European Community, one Soviet Union, one Indian, and one Chinese. As to the last two I am not so much thinking of the extent to which India exercises power over neighboring countries like Nepal, Bangladesh, Sri Lanka, Bhutan, and Sikkim, or of borderline cases like Nagaland, or merely of China's relations with Tibet. I am thinking more of internal relations inside the Indian and Chinese subcontinents, together housing almost

Figure 6.1 Six models of territorial fusion

	Subregional level	Regional level	Global level
Vertical fusion	**I** Vertical blocs	**III** Continental & oceanic regions	**V** World classes
Horizontal fusion	**II** Superstates	**IV** Horizontal subdivisions	**VI** Universal organizations

Figure 6.2 Model I: Six vertical blocs

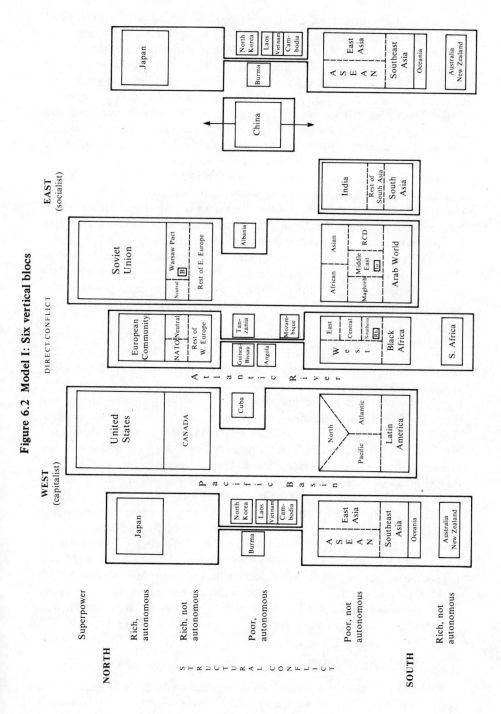

265

one half of humanity. Thus, can it be argued that China is an empire, ruled in the Mandarin language from Peking?[66] Or, can something corresponding to this be said about India?[67] I have no firm views in this connection, since it is an empirical problem calling for empirical investigation; I only put the question. At any rate, the important empires are headed by the United States, the European Community, the Soviet Union (or rather by Russia, since the internal dominance in the Soviet Union is the more important aspect of social imperialism), and Japan, with China matching them in size, and India rapidly coming up. Incidentally, all six are (very) roughly of the same order of magnitude, around half a billion—the Chinese more, the Soviet and Japanese less.

This configuration of territorial fusion can probably be seen as the worst of all possibilities. Its very essence is dominance, or built-in structural conflict from top to bottom within empires. Another essential characteristic is the precarious balance between the empires, brought about more or less by regulated arms races and systems of alliances—and also by mutual agreements not to interfere in each other's spheres of interest. This system maximizes structural violence because of the monopoly on internal dominance given to each hegemonial power, with their intimate knowledge of how to exercise that power with pinpoint precision, and because of the inability of the bottom countries to play off one top power against another.

As to manifest direct violence, this arrangement probably does not embody the most extreme possibility. It is probably true that structural violence is used as a substitute within the vertical blocs, reducing to some extent the direct violence both among bottom-level countries and between the two levels. Moreover, if the system is well regulated, if all blocs really play the game as they should, it may also in some phases be relatively low on direct violence between the blocs. On the other hand, experience seems to show that governments do not play according to such "rules," that it is impossible to keep the system neat and clean, that transgressions do take place, and even if they don't the fear that they may is in itself often sufficient to trigger violent reactions. In short, there is latent direct violence all the time, under the quiet surface.[68]

And yet this model is the dominant existing one among the six, as the empirical data in section 4.2 indicate. The "spheres of influence" configuration, with the United States having "responsibility" for Latin America, the European Community for "Africa" (and also for the Caribbean and the Pacific), and Japan for Southeast Asia, with all three competing with the Soviet Union for "influence" in the Arab world, and all four being uneasy about what the two Asian population giants, India and China, are up to, is an empirical reality.[69] But there are also potential realities, partly created as a response to model I, now to be explored.

6.3.2 MODEL II: TEN SUPERSTATES

Since I do not think that efforts to maintain model I will be successful—it belongs to another era and no longer offers "stable solutions"—the question is what alternative models will emerge. One such alternative, evidently, is horizontal fusion inside each bloc, and what this means concretely is spelled out in figure 6.3. I imagine that this has come about as a reaction to the dominance system of model I—in other words, that each vertical bloc has split into top and bottom, with the dominated withdrawing from the dominator. In the effort to do so the dominated also unify; they need solidarity and organization to stand up against their Center. This does not take place in South Asia and China, however, as the motivation to stand united is too strong.

This gives us ten potential superstates:

1. *North America* (NA)—including the United States and Canada
2. *Western Europe* (WE)—including the European Community and the rest of nonsocialist Europe
3. *Eastern Europe* (EE)—the Soviet Union and socialist Europe, i.e., the countries presently members of the Warsaw Treaty Organization
4. *China* (C)
5. *Japan* (J)
6. *Latin America* (LA)—including the twenty Latin American countries with the possible inclusion of the other (mainly Anglo-American) countries in the Carribean Center and South America
7. *Black Africa* (BA)—which is Africa with the exception of the Arab North and what might remain of the white-dominated South
8. *Arab World* (AW)—including all countries presently members of the Organization of Arab States, with the possible addition of Muslim, non-Arab states such as the RCD countries Turkey, Iran, and Pakistan (but not Malaysia, Indonesia, and Madagascar)—withdrawing from both U.S. and Soviet dominance
9. *South Asia* (SA)—India with the addition of such neighboring countries as Nepal, Bangladesh, Sri Lanka, Bhutan, and Sikkim
10. *Southeast Asia* (SEA)—the region from Thailand via the Philippines to South Korea, comprising the five ASEAN members and Hong Kong, Taiwan, and South Korea

This model divides the world into ten regions, leaving out relatively few countries. [70] Imagine now for a moment that the world crystallizes this way, as a reaction to various kinds of dominance. What kind of world would that be, what would be the relation between these ten potential superstates? A prevision (not a prediction!)[71] of these relations is of course hazardous but not impossible—and it is important to have some kind of image, even if it turns out to be relatively nightmarish. More precisely, it seems fruitful to ask which relations would be *negative* (and why), which ones would be *positive* (and why) and which ones would have a *relatively neutral character,* usually for the simple reason of distance. One such vision is given in figure 6.4.

In principle each one of these characterizations may be subject to considerable specialist argument, but I think they are generally more right than wrong.[72]

Figure 6.3 Model II: Ten superstates

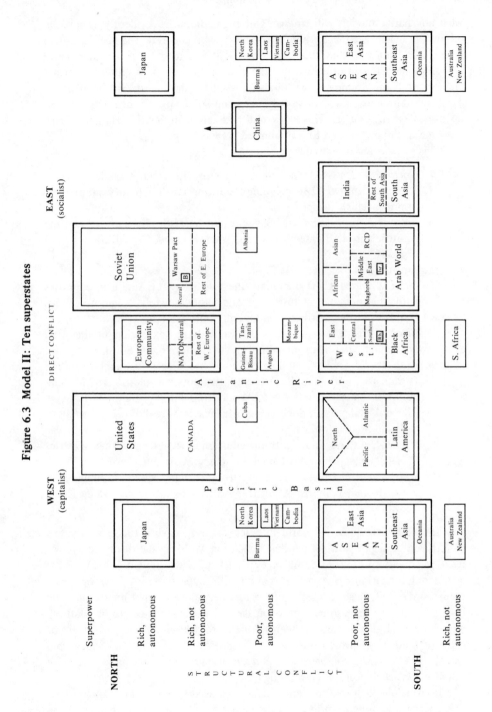

Even though there will certainly be many changes by the end of this century, some basic features of the structure may remain valid. They will now be spelled out.

With ten superstates there are in principle forty-five pairs, and I have postulated only two positive (Western Europe with North America and Latin America), nineteen negative, and twenty-four neutral ambivalent relations (among them China's relation, as of 1979, with North America and Western Europe).

Why do I so easily arrive at such negative and top-heavy structures? For two simple reasons:

1. Even with efforts to break colonial patterns from past and present most of what happens in the world still happens at the top level, with repercussions in the top-bottom and bottom-bottom relations. International interaction, positive as well as negative, has its costs, and one has to be rich and powerful to meet these costs.
2. The meaningful relations are predominantly negative simply because conflicts with the outside are among the most important solidifiers inside. The opposite relation also holds: fusion may lead to a growth that in turn will provoke fears. The superstate is often formed precisely to serve as a protective shield against outside direct or economic aggression,

Figure 6.4 A ten-superstates map of the world

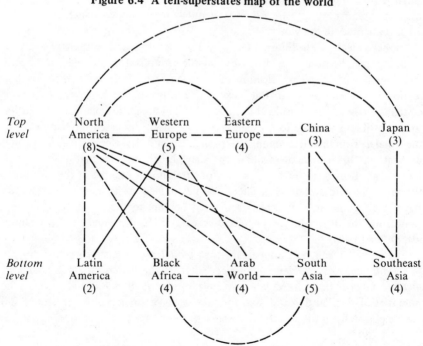

and sometimes also as an aggressive sword. Even if the intention is the former, the perception (and the consequence) may easily become the latter.

To all this can be added for almost all ten, a certain element of contiguity, of racial and ethnic homogeneity, of shared history, and the total logic then becomes extremely similar to the formation of the nation-state. Hence the patterns of top-heaviness and the predominance of negative relations are certainly not strange. What would be strange would be the opposite pattern.[73]

When I have referred to this system as a nightmare it is for the simple reason that *superstates tend to differ from states mainly because they fight superwars instead of wars.*[74] There seems to be no reason to believe that a big state has higher morality or wisdom than a small state, in spite of the fact that it should have much more human power from which to recruit the best men and women. What rather seems to be the case is that its definition of "best" tends to take on a rather domineering tinge, and that makes the total model II system far from reassuring.

On the other hand, this is not a prediction, only a prevision with a certain degree of persuasiveness. It is not a completely unlikely turn of events. But if it is not completely unlikely, then we might not live to see the turn of the century. For this is a vision so ripe with possibilities of real world wars, far beyond and above the two negative lines with Eastern Europe that people in the North Atlantic area have been trained to believe in as the major axis around which world politics rotates,[75] that it is very much to be hoped that there are also other tendencies in the world.

I have dealt with this model at such length not because it is likely or desirable but because it is in many people's minds for the reasons already mentioned. It is an exemplification of the concentric circle model mentioned in section 6.2. combined with the idea of liberation for the deprived. As such it contains elements of considerable value. It would constitute one partial solution to the problem of structural violence as it has been discussed in chapter 4, for the model contains decoupling, self-reliance, and an element of horizontal integration. But its weakness where the latter is concerned is that it does not go far enough. It does not include transcontinental, horizontal ties at the bottom of the present world system, and since such ties indeed are in existence at the top the model would still expose a fragmented bottom to the structural manipulation from the top. Moreover, it is, like everything discussed in this chapter, utterly territorial.

In short, it can perhaps be said that *model II is a partial solution to the structural violence problem of model I, but at the expense of a tremendous increase in potential direct violence.* In addition, it does not fully utilize the potential of the Third World, and for that reason also does not constitute a full emancipation from the structural violence of model I.

6.3.3 MODEL IIIa: FOUR CONTINENTAL REGIONS
MODEL IIIb: THREE OCEANIC REGIONS

We now move ahead, not only in our systematization, but also in the dialectics of this general scheme. There are two contradictions inherent in model II: its inability to resolve the problem of direct conflict because of its emphasis on the autonomy of mutually hostile units and its inability to resolve global problems of horizontal cooperation within the narrow confines set by the blocs of model I. Obviously, the answer to both problems may be in terms of expansion: sufficient expansion to contain within one unit, by ties of loyalty, by cooperation and coercion, parties that might otherwise be hostile to each other, and actors that might profitably cooperate with each other for mutual economic gains even though they do not belong to the same blocs.

In the current debate the continental regions in model IIIa and the oceanic regions in model IIIb (see figures 6.5 and 6.6) are attempts to answer some of these problems. (Incidentally, from those two charts the reader can see more clearly why Japan had to appear twice in the basic chart.) The continental models are above all an effort to solve the problem of security, but can also be, and have been, used to confront problems of development in the broad sense of this term. And the "oceanic" models can basically be seen as models for mutual economic gains but may also have some security spin-offs. Needless to say, other models can also be imagined.

According to the continental model of Figure 6.5 the world is split into four regions. Europe and North America, Latin America, Africa, and Asia. This is similar to the way in which the United Nations has divided the world into five economic regions (two in Asia), each with its own regional economic commission:

1. The Economic Commission for Europe (ECE),
   located in Geneva;
2. The Economic Commission for Latin America (ECLA),
   located in Santiago;
3. The Economic Commission for Africa (ECA),
   located in Addis Ababa;
4. The Economic and Social Commission for Asia and the Pacific (ESCAP),
   located in Bangkok; and
5. The Economic Commission for West Asia (ECWA),
   located in Beirut.

There is considerable wisdom inherent in this division of the world, and with some slight modifications it could also serve as a basis for a system of *regional security commissions* [76] in addition to the economic commissions. For so far, with the possible exception of Africa, these have been seen as foci for economic rather than security cooperation. Thus, the system coming out of the Helsinki conference is far too loose and uncoordinated.

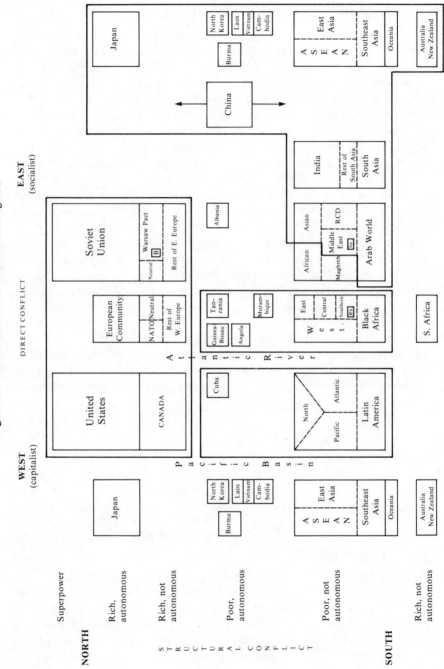

Figure 6.5 Model IIIa: Four continental regions

Figure 6.6 Model IIIb: Oceanic regions

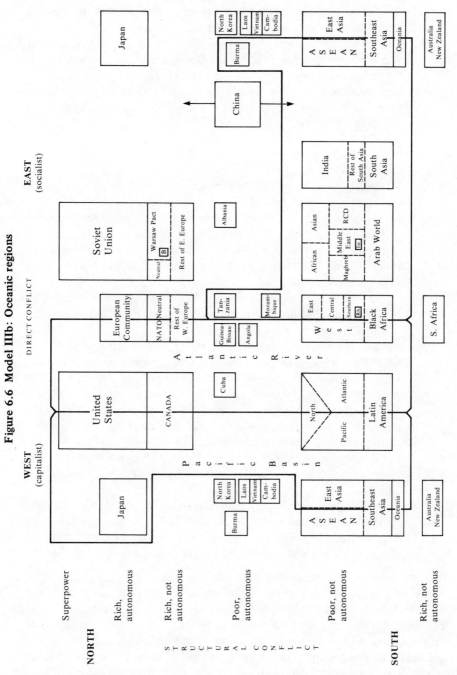

273

The basic idea can be expressed in the following ten points:

1. The world could be divided into regions so that most of the conflicts in the world are *between* regions, not *within* regions.
2. The security commission for the region could be an organization where problems internal to, typical for, and affecting the security of the region can be articulated and possibly settled.
3. Regions should be relatively contiguous and in line with general geographical thinking. Possible security commissions for regions similar to ECOSOC regions are
   (a) SCENA—for all of Europe and North America;
   (b) SCLA—for Latin America;
   (c) SCA—for Africa;
   (d) SCAP—for Asia and the Pacific; and
   (e) SCWA—for West Asia.
4. No region should be allowed to develop into a superstate capable of coordinated aggressive action toward other regions. Hence:
5. Big powers (the United States, the European Community, the Soviet Union, China, Japan) should never be allowed alone or in combination to dominate a region. Thus,
   (a) either *no* big power should be a full member of a commission,
   (b) or *at least two* big powers, split by a conflict likely to last for some time, should be members.
6. *Divided nations* (Germany, Korea, China) should have to start with both parts, with equal status, in one region, not in different regions.
7. Each country should belong to one and only one regional security commission.
8. Countries may be *ad hoc* members of other commissions, at the invitation of a (2/3) majority of the full members of the commission.
9. *Military alliances* should neither be split between different commissions nor be alone in one commission, but should be brought together in one commission to articulate and settle problems with other countries and alliances.
10. The total system of security commissions could be tied to the Security Council, approximately as the economic commissions are to ECOSOC. The sole right to exercise peacekeeping operations would rest with the United Nations, which would be the forum for interregional disputes.

Let us look more closely at these points.

A security commission would be an instrument of a security region, and with the basic properties of a security region spelled out in points 1, 2, and 4. The point is, essentially, that the threats to security in the world, the threats of the use of direct violence, are not randomly distributed. They come in clusters, and since our world is still predominantly territorial, these clusters are to some extent defined by simple contiguity. There are conflicts *within* Latin America, *within* Africa, and *within* the two parts of Asia but, with the few exceptions discussed above, no conflicts *between* these regions. There is structural conflict between North America, Europe, and Japan on the one hand and the remaining three regions on the other, but that does not mean that *this* type of conflict is best handled by having the opposed actors together in the same region. On the contrary, the whole logic argued in the preceding chapter is more in favor of *decoupling*; breaking down ties between them and promoting autonomy of the dominator as well as the dominated.

This being said, the security regions are almost defined by implication, as spelled out in point 3. But this arrangement should also be seen relative to point 4: the regions should be constituted in such a way that they cannot develop into a superstate capable of coordinated aggressive action toward the outside. Three measures are suggested to ensure this: to have no big power at all as a full member, to have at least two big powers that can neutralize each other, and to have both parts of a divided country in the same region. Needless to say, this is in a sense just the opposite of the world of the Cold War, where the principal regions (NATO, WTO) were headed by one big hegemonial power and the conflicts between regions were nurtured by the tremendous conflict energy stemming from having one part of a divided country in either camp and by definition so close to each other that there was almost continuous input of new conflict material.

In this system of commissions each country should belong to one and only one; multiple memberships should be avoided to avoid multiplication of power under the pretext that this is "realistic." On the other hand there should be no dogmatism in this connection: countries should be invited as *ad hoc* members when an issue cannot be discussed meaningfully without their full presence. This could involve both more and less than status as observer or associate member: the invited could have full rights under the relevant item on the agenda, including voting rights, but the right could be limited to that particular item. More particularly, this should also be done in order to ensure that the principle of continental contiguity is not used as a divisive tactic by one military alliance against another. Ideally, military alliances should enter into one region for the same reason as divided nations should, and that is the major reason for giving up any concept of a security commission for Europe alone (SCE) and rather arguing in favor of a security commission for Europe and North America (SCENA), as is done here.[77]

How, then, should the relationship to the United Nations be organized? In point 10 the argument is in favor of an attachment to the Security Council, much in the same way as the economic commissions are tied to ECOSOC; the UN Charter provides for this through its Articles 52–54. Thus, no major change would have to be made in the world for this to happen; this is by no means a utopian scheme. SCENA can easily be seen as an outcome of the Conference on European Security and Cooperation, for a long time suggested by the socialist countries and gradually accepted by the Western powers. SCLA can be seen as a solution to the Latin American problem of organizing security on a basis of autonomy and as an alternative to the antiquated OAS system. SCA would for all practical purposes be identical with OAU, which already is located in the "UN capital for Africa," Addis Ababa (thus permitting close cooperation with ECA); SCAP would be a natural continuation of an Asian Security Conference, somewhat as suggested by the Soviet Union, [78] and SCWA should be the carrier of a "peace process" in West Asia, not outside powers.

One could then imagine that the relationship to the Security Council could be based on the following four principles:

1. The principle of *decentralization:* as far as possible the regional commissions could be encouraged to handle security threats within the region. Threats to security that affect more than one region could be referred to the Security Council, as before.
2. The principle of *appeal:* if any issue becomes deadlocked in a regional commission or if a decision is taken that is considered unjust by one or more members, there could be the possibility of referring the issue upward, to the Security Council. Obviously, if the issue cannot be solved locally, there will always be a high probability that the reasons for the deadlock will also be found centrally.
3. The principle of *duty to report:* the regional security commissions would report regularly on their activities, and the reports from several commissions would be compared and discussed.
4. The principle of *monopoly on violence for peacekeeping:* the right to use violence, under Chapter 6 and Chapter 7 of the Charter, should be reserved for the central authority, the Security Council. The regional commissions may forward requests but not themselves authorize such actions.

The reason for the last point is, of course, related to point 4, that the region should not develop into a superstate. However modest the application of violence and however extensive the consent, once it is authorized the basis is already created for an actor capable of applying violence against others outside the region.

What concretely could the security commissions do? It is difficult to discuss this in the abstract, and it would lead too far to discuss it in detail for all five commissions. Suffice it to say that they could be permanent machineries dealing with all aspects of security, particularly in an associative context. In other words, the military affairs should be seen only as a component of the total security concept. The task would not be to control or disarm a frozen, dissociative war structure but to create an associative peace structure, while increasing predictability about all military aspects of the situation and trying to bring about freezing, thinning, or emptying of some or all parts of the territory for some or all kinds of weapons. A system of mutual observations of maneuvers as well as joint manning of inspection posts would be important in this connection, and countries should be encouraged to step forward as volunteers in offering areas that could be used as training grounds in disarmament experiments. Even a small area, symmetrically located, completely emptied for all or most types of weapons, could be a significant contribution in the European situation, particularly because of the experience that could be gained for more bold efforts in this direction.

A special reason why the linkage to the United Nations could be of importance has to do with the application of UN peacekeeping forces. In cases of extreme use of violence domestic police forces are often recruited from other regions of the national territory. Similarly, one could easily imagine double stationing of UN peacekeeping forces from all other regions but Europe and North America, with a high density in a belt on both sides of the East–West borderline that runs from north to south in Europe, starting with double stationing on the Norwegian–Soviet border and ending with double stationing on the Turkish–Soviet border. This might also have another healthy impact in our world at present: it would be a symbol of rich white Europeans coming to the rest of the world asking its peoples to help them solve problems that Europeans (and North Americans) have not been able to solve for themselves.[79]

Finally, within an associative structure the regional commission might even consider measures for nonmilitary defense (NMD) in a coordinated manner for all countries in the region.[80]

Let us now consider briefly model IIIb, the division of the world into regions that are defined not by continents but by oceans, and more particularly by the Pacific, Atlantic, and Indian oceans.[81]

As can be seen from figure 6.6 this division of the world has a weakness that the continental division does not have. Some parts of the world are less easily included, and they are rather big: Central and Eastern Europe (because they do not reach out to the Atlantic), the Soviet Union and the People's Republic of China, though they are to some extent Pacific countries and might be included there. However, this shortcoming is not fatal. No scheme for dividing the world is perfect, nor will any scheme ever prevail alone. The basic idea is merely to see the world in a different way and to break up the old continental belongingness by supplying other organizing principles. That this principle also may be beneficial from the point of view of the merchant marine countries is obvious.

With new and radical developments in shipping, such as high-speed, hovercraft cargo and passenger ships, it may again be true that oceans connect and continents set apart.[82] In that case the oceanic regions may possibly be as good for operation as I have argued the continental regions can be for security. Moreover, it seems rather unlikely that the oceanic regions would ever be able to crystallize into actors and be threats to each other. They are precisely what they are intended to be: organizing principles, foci of cooperation. But as such they have also built into themselves much of the old structure from the colonial type of imperialism. The old metropolitan center was Europe with its ample handful of colonial powers. Thus, the lines of communication tended toward Europe–

eastward from Latin America, northward from Africa, and westward from Asia. One concrete consequence of that was the systematic underutilization of the Pacific. The settlers on the Pacific coast of the Americas did not even dream of contacts across the Pacific; they were turning their backs to that ocean, looking eastward.[83] Nor did the Asians on the other side think in terms of the Americas. But the other two, the Atlantic and the Indian oceans, were amply made use of, for good and for bad.

Pacific cooperation probably has the highest development potential because this is where the underutilization has been most pronounced, as is perceived very clearly by Japan and the United States.[84] It is seen even more clearly, incidentally, by the European Community for the Mediterranean region, which leads us straight into the next perspective.[85]

6.3.4 MODEL IVa: FOUR DIVIDED CONTINENTAL REGIONS
MODEL IVb: FOUR DIVIDED OCEANIC REGIONS

These models have been added for systematic reasons, not because they have their counterparts on today's political agenda. The basic idea is simple: instead of total vertical integration within the regions defined in models IIIa and IIIb, a separation between the rich and the poor within the regions might take place.

Thus, for the Atlantic area no complete Atlantic cooperative scheme of the type mentioned above has, to my knowledge, been seriously suggested at the governmental level. What has been very much discussed, however, is the "top-dog" version of the same: NAFTA, the North Atlantic Free Trade Area. Several scenarios have been presented, one of them starting with cooperation between North America and EFTA, to which the European Community might then apply for membership! To the south, in Brazil and also in West Africa, there has been some talk about a SAFTA, South Atlantic Free Trade Area. Correspondingly, one could imagine that PAFTA, the Pacific Free Trade Area, could be split into two parts, a northern one encompassing such countries as Japan, Canada, and the United States (California), and a southern one including Southeast Asia on the one hand and Pacific Latin America on the other. Australia and New Zealand as well as the islands in Oceania might possibly belong to both, to one, or to neither. As is well known, they also have other ties of loyalty and cooperation in the world that indeed constitute "special relationships."[86]

6.3.5 MODEL V: UNIVERSAL ORGANIZATION

This is the all-inclusive model to which the United Nations aspires with all her specialized agencies. What is required, of course, is true universalism. In other words, the tradition that dominated all designs from the one put forward by Pierre Dubois in 1306—that "universalism" was always universalism *against* somebody (the pagans, the Turks, the Russians, etc.)—was also present in the United Nations, as an alliance against the Axis powers. But it is naive to believe that true universalism would substantially solve the problems of the United Nations: there are other problems of a more fundamental nature.

The basic problem is the circumstance that the UN structure is still a vertical type of integration, not only in the sense that the big and the small, the rich and the poor, the developed and the underdeveloped have been put together, but in the sense that the *interaction structure* among them, even within the UN system, remains strongly vertical. This is clearly seen in the domineering influence of the *big* powers in connection with security politics and the domineering influence of the *rich* powers in connection with development policies—both so well known that it is unnecessary to spell them out here. To a large extent the United Nations is a cloak of formal equality thrown over a skeleton of inequity and inequality[87] —much behind the half-a-billion size of the vertical blocs of model I.

Second, this universal system is big, and it shows signs of being too big. It seems somehow to lack the healthy challenge of being stimulated by some kind of peaceful competition from the outside, and it also seems to contain within itself such different units and so many contradictions and conflicts that it becomes extremely difficult to agree on common policy with real content.[88] But even if the United Nations has shortcomings for problem and conflict *solution,* it is indispensable for problem and conflict *articulation.*

However, I postpone detailed treatment of the problem of world authority in general, and the UN system in particular, until chapter 8, with some preliminary remarks on nonterritorial organizations in general in chapter 7.

6.3.6 MODEL VI: THREE WORLD CLASSES

In this model (see figure 6.7) the universalism has in a sense been preserved. There are no subregional or regional borders, but there are crystallized class connotations. The classes can be defined in economic terms (rich or poor, autonomous or nonautonomous) or in power terms (big or small, aligned or nonaligned, "tend to be poor").[89] As can be seen from the scheme, I do not believe in the commonly held idea that the world might be split into two, North against South, but find a division of the world into three classes much more likely (For big powers versus small powers, a division into two is meaningful.)

In a sense this is an expression of the strategy announced by Lin Piao.[90] The revolution in China came about because the Village revolted against the City; correspondingly the revolution in the world has to come about by the World Village revolting against the World City. China could be the leader of the World Village, in the sense of being the example, and the narrow belt around the world just referred to would be her first followers. This belt would then expand: Periphery countries in the category "poor, not autonomous," would detach themselves from the stronghold of the imperialist powers and join the category

Figure 6.7 Model VI: Three world classes

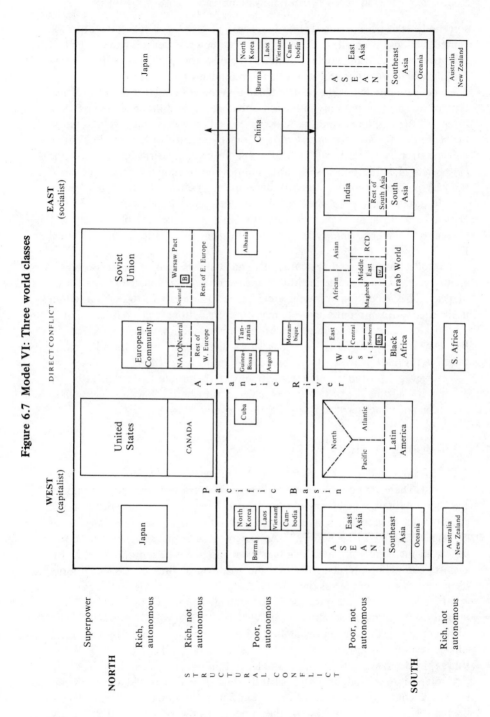

of "poor but autonomous" countries. Needless to say, this detachment can only take place if parasitic elites in the Periphery countries are decoupled from their harmony of interest with the elites in the Center powers.

But this would only be the first phase. After that comes the second phase: conquest of the World City, the New York–London–Paris–Bonn–Moscow–Tokyo alliance, the alliance of the imperialists and the revisionists (social imperialists). The last stronghold would be the North Atlantic region, the last bastion to fall, but it would eventually fall. And with its fall would come the true liberation of the world—not the artificial "mondialism" expressed in model V and articulated in a United Nations to which most of the countries in the "poor, autonomous" belt take severe exception.

Obviously, this model is almost meaningless when it is seen as a territorial model alone. It is essentially a nonterritorial model, based on efforts to explode the dominance system, whether the emphasis is on the effort to break down vertical ties or to build up horizontal ties. For that reason it cannot be seen as a model portraying some sort of world warfare where three classes of countries are involved. That is only a part of the picture; equally or more important is the corresponding picture inside all countries of the world. There is a high level of isomorphism at work here, like a set of Chinese boxes: inside the countries there are also those who are rich and relatively autonomous, those who are rich but not autonomous, those who are poor and autonomous, and those who are neither rich nor autonomous. By "autonomous," I do not mean "self-sufficient" but rather "free to set one's own goals." And just as the revolutionary ferment in model VI at the world level is seen as coming from the poor and autonomous, the same may be the case inside countries. But will China revive Lin Piao's strategy?

The struggle against the dominance system of the world becomes a very complex one: partly at the domestic level, partly at the global level. The upper classes, the center groups in the poor and nonautonomous nations, are then squeezed between national loyalties on the one hand and their own interests on the other—a squeeze that will be more and more tightly felt in the future. The prediction is that they will have to take sides: either escape to the metropolitan powers where their souls if not their bodies already belong, or identify genuinely with the peripheries in their own countries, as indicated in chapter 4.

In this model the rich, autonomous countries have so far been depicted as unified. For that reason, let us now more systematically than under model II, turn our attention to relations between the *top* powers in this scheme. As the map is drawn there are five of them: the United States, the European Community, the Soviet Union, China, and Japan. As a point of departure for a discussion of future relations among them, consider figure 6.8, which shows one way of classifying the five big powers.[91]

I have again, as under model II, put the United States and the European Community together since I see no reason to assume that the possible dividing lines between them will amount to much more than some rivalry, some eco-

Figure 6.8   A classification of the five big powers

	European *(individualist)*	*Asiatic* *(collectivist)*
West *(capitalist)*	United States European Community	Japan
East *(socialist)*	Soviet Union	China

nomic quarrels, in the years up to 2000. Some kind of NAFTA (North Atlantic Free Trade Association) or New Atlantic Charter will probably emerge sooner or later, as an umbrella encompassing the United States and the European Community. But these are small, technical details within a basically unified community. I want to discuss more important problems: what is the future of the total big-power system?

Generally speaking, I see four possible futures in the longer run:

1. *A big-power concert,* with the big powers basically in harmony and acting on a basis of consensus, setting themselves up not only as a Security Council but as an Executive Committee for the whole world;
2. *A multipolar system,* with the big powers in competition, all with each other;
3. *A (re)polarization,* along the lines of the Cold War;
4. *A new polarization,* along the Asia/Europe division.

Of course, there may also be four "three against one" formulas. However, they are seen as very unlikely, short-lived, or not very salient, like the present pattern to some extent isolating the Soviet Union (because the China–Soviet Union conflict is at present deeper than the Japan–United States or China–United States controversy).

I consider the fourth possibility in the list to be the most likely. Consider these phases after the antagonisms resulting from the American Revolution and the Napoleonic interlude had been overcome:

1. Europe basically pacified, China gradually colonized, Japan steering a different course and able to stave off European colonization (if she had not been able to, she might now possibly be much closer to China).
2. World War I and World War II resulted in an accommodation of Germany, but Russia became the Soviet Union and the East–West conflict structured the world. China joins the East after 1949, to a large extent because of the common-enemy factor; Japan is under the West. Both have special security treaties with their protectors.

3. This political configuration had a solid basis in the economic systems: capitalist in the West, socialist in the East. Japan appears sometimes as more West than the West, China as more East than the East.

4. However, this system does not last much more than about a decade. New phenomena then become apparent:

   (a) The socialism of *China* becomes different from the socialism of the *Soviet Union:* approximately expressed by the terms "communism" (spelled commune-ism) vs. "state capitalism," and more technically as mobilization/egalitarianism vs. bureaucracy/professionalism.

   (b) The capitalism of *Japan* becomes (or remains) different from the capitalism of the U.S./EC system; because they are based on "Japan-ization" and Westernization respectively, with a heavy emphasis on collectivism in the former and individualism in the latter.

   (c) Latent conflicts start becoming manifest in both pairs: over leader-ship roles in Asia, over concrete territories (China–Soviet border disputes, Japan over Okinawa and the northern territories), and above all over internal interference (Soviet in China and U.S. in Japan).

5. This leads to complete rupture between the Soviet Union and China, but not (yet) between Japan and the United States. However, conflicts are piling up around the three conflict dimensions mentioned in the pre-ceding point.

6. The question then, of course, is whether this may lead to a new conflict structure pitting European big powers against Asian big powers, instead of West against East; *in other words, a turning of the conflict axis 90 degrees.*

For this to happen the old conflict borders obviously have to be weakened further and the new conflict borders strengthened. The last phases have to be extended beyond the present.

This leads directly toward a dialectical point: one of these tendencies will tend to stimulate the other. Any weakening of one old conflict front will strengthen a new one. More positive relations between the United States/Euro-pean Community and the Soviet Union will be resented by China as "united imperialism" and "collusion between imperialists and revisionists" and prompt Japan into closer contact with China or into similar efforts to cooperate with the Soviet Union. Similarly, more contact between Japan and China might have spill-over effects in the other pair. And this certainly works both ways: if the Soviet Union and China should be able to resolve their difficulties, the United States/European Community and Japan would hardly permit tariff struggles and the like to escalate to the heights found at present. In short, there is inter-dependence in the system: the system is a structure.[92]

To exploit this point another tempting train of thought, and a more cheerful one, can be developed: that *the big-power system may develop into a criss-cross type of situation where both conflict axes are about equally strong and consequently about equally weak.* In a situation of that type the most recent arrival in the big-power club, Japan, would have ties with both China and the Western powers, and the Soviet Union with both China and the West. In addition there might even be stronger connections between the United States and China and between the two neighbors Japan and the Soviet Union. In such a case a big-power concert might be a possibility. But that situation is not likely to remain stable over time. It would be feared by the poor and the small, who would do their best to maintain at least some conflict borders to avoid such a grandiose collusion, representing nearly one half of the world population (above 1800 million).

Still another model would look into the possibilities of *big-power disintegration.* This immediately points to the strength of Japan: it is the only truly homogeneous country for which no credible disintegration scenario exists. The European Community has still a distance to go to real integration, and in the United States, the Soviet Union, and possibly also in China, center–periphery conflict may lead to disruption, whether it is the center or the periphery that chooses to secede. Japan's power status, whatever else might threaten it, is not likely to be challenged by secessionist tendencies. Internal dissent is something else, an extrainstitutional struggle for power, not a struggle aimed at disintegration.

But if we imagine that the rotation of the conflict axis is completed so that a United States–European Community–Soviet Union alliance and a China–Japan alliance would emerge, the prospects are less cheerful. In the latter case China–Japan might be formidable in their fourfold strength:

1. Together, they exceed one billion in population.
2. They are racially and ethnically homogeneous, or at least contiguous.
3. They share latent resentment against the West, against the white man—capitalist or socialist.
4. They would be interdependent in a "marriage of convenience" between Chinese "message without technology" and Japanese "technology without message."

In other words: if the class-war model of the world does not unify the big powers—and these are no longer attached to their blocs or to continental/oceanic regions, nor brought together in a more unified world—chances are that they may turn against each other, in new and unexpected configurations. In either case, the "class war" with the big powers unified or the "new big-power war," with the big powers polarized, the prospects for humankind as a whole are bleak indeed, regardless of how much the war might serve to reduce some types of structural violence.

That brings us to the conclusion in this model: we have witnessed only the beginning of the international class war; in all probability there is much more to come. For there is no sign that the big capitalist powers, the United States–European Community–Japan triangle, will give up voluntarily their imperialistic grip on the world. Quite to the contrary, there are signs that they may consolidate, constituting some kind of world capitalist directorate using the OECD as a basis.[93] Many Marxists have assumed that they would somehow go under in intercapitalist rivalries, but it looks much more likely that they will be rational enough from the point of view of their own interests to give higher priority to the minimum of cooperation needed to defend capitalism as such, regardless of whose capitalism.[94]

Further, there is no sign that the big powers in general, all five of them, will easily give up the two most dangerous big-power pursuits for the rest of humankind: a bipolarization, that may result in an equally devastating hegemony. Big powers are big—that is the trouble—and the best one might hope for in that respect would be disruption from within. As mentioned several times this may happen both to the United States and to the Soviet Union before the turn of the century. But it is hardly likely to happen to the highly unified Japan, or to the European Community or to China—both of them in a phase of consolidation and integration.[95]

Hence, it is a safe prediction that sooner or later the rest of the world will somehow come together in a world proletariat, pitted against the big and the dominant. What is new here is the word "world," for the mechanisms would be the same as I have already discussed in explaining model II (and, very briefly, model IV).

In the *economic field* this development will take the form of an increasingly unified fight against the big capitalist three—a fight that will also serve to unify them. The expanding Group of 77 in UNCTAD and the expanding series of conferences of nonaligned nations[96]—Belgrade in 1961, Cairo in 1964, Lusaka in 1970, Guyana in 1972, Colombo in 1976, Havana in 1979—are very encouraging signs of the *early beginning* of this development.[97] Trade unions of poor countries will form increasingly, using any combination of the type of strategies outlined in section 4.4—not to mention other strategies that will be developed during the struggle. The net outcome will be decoupling: more interaction among the poor, less with the rich—and also much more among the rich, possible until they produce and trade themselves to death—in short, the New International Economic Order.

In the *field of power* decoupling is known as nonalignment. It is the great achievement of the Tito–Nehru–Nasser triangle that they managed slowly to get most of the world out of the Stalin–Dulles concept, a world where everybody was aligned so that we should all stand or fall together.[98] This trend will continue, also inside Europe itself, with for instance all Nordic countries being possible candidates for nonalignment, as mentioned in section 5.4.

The big question that remains is the extent to which the world underprivileged—in the economic field pitted against the capitalist powers, in the power field against the Soviet Union and possibly China—would ultimately themselves constitute a new major power economically and militarily, giving to the world six or seven big powers instead of the present system of five (with clients) or the system envisaged in model II of ten superstates. No one knows, but if the time horizon is this century it looks rather unlikely that these parts of the world, so exploited, penetrated, fragmented, and marginalized, should be able to obtain sufficient integration to behave like the big powers from which they try to liberate themselves. Hence, I put the problem on the agenda for the twenty-first century.

6.3.7 CONCLUSION

What is the balance sheet resulting from all this? Which of these worlds is more likely, and which, if any, is the preferred world? Obviously, the answers to these two questions cannot be simple answers formulated in terms of one model as opposed to all the others, for the models do not exclude each other. It is quite possible, indeed likely, that all these six processes may take place simultaneously; and it is also possible that the preferred world within this type of scheme would have to be based on a combination of some of these models.

Thus, vertical blocs will probably still for some time deepen in penetration and widen in scope and domain. These processes may continue far beyond what is wanted by dominating and dominated nations alike, simply because of organizational inertia and old habits in either party.[99] So much has been invested in these blocs that some of the mechanisms will feed on themselves.

At the same time, however, it seems safe to predict that a certain amount of horizontalization will take place within each bloc as a response to the problems inherent in any dominance system, regardless of type. This solution to the problem of structural violence may then increase the likelihood of direct violence and, dialectically, lead to an effort to recapture some element of verticality in regional or universal vertical models. In the continental regions (which I have argued strongly for) topdog and underdog countries meet each other again, at least to some extent, but in a type of confrontation where issues may be articulated and, possibly, resolved without recourse to arms (but possibly by means of various kinds of social, nonmilitary disruption and defense). In general, vertical and horizontal integration are dialectically related: where there is vertical integration there will always be an element of structural dominance, and the reaction will be horizontal integration, at the same level (bloc, regional, or universal) or at a higher level. But horizontal integration may, in turn, lead to problems of potential direct violence and hence call for some element of vertical integration—again, at the same level or higher.

The net result of these processes should be model V *and* model VI: a United Nations sharply divided in three classes, contesting for political ascendancy. But the problem with these two models is that they are too large for our organizational capacity. Even with considerable increase in transportation and communication facilities it is hard to imagine that humankind in the foreseeable future really can learn to operate effectively at this level. Hence, just as the solution to smallness was found in bigness, the solution to bigness may be found in smallness. Parallel with the fusion processes there will be fission processes within countries and within blocs, in all probability making the history of our near future extremely complicated.

In short, I do not think that these territorial fusion processes will lead humankind toward a stable point. Rather, I see the future in terms of a number of simultaneous processes that strengthen and weaken each other and are dialectically related, leading to very complicated patterns. The only thing that seems to be relatively certain in the relatively near future, to my mind, is that model I will have to yield to model II, model V to some extent to model VI, and that there probably will be more emphasis on the intermediate, regional, and vertical models IIIa and IIIb. Beyond that I dare not venture to guess.

What then about the *preferred* world? Of course, the preferred world would be some kind of horizontal version of model V, but this would only be possible after intra- and international decoupling processes have been successful, particularly in the big countries, so that the world would consist of many more states, smaller and more equal in size. Since this is obviously not the world in which we live, I am more inclined to favor a very solid model VI element within model V, combined with models IIIa and IIIb.

But my basic point is actually that it seems quite clear from the analysis that the basic problems of humankind cannot be solved within this territorial scheme at all. It is too much based on the billiard-ball myth of the nation-state, too much based on the liberal conception that peace in any sense of the word can be brought about by some institutional manipulation of the international and supernational systems. In the search for reduction of structural and direct violence this system will probably only oscillate. *It has to be transcended; nonterritorial actors have to enter the picture.* But before turning to that, in chapters 7 and 9, let me summarize this entire chapter in a simplified manner that also includes some more concrete and immediate strategies.

6.4 STRATEGIES OF CHANGE

Any effort to summarize the latent and manifest conflicts found in the world today will by necessity be a simplification of the tremendous manifold of social conflict. However, some simplification is needed, particularly if one should try to indicate some basic strategies of change in the territorial political system of today, rather than just speculating on what might happen tomorrow and the day after. And for this purpose I shall now simply classify countries into Center and Periphery, depending on whether they are high or low on some international "division of labor" (particularly in the field of production, but also in the fields of military and political decision making), and into capitalist and socialist, depending on whether they have a market or centrally planned economy. This gives us four types of countries, with most of them falling into the Periphery, capitalist category.

To summarize the entire discussion, conflict formations[100] can now be defined within and between these countries. I have found it useful to distinguish between four main types:

1. Center–Periphery conflict formations
   (a) Imperialistic formations
       (1) between capitalist countries
       (2) between socialist countries
   (b) Big powers versus small powers
2. Intra-Center conflict formations
   (a) Capitalist powers versus socialist powers
   (b) Capitalist powers versus capitalist powers
   (c) Socialist powers versus socialist powers
   (d) European versus Asian powers
3. Intra-Periphery conflict formations
4. Intrastate conflict formations
   (a) Class conflict
       (1) within capitalist countries
       (2) within socialist countries
   (b) Territorial conflict
   (c) Race, sex, and age conflict

What is the concrete situation today, very roughly speaking, with regard to these formations?

The most important one, combining what has been said in sections 6.2 and 6.3, is no doubt the imperialistic conflict formation, based on its peculiar configuration of *four* classes, whereby the periphery in the Periphery state is pitted against an unholy alliance of the center in the Center, the periphery in the Center, and the center in the Periphery. Sometimes the capitalist and imperialistic formations are erroneously referred to as the North–South conflict; erroneously because of the participation of the local bourgeoisie (in the South) on the side of the North. On other occasions these conflicts are referred to as pure international class conflicts, with the exploited in the Center and the Periphery allied alike against their exploiters; but this is also erroneous, because the ambivalent position of the periphery in the Center is not taken into account.

Exactly because of the complex nature of this conflict formation, the large-scale, territorial strategies of change are far from obvious. The most important seems to be one type or another of a people's war, whether it takes a violent or a nonviolent form. If the imperialistic formation is really embedded in the structure, then the proletariat at the bottom can expect help neither from its own upper classes (be they commercial or political-military or both) nor from the proletariat of the Center country. The overwhelming evidence seems to indicate that this is the strategy most likely to lead to liberating results,[101] although it does not exclude such collateral strategies as efforts to demoralize the center in the Center and efforts to increase the consciousness of the periphery in the Center so that it does not participate in repressive ventures, or mention efforts to convert the periphery elite to a position more in solidarity with its own people.

I expect this formation to provide the world with more than enough drama for the coming decades, particularly since we as late as the beginning of the 1970's were not even through with the colonial phase of the imperialistic formation. Portugal was still keeping out, as she once did in connection with slavery. The same applies to southern Africa, and it is only to be deplored that the consensus in the United Nations concerning both cases seems to be inversely correlated with any efficiency of measures in the fight. Sooner or later the world will have to find forms of struggle against the colonial regime run by South Africa—and beyond humanitarian support only.

Thus, I expect more Dominican Republics and more Czechoslovakias in the time to come, to cite two relatively parallel examples from the 1960's. In addition the quest for raw materials, especially for energy, has become crucial again. Hence, the victim countries will have to join forces with others in similar positions. Not only will they have to stand up against the Center states, they will also have to stand up against or convert their own elites and join forces among themselves. For that reason it is relatively clear that the rest of this century will witness ever-increasing cooperation between and among Periphery states: cooperation among liberating Latin American states, liberating sub-Saharan African states, liberating South East Asian states, and also among liberating Eastern European states. As to the latter a *European Socialist Community,* with such members as DDR, Poland, Czechoslovakia, Hengary, Romania, and Bulgaria—like an organization of really Latin American states all of them at least to some extent freed from imperialistic penetration—is also among the obvious strategies of change. For the Western European Periphery under the U.S. Center penetration this development occurred in the late 1950's and increasingly took the form of the emergence of what today is known as the European Community.[102] It stands to reason that the rich and powerful Western European nations were earlier in finding forms of liberation and common organization than the Eastern European, Latin American, African, and South East Asian nations. But all these other fights also take place, in solidarity, and may be coordinated, as where Central American guerrilla movements turn to the post-Shah regime in Iran for support—or as when Cubans fight in lands from which their African ancestors were abducted as slaves.

However, under the general heading of Center–Periphery conflict formation there is also quite clearly a new conflict configuration taking shape. The pivot element in this formation is the United States, a country that has been fighting in one way or the other, practically speaking, over the whole world during this century. The United States managed to defeat Germany and Japan, and later engaged in all kinds of Cold War activities against the Soviet Union and China. But World War II enemies became allies in the fight against World War II allies, simply because the capitalist-versus-socialist conflict formation was much stronger than the *ad hoc* conflict formation brought about by the Axis powers for a short period, peculiar because it reflected nineteenth- rather than twentieth-century political logic.[103] As the European Community and Japan asserted themselves, the United States got into a series of complex economic conflicts with them, but all of these were overshadowed by the common concern: to protect capitalism as a system, with all its implications, including some respect for liberal values.

At the same time, however, the United States had to yield in her conflicts with the Soviet Union and China, settling with each on terms that were considerably closer to the Soviet and Chinese aims than to those originally held by the United States (concerning, for instance, the status of borders in Eastern Europe and the status of Taiwan). Thus the basis was laid for "international pentagonalism," for a five-cornered big-power cooperation at the top of the world, with a three-cornered capitalist nucleus,[104] and China oscillating.

One strategy for the fight against big-power domination of the world would be for *small powers to unite.* In doing so the old formula will probably be followed: the stronger the satellite, the more likely that it will participate in such a "revolt"; and the closer the satellites are (geographically, and in terms of having the same Center nation), the higher the likelihood that they will seek to act together. Quite concretely, this leads to the possibility of Canada increasingly dislocating herself from the United States, of the so-called rest-EFTA countries in Western Europe (Iceland, Norway, Sweden, Finland, and less importantly Switzerland and Austria) doing the same relative to the European Community and perhaps establishing contact with Canada. This would be one more source of motivation for Eastern European socialist states to do the same relative to the Soviet Union, and perhaps also to seek much more contact with small, independent states in Western Europe and North America. Groupings of these kinds might also take up more and more contact with the rapidly increasing cooperative networks between nonaligned countries, leading to a gradual isolation of the big powers. It should be remembered, however, that the big powers in their population amount to not much below half of the world's population and that their thrust of penetration is considerable.

Let us then turn to the possibilities of conflict between Center countries. There are only five of these countries, but there are at least the four ways of looking at possible conflicts between them indicated in the typology. I assume that the first one, in the old days referred to as the East–West conflict (again erroneously, because "East" and "West" are here only conceived of in the provincial European terms, not in the global sense of Occident versus Orient), is by and large in a dormant phase. In other words, I assume that there are at present no real conflict issues at the core of it. This, however, does not mean that the conflict machineries on either side of the old East–West confrontation are not in and by themselves capable of generating ever-escalating conflicts, even a hot war. It is in the nature of these machineries to expand, partly by *actio-reactio,* partly by internal dynamics, for which reason the fight against the machineries as such is as important as ever. The strategies in that connection will, however, not be repeated here. Suffice it to say that "arms control" and "disarmament" so far are not among them. Such measures should rather be seen as parts of the effort to establish big-power coalitions, nourishing their joint feeling of significance and "responsibility" in handling world affairs.

However, it is one thing to say that the classical East–West conflict has come to an end and quite another to assert that the relationship between the former antagonists is a peaceful one in a more positive sense. The major strategies for obtaining this would be exchange and cooperation, but in a *symbiotic* manner (meaning so much to each party that they prefer peace), in a *symmetric* manner (meaning nonexploitative) and with a sufficient amount of *integrative institutions* (meaning all-European institutions of cooperation, including cooperation on security). The pattern that seems to be emerging is not symbiotic or symmetric or integrative in this sense; it is relatively inconspicuous (except at the U.S.-Soviet level), exploitative in being the old trade pattern with raw materials and energy from East to West and manufactured goods and technology from West to East, with practically speaking no all-European institutions of any real significance emerging on a permanent basis. Strategies of change in this field will therefore imply not only the increase of the exchange but also a more symmetric exchange, meaning that West would have to be willing to learn more from East and take more manufactured goods from East, and both sides would have to be willing to build up relatively strong all-European institutions with, for instance, their seat in West Berlin. Obviously, a high level of free flow of information and persons also belongs for this to become a peace structure.

What are the possibilities of any conflict of significance between *capitalist powers*? In terms of cold war probably quite high, in terms of hot war negligible. In all likelihood the split between the United States and Japan will continue, and the same may apply to the split between the United States and the European Community, at least in political and economic terms, although in both cases there may be an increased tendency toward more symmetric cross-investment. But it would not be in their interest to try to destroy each other mutually, unless one of them should develop (once again) in a clearly fascist direction. The obvious candidate for this type of development would be the United States, and the only strategy of any validity against such a development within a state possessing such a gigantic power potential would have to be found within the American people themselves, with their own ability to fight against any fascist tendency. To put it bluntly: the best U.S. contribution to peace in the years to come would be to work for a better society at home and let the rest of the world take care of itself.

What are the possibilities of a cold or hot war between the *socialist powers*? Since there are only two of them at the Center level, the Soviet Union and China, all one can say is that the cold war has been going on for a long time already, with occasional excursions into hot war. The conflict is only partly over territory in North China and East Siberia, and to the extent it is concerned with such territories it does not look as if the Chinese goal is to have the Soviet Union yield territory to it, but rather to have the Soviet Union admit that the treaties of the 1860's were unequal. But two other sources of conflict are much more important.

The first conflict has to do with the allegiance of the Asian peoples within the Soviet Union, particularly of the Central Asian republic with whom the Chinese obviously identify. To the extent that these republics have a periphery status within the Soviet Union, perhaps autonomy in cultural affairs, but certainly not in political and military matters or in economic matters (the new Soviet planning regions being by far too big and too "Russified" to permit any such autonomy, in addition to the obvious centralization of the Soviet system), there will be ample conflict material.

Second, there is the fundamental problem as to which of the two major socialist powers has the more correct definition of socialism.[105] As an issue within China, it was even expressed through the cultural revolution; it has not (yet) been a manifest issue in the Soviet Union. This means that the Soviet Union might be tempted to subvert via "her" faction within China, just as China might do likewise using Asian peoples within the Soviet Union. Since both efforts would be resented extremely strongly, the conflict material here is obvious, and it looks as if the only strategy of change would be for the two giant powers to engage in a painstakingly slow and complicated process not too different from what has taken place between East and West in the European sense, in order to arrive at a structure based on equal exchange and a relatively free flow of information and people. Needless to say both strategies sound extremely utopian at present.

What is the likelihood of a European-versus-Asian conflict formation among the Center powers? All that can be said is that there are some signs in this direction, but they are not yet very strong. If it comes about it will be as unfortunate as any other bipolarization of the big-power system, but they may be less unfortunate than a Concert or Congress system among the big powers, dictating their terms to the rest of the world.

Let us then turn to the intra-Periphery conflict formations, which look more random because one's eye is so much trained on the Center countries that anything else looks unsystematic. There is, of course, a major one which has been on the world agenda for the greater part of this century, the Middle East conflict. It has imperialistic admixtures, elements of big-power-versus-small-power conflict, not to mention elements of East-West conflict, capitalist rivalry, and socialist rivalry. All these admixtures to the fundamental conflict between Jewish and Arab peoples complicate the matter extremely and make a solution to the conflict in the near future rather improbable.

One could speculate in terms of two major types of solution in this particular area, one of them on a short-term basis, the other more on a long-term basis.[106]

Thus, an Israel willing to return to what would basically be pre-June 1967 borders (with some minor adjustments), willing to let the border be policed by U.N. peacekeeping forces stationed on either side (so that if they withdraw from one party they are likely to be withheld by the other), and willing to engage in highly symbiotic, symmetric, and integrative cooperation and exchange with Arab states after some time *might* one day prove to be an acceptable element in the Middle East setting. The Camp David plan is not even this.

However, any solution along such lines is no solution to the real problem: Jews have taken territory that used to belong to the Palestinians (regardless of how many and which others also had some kind of occupancy and domination relation over this territory). A second type of solution would therefore be in terms of cantonization of this territory, including not only the Israel that has been growing since 1948, but all of British-mandated Palestine before it was cut in two in 1922. Some of these cantons would be Arab, some of them would be Jewish, and they would have gradually to emerge into a pattern of relatively symmetric exchange and cooperation, however difficult that would be. For in this area, as in many others, there seems to be no alternative to finding real solutions to the conflict. War with the present level of armament is no alternative, and no solution over the heads of the Palestinians will ever be meaningful.

There are other conflicts around the territorial world, though they are hardly of great significance in terms of their global implications. But, in general, intra-Periphery conflicts will increase because of the waning policing power of Center states, and much resourcefulness in conflict solution will therefore be needed.

Finally, there are the intrastate conflict formations, also supposed to increase in importance, among other reasons because one will learn from the other. All minorities around the world were following with great interest what happened in Bangladesh, and what happens in Spain and France today, and there will be chain reactions coming out of this. In some cases this will take the form of pure class conflict, conflict for power between classes within the same country; in other cases it will take the form of disintegration, with groups wanting to establish their own state. If these territorial conflicts are of increasing importance, because of increased class consciousness and racial-ethnic consciousness and because racial-ethnic groups very often are concentrated on separate territories, then it is absolutely mandatory that new strategies of change be found in this field.[107] More particularly, it is important that indicators of this conflict potential are developed, not in order to subdue the minority but in order to develop a higher ability to redress their grievances and meet their demands so that they do not have to shoot themselves into autonomy. For instance, it is highly important that the states of the world give up the classical definition of the conditions under which they are willing to "recognize" a new state, namely, that the new regime is in control of a territory. In order to live up to this formula any new regime candidate will *have to* establish its control violently, and the bloodshed this leads to might very well be catastrophic in more areas than former East Pakistan and Northern Ireland. Above all, the spectrum between the one-state and the two-state "solutions"—today meaning continued repression or violent liberation respectively—must be enriched. And in addition there are the conflicts between sex and age groups, but they are more nonterritorial in nature.[108]

Thus, there is no scarcity of conflicts in the world territorial system, but the two formulations for conflict believed in by so many analysts, the "East-West conflict" and the "North-South conflict," not only fail to exhaust the list, they also lead to serious misinterpretations of the nature of the conflict formations in the world today. If conflicts are to be dealt with in anything like a rational manner they have to be identified and dealt with in a more correct manner, for they affect the interests of highly concrete human beings and will continue to do so for a long time.

As to strategies of change: the summary just given has made it clear that this type of analysis essentially leads to two types of strategies, as already pointed out in section 3.4. In cases of domination there is a *dissociative strategy of liberation;* in cases of conflict between parties that do not dominate each other there is an *associative strategy of cooperation.* Either strategy has its rules, and only when carried out in a certain way are they likely to become peace strategies. It is important that both are recognized as such and that the search for less violent methods continues relentlessly, lest the territorial system always fall back on the classical paradigm: territorial units converted into fortresses, unleashing all kinds of means of destruction upon each other. Fortunately, however, the world also has a nonterritorial aspect, to which we now turn.

NOTES

References to *Essays* are to Johan Galtung, *Essays in Peace Research,* 5 vols. (Copenhagen: Ejlers, 1975-80) (Atlantic Highlands, N.J.: Humanities Press).

1. From the European point of view, that is. From other points of view the territory had been there from time immemorial, and the idea of "expanding territory" was to a large extent alien to non-Western cosmology.

2. A condition seems to be that some kind of big plastic bubble or dome could be created, and the question is to what extent such structures could stand up against meteorites from space.

3. *Small States and Territories: Status and Problems* (New York: Arno Press, 1971).

4. A euphemism for colonies.

5. Another euphemism, where the assumption seems to be that the level of Western-style political development is so low that they cannot even be referred to as self-governing.

6. In the period 1814-1905 Norway would probably have been classified in this category.

7. Federation being a loose structure, this usually means that the federation will break up.

8. This is above all the French formula.

9. One example would be the Faroe Islands, located between the Shetland

Islands and Iceland, in the North Atlantic, with 41,000 inhabitants. Interestingly enough, that small prospective mini-state is divided into fifty-two municipalities, which (apart from the biggest ones) would have an average number of inhabitants of 400. Within the Faroe Islands there are even strong autonomy movements to avoid too much Tórshavn dominance. The structure is highly viable, and what is received from the coffers of the mother country, Denmark, seems to be much less than what Danish commercial agents earn (and the Danish state earns in taxes) because the commercial cycles go through Danish agents.

10. Originally written in 1969 this prediction seems to have come true. Who, for instance, in the U.S. State Department would have imagined in, say, 1956 the possibility of Cuban troops fighting forces associated, even identified, with South Africa and the United States on the soil of Angola!

11. One problem in Oceania is, of course, that the geographical fragmentation into thousands of islands and islets so effectively reinforces social fragmentation.

12. Spitsbergen would be an example here, and it is not obvious that the Spitsbergen treaty of 1924 distributes sovereignty over Spitsbergen so asymmetrically in favor of Norway as the Norwegian government seems to believe.

13. The reader is encouraged to look at the map of the Kuwait neighborhood of the Arab peninsula.

14. Ultimately this is more an energy problem (drilling, pumping, transportation) than a water problem. The water is there, but not easily available.

15. The Japanese are particularly innovative when it comes to underwater colonies, as witnessed by their international exposition in Okinawa in the fall of 1975.

16. The Ijsselmeer in the Netherlands, increasingly reclaimed through the impressive dike and pumping systems, is a good example here.

17. Needless to say, this is a potential danger inherent in the idea of a 200-mile economic zone, and precisely the reason why it is defined as an "economic zone" only. On the other hand, the big-power, and particularly superpower, interests in preserving freedom of navigations for their own political and even military purposes is also built into the concept.

18. This argument is explored in some detail in section 8.4.

19. The United Nations headquarters in New York are, however, also a good example of how nonterritoriality can be combined with territoriality through the concept of extraterritorial rights and special police forces that increasingly give a separate identity to the United Nations.

20. It should be noted that this is not the hatred theory, the idea that brothers (and increasingly sisters) at war do so with more emotions than others. This is a structural theory: internal domination is usually more tightly spun, more intricate, more multidimensional than external domination, for which reason the struggle becomes more general and complete.

21. For some reflections on definitions of racial and ethnical groups, see Galtung, "Towards a Theory of Race Relations," *Essays* III, 13.

22. When the two coincide there is a nation-state, when they do not there is a problem—at least as long as the nation-state is built into human minds as a political program. The pervasiveness of that program seems to testify to a psychological factor, something like "fear of dissimilarity," underlying

the program. Perhaps one might even say that there are two types of conflict in human affairs: vertical conflict built around the concept of dominance, for instance as defined in chapter 4, and horizontal conflict built around the concept of dissimilarity. As is well known, very often the two combine into one empirical cluster where the two components are not so easily discernible.

23. For one modest but very useful survey of ethnic minorities, see Andres Kung and Olof G. Tandberg, *Jordens Förtryckta* (Bonniers, 1970), Tribun-serien. Although this book is by now somewhat dated, it is interesting to note how since 1970 almost all the minorities listed have made headlines in the news. Of the 80 or so minorities listed on the map of Europe (pp. 172–73), some of them now much better known than others. (For example, the Catholics in Ulster, the Basques and Catalans in Spain, and the Albanians in Yugoslavia are better known today than the Albanians in Italy, except locally.) But almost all contradictions of minority/majority are today known as manifest conflict, particularly the Chinese minorities in South East Asia.

24. A good example of latent secessionism is constituted by the Lapps in the very north of Europe, northern Norway, northern Sweden, northern Finland, and some northern parts of the Soviet Union; possibly in conjunction with similar movements among the Eskimos of Greenland and northern Canada (in the future possibly including some other peoples in northern parts of the Soviet Union farther to the east). They have been exposed to exploitation of all kinds, to penetration, are heavily fragmented and marginalized on the bases of race and ethnicity, at the same time as territories exist that traditionally constituted the basis of their economic production and social reproduction. It will be interesting to see to what extent a viable modern movement can be built around this nucleus without itself contributing to its destruction.

25. Thus, both South Africa and Israel should be seen as occupied territories. It is interesting to note the enthusiasm in a country like Norway for the Israeli commando raid on Entebbe airport in Uganda (July 1976) to liberate Israeli hostages, in a population that would have been equally enthusiastic if during the war Norwegians (who would then not be referred to as hijackers) had gotten hold of a planeload of Germans in order to liberate other Norwegians (who would then not be referred to as terrorists) from German prisons.

26. Killing people may eventually take the form of genocide, the final solution to a "minority" problem by eliminating a whole population, as Americans did with the American Indians, as Latin Americans seem to have been doing with American Indians in South America for a long time, and as the Nazis did with the Jews.

27. This point is very forcefully made by Leopold Kohr in *The Breakdown of Nations* (London: Routledge & Kegan Paul, 1957).

28. In the Ethiopian case the dominant group, the Amhars, is in the minority (perhaps 18 percent); in the Soviet Union case the dominant group (the Great Russians) accounts for about half of the population. More precisely, the census of 15 January 1970 gave the population of the Soviet Union as 241,720,000, an increase of 16 percent since the 1959 census. Of this total, the population of RSFSR was 130 million, but this figure includes

numerous minorities. RSFSR grew by only 11 percent, but the five Central Asian republics grew by 10 million, from about 23 to about 33 million, or well above 40 percent (the highest rate was in Tadzhikistan: 46 percent); 1.2 million was immigration of Russians. See *Pravda,* 17 April 1971, here quoted from *Haus Rissen Mitteilungsblatt,* III (1971), p. 33.

29. The Rhodesian formula, by no means something on which Ian Smith had any monopoly, was to protect minority rights by making the right to vote dependent on the usual criteria of income/property and education, in other words on precisely those things that are the privileges of the minority.

30. This is in itself some type of secessionism that could in principle be repeated inside Ulster by drawing a border around districts heavily populated with Catholics, but it would be in total contradiction to any principle of viability. Consequently, a more likely strategy would be to reverse the trend that created the Ulster problem in the first run, the Cromwell wave of Protestant immigration, by resettling for at least a short period of time some of them in, for instance, western Scotland.

31. For a further elaboration of this concept, see Galtung "Entropy and the General Theory of Peace," *Essays* I, 2.

32. The coupling, then, would consist in the dominant group in the structure of internal colonization being the bridgehead (the periphery of the Periphery) of the external colonization, thus tying the theory of imperialism developed in chapter 4 to the theory of internal dominance developed here.

33. And this is where the idea of a "minority" enters: proportionate representation can be permitted as long as the proportion is small enough. The dominant group may also be a minority, if the majority is divided into sufficiently antagonistic dominated minorities.

34. One reason for the apparent stability in Tanzania may be the high number of ethnic groups: if they are not too different in size, a high number may be stabilizing simply because no permanent pattern of dominance emerges as a key social axis. The figures quoted are from *Time* Magazine.

35. The definition of such groups would usually rest on linguistic criteria, religious criteria, or both. It is probably safe to assume that the stronger the correlation between such criteria, the more intense the movements and potentially more violent the struggle.

36. A similar situation may arise in Yugoslavia between the republics to the northwest (Slovenia and Croatia) and the rest (particularly Macedonia).

37. One good contribution in that direction is the book by Per Otnes, *Den samiske nasjon* (Oslo: Pax, 1972).

38. This, of course, is seen as a difficulty only if perceived by Western eyes. In less territorially inclined approaches to human organization it presents no difficulty. It may even represent a major facility: in periods of drought and other national calamities the absence of borders makes major changes of population location possible. It is probably correct to say that such calamities are and were less frequent in Europe—from which the nation-state program and the idea of strict definitions of borders emerged so strongly—and the program hence carries a certain geographical code not necessarily applicable to other regions.

39. The coexistence of Hindus and Muslims in India today, highly interwoven and with a very high level of entropy in the mixture, is a compliment to the organization of the subcontinent, particularly against the background of the bloodshed of 1947–1948.

40. On the other hand, Latin America, at least as far as the dominant white groups are concerned, can be seen as essentially two nations, one speaking Spanish, the other Portuguese.

41. It is interesting to speculate where secessionist movements in the United States might show up. One possibility is Hawaii, not so much for ethnic reasons as for life-style reasons and, potentially, different geopolitical interests from mainland. Another possibility is the states bordering on the Gulf of Mexico, particularly the black states—for instance, in a federation with Carribean countries that also originally were slave-based. Still other possibilities are California, simply because it is so rich, and the Southwest, because of the Spanish-speaking element. It goes without saying that Alaska could be added to this list when after some time its obvious economic viability (oil-based) is translated into a sense of political identity. Nothing lasts forever, including the United States.

42. Andrei Amalrik's excellent book *Will the Soviet Union Survive Until 1984?* (New York: Harper & Row, 1970) points very clearly to the vulnerability of the Soviet construction. The many bombings in Gruzia (Georgia) recently testify to the existence of some kind of grievance that one day may take the form of an independent movement. Soviet Armenia has gained strength from the contrast with the genocidal cruelty exercised by the Turks at the time of World War I; such memories are not that easily transmitted to new generations. Then there are the Central Asian republics, not to mention Ukraina. And inside the main republic, RSFSR, there are numerous minorities that one day might be striving for a higher level of autonomy than is presently granted them.

43. One of the basic points here is that we simply do not know, except for the case of Tibet. When I argued (1973, in China) that Chinese behavior in Tibet in 1951 looked rather similar to the social imperialism they accused the Soviet Union of, the answer was "Yes, but you should remember that in 1951 we were under strong Soviet influence and had a tendency to do as the Soviet Union does." The basic point about China in this connection, however, is probably the much quoted figure of 96 percent of the population as belonging to the *han* majority, thus indicating a high level of homogeneity. On the other hand, there is antogonism toward Manchurians, the symbols of the Ching dynasty, and this was undoubtedly one of the factors underlying the cultural revolution, articulated in the age old Shanghai–Peking antogonism. One wonders how many of them are back again after the post Mao counterrevolution.

44. In Western Europe the situation is probably relatively quiet as long as there is sufficient affluence with which minorities can be coopted. Since so much of the Western European affluence is based on political and economic imperialism, and social stability is based on patterns of sharing the spoils of exploitation with the underprivileged under welfare-state and more or less social-democratic formulas, it is not strange that the upsurge of national movements in Western Europe has accompanied the decline of imperialism—and will continue to do so.

45. In Eastern Europe stability is based on repression, and it is probably safe to predict that national movements will emerge much more clearly when

the regimes become more liberal, when, for instance, the Soviet Union loosens her grip on the Eastern European countries.

46. The Helsinki Agreement of 1975 is a step in the direction of a final peace treaty for Europe, and possibly as far as one could come. Hence, it is to be expected that national movements in Eastern Europe will become much more vocal in the near future.

47. On the other hand, there will also be much understanding in the Center for national movements.

48. This is one of the ideas developed by Amalrik (see note 42).

49. A functional perspective here would be to see how the parties, implicitly or explicitly, strike one item after the other off their cooperation agenda until at the end what remains is a purely formal relationship, like the gradual process of marriage dissolution. At the end there may be a "sudden jump," however, the final separation.

50. This is a basic theme of the Trends in Western Civilization Program of the Chair in Conflict and Peace Research, University of Oslo.

51. The argument here is spelled out in more detail and with a concrete case in Galtung, "Divided Nations as a Process: One State, Two States and In-Between; the Case of Korea," *Essays* V, 5. The argument is that it is high time to find more formulas located between the one-state formula and the two-states formula.

52. Often I have argued the other way: that social processes are discontinuous, "jumpy." But it is equally fruitful to look at processes that are customarily seen as being a jump across a solid dichotomy as somehow continuous, filling in the gap with all kinds of in-between formulas.

53. For an effort to spell out the "scenario" already indicated in note 30, see the article on the Ulster question in *Bulletin of Peace Proposals* (1972).

54. My experience with UN representatives from the Byelorussian and Ukrainian republics indicates that there is some dissimilarity in the sense that particularly the Byelorussians might be even more Moscow than Moscow.

55. Important, and a significant point toward the future, is the fact that almost all of them participated in the process leading up to the Helsinki Agreement of 1975. Recent popular trends against gigantism will definitely stimulate the interest in European mini-states, and one of the least known but possibly most viable seems to be the Faroe Islands, which was not a participant in that particular political process.

56. There are, of course, exceptions. Plato was very interested in numbers (*The Laws*), perhaps not so much in the *size* as in the properties of the *number* of inhabitants, particularly how many divisors the number had (5040 was a particularly felicitous number of inhabitants, according to Plato). But the Chinese seem to be very concerned with size, particularly with striking a balance between the minimum needed for economic viability and the maximum needed in order to permit direct, face-to-face democracy. The People's Commune seems to be an answer to the first problem with an average size somewhat below 10,000; the team within the brigade within the People's Commune (itself a federation of villages) seems to be an answer to the latter problem, with a size more like 250.

57. Needless to say, the macro-states would not agree with this. Much research should be done in the direction of exploring the relation between size and various indicators of positive and negative development.

58. No doubt the concept has built into it double seclusiveness: a group of similar people cohabiting in a territorial capsule, and an extrapolation of the clan hiding behind the walls of a castle. It combines ethnic arrogance with a base for aggression, and/or a feeling of ethnic inferiority with a base for defense.

59. No doubt this is what the Russians try to achieve within the Soviet Union through their demographic policies.

60. We then conceive of "culture" broadly as any pattern defining what is true or false, good or bad, right or wrong, holy or profane, and so on.

61. This is spelled out in some detail in Galtung, "The Middle East and the Theory of Conflict," *Essays* V, 3.

62. The simplest approach to this is proportionate representation.

63. This is spelled out in some detail in Galtung, "A Structural Theory of Integration," *Essays* IV, 11.

64. This is a basic theme of the World Indicators Program of the Chair in Conflict and Peace Research, University of Oslo—how to operationalize imperialism in such a way that one can talk about degrees of imperialism.

65. This is the pattern known as subimperialism, explored in the final sections of the article referred to in note 3 to chapter 4.

66. It is quite clear that the Chinese language is currently being standardized according to the version spoken in northern China, and it is not obvious that it makes much difference to the southern Chinese that this is referred to as the "northern People's dialect" rather than as "Mandarin."

67. In India there is no doubt that Hindi achieves a significance inconceivable if the capital of the country had been located farther to the south. This is explored in a project at the Chair in Conflict and Peace Research, University of Oslo: India as an International System.

68. This is less true for Latin America, although it remains to be seen what happens when the nonwhite masses come into motion in that region.

69. Most scenarios today seem to be based on fears that China and the Soviet Union will become friends again. No doubt that would change the present world political scene, but so would—and perhaps more basically—some kind of harmonization between India and China, particularly if Japan were added to it. In general, however, I object strongly to this Kissingerian approach to world politics in terms of superpowers and big powers rather than human beings. A "statesman" who never talks in terms of human beings is likely to act accordingly.

70. Most important among the countries left out are Australia and Oceania. It is interesting that Mesarović and Pestel in their book arrived at a relatively similar division of the world (see note 39 to chapter 4). It should be noted that we have great difficulties knowing how to place Afghanistan; located as it is between the RCD countries and the Indian subcontinent. The whole division of the world given here is of course related to the theory developed in section 4.2.

71. A prevision differs from a prediction by being in terms of total entities, complete structures, whereas predictions are in terms of changes along one or a few variables—at least, this is the way the terms are used here.

72. The chart was originally made in 1969 and is left here unchanged to check on how the predictions are evolving.

73. The whole argument is spelled out more in detail in Galtung, "On the

Future of the World System, Territorial and Non-Territorial," *Essays* IV, 19.

74. There are obvious reasons for this: not only do they have the capability, they also have the intention, partly derived from growing appetites, partly derived from exposure—due to their size—to a large variety of hostile forces, both internal and external.

75. And this is one reason for the very strong emotional reaction to the "oil crisis" of 1973: the world was no longer rotating around the correct axis.

76. This is spelled out in more detail in the chapter "Regional Security Commissions" in Galtung and Lodgaard, eds., *Cooperation in Europe* (Oslo: Universitetsforlaget, 1970).

77. And to some extent the development has been in this direction, with the Helsinki Agreement codifying some of the implicit rather than institutionalized processes that have been taking place in recent years—adding to the SALT and MFR negotiations.

78. Because there is no doubt that this is to some extent directed against China, it is also strongly resented by the People's Republic. It should be noted that after this was first written another economic commission operating in what traditionally is referred to as the Middle East area (now known as the Arab Region, or as West Asia) has come into being: the Economic Commission for West Asia. It does not cover the entire conflict area, unfortunately, unlike ECE.

79. Needless to say, "rich, white Europeans" do not show any inclination in this direction so far.

80. For an exploration of NMD, see section 5.3.

81. To this could definitely be added the Mediterranean as one more region, evolving more and more clearly after the 1973 "oil crisis." It should be noted that Kissinger's International Energy Agency can be seen as a North Atlantic effort clearly designed to counteract this tendency—partly successfully, because only France has remained outside the IEA (Norway being an associated member).

82. This is one more reason for including the Mediterranean area as a region, well connected from time immemorial, although not all of these potential actions have been equally pacific or well utilized.

83. The Viña del Mar Declaration was an effort to change this.

84. A very high number of cooperation agreements have been entered into recently.

85. The European Community has a distinct Mediterranean policy and was among the first to recognize the Mediterranean area as a region in its own right, before the 1973 "oil crisis."

86. There are so many efforts of these types, such as George Catlin's effort to push the NAFTA idea and the late Brazilian politician Lacerda's argumentation in favor of a South Atlantic market, tying Brazil to Angola and Guinea-Bissau and, in addition to these Portuguese-speaking areas, to the many West African countries from which substantial parts of the present Brazilian population came—as slaves.

87. But this is now rapidly changing: there are processes, often contradictory, at work both in the territorial world and in the UN system.

88. The best example of this was the failure of the United Nations to do anything in connection with the Indochina wars.

89. Thus, there are very few "nonaligned" countries in Europe or in the rich part of the world in general. Since the "aligned" conflict to a large extent is about how the rich countries can dominate the poor countries this is not strange.

90. If Lin Piao was removed by Chou En-lai, then one reasonable speculation might be that there could be a return to the Lin Piao type of policies after Chou En-lai had passed away (January 1976). Present (1979) Chinese policies seem to be in another direction, but that may change again. This perspective on big powers has also been elaborated in my articles on Japan and Korea in *Essays* V and in Galtung, *The European Community: A Superpower in the Making* (London: Allen & Urwin, 1973).

91. For an exploration of this difference, see Galtung, "Structural Analysis and Chemical Models," chapter 6 in *Methodology and Ideology* (Copenhagen: Ejlers, 1977).

92. One way of using the concepts may be as follows: a set is defined in terms of elements; in a system there are relations between the elements; in a structure there are also relations between these relations.

93. The Trilateral Commission, the Secretary General of which was a former State Department consultant and present (1979) presidential adviser (Zbigniew Brzezinski), is a typical example of this tendency. Among its members are a number of high-ranking businessmen and politicians and defense intellectuals—the latter obviously included in an effort to make use of the network of international relations institutes founded in the 1950's and 1960's, to a large extent under U.S. economic or intellectual sponsorship.

94. This point is very forcefully made by H. Magdoff in many of his important writings on imperialism.

95. It is hard to imagine that the European Community really will disintegrate from the level to which it has arrived, being such a loose *Staatesbund* rather than *Bundesstaat.* Another thing is what happens when after higher levels of integration and maturity real challenges are encountered and the structure is no longer flexible enough to absorb them.

96. The conference in Sri Lanka in August 1976 was also largely accompanied by the usual contempt in the comments of journalists from the rich world, but in a few years that will no longer be the case.

97. No doubt the Group of 77—currently counting more than 110 members including the Socialist Republic of Romania—and the movement of the nonaligned countries will for all practical purposes coincide and constitute a major force, no longer defining itself as between East and West, but in its own right. No doubt they will also soon establish their own secretariat, similar to the OECD and EC Commission, on a permanent basis. This theme is developed further in section 8.4.

98. This is in itself a part of fundamentalist definitions of conflict—well adjusted to the personalities of Stalin and Dulles.

99. A typical example of this is the European Community's efforts with the countries in the Caribbean, Africa, and the Pacific—but to a large extent thwarted by the resolute and unified approach of these countries.

100. By "conflict formation" is simply meant the parties/actors of the conflict together with the issues/goals around which the conflict is defined.

101. There is an important exception here, though: although the First World has not helped the peoples in the Third World trying to liberate themselves, they have received considerable help from the Second World, the socialist countries. Workers in Czechoslovakia producing guns by working overtime on Sundays for the Vietnamese should not be underestimated as a contributing factor to the liberation of Vietnam, regardless of what kinds of motives one might attribute to the Soviet Union in this connection.

102. This is described in some detail in chapter 1 of Galtung, *The European Community: A Superpower in the Making.*

103. Seen in this perspective the whole of World War II looks so wasteful—a gigantic effort dedicated to a purpose totally asynchronic with the middle of the twentieth century.

104. An important formulation of this principle was given in Nixon's famous speech in Kansas City, June 1971. See chapter 5, note 12.

105. For an elaboration of this, see "On Foreign Policy," chapter 6 in Galtung and Fumiko Nishimura, *Learning from the Chinese People* (Oslo, 1975).

106. This is elaborated in some detail in the article referred to in note 61.

107. For more detail, see the article referred to in note 51.

108. For there are, indeed, nonterritorial conflicts, organized around such axes as racism, sexism, and agism—the latter (the conflict between the middle-aged on one hand and the young and the old on the other) being the least crystallized of the three so far.

7. THE NONTERRITORIAL SYSTEM

7.1 NONTERRITORIAL ACTORS

Ultimately, as often said, the world consists of human beings, of individuals. But individuals are organized in collectivities that become actors and form systems. As mentioned in section 1.3, the total, the *world* system, can be split into two: the *territorial system* (T) and the *nonterritorial system* (NT)–which, one hopes, do not add up to TNT.

Actors in the territorial system are organized on the basis of *contiguity* of territorial units, actors in the nonterritorial system on the basis of *similarity* (in associations) or *interaction* (in organizations).[1] This works like Chinese boxes: inside a territorial actor, e.g., a country, there are associations and organizations (parties, trade unions, farms, factories, firms); inside a nonterritorial actor there may be states, for states also form associations (like the Francophone countries) or organizations (like the sphere of influence of a hegemonial power).[2] The basic point remains clear, however: membership in a territorial actor is based on location in *geographical space*; membership in a nonterritorial actor on location in some *sociofunctional space,* defined by similarity and/or interaction. In the first case *vicinity* is the guiding principle, in the second case *affinity.*[3]

One misunderstanding should now be cleared up. A truly nonterritorial actor is, of course, geographically *universal.* Thus, no Nordic association is a nonterritorial actor in the sense discussed here; it is only a component in a regional territorial actor (the Nordic countries) or a part of a truly nonterritorial actor (the corresponding world association, if there is any). Since our primary focus here is the world, our attention is focused on nonterritorial actors that are not regional, that do not recognize any territorial borderline at all. They may in fact not have members all over the world, but in principle they might have; they are open to all, as no Nordic association is.

Let us then go more deeply into "nonterritoriality." What kinds of units may be members of the "international organizations" that constitute nonterritorial actors? By and large there seem to be three answers, on a scale of increasing nonterritoriality:

1. Members are national governments, and the organization is *intergovernmental* (IGO);

2. Members are other national organizations or associations, and the organization is *internongovernmental* (INGO);
3. Members are individuals, and the organization is *transnational nongovernmental* (TRANGO).

I prefer not to use the term "international" for any one of these, for that term, in my view, does not imply any organization or actor at all. The "international" system is simply the system of nations (actually the system of states, or countries), in cooperation and conflict—nothing more, nothing less. For that reason I interpret IGO to mean intergovernmental (and not international, governmental), INGO to mean internongovernmental (and not international, nongovernmental), and I add to this well-known distinction the transnational (or, really, transnongovernmental) organization, the TRANGO, which relates directly to individuals wherever they are found. In the TRANGO there are no "national chapters" or similar arrangements controlling the direct relation between individuals, possibly absorbing the loyalty between the individual and the nonterritorial organization.[4]

There exists a vitally important special case of the INGO: the *business* internongovernmental organization (BINGO). It links together nongovernmental business organizations in various countries and is known today as the "multinational corporation." However, the latter is an unfortunate term for at least four reasons. First, "multi" connotes more than two nations, but often there are only two, for reasons explored in chapter 4.[5] In the case of an organization drawing on only two states the term "cross-national" may be preferred to "multinational."[6] Further, the term "multinational" conceals how asymmetric these corporations are, with one country often dominating them. Then "corporation" may not be broad enough, for there may be many other ways of organizing international business than in corporations. (Incidentally, one of these ways would be governmental, as an IGO, which in that case could be termed a BIGO.[7]) Finally, these organizations are entities of their own kind, *sui generis,* not just a multiple of companies. They are very often Business-TRANGO, for which reason the recent term "transnational corporation" (TNC) fits better.

The significance of the distinction just made between IGOs, INGOs, and TRANGOs has to do with two important phenomena located at the interface between the territorial and the nonterritorial systems. These two systems are by no means unrelated, particularly since one, the territorial, preceded the other by thousands of years and consequently must have set its stamp on the latecomer, however efficiently the latter makes use of transportation and communication.[8] The two phenomena characterizing the relation between the two systems are *isomorphy* and *homology*. The propositions are simple:

1. The nonterritorial actors tend to be isomorphic with the territorial system.
2. The nonterritorial actors tend to induce homology between territorial actors.

3. Propositions 1 and 2 are most valid for intergovernmental organizations (usually), less for internongovernmental organizations, and (almost) invalid for transnational organizations.

It is characteristic of the two most weakly nonterritorial of the nonterritorial actors, the IGOs and the INGOs, that the *world territorial structure, the state structure, is still entirely visible*. NT is a mirror reflection of T. When governments are members this is obvious, but it also applies to the typical international organization built as an association of national associations (e.g., an association of national associations of dentists, longshoremen, stamp collectors), and even to the multinational corporation. An association or organization at the national level becomes a "national chapter" or a "mother," "sister," or "daughter" company, depending on its position in the hierarchy of the nonterritorial actor.[9] Not only the *elements* of the territorial system, but also the *relations* between them can usually be rediscovered among the nonterritorial actors, which is why the term "isomorphy" is used. Relations of power (both in terms of resources and structures) and interaction frequency are often mirrored faithfully. The most powerful chapter is located in the most powerful country, in terms of location of the organization's headquarters, recruitment of staff, general perspective on world affairs, and so on.[10] Frequencies of interaction in the territorial system are mirrored in frequencies of interaction in the organization, and so on.[11] In other words, the territorial system is reproduced inside the nonterritorial actor, which for that reason is not truly nonterritorial.

This way of thinking carries us quite far analytically. Nonterritorial actors with national components—governmental or nongovernmental—can be seen as governed primarily by the principle of isomorphy. This is the baseline, as implemented in the United Nations when the major victors among the "united nations," the Allies fighting against the Axis powers, appointed themselves to permanent Security Council positions. Isomorphy is called "realism" in the plain language of power. It means that to those who have power in the territorial system, power shall also be given in the nonterritorial system. And it is probably partially true that the more an intergovernmental organization departs from this isomorphy, the less attention will be paid to it, because its decisions will be seen as not reflecting the "real world," meaning the territorial system with its bilateral relations, particularly among the strong, to which decisions will then be referred.[12]

But this is only a partial truth. A nonterritorial actor that is 100 percent isomorphic with the territorial system is in a sense only a replication of that system, except that it makes multilateral interaction possible. Some deviations from strict isomorphy will of course take place since countries are represented by persons with their idiosyncrasies, making these organizations a medium in which the smaller powers can more easily express themselves, can be listened to, and can have some impact on the territorial system. This medium is not merely one in which they can be more easily bossed.

But then there is the opposite view, that this is precisely the medium in which the territorial system of yesterday can be kept alive and even reinforced. For instance, Nationalist China had for a long time a power excess because of its position in the UN Security Council. The argument would be, however, that this is the result not of too much isomorphy but of a lack of isomorphy, because the UN served to freeze the past. One might also extend that argument to the case of the United Kingdom and France, and even to the United States, for all practical purposes defeated by what it often referred to as a "fifth-rate power," Vietnam.[13]

Imagine the United Nations brought up to date, in an effort to mirror the territorial system. The argument against it would then be that any distinction between veto and nonveto is too sharp, too absolute relative to the power distinctions in the much more subtle and complicated territorial system. Moreover, if prowess in war is used to decide who has the veto, then the United States and Vietnam should at least be on par, with Vietnam viewed as an effective challenger of the former heavyweight champion.[14]

Of course, over time the internal workings of a nonterritorial actor will acquire facets never contemplated by its social architects, the lawyers. There will be informal structures in addition to the formal ones. But existing power differentials may actually be magnified rather than reduced in an intergovernmental organization.[15]

In the INGO all this becomes much less important. Nongovernments may feel less obliged to act in the name of the "national interest" and more free to find the pattern of action and interaction that fits the values of the organization. Thus, one would assume in general that INGOs have national elements—by definition—but that the relations between them are different, for instance, much more egalitarian. The world has come to accept the idea of a big-power veto in the United Nations, whether this adequately reflects or even exaggerates territorial power, but it would hardly accept it in an international philatelic association. Needless to say, all shades and gradations can be imagined here.[16]

When it comes to transnational organizations, isomorphy breaks down almost completely: there are neither the territorial elements nor the relations of the territorial system. Transnational ties uniting individuals across territorial borders would be stronger than common citizenship. The classical example here is, of course, *membership in a nationality* as opposed to *state citizenship.* The nation, defined as a group of human beings having in common some characteristics referred to as ethnic, is the most important of all transnational organizations. (Here the unfortunate consequences of the double meaning of "nation" become particularly obvious!) Time and again nationality proves to be more important than territorially defined state citizenship, but the two are often confused because the nation-state is taken as the norm and sometimes is also a fact in our world. Thus, Jews formed such a transnational group,[17] although a much better expression would be "transgovernmental"—a TRAGO—since they are found under the protection (or abuse) of various governments. The extent to which Jews would identify themselves as "Soviet" Jews, "American" Jews, and so on would be a test of the extent to which this grouping is an INGO or a TRANGO. In some years the same reasoning may apply to women and to age groups—obviously TRANGOs in the making.

More recent examples would be international scientific unions where the dissolution of national emphasis has gone quite far.[18] Of course, people in the same discipline from the same country may know each other better, and their interaction is usually facilitated by their speaking the same language, but the search for significant colleagues, for meaningful persons with whom to work, to converse, and to exchange ideas will not be restricted by such borders. Only few and particularly repressive countries would imagine organizing their citizens to force them to speak with one voice in a transnational scientific organization.

Then there are, of course, the political parties and pressure groups that are transnational, such as the World New Left and the Vietnam solidarity movement.[19] The fact that there may also be cooperation at subnational and national levels does not detract from the transnational character of such world movements, for national identities are usually successfully washed out. A good case in point is the world hippie movement—or any movement for new life styles in defiance of the various versions of model II society, the vertical, success-oriented, power-oriented society.[20]

For these reasons I see the transnational organizations as the nonterritorial actors of the future. Only they can deserve the epithet "global actors," since only they are both based on individuals as their unit and are global in their scope.

To summarize: the idea of isomorphy can be split in two: the presence of territorial *elements,* states in nonterritorial actors, and the presence of territorial *relations* in these actors. In this regard we find the three types shown in table 7.1.

Let us then turn to the problem of *homology,* to see how nonterritorial organizations act as giant mechanisms for making all states as similar to each other as possible. Just as a state tries to find its appropriate place (often called its "natural" position) in a nonterritorial organization, so a nonterritorial organization is a vehicle facilitating the search for one's *opposite number* inside other states. Whether members are governments, nongovernmental associations, organizations, or simply individuals, any international organization will try to bring together like-minded or like-positioned elements in all states around the world. For that is their task: *to organize all of their kind,* wherever they can be found. Where their kind do not exist they can be created by, for instance, inviting

Table 7.1 Three types of nonterritorial actors

Territorial elements	Territorial relations	Nonterritoriality
present	present	low (IGOs, many BINGOs)
present	absent	medium (INGOs)
absent	absent	high (TRANGOs)

observers to international conferences who then return to their country with one message imprinted on their minds: *"Solch ein Ding müssen wir auch haben"* (We must have that too). But international organizations may become giant mechanisms through which people in the stronger states that started these organizations can imprint a message on the people of weaker states: "You must have this ministry and that profession, this hobby and sports association and that ideological movement, you must produce this and that—in order to be full-fledged members of the World." Active membership in international organizations is taken as an indicator of how deeply embedded the country is in the world system, without questioning too much who started all these organizations, on what social basis, for what purpose, in what image.[2][1]

Thus, international conferences become giant markets where isomorphy and homology can be tested, the former vis-à-vis interstate characteristics, the latter vis-à-vis intrastate characteristics. They become giant reproduction mechanisms. Power relations in the nonterritorial organization will be compared to power relations in the territorial system, to see to what extent T is reflected in NT. And individuals from various countries will compare notes to find to what extent that particular NT is reflected in their part of T—whether it is present at all, and whether their government pays as much attention to it in terms of subsidy and deference as other governments, and so on.

This entire presentation may now gain in depth if it is tied to the model of the world developed in chapter 4, more particularly to the four-nation model that was also made use of to develop a typology of warfare in chapter 5. Here this model can be used to develop a typology of such organizations (see figure 7.1). In figure 7.1 the little dots at the top of each circle represent the governments, the nuclei of the centers. Obviously, the IGOs connect these dots in various ways. The INGOs do not necessarily connect only the centers of nations; they may also tie periphery elements together. But chances are that the masses are tied to their territorial units, *that the whole concept of nonterritoriality is fundamentally an elite concept.* Even such grandiose concepts as "Europe" and even the nation-state are very much elite concepts. Why? Because such means for developing consciousness as literacy, reading beyond primary school,

Figure 7.1 Nonterritoriality as an elite concept

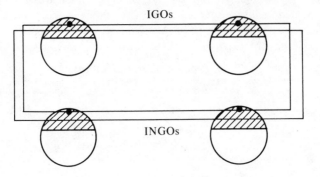

access to transportation and communication, and knowledge of foreign languages are badly distributed. Hence, without having really good data on national participation in the types of associations and organizations that also are multinationally organized, we can at least say that those individuals who participate internationally in conferences and in secretariats and the like generally belong to the elite (or the counterelite). These are the individuals who serve as links between nations, not the nonparticipant members and the even less-participant nonmembers, hidden behind the nation-state screen.[22]

Thus, if nonterritorial actors (including the transnational ones) essentially link governments and other elite groups together, then there are, in principle and in reference to the figure, four types of international organizations:

1. Those connecting Center countries (horizontal lines, top);
2. Those connecting Center and Periphery countries in the same bloc (vertical lines);
3. Those connecting Periphery countries (horizontal lines, bottom)
   (a) in the same bloc,
   (b) in different blocs;
4. Universal organizations (the whole rectangle).

The first three may be referred to as "regional" organizations (as long as we keep in mind the distinction between horizontal and vertical regions) and are not really nonterritorial actors.

In the real world, however, a particular organization is often too complex to permit classification in any single one of these types.[23] The secretariat of an organization for instance, may often be different from the rest of the organization, being transnational even when the rest is intergovernmental or internongovernmental. Much of the history of the big intergovernmental organizations is the story of how the secretariat has tried to transnationalize the national delegates (meeting in conferences and assemblies, in councils or in executive boards), teaching them "to think in terms of the world as a whole" (the "world" usually meaning the organization as conceived of by the secretariat) *and* of how the national delegates try to internationalize the secretariat by such methods as secondment, short tenure, return to governmental posts rather than a career in another transnational secretariat, and so on.[24]

The net conclusion is that the two systems, T and NT, are not independent of each other, nor should one expect them to be. The NTs of today are mainly instruments in the hands of the territorial units who know how to use them, and that does not include only the big powers.[25] But this is less true for the transnational organizations, since they are not organized in national chapters and since loyalty in them is directed to the world level and the individual level, not to the intermediate nation-state level. These members are not so concerned with "organizing something similar at home" after they have been exposed to patterns in other nations through the medium of transnational conferences. For them an institution found or founded in one country is already a world institution, not something to be used in and for one country and copied elsewhere.

But what this means is that one cannot naively assume that nonterritorial actors are on the side of the good—peace, for instance—while territorial actors are on the other side.[26] The whole matter is much more complex. In fact, it may be argued that nonterritorial actors in the broad sense are probably the most dangerous vehicles of structural violence, precisely because of the mechanisms outlined in section 4.2. Territorial actors can also exercise structural violence internationally, in the form of colonialism, although it now is outmoded. What territorial actors can still do of a destructive nature is to fight wars. In fact, wars are based on territorial concepts, since most weaponry we know, from catapults and arrows to atomic weapons, destroys territorially contiguous units. They are based on the assumption that there is a high concentration of enemies (with a low concentration of friends) at the point of impact. Wars between nonterritorial actors are conceivable, but less easily fought, at least with the present military technology.[27]

In conclusion, some words about the transnational corporations (TNCs). I have deliberately chosen not to devote a special section to an analysis of this phenomenon, partly because an extensive and very fine literature exists on the subject and partly because analytically this literature does not offer much that is really new.[28] *Basically the TNCs are the carriers of economic imperialism.* The latter is inconceivable without large-scale economic cycles in which capital, labor, raw materials, semimanufactured goods, and manufactured goods are moved and shuffled around. The administrator of that process, including all stages of financing, exploration, research and development, extraction, processing, marketing, consumption, and reinvestment at any point, is a corporation. When the cycle crosses international borders, the obvious organizational solution is the transnational corporation. The interesting analytical foci would be not only the *domain* ("In which countries does the corporation operate?") but also the *scope* ("How much of the total economic cycle does it control; does it have its own financial institutions? its own facilities for consumption?"). In general I assume that TNCs will tend to become universally monopolistic *and to control the total cycle*—and I find this last problem not sufficiently researched and more important than the problem of the size of the assets controlled (quite well researched, it seems).[29] However, it is unnecessary for one single TNC to control everything; it can do so in cooperation with others, forming some kind of loose federation among TNCs.[30] Some of them may be highly informal, like the organizations that manage to transport "guest workers" from Africa to France, for instance. To focus too much on the individual transnational corporation is to miss the point; the total system is what counts.

Much of the debate about the TNCs has been focused on their size (measured in assets and, incorrectly, compared to the GNPs of countries), the conclusion being that they have become too big, too powerful, *and potentially too autonomous.* Autonomy is not necessarily objectionable. If a TNC is autonomous it must be somewhat independent of the territorial system, and that system has not proven itself so capable of satisfying human needs that there is · no space for the emergence of new actors free from some of the constraints of the territorial system, and in addition possessing resources. After all, many would like to see the United Nations endowed with these characteristics. The problem is what effect the TNCs have, on balance. It is also important to know to what extent they are autonomous, to know, for example, whether TNC can act against the interests (as articulated by the government) of a country in which it has headquarters. The general assumption is that there is a very pronounced harmony of interest here; but to obtain that harmony the government may have to yield, not the TNC, which is of course a sign of some kind of TNC autonomy. But about this too little is known at present, it seems.[31]

We now list five major objections to TNCs,[32] all stemming from the assumption that they are not nonterritorial enough, but are in fact fundamental articulations of the territorial system. Two of these objections fall under the heading of "isomorphy" and two under "homology," and a fifth is even more closely linked to the territorial system itself.

From the point of view of isomorphy:

[1] *The TNCs serve to maintain, probably even to reinforce, a vertical division of labor.*[33] The sophisticated parts of the cycle are carried out by the headquarters in the Center (research and development, difficult aspects of finance and administration, some of the most sophisticated manufacture), the simpler parts by the daughter companies in the Periphery (extraction, simple processing, processing according to existing blueprints, marketing, local consumption). It may well be that production (for the world market, incidentally) has been moved to where many of the factors are found (particularly the raw materials and cheap labor), and even most of the consumers—a wise move when costs of transportation and insurance are considered. But the division of labor in terms of differential spin-off effects ("externalities") is still there, all the more so because the TNCs may serve as a conveyor belt for the brain drain, getting "young talent" from the periphery to the center in its most creative period. Thus, general C–P relations are replicated within the TNC, reinforced by the ease with which blueprints can flow within the corporation, obviating any need for self-reliance.

[2] *Through the TNCs, net transfer of capital from the Periphery to the Center is facilitated.* The point is, of course, that the TNC can trade with itself, fixing all the costs to the extent it covers all aspects of the cycle, including transportation, letting profits show up where taxation is most lenient, and so on.[34] Hence, TNCs can serve both types of exploitation, the in-change and the exchange varieties.

From the point of view of homology:

[3] *Through the TNCs a certain mode of production is propagated, particularly one that is capital-intensive and research-intensive.* The TNCs produce and communicate a way of producing that is developed in the industrialized coun-

tries. The methods are generally capital-intensive rather than labor-intensive, except when local labor is used for simple operations. Such methods have a well-known structural impact on the local economy, dividing it into sectors of very high and very low productivity (ultimately leading to what is known as a "population problem" in the latter sector). Moreover, the methods usually have a high research component built into them, making it "unnecessary" for locals to do their own research. This process is referred to, generally, as "transfer of technology," but it can also be seen as a way of depriving others of the chance to develop through their own efforts.

[4] *Through the TNCs certain products are propagated that are not necessarily needed in other countries.* Particularly, I am thinking of the extremely poor showing of the TNCs when it comes to satisfying fundamental needs: whether in food, clothing, shelter, health, or education, the TNCs cannot be said to have made a positive contribution to those most in need. In other words, what is wrong with a TNC like Coca-Cola is not only the division of labor between countries (probably not so important in this case, as the spin-offs from the recipe cannot be that extensive), the transfer of profits, or the high productivity *but the product itself*—the forgotten dimension in so much research on TNCs. It should be possible to produce a nutritious, highly positive drink from the point of view of health. Instead, a product that is questionable from both points of view is marketed all over the world. Even when products are at least neutral in their consequences, the argument still remains that production factors are steered away from fundamental needs satisfaction and toward the satisfaction of other needs for more privileged groups of people. Think of the amount of capital, labor, and building materials that go into a Hilton or Intercontinental hotel and imagine allocating it to the slums of the cities over which such hotels tower, and the point is made.[35]

And then there is the last point:

[5] *The TNCs will tend to try to maintain this type of international structure and to support those local groups that think likewise.* It is enough to mention the case of ITT in Chile; whether it is an extreme or a typical case, research later in this century may be able to tell us.[36] But it brings up the point about autonomy again: to the extent that the TNCs are autonomous the experience so far seems to be that they overrepresent rather than underrepresent the territorial system, being among its most eager proponents. We do not hear about TNCs that turn the division of labor upside down, produce a net transfer of profits in the opposite direction, go in for labor-intensive methods based on local creativity, and in addition put fundamental needs for the masses first. The reason is simple: all of that would be contrary to the logic of capitalism, and the TNCs are the most important instruments of capitalism of our time, ultimately pointing to a world capitalist system, *sui generis,* to succeed the international one.[37]

Something has to be done about the transnational corporations, but it is not obvious that the measures often contemplated under the heading "code of conduct" will be anything like sufficient. To the extent that such a code can be gleaned from the principles expressed in the New International Economic Order and the Charter of Economic Rights and Duties of States[38] it would mainly be directed against the foregoing points 2 and 5. It would not come to grips with the problems of vertical division of labor, the intensiveness of capital and research, and whether the products are wanted or needed at all.[39] As part of a process, control of the transfer of capital is important, even crucial; but chances are that the TNCs will be flexible enough to understand that they should yield on this point in order to retain the more subtle forms of power built into the other three points.[40]

A proposal that goes far beyond the codes of conduct so far contemplated will be developed in section 8.2, in the setting of a discussion of a world central authority. Unless something profound is done to change the very structure of these corporations they will probably be able to regroup and to devise counter-strategies to nullify the impact of any code of conduct, given the human, capital, and research resources they have at their disposal.

Hence, there is room for much new thinking in this field, not necessarily because these corporations are big and do not obey orders from states. The problem is to destroy them as vehicles of structural violence, as carriers of isomorphy with a false territorial system, and to make them serve the needs of those most in need, turning them into one of the many world cementing forces needed as a barrier against direct violence.

7.2   GROWTH, FISSION, AND FUSION

In sections 6.1-6.3 the dynamism of the territorial system was studied, its growth, fission, and fusion processes; section 6.4 offered some strategies for the steering of these processes. In the present section some of the corresponding tendencies and trends in the nonterritorial system will be analyzed, with a view to designing strategies to be presented in sections 7.3 and 7.4, focusing on world, transnational, or nonterritorial politics in 7.3 and some general strategies for the total nonterritorial system in 7.4.

To gain in perspective let us compare the nonterritorial with the territorial system as if we already had all the information neatly organized, as in figure 7.2. To discuss the future of the world system with little or no clear idea of the six processes represented there is not very meaningful. Particularly dangerous is the tendency to discuss the future of the world as if only one or two of these processes were to be of significance. In addition, the key interaction processes between the two systems must be considered.

My basic proposition is as follows: *whereas the dynamism of the territorial system will mainly consist in fission and fusion processes, the dynamism of the nonterritorial system will be in terms of growth of the system.* In a sense this is trivial: the geographical space subdivided by the territorial actors, the states or

Figure 7.2 Growth, fission, and fusion in territorial and nonterritorial systems

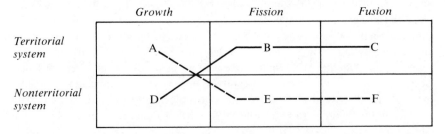

countries, is finite and relatively unchangeable (except for possibilities on the ocean floor and the ocean itself), whereas the sociofunctional space over which the nonterritorial actors are defined knows no limitations and has a very malleable topology, to say the least.[41] Hence the dynamism of the territorial system has to be squeezed into the painful exercises of disintegration and integration of the various kinds discussed in chapter 6, whereas the nonterritorial system is free to expand, adding to its numbers. Of course, there can also be some fission and fusion processes—and some of them will be very important politically, for reasons to be developed in section 7.4. But they will hardly carry the major dynamism of the system. Hence, *the unbroken line in figure 7.2 is the dynamic line, the broken line the static one.* The dynamism consists in the territorial system banging its head against the ceiling of its own limitation and boiling over in the form of nonterritorial growth—with the growth of the transnational corporations both in numbers and in assets, relative to the states, as the compelling example.[42]

The consequences of this pattern are not trivial. To start with, consider four of the factors directing nonterritorial growth:

First, when some new elements appear in social or functional space it is often surprisingly easy to build an international organization around them. I have participated in the process a number of times,[43] and I have observed that this process is easy because it so often draws upon existing nonterritorial networks. One can conceive of an organization as built around people who have some similarity in values and/or interests or around some kind of task or function. In either case organizing is facilitated by the principle of "neighborhood": many of the same people are already organized around some related task, or people related to them have already known some of the structure of that space.[44] As there are already many stones to step on, and any number of new stones (points) that can be added, the possibilities are unlimited—except by the finiteness of the human population and the limited capacity of the transportation-communication systems.

Second is the multiple-function organization, often built around one ascriptive and one achieved characteristic (for example, an association of female lawyers) or around any other combination. If people feel best when they are with their own kind they might feel even better the more characteristics they have in common, which is precisely what the multiple-function organization is about—whether it serves a psychological or a political function. As there are many functions the possibilities are legion.

Third, and more dialectic, less mechanically extrapolationist: one organization may bring about an antiorganization to counteract or negate it. However, in a longer perspective it may be that the International Peace Research Association has much more in common with the International Institute of Strategies Studies than both believed initially.[45] Anyhow, the functions of various organizations may be antithetical; the members of one may be opposed to the members of the other organization or an organization may emerge to counteract some other organization—as the Group of 77 or OPEC can be regarded relative to the OECD and the European Community, not to mention trade unions relative to transnational corporations.[46]

Fourth is the growth process that comes out of increasingly higher levels of integration. Thus, an IGO can itself be seen as the outcome of a process whereby governments have come together, first only bilaterally and on an *ad hoc* basis; then others have joined on an increasingly regular basis until the institutionalization has taken the form of an intergovernmental organization, which is then born. Correspondingly for the INGOs: nongovernmental organizations from various countries come together after a searching process for their opposite numbers abroad, and as a result an INGO is born. But when we come to BINGOs we also see more clearly that this may also operate the other way: the nonterritorial actor already exists, at least in the mind of somebody with a good national base for one "chapter" or "company," and the rest is a question of implanting it in other countries, so that both isomorphy and homology are served. But regardless of the time order of this process: *what has happened once can happen again.* The IGOs/INGOs/BINGOs can also come together, first two at a time and on an *ad hoc* basis for exchanging information and finally ending up with a super-IGO/super-INGO/super-BINGO as vast, integrative networks. The position as a liaison between a super-BINGO and a super-IGO certainly does not belong to the territorial system and is probably not even known as a position, yet it definitely exists. The person holding it would possess considerable power, among other reasons because of all the information that would come his way.[47]

Compare all this to the territorial system. The period of Great Discoveries is over; one cannot simply add a new state if one runs into difficulties or migrate to some New World. So far countries do not permit "multiple geographies," interpreted for instance as populated zones under the jurisdiction of two or more states so that everybody living there would have not merely double nationality (that exists to some extent), but some sort of mixed nationality (not British and French, but Anglo-French). Countries do oppose each other, even try to negate each other, but the way they do it is very destructive compared to the nonviolent verbal battles fought in sociofunctional space and agonizingly slow relative to the quick action possible in the NT system. There are also increasingly higher levels of integration, but the process is very slow and painful, not so easily carried out as in nonterritorial space.

One consequence is predictable, and we are already living in the ever-growing confirmation of that "prediction": the nonterritorial system will attract increasing attention, talent, and dynamism. An increasing number of persons will think, act, even live in terms of international networks of which they form some part—as pilgrims have done for millennia already. Consider what these four growth factors mean, concretely, for the case of the transnational corporations. For any new product, a new corporation. For a combination of two existing products (travel agency, bank), a new corporation. For any product one can always imagine a number of competitive products, hence any number of competing corporations, perhaps differentiated only by trade names. For corporations with some element of harmony of interests, a potential supercorporation, even concealed from the naked eye, for example, for integration along the economic cycle (one prospecting–research–development corporation, one banking institution, one processing corporation, one for transportation–communication, one for marketing, and finally one for consumption itself). It is not strange that the field is dynamic and also attracts talent and money when it can operate under such conditions. Nor is it strange that the territorial system hits back—partly because it serves imperialist interests, partly because it threatens the territorial system itself, reducing states to something stagnant, incapable of doing more than some splitting up and joining together, lost in their zero-sum games.[48]

This example also brings out the obvious: it is one thing to find and analyze the possibilities of growth, quite another to evaluate them according to the values of this book. Left to itself, given the present trends, not only will the system attain grandiose proportions by the year 2000,[49] but much of the growth will also have been in a wrong direction—strengthening the grip the northwest corner of the world has over the rest. Let us imagine that the trends continue, for good or for bad, and that the very general image given in figure 7.1 holds true: what world would that lead to?

The answer to this is very easily found: that world would have many things in common with the countries with the densest network of national associations and organizations today. It would not be difficult for a historian to write the history of, say, the British Isles in the terms suggested by this section: the decreasing salience of the territorial system and of the various counties into which that piece of territory is divided and the increasing importance of nationwide factories and firms and organizations and associations of all kinds, particularly the interest organizations of employers and employees. Part of the picture is that the system exercised considerable territorial spill-over during its age of imperialism, that some territorial part detached itself from the center (the Irish Republic), that others tried or are trying (Ulster, Scotland, Wales)—in other words, that the *territorial* structure is more salient in some parts than others, as it will also be in the world at large.[50] We know the result so far: it is not that territorial units disappear *but that they lose in salience*—except where there is some type of internal colonization and there may be a revival of the local community, meaning the small community, usually below the administrative units most countries are divided into.

But this, in turn, means that there are positive and negative experiences to draw upon from the domestic system, possibly applicable to the global system. One of them is, in simplistic terms, that there has to be some kind of political institution to steer the process. At the moment the world cannot be compared to Britain, for the countries of the world are not tied together as are the counties of Britain, nor is there any world central authority like the British central authority. The comparable condition to the world today would be what was on those isles before some kind of unification came about, but with crisscrossing nonterritorial actors growing like mushrooms. This is counter to factual history: territorial integration came first and faciliated the growth of nationwide organizations and associations later. Transportation and communication developed after nation-states had emerged and before a world central authority had been established. Consequently, some other type of political control has to be exercised, which has to have some of the same pinpoint sensitivity as the nonterritorial actors have. It has to take the form of some kind of transnational pressure group or even political party. Let us now consider that possibility.

7.3 FROM GOVERNMENTAL FOREIGN POLICY TO WORLD POLITICS

To explore the emergence of transnational political forces let us return for a moment to the bird's-eye view of history given in section 1.3. History was seen as a process starting with "primitive," nomadic tribes—with little internal differentiation, little attachment to any particular, permanent territory, and with few contact points—and ending with the division of the world into contiguous states, more or less like today. It was pointed out in section 1.2 that this process seems to be accompanied by a tremendous increase in the propensity to engage in aggressive warfare, for political and/or economic purposes. Something was gained: there was "urbanization" and "agricultural revolution," leading on to mechanization and the "industrial revolution" accompanied by the "transportation-communication revolution" and "economic growth." And something was lost: there was an increase not only in direct violence but also in structural violence. In this there is no effort to romanticize the remote past: exploitation and violence of all kinds have always existed, but not on the scale made possible by the growth in social and technological systems and the emergence of the technostructure found in private and state monopoly capitalism. The question is "Is there any way of returning to the past without doing so altogether—of preserving some of the gains, yet overcoming some of the losses?"

The approach taken to that general question in this section is based on one aspect of the present system: the tendency for foreign policy (and implicitly world politics) to be monopolized by the top of the territorial system, whether the top is referred to as "chief," "prince," or "government" (in "primitive," "traditional," or "modern" jargon, respectively). These three are each other's successors; as prince followed chief so did government follow prince, handing over to each other the two essential monopolies: on ultimate power inside the polity and on power over relations with the outside. This never meant that there were no other forms of power inside society, only that the power over that power rested with the top. Nor did it mean that there were no other contacts between societies, only that the power over those contacts also rested with the top. Thus, today there is a meaningful distinction between governmental and nongovernmental contacts, between IGOs and INGOs (bilateral and multi-lateral), but there is no doubt as to which have more power in defining the content of world politics.

To clarify this, figure 7.3 shows a process with four phases, reflecting the heading of this section: "from governmental foreign policy to world politics." (Another heading, however, might be "democratization.") In phase A we have the classical situation still dominating the world foreign-policy scene: foreign policy as something exclusively conducted between the successors of the princes where outside contact is concerned, the foreign ministries.

In phase B a democratic process is initiated. Pressure is exercised on the making of governmental foreign policy from nonelite quarters, and the government has to inform the people to some extent. The process is to some extent lifted out of its elite context, out of the corridors of power with parliamentary and party foreign-affairs committees and lobbies run by major interest groups (industrialists, the military, other sections of the government, and the like). The mechanisms whereby this process of democratization can be implemented are various: referenda, even elections over foreign-policy issues (if not clouded by domestic-policy divisions that may not be the same as foreign-policy divisions),

Figure 7.3 Toward democratic world politics

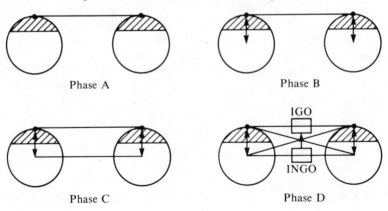

Phase A   Phase B

Phase C   Phase D

demonstrations, etc. But the process should not be confused with the "consultations" with nongovernment groups probably engaged in by most governments, bringing some segments of the political process out to a slightly wider but still highly elitist group. These still belong to phase A, as components of elitist foreign policy.

Since the phrase "democratization of foreign policy" usually evokes in the minds of people precisely the transition from phase A to phase B, the limits of the process should be clarified. Thus, obvious steps in phase B include more education on "world issues" and better articulation of the goals and interests of all kinds of groups inside any country with regard to the foreign-policy process. But these approaches, however laudable, are not what I have in mind. First of all, the "information" disseminated is likely to be generated by elites, particularly by governments, and to reflect their perspectives on the world in general and the political process in particular.[51] Second, I reject an interpretation of democracy in terms of action choices coming out of so-called mature reflection, promoted by "education" poured into individual minds. Democracy should be seen as a process, as a dialogue (or multilogue), as some kind of ordered fight and struggle for articulation and implementation, not as a study group.[52]

Thus, democratization of the foreign-policy process would inevitably include dialogue between governmental and nongovernmental actors with challenges and responses, accomplishing much more than the dissemination of information. It implies consciousness about the foreign-policy issues the country is facing, discussion all over of the options available, and forceful articulation of views. To take an example, *post hoc* discussion of a country's voting behavior in the United Nations has little to do with democratic world politics. If a UN agenda is made widely known beforehand, through the much underutilized network of UN associations and UN information offices, and is discussed in all kinds of organizations and associations, with and without government officials, we would come closer to a democratic process. Or would we?

We would be closer to a democratic process—if democracy in domestic affairs is used as a model for what democracy in world politics could and should be like. *But a basic tenet of this book is that this domestic model is an inadequate model.* The failure to see this underlies a great deal of the ills of contemporary "radical" politics: it arises in part from the failure to distinguish between foreign policy and world politics. World politics is not the same as the sum total of the foreign policies of all states, just as domestic politics is not the sum total of local governments—however democratic politics may be in the municipalities, counties, *prefectures, departements, provincias, ken, fylke, län,* or whatnot.

Imagine that democratization of foreign policy were realized according to the model of domestic politics in a relatively democratic country like, say, Norway. This would imply such measures as separate elections to determine foreign policy, since it was very clearly demonstrated by the referendum over the entry into the European Community that foreign-policy alignments may

crisscross in the most confusing manner with traditional domestic-policy alignments represented by the "political parties."[53] There might even be a separate
chamber for foreign policy in the national assembly, and some issues might have
to be cleared with both chambers because of their multiple implications. This
would lead to problems as to what would happen when the two chambers voted
differently, but such issues could be handled with some institutional arrangement as they are within existing paradigms of institution-construction. So, what
would still be nondemocratic about this arrangement?

*Simply, most of those affected by the decisions would not be participating
in the decision-making process*—and I take degree of participation by those
affected to be the basic criterion of a democratic process. Foreign-policy
decisions need not be better or more instrumental from the point of view of
world peace than undemocratic decisions. If they are genocidal, like decisions to
bomb in Indochina, there is little comfort to be obtained from the knowledge
that the decisions were arrived at democratically. If they are beneficial, this is
merely a new form of paternalism—in the name of democracy, like so many
other forms.

A typical example would be the subject of "technical assistance" or "development aid." Decisions taken here affect millions of people. Most decisions are
carried out according to the model of phase A: governments deal with each
other bilaterally or multilaterally, in "programs." Democratize the process on
the sender side, and the policies engaged in might change, but not necessarily in
progressive direction, as is believed by those who argue in favor of more popular
participation. That argument should not be used to legitimize continued governmental monopoly over the foreign-policy process. More interests and views
would be articulated and perhaps reflected in the decisions, but the receiver side
would still not be brought directly into the process.

To involve the receiver, an important change could be imagined: the
insertion into the foreign-policy process in any country of (at least) observers
from other countries, particularly from the countries directly affected by the
decisions. To some extent this is what bilateral diplomacy is about: governments
keep embassies abroad in order to provide some warning, some anticipatory
feedback into the process as a protection mechanism against wrong decisions by
foreign governments—and in order to lobby for decisions they deem beneficial.
However, embassies operate only at the governmental level and hence clearly fall
within the model of phase A. Another step would be to have representatives of
other countries as observers, associate members, or even full members in national
assemblies; but this is still both elitist and bilateral—and also unlikely.

Another, less elitist approach has already been taken for some time: the use
of foreigners, systematically and with considerable effect, to "meddle in internal
affairs." There is a very important difference between inviting a foreigner from a
Periphery country to talk about life in his country and inviting him to talk
frankly about what the Center country, the host country, should do. He might
also participate in demonstrations: in a shrinking world it should be obvious that
the problems are increasingly indivisible. We have not only a right but even a

duty to "meddle in internal affairs," for they concern our brothers and sisters and are usually full of world implications.

It may now be objected that much of this meddling can take place in the IGOs, particularly in the United Nations. For the sake of argument, let us assume the United Nations to be more perfect within its own terms of reference than it is, that is, that all territories in the world have become autonomous, that all are represented in the United Nations by representatives who are truly representative, articulating views generated through a truly democratic process within their own countries, and that it is not stifled by such vestiges of international feudalism as a "security council" with "permanent members" endowed with lasting "vetoes." In short, let us imagine some kind of perfect *indirect democracy* at work. What would be missing, as will be indicated more strongly in section 8.1, would be not only the views of actors other than states but also the structure of direct democracy. At this point it may be objected that in a world with about four billion inhabitants this is an unrealistic notion anyhow. But however problematic truly direct democracy may be, this should not serve as an argument against the creation of one (or some) of the obvious structures of direct democracy: the possibility for individuals with the same interests and values not only to find each other across borders but also to exercise political power accordingly—and this is what phase C involves.

A very simple example will illustrate phase C: imagine two border communities, one located in Norway and one in Sweden, both at a distance of hundreds of kilometers from their respective capitals but next to each other, having the same ecology and the same problems as periphery counties exposed to high internal mobility of capital, raw materials, and labor. Obviously, these communities might benefit from sharing experiences and problem-solving efforts; they might find cooperation across the borders mutually beneficial. But the political chains of command are not set up that way: Both are expected to work on their local representatives, first at the municipal level, later at the *fylke/län* level, and then at the national assembly level, with the hope that the shared concern ultimately will be put on the agenda of the Nordic Council. In short, whereas proximity should lead to phase C solutions, even Nordic structures lead to phase B solutions with a strong admixture of phase A, since the agenda is articulated mainly in the elite centers.

One possibility is for the two groups to take matters in their own hands and simply go ahead, not waiting for top-heavy machineries to grind out more or less adequate solutions. One way of going ahead would be to establish transborder councils for joint articulation in both capitals. In other words, the old model of separate articulation would be replaced by joint pressure. Nongovernmental, even nonelite ties would be established; they would be foci for the sharing of experience and the hammering-out of joint programs, which would then be fought for by joint pressure groups in the centers of decision making.

In phase D this process would have been carried an important step further. International ties among individuals and groups with similar values and interests would be used not only to articulate but also to act, not only to harmonize action nationally and internationally but also to act jointly at the world level. The question "In what forum or forums shall they act?" then arises. There seem to be two general answers to this question.

First, inevitably they will act on the intergovernmental organizations. Such action can take many forms, and it seems urgent that as many as possible be tried as quickly as possible in present world politics. There may be lobbying, pressure groups, and demonstrations. But these are still relatively primitive forms compared to a form that recently has found more frequent expression: the parallel conference, or even in some cases the anticonference. An international group with strong views on issues to be discussed, perhaps even with an attempt at solution, in an international governmental conference organizes its own conference, which may coincide in space, time, or both with the "real" conference. I am thinking of such recent examples as the plethora of conferences that descended on Stockholm in June 1972 in connection with the general problematics subsumed under the term "ecology." Only some of the conferences constituted the UN Conference hosted by the Swedish government.

In principle such parallel conferences are ways of articulating views that are not necessarily antithetical to governmental views but that might be difficult for the government level to support. In this INGOs may cooperate with the governmental level by inviting participants to their conference, providing them with information and viewpoints that their respective national bureaucracies have been unwilling or unable (or both) to produce, and even inviting them to further dialogue. That dialogue may then take increasingly insistent forms, in situations of real crisis also backed up by demonstrations of a highly demanding character.[55]

If we now extrapolate from this model, one possible consequence is already visible on the horizon: the *world political party.* Increasingly often, similarly organized groups will come together at such events, well distributed in space and time. Increasingly often they will find that the stands they take have important similarities, and these similarities will crystallize into world ideologies (as they have already done to a large extent). The result will be the nucleus of a world political party. A very good recent example in this regard was the world movement against the U.S. war in Indochina, a movement that had a clear target but that was deprived of a significant world forum. The impotence of the United Nations in those years (because of U.S. pressure) was reflected very well in its inability to serve as a forum for this movement.

However, there is a second aspect of phase D politics that transcends the formulas so far emerging: a transition from international, nongovernmental pressure groups on international governmental bodies to a new role for INGOs and TRANGOs in world politics. An increasing part of world politics should gradually be taken over by nongovernmental bodies, both within and between countries. Let us look at some practical examples.

One of them concerns the age-old issue of *recognition* of emerging states. The privilege of recognizing new states traditionally rested with the prince and was in an unquestioning manner taken over by the prince's successor, the government, and particularly by the foreign-policy decision-making elite. The elitism of the system is reflected particularly well in the idea that the most important recognition is recognition by the leading power—thus the courting of the big powers in order to obtain recognition from them. [56] What I am suggesting in this connection is not the use of universal intergovernmental bodies like the United Nations as the new primary source of legitimation. In the U.S.–China policy of 1971 one could see a clear effort to run ahead of the United Nations in maintaining a position as the prime legitimizer. The approach I advocate, however, is the use of nongovernmental bodies for legitimation.

Why should not trade unions, universities, high schools, professional organizations, states, provinces, and municipalities also pronounce themselves on the recognition of new states, such as Bangladesh or, in earlier years, China? Why should one accept the monopoly of a handful of people in this important connection? A government is only one group in a population. There are also other groups that are equally or more affected by international affairs. They might have other views that deserve articulation and that should also serve as inputs into the political process, not only via local governments but directly.

There is one particular reason why this is very important. As mentioned in chapter 6 one old formula used by governments for granting recognition is the existence in the other state of a government firmly in control. In other words, the legitimizer requests that the power to be legitimized has the same structure as he believes he has himself. But this leads to a terrible problem, because in order to arrive at this form of control a new regime literally has to shoot itself into power. The road to recognition has to be paved with battles and blood, at least in those cases where the old regime is not so rotten that it falls with the first blow. The mechanism of recognition, hence, is a mechanism inviting direct violence.

Other groups within a country, however, might not be guided by this perspective. Thus, trade unions might conceive of the problems of other countries in terms of how ordinary people fare and might extend their recognition on a basis more concerned with structural than direct violence. Such groups as intellectuals, professionals, and workers might also look at the problem from less governmentally biased angles. They might, for example, more easily have been able to recognize the forces struggling in East Pakistan before events took a bloody course, finally leading to the intervention of the Indian Army.

Needless to say, such a broad basis might lead to confusing recognition patterns, which is exactly the idea. Groupings within a country in favor of recognizing an embryonic state should be free not only to express this but also to act accordingly, to take the contacts they want and to pursue them. The government is one such group: under such a set-up it might issue signals and directives, but not orders binding all citizens.

Another example can be found in the field of *cooperation.* Consider the negotiations concerning all European cooperation: they constituted an almost perfect case of elitism. In fact, they were probably even more elitist than the

Vienna Congress more than one and a half centuries earlier. There was almost no nongovernmental participation whatsoever: no official forum in which workers, housewives, the young, the old, and similar groups could articulate what they might like a future Europe to be. [57]

The assumption is that, as governments know better, whatever input there might be from such groups should run through governmental channels. Again, we should aim higher than to phase A and phase B structures in our quest for more democratic world politics; ultimately this will lead to the formation of nonterritorial organizations that will act like world political parties. If that happens, the NT system would have been significantly expanded in a way that might reduce structural violence without adding to the direct violence, thus contributing to the solution of some of the problems discussed in section 6.3. The next step, then, would be integration into a world central authority, to be discussed in section 8.1.

7.4   STRATEGIES OF CHANGE

The battles that will increasingly be fought in the nonterritorial system do not catch the headlines, *for this is the invisible continent.* There are exceptions, though, like the "superpowers" among the NTs, the United Nations, and the TNCs. Much of what follows here derives from those examples but is guided by the general strategy of development put forward in section 4.4 and the theory of nonterritorial actors and their growth processes from the first two sections of this chapter.

People live with their bodies in solid geography and are fed by soil, air, and water—not by "sociofunctional space." Consequently, in the first run, changes in the nonterritorial system will have to serve the best strategies for changing the territorial system. Beyond that the system should develop a life of its own as long as it is not used to reintroduce patterns of dominance. Since self-reliance is assumed to be the basic strategy for the territorial system, where structural violence is concerned, the major task in the years to come is to act on the nonterritorial actors dynamically—to destroy them as vehicles of structural violence, as carriers of isomorphy with a distorted territorial system and of homology with powerful and equally distorted states—without destroying them as a world-cementing force functioning to some extent as a barrier against direct violence.

In what direction, then, should one try to steer the three processes of growth, fission, and fusion?

As to growth: there is a need for more transnational organizations, TRANGOs as opposed to INGOs and IGOs. Only through them can a global identity be given an organizational form. Even if this is a Western individualistic cultural bias, it may nevertheless be a bias to some extent worth disseminating. However, I would temper the suggestion with the following consideration: the weak, dominated countries should make use of national chapters and even band together in solidarity; the stronger countries could do more to dissolve that national identity, particularly the regional identity, and think and act more in general human and global terms, for such terms exist.[58] The tactics have to vary according to conditions. Of course I would argue in favor of more world movements, built around values of the type the present book is based on (see chapter 2), which would then be on the world political left. The world political right is already so firmly entrenched, built into the structure itself, that in this strategy there is no one-sidedness (not that one should be afraid of that), only a mild antidote to the present system.

Further, in the field of corporations there is a need for corporations dealing with the satisfaction of fundamental needs, but on a noncommercial, noncommodity basis, in which case it would probably defy anybody's image of a corporation. (That they also should be globalized along the lines to be indicated in section 8.3 goes without saying.) The argument would be, to refer to that example again, that the basic thing wrong with the Coca-Cola corporation is Coca-Cola itself. It drains resources away from some tasty yet nutritionally valuable product that could be sold at heavily subsidized prices. Seen in that perspective, much of the staff, the bottling plants, and the like appear in a better light, potentially: one might even imagine turning the sales agents into propagandists for better nutrition.

As to fission: the major dynamic process to be steered politically would be fission, and the general course is clear: it should go in the direction of self-reliance. Concretely, this means that *it would be in the Third World interest to look critically at each single international organization in which they participate, governmental or nongovernmental, business or not, and ask whether it impedes or facilitates their self-reliance, their capacity for "relying on own forces."* If it is found that the organization is too isomorphic with the present territorial system, there are clear strategies to be pursued (derived from phases 4 and 5, table 4.5), starting with the weaker and ending with the stronger:

1. Organizing better contacts and more interaction among Periphery countries within the context of the organization;
2. Making the organization more symmetric by demanding fair representation among the officers, in all committees, and so on, possibly also by demanding rotating location of headquarters;
3. Creating a subordinate organization within the organization open only to the Periphery—like the UNCTAD 77;
4. Creating an independent organization, outside the universal organization, like OPEC or the (weak) organization of nonaligned countries, possibly later to become a Third World secretariat;
5. Withdrawing completely from the universal organization and organizing their own with a view to possible reintegration later.

Strategy 5 would be the ultimate threat, to be used in extreme cases, but generally it is an unsubtle strategy because it is so unflexible and reduces options. Strategies 3 and 4, however, should probably be used in a great number of cases, including those of the United Nations and organizations that are completely ideologically "sound." Liberals and radicals from small, white, Western, capitalist countries may also reduce the chances of Third World self-reliance by being too hard-working and effective on behalf of others. In the short run, left-wing Western missionarism may be preferable to the right-wing version, but may, in the long run, be equally devastating. Basically, their task is to help the Periphery by working inside the Center countries.

In any organization, then, from sociology to Esperanto to the United Nations, the prediction and prescription would be for the world Periphery to find their own organizational formula if they decide that an organization of that kind is needed at all. They would, for instance, detect an even stronger Western bias in Esperanto than in sociology—and one more difficult to eradicate. The universal organization might be kept for dialogue and for whatever purpose would remain, *as long as the Periphery has a chance to form its own consciousness and develop its own forms of cooperation—in other words, to control the organizational infrastructure that is the condition for collective self-reliance.* This process would be halfway fission; it would lead to a proliferation of regional "nonterritorial" actors, which later on might reintegrate in the universal body if it is decided that their task has been performed, thus combining dissociative and associative methods in a highly flexible strategy.

As to fusion: under this formula there may be some key to a reduction of the overspecialization and division of labor going on in the world today. A fusion of organizations for nurses with organizations for physicians into an organization for health specialists might become unwieldy, but it could then split again according to some of the subject areas (although that would not be so good either) after the sexist division had been overcome. The same could be said for the social sciences, the study of mankind: whether divided into disciplines and subdisciplines or into interdisciplinary problem areas, mankind is subdivided in a way that must be alienating and that has had profoundly harmful effects on social scientists, but we are surrounded by so many others deformed in the same way that we fail to discover it.

These strategies could be pursued in a nonviolent yet firm and articulate manner in one general conference after another, across the board, in all organizations. They would be meaningful almost everywhere. It is important to do this work and to turn the great advantage of the flexibility of the nonterritorial system into a positive factor for development; for such battles may be more easily fought and won in the nonterritorial than in the territorial system where the machineries of violence are located. In doing so the principle of isomorphy may be used to work the other way: the nonterritorial system may lead the territorial system to some extent in the direction of more equity, autonomy, self-reliance, solidarity (among the weak), and participation (of the marginalized). It is difficult to prove, but there is hardly any doubt that the way in which the United Nations has been changing in recent years has had some effect of this kind, although the major impact is still to come, as otherwise the status-quo powers would not have cared to protest the "unrealistic" resolutions so frequently.[59]

There is still one major element missing, or at least not made explicit enough, however. These organizations are by far too elitist. Mass participation is in general very far below some of the most impressive transnational enterprises of all times: the pilgrimages of the Muslim world to Mecca.[60] At least two factors were and are at work there: a tremendous emotional appeal to the total human being and—more prosaically—very well organized and inexpensive transportation. Some of the other religious INGOs may be able to organize something similar (like the Divine Light Mission), but most of the INGOs, not to mention the TNCs and the IGOs, attract only very small elite groups for their meetings.

One key to this, of course, is cheap transportation, and one key to that would be world cooperation (in IGO form, pushed into action by many INGOs operating in effective concert) in order to lower the prices of surface transport or at least to make some special, very inexpensive, "third-class" services available (slower, less comfortable trains and ships, for instance). This is particularly significant in view of the importance of generating mass concern for world politics—in short, to put into action some of the ideas indicated in the preceding section.[61] The same applies to telecommunication.

But pilgrims would travel even if transportation costs were higher because of the *command,* thus contributing to the "cementing force" that for centuries seems to have served as a much more effective bulwark against war among Muslim than among Christian countries. Is there something else that could have a corresponding appeal? Maybe the transnational political parties discussed in the preceding section—in other words, meetings not of national delegates but of ordinary people who may not even be registered nationally by any party but who identify at the transnational level. And, quite definitely, *nations.* A nation can be seen as a potential nonterritorial actor, except insofar as the nation-state idea of putting everybody belonging to the same nation in the same country has been implemented. In the future world one might think in terms of nations as being scattered around, of states as being pluralistic and multinational (and nations as being multistate). Each nation would have its Mecca, its shrine; like emigrants its peoples would flock to it at regular or irregular intervals. I mention this not because it is a necessity or a strategy, but simply because it is probably going to happen anyhow, if for no other reason than that people travel more than before and very often settle in new places. In this there may be a wish for new experience and for more diversity, as well as for better economic opportunities. But to the extent that it takes place it makes sense. If no nation is systematically exploited in this more "entropic" world, that world would probably be much safer from a peace-theoretical point of view than a well-sorted nation-state world.

And that brings us to a conclusion about the significance of the nonterritorial system. Some, by no means all, of the direct violence in our world is related to the predominance of the territorial system, a system that feeds us but also kills us. This presents us with a problem whether we like it or not: how to reduce the significance of the basic territorial unit, the state as we know it today. The answer is not to go back to what was before more permanent territorial settlement—nomadic forms of life.[62] Nor is the answer to return to the territorial system in earlier forms, the mini-states—although that would be more feasible. Nationwide, regional, global cooperation are also indispensable, as argued in chapter 6 and as will be developed further in chapter 8.

Rather, the solution is something similar to the mathematicians's answer to the problem of getting square roots of negative numbers: he adds another type of number, imaginary numbers, to the real ones, getting *complex* numbers as a result. Immediately a vast range of possibilities opens up; things can be done that could not be done before. Correspondingly, the idea here is in terms of a complex world with nonterritorial organizations crosscutting self-reliant territorial units; the nonterritorial units being so strong that they can even serve as a base (together with the territorial units) for a central authority with the capacity not only to articulate problems and conflicts but also to solve them. The argument is in favor of an entirely new, different type of nomadic existence where nobody is forced to move because the territorial units are not sufficiently self-reliant, but where the identification with the territorial unit is not so blind and parochial that it degenerates into local, national, or regional chauvinism. There will always be territorial vectors, to continue the mathematical metaphors, directing some of the loyalties; but at the same time there will be nonterritorial vectors pointing in other directions, for instance, to the underprivileged and exploited everywhere. There will be an overlayer of global identification; all of it adding up to a much less primitive pattern of identification than, for instance, patriotism.

Is this utopian? Definitely not, and we know it is not utopian for the simple reason that it has happened already inside so many states, some of them of a size comparable with the order of magnitude of the world itself. The problem is to achieve this state while counteracting effectively the dominance system, also insofar as it has made its imprint on the nonterritorial system. That job has not been carried out inside countries either, although in some more than others, and there is probably much to learn from the histories of nation building where this is concerned,[63] particularly from the federal states. In many cases the threat of direct violence has probably been reduced at the expense of increased structural violence made possible by the higher level of integration; in other cases reduction of the two may have gone hand in hand.

Another problem of key importance here is what happens to personal identity as the horizon of relevant world units expands, if only on the TV screen? One need not be too pessimistic: if people have been able to derive some type of identity from their identification with such territorial giants as the United States, the Soviet Union, and China (an identity by far transcending identification with the local community or state/republic/province or with any organization to which they may belong), why not also the whole world?[64] Could it not be that some of the feeling of loss of identity today does not derive so much from the erosion of national identity, due to the way the rest of the world and the nonterritorial system penetrate, as to the absence of some kind of landing platform, some anchoring in the ultimate unit, the whole world itself? Today identities may be forking out in all kinds of directions for those who have psychologically outgrown their territorial cells; tomorrow the forking paths may come together again at the ultimate level. Just as national identification is not with governmental machinery, this does not mean identifying with a bureaucracy such as the United Nations, but with people with causes and purposes—only world-encompassing ones.

But there is something more to gain from the nomadic parallel than merely a certain detachment from the territorial unity, achieved mainly by means of psychological mobility. Nomads also moved because they had to, because the ground on which they lived could not sustain them any longer. That type of mobility is very well known from most countries today, because the center-periphery gradient in most countries (with the capital and other cities colonizing the countryside) makes the periphery look like a wasteland where nothing happens, a mere effect of causes located in the cities.[65]

Why should this not also happen on a world scale? *Ultimately, mobility is a great equalizer,* perhaps the best there is, also because it might drag the center down when the masses of underprivileged descend on the cities of the states and the world-city of the world—the Center of the capitalist world. Very much of what the latter do in terms of development and family planning can be seen as strategies to stave off this tidal wave, particularly out of fear that it might one day take on very ugly violent forms.[66] That fear may be realistic, but not the strategies if that is the purpose; so far, they mainly tend to aggravate the situation, and motivations of the kind mentioned are a little too visible. Hence, great transnational migrations of the type mentioned belong to the possibilities of the future world even after a policy of self-reliance has gained more of a foothold, for there are asymmetries in the world geography, and five centuries of consistent center–periphery gradient building (with the center in the West) are not easily reversed. Much of the migration would flow along old territorial gradients (as Algerians continue to seek work in France), and much of it will take new forms (as many more Mexicans settle in the southwest of the United States, Chinese in Siberia, and Indians in Australia).[67]

Since one of the territorial prerogatives is to control movement in and out of the country, this movement would constitute a major challenge of the territorial system, even a partial breakdown. There will be all kinds of last-ditch efforts to stop it with all kinds of methods, ranging from increased "redistribution of wealth and resources" to genocidal attempts, but such efforts will be weakened to the extent that there is a growth in true global identification. After all, in times of extreme distress one part of a country usually receives and helps masses of refugees from areas of disaster due to natural or social catastrophes. Many might disagree, but a development of this type appears to be so likely that

a far better strategy would be to prepare for it, training populations in overcoming prejudice, adjusting local institutions like schools to a multinational
population, and increasing immigration quotas—not only for the many refugees that will come from the center in the Periphery, as argued in section 4.4.
For ultimately this kind of mobility is also an aspect of the increasing salience of
the nonterritorial system, loosening some of the territorial grip on people, if not
on all of them all the time, at least on some of them some of the time.

NOTES

References to *Essays* are to Johan Galtung, *Essays in Peace Research,* 5 vols.
(Copenhagen: Ejlers, 1975–80) (Atlantic Highlands, N.J.: Humanities Press).

1. For further development of this theme, see Galtung, "A Structural Theory
   of Integration," *Essays* IV, 11.

2. Let T, A, and O stand for territorial, associational, and organizational
   integration respectively, and TAO, for instance, for a territorial unit built
   around associations of organizations. TO might be a proper way of looking
   at Japan, as a country built around economic organizations; TA might be a
   perspective on Norway, where the basic unit seems to be associations (trade
   unions, professional associations, political parties, value-oriented associations
   of all kinds), and TT or T^2 would be the appropriate perspective on a federal
   country. All nine combinations are empirically meaningful, but AT and OT
   perhaps less so than the others as the territorial focus is so predominant
   that there is much less integration between than within territorial units.

3. The word-pair is taken from the former Israeli foreign minister, Abba Eban.
   It should be noted that there are two kinds of affinity, though, A and O.

4. Anyone who has tried to organize a conference, or anything else for that
   matter, with Soviet citizens knows what this means in practice. The whole
   idea of a transnational organization presupposes that state borders are
   penetrable both ways, between individuals within and organizations without.
   This condition does not obtain in the Soviet Union, nor in many other
   countries.

5. For imperialism to function, two parties are sufficient, one Center and one
   Periphery country—e.g., the United States and Canada.

6. For some terminology of this kind, see Galtung, "On the Future of the
   International System," *Essays* IV, 18; also published as the first chapter in
   Jungk and Galtung, eds., *Mankind 2000* (Oslo, 1968).

7. And this is one of the highly underresearched areas in the world economic
   system: the role played by the Soviet state enterprises abroad. One hypothesis might be that a key role is to negotiate long-term deals with raw
   materials and unprocessed agricultural products flowing into the Soviet
   Union for resale on the world market when prices improve (sugar from
   Cuba, cocoa from Ghana, gas from Iran, possibly wheat from the United
   States).

8. Thus, I would maintain that the most important aspect of the industrial
   revolution was not mass manufacture—that had happened before, e.g., the
   famous pottery factories in Arezzo—but increasingly rapid and efficient
   communication and transportation, making the mobility of all production

factors (capital, labor, raw materials) and the products themselves possible over ever-expanding areas, ending up with the modern transnational corporations and their *global reach*—the excellent title of the equally excellent book on them by R. J. Barnet and R. E. Müller (New York, 1975). The real watershed in recent history can be spelled out in such terms, in addition to the concentration of power over capital, including capital goods (means of production). See the UN report on these matters: "Report of the Group of Eminent Persons to Study the Role of Multinational Corporations on Development and on International Relations" (E/5500/Add.1, Parts I and II); the group was established by an ECOSOC resolution of 2 July 1972 (1721 - LIII). See also Document E/5500 of 14 June 1974.

9. It is interesting to note how many sinister phenomena operate under the guise of such female terms as "mother," "sister," and "daughter" company, etc.

10. For some data on this, see Galtung, "Nonterritorial Actors and the Problem of Peace," in Saul H. Mendlovitz, ed., *On the Creation of a Just World Order* (New York: Free Press, 1975), or Galtung and Skjelsbaek, "Nonterritorial Actors: The Invisible Continent," *Essays* IV, 12, and Anthony J. N. Judge and Kjell Skjelsbaek, "Transnational Associations and Their Functions," in A. J. R. Groom and Paul Taylor, eds., *Functionalism: Theory and Practice in International Relations* (London: University of London Press, 1973).

11. On the other hand, there will always be some discrepancies. After all, it is easier for the Periphery to interact inside an organization, particularly during conferences and conventions. See Chadwick F. Alger, "Non-resolution Consequences of the United Nations and Their Effect on International Conflict," *Journal of Conflict Resolution* (1961), pp. 128–45.

12. For some data on the extent to which bilateral contact in the territorial system follows the principle of first big with big, then big with small, and finally small with small, see Galtung, "East–West Interaction Patterns," *Essays* IV, 7. Typically, so-called disarmament negotiations have also been taken out of the General Assembly to forums, usually Geneva-based, with a higher proportion of the big, and tend to end up in bilateral negotiations between the superpowers, e.g., the SALT talks.

13. It is ironical to think of all those defense intellectuals, no doubt rating themselves as first-rate intellectuals, who talked about that fifth-rate power. They proved to be fifth-rate intellectuals talking about a first-rate power, because their thinking about power was so primitive (in my view a failure to understand the role of autonomy power in addition to conventional balance power, power-over-oneself as opposed to power-over-others).

14. In international politics it is, fortunately, not the round-robin method with everybody competing with everybody that is used; the system is more similar to the way champions emerge in boxing (by challenging the champion).

15. One reason for this is that everything is so transparent and so explicit. Although it is fashionable to have people from small countries as chairmen and presidents, it is hard to imagine an intergovernmental organization without all or most big powers on the board, if they are members at all. In a transnational organization no such position would come automatically. Of course, it is possible for the small to meet behind their backs, but organizations have formalized procedures for decision making that usually are seen as having to be acceptable to big powers to be "realistic"—an assumption that

fortunately has been challenged quite often is the United Nations recently. The territorial system does not have a similar system (if it had, it would be an IGO); it relies instead on a complex web of bilateral pressures, and occasional eruptions of more naked power.

16. Such gradations are often introduced in functionally specific organizations, e.g., that contemplated for the seabed, defining functionally specific big powers (according to length of coastline, shipping tonnage, importance of fisheries, etc.).

17. I say "formed" with some qualification. Since the creation of a Jewish nation-state, Israel, it is doubtful whether Jews differ very much from others in this regard, except insofar as a great proportion live outside the borders of that state. One Jewish argument was, of course, "Why should we be different from others, why should it fall on us to be some kind of cementing force in a world of states?" The argument is highly understandable, and yet the day may perhaps come when the nation-state program is given up by most nations in favor of a nations-world, possibly with some small territory for each nation, a shrine like Vatican City, but otherwise mixing with each other all over the world.

18. In two such associations particularly known to me, the International Peace Research Association and the World Future Studies Federation, some national identities are, of course, still discernible because the topics—peace and the future—have not been universalized in the way mathematics and chemistry have been. National interests and styles are reflected to some extent. And yet correlations with national background are remarkably low, as also applies to Pugwash—with the possible exception of the Soviet participants, who are remarkabbly uniform in their presentations. Their papers look identical, as if they are produced by the same national secretariat, and names are allocated at random to comply with Western models in the TRANGO direction (according to the best sources this is exactly what happened some years ago).

19. 1968 was a remarkable year in this sense. Suddenly it became obvious how little in terms of organization is needed to constitute such movements. In all continents students revolted; but they were successful only in China—if one assumes that the Cultural Revolution was a part, *partly,* of the same phenomenon. Obviously modern mass media do, unpaid, more to coordinate such groups by making them and their actions mutually visible than they would ever have been able to do themselves, and in a homogenizing world (because of industrialism and various forms of capitalism) problems are similar enough to make their experiences mutually relevant.

20. This would constitute a more conscious type of revolt than the more ubiquitous "revolts" that are merely efforts to obtain adjustments within a model II society. This is where the Chinese part from fellow student revolutionaries in many other countries. "On the Cultural Revolution," chapter 3 in Galtung and Fumiko Nishimura, *Learning from the Chinese People* (Oslo, 1975).

21. And who started all these organizations. That we know something about, and it is more than clear what message is conveyed through that channel: the northwestern corner of the world (see the references cited in note 10).

22. In other words, among these are the people who, often unwittingly, are necessary conditions for imperialism to function at all. In saying so, however, I am of course not thinking of all kinds of international organizations.

Obviously, economic imperialism is above all carried by the BINGOs (the MNCs, or TNCs as the name would be now); political imperialism by IGOs and by the internationals of the parties (better organized on the left than on the right because the latter have the whole BINGO complex to back them up); military imperialism by all the military alliances and international cooperative systems with their special kind of daughter companies known as bases; social imperialism by the latter two but also by all kinds of experts belonging to international or regional professional communities, shaping societies in their image; cultural imperialism mainly by INGOs, but also to a large extent by the cultural agencies run by governments to propagate the national culture abroad; and communication imperialism by the news agencies and the like.

23. Thus, very often an organization wants to become universal, and may even pretend to be so, but in fact ends up connecting Center countries only—if for no other reason than that the resources of the world are so distributed that only they can afford to participate. Another reason may be added, though: most Westerners fail to contemplate how utterly Western is the entire idea of detachable individuals leaving their home context to exchange experiences and views in an abstract, theoretical form in a conference. The difficulty in getting Chinese participants to Western-style conferences is related to this: how can any one individual represent collective Chinese reality, and how can any reality be represented in words alone?

24. The Soviet Union is particularly famous for this in the United Nations. As it is itself a Western country, I prefer to interpret it as control over individuals rather than as a rejection of the Western organization model.

25. On the contrary, there are some indications that the NTs are particularly well used by the smaller, Western, capitalist countries. Thus, if we look at the number of INGOs per capita, eight of the ten top countries on the list fall into this category (but not for IGOs per capita, because all countries have to be members of a certain number, so the size of the population pushes a number of Third World countries up on the top of the list). As to number of international officials per capita, however, the capitalist northwest dominates. See the references cited in note 10.

26. This error is, I hope, avoided in the present chapter and in the following chapters, as well as in my essay "Nonterritorial Actors and the Problem of Peace" in Saul H. Mendlovitz, ed., *On the Creation of a Just World Order*, (New York: Free Press, 1975). However, I readily admit to much more skepticism about the NTs than I had some years ago, perhaps seeing better the role they play. What remains is the idea that they can be changed and therefore constitute a tremendous potential, for peace and development.

27. On the other hand, a recourse to cloak-and-dagger techniques, singling out special individuals rather than territories for destruction, is conceivable, even with "modern" technology—e.g., some kind of mini-rocket steered by homing devices placed surreptitiously on those designated as victims.

28. In addition to Barnet and Müller's *Global Reach* I recommend Louis Turner's *Invisible Empires* (London: Hamilton, 1970). Both have excellent bibliographies. In some years the UN research center on transnational corporations will no doubt be a major source of insight and information in this field. Their guide to research in the field is already useful: *Survey of Research on Transnational Corporations* (New York: United Nations, 1977); based on questionnaires to researchers and institutes.

29. These three propositions would follow from the expansionist nature of capitalism: to try to cover the whole world and to cover it alone—not only to control the prices, but because expansionism is built into the capitalist production process. The tendency to control the total cycle is, of course, not new; it is also found in the plantation economy, and others, but the scale is new. It is no longer merely a question of forcing workers to buy in the company stores but of controlling the consumption patterns of entire populations.

30. Japan can be seen as one such cooperative federation when operating abroad. There is not only the individual *zaibatsu*; all of Japan is a *zaibatsu.*

31. Take the case of Exxon, reputed not to have supplied fuel to the U.S. Sixth Fleet in the Mediterranean during the Yom Kippur war in October 1973 for fear of offending the Arabs. It looks as if this disharmony of interest between a U.S. corporation and the U.S. government was solved in the direction of the former.

32. This is inspired by a discussion of multinational corporations in the third week of the World Future Models course at the Inter-University Centre, Dubrovnik, January 1975. I am indebted to the organizer of the seminar, Professor Nasrollah Fatemi, and to Mr. F. Reinauer-Second for particularly important criticism.

33. This point was repeatedly made by the late Stephen Hymer, whose premature death was a great loss to the critical research in this field.

34. This is a basic point in the critique of the TNCs, but of the five on the list I tend to rank it last in real significance.

35. "But nobody would invest in a slum" is the answer, which is true within short-run capitalist rationality. In the long run the use of the social surplus for such purposes would liberate the population from the shackles of poverty, thereby increasing production and productivity—provided that the economy would permit the absorption of more labor in more creative capacities. The truth is, of course, that the capitalist economy in the Periphery in general would not allow this, being based on uneven development inside the country. As a consequence the combination of luxury hotels and slums is an essential, not an accidental part of the system.

36. One of the lasting achievements of the late Salvador Allende will be his UN speech on transnational corporations in general and on the ITT in particular—showing the power of the United Nations as an articulation forum. From the report in the *International Herald Tribune,* 5 December 1972: "Mr. Allende also harshly criticised the large, multinational corporations, which he accused on 'economic aggression' against Chile. He attacked in especially strong terms International Telegraph and Telephone and Kennecott Copper Corp., which he said 'had driven their claws deep into my country, [and] proposed to manage our political life.'"

37. Immanuel Wallerstein's monumental study *The Modern World System,* with the first volume covering 1450 to 1640 (New York and London: Academic Press, 1975), is of course the key work in this field today.

38. For a critique, see Galtung, "Self-reliance and Global Interdependence: Some Reflections on the New International Order," *Papers,* no. 55, Chair in Conflict and Peace Research, University of Oslo, 1976; also CIDA (Ottawa, 1978).

39. One reason for this may be that the Third World elites drafting such resolutions want/need products themselves, another that this type of cri-

ticism would be even more resented because it goes deeper. One thing is to criticize somebody for exploitation, even for cheating; quite another is to intimate that the entire production process is based on a major fallacy, that most of the products are in the "pink toilet paper category" and are the consequence of wrong priorities in a distorted system. My own impression from many meetings of that kind is that non-Western elites often are extremely tactful and polite and prefer less contentious dimensions of argument, not only for political reasons.

40. Which is the point that can be made about the Lomé Convention; see "The Lomé Convention and Neo-capitalism," *Africa Today* (1976).

41. This argument, as well as much of the rest of this section, is developed at greater length in Galtung and Skjelsbaek, "Non-Territorial Actors: The Invisible Continent," *Essays* IV, 12.

42. Of course, if countries could expand into unclaimed territory or could continue conquering other countries, corporations would not have had to go multinational. But these two processes have by and large come to an end, not the least because they are partly unnecessary; conquest can continue through the overflow into an isomorphic nonterritorial system.

43. For instance, in the founding of the International Peace Research Association and the World Future Studies Federation.

44. The world master in this, no doubt, is the assistant general secretary of the Union of International Associations in Brussels, Anthony Judge, to whom I am indebted for much of the thinking underlying this chapter.

45. A contradiction is never total, always along some dimensions that carry the burden of defining the conflict, to the exclusion of others. Thus, strategists and peace researchers may share a lack of concern for cultural, civilizational factors, being more focused on structural and other political variables.

46. "Global Unions to Counter Global Companies" was a headline in a December 1972 issue of the *International Herald Tribune*. The article stated that "the goal is for workers in all countries where a global corporation has plants to join forces so the company cannot 'play one nation's workers off against the other as they now do'" (quoting an official of the International Metal Workers Federation). Particularly urgent in this connection was the idea of having "plans for dealing with workers at Ford, Chrysler, GM, Singer, General Electric, Fiat–Citröen, SKF, Toyota, Nissan, and Brown–Boveri... because of the towering power of the international giants which they claim would, within the next decade, control 75 percent of the world's manufacturing output." According to the theory of the present book, however, there is a dilemma here, also expressed as a question in the article, "Would the richer workers support the demands of those in a poor country?" As long as the division of labor persists, no, for the cheaper the factors and semimanufactures as they arrive for (further) processing, the higher the profits to the rich countries, with a share to the workers. But if the division of labor breaks down and daughter companies start competing with the mother company in the mother country with the same product produced more cheaply, there will be either protectionism or a demand for higher pay to workers in poor countries, in order to make those countries less competitive. Either task can best be handled for Center capitalism by a social-democratic regime because it is better at coopting the workers effectively.

47. Thus, the general secretaries of the ICSU (International Council of Scientific Unions), the ISSC (International Social Science Council), and the Inter-

national Union of Philosophy and the Humanities share considerable information among themselves. Imagine that they had a secretary general and
that the ministers of science of all countries also had one. It is the meeting
between two persons of that kind (or, maybe it would be the same person?)
that constitutes one of the key linkage points in the world system, at the
interface between T and NT.

48. Some examples of NT growth can be added to stimulate imagination.
Adding to the obvious "examples of parliamentarians and international civil
servants: there are many untapped possibilities in this world for tying
together people occupationally concerned with the politics of peace and
war. More concretely, we are thinking of heads of state, heads of government, foreign ministers, defense ministers, generals and other top military
personnel, and ambassadors and other top diplomatic personnel. The purpose would be clear: not so much to facilitate their communication as to put
them in a setting where they are forced to think, and even act, from world
perspectives wherever such perspectives are relevant" (from "Nonterritorial
Actors and the Problem of Peace"—see note 10—pp. 168-69).

49. One prediction might be in the neighborhood of 1,000 IGOs and 10,000
INGOs—ibid., p. 161 (for TNCs insufficient data were available). The figures
gain in perspective when compared with the static nature of T after the
expansion of the early 1960's, due to decolonization, nears its completion.

50. Thus, China will probably stick to her millennium-old tradition of impene-
trability—not because she is socialist/communist but because she is China.

51. This was one of the most important experiences during the campaign for and
against Norwegian membership in the European Community ending with the
referendum in 1972: the discovery that the counterexpertise so often
possessed more accurate and more relevant information. It was not necessarily that the official information was erroneous but that the range of issues
and the perspective were too narrow. It was a question of paradigms of
thinking—and acting.

52. This is the most harmful impact of public opinion polls: they tend to reduce
democracy to a reading of opinion when the process of attitude formation,
the open and free debate where every assumption can be challenged, both
ways, is a much more important characteristic of democracy than the final
distribution in a statistical table.

53. For some data and analysis, see the excellent article by Ottar Hellevik, Nils
Petter Gledistsch, and Kristen Ringdal: "The Common Market Issue in
Norway: A Conflict between Center and Periphery," *Journal of Peace
Research* (1975), pp. 37-54. Above all, the article demonstrates that more
important than party adherence was social position on a center-periphery
gradient—the periphery being against, the center in favor—but several of the
parties had adherents from various points of the scale of social position
causing internal strife when the leadership had taken their—usually typically
centrist—position.

54. In general this would make use of an INGO network, but perhaps only an
emerging INGO or TRANGO that will be born in the process. In a homogeneous setting like the European Community this is more easy. But precisely because it is more easy it does not seem to happen very often in a
spontaneous way that captures general attention because such initiatives are
so easily absorbed by the established pressure group system, the political
parties already existing. On the other hand, the goal is to arrive at some

system of that kind on a more worldwide basis, so the European Community experience also gives some advance information about the less laudable consequences.

55. As one example could serve the demonstrations against the Organization of American States (I give the name in English, because it is a highly U.S.-dominated organization) in Bogotá in April 1948, leading to the famous *Bogotazo*.

56. Thus, some surprise was expressed when in August 1975 Pakistan was the first to recognize the regime in Bangladesh that came into power by killing the founder of the country, Sheikh Mujibur Rahman—instead of waiting for the United States to act.

57. Thus, both the population conference in Bucharest in August 1974 and the women's conference in Mexico City in June 1975 had big nongovernmental forums attached to them; the United Nations seems to be much less afraid of people than the European governments. There may be a good reason for that: the quickly crystallizing alliance between increasingly progressive Third World countries (the UN majority) and progressive forces in the countries in the capitalist Center.

58. In the West the nuclei of such ideologies exist in Christianity, humanism, and socialism—if they could be liberated from explicit or implicit assumptions about the world as somehow unicentric, with the West in the center. Such minimalist ideologies do not need to be very explicit. They emerge as an implicit understanding, better so when the organization is really transnational. And the best point of departure for an ideology of that kind would be to build it around conceptions of human needs, material and nonmaterial, basic and less basic.

59. For a very thorough analysis of the development of the UN system in this kind of perspective, see the excellent work done by Kurt Jacobsen at the International Peace Research Institute in Oslo, *The General Assembly of the United Nations* (Oslo: Universitetsforlaget, 1978).

60. And to a lesser extent of the Christian and Jewish worlds (to Jerusalem) and the Hindu world (e.g., to Varanasi).

61. Interrail and similar arrangements may contribute much to the formation of transnational groups and to increasingly dense INGO networks that give contacts for inexpensive or free accommodation. These belong to the trivia of transnationalization from the point of view of grand theory, but they are necessary conditions nevertheless.

62. In other words and emphatically: it is not to try to slide down the curve in figure 1.1, "turning the clock backward." History's clock is rarely if ever turned backward, but some of the features of earlier times can be recreated.

63. I am thinking particularly of the project directed by Professor Stein Rokkan at the University of Bergen.

64. Some would answer that it is not comparable because of the absence of an external threat, but the national identity exists also in the absence of such threats. Moreover, the idea that the combined weight of direct violence, poverty, repression, and ecological imbalance might one day add up to a functional equivalent for the world as a whole is hardly so farfetched.

65. For one analysis along such lines, see Galtung, "Human Settlements: A Theory, Some Strategies and Some Proposals," *Papers*, no. 19, Chair in Conflict and Peace Research, University of Oslo.

66. Of course, Mexicans and Chinese would bolster such claims with reference to what happened around the middle of the nineteenth century in either region—the Indians with reference to the incongruity between overpopulated, underdeveloped India and underpopulated, overdeveloped Australia.

67. Experience seems to indicate that this is a slow process, although a key actor in the world, the United States, was populated that way. No doubt that has contributed to a certain pattern of self-righteousness in that particular country, given the high proportion of the population with direct or indirect (through ancestors) negative experience from some other part of the world, easily believing that those left behind are suffering from the same political and/or economic difficulties.

8. WORLD ORGANIZATION

8.1 A WORLD CENTRAL AUTHORITY

The dominant terminal peace model of this millennium seems to be the world-state, the idea of transforming politics to *Weltinnenpolitik*[1] on the model of a successful nation-state. This model is a typical Western cultural product, much less prominent in non-Western cultures and political thought.[2] It is the logical extension of certain features in Western culture: of the Christian doctrine of *one* God for all humanity (monotheism and universalism),[3] with the missionary nature of Christianity;[4] of the ideas of universally valid "laws," in moral, legal, and natural science, and ultimately also in social science; based on the export of political and economic institutions along the channels established by Western imperialism after the Great Discoveries.[5] Thus, the very idea of a world-state should invite and stimulate critical skepticism—and not only in non-Western circles, since historically this idea has been so clearly based on Western cosmological, cultural, political, and indeed economic and military premises. The proposals have looked like the West, or some part of it, writ large; substituting "world" and "country" for "country" and "district" in some national constitution to make it a world constitution. Since the models can often be seen as concentric expansions of Western processes, they also coincided with Western notions of "progress,"[6] and with Western imperialism.

And yet some kind of world-state is bound to come about—not because of any immutable law or principle, but because of the problems and conflicts brought about through the contradiction between the expansion of man and the finiteness of nature. A world where man and his institutions bump into each other and into nature at every turn requires a different organization than a world of roving tribes who have plenty of space, catching only occasional glimpses of each other. Some kind of mechanism for problem and conflict articulation and resolution is indispensable. The question is *what*.

We are almost bound to attempt to answer this question in terms of projections from empirical models at a lower level, using the states we know. The trouble with this kind of extrapolation is that once more the range is narrowed down to Western forms, since Western "nation-building" formulas have dominated the world scene so much that we have difficulties conceiving of

341

the state in other terms. If the world is to be organized like a state, and the answer to the question "Which state?" is in terms of unitary, federal, and confederal models (like France, the United States, and Yugoslavia the way she is developing now), the range is still far from sufficient. To formulate just one basic problem: all these ways of integrating people are still vertical, however "representative" they may be. There is a built-in division of labor between ruler and ruled, center and periphery. Along this axis, power flows—ideological, remunerative, punitive—and often takes the form of forceful repression. One might now say that if the smaller unit, the state, has not solved this power problem, then it is not to be expected that the biggest unit, the whole world, will do much better. But that again is extrapolationist thinking, ignoring the fact that the state formations that serve as models took place at a period in European history (the early modern period) characterized by mixtures of feudal and precapitalist social structures, of conservative and liberal societies.[7] We have to try to liberate ourselves from its built-in assumptions.

One such implicit assumption, for instance, is the thesis of proportionality between the size of the state and the size of force at the disposal of the central authority. "The larger the size the more internal and external enemies, hence the higher the need for force" seems to have been the thesis on which this ratio has been based. The doctrine has been monopoly over ultimate power inside with at least a balance of power with the outside. To the extent any excess force has been converted into imperialist expansion one way or the other the thesis may be true, even self-fulfilling. In general, the larger the size the more disagreement and disharmony. But "the larger the size, the more resources that can be converted into force" is a more plausible formulation, using the first thesis as a rationalization. It becomes like a program: force has to be proportionate to resources, resources have to be partially converted into force,[8] which then plays into the argument in favor of small states (see section 6.2).

No world central authority can make use of such assumptions. First, in principle there is no "outside" to balance; with the outside nature, there are only problems, outer limits, not conflicts. Second, to have ultimate power on the inside, the central authority would have to exceed in force not only the biggest state component, but also any coalition as is done in the Soviet Union. Leaving aside the problem of resources, if such an arsenal of power were assembled in the name of a world-state, backed up, for instance, with Western universalist self-righteousness, world repression would take on gigantic forms never before seen in history because modern technology would also be involved.

Generally, then, we must take care lest space-bound and time-bound assumptions relating to Europe some centuries ago be given excessive prominence in any conception. More concretely, we must attend to

1. The problem of the *rationale* for a central world authority;
2. The problem of *representation for articulation and decision* on problems and conflicts;
3. The problem of *power for resolution* of problems and conflicts.

These problems will have to be dealt with in the order given, but they are so interrelated that the distinctions are not very neat ones.

8.1.1 THE RATIONALE

The twin aspects of expanding man and finite nature, namely, scarcity and interdependence, are more than sufficient as a rationale for a central world authority.[9] It is important to state what rationale is excluded by this assumption. Excluded is the idea that a form already exists, a structure *cum* culture, of such perfection that it *will,* by inner necessity, expand until it covers the whole world—or *should* do so if this process is somehow lacking in automaticity. In earlier days Britain and France suffered from this, before them Spain and Portugal. The two major expressions of Western thinking today, liberalism and Marxism, also seem to have this assumption of universality somewhere, although in different forms. Since liberals tend to find answers to problems in new institutions and Marxists find answers in transcendence through revolution, they will think in terms of world institutions and world revolution respectively. The former has led to an image of the world as a projection of institutions found at home, the latter to a replication of revolutions also found at home.[10] Both become parts of Western export for copy abroad, skeptical of deviations from the model, as in Japan and China, watching for signs of "normal" development.

The liberal will see the good world as the good state writ large, as mentioned; the Marxist will see it as a set of countries that had undergone the correct revolution and become socialist. The former will exaggerate the benefits to be expected from a strong world superstructure in terms of its impact on states; the latter will belittle these benefits and see the key to progress as located in basic changes at lower levels. My inclination is in the latter direction: the world is so distorted that an impressive framework of world institutions may conceal rather than solve the issues and may perpetuate, even reinforce, rather than change structures. But something can nevertheless be achieved through institution building at the world level, even if self-reliance through decentralized local actions are seen as much more important.[11]

For there are *problems* that require global *planning* and *execution* and there are *conflicts* that require world *articulation* and *resolution*—although most problems and conflicts, fortunately for humankind, can be solved at lower levels, in ways compatible with ideas and ideals of decentralization and small units. Consequently, one should try to some extent to reason *from* the nature of the problems and the conflicts, and *from* the basic values, *to* the forms of a world central authority, not from some preconceived scheme taken from existing social repertories.

The distinction between problem and conflict is a useful one for that purpose, although not very sharp. By and large, problems are technical, conflicts are political—and most issues have elements of both. In a conflict there is always an incompatibility somewhere—of interest or goals. In either case some kind of authority is needed, technical or political—the former based on skill, the latter on power. By and large I agree with the thesis that there should be some overlap here: the skillful should to some extent be powerful, and the powerful skillful, or, at least, the two types of authority should be found under the same institutional roof.[12]

The United Nations is based on that assumption. There are technical organs (specialized agencies, etc.) to solve problems, and political organs (such as the Security Council and the General Assembly) to solve conflicts. The assumption is that there will be a spill-over effect from one type of authority to the other. To what extent this works, and to what extent the United Nations is a "success" in general, is not for me to argue here, however.[13] The United Nations was, when it was founded in 1945, an expression of world images held at a certain time, after the defeat of the Axis powers, and mainly in a certain place, the white, Western corner of the world. The underlying social philosophy was actor-oriented; it was liberal almost to the point of being structure-blind. Moreover, it was built on the assumption that there would be a sufficient consensus for a big-power concert to be operative. Like everything human, the United Nations undergoes changes; nothing is eternally durable. However, the circumstance that the world has an overabundance of problems and conflicts and a weak United Nations should not lead to the liberal fallacy that the world can be saved through an effective, much stronger superstructure, through, for example, the idea of countering each problem with a new UN agency. Needless to say, to that fallacy there is a corresponding Marxist one: the idea that in a world of socialist states the supernational level somehow will take care of itself. There is little between not wanting a heavy or forceful central authority and wanting virtually none at all. The problem may not be how to get more of the UN system, better endowed, but how to get a different, more adequate world central authority, building on the United Nations and her agencies.

8.1.2 REPRESENTATION FOR ARTICULATION

Problem and conflict *articulation* are ways of making the world society transparent, of sharing experiences in general and reports as to where and how the shoe pinches in particular. For this to happen the world central authority has to be *representative* in such a way that problems and conflicts can be reflected. A *world* authority, hence, is something quite different from an international or, more precisely, intergovernmental organization like the United Nations. An intergovernmental organization will capture only some of the world's problems and conflicts, namely, those that governments will bring up. Conflicts between government and nongovernment—between the rulers and the ruled—will not necessarily be reflected—like problems of secession or of governmental repression of its own people, for instance through transfer of technology that mainly favors the elites. Hence, a world authority has to give representation to more than governments if it wants to reflect more of the world than the governmental aspect of the territorial network of states.[14]

Which actors, then, should be represented? No universal formula can be put forward, for the world changes and new actors will constantly come into being. But we know there are *present* actors and *emerging* actors, *territorial* and *nonterritorial.* Who are they?

The *present, territorial* actors are clear enough: they are the *states* or countries, today represented by their governments. If they, and particularly the most powerful of them, dominate the United Nations of today that does not mean that they have to dominate a world central authority of tomorrow, any more than national assemblies (based on parties) are dominated by district powers.

Then there are the *emerging, territorial* actors, which for simplicity may be referred to as the *minorities.* They are subnational, but may be found in several states, as are Jews, Chinese, and Kurds. They are usually exploited, are racially and/or ethnically different, and are segregated territorially.[15] Whether in fact they will "emerge" and constitute states in the future is another question, and not necessarily important. The point today is that they have problems and conflicts that are inadequately articulated, not to mention resolved. For this reason they should be represented at the world central authority by themselves so that they can articulate their problems *together.* They should not be fragmented, each exposed to its own repression and false representation by those who repress them.

Then there are the *nonterritorial* actors, which are considerably more problematic. They are less clearly defined, especially as to the extent to which they are replications or reproductions, even reinforcements, of the territorial system of actors. This is most clear for the IGOs, where the territorial system to a large extent finds an isomorphic expression, as mentioned in section 7.1. Thus, the *power* aspect of the territorial system is mirrored in the UN three-tier distinction between ordinary General Assembly members and Security Council members with a veto, with the rotating Security Council members as some kind of a bridge between the categories. And the *economic* aspect of the territorial system finds its clear expression in the World Bank and related agencies.[16] To be on top of the nuclear stock pile, or of the vertical division of labor, gives *de jure* or *de facto* veto in IGOs, as it may do in the territorial system.[17] In fact, sometimes it may mean even more in the IGOs because there are procedural rules and because "representatives" are more easily disciplined by those who dominate IGOs than "people" are by their elites. "Representatives" are, after all, expressions of the same mode of thinking and acting and more similar to each other than elites to people.

For this reason IGOs should not be represented in a world central authority; that would be tantamount to a replication of the territorial system. Quite another matter is the cooperation between secretariats of IGOs, often or usually much more transnational in their orientation than the IGOs as such, with their national delegations. A strong network of secretariat cooperation, under a control mechanism to be discussed later, is indispensable. Such a network is actually emerging today and very strongly: I am thinking of all the forms of cooperation between the UN specialized agencies.[18]

But INGOs should be represented. They are a part of world reality, and although most of them are even more expressions of Western ideas and interests than the world itself, this will in all probability change. One difficulty is that the distinction between "governmental" and "nongovernmental" does not make much sense in socialist countries, but there is a corresponding distinction between organizations represented by ministry officials or not. These are the *present, nongovernmental* actors, and the international system already has had some experience in dealing with them.

What about the *transnational* organizations? These are organizations of individuals with nothing like national chapters, not to mention a replication within the organization of interstate relations of dominance of all kinds. These are among the *emerging, nonterritorial* actors—people's movements, youth movements, women's movements, even as world political parties, however embryonic that form. Today most of these movements would still be organized with national chapters, however.

In short, the scheme would be something like that shown in figure 8.1.

For all of them there will be problems of recognition and accreditation. For states there is already a tradition. For minorities I have indicated three criteria. For the nonterritorial a minimum dispersion all over the world must be a condition, and for the transnational association something approaching a world party system might constitute a criterion.

That brings us to the problem of selection of representatives, but first some words about the frequent suggestion of a *People's Assembly*. There is, for instance, the idea that for each one million human beings around the world there should be one elected representative. The valuable element in this proposal is the idea of *direct election* to the world central authority, which can function in a satisfactory manner as a vehicle of articulation only if *vox populi* has effective channels. But this raises two problems: how is this voting process defined, and what is the unit represented?

Figure 8.1 World actors to be represented

	Territorial	*Nonterritorial*
Present	*National* States	*Supranational* Organizations
Emerging	*Subnational* Minorities	*Transnational* Associations

In all proposals I have seen, the voting unit is territorial, usually the nation-state. Thus, Norway would have a right to four popularly elected representatives, China 1000 or so. Inside the state there are similar arrangements, with territorial representation (e.g., districts, in a senate) or nonterritorial representation (e.g., parties, in a house of representatives) guaranteed. The general idea would be to repeat this *between* states. But so far only *territorial* units have been represented at the world level, and only by *selection,* not by election.

State representation by direct election would solve one of these problems but also serve to reinforce the state structure of the world by legitimizing it better. Experience from Western European organizations with parliamentary assemblies (the European Community, the Council of Europe[19]) seems to indicate that the national identification is still strong, although voting along party lines is frequent when the parties are sufficiently similar as to structure, the interests they reflect, and the stands they take. This is not an argument against having direct elections, only an argument against believing that the territorial flavor will be washed out by such arrangements. Nor should it be. The territorial basis of organizing the human endeavor is entirely legitimate as long as it is not carried to the absurdities witnessed in the present world.

So the question is rather "Why organize direct elections only for representatives of states?" My argument would be that there should be *direct election for all four types of actors* to be represented; national, subnational, supranational, and transnational. There should be direct election of representatives from France, from Bretagne, from INGOs with national chapters in France and from transnational associations to which French persons belong. French people should elect their representatives and also participate in worldwide party elections. That elections may not be free in many places in the world, that it may be impossible to hold them for a subnational unit fighting for its liberation, or impractical to hold them for big supranational entities are not sufficient arguments against the principle of direct representation as an ideal, to be approximated as well as possible.[20]

The ratio of selected to elected representatives (and I count appointed parliamentarians among the former), as well as the ratio of bloc to individual, independent voting, will probably have to be worked out by each state, minority, organization, and association separately as an expression of its internal organization and linkage to the world community. But the general direction of change should be toward elected representatives and individual voting (i.e., as an expression of that individual representative's constituency). The only constant factor would be the number of votes accorded each actor in proportion to its members, as in trade union conferences. The European Community, for instance, would have something like 260 votes regardless of level of integration. This process should not be referred to as "weighted voting." It is today's voting that is weighted, in favor of the small and in disfavor of the big states, and usually also in favor of the rich and in disfavor of the poor,[21] as in a stockholders' conference.

One obvious difficulty is that whereas the number of countries is fairly well defined, with relatively clear criteria, the number of subnational, supranational, and particularly transnational actors is considerably less well defined. But I am not so worried about that. It is possible to run a parliamentary democracy not knowing how many parties will appear for each election, essentially using self-definition as a criterion. Of course, to be represented, parties have to have votes, and all countries, in one way or another, request a minimum number (in absolute or in percentage terms) of votes for representation to take place. Precisely here popular direct election reenters. A party hoping for representation will have to demonstrate, or at least indicate convincingly, that there is a sufficient number of people wanting to be represented through it. Needless to say, this raises all the problems of who can finance elections of one kind or another, particularly at a world level, and who are permitted to hold them. For that reason one might start with some of the transnational actors already in existence and gradually work in the direction of a meaningful party system.[22]

Again, I would be much more worried if too few actors were permitted access to the articulation mechanisms than if too many should come in. To articulate is not the same as to resolve. To articulate is more like the Pacem in Terris conferences,[23] a parade of issues, even a forum for mutual recognition of problems as valid; "I accept your problem if you accept mine." Resolutions can be passed expressing general concern, as in the UN General Assembly, but that is not the same as to solve a problem or a conflict. However, better a genuine articulation than a distorting, false "solution."

Concretely, therefore, what I have in mind would be three assemblies added to a House of States: a House of Minorities, a House of Supranational Organizations, and a House of Transnational Associations. If the House of States were something like a senate, then the House of Minorities would be for emerging states, the House of Associations would be like a parliament or congress, and the House of Organizations would represent functional groups, as in a corporate state. The assumption is that each of these assemblies would see the world from different angles, cut the problem and conflict pies differently, and catch different conflicts and problems in their conceptual and political nets. The houses would be relatively open-ended with regard to membership, probably with less stability than the present house of states, the General Assembly. Some might move from one house to the other—if minorities become states, for instance. Many might not attend, like the members of both houses of the British Parliament. But all four houses would discuss and pronounce themselves on the same agenda, an agenda that would have to be agreed upon by an interhouse coordinating committee. At that particular point there may be much to learn from the U.S. Congress.

So much for articulation and for resolutions. What about decisions as to how to solve problems and conflicts?

I stick to the idea that this is for the time being best done by using the present territorial units, the mutually exclusive and exhaustive system of states that span the world. This system has the advantage that people can be identified by location of *birth,* (major) *occupation,* or (major) *residence;* and since they can be located they can also be registered for voting once *and only once* in each election. To base decision making on minorities and nonterritorial organizations would always give extra votes to those who have multiple memberships, thus adding to their structural power. But having said this, voting based on territorial units as it is done today in the United Nations leaves very much to be desired. The House of Associations would probably gradually develop into a House of World Parties with transnational voting patterns offsetting the bloc voting to be expected in a house of states.

The general structure is now clear: four houses for *articulation,* with some mobility between the houses; one house (later two) for *decisions,* expressed as resolutions after problems and conflicts have been adequately articulated in all houses, with a voting formula as sensitive as possible to the distribution of the population in the world. Two more ideas should then be added.

First, for articulation it is often insufficient to wait for the parties directly concerned to articulate the problems and conflicts. The level of consciousness may be low, both of the factual state of affairs and of the evaluative light to be shed on these affairs. For that reason some kind of *Board of Review* consisting of world citizens of special repute—politicians, lawyers, social scientists, or just anybody—could be instituted.[24] This is not a plea for an expertocracy or a Council of Wise Men, of philosopher-kings, but a plea for better utilization of the types of insights that are presented every day around the world in countless conferences. They would not decide, they would articulate and suggest. Obviously membership should be limited; insight more than representation and factual knowledge should be sought; and if there are quotas these should probably be by age rather than by other criteria to see to it that the freshness of the young as well as the experience of the old are represented. No effort should be made to arrive at any consensus. These people would serve the task entrusted to them best by using their skills and being as true to their own values as possible.

Second, there is no reason to doubt that all of this might very easily develop into a big bureaucracy far above the heads of people in general, as the UN system has done today. For that reason it is absolutely mandatory that there be excellent two-way communication between the World Central Authority with its houses and the world population at large.

Newspaper reports of proceedings at the World Central Authority would not be sufficient. In addition the electronic global village should be used for what it can offer, to televise major proceedings via satellites to millions and millions of viewers in all countries. But TV has the basic shortcoming that it is feudal in its structure. More particularly, it offers no occasion for immediate feedback. Hence, world central authority delegates should do what is commonplace in democracies: report back to their constituencies, wherever they are, in person, willing to stand up to searching and critical examination. TV communication should be improved, to get some idea of world opinion on special occasions. The potential for all-world TV programs over satellite should be utilized for world debates of important issues, with some opportunity for call-in from viewers.

For this is where communication from the grassroot level up is indispensable. Delegates should, as much as possible, be subject to constituency instructions and to recall if they fail to live up to them. This is another reason that visibility of proceedings is so important. The only difference in that regard between an appointed and an elected delegate is that the latter will receive instructions from an electorate that may be nonexpert, nonbureaucrat—and hence pay more attention to basic principles and values and less to technicalities, or more to conflicts and less to problems, to put it that way. Since both are needed, the ideal delegations should have both kinds of elements. But for the participation of humankind as a whole in world decision making, information on world authority agendas in advance, thorough discussion down to the grassroot level, and instruction of delegates are indispensable ingredients. A bureaucracy that appoints and reports back *post festum* is no substitute, and can never be.

8.1.3 POWER BEHIND RESOLUTIONS

A world central authority has to have *some* power, some means of obtaining fundamental compliance. The question is "What type of power?" Drawing on general power theory (see section 2.4), this can be turned into two questions: "What *kind* of power, resource power or structural power?" and "In what *channel*—ideological, remunerative, or punitive—should power be exercised?"

It is easiest to answer the last question first. All three channels are needed, to some extent, but the emphasis should be on remunerative power. I shall argue this by arguing against any heavy emphasis on ideological and punitive power.

The argument against excessive ideological power is that it runs against values of pluralism, of diversity. It implies a world ideology, some kind of universal church, a common way of conceiving of things, past, present, and future. Compliance is obtained through sharing a maximum number of values and ideas instead of a minimum. It presupposes a model of man with heavy emphasis on similarity among people, to the point where diversity vanishes. It neglects the dialectics of dissimilarity, how all churches develop counterchurches that start out as sects and eventually take over, only themselves to be negated. It neglects the awesome consequences of trying to maintain the illusion of maximum similarity in the face of massive evidence to the contrary, particularly because force is usually resorted to to root out the dissidents. A maximalist ideology tends to become an ideology that conceives of those who fail to share it as worse than wrong; they are seen as *false*, as aberrations in the evolution of man, diseased rather than misled people, and hence subject to therapy or elimination—to psychiatric hospital rather than prison, to extermination rather than execution.

In short, I do not see the necessity or even desirability of developing much of a world ideology. The absence of a world ideology today is perhaps one of the most positive features of the present system. However tempting it is for intellectuals of various persuasions to hammer out a tight verbal system with internal consistency, it is hard to believe that it serves a valid purpose. World changes will take place, they are bound to come—but they will be in many directions and often contradictory. The guideline should not be maximalist but some minimalist kernel of values, like "absence of direct and structural violence" and "ecological balance." In other words, compliance should not be obtained by commands appealing to a commonly shared *Weltanschauung.* Such a solidarity may be the reason that China works today, but the world is not that uniform. This also applies to fields like science and technology that are now far too antipluralist.

Nor should compliance, principally, be obtained through punitive means, ranging from economic/diplomatic/communication sanctions to military operations. There is an obvious scope for a world police force, on a permanent basis—for instance, of the order of magnitude of 10^5 to 10^6 men and women and with destructive capability of the type authorized in the UN peacekeeping operations to date. But the magnitude of such forces would have to be derived from other considerations than balance-of-power thinking. More precisely, it might be derived from considerations of what is needed to back up laws to protect ecological balance and to counteract the most blatant cases of structural violence, for example, the suppression of minorities. In other words, a world police force should be geared less to the containment of direct violence and more to the promotion of the other two values, in ways to be specified in section 8.3.

The basic power channel of the World Central Authority would be the channel of remunerative power. I see a world central authority as having enormous resources for constructive use at its disposal, which means capital, goods, and know-how. The authority should be able to disburse all three where they are needed in accordance with global planning (long-term) and budgets (short-term). Most of this would be fixed and institutionalized, but there could also be above-normal remuneration to those who comply particularly well with the international norms. In short, I am thinking of a system of positive sanctions much more than negative sanctions, for the simple reasons that the latter do not seem to work as an instrument of compliance and the former are at the same time vehicles of global development.

Thus, the power is seen as coming in the form of technical adequacy, ability to solve problems, and positive sanctions on top of this. It is very hard, in the light of past experiences in big countries, to believe that a world central authority could try for more than this without either being pulled into the Charybdis of tyranny or dashed upon the Scylla of failure.

As to the first question, what *kind* of power, there are in principle two answers, structure and resources. A world central authority could derive much of its authority simply from being central, making the rest of the world peripheral and marginal. But how much centrality is compatible with a democratic structure of the world? For instance, a world central authority can only to a very limited extent be based on secrecy and on distance to its citizens. The World Central Authority should not be like a new actor standing above all others; rather, it should be like a medium in which they can all associate freely, as shown in figure 8.2. Without engaging in metaphysics, we can find a parallel here with the Christian and Buddhist concepts of God: God as suprapersonal and God as transpersonal. A "pantheistic" rather than a "monotheistic" concept of ultimate authority underlies the preferred model.

But there are still problems of remunerative power and punitive power to be considered, which will to some extent be the subjects of the next two sections. Let us start with a major potential source of remunerative power, in line with the idea that this will have to be the major form of power at the disposal of a world central authority.

8.2   FROM MULTINATIONAL CORPORATIONS
TO GLOBAL COOPERATIVES

A basic field in connection with world organization will always have to be world production, particularly for the satisfaction of fundamental needs. One approach to this is through the problem of controlling multinational corporations. The argumentation is well known, particularly as multinational corporations today are major vehicles of the dominance system. But the problem can, as mentioned in chapter 7, also be seen from other angles, not only asking about the question of control but also the question of *what* to produce, for whom. We shall explore both, as well as some other problems, particularly problems relating to world transportation and communication.

The first-order approximation to what I am suggesting is easily formulated: *globalization of the major world corporations.* Just as the emergence of the nation-state society led to the nationalization of some key types of economic

Figure 8.2 Two models of world central authority

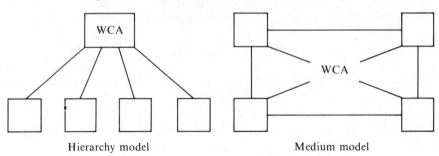

Hierarchy model   Medium model

activity within its border, particularly in the fields of transportation and communication, the emergence of the global society will have to lead to the globalization of some types of production. But all formulas become absurd when carried to the extreme; what follows is therefore aimed only at key world economic activity, of the kind that involves economic cycles (with extraction of raw materials, production, consumption, and transportation–communication, financing, research, and administration) that are particularly world-encompassing and/or economic activity basic to the survival and continued development of humankind, possibly adding transportation and communication to the standard list of food, clothes, shelter, medical service and schooling.

There are at least three arguments in favor of globalization:

1. It may ensure rational planning in a global community based on a finite nature, including constructing economic cycles that satisfy fundamental needs and equalize benefits better than the present system.
2. It may ensure, even enforce, a form of production that does not lead to the present excessive costs in terms of depletion and pollution but is compatible with new norms of ecological balance.
3. It may detach production for fundamental needs from competition for market demand and tie it more to supply for real needs.

It should be emphasized that globalization differs from nationalization, for nationalization may also be an important tool in international competition of an unhealthy kind, by giving more power to the state, however much it supersedes unhealthy domestic competition (one typical example being the arms trade). Thus, there is no assumption that all competition is unhealthy; only that competition is unhealthy that leads to exploitation, to the creation of artificial needs, to nonsatisfaction of fundamental needs, and to ecological imbalance.

Let us take as a concrete example what used to be the biggest of all the multinational corporations, GMC, the General Motors Corporation, and ask what human beings as world citizens might like to do with it.

To start with, let us reinterpret the G, and spell it GLOBAL. Ownership would be transferred from U.S. (and other) stockholders to, for instance, a UN production authority or a world production authority. This leads to the problem of expropriation with or without compensation and all the other well-known problems of nationalization. We assume that it will be carried out with compensation, which means that the World Central Authority must have considerable resources at its disposal, acquired in ways discussed hereafter.

Ownership by a world production authority should not be confused with decision making. The decision making should be in the hands of representatives of those affected by the economic cycles engendered by the organization—those who extract raw material, those who process it (workers, technicians, researchers), and those who consume. It should not be restricted to those who own (i.e., have invested capital) or those who are employed—the conservative and liberal formulas, respectively.[25] The World Central Authority should be so organized that adequate representation can easily be found from and by those affected by its activities.

This transfer of ownership from multinational to world level can come about by means of some type of gradualism. The alternative to doing it overnight is not satisfaction with the status quo, but to do it more gradually. Thus, licenses to operate internationally, to use the international medium, so to speak, could be granted under increasingly strict conditions: increasing fees, progressive taxation, report duties, increasing power given to board members appointed by international authorities (from observer status to full membership, even top ranks), increasing percentage of capital controlled by world authority, and so on. A number of procedures could be imagined, and for many of them nationalization processes in past and present would offer important positive and negative examples, for limitation as well as for warning.

But I do not think that transfer of ownership is all there should be to it. A Global Motors Corporation, producing exactly the same goods as the present GMC would be a good parallel to nationalization experiences (whereby, for instance, weapons of destruction are produced by state rather than private capitalists) but not a pointer to a better future, as far as the output, the "motors," is concerned. For that reason let us keep M, and spell it MOBILITY. It has to be reinterpreted, for if the new organization I have in mind should produce exactly the same things under its new and more representative decision making, not enough would have been gained.

What are the real needs in terms of mobility? As pointed out many times, one is a very inexpensive and nonpolluting means of mass transportation. If our sight is lowered socially so that top priority is given consistently to the needs of the most deprived, our attention would turn away from the costly, risky, unnecessarily polluting motor cars today associated with the label GMC (and other corporations). It would not point only in the direction of inexpensive collective transportation, such as buses of all sizes, down to the big cars running on a half regular, half *ad hoc* schedule in Mexico City and Caracas. One could also think in terms of individualized transportation that is inexpensive, safer, and no threat to the environment, like the donkey mentioned by Illich or a revival of sailing ships.[26]

Maybe the answer lies in some kind of battery-driven Tivoli car with solid *cautchouk* protection, making collisions fun rather than lethal, leaving those who want to race to special tracks where they can engage in their dangerous pursuits and display their prowess for all who want to join in admiration. The absurdities in what today is produced under the label "car" include such items as potential speeds up to 200 kmh and above in countries where the speed limit is 80, 90, or 100 kmh, not to mention bumpers that serve only some misconstrued conception of what is esthetic, costing even more to replace than what they are supposed to protect, but keeping dealers well afloat in their business.

I do not claim to know where the answer lies, but find the task of producing the low-cost, low-risk, low-threat means challenging. It will be hard to beat the bicycle, that ingenious device offering fresh air, exercise, and transportation all at once. One should not be deluded into believing that batteries provide the answer to pollution if they have to be charged from sockets drawing on electricity supplied by nuclear power plants or hydroelectric power plants, with pollution and depletion somewhere in either case. But the world will soon learn how to make pollution-depletion budgets, and some day perhaps master completely new forms of energy, making the old dream of magic carpets possible. There is no reason to assume that innovation is coming to an end.

Then the letter C–let us spell it COOPERATIVE. The world has seen enough corporations, meaning centrally run, big organizations, with all decision making and profit making gravitating toward the center. What is envisaged would also be big, and that may be wrong. There is something wrong in economic cycles that cannot be understood, not even perceived, by all those who are involved in them; and there is something basically sound in the self-reliance of the small unit, the Chinese People's Commune or the Asian *sarvodaya* village. But some things must probably also be produced on a level of bigness, for instance, energy, communication, and transportation, perhaps also some food (but not enough to threaten self-reliance)–not so much because of alleged economies of scale as in order to tie humankind together in some strong interdependencies. Although this will lead to some uniformity, it is hardly an encroachment on individual rights or pluralism if not everybody can have his own voltage. On the other hand, as self-reliance of the local community in the most basic needs is also an important goal, there is an important political issue right under the surface here.[27]

When I say "cooperative" I do not mean only that decision making should involve all who are concerned but also that they should be involved in the sense of having a material personal interest in it. Not only he who works in the factory could get the product at a discount, but also he who contributes in the decision making, the buyer, he who shows up at consumers' meetings, and so on. Above all, decision making could be decentralized, with the organizations found along the economic cycle evolving their own form and style. This could be done with due respect for harmonization, but not under the assumption that one of the units is decisive and should set the tone for all the others because, for instance, it is located in a certain country, employs the highest rate of university-educated personnel, or the like. But the countries participating in the global cooperative will of course be the first to benefit from it.

From General Motors Corporation to Global Mobility Cooperative–does that make sense? Only if one can point to some transition mechanisms with power behind them, a means of bringing about compliance. I have three such mechanisms in mind, for any multinational organization for economic activity depends on three sources of cooperation. It needs some element of government approval to operate on the territory where that government is sovereign, it needs employees to produce the product, and consumers have to cooperate by buying the product—for I am not thinking in terms of the "planned" economy wherein quantities have to be produced whether they are consumed or not.

[1] The pressure that *governments* can put on present-day transnational corporations is simple. In order to operate in a given territory corporations have to conform to certain standards, already referred to as a "code of conduct." The idea is to build into such a code the ideals of organization for global production. Such standards could be specified in a convention, and signatory states would pledge themselves to grant permission to operate only when the standards are respected, which means standards of ownership, of production, and of decision making. Needless to say, in the beginning only the more progressive governments, perhaps particularly those that have a tradition of supporting nationalization, would be likely to take such important steps toward globalization.

[2] The pressure that *employees* can bring to bear on their companies goes far beyond the conventional strike, which also may be used in some places to bring about a change toward globalization. Employees may walk out if this change does not take place. But they may also make the claim much more clear by, say, occupying the organization during a weekend and using it for (symbolic) production for more fundamental and more global needs. Above all: the researchers found in any big transnational corporation may refuse to produce classified knowledge marketed as licenses, patents, and the like and simply start publishing any invention and innovation of any use anywhere in the world for the satisfaction of real needs. In short, the Daniel Ellsberg of the multinational corporation would not sell to the competitor for his own benefit but give "his" work product back to the people to whom it belongs. For what any researcher, standing on the shoulders of all others, has added is so little relative to what already was that no invention is "his," and even less is it the property of the organization that happens to pay his salary. When in addition the invention is in a field relating to basic human needs, any monopolization is criminal and should be defined as such in global law.[28]

[3] The pressure that *consumers* can exercise is partly positive in terms of organized demands for certain products or product specifications and partly negative in terms of organized buyers' strikes. Both lie outside the very narrow band of articulation provided by classical capitalist society where to buy means "yes" and not to buy means "no"—with no articulation, no organization, no alternatives, no power behind it. Modern capitalism has added to this "marketing research" as a method of sensing the mood of an inarticulate aggregate of individuals, typically drawing on the atomizing, individualizing methodology of survey research. State capitalism seems to have added nothing, short of the dubious idea that a state bureaucrat possesses more insight than a private capitalist, because he is accountable to the party and not to stockholders. But holders of political and economic stock are not that different, and there are no substitutes for enlightened consumers. Such consumers must transcend the

present tendency to criticize products for details instead of fundamentals, among them the basic question of whether the product is needed at all and whether production capacity should rather be used for some other so far unproduced or underproduced product. What I have in mind is essentially a breakdown of the sharp division of labor between producers and consumers found today and reinforced in a strange manner by the movement for "industrial democracy," meaning some kind of equality among producers only.

Together these three sources of power should carry far, though there should be no illusion that any fight for the transformation of some of the world's major productive forces would be an easy one. As an example, take world aviation, a typical candidate for globalization and a good example of an industry that depends on a high level of global organization. That organization is to a large extent found today, through ICAO and IATA, and especially through the cooperation of skilled professionals in the air and on the ground, across borders of most kinds, around the world. But all basic decisions are made by the companies, to some extent by the personnel who work in the companies (using a high number of strikes), and above all by governments—never by passengers. Only when competition and the need for self-aggrandizement of companies and governments lead to absurd results have public reactions been heeded, as in the case of the SST. But there has been indirect sensitivity all the time because some companies have not been IATA members (particularly the case of Loftleidir). Because of the tremendous upswing in charter flights, public interest has been expressed and taken care of in an unmistakable manner. The public interest has, above all, been one: cheaper transportation as the Laker case proves.[29]

But the public is like a dormant giant—it is not easily brought to realize sufficiently its own powers. So imagine a strong transnational World Air Passengers Association, WAPA, capable of launching consumers' strikes against selected air companies, indeed also against substandard airfields. The association would have an office at each airport for processing complaints and suggestions, would raise not only matters of fare *level* (why should the passengers of today pay for more expensive, even if faster, transport for passengers of tomorrow?) but also fare *structure* (why does the fare structure still reflect so much of the vertical, imperial organization of the world?). It should, jointly with citizens in general, start questioning seriously the whole use of conventional airplanes and ask for such alternatives as VTOL, helicopter, and zeppelin transport to reduce noise and other forms of pollution. They should strip general air transport of unnecessary trappings like on-board meals (luncheon packages might be available), all kinds of costly "maharajah, red carpet, VIP" treatment designed to lure customers, and so on. Needless to say, such things may still be available to those who want to pay for them, but at an extra cost. The general point is clear: air transport should be for the common man who pays for himself, not for diplomats, business executives, and organization men in general who are reimbursed by their organizations and catered to in an atmosphere that has to exude some element of power and affluence.[30] It is unnecessary to emphasize the necessity of transportation to the nonterritorial continent. Cheap transportation—as for the Muslim *Hadj*—is a way of democratizing that mode of human existence.

From these two examples, the production and use of means of transportation on the ground and in the air, one could proceed in many directions. The most obvious is in the field of *means of communications,* where a pattern has already emerged highly isomorphic with the model I system of section 6.3. In chapter 4 I have already indicated how satellite communication might constitute the bridging element in a completely new phase of imperialism, after the international organizations no longer serve the purpose.[31] Control over world communication is firmly on the agenda, with two basic guidelines.

First is *the right of privacy,* meaning the right not only of individuals but also of collectivities not to be communicated to. For states this principle has already been laid down in a UN resolution, but many of the states that are most eager supporters of this principle are not willing to grant their own minorities the same right—or their organizations or associations, for that matter. There is, certainly, a problem here. On one hand there is the basic right of the individual to seek and obtain messages, on the other hand is the right of the collectivity to protect itself (through decisions democratically arrived at) against the use of communication for subversion or "superversion."[32] But that dilemma dissolves if we introduce the *freedom to move.* A state might demand that messages be not broadcast in its direction, but it should not be able to prevent its citizens from obtaining those messages through travel. As in a family whose majority demands that a teenage son limit his listening to pop music programs at home, limitation is different from prohibition, for the teenager may enjoy such programs elsewhere. The principle of diversity implies the freedom to seek new messages and also the freedom to close them out.

Second is the *globalization of means of communication across national borders*—along the lines indicated before, with a *world communication authority* alongside with a *world transportation authority*—and under the control of the World Central Authority with its four houses. Needless to say, lest this should become a bureaucracy beating anything the world has ever seen, the task of these world authorities would be to adopt broad, coordinated guidelines for decentralized activity—similar to what is done today all over the world in the field of health, under the auspices of the World Health Organization. (This organization, incidentally, has almost the right name, as the reference is to "world," not to a particular organization like the United Nations, but it should be bolstered with the term "authority.")

In connection with communication I would like to give a detailed, concrete image of how telesatellites could be used to build more global consciousness. It is such a precious instrument and so often terribly abused for the dissemination of propaganda for commercial products and violent behavior. Of course, one important field would be to organize some kind of global newscasts, at least

"The World Seen from the United Nations," a five-minute segment to be included in national newscasts.

But the whole idea of relating to the world via the concept of "news" is much more problematic than it may look. Newspapers have been criticized for a tendency to overaccentuate elite persons and their actions in the preceding twenty-four hours, particularly when there is some dramatic, preferably negative, element to be reported. TV as a medium has the advantage that it can show processes and give better images of ordinary people, not only of leading actors on the national or international scene. For this reason TV has a potential, at least, for being less person-oriented and more dynamically structure-oriented than other news media. The problem of how correctly TV news reflects world events will not be developed further here. We shall rather look at the opposite side of the picture: how can TV, effectively used during an international crisis, be an instrument of conflict resolution? In other words, the problem is not only how TV reflects the world but how TV can positively act on it to have a beneficial impact.

Let us assume that during international crises (1) larger segments of the population than just the top decision-makers should be given a chance to express themselves, and (2) that there is a general scarcity of good ideas as to how to proceed in such crises; that decision-makers are often very effectively isolated or isolating themselves; and that they are often subject to some kind of regression to highly polarized and even primitive forms of behavior. *The concrete suggestion, then, is to make use of modern space technology to set up, over a telesatellite communication system and between cooperating TV companies in as many countries as would care to participate (and under the guidance of a central authority), an international panel of experts in order to tap their brains. Further, this panel should then enter into TV dialogue with some national panels, recruited as representatively and as symmetrically as possible.*

Technically, it should not be difficult. There is experience in worldwide TV cooperation via satellite or a system of satellites, for instance, the around-the-world program presented in June 1967 in a number of countries (unfortunately, the Eastern European countries withdrew from the cooperation). However, this program, technically interesting as it was, was not a very serious one. It was a strange mixture of public relations for the countries concerned, conveying relatively stereotyped images of themselves, and a collection of curios. It did not address itself seriously to any problem, nor could it have done so since it was the first venture of its kind.

But technically it has been proved repeatedly that worldwide TV cooperation over satellite is feasible, although there are difficulties on the world level (with countries located as far from each other as Japan, the United States, Sweden, and Australia). On the other hand, it is obvious that such panels would be most interesting if the participating countries could be found on both sides of important conflict borders, so that both or several points of view might be presented. Although this might create additional technical difficulties since the machineries used are also often polarized by conflict borders, the difficulties should not be insurmountable, given some good will, unless the crisis is acute.

Thus, in practice, one would think in terms of a cooperative organization like Eurovision, at least, extended eastward, in the spirit of all-European cooperation, to set up a joint program of experts or generally insightful people to pronounce themselves on the eve of some kind of international crisis. One model here is the Pacem in Terris II conference that was convened in Geneva at the end of May 1967. At this conference, judged by many to be a failure because it did not produce unanimous solutions or resolutions, a number of highly well informed and imaginative personalities presented ideas and suggestions in connection with ongoing conflicts. It is obvious that very many of these ideas, perhaps most, would not have any chance in the present world, sometimes because they were completely unrealistic, sometimes because they were objectionable from the point of view of one or another party to a conflict.

But this is not essential. Very few thought processes lead to anything that can be implemented immediately as policy action, and thoughts are also often stimulating in another direction than originally intended by their producers. The important thing here is rather to have some sort of idea factory that can function in the open. There are more than enough think tanks functioning in separate institutes, in ministries, in the United Nations, and so on, well hidden from the public eye—thereby reducing popular participation and popular awareness. In front of the TV, the viewers can make up their own opinion, accept some ideas and reject others, and if they accept some, they might even constitute potentially important popular pressure on the decision makers. For the people would know more about what their leaders know, and the leaders would know that people know—which is even more important. Needless to say, it would be problematic to decide who should participate on such a panel. But in concrete terms one might think of, say, ten countries participating with two persons from each, with an obligation to speak one of the official UN languages. In each country there would be simultaneous translators available to translate these languages into the language of the country itself, so that there should be no linguistic difficulties in connection with the local participation.

The twenty or so participants would then be asked to present their views on the conflict, with one extremely important normative constraint on their utterances: to reduce condemnation, general guilt distribution, and even analysis to a minimum and to increase positive proposal making and views of what the future could be like to a maximum. In other words, the suggestions and the discussion should be not merely "constructive" in a vague sense but concretely proposal-oriented, with as detailed suggestions as possible, and future-oriented rather than past-oriented. One should not try to bring forward once more the news analyst, the intellectual commentator who knows a lot of details about what has happened and what is happening. Rather, one should stimulate the imaginative generalist, or the specialist for that matter, known from the past for having concrete proposals in mind that have a bearing on practical situations and problems. This holds for the central panel as well as for the local national panels that would have a two-way discussion with the central panel, visible to the rest of the world.

Such people are not easily found. They are not overrepresented among scientists, who often have a predilection for data; and as data do not exist in the future, which is the realm of prediction and probability, scientists have a tendency to focus more on the past and the present than on the future. Thus, it is more likely that the ideal participants would be found among persons who are writers in a more general sense, former politicians and diplomats (as current officeholders would probably be barred from participating in order not to be forced to say anything that would be binding on organizations they represent) and generally well-oriented people. Obviously, the composition of the panel will have to vary from one conflict to the other, but one could also build up a relatively permanent nucleus of generalists.

After a presentation of proposals, the panel could discuss the proposals in order to elaborate them further, all the time being literally in the world public eye. A premium should be set on the person who is able to extract from somebody else's proposal valuable elements, build on them, elaborate them, and bring them further in an associative *or dissociative* process. People who are able only to find negative elements in proposals put forward by others in order to use those elements as pegs on which they can hang their own killing arguments should be eliminated. The latter type of intellectual game should be regarded as a luxury that we cannot afford in times of serious crisis. *Dicere* and *contra dicere* may be indispensable in courtrooms and seminar rooms, but they may also lead to highly destructive intellectual habits, well developed in the teutonic and gallic traditions.

One should not try to press the panel to come to a unanimous conclusion, since that conclusion would probably be a rather diluted compromise. The interesting thing would not be what twenty people could agree on, but what twenty individuals could help each other develop as possible constructive courses of action. Since there is a general tendency, during time of crises, for decision makers to try to manipulate mass media to dominate public opinion, a network of TV panels of this kind could constitute a democratizing element, a kind of counterpoint to decision makers and above all a counterpoint that would be watched by the population at large. This might mobilize not only attitudinal support for one view against another among the population, but also a correspondingly creative process in the population in general. Other people might feel they had ideas; and in countries that permit freedom of expression of such ideas, newspapers and other mass media should be encouraged to serve as additional forums for such contributions.

Participants should not be able to make deals among themselves so that more than two-thirds of them support or put forward the same point of view. Since there is little doubt that, with the present-day communication structure, such a panel would have some influence, it should be operating under some rules of procedure. One possibility might be a pledge not to do so; another that participants did not know long in advance that they would be picked; a third isolation of participants in studios before the debate to forestall cooperation among them. On the other hand, they must be given some warning in order to think through what they would like to present as proposals. For the same reason they should probably be picked from among persons known for independence, autonomy, and creativity, not among persons known as loyal spokesmen of already existing groups, interest organizations, and so on. It is presumed that such groups would already have their means of expression in a crisis, for instance, through a party press, and that what should be stimulated should rather be a maximum of nondirected creativity.

Under whose auspices should such a program be run? As presented here, it would be, probably, in the name of some kind of global cooperative TV organization. However, there is a certain conservative element in that plan. Since TV originally had a very low level of geographical penetration, essentially limited by the range from some mountain top or even the top of a high building to the surrounding horizon, TV, much more than radio, became a territorial concept. TV corresponds to the nation-state as a glove to a hand: they are both expressions of the principle of territorial contiguity, whereas the radio pays considerably less respect to the geographical constraints on which nation-states are based. For this reason one would also expect governments to make considerable use of TV companies as instruments of internal propaganda and control, of domestic news management and moral formation in times of crisis; these factors may counteract proposals for international cooperation of the type put forward here. In other words, not only TNC profit motives but also governmental political interests may stand in the way of global cooperatives of the type envisaged here. But some other formulas could be used.

One choice would be to put programs of this type under the auspices of an existing intergovernmental organization—preferably a universal one, although regional organizations might also be interesting. One could imagine that from the beginning such things might take place on a regional basis for technical reasons, but under UN auspices. Another possibility would be that the United Nations have a specialized agency for news communication and that the panel be asked by that agency to comment on particularly critical news items, on an *ad hoc* or a regular basis. Such a specialized agency would of course have this as only a minor task. Its major task might be, for instance, to serve as an international news agency, with an effort to arrive at a maximally objective form of news communication. If this is impossible, and it very often seems to be impossible to find any kind of "objective" platform from which conflicts can be adequately reported, a specialized agency of this type might at least be able to report to all countries what the conflict looks like according to the views presented by the parties to the conflict, for instance, by quoting editorial articles. With such an agency in operation, communicating all over the world, individuals anywhere would know that if their government presents only one side of an issue, it is deliberately withholding the other side.

Another possibility, somewhat in the same direction, would be to make use of INGOs. In a not too remote future, certain professional groups or groups with a particular value-orientation will probably ask for their own TV channel, for programs relayed over TV satellites separately or jointly owned, wherever in the world they happen to be living. In such a world privacy would be a concept relating more to uninterfered-with electromagnetic frequency than to geographical location, since geography would be insignificant relative to position in "electromagnetic space." It might be interesting to think in terms of bringing different INGOs together through cooperation in panels of the kind envisaged, and the programs could then be presented in the name of some kind of super-INGO, for instance, by some international council of scientific organizations. However, this is obviously still for the future.

There is little doubt that such discussion programs would be listened to. They would constitute a major element of attraction in times of crisis, exactly because people feel so lonely, so noninstrumental, and so much victimized by the propaganda machineries they are exposed to. As the situation is today there is a contradiction between the global nature of the means of communication and the way in which they serve parochial political and commercial interests. It is high time that this contradiction is overcome, and global cooperation with popular participation would be one way of achieving it in this tremendously important field.

8.3 FROM STATUS-QUO PEACEKEEPING TO WORLD POLICE FORCES

The classical instrumental approach to peace, often seen as *the* peace structure, is the balance-of-power approach, which is not so different from the arms control/disarmament approach, as indicated in section 5.2. The whole approach is basically dissociative: the antagonists are kept away from each other under mutual threats of considerable punishment if they transgress, particularly if they transgress into each others' territory. Often the balance of power is accompanied by other dissociative social measures such as mutual prejudice (social distance), not to mention such classical approaches as the use of geography in the form of distance (an ocean, a desert) or impediments (a river, a mountain chain). If the two social forces mentioned, the threat of destructive behavior and an attitude of hatred and/or contempt, are insufficient to keep the antagonists apart, *third parties may be called in* (or call themselves in) to exercise peacekeeping operations in patrolling the borderline. If the two geographical factors prove insufficient, *technology may be used to supplement geography,* in the form of mines, electromagnetic fences, and so on, as mentioned in section 3.4.

The dissociative approach has some merits. It is equitable, if not egalitarian, since it prescribes a social vacuum or close to a vacuum, and in a vacuum there can be no exploitation. In creating a vacuum it also permits diversity among the parties. But its demerits are more conspicuous.

First, and basically, *in this structure arms are targeted.*[33] There has to be not only a capacity to destroy but also some credibility that the capacity will be used, and no doubt as to who the enemy is. The impact of this in terms of creating a garrison state within and a world of fear without is well known. But more basically: all the reasons supplied in the first sections of chapter 5 on why arms races do not stop are, *a fortiori,* valid for this structure. There is power but little balance, at best a precarious, dynamic balance. And this dynamism in the arms race is contagious: because of the coupling of the world's conflicts it spreads to other parts of the world, through vertical and horizontal proliferation or simply through imitation.

Second, *the world is no longer fit for this structure.* Geography has become largely irrelevant, there is no geographical distance or impediment that technology cannot overbid. Technology can then be met with more technology, but that is tantamount to an arms race. Prejudice can be counted upon in crises, but not in general: people start knowing each other too well. The weapons have simply become too dangerous to be used. Of course, there is for that reason also a proliferation of small-scale weapons. But the argument nevertheless holds, to a large extent.

It is in this context that the call for *third parties* to supplement the dissociative strategies engaged in by the first and second parties arises. When a war breaks out between two groups, a status quo has been interrupted; one approach to the problem of war is to try to reestablish the *status quo ante.* This actor-oriented approach aims at preventing *actors* from engaging in "evil actions." It does not immediately ask the question of whether the *status quo ante* is worth reestablishing and maintaining or is possibly even inferior to a violent encounter because of the *structural* violence built into it. That question lies outside the competence and even the scope of that approach, whose intention is to "keep the peace," meaning "maintaining absence of direct violence," not working for structural change.

If the two parties at war can keep peace themselves, get disentangled from the deadly embrace, and get back to the *status quo ante* (and they sometimes can[34]), then no need for third parties arises. But if we assume that the peacekeeping is carried out by third parties, three questions immediately arise:

1. What kind of first and second parties are there?
2. What kind of third parties are possible?
3. What are the means at the disposal of the third parties to maintain the status quo?

We shall see that it is impossible to discuss these questions without a typology of wars and the underlying conflicts similar to that developed in section 5.1 on the basis of the theory from chapter 4.

For the basic dilemma of peacekeeping as defined here is not how to find a third party, legitimize its actions under some formula of collective security, and make it capable of performing its roles adequately. These are the problems that, characteristically, have attracted most attention.[35] The basic dilemma seems to be how peacekeeping as an approach can differentiate between horizontal, vertical, and "diagonal" wars, and not just treat them all as "wars," "trouble," "shooting in the streets," and so on.

There is hardly any doubt that a good case can be made for peacekeeping in a *horizontal* conflict, a conflict with no element of dominance—a conflict, that is, over goals rather than interests. When associative mechanisms (see section 3.4) have either not been tried or have been found insufficient, the next approach will either not be tried or have been found insufficient, the next approach proves insufficient, improve it with *technology;* and if the social forces of social distance and balance of power prove insufficient (as they have, by definition), the assistance of *third parties* might be tried to keep the belligerents apart.

The difficulty is that only a few wars are horizontal. In our typology types 1 and 2 are horizontal, and under types 4 and 5 horizontal internal wars can be imagined. In these cases peacekeeping cannot, deliberately or not, be a means to maintain a dominance structure; it is truly a third party. But if it intervenes and freezes a status quo in a *vertical* conflict between periphery and center, then, wanting it or not, *it is simply a party to the conflict, siding objectively with the side most interested in preserving the status quo.* This is elementary, but too often forgotten.[36]

Let us then introduce the distinctions among intranational, intraregional, and international peacekeeping.

Intranational peacekeeping is nothing new: it is what the state is supposed to perform, one of its major functions. The state intervenes in vertical as well as horizontal internal conflicts, and it is unnecessary here to explore further how state intervention in vertical conflicts, e.g., using soldiers against (or substituting for) striking workers, traditionally makes the state a second rather than a third party to such conflicts.[37]

Intraregional peacekeeping is nothing new either. Within its sphere of influence the country with *de facto* power monopoly, the hegemonial power, has always exercised horizontal and vertical peacekeeping. It has kept peace among Periphery countries and has stopped the Periphery from launching attacks against the Center. What was said for intranational peacekeeping applies also here.[38]

What is new is *international peacekeeping,* under the UN Charter,[39] or as earlier envisaged by the Covenant of the League of Nations.[40] It is immediately seen that under the present type of world "order" it must be very limited in scope. It cannot in general intervene in the two types of internal wars. Under the doctrine of nonintervention in *internal* affairs the nation-state has a monopoly on peacekeeping inside its domain of jurisdiction. Further, it cannot in general intervene in intraregional wars, whether between two Periphery countries inside the empire or simply imperialistic wars. Under the doctrine of regional peace-keeping (Chapter 8 of the UN Charter) the region also has a monopoly on peacekeeping inside its domain.

This rules out wars of types 3, 4, 5, and 6 in our typology. But the subversive wars and the internationalized class wars are also highly problematic since the internal component is so high. They are basically internal wars, except that there is also an element of international assistance or coordination. There may be a case for patrolling waterways, for enforcing nonintervention and things of that kind, but that is not the same as peacekeeping. Hence, types 7 through 12 are, in our present world, most likely to be dealt with under the formulas of intranational or intraregional peacekeeping mentioned before, shielding off the international community from efforts to penetrate too deeply into "internal affairs."

Types 1 and 2 remain as candidates for truly *international peacekeeping,* which brings us to the third dilemma of international peacekeeping: *it is intended for the weak, not for the strong.* Elements of the instrument are used in the conflict between Israel and the Arab states, between India and Pakistan, but not between the United States and the Soviet Union. It can be used in wars between Periphery states if they are not both within the same region but not, so far, between superpowers, probably not even between big powers. Why? It is not only because the United Nations is weak, but rather because if it were effective the big powers would no longer be superpowers.[41]

The rationalization may be in terms of the level of sophistication in weaponry: no one else is sophisticated and strong enough to keep peace between us! But the other interpretation is deeper and more in accordance with the facts, for the aim of peacekeeping is not necessarily to produce a counterweight sufficient to keep the belligerents apart if they really want to fight: to be a big power, and *a fortiori* to be a superpower, is *to have the right to be one's own peacekeeper.* A superpower is fully responsible, not needing to be looked after. Should it nevertheless go to war, it is because war is unavoidable. There may be a small probability of miscalculation and technical error, but that can be smoothed out through systems analysis and through Center– direct negotiation, for example, in arms control and disarmament negotiations. At any rate, it is nothing for lesser powers to try to meddle into, singly or combined in the General Assembly.[42]

To be a lesser power, in this type of thinking, also carries with it the connotation of a lower level of rationality, of politicians who give in to their emotions, of lack of experience in handling the tools of war, of a certain volatility—all factors that make most Periphery–Periphery wars less necessary and more avoidable than Center–Center wars. Hence comes the case for peace-keeping *by making the world one region under superpower condominium,* under

UN auspices, and leaving the concrete job to lesser powers, as it has been done so far.[43] But in so doing the entire peacekeeping instrument easily becomes an expression of the top-heaviness of the world, limited to only some cases of type 2 (Periphery–Periphery), out of the twelve types of wars. A rather severe limitation indeed!

Let us now retrace our steps and try to indicate some measures to get out of these three dilemmas. The world cannot do without a peacekeeping instrument, but it cannot do *with* one with so many structural weaknesses, either. Let us search for some formulas out of the dilemmas, in the opposite order of their presentation, asking the question "What should a world central authority do?"

First, *horizontal peacekeeping must be made more symmetric.* If there is peacekeeping in the Periphery, by the big powers or by the superpowers themselves, or condoned by them under a UN formula, *then there must also be a provision for Periphery peacekeeping in the Center.* The idea is much less impractical or utopian than it may sound. Many scenarios for the initial phase of a major war in Europe are based on some type of transgression across the East–West borderline that runs from North to South, from the border between Norway and the Soviet Union down to the borders between Bulgaria and Greece/Turkey. To station non-European UN troops along this border, or a critical points, would be an extremely important symbol of symmetry and global sharing of problems.[44] In section 6.3 this was mentioned as good for Europe; here it is repeated as a new perspective on *world* peacekeeping.

But this type of symmetry, that many would find artificial, is not the only possibility. *Symmetry can also be obtained by locking the traditional world Center out from peacekeeping in the Periphery.* This is what the OAU to some extent has done,[45] it is what the future Organization of Latin American States[46] might do in its domain, it is what India might aspire to do in South Asia, and so on. As shall be argued later, I find this regionalization suboptimal, for if peace is indivisible, then peacekeeping should be even more so. What would prevent such peacekeeping regions from turning against each other? Very little, as I have tried to show in chapter 6. Hence, I would prefer, as usual, *symmetry through exchange to symmetry through dissociation.*

Second, *there is the problem of extending the sphere of applicability of international peacekeeping.* This means, unequivocally, to break through these artificial walls humankind has built around itself called regions and states. The doctrine of nonintervention will have to go or change, which will be an extremely painful and drawn-out process. Nonintervention is based on the illusion that in our world the normal war still is of types 1 and 2.

That the doctrine has to go is more than evident from a case like Bangladesh: under that doctrine genocide of a nation aspiring to some kind of statehood (whether it be full autonomy or autonomy inside a federation) can be attempted unimpeded by any effort to carry out "peacekeeping."[47] Or, to take a contrived example: imagine that Hitler had said in 1936 that he really had no territorial ambitions at all, that all he wanted was to kill all the Jews he could lay a hand on? Would that constitute a case for intervention? The point is simply that with wars of types 4 and 5 becoming more important the doctrine of nonintervention will become increasingly anachronistic. Fortunately, Idi Amin's invasion of Tanzania gave Tanzania a pretext to invade Uganda.

The same can be said about the monopoly on peacekeeping held by regions dominated by hegemonial powers. Such regions, like the U.S.-dominated Organization of American States and the Soviet-dominated Warsaw Treaty Organization, are empires badly disguised, and their nature was clearly revealed when they were used to uphold the structure of dominance in the Dominican Republic in 1965 and in Czechoslovakia in 1968.[48] With the assistance of some of the satellites in both cases, a war of type 6 was fought, under the pretext that the "other side" was launching something of type 8—subversive warfare—the evidence being less than slim in either case.

The fight against *intrabloc* monopoly on peacekeeping is easier than the fight against *intranational* monopoly on peacekeeping. Today all over the world there is a certain sentiment against blocs dominated by one hegemonial power. Hence, by the end of this century there may be no such blocs left. They may all share the fate of the *pax britannica* and the *pax gallica* systems, although some residues of both are still lingering on.[49] If one now imagined a general horizontalization of regions, internal collective peacekeeping within such regions, as for example the OAU, would obviously be different from the two examples mentioned. But the peacekeeping would still have to be authorized by the United Nations; it should be decentralized rather than regionalized, as was spelled out in section 6.3. In such regions international wars would be horizontal, not vertical, which would simplify the problem tremendously.

Where the intranational monopoly on peacekeeping is concerned we run up against a much more deeply entrenched system, since it is a system with considerable tradition and sophistication. More particularly, I am thinking of how easily a population can be made to turn against foreign intruders, however much they are "third parties" operating "legitimately." Hence, the criterion must somehow be exactly the extent to which the third parties are wanted. Not only governments should be entitled to articulate the wish for a peacekeeping operation, but other groups should also be entitled to do so. Of course, this has already been seen in the form of representatives, often smuggled out of the oppressive system, organizing lobbies and so on. An obvious point, hence, is that the world *must* find an institutional way of representing such groups, which is not going to be easy. We are thinking of a form whereby Biafra, Bangladesh, Euzkadi, and the Catholic minority in Ulster would all be (or would have been) able to raise their voices to a world authority, not only to Nigeria, Pakistan, Spain, and Britain. Thus, the four groups would have highly different views on the issue of intervention by an international peacekeeping force. Any international authority that is an intergovernmental authority cannot be relied upon in such issues; it is also rapidly becoming an anachronism because of its structural inability to cope with such problems. Hence, there is one more argument in favor of the House of Minorities advocated in section 8.1.

Third, *there is the whole problem of the role of peacekeeping in connection with vertical conflict,* with conflicts arising from structural violence. Briefly stated, one could imagine three positions on this issue:

1. *The formalistic stand* is that trouble is trouble, any war should be handled in the same way; besides, there will be no agreement as to what kind of war it is anyhow. *Conclusion:* third-party intervention also in vertical conflict, to keep them apart.
2. *The "let-it-work-itself-out" stand* is that a vertical war is the acting out of internal contradictions, which have to work themselves out. Ultimately the progressive forces will win; the rest of the world should stay out. *Conclusion:* no third-party intervention (because it would support the second party, the dominant party).
3. *The "use-peacekeeping-on-the-side-of-peace" stand* is that to keep peace in the sense of the absence of direct violence is not enough. One should also make peace in the sense of abolishing structural violence. *Conclusion:* third-party intervention, on the side of the first party, the dominated party.

I reject the first position as mechanistic and in practice counterproductive to the cause of peace because it preserves structural violence, and thereby also direct violence, in the longer run, e.g., by "protecting civilians" in the Dominican Republic in 1965.[50] I also reject the second position, among other reasons because it may lead to extremely drawn-out wars with no guarantee of a result. It is cynical to tell freedom fighters in southern Africa that they must "work it out themselves," fighting with simple arms against fighter-bombers and napalm.[51]

But the third stand is also problematic, among other reasons because of the difficulty in deciding whether there is a clear case of dominance and how it operates. In some cases it is extremely simple. Thus, the United Nations could have intervened, for instance, in southern Africa on the side of the freedom fighters (that the diagnosis is "extremely simple" is revealed by the near unanimity of UN resolutions). But other cases may be more problematic.

But even in such cases many other forms can be found. Thus, the modern war of liberation proceeds precisely by liberating territories and turning them into models of what the future state shall be once they have been liberated (from structural violence).[52] International peacekeeping should consist not only in giving funds and know-how of various kinds to these territories but also, as a minimum, in helping protect these territories.[53] A peacekeeping operation in a *horizontal* conflict would be a two-way wall separating the parties. *A peacekeeping operation in a vertical conflict should be more like a one-way wall, permitting the freedom fighters out to expand the liberated territory but preventing the oppressors from getting in.* Many other formulas could be imagined. Needless to say, they will not easily pass the filters posed systematically against them by international law, so dominated by governmentalism and the actor-oriented perspective, with all its built-in vested interests and status-quo-preserving assumptions about the prevalence of horizontal relations, in conflicts and in wars.[54]

Third-party intervention in order to prevent *structural* violence, not only *direct* violence, is bound to rise higher and higher on the political agenda. I mentioned the case of a Hitler bent on killing Jews yet protected by the doctrine of nonintervention, if not necessarily in practice. But he might have said, "I do not want to kill them suddenly, only slowly, by exposing them to malnutrition, protein deficiency, slum conditions, no health facilities, no education, and the most menial and dangerous work." In that case he would only have put into words what many societies practice anyway. Why should this be less of a case for intervention? Are we bound to wait for the elite in that country or its legislative assembly to be sufficiently aroused by compassion or self-interest to change conditions?[55]

Or, does structural violence have to be converted into direct violence that can be seen as a threat also to the elites and to the outside world in order for intervention to take place? Is this conversion mechanism really in the interest of the world, when clear indicators of structural violence can be established and verified before the eruption comes? Or is it only one more expression of the excessive weight given to the actor-oriented perspective as opposed to the structure-oriented perspective? However that may be, sooner or later the peace-keeping instrument will have to be made less biased and be directed not only against the destruction of human life in battle, but also against its destruction in slums.

To take another problem: so far, the UN peacekeeping forces seem to have been able to draw on considerable good will and enthusiasm in such nations as Canada and the Nordic countries. To what extent is that enthusiasm conditioned by the low likelihood that these forces will ever be used on their own territory?[56] Would enthusiasm decline if that condition were no longer valid? How could support nevertheless be maintained, if it should be maintained—as I think it should?

With such improvements as indicated, peacekeeping may still be a very valuable instrument. That it is insufficient alone is commonplace; nobody ever argued that it should be used alone. But it is not enough to say that along with a status-quo-oriented peacekeeping operation doing exactly that, "keeping peace," there must also be peacemaking (meaning mediation/arbitration) and peacebuilding efforts (meaning structural changes when taken seriously, some cosmetic attitudinal and behavioral changes when taken more frivolously).[57] Experience shows us convincingly that although these are useful analytical distinctions, the concrete activities cannot be separated in the field.[58] More particularly, the peacekeeping operations have in and by themselves to be peacebuilding and peacemaking, for instance, along the lines indicated before.

Thus, there is a scope for *world police forces,* forces different from the UN peacekeeping forces we have seen so far,[59] except for some of the minor operations centered on truce supervision and observation in general.[60] For such operations they should have the equipment it takes, which probably is to be evaluated in terms of human software rather than (but not to the exclusion of) electronic and other hardware.[61]

However, in concluding this section it should be emphasized that most of the thinking on world police forces has presupposed a conflict model rather than a problem model. Police have been seen in a third-party role—to which is added, very explicitly, the idea that *a third party should side with the party that is right if there is such a party, as there is, even often,* and even when this implies intervention in "internal affairs" in extreme cases. But there is also a role for the police in connection with, say, the problems of the environment, supervising that world norms against pollution and depletion are adhered to. Of course, this may also be seen as a conflict—between "capitalists" and "people"—and to some extent rightly so. However, the role of a helicopter-equipped antipollution task force in a case like that of the *Torrey Canyon* is not first of all to arrest the captain and some other people but to contain the damage, to warn, and to mobilize. It may very well be that a creditable, profoundly loyal, and dedicated world police might emerge more easily as an outcome of such activities than as an outcome of peacekeeping operations.

But, it will be objected, a police force does not serve to prevent a major war between major powers or an attack by a big power on small powers—which is true. No instrument serves all purposes at the same time; the dentist's drill is not good for road work. National police forces, even in a country like Norway, would be inadequate if all criminals and all political extremists joined forces, but the cost of making the police capable of handling such situations would be the police state. A world police force capable of handling even superpowers would transcend any image of the "police world"; it is almost inconceivable (unless all other countries in the world put their forces at the disposal of the World Central Authority). The defense against such cases of direct violence has to be built with other means. Some indications of what is needed are given in chapters 5 and 6 and in all the structural measures contemplated in chapters 7 and 8.

8.4 STRATEGIES FOR CHANGE

The key to the future is the integration of the territorial and the nonterritorial systems, keeping in mind all the time the fight against both direct violence and structural violence with its two major expressions—poverty and repression—and the problems relating to ecological balance. A world central authority as a central guidance system is indispensable, but certainly not sufficient. Too much centralism will reintroduce structural violence in another form, the form usually lamented by the political right: making clients out of countries, local communities, and people. But this has certainly not taken place yet. Countries may be clients, but of big powers, not of the United Nations; local communities and people may also be clients, but of their own governments—and in most cases of those who own some of the means of production. We still have not reached the region of compromise in the "neither too much nor too little" formula; there is still a good distance to go from the "too little."

There is, however, another problem which is rather pressing even today. The United Nations subdivides territorial space into countries and nonterritorial space into functions, building UN agencies around some of them. I have argued in favor of giving more scope to the nonterritorial actors, partly because they are so dynamic in terms of their growth and partly because they can be turned into excellent instruments for problem solving and conflict resolution. But that does not solve one important problem: the subdivision and fragmentation that are brought in with the proliferation of such actors. Countries have the same problems of excessive subdivision into ministries or departments, caused by and leading to sector thinking, and the instrument of interdepartmental committees is hardly sufficient to overcome this fragmentation (nor is the interagency committee).

The answer is probably not to stop nonterritorial growth and its impact on the world central authority, but to strengthen the institutions and organizations whereby all the various functions can be integrated. Ultimately this locus is in the human beings themselves, but they are easily manipulated. The local community offers a much better answer to the problem of how to keep things together, if the local community has a reasonably high level of self-reliance. But the same problem can also be posed at the other end of the world spectrum: in the world central authority itself.

Hence the importance of keeping a General Assembly as the place where all problems are discussed, not yielding to any temptation to have one general assembly for political/security matters and one for economic/development matters. There may be separate committees and assemblies; but somewhere there should be an assembly that has to deal with it all and see it in perspective, constituted in such a way that it can articulate all important problems and conflicts. Fragmentation of the total situation into energy, raw materials, population, and so on will serve the rulers rather than the ruled.[62]

In that spirit let us try to envisage some ways of building on the present UN system to turn it into a more adequate world central authority. In doing so let us take the longer view—the year 2000 or something like that. It is not a question of the many important reforms that can be implemented with a time horizon of five years or the decade. For this reason the methods proposed here are, precisely, strategies rather than tactics. Whether, in fact, they will ultimately come about in continuity with the present UN system or whether some new discontinuous jump will take place (as from the League of Nations to the United Nations) remains to be seen. It is hard to believe that something like what is envisaged here will not sooner rather than later be a permanent fixture of any world central authority.

There is no reason to repeat what has been said in sections 8.1, 8.2, and 8.3 about organization, globalization, and control of violence. Those were the broad outlines; here is the place for specifics.

8.4.1 ORGANIZATION

I have argued in favor of regionalization not only in economic affairs but also in the field of security (section 6.3) and in favor of adding more houses to the United Nations. Both of these can be seen as very gradual processes. Imagine that both take place at the same time as more specialized agencies are added and located in the Third World: The old United Nations, a big-power dominated, territorially based organization, will still be there but will be surrounded by so much organizational growth that it will lose in salience. As a consequence the Security Council and the big-power veto will also gradually lose significance because there will be so many other places to present the same issues.[63] If the rule that big powers can be members of one and only one region is adhered to, their veto in the universal organization can be repeated in only one region. The Security Council in its present shape will probably die a slow rather than a quick death and gradually be replaced by some kind of executive committee with rotating membership—the general practice in democratic organizations. The strategy would be to get around it rather than to attack it directly.

But the Security Council is only an anomaly from the past that might even have played a positive role in getting a world authority off the ground. More important than architectonics at the top would be to strengthen the contact between the United Nations and the citizens of its states. One way of doing that would be to have *UN embassies in all member states,* complementing the permanent delegations that states have to the United Nations, making the tie more symmetric. The UN embassy should be of major importance in the local capital; it should house all the local UN agencies, possibly the local UN association, and today's resident representative (of the UNDP) would be tomorrow's UN ambassador, preferably taken from another region of the world, and an obvious candidate for the position of *doyen* of the *corps diplomatique.*

As a matter of fact, the whole *corps diplomatique* could be partly globalized. It could be made into a locally based General Assembly in miniature—somewhat as the Finns made use of all the ambassadors to their country in the preparatory stages of the Conference on Cooperation and Security in Europe. Bilateral diplomacy is to a large extent moribund anyhow. Its reporting function is often performed much better by international journalists, social scientists, and other experts. Its negotiation function is to a large extent being taken over either by the IGOs or by opposite-number direct negotiation (e.g., foreign ministers or ministers of education working it out during a conference, later on perhaps reporting to their ambassadors). The task of taking care of the country's citizens when they need help can be performed by the consular service. (It can also be performed by INGOs, as many people will report to colleagues and associates when in distress, rather than to their own consulates; there are also often organizations present from their own country like charter companies, banks, and so on.) There remains the task of being host and guide to visiting dignitaries from the home country, sporting a superb *cuisine* for national cooking—but even that is threatened through the spread of "ethnic" restaurants all over the world.

Consequently one could envisage an arrangement similar to what the airlines have at the airports (but do not practice in the cities, unfortunately): a big building where each country has a couple of rooms for its representatives, sharing common expenses, cutting out all the trimmings from the period when the embassy had virtual monopoly on the contact between countries A and B (the garden, the top salaries, the pompous pretentiousness)—with a couple of rooms they could rent for cocktail parties (which serve a useful function), and a meeting room—with, of course, the UN embassy on the top floor.

What would be discussed in those meetings, where local politicians and civil servants would be present? They might be dedicated to issues on the General Assembly agenda from the point of view of the host country, with a view to learning that country's views better and to informing the country of others' views. They might, if the host country receives technical assistance, peace-keeping help, or some other major UN service, discuss how best to implement UN decisions and coordinate them with whatever bilateral arrangement might exist in the country, making it possible to draw on the world experience as a whole.

But above all *the major purpose would be to multilateralize international diplomacy,* to increase mutual visibility and transparency—communication some-what akin to what happens in the Quakers' diplomat seminars, only more formalized and with some real function to play. It is very important to conceive of the arrangement as a two-way flow: not only what the other countries can do in or for the host country, but also vice versa—a concept that will be much more meaningful when the world slowly comes around to think in terms of maldevel-opment (out of which underdevelopment is only one case, the other being the overdevelopment in many of the rich, industrialized countries) and a common concern for development in all countries. Much of this concern is already there; an institution of this kind could give it more life, provided diplomats were trained to think and act more in terms of world and human interest and less in terms of national interest. For this purpose, the training of diplomats as generalists rather than sectorial specialists should be retained for this type of institution to serve as an integrative focus, keeping countries and specialized functions together again.

One might also go one step further when it comes to UN penetration into member states: have UN personnel participate as observers, perhaps also as trainees, *stages,* in legislative and executive organs of the host country. What would be more natural than a very close cooperation between the UN embassy in a country and the UN office/desk in the foreign office of that country? Why could not the UN ambassador be present when the foreign affairs committee in the local parliament discusses UN affairs? Or, be present in parliament as observer—perhaps one day even with the right to speak when called upon, like visiting heads of state, sometimes invited to address national assemblies?

Even more important than this type of elite integration would be the use of the local UN embassy for some kind of reporting on the state of affairs in the host country, as all embassies do anyhow, focusing on the level of violence, poverty, repression, and ecological imbalances. Ultimately, such items are reported one way or the other, but so far the country itself has control over most of the information to be published about the country in UN reports. This will have to change, and the UN embassy could play some role in that connection as a monitoring agency for norms embodied in UN resolutions and declarations—not to mention in the charter itself. This goes beyond what countries would permit today. On the other hand, what they permit today—except some of the most repressive countries—is also far beyond what they permitted a generation ago, in terms of having national myths shattered through the reports and comparisons made in international organizations.

Still more important would be the use of the UN embassy as an institution to which local citizens could report infractions of arms control/disarmament agreements (see section 5.4), extreme cases of poverty hidden by the host country, infractions of human rights norms, and cases of ecological imbalance. That many, perhaps most countries would not permit such activity is no argument against starting with those countries allowing it. The idea is significant: there is a world central authority with a right to know when world norms are infracted inside a country and with a right to publicize the fact that it knows. It may not be able to do much, but experience from agencies like Amnesty International gives some reason for hope in this field—and their experience would of course have to be drawn upon.[64]

Finally, one question that sooner or later will have to be solved in a more satisfactory manner than at present: where should the UN headquarters be located? In one of the divided capitals of the world, such as Berlin or Jerusalem?[65] In a floating city? In a federal territory carved out of one of the underused parts of the world? In a Third World capital, because the Third World contains the majority both of countries and of people? In rotating locations? I do not know, but the present place is too symbolic of what is, fortunately, a recent past, the total world domination by its northwest corner.[66]

8.4.2 GLOBALIZATION

There are at least three good reasons for globalization: to institutionalize the idea of *man's common heritage,* of *commons* belonging to men and women everywhere, not subjected to private or national interests; to see to it that these commons as much as possible are used for the satisfaction of human needs (starting with the most basic needs of those most needy); and to provide a world central authority with revenue independent of powerful member states that might punish or reward the authority according to whether or not it serves their interests. These reasons are exactly the same as for nationalization inside a country—except that inside a country resources may also be appropriated for fight and defense against other countries.

Here is one list of possible commons:

    I. From the territorial system
  1. Underused territory (polar regions, Spitsbergen, Greenland, possibly some desert areas)
  2. Seabed outside national jurisdiction (but with some mixed national/international jurisdiction in the "exclusive economic zones") to earth center
  3. Ocean column above the international seabed (including permanent fixtures, floating islands and cities)
  4. International air space
  5. Extraterritorial space
   II. From the nonterritorial system
  1. Subnational actors (persons, communities)
  2. IGOs—by making them UN specialized agencies, subject to certain rules
  3. INGOs—by giving them consultative status, etc., to specialized agencies, subject to certain rules
  4. BINGOs, multinational corporations—by placing them under some kind of world central authority control
  III. From the cultural system
  1. Scientific knowledge
  2. Art products
  3. Monuments, sites
  IV. From nature
  1. Live nature (particular parts of flora and fauna)
  2. Non-live nature (sights, scenic spots, etc.)

It is important to conceive of globalization in terms of *degree*. In some cases globalization may merely mean a statement from a central world authority to the effect that something is *regarded* as belonging to humankind as a whole; in other cases it may entail the right to levy taxes; and in still other cases it may mean complete ownership. In some cases all three reasons for globalization may come into play, in other cases only one of them. Let us look at some examples from our list, starting with nature, since that is the part least explored in this context.

There is a difference between declaring that threatened species like the whales cannot lawfully be killed by citizens of any country and declaring that they belong to humankind as a whole represented by a central authority—meaning that killing them is a crime against that authority and humanity as a whole. The difference is very clearly seen in connection with national parks: poachers do not commit an abstract crime, for there is an offended subject, the public. Of course, there has to be a direct relation between the public and the authority on the one hand and the protected species on the other, which is precisely what the national park establishes. Correspondingly, one way of protecting the whales might be to organize frequent tourist excursions to their waters, just as a way to protect seals is to make the barbarism with which they are killed visible to everybody.[67]

What about sights, sites, and art products? The argument varies from case to case, but the general reasoning would be as follows. Imagine a country with a magnificent natural sight, a waterfall, for example, and imagine that all the citizens are of the opinion that it should be converted into hydroelectric power. Is it obvious that they have a right to do so? Or, could one argue that the world as a whole has a legitimate interest here, not only the few who engage in what is called mass tourism, but everybody, including future generations? Or, imagine that the local population agrees that a monument should be torn down because it stands in the way of a school or health clinic. Is it obvious that they are entitled to make that decision and implement it alone?

Is it obvious that the great products of human art belong to the country in which the artist was born? Voices can be heard against the idea that private publishing companies should derive profits from selling reproductions of paintings long after the artist has passed away, but is it better that the government makes money or bolsters its prestige by exporting art products as symbols of national strength, in exhibitions, cultural exchanges, and museums for tourists? Henrik Ibsen is to some small extent a part of Norwegian foreign policy even though he lived twenty-nine years abroad and had his property auctioned away; he became a monument in his own country when still alive, partly because of his longevity, and he is part of the Norwegian GNP.[68] But he wrote for humanity about profoundly human problems—from a very bourgeois perspective, but a rather universal bourgeois perspective. Some formula should be found whereby such art products belong to humanity also in a material sense, for example, by UNESCO acquiring publishing rights and organizing permanent and itinerant exhibitions of works that are "globalized"—unless the artist explicitly should be against it.[69] The principle of man's common heritage would receive great impetus and be broadened from the more materialistic and power political concerns currently dominating the issue.[70]

Scientific knowledge constitutes a particularly crucial category in this connection, as does *nature* that can be used for the satisfaction of basic needs—especially the arable parts of the world. Should any organization, profit or nonprofit, private or governmental, national or international, be entitled to classify and even to withhold knowledge that can be used to produce more and better food, shelter, and clothes, to give health to people or new methods of education? Is a country that happens to have an excess of arable land entitled to turn it into highways and airports or let it deteriorate into wastelands when there are countries with a severe food deficit because they lack arable land? The case of scientific knowledge calls for general availability, for the abolition of patents, and for the protection of the producers of knowledge against economic or political retribution from companies and governments when they make their knowledge public. The case of arable land might call for the same type of control of natural resources on a world basis as many countries already have on a national basis. National control as envisaged in the New International Economic Order is probably a necessary, but not sufficient, step.[71]

Moving up the list we then come to the nonterritorial and territorial systems. In the preceding subsection, I have discussed some of the ways in which a world central authority, even building on the present United Nations, might penetrate the major parts of the territorial system, the member states, and then turn to the idea, now very current, of establishing international sovereignty over the unclaimed or underused parts of the world geography.[72] It is important to keep the double rationale in mind: to deny countries the possibility of using them improperly (e.g., for military purposes) and to give the international community a chance to use them properly (e.g., for basic needs). In addition there is the idea of securing some independent revenue. A test case is the effort to establish an International Seabed Regime, coupled to the norm against "emplacement" of arms of destruction on the ocean floor[73] and to the idea of revenue from the exploitation of seabed resources. But the second reason is often not kept sufficiently in mind: it would be a tragic irony if the first real effort to globalize a common should end up in a gigantic effort to process nodules into arms that are used to put down insurgency in the Periphery countries, at the same time as they receive some revenue from the authority.[74]

Obviously, the purpose of globalizing the seabed would not be met unless the raw materials were systematically processed in the direction of fundamental needs satisfaction. The best use of the seabed might well be to cultivate it, for food production or for something that could be turned into clothes, shelter, and health. For this to happen the ocean has to be included, because it is much richer and together with the seabed constitutes an ecological system. Globalization of the oceans will have to be the next step to follow rapidly after the seabed globalization, together with the other items on the list from the territorial system.

Income can be derived from these globalized commons in several ways: as direct income from production, in the form of royalties of various kinds, and by taxes for the use of the commons—on ships for using international waters, on airlines for using international air space (not to mention rocket-launching countries!), on communication networks for using outer space, and so on.[75] The taxes could be very light, as the principle is probably more important than the total income to be derived from taxation. Much more could actually be derived from taxing transnational corporations, on the grounds that they are depending on the whole world system and some kind of order to operate at all, which might also constitute a more valid answer to the problem of to whom they should pay taxes. Their transnational nature implies that they should be accountable to a transnational party, not only to a multiple of nations. What should be taxed would somehow have to be the value of what flows internationally of factors and products.[76]

In passing it should also be mentioned that more income for a world central authority could be derived from the member states, simply by raising the annual assessment.[77] It could also be converted into something more similar to national taxation by having each country declare its net income in the preceding year, giving exemption for natural disasters, emergencies, misery, and so on. It could be administered by a strengthened ECOSOC; as such national statistics are made by many countries, they could be standardized, supervised by the local UN embassy, and used as a basis. That there would be efforts to cheat is obvious; in a sense that would even be a sign that a world central authority had come of age.

As I have already discussed globalization of BINGOs using international institutions, let us turn to the possibility of globalizing subnational actors, IGOs and INGOs. In a sense it already exists: the United Nations and her agencies serve as norm producers about what a proper international organization should look like[78]—although the norms are sometimes broken by the UN organizations themselves, for example, by the Washington-based UN organizations in the field of monetary affairs, mainly reflecting world capitalism.[79] Such norms could be made more precise, but that might also contribute to some rigidity.[80]

Other possibilities would be explored. There have been several initiatives around the world to establish world citizenship or to "donate" communities to the world—to globalize or *mundialize* them. The difficulty is that these have remained symbolic acts devoid of institutional consequences. If there were a way in which such communities could pay some taxes directly to the United Nations—not only voluntary contributions to the UNICEF fund—or if the United Nations could make use of their enthusiasm, some momentum might come out of it. In general there will not be many consequences before the national government will put a stop to the movement. But it might help to transnationalize, deriving some strength from international solidarity, which is the reason I have put this under the heading of nonterritorial possibilities. More particularly, all the town-twinning schemes could become more meaningful if they did not only serve as a basis for better mutual knowledge and binational ties but became the nucleus of an "association of globalized cities"—for instance pledging themselves to pay 1 percent of municipal taxes to the World Central Authority.[81] It may be argued that this would leave out the villages, but if they were organized more like federations of villages, as argued elsewhere, they could also become more visible on the global scene.

This model could then, conceivably, also be applied to some of the international organizations, for instance those of the professions, and particularly of the scientists. In the Hippocratic oath there is already a good expression of what globalization of the medical profession might entail;[82] and there are significant moves across the whole gamut of professions to establish similar codes of ethics.[83] Such codes should contain at least two basic elements: a pledge to devote oneself above all to the satisfaction of true human needs, or at least not to counteract them, and a dedication to the whole world, to serve humans everywhere, and particularly those most in need. Efforts to establish codes with a content of that type are predestined to meet with very heavy resistance, which may even serve to crystallize the issue by driving a wedge between those with primary loyalty to their own country and those who feel ready to declare their transnational loyalty and try, on all occasions, to give meaningful expression to a pledge of that kind.[84] One might also add that this should not be interpreted as a move against national loyalty and basic research with no particular immediate applicability of any kind. It is meant rather as a guide in case of conflicting loyalties and allocations.

Then, there are some other groups of people one might also like to see globalized: heads of state, heads of government, foreign ministers, ministers of defense, diplomats, military forces, and others traditionally specializing in zero-sum games in the territorial system, referred to as being "in the national interest." The idea is much less absurd than it might sound, for it is no longer obvious that they are only playing zero-sum games. At the regional level they very often cooperate quite well, and the World Central Authority could at least give them the universal setting in which they might be able to develop more cooperative enterprises at the global level. Most foreign ministers come to the General Assembly; they could coordinate better and make it into a joint meeting. Heads of state could also come and could provide the world with one annual summit meeting,[85] building up an increasing pressure for some tangible results. As to the partial globalization of diplomats, sufficient indication has already been given of that, so let us turn to the military.

8.4.3 INTERNATIONAL CONTROL OF VIOLENCE

Some indications have been given in section 8.3 about the conditions for the application of world police forces to contain direct aggression and to join in the fight against structural aggression. The only point to be added here is that this presupposes some experts in the control of violence, who have to be properly "globalized," although they may operate regionally, as indicated in section 6.2. Their dedication has to be to human beings, to save them and protect them from all kinds of violence; and their loyalty has to be global, not national or regional. To obtain this it is hardly enough to make up an international force by mixing together national contingents, although that was the only way to get the idea off the ground. The sum of ten different national prejudices is not global identification.[86] There probably has to be a prehistory of common training and experience, in other words an argument for permanent forces rather than standby forces, earmarked for UN service, in the order of magnitude of 10^5. This force has to be an elite force, not in the sense of commando forces, special forces, red devils, and green berets, but in the sense of combining the best of police and military techniques in control of violence—including control of themselves—with peacemaking and peacebuilding functions.[87]

There is a problem here, though: the more perfect they become, the more they will tend to take over functions that should be carried out locally, depriving local forces of the chance to grow through the challenge of carrying out their own peacekeeping mediation and cooperative ventures. In general these experts will probably be better at dissociative than associative strategies, better at keeping the parties apart and policing two-way or one-way borders than at building cooperative networks between the parties, if that is the answer. But even the dissociative work should be done with full insight into the other aspects of the fight against violence, and it is around this broad range of professional expertise that real globalization can be built. It must be a major goal to do this in such a way that national armies appear violent, amateurish, somewhat child-ish, and parochial in comparison, just as one purpose of peace research is to give people an alternative to military research. Both attempts will meet with resis-tance from predictable quarters.[88]

In conclusion, some words should be added about a last but certainly not least important profession in this connection: *the international lawyers.* Law is an image of a structure crystallized into written norms (or sources for the deduction of such norms). I say "image" because it is not necessarily the empirical, factual structure—that would imply that norms are not broken. I say "structure" because the actors, the "juridical persons," are nameless; they are defined in terms of their rights and duties and judged in terms of their actions. In this particular sense, law in general is structure-oriented; it is actor-blind in the sense that it is not particularistic to specific, named actors. On the other hand, however, law tends to be blind to the significance of such structural variables as those developed and used in the present book (see section 2.3). Thus, norms against exploitation, penetration, fragmentation, and marginaliza-tion are at least unknown to me, and lawyers will probably tend to conceive of such categories as "sociological," "meaningless," or "utopian" (the last term being applied to their negations). Lawyers will therefore tend to be caught in such traps as defining equality in terms of equal fisheries limits, blind to the circumstance that this can lead to the most inequitable structures when one country has long-distance trawlers and the other has wooden canoes.[89] Similarly, their efforts to approach the problem of equity will probably be oriented toward terms of exchange rather than toward division of labor and so on. Thus they will tend to construct structure images that belong to the past rather than being pointers to the future. *Conclusion:* there is a scope for the globalization of lawyers, for making them more mindful of forward-oriented values, so that they can build images of future structure and lead rather than lag behind the development. This also applies to other professions.

8.5 SUMMARY

Let me now try to summarize what has been said in the last three chapters; on the territorial system, the nonterritorial system, and the problem of a world central authority. The essence can be put in four paragraphs, four theses.

[1] The primary task is to try to reduce the enormous amount of structural violence built into the world system, within and between countries, if at all possible without incurring direct violence.[90] Fundamentally, this battle has to be fought in the territorial system, through the formula of collective, national, and

local self-reliance. It does imply partial withdrawal from an exploitative world structure, through collective self-reliance among Third World countries relative to the United States, the European Community, and Japan (and also the Eastern European countries relative to the Soviet Union). It may also imply a strengthening of local communities everywhere relative to their centers, particularly where some ethnic factor is involved. Politically this adds up to strong intergovernmental organizations for the Third World as a whole or on a regional basis; to Third World countries with more ability to withstand pressures from the outside; to increased use of federal structures; and in some cases to secession and disintegration of existing states.

[2] The nonterritorial system is also a carrier of structural violence, being used, as it is, by the Center countries. It has, however, three great advantages relative to the territorial system: it is much more dynamic, being based on rapid emergence of new actors rather than painful fusion and fission processes; it is more flexible, being tied to sociofunctional rather than geopolitical spaces, and its conflicts can to a large extent be handled without recourse to violence. Hence it is argued that the nonterritorial system should be used systematically and skillfully in prefiguring changes in the territorial system (as the formation of the UNCTAD 77 gradually can be seen to lead toward a Third World secretariat). Hence a great number of suggestions in the spirit of dialectics, both breaking down some of the existing structure of the nonterritorial system and building up a new structure more capable of serving basic needs and of giving priority to those most in need, among countries, among people.

[3] The net outcome of this would be *a world where each part is a center,*[91] *spun together in a dense network of nonexploitative, participatory international organizations of various kinds. This would be the world of our dreams: many and smaller units (today's problem being the macro-state rather than the mini-state), woven together in a web of multilateral ties, substituting for the bilateral approach to global cohesion a much more multilateral approach.* Utopian? Not at all, as this is how countries are kept together in this world—not by counties, *departements, provincias, ken,* and *fylker* having bilateral relations, but through the integration of them all under multilateral, national umbrellas constituted by associations and organizations, trade unions, companies, and ministries; bilateralism is insignificant.[92]

[4] And yet, I have argued against the final, logical conclusions: the world government,[93] except in the shape of a weak one whose power is based on rewards rather than punishment and essentially of a federal nature—"some kind of Swiss constitution with a highly diversified but somewhat Chinese content" to put it in a formula almost doomed to be misunderstood (but I take the risk nonetheless, as it communicates something). This world central authority would have a role as a major articulator of problems and conflicts, and then try to seek the solution as far down in the system as possible. To do this, both territorial and nonterritorial actors have to be represented, and both the established old ones and the emerging new ones. Today the territorial system is no doubt stronger

than the nonterritorial one; tomorrow they may become equal; the day after tomorrow the nonterritorial system may carry the burden of political articulation and decision making (as it does inside most countries). Hence the World Central Authority has to be made in such a way that it can accommodate world dynamism in the years to come.[94]

The years to come will be the years that will witness how the Western-dominated system that started with the Great Discoveries is coming to an end. To express it mildly: these will be difficult years and will call for a maximum of concerted action by individuals. And that is the theme of the final chapter.

NOTES

References to *Essays* are to Johan Galtung, *Essays in Peace Research*, 5 vols. (Copenhagen: Ejlers, 1975-80) (Atlantic Highlands, N.J.: Humanities Press).

1. The felicitous expression comes from C. F. von Weizsacker. It is one of those rare examples of how a concept expressed in a word or two can be much more productive in creating images than a whole theory.

2. I, at least, am ignorant of consistent world models for "eternal peace," expressed in political terms, produced in non-Western parts of the world. Rather, this seems to be a particular Western concern, this idea of devising peace plans for the whole world—the present book being one more example. See "Social Cosmology and the Concept of Peace," *Essays, V,* 16.

3. See Galtung, *Social Cosmology and Western Civilization,* Trends in Western Civilization Project (University of Oslo, 1979). Centralism is seen as a key aspect of Western civilization, the center being in the West.

4. See Matthew 28: 18-20.

5. The idea of referring to something as a "discovery" the moment somebody from the West sets his foot there is, of course, also a part of Western imperialism, as is the numbering in the expression *"Third* World."

6. One of the best examples of this kind of thinking is probably from Macauley, when he sees the British Empire as a procession of peoples with the white dominions in front, followed by colored people decreasingly similar to Britain in institutional, cultural, and racial terms, ending with the primitive pagans—all of them being reviewed by Queen Victoria, who gives hope to all of them as they pass through history, evolving toward the highest of all stages—Britain herself.

7. In the terms used in section 3.1 these were societies of the model I variety being strongly eroded by model II aspects. They were all vertical, increasingly city-oriented, increasingly centralizing societies. The political-administrative centralization of the nation-state went hand in hand with the economic centralism brought about by rising capitalism, particularly when industries and head offices were located close to the administrative centers. The strong interest in federal structures after that time already gives testimony to the need for some alternative.

8. This is known as *rank concordance:* the idea that if you are high on one dimension you should be high on others as well; if you are low, stay low because it is presumptuous to get higher. For an analysis of this as a factor in

social dynamics, see Galtung "International Relations and International Conflicts: A Sociological Approach," *Essays* IV, 9.

9. Of course, it is quite possible to have scarcity without any need for interdependence (vast, resource-poor, sparsely populated stretches) and interdependence without any scarcity (the opposite pattern). In a sense it is good for us that in the present phase of world history the human density and the resource scarcity pull in the same direction: toward some level of globalization.

10. These are among the basic similarities between liberalism and Marxism as analyzed in Galtung, *Two Ways of Being Western: Some Similarities between Liberalism and Marxism,* Trends in Western Civilization Project (University of Oslo, 1979).

11. In the theory of federalism this is known as "subsidiary federalism": always try to have a problem solved at the lowest possible level in a hierarchy of levels. It should be pointed out that a key variable here is the type of technology chosen. Thus, in the field of energy the basic argument against nuclear power stations would not be that they pollute and deplete but that they centralize, whereas the key argument in favor of a solar-tidal-wind-wave-geothermic-biogas mix might be not so much that it neither depletes nor pollutes much but that it is compatible with a highly decentralized structure. For the environmentalist the relative weight of the arguments would be turned around, also focusing on diversity in the latter case.

12. This is the basic argument in the Mitrany type of functionalism: there will be a spill-over from one sector to the other with the successful sectors to some extent compensating, or inspiring, dragging along, the less successful sectors. Missing in the functionalist analysis are at least two rather important points: an analysis of the structure of these institutions in terms of the verticality they engender and an awareness of the asymmetry. Success is taken for granted, failure becomes a scandal, and one does not compensate for the other.

13. I hope that one day somebody will make a good content analysis of the changing attitude to the United Nations in Western press media as the Western control was slowly eroded by the "tyranny of the Third World majority"—a very strange Western expression for democracy. In a system governed by interests considerably more than by values it goes without saying that "success/failure" will be measured by interest rather than by value standards—by "What is in it for me?" rather than by "How does it stand relative to value-standard X,Y,Z?" When interests are contradictory, one country's failure is the other country's success.

14. See the article by Roy Preiswerk, "Can We Study International Relations as if People Mattered?" *International Relations in a Changing World* (Geneva: Institut Universitaire des Hautes Etudes Internationales, 1977). Of course, organizations may also turn out to be abstractions far removed from human beings, but they usually have less solid layers of establishmentarian control built around themselves than do states.

15. See the analysis in section 6.2.

16. The best analysis continues to be Theresa Hayter, *Aid as Imperialism* (London: Penguin, 1971), but there are also good recent analyses of the World Bank's effort to turn to the countryside, investing in it in order to (as I see it) integrate it better into world capitalism.

17. A good example is the joint superpower behavior in the Law of the Sea conferences: they command the military sea power, the merchant sea power and the technology for off-shore, even ocean-floor, exploration and exploitation. Yet is is interesting to observe how much less impressed the other countries are by them than they were only a decade ago, and how much they conspire to expose the two superpowers rather than each camp trying to produce cover-ups for "their" superpower.

18. I, having been working with some of them (such as FAO, ILO, UNIDO, UNESCO, WHO, UNCTAD, UNEP, UNU) am struck by how unaware they nevertheless often are of each other's activities. See Galtung "The Technology That Can Alienate," *Development Forum* (July–August 1976), p. 8.

19. This double identification is, of course, found not only in intergovernmental organizations but also in countries: district identification as opposed to party identification. Thus, one should not exaggerate the novelty of the intergovernmental assemblies. What is new is the system set up for direct election to the European assembly, but it may not necessarily make much difference in the assembly itself unless some *sui generis* party formation takes place, making it possible for people to vote according to issues at the *inter*governmental level.

20. The staff at the Canadian Peace Research Institute in Ontario, Canada, has made an impressive contribution to the problem of voting formulas for direct election to a world assembly, e.g., in the United Nations.

21. Thus, the Security Council defines an upper class of big powers, the World Bank, and related organizations of rich countries. But the General Assembly gives more of a say to the people of small than of big countries, provided they (the people) have an influence on their own governments. The picture is not so simple.

22. One of the best nuclei around which to make a transnational party today would probably be related to the transnational corporations. Employees in such organizations have obvious interests to defend (but see comments on that issue toward the end of section 7.1), as do the consumers–and the TNCs themselves. The important point is that this issue can never be fully articulated in an intergovernmental assembly for governments, which will tend to strike bland compromises between divergent interests inside their own countries, or to be the spokesmen of only one of the parties. There are other issues that may be quite well handled at the intergovernmental level, e.g., in talks between exporters of raw material and exporters of manufactured goods (and services)–as is done in UNCTAD, where this is formalized in the A, B, C, and D division of countries into groups–or in the sixth and seventh special assemblies of the UN General Assembly. But there is also the danger that the availability of this machinery may serve to define the issues badly, as intercountry rather than–also–intraclass issues, as is true for most issues under the heading of imperialism.

23. One such conference, in Geneva in May 1967, served exactly this purpose. The Pacem in Maribus conferences so well organized by the International Ocean Institute in Malta–an organization inspired by the leadership exercised by Elizabeth Mann Borgese and Arvid Pardo–is another excellent example. The Pugwash conferences are not: there is too much of a tendency to narrow the range of issues to those on superpower agendas. The range of participants is good, but not the range of issues. Thus, Pugwash still has difficulties coming to grips with development issues, and offers a nice illustration of how little automatic transfer there is from having courageous,

original stands on a certain set of issues—related to East–West conflict and arms control—to having similar stands on other issues. Part of this is due to the overrepresentation of natural scientists in the Pugwash leadership.

24. UNITAR was trying to do something like this with its Commission for the Future; the Club of Rome is trying something of the same. One such meeting is very effectively satirized in Arthur Koestler's brilliant *The Call Girls*. For anyone participating in a fair number of such exercises it will be hard not to grant him more than a grain of truth, particularly in his portrayal of how isolated these groups are from human beings in general and political life in particular.

25. In conservative societies those who are owners would have the power. In liberal societies this power would be shared with those who are employed and increasingly so in the social-democratic/socialist formulas. Under Yugoslav formulas of self-management the distinction between owner and employee is almost washed out, but the borderline between producers and consumers is as clear as ever. Under Chinese formulas of *self-reliance* this borderline also appears erased, involving all affected by the economic cycle in basic decision making one way or the other (see section 9.2).

26. Illich's book *Energy and Equity* (London: Calder and Boyars, 1974) is easily the best that has ever been written about energy and transportation from a social angle. It should make transportation engineers and the current crop of energy specialists blush in humility when they consider how unable they are to reflect any of the social insight contained in an average Illich page.

27. The more basic the need, the more important that the sources of need satisfaction can be obtained locally to avoid any kind of blackmail. This is what the centralizing nation-state has understood so well, partly in centralizing production and/or distribution, partly by stimulating local dependence on nonfundamentals (e.g., centralized newscasting).

28. Estimates differ, but according to the research done by the Transfer of Technology division of UNCTAD as much as 40 percent of patents are in the field of pharmaceuticals. See Peter O'Brien, "Developing Countries and the Patent System: An Economic Appraisal," *World Development* (September 1974).

29. This is seen very clearly when one compares the occupancy of Aeroflot flights (tickets often available at considerable reduction) with IATA airlines on the same routes. The reason why ordinary tickets are so expensive is hard to tell. It may be that the official reason ("We have to keep regular schedules, a certain density in time and space, and that costs") is partly true; but another side of the issue may be that the governments and corporations of rich countries can well afford the rates and that the price elasticity for them is negligible. They will fly anyhow with the current interaction and interdependence level. This may be considerably less true for the Soviet Union where everything is governmental anyhow and the need to travel internationally is much lower.

30. The major purpose of the Concorde is to define, once more, the *crème de la crème* when too many have managed to get into the ordinary *crème*.

31. And they will go one day: the type of criticism of them found in section 7.1—based on chapter 4—leading to the type of strategies discussed in section 7.4 is too widespread.

32. Like the Third World effort to create their own press agencies as a protection against the First World press agencies (the Second World agencies being

considerably less important—too dull, too obvious in their propaganda), this may serve as a very thinly veiled formula to gain more governmental control over communication of any kind. It is not difficult to understand that Third World governments may like to keep out *Bild-Zeitung* or the *Daily Mail,* but if this is done at the expense of also keeping out *Le Monde* and the *International Herald Tribune* the price is excessive.

33. The assumption here, then, is that the dimension targeted/distargeted may be more important than armed/disarmed. Targeted arms are mobilized. Distargeted arms may under some conditions be almost nonexistent arms.

34. Norway and Sweden in 1905 may serve as an example here.

35. In the spate of books that came out as a result of the UNEF, ONUC, UNFICYP operations. For another approach, see Galtung and Helge Hveem, "Participants in Peacekeeping Forces," *Essays* II, 10.

36. The Cyprus operation in 1964, lasting until 1974, may be an example of this. The relation between Greek and Turkish Cypriots was too asymmetric; if not necessarily inequitable in economic terms, unequal in political terms— even if for no other reason than the purely numerical.

37. This is, of course, a basic Marxist insight in the theory of the state. But it is interesting to see how governments, and ministries, in more liberal regimes may find it opportune to produce power using third-party positions in conflicts between interest and value groups as raw material. A typical delegation to an intergovernmental conference, for instance, would present the employees of the government (e.g., the foreign ministry) with many such chances if the delegates representing interest and value groups are sufficiently divided by conflicts.

38. Thus, it is in the interest of the hegemonial power to have a number of conflicts among the client states to be able to present itself as the great protector against "useless" bloodshed. Needless to say, European imperialism tried to present itself in this way, always looking for enemies of those who had the courage and capacity to stand up against the intruders, to be able to present themselves as protectors of the small.

39. Chapters 6 and 7—or "Chapter 6½" as the compromise formula used in some cases is often referred to.

40. Would the Abyssinia (as the Italians still call Ethiopia) operation have been stopped under the UN charter? The answer is clearly "no." Whatever can be said about Mussolini's operation, it is entirely dwarfed by what the United States did in Indochina; and the United Nations proved just as unable as the League of Nations to stop that operation.

41. To be a "superpower" or a "big power" means, among other things, the refusal to accept that others have power over one's own exercise of power. It means autonomy, which is incompatible, according to the law of the jungle, with submission to dictates by an army of small powers.

42. And yet this is probably precisely what is going to happen, and perhaps sooner rather than later.

43. Thus, it is interesting to note that the idea of some kind of joint U.S.-Soviet Union peacekeeping after the October 1973 Arab-Israeli war was never implemented. There may be many reasons for this, one of them certainly that the risks are too high when the conflict in West Asia is so directly coupled to the superpower conflict. It is better to use forces from countries that have no conflicts among themselves, especially if they are to be

stationed at opposite sides of a conflict border. Superpowers have other ways of interfering, less risky for themselves. But there is also in this an element of arrogance: "Your conflict does not merit our presence."

44. However, to station troops along conflict borders is only rational if the conflict is international. Thus, the MacNamara line, the "electronic fence" between what was then North Vietnam and South Vietnam, presupposed a very heavy load on the North–South component in the conflict, and correspondingly low on the South–South component. A really watertight border would reveal too clearly the extent to which the war was internal to the southern part of the country. Correspondingly, a too perfect system to prevent border transgressions in Europe has already revealed very clearly the extent to which the East–West conflict is an East–East and West–West conflict; to station such troops would make it even more clear.

45. For instance, in the conflict between Algeria and Morocco.

46. Or the Organization of Eastern European States—the European Socialist Community—to mention one where it is the Soviet Union that will be excluded. The United States and the Soviet Union should rather be regarded as permanent peacekeeping operations within their own borders.

47. This depends, of course, on the extent to which neighboring countries or the international community in general has corresponding "problems" and for that reason would feel that resolutions or action justifying "intervention in internal affairs" may one day be turned against themselves.

48. For a more detailed treatment of this, see Galtung, "Big Powers and the World Feudal Structure," *Essays* IV, 10.

49. Ulster and Chad are good examples.

50. In general this is so important to big powers as a pretext that it is in their interest to see to it that there always is a sufficient number of expatriates stationed in any conflict-loaded area within their "sphere of interest"—just as it may be in the interest of those who are natives to the area to keep the number of expatriates low and move them out quickly when a conflict is surfacing.

51. The Soviet Union has drawn one simple conclusion from this: supply the freedom fighters with modern arms. In a historical perspective this may well stand out as the most significant contribution from the system started by Lenin in 1917, much more important than the social model realized inside the country and regardless of what ulterior motives the Soviet Union might have had.

52. This, of course, is the model found in the Chinese, Cuban, Algerian, Vietnamese, and Guinea–Bissau/Mozambique/Angola revolutions, to mention only some.

53. The Cuban action in Angola in 1976 should be seen in this light, a very clear example indeed of how far the world has moved during the last twenty years. Who would, in 1956, have predicted that soldiers from that humiliated and subjugated island in the Caribbean would twenty years later side with the Soviet Union and a progressive Angola regime against the forces siding with the United States? And yet the world will have many such surprises in the years to come.

54. Historically, international law must probably be seen as a system that emerged in a context of states relatively well balanced in strength—just as the system of international trade based on the theory of comparative

advantages. When extended to highly asymmetric, vertical situations, either system reinforces the verticality, a consequence that may have been applauded although not necessarily intended.

55. Given the pattern of recruitment into positions of power, and what happens to people in positions of power, this will tend to take some time.

56. I am indebted to Yash Tandon for this important point.

57. See the article referred to in note 37.

58. Moreover, if peacebuilding has to be done locally and it is to have the quality associated with *self-reliance* (see section 9.2)—at the same time as peacekeeping comes from the outside—there may be an insoluble contradiction here. To have the soldiers with the blue helmets or berets not only keep and make peace but also build it in the sense of being the catalysts, even the executors of profound changes, is to invite an intervention that may make colonialism pale in comparison. On the other hand, merely to engage in peacekeeping may have the undesired status quo consequences pointed to. The field waits for somebody to transcend this contradiction, as Gandhi did with his *satyagraha* brigades, where a basic point was precisely that the local population will have to carry out their own "peacekeeping, -making, and -building." See the article with that title, *Essays* II, 11.

59. For an image of how closely related they are, see Galtung and Ingrid Eide, "Some Factors Affecting Local Acceptance of a UN Force: A Pilot Project Report from Gaza," *Essays* II, 9.

60. For a good account of one of these operations, see the book by Odd Bull, the UN commander of the truce supervision in the Middle East for many years.

61. An analysis of this is given in Harbottle, Rikhye, and Egge, *The Thin Blue Line* (1975).

62. This is seen clearly by the Third World countries, for which reason there is much insistence on an integrated approach. However, this type of issue integration should not be in economic fields alone, but across all fields— which is to some extent taking place in the UN General Assembly, but could be even more successful if the ECOSOC deliberations were given more prominence.

63. What is needed, however, are more world disarmament conferences, treating disarmament the same way as food, population, women, and science and technology are treated: openly. The Western resistance to this Soviet proposal shows clearly who feels they have most to lose by open articulation of such issues. The 1978 UN special session should be seen as a beginning only.

64. On the other hand, Amnesty International also has a tendency to be overly actor-oriented, treating each case of infraction of human rights as a separate case. Of course, there is one unit of analysis at a higher level of abstraction: the authoritarian regime. But regimes are parts of international structures of dominance, making for some correspondence between structures of dominance in general and structures of repression in particular. There is even a pattern of subimperialism at work here: the intermediaries in economic-political investment may also be the intermediaries in forging and using the tools of repression (the role of the Czechs in building the G2 in Cuba in the early sixties; the role of the Brazilians in building up patterns of torture in Chile).

65. Under such formulas the cities might, possibly, also be reunited or opened to all as international cities.

66. In the United States there is probably still a very low level of understanding of the significance of the Indochina wars. For some reflections on this, see Galtung "The United States in Indochina: The Paradigm for a Generation," *Essays* V, 8.

67. It is interesting to see what effect this action has had on Norway—a country that combines the killing of baby seals with a high level of international moralism in general, and is better trained as a sender than as a receiver of such actions, demonstrations, and resolutions. One reaction is underreporting of the actions, another is efforts to undermine the credibility of the activists—well-known strategies, but usually engaged in by other countries. At the same time it may be surmised that slowly and surreptitiously steps are taken to comply with the points raised but in such a way that it cannot be seen as an effect of the demonstrations. Governments do not admit that they act "under pressure."

68. The work, sponsored by international organizations, to save the monuments threatened with inundation by the building of Aswan Dam/Lake Nasser is impressive. Would that also have been done one, two, three generations ago?

69. According to the excellent biography by Hans Heiberg.

70. As seen clearly in the Law of the Sea conferences. No consideration at all seems to be given to esthetic aspects, as could be expected in a world dominated by such a profoundly materialistic culture as the Western one.

71. This is spelled out in Galtung, "Self-reliance and Global Interdependence: Some Reflections on the New International Economic Order," *Papers,* no. 55, Chair in Conflict and Peace Research, University of Oslo, 1976, and CIDA, Ottawa, 1978.

72. There are not so many left, though—the polar zones and neighboring areas and the ocean floor, in addition to extraplanetary bodies.

73. Spelled out by Elizabeth Mann Borgese and Arvid Pardo, separately and jointly, in numerous papers.

74. See Galtung "Human Needs, National Interests and World Politics: The Law of the Sea Conference," *Essays* V, 13.

75. A real test of strength would be for a world organization to try to tax the United States and the Soviet Union for littering extraplanetary space with all kinds of spacecraft—or merely for using outer space.

76. That transnational corporations would respond by raising the prices of their products is not so important. The world authority could respond by spending the revenue on what is needed for satisfaction of basic material needs, thus shifting resources from nonbasic to basic products.

77. This point has often been made, very effectively by, for instance, Dudley Seers in numerous articles. For a relevant early formulation, see his article "International Aid: The Next Step," *Journal of Modern African Studies* (1964), pp. 471–89.

78. One such norm, an important one, is the idea of having a fair global representation in any kind of committee and conference (of at least the First, Second, and Third worlds—with the Third subdivided in the three major continents) and a fair sex distribution. To a participant in conferences organized by UN bodies and by such Western organizations as the Council of Europe and the OECD, it has become very clear how spurious the sense of efficiency that the latter develop relative to the United Nations actually is. It is often the efficiency of having a discussion with one's own mirror image.

79. They are, of course, also the agencies with most capital at their disposal.

80. One example would be too rigid norms of geographical distribution. For instance, if a country consistently fails to fill the quota available to it there is no reason that the openings should not be temporarly allocated to some other country.

81. This might tie cities—human habitats—more closely to the world system, but not necessarily human beings, for they may not identify much more with what their municipality does than with the actions of their countries.

82. This is one reason why we are so much more shocked when a physician engages in crimes against humanity, e.g., in Auschwitz, than when such actions (e.g., the preparation of anti-body weapons, of napalm, etc.) are engaged in by natural scientists—of whom we even seem to expect immoral or amoral behavior.

83. For one effort in this direction, see J. Galtung, *Papers on Methodology* (Copenhagen: Ejlers, 1979), chap. 4.

84. The Pugwash movement might play an important role here if it had not been for the heavy role played by natural scientists in governmental superpower service.

85. For some reflections on this, see Galtung, "Summit Meetings and International Relations," *Essays* IV, 2.

86. On the other hand, if there is anything that is the thesis of the present book then it is that global identification should not become identification with global institutions, but simply with human beings everywhere—with concrete human beings, not with abstract globalism.

87. This topic has been dealt with more extensively in section 8.3; what is mentioned here is more a summary in order to put it in the context of a more nearly total strategy.

88. There is a difference, however: whereas the military have successfully penetrated UN peacekeeping operations, they have not been able to penetrate peace research, which so far has quite successfully resisted efforts by the superpowers and the military sectors to penetrate and pervert it. The policy of neglect on the part of the latter has been very advantageous from the point of view of peace research.

89. See note 54.

90. I refuse to think in terms of trade-offs of one against the other as is done by conservatives who make use of structural violence to prevent direct violence, or by radicals who want to apply "some" direct violence to get rid of structural violence. One characteristic, almost by definition, of peace research is to search for ways of transcending this contradiction, well knowing that the number of formulas, even on paper, in this field is very limited.

91. From the Cocoyoc Declaration, circulated as a document of the General Assembly under the symbol A/C.2/292.

92. Probably even too insignificant, and this should not be held up as an ideal. Bilateralism between exploited, peripheral units may be preferable to centralizing multilateralism, for in the multilateral interaction network there will usually be some unit in the capital that is somewhat more equal than the others. (See section 9.2 for the self-reliance rationale for this.) On the other hand, the world community already has many counterforces in operation, resisting too much centralization—probably more than most states.

93. It is interesting to see that the European Community is also very hesitant,

and probably wisely so, when it comes to taking that kind of step; the level of integration being below what one usually would associate with the term "government." On the other hand, it may be forced by world contradictions, e.g., massive Third World confrontations, to take some step of that kind. This would not apply to the world in general because of the—so far—absence of external enemies.

94. For this purpose one might learn both from some parliamentary democracies and from the dynamism brought about by cultural revolutions. And one may also have to do something very concrete: move the headquarters away from the atmosphere of the cold war, as suggested on 28 September 1960, in the General Assembly, by Soekarno, the first president of Indonesia. One idea might be to move it to one of the "trouble centers" of the world, possibly as a way of globalizing it. Berlin has been mentioned, but that would certainly not be a move away from the "cold war atmosphere." Jerusalem has been suggested (e.g., by a Norwegian priest, Martin Hegdal, in "FNs hovedkvarter til Jerusalem?" *Nationen,* 14 November 1970). Jerusalem is on neither the East-West nor the North-South axis, but being on the cross-roads of three occidental cultures—Judaism, Christianity, Islam—it may be too biased culturally.

$9 \cdot$ INDIVIDUAL ACTIVATION

9.1 A THEORY OF PROGRESSIVE ACTION

In the preceding pages there is no scarcity of proposals. Typically, these proposals focus on what should be done and why it should be done—but not on who should do it, how and when and where. What is missing is the actor-designation (whether of *actual* or *potential* actors); a clear image of the *transition path*, including the first steps; and some idea of the *concrete context*. This is not to say that proposals that fall short of these criteria are worthless, even when the receiver remains anonymous and "somebody should do something" is the whole message. A proposal of that kind is like a cry, more or less well articulated, often despairing, and should perhaps be considered incomplete rather than wrong. The declaratory part, the preamble so to speak, is there; but the proposal falls short because the operational part is missing. Without the operational part the proposal becomes a vision only; with nothing but the operational part, the proposal becomes a bureaucratic directive to designated people to do something without informing them of the goal and the rationale for their action. It is in the combination of the vision and the directive that the possibility of developing good action proposals lies.

Since our focus is on the designation of actual and potential actors let me first say a few words about *how* and *when*. Transition paths can be worked out by using the scenario technique as a heuristic device. One assumes that the goal has been arrived at, and one asks; "What happened before that, and before that again?" Paths into the future can be mapped out this way as soon as they become linked to the present, to here and now, as indicated in section 1.4. That carries directly into the third missing element in most peace proposals: *when* and *where* to start, the concrete context for action. The scenario is useful only if it becomes a program with a *specific point of departure*. A rigid program is probably worse than no program at all, but a concrete program stimulates thinking and action much more than a distant vision. What matters is to have a direction in which to start.

The basic problem is who shall do it: the actor-designation. To designate an actor is to scan the social horizon to find the material for one. Two scanning devices seem particularly significant, building on the role of consciousness and organization in the theory of revolutions developed in sections 3.4 and 4.3: (1)

393

motivation—who are the actors who might be motivated to implement a proposal? (2) *capability*—who are the actors who might be capable of implementing the proposal?

If we assume that progressive action proposals in general involve a basic change in the status quo because it is intolerable, filled with direct and structural violence, then it follows that the most capable actors usually will not be highly motivated. They may prefer remaining on top of an unpeaceful status quo to an uncertain position in a possibly more peaceful future. Similarly, the most highly motivated actors may not be among the most capable, leading to the prediction that the status quo will prevail. But if this is the case today, then it was probably also true yesterday and before that. And yet, the world is changing all the time. Some changes do not depend on motivation and capability, as they are not the outcomes of volition. Also, there are actors who are both motivated and capable of positive change, often because they align themselves with the nonplanned changes and because new consciousness formation and mobilization take place. There is no reason to assume that the world has come to rest in a state of peacelessness.

The sources of *motivation* can conveniently be divided into the classical push and pull forces, depending on whether the emphasis is on why one should get away from here or on what one should try to build for the future. In both cases I am thinking of conscious forces.

The *push forces* from the present may be seen in terms of absolute or relative deprivation, leading to a state of despair from which forces for change are spontaneously generated. For a sense of absolute deprivation to develop it is not enough that basic needs—material and/or nonmaterial—are left unsatisfied; they also have to be seen as satisfiable, for example, by changing social structures. Relative deprivation may come about by comparing one's one low position in the structure with somebody else's high up or may arise in an actor high on literacy, knowledge, and education but low on power and wealth (whether the actor is a country or a person).[1] It may be rooted in time, as when improvement of conditions has led to rising expectations that are suddenly frustrated. It may be located in space, for instance, in a demonstration effect between countries.

Social disequilibria, frustrated expectations, and demonstration effects become like blockbusters working on the human mind, at a private level as well as at a collective level. They may propel the individual into self-centered action to improve his own lot; and if he is sufficiently self-seeking the motivation will peter out with the solution of his own personal problem. But it may also lead to more genuine political consciousness and group action, not only as a coordination of individual desires, but also because needs of groups and classes of individuals and countries are reflected. Political man and woman are capable of solidarity, of collective identification beyond private goals.

Then there are the *pull forces,* the images of the future, the visions of what could be done. Who are the visionaries? Of course, they are largely the people and countries motivated to get away from the present. The visionaries are often the people who have insight without power, and there is usually antagonism between them and the people with power but devoid of insight.

Let us then turn to *capability*. That capability or power is not necessarily translated into basic action is seen clearly in the field of arms races. Countless conferences are being held involving precisely the top actors in the military–political–industrial complex, yet the result is negligible—certainly not for lack of power, but for lack of motivation. On the other hand, there are such actors as those scientists who keep the systems going by developing new weapons systems so that the arms race may jump from one phase to the next, in what looks like a stable interplay between qualitative changes in the machinery of destruction.

But what looks stable is in reality a highly unstable equilibrium, supported only as long as scientists cooperate with the system. The moment they withdraw from weapons research and development, the system will change dramatically. *Capability in this case lies in the ability to upset an unstable equilibrium,* turning the apparently static nature of the system into a dynamic force. What holds for scientists also holds for underprivileged and exploited people and countries: solidary mass action is needed to upset the system. *There is political space.*

Many people have thought throughout history that the major key to upsetting an intolerable but unstable equilibrium is to eradicate one particular person, for instance through tyrannicide. The assumption has been that the vicious circle can be eliminated by eliminating one or a few persons. This analysis leaves out the other side of the equation: it is not only that the evil person creates the evil system; it is also that the wrong structure calls for the evil person, and he who understands this fully can quickly fill the vacuum created by the bullet or the poison pellet. Change has to have structure as its target, not merely persons. And the structure is upheld by everybody in it. There is always some complicity on the part of the victims, some element of cooperation with the tyrannic person or country, and that cooperation *can* be withdrawn.[2]

A second key to capability lies in long-term trends. Thus, today in some countries the right of the government to enroll its citizens into armies and the duty of these citizens to fight and die in wars are increasingly being questioned, not only in words (as always), but in deeds of protest and withdrawal.[3] This is particularly clear in the United States and in the Bundesrepublik. If this is a trend the forces upholding it and resisting it should be analyzed. If one believes the results to be productive, the analysis would focus on how the support can be strengthened and the resistance weakened. But, needless to say, more important trends in the world today are directed against structural violence in the form of peoples' wars and national wars of liberation, in the whole trend of events that so far have culminated with the OPEC 1973 action and the fall of Saigon on 30 April 1975.[4]

In other words actor-designation would build on a social analysis not only to find who would be motivated but also to find who would be capable of upsetting malignant, but unstable equilibria and/or of supporting benign trends. In both cases, the forces concerned have to be so strong that counterstrategies, even repressive terror, cannot easily wipe them out. If those who are motivated are incapable and those who are capable are unmotivated, a peace proposal will have to proceed one step further: how can motivation be increased at the strategic points in society? How can those who are motivated develop latent capabilities? For instance, how can scientists cooperating with "defense establishments" be motivated to see their activity in another light, and how can they turn that motivation into action? How can impoverished peasants organize and throw off the yoke on their shoulders?

Scanning the society with this program in mind will usually bring out some suggestions as to potential actors. Who they are, and how many, depends on one's social theory. At this point an important point should be made about social theories: actors will differ in degree of motivation and capability, *but a social theory that designates only a limited category of the inhabitants of society as the carriers of the new (and better) times to come is a dangerous theory, regardless of how well it may have corresponded with facts in the past.* Whether favoring industrial workers (Marx, Lenin), peasants (Mao), or students (Marcuse), any designation that focuses on one group of people is almost bound to introduce a new vertical distinction in society between those designated to be the *force motrice* of history and those not. The former are predestined to become an elite, the others become at best spectators, at worst suspect.[5] One cannot designate a chosen group (or people) without implicitly rejecting others. *Moreover, everything this new elite does is by definition progressive.* The net result of such theories is only that a new *Herrschaft* is constituted, often as capable of direct and structural violence as any *Herrschaft* it was set up to overthrow. In other words, a theory of that kind, for example gambling on professionals (liberal version) or the proletariat (Marxist version), is an instrument of marginalization, introducing a distinction between first-class and second-class people. Consequently, it cannot be a peace theory.

The answer to this dilemma is not to abandon actor-designation and return to the peace proposals without any address, and, for that reason, also without a market. Nor is the answer to assume that *everybody* should feel called upon and capable of doing everything; that would be an expression of historical, and structural, blindness. Motivation and capability are differentially distributed; and even if propaganda and other ways of raising consciousness (e.g., confrontation) can affect the former, only concrete social action, organization and mobilization, can affect the latter.

Hence, the answer lies rather *in having tasks for everybody,* in giving unifying participation to everybody, perhaps not of equal immediate significance, but of direct relevance. Any theory that systematically leaves out groups, *a priori,* is from this point of view bad theory. Good theory should not designate enemies, nor should it relegate some into apathy and elevate others into elite positions by virtue of their "role in history." As far as humanly possible peace proposals should be directed against the peacelessness in social structures, not against fellow human beings. Strategies for change should be inclusive, not exclusive—if there are enemies they should designate themselves through their action, not be outlawed by some theory. For this reason dogmatic, linear or nonlinear, theories of history (written History) may become very dangerous tools of oppression.

Liberal theory has a tendency to overdesignate elites as actors; Marxist theory has a tendency to overdesignate the proletariat (or the elite with a proletariat origin). As usual the stand taken here will be a combination of the views embedded in the actor-oriented and structure-oriented perspectives respectively. New social forms, with more freedom and equity and less violence do not come into being by themselves; they are not the result of automatic processes. Human choice and will enter, but I have tried to point out that abstract values and goals are not enough: values and goals have to be internalized in actors who are strategically located. The liberal emphasis on *values* is necessary but not sufficient because it does not locate actual and potential actors in the social structure. Correspondingly, the Marxist emphasis on *contradictions* is necessary because each social contradiction can be translated into a motivation for change (through perception of absolute or relative deprivation), but it is not sufficient. To stimulate all kinds of contradictions toward "maturity" through consciousness formation and mobilization may lead to much dynamism, but not necessarily in the same direction and not necessarily in the right direction. Some overall direction is needed, in the sense of both coordination and goal setting. Sometimes this comes about through the dictatorship exercised by a group, a class, or a party; sometimes it is the outcome of a natural or social catastrophe, for example, a world war or imperialist plunder crystallizing society; sometimes both reasons operate.

To summarize: the point of departure is the social structure—locally, domestically, globally. Within the social structure contradictions arise that I have referred to many times as verticalities—basically in the form of exploitation supported by penetration, fragmentation, and marginalization.[6] Each structure divides people into exploiters and exploited. But as human beings participate in several structures one man may be an exploited worker in one structure and an exploiting middle-aged husband in another. In the global and domestic structures not only people but *peoples* may be exploited.

The set of exploited peoples everywhere (the Lapps in northern Norway, the Catholics in Ulster, the American Indians, women, peoples in Latin America, Africa, and Asia) *is the Third World.*[7] Thus, the Third World is a structural concept, not a geographical one. It is not what was left after the Old World had conquered the New World in North America, nor what is left when one subtracts developed capitalist and socialist countries, nor what is left when one subtracts superpowers and the other industrialized countries (the Chinese concept). The Third World has its pockets in the Old World and in the New; the latter have their pockets in Latin America, Africa, and Asia.

In general, structural reasoning leads to more complex maps of social reality than classroom geographical maps are able to reflect. Moreover, contradictions are multiple; there is no single overriding contradiction (e.g , capitalism) that contains the key to the elimination of all the others. As no single contradiction contains the essence of all the others, there is no single exploited class that constitutes the single answer to the question of actor-designation either (e.g., the industrial proletariat).[8] With a multiple theory of contradictions there is also a multiple theory of actors who can be carriers of new values: the exploited everywhere; the Third World in the sense given, particularly the rural masses; women; the very young and the very old; all those who are made into clients under the tutelage of bureaucrats and professionals—perhaps intellectuals in general—not to mention pupils and students; and certainly also industrial workers.[9]

Whether because of Marx himself or dogmatic Marxists, great damage has been done by those who insist on one singular, overriding contradiction and one singular, overriding actor for progressive social change. My view here is more like what I perceive to be the Chinese view: contradictions are multiple, even unlimited in number, and will always be with us. But in each concrete case—with specific answers to the questions of *where* and *when*—there is usually one contradiction that is more important than the others and should be attacked *first*. However, and significantly, in deciding which contradiction is most important I would look at *how much* it impedes the satisfaction of *how basic* needs for *how many*; not at some theory about possible linkages between one contradiction and others. It is on that basis I arrive at the conclusion that capitalist imperialism is contradiction number one[10] in the world today and consequently that its destruction and elimination is a positive act needed to build something different—to let one hundred, one thousand, ten thousand flowers of alternative systems emerge and blossom—not on the basis of a theory of history.

9.2 SELF-RELIANCE: THE OVERRIDING STRATEGY

In section 9.3 the ideas from 9.1 will be followed up, giving some indication of transition paths and possible actors for many of the numerous proposals given in the preceding chapters. Many of these will be tactical rather than strategic considerations. There is a need for one overriding strategic concept, and the one that comes closest is, in my view, the idea of *self-reliance*. One tremendous advantage with the term "self-reliance" is its open-endedness. The term has a certain nucleus of content, but it is up to all of us to give it more precise connotations (certainly the only self-reliant way of going about defining the term "self-reliance"). The following is one suggestion, one effort to fill it with content, even to build some kind of ideology around it.

Roland Berger has this to say about the Chinese origin of the idea:[11]

In his August 1945 speech Mao Tse-tung used the phrase "tzu li keng sheng" which literally translated is "regeneration through our own efforts." This more accurately conveys the true meaning of the policy than the term "self-reliance." "Regeneration through our own efforts" also makes it clear that this is a policy radically different from "self-sufficiency" or "autarchy." It is in fact the mass line applied on the economic front and stems directly from Mao Tse-tung's consistent emphasis that "the people, and the people alone, are the motive force in the making of world history" and that "the masses have boundless creative power."

Although nothing in what follows is contrary to what has just been said it would be less than self-reliant to give to the Chinese any kind of monopoly of this precious idea. After all the idea of local self-reliance, in the sense of the small community relying on its own forces, is as old as humanity itself: This was the normal form of human existence. Then something happened: the world-encompassing center–periphery formation built as a program into Western civilization[12] (with the West in the center, of course), put into (1) *cultural practice through the spread of Christianity and later on Western science and other forms of Western thought,* into (2) *socioeconomic practice through capitalism,* and into (3) *military–political practice through colonialism*—all wrapped together in the imperialism of the nineteenth century and the first half of the twentieth century and the neoimperialism of our part of the twentieth century.[13] The neoimperialist experience informs us that center–periphery formation is a much deeper phenomenon than political–military colonialism. *One* basic theoretical assumption is that its roots lie in the economic infrastructure, for example, in the centralizing networks and economic cycles spun by the transnational corporations. *Another* assumption, to which I myself subscribe, working backward with the given list (and working backward in history), is that the roots are cultural–civilizational, and of a double nature. On one hand, *one* civilization in the world, the Western one, not only considers itself the center of the world (as is natural) but also universally valid, the center from which messages of all forms radiate to a periphery eager to receive the Western truth in material and nonmaterial forms. On the other hand, because of a number of geographical and historical circumstances the rest of the world has to a large extent let itself be impressed by the West and has to some extent accepted a position in the Periphery in exchange for some of the Center products, material and nonmaterial, that the Center has considered not only its right, but its duty to distribute all over the world. In other words, I postulate an element of Periphery complicity in the form of a submissiveness it is up to the Periphery to withdraw. In this factor a basic source of change is located.

This analysis serves to place self-reliance in a historical context. Self-reliance is not merely an abstract recipe, a way of organizing the economy with heavy emphasis on the use of local factors, but a highly concrete fight against any kind of center–periphery formation with the ultimate goal of arriving at a world where "each part is a center."[14] As the essence of center–periphery formation is vertical division of labor, with exchanges across a gap in level of processing where trade is concerned, a gap in level of knowledge where science is concerned, a gap in level of initiative where politics is concerned, and so on—the difference between the sender and the receiver, the leader and the led—the basic idea of self-reliance is to get out of this type of relationship. Three supporting mechanisms (of exploitation) have to be attacked—penetration, fragmentation, and marginalization—which leads one straight into the practice of self-reliance as a way of fighting center–periphery formation.

Penetration, or dependency (the Latin American *dependencia*), is essentially a power relation: it means that what happens in the periphery is a consequence of causes located in the center. Thus, it gives broader scope to "power" than is usually given in actor-oriented analysis where the "cause" referred to has to be somebody's *intent* to exercise power; it also takes in the type of power that is built into a structure. Because power of any type can be seen as being one or more of three kinds:[15] normative–ideological, remunerative, and *punitive* (persuasion, carrot, and stick power, to put it simply), the fight against penetration also has to have three ingredients. To withstand normative–ideological power emanating from some kind of center, *self-confidence* and self-respect (the Latin American *dignidad*) are needed—a faith in one's own values and culture and civilization, in both the traditional way *and* in the ability to create new culture. To withstand remunerative power absolute self-sufficiency or autarchy is not needed. On closer analysis it is clearly seen that the point is *to be able to produce for basic needs, particularly food, so that in a crisis food cannot be used as a weapon.* Another aspect would combine the fights against cultural, ideological, and remunerative penetration in the struggle for independent taste formation, being less susceptible to "tastes" generated from the center and satisfiable with center goods only. Finally, to withstand coercive power a certain *fearlessness* is needed, both as an attitude and as a structure of defense, as an attitude and practice of invulnerability.

Thus, with the focus on such expressions as "self-confidence," "*ability* to be self-sufficient," and "fearlessness" and "invulnerability," it is clear that self-reliance as a doctrine is located more in the field of psychopolitics than in the field of economics. It would be a gross misunderstanding to reduce it to a formula for economic relations alone, although that would be in line with the economism of our times and with the assumption that the root of center–periphery relations is in the economic infrastructure alone. More particularly, self-reliance is not a new way of "bridging the gap," of "catching up" in the sense of equalizing GNP per capita or some similar measure. There are at least two good reasons that such a goal is not compatible with the idea of self-reliance: It means taking over the *goal structure* of other societies, which then become models to imitate; and it probably also means taking over the *means* used by the rich industrialized Western countries, including center–periphery formation within and between countries. The Third World does not become self-reliant by imitating the First and Second worlds, nor by exploiting some kind of Fourth World; the Fourth World, by exploiting the Fifth World (whatever that might be), and so on.[16] Self-reliance cannot be attained at the expense of the self-reliance of others; it implies the autonomy to set one's own goals and realize them as far as possible through one's own efforts, using one's own factors.

In general terms the way to fight penetration is not through counterpenetration, trying to do to the Center what the Center has always done to the Periphery (persuasion, threats, and promises), but through becoming autonomous. There is much evidence to indicate that this is best done in a process of struggle; that the struggle itself generates patterns of attitude and behavior and new structures that not only serve to break down ties of penetration but also to build true self-reliance.[17] Much of the success of the Chinese revolution was no doubt due to their ability and opportunity to combine liberation with positive self-reliance during the long years of struggle. Whether this type of experience is a necessary condition for true self-reliance later is another question, however. The Chinese, Vietnamese, and partly the Cuban experiences seem to indicate that it may be closer to a sufficient condition.

The dual character of self-reliance—breaking up old relations in order to build new ones—comes out equally clearly in the efforts to counteract fragmentation and marginalization. The point is to break up the Center monopoly, or near-monopoly, on *interaction* by initiating new patterns of cooperation and to break up the Center near-monopoly on *organizations* by creating new organizations. These are both active, outward-oriented aspects of self-reliance, showing clearly how different it is from self-sufficiency as a concept. The point is not to avoid interaction but to interact according to the criterion of self-reliance, which means in such a way that no new center–periphery relationship emerges. In practice this means a preference for horizontal interaction—particularly trade—with others more or less at the same level and a preference for organizations with others at the same level—"level" meaning something like "degree of peripherization" rather than the highly misleading GNP per capita. The dual nature consists in using the same horizontal organizations of people, districts, countries, even regions in the same position relative to dominance from the center as solidarity organizations in the struggle against the present pattern *and* as the ties out of which a more equitable future world can be built.[18]

So much for the general *concept* of self-reliance as a pattern of regeneration through one's own efforts, of fighting dominance by starting to rely on oneself, meaning individual self and the collective Self of others in the same position. But concretely what is the *practice* of self-reliance? Two principles seem to be at work here in addition to everything said before: the *principle of participation* and the *principle of concentric circles.* These principles are crucial as guidelines, but like all such principles become ridiculous when they generate into dogmas.

Self-reliance is a dynamic movement *from* the periphery, at all levels—individual, local, national, regional. It is not something done *for* the periphery; basically, it is something done *by* the periphery. Thus, control over the economic machinery of a country by national, and even by local, state, or private capitalists in order to produce for the satisfaction of basic needs is not self-reliance. It may be to "serve the people," but it is not to "trust the people"—to use the Chinese jargon. Self-reliance ultimately means that the society is organized in such a way that the masses arrive at self-fulfillment through self-reliance—in participation with others in the same situation. Obviously this points directly to a decentralized society, e.g., in the form of the 70,000 (or so) Chinese People's Communes with their subdivisions (brigades and teams), and sufficient autonomy locally to permit participation down at the grassroot level.[19]

Hence self-reliance should ideally be seen as something originating in the antipode to the metropoles in the Center: the vast rural lands in which the larger part of the world population still lives. Concretely it takes the form of using local factors—local creativity, raw materials, land, and capital. Often the center has drained away so much of the conventional raw materials and the local capital that the task is to find forms that stimulate local creativity. This should not be confused with labor: intensive forms of production which may constitute a solution where there is scarcity of capital and excess of labor. Such factor substitution is entirely compatible with centralized management and manipulation, professionalism, and bureaucratization. Rather, the point would be to opt for those forms of production that permit local grassroots initiative and innovation yielding results compatible with local conditions, tastes, and culture. The point would be that the loss in efficiency caused by sometimes reinventing something already invented elsewhere is more than offset by the gain in self-confidence in accepting the challenge of being the innovator. To be the able recipient of a technology developed elsewhere casts the person/community/country/region in the role of the good pupil, a role that is very difficult to unlearn and the very opposite of being self-confident.[20]

The basic economic principle, then, would be to use local factors and produce for local consumption. Before producing anything, however, the basic question during times of crisis should always be asked: "Do we need this product?" The argument that it can be used for *exchange* even if we do not need it for any use presupposes that there are other communities that are not based on self-reliance, as capitalism assumes that there will always be a periphery somewhere that can serve as a "market." Moreover, only with the masses in command is there a sufficient guarantee that first priority will be given to production for the satisfaction of the basic needs of those most in need, emphasizing use-value over exchange-value.[21]

If the answer is "Yes, we need this product," the task would be to try to produce it from local factors rather than to get it in exchange for some factor held to be available in excess quantities (labor, raw materials) or in exchange for some locally produced product. In so thinking, and acting, there is no doubt that self-reliance is profoundly anticapitalist, for capitalism is based on mobility of factors and products in world-encompassing cycles. Capitalism generates trade, which in turn is good for the traders.[22] If it had also been good for development all over the world that would have shown up already, for there has been an enormous increase in world trade during the last centuries. Hence the theory is that self-reliance will serve the purpose of development better, for reasons to be given.

But what happens if the product needed cannot be produced locally, from local factors, in a federation of villages with no industrial experience or base in the conventional sense? One does what people do in times of crisis; one finds some new ways of using raw materials to get the product nevertheless (the Cuban use of sugar cane as general raw material for a vast variety of products), or one changes the product so that it still serves the purpose but makes better use of local factors (the Chinese use of hydroelectric energy for tractors in some regions).

However, there are obvious limits to local efforts, given the asymmetries in the world economic geography, which are numerous indeed—the most important one probably being the asymmetry of water distribution. Canals can be dug by people rather than by machines, but pumps are among the best devices made by man, and one should not necessarily wait until the industrial base for making pumps has been developed. The problem is *where* to go to get the pumps when they are indispensable and cannot be produced locally. This is where the principle of concentric circles enters: start the search for a partner in this type of cooperation with another community at the same level in the same district; if that does not work, have the district cooperate with another district in the same province; if that does not work, have the province search for another province in the same country; if that does not work, cooperate with another country in the same subregion (meaning Grupo Andino, ASEAN, West or East African communities, etc.); if that does not work, try the larger region (meaning the ECLA, the ECA, ECWA, ESCAP regions); if that does not work, try for Third World cooperation; and ultimately, if that does not work either, try some type of limited cooperation with the "developed" countries.

In a simplified version this leads to three levels of self-reliance: local self-reliance, national self-reliance, and collective (subregional, regional, Third World) self-reliance. The relations among these three levels pose important problems to be studied. Thus, far from being antithetical to trade and exchange and cooperation a consistent policy of self-reliance may even increase the exchange level in the world because it will engender much more cooperation between neighbors in geographical and social space. The point is not to cut out trade but to *redirect* it and *recompose* it by giving preference to cooperation with those in the same position, preferring the neighbor to the more distant possibility, cooperation to exchange, and intrasector to intersector trade. Working outward from oneself and oneSelf, in a set of oceanic circles as Gandhi might have said,[23] is just the opposite of the prevalent pattern today that links the periphery of the Periphery to the center of the Center through a series of costly middlemen with obvious vested interests and power to fight for the status quo, including the intellectual power to rationalize the status quo through concepts like comparative advantages.[24]

At this point, let me summarize in a negative way by listing what self-reliance (SR) is not:

1. *SR is not an abstract, general formula.* Self-reliance is a part of a historical process, at the same time the fight against a certain global and domestic structure and a way of building a new one.

2. *SR cannot be led from above.* Self-reliance may probably be *initiated* from above, but it is meaningless without mass participation. Through collective self-reliance necessary conditions may be created at the national level and through national self-reliance necessary conditions may be created at the local level, but it is only at the local level that self-reliance, properly speaking, can unfold itself as mass action.

3. *Self-reliance is not the same as national/local processing of raw materials.* This is usually a necessary condition, for one basic idea is to contract economic cycles and to use local factors. But national processing is entirely compatible with national capitalism and penetration of the national periphery from the national centers, just as local processing is compatible with local capitalism and all that implies in terms of division of labor between owners/labor-buyers/decision makers and workers of all kinds, both in terms of deciding what to produce, how to produce it, and what to do with the surplus created. Moreover, capitalism as it is known today is expansionist by nature and will tend to overflow the borderlines of any self-reliant unit, turning other units into sources of factors and markets for capital and products, all of which would be incompatible with the self-reliance of those units.

4. *Self-reliance is not the same as producing for the satisfaction of the basic needs of those most in need.* Those are excellent priorities, but they are also compatible with managerialism and clientelization. SR implies another subject–object relation, that the masses are more the masters of their own need satisfaction, not developing the "psychology of depending on the government for relief."[25]

5. *Self-reliance is not the same as self-sufficiency or autarchy.* SR implies a redirection and recomposition of trade and cooperation, not the building of tight walls around all units—although it may be argued that self-sufficiency in food is worth striving for.

From this indication of the practice of self-reliance let me briefly indicate what seems to be the theoretical rationale for self-reliance in the present situation of gross asymmetries in the world, between the Center with its subcenters and the vast peripheries. More precisely, there are at least thirteen hypotheses linked to this kind of structure that seem to have sufficient *a priori* credibility to be worth gambling on:

[1] *Through SR, priorities will change toward production for basic needs for those most in need.* With the masses in control of the productive machinery, especially in the countryside, such ideas as using land for cash crops in order to "earn foreign currency" (for the elites to buy consumer goods, means of

destruction, and some means of production) would less easily emerge, unless the control over the economic cycle were sufficient to guarantee that basic needs would not remain unsatisfied.[26]

[2] *Through SR, mass participation is ensured.* A necessary condition for mass participation is a high level of control over the local economy, which is one of the many ingredients in SR. If the economy is steered by remote control, often of impersonal forces, participation will remain formal; it will, for example, only take the form of participation in municipal elections, electing committees with as little control over the economy as the local stationmaster over a long-distance express train (as the train directs his use of the control signals). Thus mass participation becomes the alpha and the omega of self-reliance, both as necessary and as sufficient conditions.

[3] *Through SR, local factors are utilized much better.* This aspect of SR picks up the accusation against capitalism that, in addition to being exploitative, capitalism is also irrational in terms of its own criteria; it makes inefficient use of local factors. Trade is the easy solution once the infrastructure exists as a substitute for search and re-search, for new ways of growing food, for new types of foodstuffs, and so on. Nobody who has been through a crisis such as a war economy is in any doubt as to what this means: a mobilization of resources, some of them known before but unused or underused and others even unknown. The argument against this approach is often heard: "We do not want to live in a war economy." It is true that psychologically this kind of economy has been associated with crisis in the rich part of the world, but for the poor in the poor part of the world the "normal" capitalist economy has been a state of permanent crisis. The alternative, self-reliance under one name or the other is at least capable of satisfying basic needs. But it is quite clear that the psychology of the "developed" countries, and of the overdeveloped pockets in the "developing" countries, would have to undergo some changes for SR to be acceptable. These changes will probably come about in two ways, *negatively* as the result of crisis produced with the coming redirection and recomposition of world trade (which will come even as a consequence of the much more moderate New International Economic Order) and *positively* as a desire for an alternative way of life where self-fulfillment is seen as something coming out of self-reliance rather than from mass consumption in an affluent, but clientelized, society.[27]

[4] *Through SR, creativity is stimulated.* I have mentioned that the transfer of technology, however good the terms, casts the recipient in the role of the learner—learning how to produce, even learning how to consume. Possibly this is the most devastating consequence of the present world order and the consequence most difficult to remedy. The way to correct it is definitely not through schooling alone, as that would, with the present pattern, only increase the dependency on Western centers rather than instill faith and pride in one's own culture and confidence in one's own ability to innovate. The road to innovation probably goes through innovation and benefits from partly closing oneself off from some of the innovations and "advice" coming from global and domestic centers.[28]

[5] *Through SR, there will be more compatibility with local conditions.* That factors will be better utilized has already been mentioned; that ecological concerns stand a better chance will be indicated. The conditions I have in mind here are not economic/ecological but structural/cultural. Self-reliance does not build walls in the sense that people are no longer given access to knowledge about production and consumption patterns outside the community/nation/ region, but it should foster, indeed be based on, more self-confidence. One important aspect would be to reverse the relation between technologies of production and consumption on the one hand and the local structure and culture on the other, no longer assuming (as Western social science has tended to do) that the latter have to yield to the former, and institutions search and re-search for technologies that are compatible with the structures and culture one wants to have. Thus, if people want to be together and talk with each other when they are working then individualizing and noisy means of production should not be chosen; there would be a search for other technologies. Under the condition of SR the local population will tend to trust their own intuitions more and respect foreign technology less.

[6] *Through SR, there will be much more diversity of development.* This is almost a tautology: when development comes out of local conditions, according to the principle of concentric circles, local factors *and* local culture, values, and traditions will force much more diversity into our world. Self-reliance is incompatible with imitation of model countries and also counteracts the silent subversion of local culture by the culture and structure that always accompany the import of foreign technology and material things in general. One of the most important proofs of this hypothesis was given by China. Had China relied on technical assistance from either or both of the standard model countries in trade and in transfer of technology as the basic factor in her development, the world would have been given one more big copy. Instead, world diversity increased tremendously, to the inspiration of all in search of a richer basis for inspiration. For SR does not rule out the exchange of ideas; it is rather a question of redirection and recomposition of the idea flow, learning more from cooperation with equals than from imitation of (self-appointed) models.

[7] *Through SR, there will be less alienation.* This also borders on the tautologous: with self-reliance economic cycles will contract because of the principles of local production (as far as possible) and of concentric circles. However, it should be pointed out that local economic cycles can also be highly alienating if there is no mass participation and no focus on production for one's own needs, particularly for the basic needs. The point is rather that a negative factor is eliminated: the vertical, world-encompassing cycle, practically speaking considerable power. Thus, SR is incompatible with the transnational corporations as we know them today but not incompatible with some type of regional, horizontal organization for economic cooperation, as long as it does not impede the type of mass participation whereby people in general produce and consume in such a way that nonmaterial needs are also satisfied (for creativity, togetherness, sense of competence).[29]

[8] *Through SR, ecological balance will be more easily attained.* When ecological cycles contract, the consequences of production and consumption in terms of depletion and pollution will be not only more visible but also more direct. The farmer who by and large produces what he consumes and consumes what he produces has the gut knowledge that pollution and depletion will be detrimental to him and his offspring, and this very knowledge initiates the type of negative feedback that may prevent ecological problems from surfacing at all. Depletion cannot be relegated to some far-off corner of the world, because in that corner they are also practicing self-reliance and do not let raw materials out except to neighbors at the same level. Pollutants cannot be dumped on somebody else's territory, including "empty" nature, if SR includes, as it should, a spirit of compassion and partnership with nature (which does not follow from the economic principles alone).

[9] *Through SR, important externalities are internalized or given to neighbors at the same level.* This is, of course, one of the most important arguments in favor of SR: by relying on one's own forces a genuine development of oneself, individually and collectively, takes place. Much less is lost by reinventing something already invented elsewhere than by casting oneself in the role of a learner and imitator. In more conventional terms: the research and development facilities may be clumsy, but they are one's own; it is from one's own mistakes, not from those made by others, that there is the most to learn. Through the mechanism of exchange with others at the same level (say, primitive tractors for primitive transistors) externalities are given to others at the same level instead of being added to the high level of the Center countries. The principles of redirection and recomposition would under inspired leadership distribute the externalities more evenly inside today's vast global Periphery.

[10] *Through SR, solidarity with others at the same level gets a solid basis.* In the simplified version of the principle of concentric circles, the distinction made between local, national, and collective (Third World) self-reliance, the focus is already on Periphery solidarity. For the time being this is best articulated at the intergovernmental level; and through increased trade and particularly through increased cooperation in innovative behavior of a type that respects local conditions, a horizontal infrastructure will emerge as a basis for true autonomy. Through mutual aid the Periphery of today will be weaned off its dependency on the Center of today through partial withdrawal from the Center and increased reliance on itself, in which case the terms "Center" and "Periphery" as applied to the global system will no longer be valid. But they may still be highly valid as applied to the domestic system of the countries in today's Center and Periphery. The principles of self-reliance are as valid for cooperation between districts/states/provinces/departments inside countries as for cooperation between countries. To wean districts off their dependence on capitals is a process that involves the same patterns of thought and action as the corresponding global action. I agree, however, with those who argue that the basic contradiction in the world of today resides in the structure of global capitalism and that after that contradiction has been overcome a necessary condition for

attacking the domestic structures, which often take the form of internal coloniz-ation, will obtain.

[11] *Through SR, ability to withstand manipulation due to trade depen-dency increases.* Dependency on import (e.g., of foodstuffs or oil) and on export (e.g., of manufactures and capital) constitute important subclasses of the entire dependency syndrome. Decisions made in one country (to double prices, to stop export, to deny import) have profound effects on other countries in ways that are well known today. When the effect is submission to the will of another country, one can talk about manipulation. The obvious countermeasure is, as pointed out, to inoculate oneself against this type of power by developing a capacity for self-*sufficiency* (not only self-reliance) *in times of crisis* (i.e., when the weapons of export and/or import denial are used), particularly in the field of *basic commodities.* It may well be that this will lead, in some cases, to a double economy—a regular one with import of foodstuffs and oil and other commodi-ties and a reserve economy for which new patterns of growing food and new forms of energy production, conservation, and conversion are developed. Better still would be a combination in times of noncrisis of both economies, a "walking-on-two-legs" policy, because of the obvious benefits to be derived from this type of diversity. Moreover, it will blur a distinction between the patterns of production and consumption in ordinary and extraordinary periods, thus con-tributing to changes in lifestyles and patterns of development. Innovations along such lines as kitchen gardens everywhere (including on the roofs of high-rise city buildings), three-dimensional agriculture, acquaculture, biogas energy generators, and the use of human manure combined with waste products from agricultural production and consumption should not be seen as crisis devices to be dispensed with when the crisis is over but as good in themselves for the many reasons already mentioned. And one of the reasons, as mentioned, is to increase the power of today's Periphery—collective, national, local—by making it less suscep-tible to import–export manipulations, more able to withstand pressure.

[12] *Through SR, the military defense capability of the country increases.* A decentralized country with many units capable of sustaining themselves in times of crisis, having not only their own food and other essential commodities but also their own leadership, guidance, and will to resist, is a much less vulnerable country. Vulnerability, one of the key (and therefore least analyzed) parameters of any military balance, makes some countries virtually indefensible today, Japan being an extreme example because of its very high import–export dependency and heavy concentration of all kinds of institutions for the produc-tion of goods and decisions along the Tokaido line. In a country where the economy is organized according to the principles of local self-reliance, there is little or no domino effect to be obtained by knocking out a center such as the capital (often the economic–political–military–cultural–structural–communica-tive capital all in one). A SR country would have to be conquered part by part, but these parts will have much higher capacity to organize paramilitary, guerril-la-type resistance as well as nonmilitary forms of defense even after an occupa-

tion has taken place. Knowledge of this may deter effectively a would-be attacker, as it may have done in both the U.S.-Cuba and the Soviet Union-China cases. A country knowing its own invulnerability to be high may also be less tempted to enter into preemptive military adventures, threatening postures, military encirclement through alliance formation and bases, and "forward defense lines" (in order to have the fighting take place far away from one's own vulnerable homeland) and, consequently, may become a much less aggressive country. In other words, just as there is a basic compatibility between capitalistic growth and modern hierarchical, technocratic military organization there is also a basic compatibility between self-reliance as the basic mode of production and paramilitary-guerrilla-*satyagraha* forms of defense whereby the civilian population is mobilized and becomes less vulnerable and less clientelized through dependence on vertical military organizations that in turn depend on Center countries for supplies of military hardware and software through hierarchical "alliance" systems.

[13] *Through SR as a basic approach, today's Center and Periphery are brought onto a more equal footing.* The word-pair "developed/developing" is a part of the Western syndrome whereby West defines itself as completed and the rest of the world as a periphery waiting to become like West. The word-pair "underdeveloped/overdeveloped" does away with this asymmetry, defining either as *maldeveloped,* one because there are too few means available for the satisfaction of human needs, the other because there are too many.[30] Needless to say, there are underdeveloped pockets in the overdeveloped countries and overdeveloped pockets in the underdeveloped countries.

Collective self-reliance in today's Center is more than a mechanism of defense against collective self-reliance in today's Periphery: "If you deny us raw materials, we shall use synthetics; if you quadruple the prices of your oil, we shall develop nuclear energy and other alternatives (in addition to making use of Norwegian oil resources)," and so on. This highly foreseeable consequence is by and large to the good because it will, not unlike an economic boycott, force the Periphery into even more self-reliance, thereby gradually making the terms "Center" and "Periphery" obsolete. The same, incidentally, applies to the present pattern of Center countries to withdraw or withhold money and personnel to intergovernmental organizations, including falling back on their own organizations (EC, OECD, *ad hoc* meetings, etc.): it will pave the way for a Third World secretariat, even a Third World United Nations in addition to (not to the exclusion of) the present system. But self-reliance in the Center, particularly when practiced at the local level, also gives the overdeveloped, capitalist West a chance to regain much of what has been lost in recent times: a sense of mastery of local destiny, mobilization of local creativity, less dependence on professionals, less clientelization generally speaking, new technologies (intermediate, soft, appropriate, human) with smaller economic cycles that are more aligned with middle-range ecological cycles, mass participation, societies less vulnerable to military attack: in short, the list we have just gone through. Some lowering of the purely material standard of living is a very low price to pay for that—and as the contradictions sharpen the probability that Center populations (not only some intellectual elites) will consider that trade-off favorably will probably increase rapidly.

It is felt that these arguments carry a certain weight and are already being reflected, increasingly, at the global, domestic, and local levels of political thought and action. If they are put into practice, there will be implications for world interaction in general and world trade in particular, as indicated in figure 9.1. The most important dynamic tendency will be in the direction of decreased Center–Periphery intersector trade (i.e., across genuine gaps in the level of processing) as an expression of increased Periphery tendency to process their own raw materials and use their own tertiary sector, their own services. As a consequence of this and equally much as an expression of self-reliance one may hypothesize increased intrasector trade—raw materials against raw materials, (semi)manufactures against (semi)manufactures, services against services—both in the Center and in the Periphery. In doing so the Periphery will not only preserve more of the positive externalities for the Periphery and distribute them more evenly among themselves; they will also be better protected against terms of trade fluctuations, as there will be more focus on intrasector trade. What will happen in the other three cells in the figure is hard to postulate but the general hypothesis is certainly that increased self-reliance involves redirection and recomposition of trade and, consequently, will have an impact on the total world trade picture. Whether the total world trade volume will go up or down or remain about the same under a system of self-reliance is another matter, however—there is hardly any basis for knowing.

The same, needless to say, applies to everything else just said: it is highly hypothetical. The thirteen rationales should be seen as hypotheses about positive effects that would derive from a policy of self-reliance, and there are also hypotheses about negative effects. Five of them are as follow.

[1] *Through SR, inequities may yield but inequalities will remain.* There are many types of inequalities, due to different factor endowment, different ability to mobilize the creativity of the people, different levels of mobilization of the population in general for action, and so on. Self-reliance takes care of

Figure 9.1 Implications for world interaction

	Intrasector trade	*Intersector trade*
Center-Center	UP	?
Center-Periphery	?	DOWN
Periphery-Periphery	UP	?

inequality only insofar as it is interaction-induced, derived from the accumulative effects of unfavorable (to the Periphery) terms of trade and/or spin-offs from vertical division of labor or from externalities in general. Through SR, center–periphery relations will be cut down (and if the center reacts sufficiently angrily they may quickly be cut down almost to zero), but that only guarantees that whatever inequality remains is not interaction-induced. Consequently there is also an argument for mechanisms of global redistribution that will "take from the rich and give to the poor" at the same time as the poor become more autonomous. The politics of coordinating this redistribution will be extremely complex, to say the least, which will argue in favor of small revisions of the present system whereby the Center will promise some transfers (not only stabilization of the terms of trade) in exchange for keeping the present (inter)-national division of labor.

[2] *Through SR at the collective level and at the national level, local exploitation may solidify because the basis is unchanged.* The term "self-reliance" should not be used unless there is genuine mass involvement. National and collective self-reliance should be seen as means toward this goal. They are necessary, for local units would be much too exposed to, say, transnational corporations unless there is some national protection available, just as the single Periphery country would need collective solidarity in order to bring about changes in the global structures of trade, politics, military action, culture, and communication. The argument is not in favor of anarchy in the sense of a world divided into small, local communities but in favor of a world where more power, initiative, and better level of needs satisfaction are found in the periphery at all levels of organization: individuals, groups, local communities, countries, and regions. What is not wanted is the use of the rhetoric of self-reliance to blur contradictions between local elites and the people in general.

[3] *Through SR, organic ties between units will be reduced.* SR should be interpreted to mean not isolationism but redirection of interaction in general, as argued many times. Nevertheless, the argument that the world might be cut in two, the former Center and the former Periphery, carries a certain weight because the tendency in that direction would have to be counteracted in a conscious manner compatible with the SR idea. SR policy calls for a certain amount of *de*coupling on more equal terms, for some time, but it also calls for *re*coupling on more equal terms, for intrasector exchanges. The time for *re*-coupling is not necessarily when the former Center is willing to import manufactured goods on equal (tariff and nontariff) terms; that is a very limited perspective on the matter. Equally important is probably the level of general population autonomy, of sufficient self-confidence no longer to be afraid of meeting challenges from other self-reliant units.

[4] *Through SR, mobility between units will be reduced.* SR should not be confused with a system of serfdom tying people to a geographical community, nor with a nomadic system. SR should be compatible with mobility, especially according to the principle of concentric circles—meaning a preference for ex-

change with people in units that are geographical and social neighbors. The Chinese seemed to be practicing a high level of mobility between People's Communes as a way of exchanging experience, but mobility might also be seen as a way of providing individuals with new experience and, consequently, with the raw material for a richer life. What would not be legitimate under an ethos of self-reliance, however, would be to build the systems, particularly the economy, in such a way that the unit *depends* on an input of experts and/or cheap labor from the outside (or *depends* on the export of such people because of the postal remittances they send back). Again, it is obvious that any antimobility principle becomes sheer repression if it is adhered to too dogmatically, among other reasons because of the need for communication between such groups.

[5] *Through SR, a new vertical distinction will be created between self-reliant and nonself-reliant units.* The argument is very often heard that not all units can be self-reliant and that "it was easy for China to be self-reliant with those masses of land and people and history." The argument usually confuses self-reliance with self-sufficiency and also overlooks the important circumstance that China practiced self-reliance inside the country, probably with the consequence that intra-Chinese trade was lower than it would be in a capitalist economy of the same size and the same level of conventional development. Nevertheless, it is obvious that there is a problem of delineating the self-reliant units. Sometimes they will be subnational, sometimes national and sometimes supernational (Nordic countries, Grupo Andino, etc.). As SR is both a psychopolitical and a socioeconomic category, old cultural borders, ethnic groupings, and so on will play a considerable role. Since the "integration" of ethnic minorities (that sometimes add up to majorities) during state formation is a part of the general center–periphery syndrome, the idea of self-reliance should also be considered in the context of the striving for increased autonomy by such groups—and there are many of them around the world.

Finally, one major consideration: self-reliance as an economic doctrine is a system in search of a technology. By "technology," I mean simply the material components that enter the economic cycle, particularly the technologies of extraction, production, and consumption. Today one might also include the technologies of antipollution and recycling in general. Self-reliance introduces severe constraints on the choice of technologies. Thus, ideally they should

1. Be generated locally,
2. Be compatible with local social structures,
3. Be compatible with local culture,
4. Make optimal use of local factors,
5. Be compatible with the idea of local ecological balance,
6. Deliver the goods, for the satisfaction of basic needs.

This may look like an overdetermination of the system, but the idea of self-reliance presupposes that no system is closed in the sense that basic parameters will remain the way they are under present conditions. On the contrary, it is assumed that self-reliance will generate forces, particularly creativity, that will serve as major inputs to the units. Whether and under which circumstances that hypothesis is valid, then, becomes a major question for the practice and theory of development in the future.

9.3   PEACE ROLES OLD AND NEW

We now have a general theory of progressive action and an effort to condense the contents of this book into one concept: *self-reliance*, at the local, domestic, and global levels. But we are concrete human beings, not abstract structures or paper plans. How do we act? What do we do here and now? The following is not a summary of the many suggestions for actions given in the text, but some reflections on how one works concretely for peace–development–self-reliance. I have chosen to present them in six points, not particularly well systematized, for a reason that will be spelled out in the first point.

[1] *History is a process, not a structure.* There are many ways of stating this simple and important point. Human action unfolds itself in time. Whatever we do today is a part of the stream of history. We are not starting the work for a better future today, nor will that job be completed in a generation's time, by the year 2000, or at some other goal point. We are continuing what others have done before us, not as a transition from X to Y but as very small parts of something more gigantic. We shall always be underway. Goals formulated in this book and similar goals are neither fixed nor constant; they are parts of the stream of history and will change as we go along. Hence, let us not overdramatize. Humankind has been working at the job of improving its existence for a couple of million years and will continue to do so for some time. We shall do our part, but it would be an expression of "time centrism"[31] to assume that the major turning point of history is just around the corner.

[2] *Consciousness is a key dimension.* In the world today there is no scarcity of action. No doubt much will be gained when more people can become more active, liberated from the shackles of insecurity, poverty, repression, and alienation. But a much more active world is not necessarily a much better world, for the simple reason that action may be in the wrong direction; one individual's increased activity may be canceled by his neighbor. There must be some guiding, crystallizing element, and that is what I have referred to as consciousness. Think of what countries have been able to do by mobilizing their inhabitants in times of war and times of peace, crystallizing and aligning their action through some shared consciousness. Today we might react negatively to much of that because of its parochialism and its dedication to such abstract goals as nation building, but as a historical force it has ranked and still ranks among the strongest in human history.

Hence, the basic need right now is the cultivation of a global consciousness that I have tried to identify with a dedication to the human race, concretely in terms of the needs for security, economic well-being, freedom, and identity within the limits set by our ecology. One little point to be added gives this goal teeth and substance: to satisfy the human needs of everybody, yes—*but starting with those most in need.*[32] If we have limited resources, as we do, we must start building security for and with the least secure, start raising the level of economic well-being for the most miserable among us, start relieving the repression of the most repressed, start giving more meaning to those who have the most alienating, boring type of existence. We others can wait. Even if we do not wait, we have no right to proceed in such a way as to deprive others of the resources for their need satisfaction. In short, all the work done today to bring into being a global consciousness based on identification with human beings everywhere, thereby crystallizing and aligning human action, is work for peace and development.[33]

[3] *All levels of action are relevant.* Look at the key dimensions of our existence, at space and time; there is "here and now" and there is "the whole world in the future." Some people are best at the micro-level, some are most effective at the macro-level; one does not exclude the other. The concept of local self-reliance makes the localism of the here and now much more relevant, not as an experiment to be replicated at higher levels, not as a training ground, but simply because it *is* development; it is not "only" local. "Local" is where people live. To bring about a modestly decent family life is difficult enough—and yet there are few places where security, well-being, freedom, and identity can so effectively be realized. To ensure that the domestic and global structures in which these small units are embedded do not make such a life impossible, the struggle for higher levels of self-reliance is a necessary condition. Human beings have limitations; nobody should blame anyone else for not being able to be active at all levels and in all the right directions at one time. Mutual respect among those who at least do not counteract human self-reliance anywhere is itself a positive force, because less energy is lost in unnecessary struggle and a basis is laid for solidarity, for example, among the leaders of progressive countries in the First, Second, and Third worlds; progressive mass movements; and ordinary, decent people everywhere. There is also the level of time: some people act now, others plan for the future, acting on paper. Obviously, these activities are equally complementary. Action can be concrete and it can be abstract; the former alone leads to actionism, the latter alone to abstractions. The two have to be tied together as they often are in political movements. The basic components for action are there but require much more clarity about the goals.

[4] *Avoid vertical division of labor.* If all action compatible with a very minimal ideology based on human need satisfaction everywhere, starting with those most in need, is positive, then none should by definition be seen as more important or prestigious than others. Intellectuals who work with large chunks of space and time, with visions of the whole world in the future, are indispensable, as is the mother who embraces her newborn child and in the single act of giving her breast provides security, well-being, freedom, and identity all in

one. But the former should not be given too much more power or prestige just because they are less numerous, have more education, and are less substitutable relative to more people (the mother is also insubstitutable, but in a very limited circle). More particularly, patterns should be avoided whereby the intellectuals only make grand designs or serve as catalysts or as the staff of look-out institutions, then step aside, leaving the hard job to the masses, later reappearing as ministers of planning. There is room both for the professionals and for the populists, for elite persons and for masses in our contemporary vertical society; and the latter should not be the tools of the former. The tremendous dedication to promote human self-reliance and self-realization found at all levels of human society every day should be given much more prominence, lest progress become identified with making plans and models of progress.

[5] *Actor-oriented and structure-oriented peace roles are both relevant.* No doubt the old peace roles were predominantly actor-oriented: the often lonely, particularly devoted and capable individual who could negotiate and mediate; the statesman who could navigate in troubled waters. Out of this came the obvious idea of trying to cultivate the skills of such people by codifying what goes into successful peacekeeping, peacemaking, and peacebuilding. The same occurred for development: entrepreneurial skills were analyzed, schools of management created, experts trained by bilateral and multilateral aid agencies back in the 1950's and 1960's. The approach is usually structure-blind, based on the assumption that the structure is capable of carrying peace and development further if only the right individuals with the right training are given the opportunity at the right point in space and time. In a professionalizing society all such efforts were seen as natural.[34]

But the slogan on which this was based only serves to highlight the problem of this section: "peace as a profession." For here we immediately run into the four characteristics of structural violence. He who has a profession is already a member of a caste with a monopoly on the exercise of that profession. And all the others are fragmented clients whose consciousness is penetrated precisely because the professional is regarded as the only person with *competence,* presumably not only knowing better but also knowing what constitutes knowledge. In every concrete work situation the professional will have the important and challenging tasks, while other people will be used as assistants. Thus, every profession is in and by itself some form of structural violence. Not all are equally peaceless: there are those with more and there are those with less structural violence built into them. Among the most violent one could mention the U.S. Air Force: On big posters at the Nouasseur base in the neighborhood of Casablanca one could read, written with very big characters, "Peace Is Our Profession." When that is the interpretation of "peace as a profession," it does not seem to be worth having.[35]

One important aspect of the idea of "structural violence" is perhaps that by means of this concept a social net is constructed whereby birds of many feathers can be caught and kept, not only the good old scapegoats such as "capitalists" but, for instance, also us, the intellectuals. With this concept an instrument is created whereby intellectuals, including peace researchers, can be seen as carriers of violence, just as much as any other professional always claiming that "I know . . ." He is in a neomonopoly position to give answers and to formulate the acceptable questions. Can one define peace-strategic roles that are compatible with such an expanded concept of peace, and really distribute democratically the tasks of peace? The following is a short list of four roles—not definitions, not even examples, but rather illustrations to make the point more clear.

(a) *Citizens' initiatives.* First are the citizens' initiatives. Hans Eckehard Bahr and others at the Bochum University have written important books about this theme, such as *Politisierung des Alltags.*[36] Citizens' initiative constitutes some kind of proof of the falsehood of a sharp dichotomy between evolution and revolution: these initiatives transcend that dichotomy. As we are always living under the pressure of false dichotomies, what makes this a false one? It is almost always assumed that the revolutionary process takes place at the level of the nation-state: one can imagine a revolution in Germany, but not in Niedersachsen. A revolution in Rheinland–Pfalz even sounds like a semantic impossibility. The problem however, is not "Federal Republic versus Rheinland-Pfalz," not a question of size or territory.

Rather, the point is that we have come to know other forms of revolution. Since 1968 there have been revolutions at the micro-level, in the schools, in the prisons, in the hospitals, in universities, at institutes—for instance, at the International Peace Research Institute in Oslo. Thus, when the definition of structural violence was applied to our own institute one saw more clearly how there is a small caste of researchers who fragment assistants and secretaries, even to the point of penetration and exploitation. What does one do then? One might try such efforts as equalization of salaries, giving for instance to a secretary with seven years' professional experience exactly the same salary as to a Ph.D. with seven years' "experience"—which in the latter case means "experience in university life, combined with studies." One may try to have researchers do more typing and let the secretaries participate more in research. Some experiences have accumulated, and perhaps a certain creativity has developed, but not too much progress has been made. Maybe one can say only that we have seen clearly how the concepts of "violence," "revolution," "peace," and so on have to be developed in such a way that they also focus the attention on oneself, not only to be traps in which to snare others—but that is already something.

Citizens' initiatives can be seen as a plurality of revolutions at the micro-level: they are concerned with city blocks and wards, with factories and institutes, with organizations in general, and also with the family. When in a small family father and mother say to their two-year-old child, "What would you like to have for dinner today? There are two possibilities," instead of saying "Here is your food!" then that has something to do with the opposite of marginalization, which is participation, and also with solidarity, autonomy, and equality. In fact, a large quantity of micro-revolutions is not incompatible with a bigger revolution (but may be a condition or a consequence of that one), nor is it incompatible with general evolution. All such dichotomies tend to be false, for they are almost never dichotomies but trichotomies or polychotomies, and there are almost always possibilities of combination, there is always a *tertium.*

By means of such citizens' initiatives a fight against structural violence is launched, experience is gained, autonomy is realized, peace is created. Broad masses in the population learn *that,* and to some extent *how,* peace can be made. And the important point in this connection is not that structural violence is dangerous because it may one day express itself in direct violence. That was the old problem formulation, the one that also has found its place in the charter of the United Nations. The point is that structural violence *is* peacelessness, *is* violence, which makes a fight against structural violence active peace politics regardless of the level at which it is carried out. The method of fighting is in itself a fight against structural violence: through active participation people are no longer objects of conflict, but subjects of conflict.[38]

And when that has happened, we would no longer live in a society where there is a clear division of labor between the subjects and the objects of a conflict. Thus, small children are in general shown only the glossy surface of social life. It is almost always true, particularly in middle-class families, that the family as a whole and the parents in general present themselves to others, in everyday life, in a conflict-free state: conflicts are something one deals with when the children are not present. One saves the children from the conflict, keeping them unconscious and at a distance, so that they grow up with a very limited possibility of conflict participation. When they achieve school age, conflicts are also taken away from them and processed as raw material by teachers, parents, and organizations, always insisting that the children are not mature enough for participation in this process. Then they become about eighteen years old and they get into conflict, but by this stage the possibilities of their understanding conflict through their own experience have been so curtailed that their conflict resolution repertory for that reason is very limited. As a conclusion they become highly manipulable, as objects rather than subjects.[39]

The most significant point about citizens' initiatives, hence, is precisely the collection of *own* experience. A person who comes from the outside, a "third party" saying "Here I am, I know quite a lot about conflict, and you seem to have a very interesting one, let me solve it for you!" is, structurally speaking, a thief, for he takes away from others a possibility for personal, and thereby social, growth. At this point one could actually mention, at the international level, how Finland—although it certainly is a country very much to be admired— has developed a high capacity in the import of other nations' conflict as raw material for processing in Helsinki. Just as efforts to solve conflicts have such important spin-off effects as the blooming hotel industry in Geneva there is also a conflict-resolution industry in the Finnish foreign office with obvious consequences for its qualitative and quantitative growth.[40]

One might speculate a little bit about the conditions of success for such citizens' initiatives. Concretely they usually take the form of *action,* even of *confrontation.* But these are phenomena that have to take place in time and space, not abstractions like paper solutions and verbal theories. Preferably, time and space should be defined in such a way as to have immediate relevance for the issue. Thus, if the issue is the devastation of an old quarter of a town with highly unprofitable but also highly stimulating, soothing, inspiring houses, *time* could mean when the issue is debated in the city parliament or when the bulldozers are about to start working. *Space* could be outside the city parliament or in front of the bulldozers. In either case it is quite clear how the correct choice of time and space facilitates communication to the opposite party, to the neutrals if there are any, and to one's own side. The abstract action with no inherent time and space link to the issues is very often a kick in the air: the empty demonstration gathering at some square frequently used for that purpose and at a good demonstration hour—for instance, right after schools and working places are closing down for the day. Such demonstrations tend to be ritualized citizen action, not instrumental.[41]

One obvious problem in connection with citizens' initiatives is that the *international* calendar of events is so removed from citizens' lives. A foreign minister has his diary studded with significant events, but the entries in the citizens' diary are more likely to deal with birthdays, parties, and other events of daily life. Hence, what is more than anything else needed in this field is some kind of convergence between the diaries, some way in which citizens' daily lives have an immediate link to international affairs. My experience so far is that one important way to achieve this is the referendum on international policy, for instance, the referendum that took place in Norway on Norwegian entry into the European Community—possibly the most mobilizing political event in modern Norwegian political history.[42] Again, it is obvious that too many such events will also have a ritualizing effect.[43]

(b) *Noncooperation.* The second possibility is, under certain circumstances, to refuse to participate in certain social positions with a particularly pronounced component of violence. It would not be a bad idea if a list of transnational corporations were established, so that one could clearly see which of them (according to the four criteria of structural violence given above) are responsible for most of the structural violence in the world. One could then appeal to everybody who wants a position in an organization of this type to abstain from that move, by pointing to the twenty or so corporations on top of the list. Similarly, there are governments with whom it is important not to cooperate, and within these governments there are some ministries that are worse than others.[44]

In short, it is important nowadays that governments be not regarded as sacrosanct. Actually, one should regard them only as groups within our societies, with no mystical source of legitimacy above the ability to do a good job, not only for one's own population but the world in general. This legitimacy has to be proven over and over again because it should be doubted every day, as we saw so clearly in the Watergate affair in the United States. Of course, the Watergate scandal was only an expression or an idiom in which a much deeper scandal could be expressed, something built into the very structure of that gigantic society. But it was useful to expose misdeeds at that point, particularly because the roots of the scandal were so deep, although it probably mystified the deeper scandal.

(c) *Increased transparency.* Any good journalist and social critic sees it as his task to make the workings of society more transparent for the citizens living in it. However, much more dramatic forms than analysis—and that is what peace research usually limits itself to—can be found, and one might think particularly of Daniel Ellsberg. As a matter of fact, there are interesting parallels between Ellsberg and Ossietzky: neither of them functioned as a spy or an agent for a foreign power, Ellsberg even defined himself as a "spy for humanity."[45]

But before that Ellsberg was certainly an exponent of the "peace is our profession" ethos in the sense of the U.S. Air Force. He participated in the formulation of equations and diagrams with military input and military output; the destruction potential and the destruction made, particularly in terms of people killed; for instance, measured in megabodies, one million dead. (The Vietnam wars had perhaps brought it so far as to two megabodies, all together.) Ellsberg was a part of this monstrous death factory, as were other intellectuals in Boston, at Harvard University or the Massachusetts Institute of Technology; he was a "specialist" like the others. They conceived of themselves as first-rate intellectuals fighting against a fifth-rate power, only to see later that they were fifth-rate intellectuals engaged in a fight against a first-rate power.

They worked on the increments of the variables and expressed the relation in curves, using their expertise about military input and megabody output, and established an upper limit, the famous "unacceptable damage" for the military output. But then they experienced that this limit was a very different one in a society with total mobilization of the creativity of the total population, something quite different from the analogue they had consciously or unconsciously been using, contemporary American society. This came as a shock to Ellsberg— one could even express it biblically by invoking the analogy of Saul on the road to Damascus—the conversion was total and now he is, as he says himself, a different human being.

So, how would it be if instead of *megabodies* one made use of a *megadan* ("Dan" for Daniel Ellsberg)? That would be one million people in foreign offices, in defense ministries, in the transnational corporations, in each and every organization that somehow disposes over the means of structural and direct violence, implementing them and improving them. At times of crisis they would publish secrets, as Daniel Ellsberg did for the Vietnam conflict with the Pentagon Papers. For these papers were made secret not in order to protect or promote humanity but in order to protect the United States and more particularly its government, not to mention its president. Most secret documents are of that kind.

Thus, Ellsberg's role was a new peace-strategic role; and mobilization of all the Ellsbergs of the world would be a rewarding as well as an important task. With that mobilization the monopoly of governments on secrets would be threatened, which would by and large be a most positive and significant contribution to peace. Thus, if the Norwegian Nobel Peace Prize Committee had had as much courage as it had in the year 1935/36 when Carl von Ossietzky was given the Nobel Peace Prize, then Ellsberg would undoubtedly have been the recipient of that prize.[46]

(d) *Toward new science and technology.* Fourth, there is much work to do in the field of new technologies and new branches of science. Consider that so many scientists in one major country in the Western world, believing in humanity and Christianity, were made use of for the Vietnam war. Research at the Massachusetts Institute of Technology was to a large extent financed by the Pentagon, but it is more general than that: there was an almost incredible intellectual mobilization for the war we today know extremely well, a war about which we probably know most of what there is to know. What strikes one as horrifying is the compatibility, even identity between war and science—the way in which one has come to conclude that there is something in modern science that in and by itself makes it disposed for war.[47]

In our model of science the vertical division of labor is already built into the structure. This leads to the question of whether this is a good social model at all. It promotes a small elite that designates itself as scientific, regarding others as clients, as students who understand little and whose consciousness it has a right, even a duty to help form. This is the problem not only for peace research, but for any science; and it is not enough to engage in popularization, since that is only a form of paternalism. Another solution would be to develop scientific concepts less based on division of labor so that everybody is included, everybody can participate.[48]

Such attempts were made in Maoist China; in our vertical society not even efforts are made in that direction. Not only should science and technology be geared toward the satisfaction of basic material needs for food, clothes, shelter, health, and education for all—starting with those most in need—but efforts should be made to generate forms of research whereby everybody can participate as a producer of knowledge.

[6] *Peace action has to be generated spontaneously.* At this point I stop. It is not for me to produce endless catalogs suggesting praxis for other people to engage in. The task is to do it, to seek activation, to be active. And there is no substitute for the form of activation that springs out of one's own consciousness, triggered by the injustice of a social situation, tempered by the fear that it will get worse rather than better, motivated by a vision of an achievable, viable alternative—and crystallizing into plans for action in solidarity with others in the same situation. In the process, experience is gained, tested against one's assumptions, and the unity of research and action mentioned as desirable in section 1.3 are brought about—in this our difficult and wonderful world.

9.4 SUMMARY AND CONCLUSION: THE LIGHT IN THE DARK

The basic focus of this book is the human individual, in a social setting, domestically and globally. Each person has the right to self-realization, an inalienable right of personal growth. As a minimum there are the *fundamental material needs* of food, shelter, clothing, health, and education, and the almost equally fundamental intangible needs of *identity* with self and others, society and culture, and of freedom, of access to the means of expression and impression, in the sense of *choice.* Hence, the beginning of any political analysis is where we stand on such dimensions, not in an average sense but for any single one of us: how many have more than the minimum of food, of shelter, of health, of education, of basic freedom? What we find is that we are dismally short after millions of years of human history—and not even progressing. The number of members of humankind with fundamental needs unsatisfied is increasing, the repression of identity and freedom seems to be increasing, and the direct violence of all kinds of wars is on the increase. All together, the indications are that humankind is heading for some kind of suicide. At the same time there is the finiteness of the natural base on which we live: resources are being depleted, pollution is making itself felt, ecological cycles are destroyed. Humankind seems to be painting itself into a corner, as mentioned earlier.

The basic diagnosis of these evils is structural. When humankind is the victim of so much suffering it is not only because of the direct violence of wars but also and even more because of the structural violence built into the social structure, within countries and between countries. Basic to this structure is the concept of *exploitation,* which is defined as the *vertical division of labor.* Some people do one kind of job, others do another kind; they are linked together and cannot function without one another, but some get much more out of the relationship than others. Some are enriched partly because others are impoverished. Thus, inside a country there are those who solve problems—the managers, the professionals—and those who implement solutions—the clerks, the workers. There are those who make decisions and those who obey. Between countries, there are those who participate in the international division of labor by digging holes in the ground to provide others with raw materials; and there are those who process these raw materials, imprint form, culture, and their decisions on them, and market their processed goods, also in the countries whence the raw materials came, greatly benefiting from terms of trade and spin-off effects. Some impose their social forms on other countries by political and military means, making others into copies of themselves, dividing the labor between those who decide and those who have to obey.

Particularly important is the combination of the vertical divisions of labor between *and* within countries. In this combination the Center country establishes a bridgehead in the Periphery country and works through this bridgehead, making the bridgehead an extension of its own center. Where the division of labor is primarily economic—between the providers of raw materials and those who process them between countries, and between those who implement solutions and those who work out these solutions within both countries—the pattern is known as *capitalistic imperialism.* Where the division of labor is primarily political/military—between those who provide the social model and those who have to accept it, between those who decide and those who have to obey—the pattern is known as *social imperialism.* In many cases, such as in the relationships between the United States and many Latin American and Southeast Asian countries, there is a mixture of both—but this probably applies less to the relationship between the Soviet Union and her satellite countries.

Imperialistic relations are based on exploitation and on penetration—on the formation of bridgeheads inside other countries. Particularly important in forming these bridgeheads are the various international organizations. The governmental international organizations, the nongovernmental ones, not to mention the transnational corporations, all serve one basic function: that of homogenizing and harmonizing elites. In so doing they provide the elites in the dominating countries—capitalist or socialist—with bridgeheads in the form of local chapters, or daughter companies. Even the United Nations and its specialized agencies have this aspect, but it has of course also the opposite aspect: to serve as a world forum for the articulation of grievances, making the world more transparent to the extent that the representatives really represent the masses of their countries. Very often they represent only the bridgeheads, thus adding to Center power over humankind.

In addition to *exploitation* and *penetration* the current world structure is also characterized by *fragmentation* and *marginalization.* Fragmentation means the way in which those at the bottom within, as well as between, countries are kept apart and often made unable to act in a coordinated manner against their exploiters. Marginalization means the way in which they are even kept outside what is going on, made marginal, second-class, to the entire domestic or global society, as are suppressed races and colonial peoples.

As a result, humankind is divided into a small group in the center who enjoy both personal and socioeconomic growth and a vast majority in the periphery who are denied either, whose work is drudgery, whose lives are endangered through lack of essentials, who die halfway through their lives or earlier, unfulfilled, often suppressed and deprived of any type of human rights. The division is partly between countries, partly within them. In addition, there is also a basic conflict between the capitalist and the socialist configurations—not only within them—seemingly about what kind of domination is preferable.

So, both within and between the capitalist and socialist types of imperialism, conflicts are rampant. Means of coercion are needed to build these repressive structures, to maintain them, and to fight them. Thus the world gets a *war system* in addition to the *dominance system,* in the form of the East–West arms race, and in the form of imperialistic wars, of the types exemplified in Indochina and Hungary and in the suppression inside the Soviet Union, in Northern Ireland, in the Basque countries, and in what was once East Pakistan. Thus the war system partly serves to establish structural violence and emerges partly as a response to it—and partly as a response to the response. These are the phases of violence: direct violence to establish structural violence; the structural violence itself, which may last for a very long time; direct violence to destroy it (revolutionary violence); and direct counterviolence to protect it (counterrevolutionary violence, "counterinsurgency"). In addition there is the more "horizontal violence," between equals, as between the heads of empires, to protect the empires.

By and large the world has the following empires today: the United States, concentrating on Latin America; the European Community, concentrating on Black Africa; the Soviet Union, over many peoples inside her own territory and over most peoples in Eastern Europe; and Japan over much of Southeast Asia in purely economic terms. The two most populous countries in the world, India and China, also have some aspects of internal imperialism (Naga, Tibet) and external tendencies. There is structural violence within these empires, neverending waves of direct violence within them, and threats of direct violence between them. Thus exploitation, penetration, fragmentation, and marginalization stand in the way of both personal and social growth, except at the top of the empires. On the other hand, exploitation has now come so far that whereas those in the periphery are exposed to perennial *underdevelopment* those in the center are now threatened by *overdevelopment,* a type of "growth" that stands in the way of rather than serves their own self-realization. Some results are overfeeding, gadget-oriented, empty lives, a supercomplicated, alienating society, and psychosomatic diseases.

The basic remedy for these evils is the demolition of exploitative structures. They cannot be permitted to continue. The strategy would, by and large, have to be as follows: to build down vertical trade relations by holding onto raw materials and importing fewer industrial goods, relying on individual and collective *self-reliance* for those suffering under capitalistic imperialism. For those suffering under social imperialism the formula will have to be to organize resistance, to build down obedience or put up only the empty pretense of obedience. In both cases one may have to wait until the suppressing country or countries are weak, preparing for the moment to come. Weakness may come about through overextension, for the suppressors are not only bigger than the suppressed (because they are integrated rather than fragmented), they are also very often overextended. Weakness may come about by withholding from them what they like most: raw materials or raw obedience, a demand for economic products or a corresponding demand for ideological products. Ultimately the weakness may also be brought about through the finiteness of nature: the exploiters, particularly the United States, also exploit nature so much that they may one day be hit by simple natural scarcity or pollute themselves if not to death at least into considerable difficulty.

When these methods threaten the exploitative structures, the exploiters themselves or their bridgeheads, as in Chile and Czechoslovakia, will hit back. To counteract this reaction, direct violence should be avoided as far as possible and methods of nonviolent revolution and nonmilitary defense should be developed. In the Center countries nothing should be spared to demoralize and weaken those who might possibly make use of methods of direct violence to maintain the patterns of structural violence, between countries as well as within countries.

For there is also structural violence within countries, and it does not only take the form of capitalism. A more modern form is brought about through schooling: the interesting, problem-solving, personality-expanding jobs are monopolized by those who have higher education, the other jobs are given to the rest. Again, the only workable remedy is probably to break down the structure, eradicating the distinction between owners and users of means of production and the distinction between professionals and the hewers of wood. That this is not only meaningful but possible is shown very clearly through the experiences gained in China during and after the cultural revolution. China is the only society where the contradiction between growth and equity is transcended, possibly at the expense of a trade-off between equality and freedom.

The basic goal would have to be a world of humans, living equitably in a world of social units, some big, some small, none of them exploiting the other. For this to be brought about, a high level of self-reliance, in some cases even self-sufficiency, is necessary (particularly when it comes to food). Exploitative relations must be banned, as today are banned slavery and (political) colonialism. The economic cycles of production will have to be not only less exploitative than today—within and between countries—but also less encompassing, more local. This is the only way in which the participants—the producers and the consumers—can fully comprehend what is going on and not be alienated by their own participation. It is also the only way in which they can fully see the depletion and pollution in time to counteract it. Thus, the way out is not only an intermediate technology, but also an intermediate economic cycle—somewhere between the devastation caused by transnational corporations and the impoverishing effects of the primitive and traditional economic cycles that are quite unable to sustain the world population of today. That population will also have to be limited, not by limiting the poor alone but by establishing all over the world the norm that from two persons shall come not more than two persons.

But what will keep such a world together, a world where many of today's superstates will have to be broken into smaller units to permit the individual genuine participation in what is going on? Three things will: direct relations, nonterritorial organizations, and a world central authority.

The direct relations should provide the world with a dense network, linking the units by ties of trade and all other forms of exchange. But trade will take place according to a code of equity, not only to *mutual* benefit, but to more or less *equal* benefit. Fundamentally, the units will be self-reliant in the sense that they can weather a crisis, can survive if others withdraw from them. In short, they will no longer be dependent.

The nonterritorial actors are already numerous and should be permitted to grow in number, but only if they do not contribute to the present patterns of capitalist and social imperialism. International organizations that are merely reproductions of the general world pattern—meaning that those who dominate on the outside also dominate on the inside of the organizations—should be changed, even split, with the dominated going it alone. Thus, the world will have to see a separate organization of Latin American states (without the United States), a separate organization of Eastern European countries (without the Soviet Union), a stronger organization of Southeast Asian states (without Japan), just as it has witnessed the emergence of a European Community (without the United States). This will have to be repeated inside international organizations, pitting poor countries against the rich, the nonaligned against the aligned, the small against the big. The forums, such as the United Nations, where they can meet and solve problems must be preserved. Thus, a combination of integration and disintegration is needed, using nonterritorial organizations both to keep the world together and to facilitate the liberation of the dominated.

A world central authority will have to serve the double function of *articulating* problems and conflicts and *solving* them. For articulation purposes the United Nations has to be made more representative, not only of states but also of minorities within states and of nonterritorial organizations. For the solution of problems and conflicts the United Nations will have to rely on services rather than force and on old and new world authorities (new ones are needed in such fields as housing, resources, energy, ocean regimes, and disarmament) rather than on big international peacekeeping forces. The latter are warranted on a limited scale, but they may also pose a major threat to humankind if they grow too big and are supported by some kind of joint world self-righteousness.

So, here we stand, in a world grossly maldeveloped, especially during the last centuries, although at the same time a world holding great promises because of the tremendous creative and productive ability of all of us. It is now up to us better to see the dangerous situation in which we are, to analyze it correctly, and to find the proper images of the future and the strategies that can lead us in a new direction. Above all, it is now up to all of us to act more and to act more correctly. It gives great comfort to know that the world is moving today, that giant forces are put into motion, that imperialism can be beaten in the plains and the forests, the mountains and the cities of Indochina; that five centuries of exploitation hauling cheap raw materials and energy out of the "Third World" can be reversed, to some extent and for some time, through actions of solidarity; that the grip the northwestern corner of the world has on Africa is loosening every day; that there is not only a deadening structure of imperialism but also a process of liberation, however erratic and problematic. Movement there is. There is light in the dark, and from that light we can take our leads, every one, weakening the oppressors and strengthening the oppressed of this our earth.

NOTES

References to *Essays* are to Johan Galtung, *Essays in Peace Research,* 5 vols. (Copenhagen: Ejlers, 1975–80) (Atlantic Highlands, N.J.: Humanities Press).

1. This combination, or any similar high–low combination, is known as rank disequilibrium. For a general theory of its implications, see, for instance, Galtung, "The Dynamics of Rank Conflict," *Essays* III, 6.

2. This is the basic insight on which Gandhian forms of resistance are based, as pointed out in sections 4.3 and 5.3.

3. Thus in Germany as much as 10 percent of the age class has been registered as CO's.

4. Rereading this I wonder why I did not write "liberation of Saigon." There is a reason though: there was little in terms of a spontaneous uprising inside Saigon. In the longer time perspective what happens may prove to be liberalizing also for that particular part of the Vietnamese that inhabited the Saigon I know from a study there in January 1968. In the short run the "fall of Saigon" is probably a more correct term.

5. I have dealt with these themes at some length in "East–West Security and Cooperation: A Skeptical Contribution," *Essays* V, 2, and *Journal of Peace Research* (1975), pp. 165–78. and "Deductive Thinking and Political Practice: An Essay on Teutonic Intellectual Style," *Papers on Methodology* (Copenhagen: Ejlers, 1979).

6. For details, see section 4.2.

7. In other words, this is an effort to define the Third World more in terms of people rather than countries—in line with the basic theme of this book.

8. For this is the basic thing we could learn from China. See Galtung and Fumiko Nishimura, *Learning from the Chinese People* (Oslo, 1975).

9. It is high time to start thinking in terms of the alliances among all these types of topdogs, particularly the very powerful technocratic alliance between bureaucrats, capitalists, and professionals/researchers on which the dominant structure in modern society to a large extent is based.

10. I do not agree with the Chinese idea that "social imperialism" is worse than "capitalist imperialism": the latter affects more people in more countries and in terms of even more basic needs. The former may affect the Chinese more, however.

11. Roland Berger, "Self-reliance, Past and Present," *Eastern Horizon* IX, no. 3, pp. 8–24. See also Ashok Parthasarathi, "The Role of Self-reliance in Alternative Strategies for Development," a paper prepared for the Twenty-fifth Pugwash Conference (Madras, 13–19 January 1976), with a summary by the secretary-general of Pugwash. One particular aspect of self-reliance is analyzed in Surendra J. Patel, "Collective Self-reliance of Developing Countries," Background Paper no. 8, WFUNA Annual Summer School. Also see the Cocoyoc Declaration of 1974 for the general philosophy of self-reliance. I have chosen not to try to reflect the recent changes in China after the death of Mao Tse-tung and the demise of the so-called Gang of Four as I am not at all convinced that the new course will be long lasting. Rather, it is probably in a zig-zag pattern oscillating between distribution-oriented and growth-oriented policies that the key to Chinese development strategy can be found, and this is quite consistent with the self-reliance policy of "walking on two legs." That mistakes may be made and that struggle takes place would be normal in human affairs. However this may be, more time is needed to see more clearly what the social meaning of all this is, and in the meantime there will always be much to learn from recent Chinese history.

12. This is a basic theme of the Trends in Western Civilization research program of the Chair in Conflict and Peace Research, University of Oslo.

13. The standard term is "neocolonialism," but the phenomenon is broader in scope; it is actually imperialism no longer supported by military–political colonialism in the classical sense.

14. From the Cocoyoc Declaration: "The ideal we need is a harmonized cooperative world in which each part is a center, living at the expense of nobody else, in partnership with nature and in solidarity with future generations."

15. Power is then seen as a *relation* between a sender and a receiver, not as something existing in the sender alone. The latter would be power potential.

16. Extreme care should be taken in using concepts like the "fourth world" that are usually introduced to indicate divisiveness inside the Third World. On the other hand there is no reason to conceal that dominance relations also develop inside the Third World. If one should talk meaningfully about the "fourth world," however, it would probably make much more sense to see it as located within all Third World countries—the vast periphery of the Periphery—than to see it as a group of countries such as the twenty-five designated as the least-developed countries.

17. This is probably a contingent relation, though. It is hardly absolutely necessary, but that it is not absolutely sufficient is seen from the Algerian case today, and probably also from the Soviet case. In both cases a tremendous struggle preceded independence and transition to socialism, but the systems can hardly be characterized as self-reliant.

18. Thus, the UNCTAD 77 is certainly more than an organization for global articulation and collective bargaining; it is also a setting within which new cooperative structures are emerging.

19. This is developed in some detail in Galtung and Nishimura, *Learning from the Chinese People,* chap. 4.

20. At this point a Western preoccupation with the loss of efficiency in multiple innovation, or reinnovation, enters. Great efforts are exercised to avoid this through "coordination and documentation." Without denying the value of that approach in some fields it should be noticed how this serves the function of reinforcing the Center as Center because it has the largest capability (e.g., in pure R & D, science and technology terms) for creating new science and technology.

21. However, no absolute dogmatic position about producing only for use, never for exchange will be taken here. When one produces for the use of others there is always an exchange element present that makes it hard to draw an absolute borderline. But the concept of production for socially beneficial goals, including the satisfaction of basic material needs of oneself and others, might be seen as a basic ingredient in self-reliance as a concept.

22. This is probably one of the few absolutely safe statements one can make about capitalism, from which it follows that capitalist patterns will be maintained not necessarily only by countries with a dominant private sector but by countries that base their economies to a large extent on trade, whether most of the economy is in the private or the public sector.

23. Gandhi may be seen as one of the ideologists and practitioners of self-reliance, through the *sarvodaya* concept at the (local level) and *swadeshi* concept (at the national level) inside a pattern of local capitalism, but of the type normatively regulated through what Gandhi referred to as the "horizontal" aspects of caste, the trade union aspects.

24. The concept is probably, as Myrdal has argued, meaningful for countries at the same level of development, making exchanges of products at roughly

speaking the same level of processing, thus balancing the externalities and keeping terms of trade relatively stable.

25. Berger, op. cit., p. 9. The quotation is from a cable by Mao to some local headquarters in 1948.

26. See the very interesting analysis by K.N. Raj et al., *Poverty, Unemployment and Development Policy: A Case Study of Selected Issues with Reference to Kerala* (Trivandrum, March 1975), where it is argued strongly that food should be produced locally in order not to become too expensive for the people and in order to utilize fully marginal resources.

27. It is probably only when the quest for a less consumptive new life style in rich countries is seen as a quest for a higher quality of life (and not as a reaction to changing trade patterns) that sufficient momentum will be generated.

28. The individual-level paradigm for this is, of course, the way in which most people grow up through a phase of withdrawal from parental authority, establishing their own personalities through more autonomously guided trial and error. From the parental point of view this is known as "the difficult years" and "the puberty crisis."

29. These more ephemeral, higher, and nonmaterial needs are more difficult to define and for that reason are usually left out of economistically guided analyses. The result is clearly seen in the high level of alienation in the working conditions of developed countries, one eloquent testimony being Studs Terkel, *Working* (New York: Avon Books, 1972).

30. See Galtung et al., *Measuring World Development,* Chair in Conflict and Peace Research, University of Oslo, 1974.

31. Again an aspect of Western civilization: *here,* in the West, is the center of the world; *now,* right now, is the center of time.

32. In a sense this may be seen to be the most important point in the Christian ethic, translated into economic practice in the economic systems of socialism, but easily perverted into something far more materialistic than originally intended.

33. The Cocoyoc Declaration is a typical effort to produce ideology of that type.

34. An example was the International Peace Academy, which started operating in 1970 with sessions in Vienna—originally as a broad forum for the development and exchange of information and views on all kinds of matter related to peace, later turning more narrow, focusing on peacekeeping only in a professionalizing manner.

35. Peace should never be professionalized, for when that happens a closed group is formed, a guild, a caste, with high technical competence but increasingly removed from the people they are supposed to serve. Technical efficiency, command of the means, becomes more important than the ends: the well-being of everybody. This is particularly clearly seen in the unquestioning way in which military men develop such horrendous doctrines as countervalue strategies whereby masses of fellow human beings are held as hostages, possibly to be exterminated in a nuclear holocaust.

36. Luchterhand, 1972.

37. For more information about this see the article written by Nils Petter Gleditsch in the report for the years 1970–1972 from the International Peace Research Institute, Oslo.

38. This is the major theme in Galtung, "Conflict as a Way of Life," *Essays* III, 15.

39. For a further exploration of that theme, see Galtung, "Schooling and Future Society," *Papers,* no. 7, Chair in Conflict and Peace Research, University of Oslo.

40. Thus, an expansion program of considerable magnitude was initiated by that foreign office in 1971 when it became clear that they were to play a major role in the all-European process.

41. This is particularly true to the extent that the authorities learn patterns of dealing with them: treat them with respect, permitting or even encouraging the demonstration process, and then pay no attention to them whatsoever.

42. The referendum was held in September 1972 and was a very close race (53 percent against, 47 percent in favor) as an indication of how heated the political debate had been.

43. I am thinking here of the Swiss referenda, often having very low rates of participation but giving the population a chance to pronounce themselves on details of policy-making not found in other countries.

44. Working along such lines is an integral part of the World Indicators Program, Chair of Conflict and Peace Research, University of Oslo.

45. That does not mean that they were accepted as such by their contemporaries who tried to see them as spies for "the enemy"—not only to blackmail them but also, partly, because this was the only alternative to loyalty and apathy known to the authorities in either case.

46. Lacking that courage, it instead gave the prize to Henry Kissinger, and later to Eisaku Sato and to Menachem Begin and Anwar Sadat, leading to a major depreciation of the value of that prize.

47. This point is repeatedly made by Herbert Marcuse.

48. See Galtung, "Social Structure and Science Structure," chapter 1 in *Methodology and Ideology* (Copenhagen: Ejlers, 1977).

Appendix WORLD SOCIAL INDICATORS

A.1   INDICATORS AND OPERATIONALIZATION

Today many people do not understand how vitally significant discussions of "social indicators" are, or how powerful the people who define them. The discussions are found in intergovernmental organizations and in ministries, at universities, research institutes, in political parties, and the like.[1] Mostly, however, they are conducted at a technical level among experts. The topic looks innocent enough—"only" statistics and mathematical formulas. But each social indicator represents a goal,[2] openly or in disguise, and when the ruling indicators are decided by the ruling people in the ruling countries, they are likely to reflect the rulers' vested interests. Thus, "per capita gross national product" probably looked like an expert abstraction when it first emerged.[3] By now the indicator has become an institutionalized goal; and since this indicator measures the level of processing and marketing in the economy—and not, for instance, the degree of satisfaction of fundamental needs—it serves to keep today's ruling countries in ruling positions.[4] If waning their power is also waning.

Such dimensions should not be decided on by scientists, experts, politicians, or other elite persons. *People themselves should decide the goals, their implementation and operationalization.*[5] But in a world so distorted by vertical division of labor and professionalism as today's world, it becomes important that counter-elites also work out indicators that show by contrast how narrow and politically biased current indicators are, to make the debate both broader and more public.

The present effort attempts to broaden the spectrum of social indicators to include goals of the political left,[6] not only by broadening the *scope* of social indicators but also by extending their *domain,* from indicators for the country to indicators for the world, creating *global* indicators. The current idea that the state of the world is equal to the sum (or the average) of the states of its component countries is a reflection of a liberal, actor-oriented, structure-blind view of the world. For the world also has a structure; it is not only a set of actors.

As a prerequisite for any choice of dimensions, we need an *image* of the world. The image suggested as a general point of departure is of a world of levels,

431

as follows:

Level 0:   Nature (N)
Level 1:   Individual actors (I)
Level 2:   Collective actors of two kinds
           territorial actors (T)
           nonterritorial actors (NT)
Level 3:   World (W)

such that the equation for the world, in terms of actors, is

$$W = N + I + T + NT.$$

Thus, the world consists of finite nature, in and by which individuals live. These individuals are, however, organized as territorial and nonterritorial actors, both of which interact and form structures. From a global point of view the most important territorial actors are the *countries,* territorially contiguous polities; and the most important nonterritorial actors are the multinational associations and organizations, whether *governmental* (intergovernmental organizations, IGOs), or *nongovernmental* (internongovernmental organizations, INGOs), *nonprofit* or *profit* ("business," BIGOs in the governmental case and BINGOs in the nongovernmental case) or *transnational* with individuals rather than national governments or other national groups as members (TRANGOs, TNCs).

Our "world social accounting" could then have five parts:

1. $W,N =$ the world as an *ecosystem,* including man, with its balances and imbalances.
2. $W,I =$ the world as a *society of individuals.* (If the world were one country, what kind of country would that be?)
3. $W,T =$ the world as a *community of countries.* (What does this world look like?)
4. $W,NT =$ the world as a *community of organizations.* (What does this world look like?)
5. $All =$ the world conceived of as nature, individuals, countries, and organizations. (How do they all interact?)

Under the first heading one would study depletion and pollution of the water, oxygen, and protein sources; the sources of energy; the world temperature situation; and so on. Under the second heading one would, for instance, look into world demography and ask questions about the world demographic and occupational distribution, disregarding the collectivities intervening between world and individual levels.[7] That topic would come under the third heading, as the world would appear as a set of countries, and under the fourth heading, as a set of organizations, and the distributions would be investigated. Finally, this would all be put together, in ways to be specified later.

This world is like Chinese boxes: actors within actors. Because our basic concern is with the *good life* of individual human beings, given a finite world and the organization into collectivities with distributions and structures, we are immediately led to the problem of the *good collectivity*. But the fact that the world is itself a collectivity of collectivities leads to the problem of the *good world*. To address this problem sensibly we must reason from the individual through the collectivity to the world, and not vice versa. The other way round one has so often led to nonhuman, even antihuman, abstractions. For instance, if we start by saying that the good world is a world without war, that it is found in a hierarchical world where a group of strong countries dominate the rest and where the countries are built according to the same model, with groups of strong people dominating the rest, then the net result is a world with a tiny minority of the strong in strong countries living very good lives and a majority of the weak in weak countries leading lives of squalor. Many other examples could be given of the danger in starting with collectivities—GNP per capita among them.[8]

Hence, we are led to the problem of analysis at different levels, including analysis of the relations between the levels. Just as we should use the same dimensions for analyses of the present, the preferred, and the rejected worlds—for data, theory, and values—we should also use the same dimensions for analyses at the individual, the collective, and the world levels. The world cannot afford any longer this fragmentation of knowledge, and one way of countering it is to develop a common language for empirical, theoretical, and axiological analysis, regardless of level.[9]

In this effort, it is found that the real distinction is one of basic perspective rather than the weight given to data, theory, or value, or level of analysis. I have referred to these perspectives as the *actor-oriented* and the *structure-oriented* perspectives, respectively.[10]

According to the actor-oriented perspective, any collectivity is a set of actors that can be classified and enumerated in various ways. More particularly, the actors can be classified according to two types of attributes: as *being* what they *are* and as *having* what they *have*.[11] In either case *distributions* can be defined, and the appropriate social indicator will be some kind of *statistical parameter*. The language of operational discourse is *arithmetic*.

These simple thoughts then give rise to five kinds of goal dimensions for a collectivity, to be explored in some detail.

1. Based on level of "being": *personal growth* (antonym: *alienation*)
2. Based on dispersion of "being": *diversity* (antonym: *uniformity*)
3. Based on level of "having": *socioeconomic growth* (antonym: *poverty*)
4. Based on disperson of "having": *equality* (antonym: *inequality*)
5. Based on covariation of "being/having": *social justice* (antonym: *social injustice*)

The antonyms in parentheses stand for what is generally regarded as bad. Thus, the basis here is a view of a collectivity as a distribution of actors; a distinction between what an actor *is* and what he *has;* and a short list of the simplest parameters that can be used.

According to the structure-oriented perspective, any collectivity consists of social positions connected by interaction relations and interaction patterns, together forming a structure. Development does not consist primarily in changes in the distributions of attributes, but in structural changes. Some representation of the structure will have to be developed, for instance in the form of *graphs,* and the appropriate indicator will be some kind of graph parameter. The distinction must then be drawn between structural properties that relate to the *interaction relation* as such (e.g., to an exchange relation) and to the *interaction pattern,* where more than two positions are involved. The language of operational discourse is *geometric.*

Four kinds of goal dimensions for a collectivity are also to be explored:

6. Based on interaction relation: *equity* (antonyms: *inequity, exploitation*)
7. Based on interaction relation: *autonomy* (antonym: *penetration*)
8. Based on interaction pattern: *solidarity* (antonym: *fragmentation*)
9. Based on interaction pattern: *participation* (antonym: *marginalization*)

Once more, the antonyms serve to anchor the dimensions at two points. Thus, the basis here is a view of a collectivity as a structure, consisting of the interaction *relation* (which I take to be bilateral) and interaction *patterns* (which I conceive of as multilateral). This perspective should then be added to the equation above.

A tenth goal dimension arises from the inclusion of nature in the equation for the world:

10. Based on the ecosystem: *ecological balance* (antonym: *ecological imbalance*)

This presentation is so brief as to be almost meaningless. The theoretical rationale, given elsewhere,[12] applies to collectivities of individuals as well as to collectivities of collectivities—across levels, that is. Now I shall try to inject meaning into these concepts through operationalization. But first, some exploration of the problem of operationalization, in general. Operationalization has to be argued; it is not self-evident. It can very easily become an empty, distorting exercise. To operationalize a dimension is to indicate a procedure whereby the position on that dimension can be given an algebraic, usually numerical, expression. There are at least five good reasons for operationalization.

[1] Operationalization forces *precision* on us. We have to specify exactly what is meant by the dimension; we are forced away from slogans. If the result is supposed to be a number, no vagueness is permissible. Obviously, this demand for precision may lead to caricatures. Usually, or at least very often, an operationalization is able to capture only one aspect or connotation of a goal dimension, and not the many surplus meanings that richer minds have been able to infuse it with. But this can be seen as an argument for *better* conceptualization, exploring separate subdimensions of a concept, and for *better* operation-

alization, rather than for no operationalization at all. Operationalization, carefully practiced, may become a way of making slogans and catchwords more meaningful; at the expense of fragmenting them into components.

[2] Operationalization is a potential instrument of *practice.* Operationalization not only makes the dimension more precise and communicable; it can also indicate processes and component actions needed to increase the level of value-realization along the dimension. It should indicate practical operations, not only operations with numbers. Above all, it should not merely be a formula chosen ritualistically from the storehouse of descriptive statistics. When *good* operationalization has been found, communication about the value for the purpose of practice and action, not only of theory and philosophy is facilitated. Thus, one reason that economic growth is so dominant in people's minds is its operationalization in terms of annual increment in GNP, GDP, or NI (national income), in absolute terms or per capita. *The formula for GNP is also a formula for how to increase GNP.* It does not adequately reflect women's work in the home or farmer production for own consumption. It is secondary- and tertiary-sector–oriented, measuring the degree of processing and marketing, that is, the power position of a country in the international vertical division of labor. This is easily forgotten. But it does explain quite well the popularity enjoyed by the measure in rich societies. Correspondingly, *one* reason that economic equality is less on people's minds is the lack of good operationalization. True, it is mainly the other way around, that vested interest in economic growth leads to operationalization (and vested disinterest in equality to little concern with its operationalization). But operationalization may also stimulate interest. Thus, to take a third example: most people would like to have "richer lives" leading to personal growth, but this desire might more easily be translated into action if someone offered an operationalization that also had the merit of being practice-indicative.

[3] In a sense underlying the preceding point, operationalization makes *comparisons* possible. I am thinking of two types of comparisons: *synchronic,* whereby a country is compared with other countries at the same time, and *diachronic,* whereby a society is compared with itself over time, including itself in the future. Both comparisons make sense in a world bent on achieving these goals: a society may evaluate itself relative to others (synchronic), and/or it may check how it is doing over time (diachronic). In either case operationalization may serve as a stimulus for action; if in addition operationalization is practice-indicative, its practical value should be obvious.

In connection with this last point there is a particular mechanism worth mentioning as a typical example of the significance of operationalization. What propels societies into action when they are carrying out their synchronic and diachronic comparisons seems to be not so much comparisons based on *one* goal dimension alone as comparisons based on *two* dimensions. This is where rank disequilibrium[13] and rank incongruence[14] enter as powerful motivators for concrete action. The basic comparisons, synchronic as well as diachronic, are bivariate, not univariate.

Figure A.1 Three cases of international comparisons

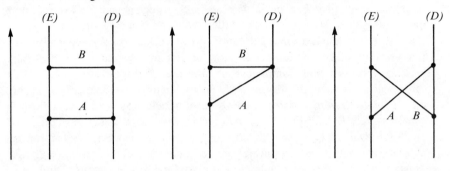

Thus, imagine the concern is with educational growth (*E*) and economic growth (*D*), as two aspects of socioeconomic growth. If country *A* lags behind country *B* on both, this may not lead to any action in *A*: country *B* may simply be seen (by policymakers in *A*) as more "developed." But if they are at the same economic level, and *B* nevertheless is far ahead in education—or worse still, if *B* is below in economic level, yet above in education—then a strong motivation to "catch up" may be the result. The more similar they are, the more will one dissimilarity stand out, and the motivation may be acute. Correspondingly, if *A* compares itself diachronically with itself and finds economic progress but no growth in education—educational rates may even have fallen—in that case a very strong motivation for "restoring the balance" may ensue.[15]

The three situations can be pictured as in figure A.1, regardless of whether the comparison candidate *B* is another country or the country itself at some other period in history. Such precise comparisons can be made only if an operationalization exists, otherwise they will become mere intuitive guesses, more or less educated. And for the comparisons to be made there must be some comparison market in which *A* and *B* meet. For *A* ≠ *B*, the international system is that market, particularly the international organizations. For *A* = *B*, history is the market; the intranational system equipped with memory.

[4] Not only the relative values of indicators but also their *absolute* value may often stimulate, even impel, actors into practice. Low GNP per capita, as an indicator of poverty, has long served as a signal that gets bureaucracies (i.e., highly institutionalized actors) moving into action, and so do indicators of ecological imbalance. Why should not the same happen in connection with indicators of much more complex goal dimensions, such as personal growth, diversity, equality, justice, equity, autonomy, solidarity and participation? Why should not minimum levels of tolerance be established? Again, the elaboration of such indicators and minimum levels is obviously more of a necessary than a sufficient condition for action, but that should not serve as an excuse to postpone this significant task.

[5] There is the need for operationalization as a tool for exploring empirical relations and for theory formation, with a view to *critical and constructivist analysis*. Even operationalization that does not yield more than weak levels of

measurement (such as nominal and ordinal levels) can be used as an empirical basis for theoretical work. As typical examples, the two types of analysis already briefly touched upon may serve: bivariate synchronic analysis (BSA) and bivariate diachronic analysis (BDA).[16] In the former there are two dimensions, and countries are measured on both at the *same* point in time to see how they *cluster*. In the latter there are also two dimensions, but this time one country is measured on both dimensions at *several* points in time to study its *trajectory*.

Thus, imagine good operationalizations exist for economic growth and for economic equality. By means of BSA one would gain insight into how these variables correlate, whether the tendency is for the rich to be more or less egalitarian than the poor, and so on. By means of BDA one would gain insight into how a country may change through time—is there first growth on one of them and then on the other, or is the growth more "balanced"? Any generalization from a BSA to other points in *time*—claiming invariance to a finding with no understanding of context and historical factors—and any generalization from a BDA to other societies, other points in *space,* must remain conjecture. Multivariate rather than bivariate analysis will not make generalization less conjectural.[17] Of the many ways of gaining insight, none is perfect, but these two methods seem to be among the fundamental ones, and some level of operationalization is a necessary condition for doing any empirical work with them at all. Another necessary condition, usually not fulfilled, is that the indicators be linked to each other and not represent separate, completely disparate departures that do not converge empirically, theoretically, or axiologically. Dimensions as well as indicators have to derive from some common bases if they refer to the same basic concern.

It is, then, my contention that the two bases I have chosen—the actor-oriented and the structure-oriented perspectives—do that job for us. In operational terms, the former leads us to distributions and the latter to structures represented by graphs. I shall try to show that even simple aspects of these distributions and graphs can yield sensible operationalizations of very lofty goals.

A.2   OPERATIONALIZATION OF ACTOR-ORIENTED GOALS

The wrong approach would now be to copy slavishly the most consistent family of parameters available from mathematical statistics, the moment-based family comprising arithmetic mean, variance, and product-moment correlation coefficients. These are all based on mathematical operations that make for great mathematical elegance and pay fat dividends in theoretical statistics[18] (e.g., in the theory of statistical testing), but they are not indicative of any practice. No government—or anybody else for that matter—would ever carry out anything corresponding to the operations underlying the calculation of a variance, not to mention the Pearson type of correlation coefficient. No, we must look for more adequate parameters and be systematically critical in our search.

Let us, then, consider operationalization of the values one by one.

A.2.1 PERSONAL GROWTH

There is "outer man," the body, and there is "inner man," the personality, the mind, the soul—and by "personal growth" I refer to both. In the words of Christian Bay, again, the Most Basic Rights are "(1) to stay alive, (2) unmolested and (3) free to develop according to inner propensities and potentialities, in that order." I shall also treat them in that order.

The extent to which a person "stays alive" is measured by means of *life duration,* which clearly is one crucial social indicator. It can be made age- and sex-specific, but it probably serves its purpose quite well as generally calculated. Of particular interest, also, is *infant survival* (the reverse of the usually given negative indicator, infant mortality). Age at death is a basic human concern.

However, in a sense more significant than these indicators of the general state of health are the indicators of factors that prevent people from staying alive. Clearly, these are indicators of *violence.* Violence can be *direct,* as when people are killed; it can be *structural,* as when life expectancy depends heavily on position in the social structure.

The simplest indicator of *direct violence* is probably still *homicide and suicide per capita,* depending on whether the killing is attributed to others or to oneself. The difficulties with these rates are well known, but considerable effort goes into collecting the data and the vast literature indicates their usefulness as indicators.

Indicators of *structural violence* cannot be that simple, for it is not merely a question of counting the number of deaths of a certain type. Of course, there may be special diseases, for example, those caused by pollution or accidents of certain types, for which this approach could be used. But, generally speaking, structural violence is a concept at a higher level of abstraction. The basic idea is that there is such a concept as "premature death." This we know, because we know that with some changes in social structure, in general and health structure in particular, life expectancy can be improved considerably. More particularly, it may be possible to give to the whole population the life expectancy of the class enjoying appropriate health standards, that is, the "upper classes." The level enjoyed by them would be an indicator of the *potential* possibility to "stay alive" in that society; for all but the upper classes that would be above the *actual* possibility to stay alive. The difference, *when avoidable,* is structural violence. What it means is that a person has less possibility of staying alive than he or she would have had if born into a different position in the social structure. The difference, in very concrete terms, is not a lost life but so many lost years of life. If, for instance, in some country whites have a life expectancy of 65 years, blacks 55 years, and Indians 45 years, then twenty years of living, or almost one third of their lives, are taken away from the latter. Clearly, this is under the assumption that all groups will have the same life expectancy when growing up under the same conditions.

To develop indicators of structural violence of this type is of prime importance in order better to realize the magnitude of the problem. To do this the following components are needed:

1. A basic structural variable, such as race or class,
2. Demographic distribution as a function of the variable,
3. Life duration as a function of the structural variable, the *actual* level, and
4. Attainable life duration under the assumption of egalitarian social structure and health structure, the *potential* level.

Of these components the first and the fourth are "subjective." The second and the third are given once the first component has been defined. Clearly, it has to be defined in a meaningful, commonsense manner—as indicated—and may not easily be comparable from one society to another. Comparisons over time within the same society may, however, be more meaningful, as our basic concern would be with how societies change and transform. As for the fourth component, one could operate under a number of assumptions.

In any case the typical model of potential level would be "flat," that life expectancy does not vary with position in the structure. But *which* flat level is another matter. The average for the "upper classes" will depend on how those classes are defined and also on how attainable a general distribution of their life chances appear to be. This need not worry us, however, for structural violence can be estimated relative to a general life duration of 65 years, 70 years, 75 years, and so on. What matters is the departure of the actual life duration from any potential line and how that departure is weighed by the population distribution.

In general it might be useful, as I have indicated, to have the amount of structural violence converted into *lost lives,* not only into *lost years alive* as in the preceding example. It is important to bring out clearly the truth in the saying that "war in the Third World is called poverty," and the fact that this form of war is not unknown in many rich countries.

Let us then move from "stay alive" and *mortality* considerations to "unmolested," which should lead us to *morbidity* considerations. A person can stay alive but be heavily molested by psychic and somatic diseases. One way of bringing this in would be a traditional way, by means of *morbidity rates* of various kinds. The difficulty is to find indicators that do not simply reflect the level of health service in the country, and for that reason these indicators are probably only meaningful for more developed countries. The structural approach taken to mortality may also be applied to morbidity, using morbidity rates instead of life duration in the calculation. Accidents in the home, at work, or in traffic may also be analyzed in this perspective to get at the structural component and not only the actor-oriented aspect, although the unit to which the accident applies would still be the individual human being.

If we then move on to "free to develop according to inner propensities and potentialities" there is, of course, a morbidity area located between outer and inner man: *mental illness.* Rates for this area are among the most problematic but are equally indispensable. The consumption of alcohol and drugs, to the extent that it impedes personal growth and does not serve to facilitate it under certain conditions, should also be included, particularly since there are such concepts as "alcoholics" and "drug addicts," meaning people rendered unable to function properly by (almost) any standard.

So far all I have said deals with the factors impending personal growth, from the most obvious, death, through types of somatic and psychic diseases. What about the positive approach, to somatic as well as mental health? Centuries of research in the field do not seem to have led to much of a tradition in this field. This may be a positive note, for very specific norms as to what constitutes positive somatic and mental health would easily run against norms of diversity, as they might lead to a uniform quest to live up to the standards. Still, there is one approach that, albeit more structure-oriented than actor-oriented, should be mentioned. It touches on "inner man" in a very special way, but it is meaningful if personal growth is seen as the opposite not only of personal extinction, somatic death, but also as the opposite of "alienation," as in the general theory.

In starting with the "inner man" we start then in a sense with the most difficult value, for it is extremely difficult to conceptualize, let alone to operationalize. It relates to the individual, yet should be comparable across individuals so that an average can be calculated for the collectivity as a whole. To many this may sound cynical, even abusive, a travesty on the concept of personal growth. So let me try to indicate how the search for operationalization may also have the opposite implication.

Looking at four terms frequently used to give some connotation to what is meant by "personal growth,"

> self-realization (connotation of fixed potential)
> self-individuation (connotation of Western individualism)
> self-expansion
> self-actuation

I believe that only the last pair yields a basis for operationalization. Moreover, one key was found to be located between the actor-oriented and the structure-oriented perspectives, in the so-called allocation process.[19] In short, are human beings made to fit into predetermined positions, in which case they have to be substitutable, replaceable; or are positions something to be built around irreplaceable people? Can people outgrow structure?

Two approaches are now available for the operationalization of substitutability, one in *extension* and one in *intension*.

The extensional approach is the easier one: simply find for each individual in a collectivity how many could substitute for him in his *work* relative to the total (work) population. Most persons are insubstitutable within the family (otherwise we would not call it a family) and often also in many other settings (among friends, in associations). But we focus on the most fundamental setting: the economically productive status. In some positions very many could substitute, in others very few—even down to none if the person has overpowered the position completely. That lower limit is *insubstitutability,* and that is the precise version of the goal to be pursued, "personal growth," according to this perspective. *The average along the substitutability dimension would be the social indicator we are looking for.* But I repeat that it is not very meaningful unless a dispersion measure is given. A high average may conceal a high level of alienation at the bottom.[20]

Then there is the intensional approach, looking for the *number of characteristics* a person has to satisfy to fill a status, rather than for the *number of people* who can be used to fill it. The more characteristics, in general, the lower the substitutability. The difficulty with this approach is that there is no upper limit defining insubstitutability, which is our positive value. Besides, as it is both easier and more meaningful to count people than to count "characteristics," I would generally opt in favor of the former.

A.2.2 DIVERSITY

This dimension is also problematic, although perhaps less so than the preceding one. Basically, diversity has to do with *structural and cultural variation* found within a society. Leaving aside the cultural aspect, diversity has to do with the number of structural types found as an answer to a functional problem and with the freedom of choice between them. As an example, take marriage. From one point of view we can distinguish four types: the monogamous, the two polygamous types (polyandric and polygynic), and group marriage. From another angle one may distinguish three types: the heterosexual and the two homosexual types. Combining these two typologies we would arrive at a maximum of twelve types. Or, take educational systems. In principle we might distinguish three types, using Margaret Mead's typology;[21] post-, con-, or prefigurative, depending on whether the flow of knowledge and insight is predominantly old-to-young, young-to-young, or young-to-old. Should we now simply count the number of different types and let that be the measure of diversity for that dimension? In that case, who is to decide whether the types are sufficiently different to be counted? And how do we know that there is "freedom of choice"?

The only way of deciding and knowing is to leave this to the *members of the collectivity* themselves. If, in fact, they choose different types, then that proves that free choice exists. In that case one measure of diversity would be the measure of information taken from information theory:

$$- \sum_{i=1}^{i=N} p_i \log_2 p_i$$

where p_i is the proportion choosing type i. In addition there should be some measure of the degree of freedom for ideas and people to move so that the choice is based on information and selection and is not something frozen into society by birth.[22] However this is, diversity would be minimum, *zero,* if all members have concentrated on one type. In that case the other types would only be a theoretical *potential,* defined and expressed in the culture, not part of empirical reality. It is the latter diversity this measure reflects: the diversity that exists and therefore may enrich people in that society, not the diversity that *may* exist. Correspondingly, diversity would be maximum, *unity,* if all p_i were equal, if the population were evenly divided between the types. In that case there would be maximum variation, minimum order, and uniformity. Thus, there is more diversity with a population evenly split between *two* types than in a society where the population is unevenly split among *ten* types. Whether this is reasonable is debatable; the whole measure is problematic.

The measure has the advantage of drawing our attention to an important circumstance. *No dictatorship is needed for the measure to attain minimum value: social uniformity can also be obtained through the mechanisms of democracy.* A compromise among several potential types, leading to the elimination of all but one type, is still *structural uniformity,* however much it takes place in a setting granting the freedom to express *cultural diversity,*[23] also after the compromise has been arrived at by majority vote.

A simpler measure would be based on the highest proportion, p_{max}, which obviously can vary between 1 (uniformity) and $1/N$ (even distribution, maximum diversity). The measure would be $(p_{max} - 1/N) / (1 - 1/N)$.[24] Like the other, it measures the dispersion of *actors* on *structural* types.

A.2.3 SOCIOECONOMIC GROWTH

Because this is the dimension that has dominated, practically speaking, all operationalization of "development," there is a very rich tradition to draw upon. I have chosen not to criticize or to modify that tradition but to incorporate it into the much wider framework of ten dimensions. The measures are incomplete rather than incorrect. If there is a value somehow available to the members of a collectivity, then it does make sense to divide the amount of that value by the number of members to get some impression as to how much is essentially available, on the average, to the individual member. In other words, I recommend *arithmetic means*—of which *percentages* or *rates* are special cases—as a basic parameter only if at the same time the bottom level is considered. And one way of doing that is to use as indicator the percentage above ("not below") a minimum.

One distinction often blurred by all these averages, however, is that between *distributive* and *nondistributive* (collective) values: values that in a concrete sense can belong to an individual (like literacy) and values that belong to the collectivity (like a well). To apply per capita measures to nondistributive values is an individualization to fit a certain social cosmology, where everything is distributed. It shades into the ridiculous when the number of kilometers of paved roads is divided by the size of the population. A supply of nondistributive value must be seen relative to demand, and demand should at least be expressed in terms of real consumers. The number of churches should be evaluated relative to the number of church seekers, production facilities for wigs relative to the incidence of baldness, and so on. To do this, more refined statistics will have to be made available, producing other denominators for these rates than the total population.

In my own research[25] I have found the following indicators of socioeconomic growth particularly valuable:

I. *Satisfaction of fundamental needs* = material personal growth

   1. Food

      F_1 = Percentage with calorie intake not below age-, sex-, and place-specific minima, and average calorie intake

      F_2 = Percentage with protein intake not below age-, sex-, and place specific minima, and average protein intake

   2. Clothes

      C = Percentage not below place-specific minimum, and average (e.g., cloth per capita)

   3. Shelter

      S = Percentage not below place-specific minimum, and average (e.g., rooms per capita)

   4. Health

      H_1 = Infant survival (i.e., surviving the first year)

      H_2 = Life duration for males, and percentage above minimum

      H_3 = Life duration for females, and percentage above minimum

   5. Education

      E_0 = Percentage of literates in relevant population

      E_1 = Percentage of age group enrolled in primary education

      E_2 = Percentage of age group enrolled in secondary education

      E_3 = Percentage of age group enrolled in tertiary education

      E_4 = Percentage of age group in post-tertiary training

II. *Economic growth*

   1. "Development"

      D_1 = GNP, GDP, NI

      D_2 = GNP per capita, GDP per capita, NI per capita

   2. Nonprimary growth

      N_1 = Percentage of working population in nonprimary sectors of economic activity

      N_2 = Percentage of economy derived from nonprimary sectors of economic activity

3. Industrialization

I_1 = Industrialization: like N_1, but including only secondary sector

I_2 = Industrialization: like N$_2$, but including only secondary sector

4. Tertiarization

Same indicators for the tertiary sector

III. *Social growth*

1. Urbanization

U_1 = Percentage living in units of more than 20,000

U_2 = Percentage living in units of more than 1,000,000 (metropolitan)

U_3 = Percentage living in units of more than 10,000,000 (megalopolization)

2. Transportation

T_1 = Kilometers of railroad track

T_2 = Passenger kilometers per capita

T_3 = Tonnage kilometers per capita

3. Communication

C_1 = Mail per capita

C_2 = Telephones per capita

Then there are cars and roads, radios and movies, parks, libraries, and so on. There is no limit to this list. And, indeed, there is the very problematic employment situation.[26]

It should be pointed out that for the fundamental needs we have in most cases a double set of indicators: a percentage of people with the need satisfied, and average goal consumption.[27]

In addition to these *growth indicators* there would also be the same number of *rates of growth indicators.* Since social systems are fairly inert, changing slowly relative to the capacity of human perception, there is the tradition of using change per year as a measure of the rate. This also applies to other than socioeconomic growth indicators.

The distinction between "economic growth" and "social growth" is not a very important one. Economists and sociologists working on development problems—not to mention politicians and administrators—would have to use all three types of indicators. The distinction is also too blunt, but I assume that it is more right than wrong.

What one should guard very strongly against, however, is the identification of what is here called "social growth" with *social development.* Thus, I would define "social development" in terms of *all* goals, with the exception of personal growth, combining socioeconomic growth and political growth. I would then see social development as a necessary (and sufficient?) condition for personal growth, much like Plato's just state, supposed to produce just persons. To reduce social development to a question of acreage of parks per inhabitant or of books on shelves in libraries, is to trivialize matters, to attempt to escape from politics into the safety of administrative routines, and even to overconform to an actor-oriented perspective of social affairs.

Equally strongly one should resist the tendency to refer to "economic growth" as *economic development*. There is nothing wrong with the term "development"; but no matter how widespread the usage is, I am firmly against juxtaposing the terms "economic" and development." Economic growth is only an aspect of one aspect of development; and it could even be contrasted with development, as has so often been done. As is well known, there can be economic growth without personal growth (material or nonmaterial), without diversity, without much social growth, without equality, without justice, with exploitation (inequity), with penetration, fragmentation, and marginalization—in short, there can be socioeconomic growth without development.[28]

Finally, what is here called "social growth" is often referred to as "modernization." Societies can become modern without becoming rich, and vice versa. But it should *not* be referred to as "Westernization"—that term should be reserved for much deeper-lying aspects of social organization and be contrasted with, for instance, "Japanization" as a completely different way of becoming rich and modern.[29]

A.2.4 EQUALITY

Obviously, the approach to indicators of equality would now be to develop *dispersion parameters,* with zero or low dispersion meaning equality and high dispersion meaning inequality. For *distributed,* "private" goods this is relatively unproblematic as soon as the dispersion parameter has been chosen: the dispersion parameter will then measure the extent to which it has really been distributed. For *nondistributed,* "public" goods, it should be defined in terms of *access to* (schools, hospitals, movie theaters) rather than in terms of *possession of* (education, longevity, TV sets). Sometimes this would be measured in terms of *distance,* which in turn is a composite of kilometers, time, money, and other types of cost needed to have access.[30]

When it comes to parameters, one should beware the use of measures of standard deviation and variance, partly because they do not reflect empirical operations but only manipulation with numbers and partly because too much weight is given to extreme cases. The Gini coefficient[31] is somewhat better. In the future more parameters of equality and inequality will definitely be developed, so let me here and now mention some general desiderata.

First, they should be a measure of the discrepancy between a potential reality of equality and an empirical reality of (varying degrees of) inequality.

Second, the model of equality should be in operational terms.

Thus, one model of equality when it comes to land reform is in terms of soil acreage (taking quality into account)—*equality simply meaning ownership of equal size.* Another model is in terms of power to decide over the use of land—*equality meaning equal sharing of decision making.* In the first case acreage is distributed, in the second case not. Inequality can be defined by looking at the distribution of the size of the farms, for instance, with the top 10 percent of landowners controlling 50 percent of the land, the next 10 percent controlling 30 percent and the last 80 percent controlling 20 percent. Or it can be defined in terms of power in decision making over the use of the total amount of land available for tilling, probably leading to much more extreme types of inequality. For the *latifundista* not only controls his own sizable part of land; he also—directly and indirectly—controls the *minifundistas,* making their share of total acreage an upper limit for their share of control.

What the Gini index does is to measure the area between the two Lorenz curves of equality and inequality. The example is chosen to show how the parameter measures a form, the concrete content of which depends on how the variable is defined. The goal of equality would lead to two very different types of land reform, depending on which variable is chosen, soil or power. In the first case, one would get the classic reform of land taken from the rich and given to the poor, decreasing the discrepancy between the curves of potential and empirical reality in land distribution. In the second case, one would get the modern type of land reform, with not land but power over land being distributed, retaining the dimensions of the latifundia, even expanding them. Under the first condition, the goal would be to make each farmer a self-sufficient, autonomous owner of his own land (he who tills the land shall also own it); under the second condition, the goal might be large-scale industrial farming with each worker having an equal share in the decision making under one of the many schemes of industrial democracy (he who tills the land shall also decide over it). Obviously, a transfer of power to a central bureaucracy would lead to neither the first nor the second solution.

In conclusion, another approach to equality should be mentioned, since it is humanly more important than reduction of the Gini index. I am thinking of a systematic focus on the most deprived, on the part of the population registered below the minimum on the indicators of fundamental human needs. In this approach economic development would be the extent to which fundamental needs (food, clothes, shelter, education, and health) are satisfied over and above the minima. Instead of averages that conceal the dispersion *and instead of dispersions that conceal the absolute state of affairs,* it is the proportion above the minimum level that counts as development. The indicators are given in subsection A.2.3, for socioeconomic growth; conceptually they are measures of level as well as of dispersion.[32]

Essentially this is a human-rights approach, an effort to measure the extent to which fundamental development ideas and ideals have been implemented in the society *as a whole,* by focusing at the lower end of the distribution. A shortcoming of the approach is its failure to take into account the upper part of the distribution. Thus, the question may be raised whether equality is possible in a society where all are literate, but without any upper limit to education attained; or in a society where all are adequately fed, clad, and sheltered, but with no upper limit on the consumption of such goods. For this aspect more general dispersion measures are needed, as already mentioned, reflecting more of the distribution. One approach would be to use the percentage above a maximum on consumption; another would be to measure the distance (in calorie consumption, life duration, income—whatever) between the top a percent and the bottom b percent ($a = b = 25$, or $a = 5$ and $b = 50$, would be a good example).

A.2.5 SOCIAL JUSTICE

The approach to indicators of justice would be to develop *covariation parameters,* in order to study the extent to which "being" can be said to relate to "having." A low or zero value would mean social justice, a high value would mean injustice. If there is total equality—zero dispersion of "having"—then there cannot be any injustice, for there is no dispersion to be unjust with. But if there is a nonzero dispersion along the "having" variable, then it is highly meaningful to ask whether it is due to covariation with the "being" variable or is independent of the "being" variable. The latter is also a possibility, as there can be inequality without any injustice. People may be rich or poor for reasons unrelated to, for example, their skin color. Hence, there is no doubt that social justice defined this way is a problem of covariation and that it is logically distinct from equality.

The traditional approach to covariation takes as its point of departure the central tendency of one variable for each value of the other variable, that is, the *regression curve.* In our formulation this would generally be the average of "having" for each value of "being." The simplest correlation measure possible would be some measure of the variation between the averages. If there are only two values of "being" (male–female, white–colored), the best measure would be the *percentage difference,* provided the averages are measured as percentages. Another measure would be the *generalized percentage difference* when there are more than two values,[33] or the steepness of the regression line fitted to the regression curve, that is, the *regression coefficient.*

These are not correlation coefficients in the traditional sense, but correlation coefficients do not measure exactly what we are interested in. To the extent they are based on variance, they are poor measures of inequality for the reasons given, although they do account for dispersion of "having" in terms of the variation in "being." Justice is not primarily a question of equality, but a question of whether one group is, on the average, better off than another group, which is reflected quite well in the difference-between-averages approach I have advocated. When the difference is zero there is justice, according to this operationalization. When the difference is considerable there is injustice; and when the injustice is institutionalized there is discrimination. A negative difference or correlation, so-called compensatory justice, is only another form of injustice, however instrumental.[34]

It may be objected that this measure is too crude. It may be said that it is only the *first* approximation to justice and that in the *second* approximation one should also require the two dispersions to be equal (in other words, "homoscedasticity"). Imagine the comparison is between two racial groups and that the formerly underdog group has gained independence and has secured for a small minority of its members a very high level of having, so high that it has raised its group average up to the level of the formerly dominant group, leaving the vast majority of that group way behind. Is this justice? In the sense of the operationalization, yes, but considering it also leads us immediately to the idea that as a next step one might require equality between dispersions, as a third and fourth step equality between the skewness and "kurtosis" parameters, and so on until, ultimately, the two distributions have become equal.[35] But the latter is a very strong requirement, possibly even unnecessarily strong.

This general statistical approach has the merit of measuring *degrees* of justice and injustice. It does not rest content with a declaration that "there is justice" or "there is injustice" in the collectivity. On the other hand, too much emphasis on degree, on quantity, may lead the attention away from differences in quality. Thus, underlying this statistical approach is the implicit assumption that some individuals low on "being" may be rich on "having" and vice versa; that the correlation between the two is not perfect, not a "law."[36] In other words, there is some sort of assumption about upward and downward mobility, allowing for drifting up and down. There is of course an implicit operationalization of *total social injustice,* as in the condition of total separation in two clusters, which may or may not be reflected in a maximum value of the covariation parameter. *But this condition is often the most important one, because it is the condition that really defines a society with first-class and second-class citizenship, particularly when the separation is protected by concrete legal rules and institutions.* The indicator introduced is a way of detecting this type of condition and also a way of measuring departures from it toward less unjust conditions. But it does not catch how strongly injustice is protected.

As a special case under social justice comes *equality of opportunity,* to many a cornerstone of democracy.[37] I would operationalize it as any other case of social justice, using as "having" dimensions *"having access to nondistributive value,"* and as "being" dimensions family background and geographical location. Whether equality of opportunity in fact leads to social justice in the broader sense—to justice in terms of occupations, for example—is another matter that can be explored empirically precisely by means of these statistical tools.

This is where, in general, the justice approach is more satisfactory than the equality approach. Under the heading of equality all one can do is measure its degree of presence or absence. *The measures of inequality are nonstructural;* they do not relate inequality to anything. Under justice, "having" is systematically related to any dimension of "being," singly or in combination, to find out which underlying dimensions account for how much of the inequality encountered. This is basic; and empirical exploration in such terms should be encouraged to map the inequality and injustice, as long as this is not confused with tracing its institutional and structural causes. The empirical operationalizations chosen are of such a kind that the whole variety of multivariate analysis techniques (MVA) would be at our disposal, thus following one of the guidelines mentioned in subsection A.2.2.

One final advantage of social justice in terms of averages rather than dispersions is that averages are much more easy to come by, both for bureaucracies and for those trying to get information from bureaucracies. One should therefore require that statistics on "having" be systematically broken down on categories of "being," that income, education, and health statistics, for example, be given separately for different districts, for the two sexes, for different occupations, different races, or ethnical groups, and so on. In this way statistics on social justice versus injustice would also give us information on the level of equality versus inequality in the society studied. In short: *disaggregation* is required.[38]

A.3   OPERATIONALIZATION OF STRUCTURE-ORIENTED GOALS

When it comes to operationalizing these goals there is less of a tradition available to guide us. Characteristically, social science is better at parametrizing distributions than structures. The measurement of society has been based on arithmetic rather than on geometry, because it has been based on the actor-oriented rather than the structure-oriented perspective. But that does not mean that the situation is impossible. Several of the values mentioned are relatively easily operationalized, using the theory of graphs, converting into arithmetical terms, or even into statistical distributions the properties of geometrical structures. *The point is merely that the distribution will have to reflect a structure, not only properties of individual or collective actors.* For instance, take "equity," or the negation of exploitation: some kind of balance parameter is needed here that can never be defined in terms of one actor alone. At the very least a bilateral interaction relation is needed.

A.3.1   EQUITY

Conceptually the dimension of equity is not too problematic, but to narrow the richness of the concept down to something that can be operationalized looks difficult at present. Our point of departure would be the total cost–benefit budget when A and B are related to each other in an interaction relation.[39] The case of A and B as countries is easiest to handle, as in table A.1.

What is needed is a focus on what takes place *between* as well as *within* the actors; a focus on *benefits* that accrue to them, as well as on their *costs*. For

Table A.1   The interaction budget: An example

	A		B	
	Cost	Benefit	Cost	Benefit
Inter-actor effects	regular terms of trade analysis			
Intra-actor effects	pollution	spin-offs	depletion	little or none

each actor the net benefit would then be calculated (it might well be negative, for one or even for both of them, as in a war), and the two net benefits would then be compared (in a war it may be true that all parties lose; but war is about who loses least). The more nearly equal they are, the more equitable the interaction relation. The average of the difference between the net benefits, for all bilateral interaction relations, would be a measure for a *set* of interaction relations, that is, for a structure. This is the measure we are looking for.

Take the example of interaction between two countries exchanging raw materials for processed goods, as in table A.1. Imagine that the exchange takes place at "market value"—both countries agree that what crosses the borders in either direction has the same value. The basis for evaluating *equity* (not terms of trade) is, however, broader: the intra-actor effects are included, and they can be positive (benefits) as well as negative (costs). For the industrialized countries the positive effects are the "spin-off" effects from processing, and the negative effects are usually summarized under the heading "pollution." For the nonindustrialized country the positive effects may perhaps be in terms of learning, but these are usually small, whereas the negative effects are considerable, in terms of depletion, erosion, and so on. Extraction is easily status-quo-preserving for structure.

One approach to operationalizing all of this would be in terms of *replacement value*,[40] asking for each *intra*-actor benefit, "How much would we have to pay to obtain this without *inter*-action?"; and for *intra*-actor damage, "How much would we have to pay to undo this damage?" The difficulty with these measures lies in the circular reasoning they may lead to: market prices are somehow accepted as basis for measurements, and these prices are themselves expressions of an inequitable structure. However, as a first approximation such calculations may be useful and should be carried out.

As another example, take the interaction between worker and manager, with the former selling manpower for salary, but performing highly routinized work because his position is high on substitutability. For the worker the job is personality-contracting, for the manager it may be personality-expanding. These factors are more difficult to monetize, but it does make sense to ask how much the director would have had to pay for similar experience and challenge, or the worker needed to compensate for the psychological (not to mention the physical) losses incurred during long and tedious working hours. Again, operationalization may be difficult, but not impossible, and it would be clearly practice-indicative in either case.

All that has been said so far gives at best only an operationalization of equity in economic interaction. But the example of the director and the worker points further, and the same basic logic can be used for any type of interaction.[41] The fundamental question would concern intra-actor costs and benefits, not only inter-actor effects of the interaction. The next question, in an effort to operationalize, would concern what it would "cost" to obtain these benefits if the interaction had not taken place or to negate the costs when the interaction did take place. Obviously, these costs cannot all be monetized.

To return to the example involving two countries trading with each other: *degree of processing* is a fundamental variable here, since processing entails positive and negative spin-off effects. If we now assume that degree of processing is important, then a simple measure of division of labor can be developed, although it is far from unproblematic. Let us refer to "degree of processing" as D; assume it varies from 0 (pure extraction) to 1 (total form); and study export, E, and import, I, as functions of D. Thus, $E(D)$ would give us for a country the value of the export for each level of degree of processing, and similarly for $I(D)$. The quantity

$$\int_0^1 E(D)\,dD - \int_0^1 I(D)\,dD$$

is simply the trade balance and says nothing interesting. But if we split the integrals, for instance as follows:

$$D(D = 0), \quad \int_{>0}^1 E(D)\,dD$$

$$I(D = 0), \quad \int_{>0}^1 I(D)\,dD$$

they may become much more meaningful, as they now give the value of raw material export and import and the value of processed goods export and import.

Let us symbolize these values as follows:

	Raw Materials	Processed goods
Export	b	d
Import	a	c

Some countries tend to trade along the main diagonal, some countries along the bi-diagonal in this matrix; and some countries have no such set configuration.

Obviously, $(a + d)$ measures the extent to which the country is a processing country, $(b + c)$ the extent to which it is an extracting country. The measure[42]

$$TCI = \frac{(a + d) - (b + c)}{(a + b) - (c + d)},$$

the *trade composition index*, is a measure of where on the axis from -1 (pure extracting country) to $+1$ (pure processing country) the country is located. The measure is admittedly crude because it allows only a simple dichotomy along the D axis; however, it meaningfully distributes the countries on a major axis of world trade politics. In fact, the traditional Yule's Q correlation coefficient, treating the distribution of the total trade as if it were a frequency table (and in a sense it is, counting monetary units):

$$Q = \frac{ad - bc}{ad + bc}$$

gives a better dispersion. In either case Japan comes out on top, and then follow the Western industrialized countries. At the bottom we find a heavy cluster of "developing" countries.

This measure, in additive as well as multiplicative form, gives the position of a given country in today's *world vertical division of labor*. A better measure would actually be a generalization, such as the difference between the averages of the export and import distributions:

$$TCI^* = \tfrac{1}{2} \left[\int_0^1 DE(D)dD \ - \ \int_0^1 DI(D)dD \right]$$

which also ranges from 1 to -1. If a two-point distribution is assumed for $E(D)$ and $I(D)$, TCI^* reduces to the measure TCI. Such a two-point distribution can be defined by using the SITC code, referring to 0–4 as raw materials and 5–8 as processed goods, roughly speaking.

Both measures could now be calculated on the basis of world trade, regional trade, or dyads, that is, pairs of countries. Obviously, if the trade between two countries is considered, the algebraic values for the two countries will be equal, because what is export for one is import for the other. But whatever the basis, the distance between them, and the generalized distance (the average of the absolute distances for all pairs), or any other measure of dispersion along the TCI axis would be a measure of the "total degree of division of labor." I do not say "total degree of inequity," or "exploitation," because the relation between division of labor and exploitation/inequity, as indicated before, is a complex one, and these are obviously measures of division of labor.

The complexity hinges on the definition of "degree of processing," D itself. We define D as the degree of imprint of culture on nature, *culture being defined as pure nonmaterial form* (like a piece of mathematics, a symphony) and nature being defined as very close to minimum processing. Form is matter reduced almost to zero, form being the essence of the "product."

How, then, does one define degree of processing, given these considerations? Here are four attempts:

1. *On the basis of capital,*[43] relating the price of the processed product to the price of the raw materials that went into producing it. The difficulty is that any such measure builds into the analysis the structure of the market with all its political implications.[44]

2. *On the basis of labor,*[45] relating the work that went into the processed product to the work that went into the raw materials. The difficulty is that any such measure depends heavily on fluctuations in technology, on how easily available the raw materials are, and so on.

3. *On the basis of protection,*[46] studying the amount of protection of various types (tariff barriers, nontariff barriers) given to products at various levels of processing. Typically, the tariffs for raw materials are zero, for semiprocessed goods 5 to 10 percent, for more processed goods 10 to 20 percent and so on.[47] Nontariff barriers may be more difficult to estimate in precise terms, but hardly impossible, looking at the empirical effect of quotas, all kinds of standards, and the like. If one considered only tariff barriers (now yielding to these nontariff barriers), the assumption would be that those who have decided on the tariffs knew what they did, that if the duties levied on two products are 10 percent and 15 percent respectively, then the degrees of processing relate to each other in the ratio 2:3. The problem is, however, that these barriers change in space and time even when degree of processing cannot otherwise be said to change and that they reflect the relative power and countries and groups within countries.

4. *On the basis of information theory.*[48] If processing is giving form to nature, then it should be possible to develop a measure of the degree of form, using the information-theory notion of the number of dichotomous choices that went into producing that particular product, given the raw material. In a sense this would be the ideal measure, but it is not easily available.

There is also a fifth approach: to try to relate the degree of processing to the spin-off effects, simply stating that the effects are proportionate to the degree of processing. However, this leads to the difficulty that any proposition about a relation between degree of processing and spin-off would be a tautology, although a very simple one, not the highly complex semicircular relations the first three measures just given would lead to. Hence, there seems to be no way out except to try to develop a measure similar to the fourth and described here.

A.3.2   AUTONOMY

Autonomy is for the power aspect of the interaction relation what equity is for the exchange aspect, which means that the two are closely related.

Autonomy is power-over-oneself so as to withstand what others have of power-over-others. If we distinguish among ideological, remunerative, and punitive power and assume that these work only under the condition of a certain submissiveness, dependency, and fear, and that the antidotes are *self-respect, self-sufficiency,* and *fearlessness,* respectively, then these "antidotes" form the three components of autonomy as I see it.

The first component, *self-respect,* has to do with value production, which in turn is a part of cultural production. The problem is the extent to which this production is indigenous and not based mainly on cultural import. When the Chinese alleged that the "social imperialism" of the Soviet Union was a threat to their autonomy, what they expressed was the strong feeling that explicit and implicit goals were impressed upon them (e.g., Model II society, as opposed to Model III society). The same can perhaps be said about Eastern Europe today, where essentially Western European goals are pursued, only at a higher level of state ownership.

Does that mean that *cultural diversity* is an indicator of identity? No; that one culture, including the goals, is similar to other cultures is no proof of submissiveness. It could also be the result of genuine discussion and a conscious decision to accept those goals. Further, diversity in the form of acceptance of old culture, of ancient indigenous culture as an alternative to cultural pressure from the outside, is no proof of autonomy: it may just mean submissiveness to earlier generations rather than submissiveness to other, contemporary cultures. Cultural colonization can take place in time as well as in space.[49]

Hence, one indicator would probably have to be the extent to which present *cultural production* is carried out elsewhere, in the form of import of books (relative to local production), of foreign authors (relative to local), of foreign import in school and university curricula (relative to locally produced curricula), and the like. This is not totally satisfactory, but it is certainly a better indicator than cultural diversity.

As to the second component, *self-sufficiency,* there is an old tradition: the proportion of the GNP (or some similar indicator) that is not trade-dependent. Thus, the present superpowers—the United States, the Soviet Union, China—are on the top of this list, which is undoubtedly related to their autonomy. The measure can be used as long as one remembers that it is overly quantitative and does not take into account that the country may depend qualitatively on few imported items, such as oil. On the other hand, if these items are cut out (during a war, for instance) the country may show great power of endurance, of improvisation, of mobilizing untapped resources, and the items may prove to be less important than originally considered. Hence, it is really only after a crisis, an *experimentum crucis,* that the degree of self-sufficiency can be known, since one crucial factor is the population's ability to accept a decrease in its living standard, in addition to imaginative improvisation.

As to the third component, *fearlessness,* we would again have to proceed in a roundabout fashion to measure the level of *invulnerability,* which would be the objective counterpart of fear. In one sense, a "traditional" society and a "modern" society relate to each other as do primitive and more advanced organisms. A traditional society would typically consist of many parts such as villages, themselves largely self-sufficient. The modern society has a center and periphery, and the two are highly interconnected so that the periphery will have greater difficulty surviving without the center. Destruction of a part of a traditional society, in war or in a natural catastrophe, may lead to spontaneous regeneration (as in a "primitive" organism) because each part is like the others, and the others can continue more or less as before.[50] The destruction of the center of modern society may lead to total social destruction because of the high level of *interconnectedness, division of labor,* and *centralization.* For that reason "modern" society will try to protect itself by making its center less vulnerable to attack. In so doing, it would have to account for the three factors just mentioned, to bring about a more decentralized society in which the various districts are less interconnected (so that destruction of one does not destroy the rest) and require less division of labor. The less vulnerable society may be more like the traditional society—and modern society may be an aberration because of its vulnerability, which is so high that modern arms races are seen as the only defense in spite of the tremendous risks at that vulnerability level.

The operationalization of invulnerability,[51] the objective aspect of fearlessness, would analyze the degree of centralization, interconnectedness, and division of labor. It should be possible to express this as a one-dimensional indicator, derived by means of panels of well-instructed judges asked to rate societies on, for instance, a five-point scale ranging between these two extremes.

A.3.3 SOLIDARITY

Solidarity as here conceived of is considerably easier to operationalize. Again, all that can be hoped for in the first run is to operationalize the objective aspect, not the subjective feelings of solidarity. The concept concerns the interaction *pattern,* not the actor attitudes, and only the *bilateral* relations, not the multilateral relations.

"Solidarity" is defined as the degree of togetherness *at the bottom* of the social structure. In order to talk about solidarity one first has to know the division of labor: who exploits and who are exploited, who are on top, who at the bottom. Togetherness at the top is seen as one aspect of structural power, another aspect being fragmentation at the bottom. Hence, solidarity is the extent to which there is no difference in togetherness at the top and at the bottom. It is not enough to say that bilateral interaction at the bottom exists; it has to be commensurate with the corresponding indicators at the top. If it is, if workers associate as much as directors, and poor countries as much as rich countries, then solidarity has been realized; there is a certain balance in the structure. There has been a transition from a feudal structure to a class structure, not only with class consciousness (which would be the subjective aspect of solidarity) but also with class mobilization.

One approach to the operationalization of solidarity would be to calculate, for each position in the interaction structure, the so-called *associated number:* the *maximum number of bilateral steps* (i.e., interaction relations) one would have to take from that position to the position furthest away.[52] Another approach would be to calculate the *average number of steps* to all other positions, in order not to give too much weight to long "tails" stretching out to distant positions. Thus, in the simple three-actor structure where one center actor rules over two fragmented periphery actors, the associated number for the center is clearly 1, while for the periphery it is 2. In general, the positions with *minimum* associated number are referred to as the *center* and the positions with *maximum* associated number as the *periphery* of the structure. Correspondingly, for the average number of steps, one would talk of minimum and maximum *ranges* rather than *numbers.*

The next step would then be to look at the distribution of associated numbers or averages. This distribution also has an average that is a crude measure of how far, on the average, one has to go in that structure to reach the position most removed. The lower the average, the more connected the structure and the more direct the relationship; the higher the average, the less connected and the more indirect the relationship. Thus, the magnitude of this average can be related to the problem of indirect or direct democracy.

That distribution also has a dispersion, which is what we are looking for. In this case I would not object too strongly to variance-based measures of the dispersion. However the dispersion is measured, the higher the dispersion, the more asymmetric the structure; and the lower the dispersion, the more symmetric the structure—down to zero, where the structure would be completely symmetric. The value of (bilateral) participation would then be realized. In this case all positions would have the same maximum (or average) distance to other positions, so that they are the same where access to each other is concerned. There is no longer any center or periphery in this sense, hence no longer any fragmentation. Whether that distance is short or long is a matter that depends on how saturated the structure is.

The weakness of this measure is that any interaction relation, weak or strong, is counted equally. The measure is binary; a relation exists or it does not. But there are other operationalizations that would reflect both the structure of interaction and the quantity of interaction. Thus, consider the total export from a country or from a group of countries and study the distribution of the percentages of the export in various directions, p_1, p_2, p_n. From this distribution several measures can easily be derived.

The first measure, *export concentration,*[53] would be based on the ordering of the p_i according to magnitude. The largest p_i, or the sum of the three largest, would be the measure. If it is very high, export is evidently going to only one, or three, countries. It is highly concentrated, which in turn means that the country in question is some kind of appendix to these countries. However, it does not necessarily follow that the country is alone in this: it might be that all countries have very high levels of export concentration. For that reason the distribution of export concentration measures should be studied, and standard scores computed. Another term for this might actually also be "vulnerability," since it is reasonable to assume that the higher the concentration, the more vulnerable the export.

The second measure, the *Eigenhandelsquote*,[54] is based on *adding* trade figures rather than ordering them. Groups of countries are defined, for example, as MDCs and LDCs or by region. The *Eigenhandelsquote* would be the percentage the export inside one's own group comprises of the total export from the countries in the group. It is a measure of the tendency to export to one's own kind. Characteristic of countries at the bottom of the world system is not only that they trade less in total, but also that they trade less among themselves. Whereas export concentration measures the degree of concentration upward, the *Eigenhandelsquote* measures the degree of fragmentation sideward at the bottom. Just as for the export concentration, it is the relative *Eigenhandelsquote* that gives the best image of the level of solidarity or fragmentation.

Similar figures could then be calculated for the import or for the total trade, which would be the sum of the two (or the average). The measures are meaningful not only for goods or other economic entities but also for other types of interaction, such as the movement of people (labor) and information (news).

A.3.4 PARTICIPATION

The interaction structure consists of relations and patterns, and participation is to the multilateral interaction pattern what solidarity is to the bilateral interaction relation. Solidarity connects the periphery and makes for a more symmetric structure; participation brings the marginals into the patterns and makes them more generally participatory. A fragmented structure makes actors into appendices; a marginalized structure cuts them out from multilateral participation. The two concepts are logically independent; although there is often a high correlation between being peripheral and marginal, the concepts relate to different aspects of the total structure.

The simplest way of measuring participation would be to count participation in organizations, even in the form of membership cards. There are two difficulties, however. Organizations are *institutionalized* multilateral interaction. The crowd, the clique, the network may be much more important as ways to counteract marginality, which means that the type of data collected by anthropologists and sociologists would be needed for operationalization. Also, there are many organizations that in their very structure are the exact opposite of what here has been referred to as "development" (because of heavy division of labor), which means that participation as here defined is only a limited segment of the total process. It is nevertheless included as a separate dimension, particularly since the distribution of the number of memberships in an organization is usually extremely biased. Integration at the top of society is a question not only of more bilateral interaction but also of more memberships—to the point where society may become a real dichotomy between a saturated, participant network on the top and a second-class group of peripherals and marginals.[55]

A.3.5 ECOLOGICAL BALANCE

Finally, some words about the relation to nature, although it is not a "structure-oriented goal." All I can do here is to give some comments from a social-science perspective as to the direction in which I might like to see "ecological balance" operationalized.[56]

"Ecology" refers to something in which man is included; it is a concept not of man *versus* nature or of man *in* nature but of man *and* nature—of human beings as a part of nature. It may be argued that only biological man as part of the biosphere is included, but the concept opens for consideration not only *overpollution* and *overdepletion,* but also of *overpopulation.* Moreover, it considers not only whether nature is adequate for man but also whether man is adequate for himself and for nature—and nature's adequacy for nature.[57]

Further, equilibrium refers not to a stationary state but to a moving balance. Certain variables change, such as all the other nine goal dimensions. Others do not change, or do so only within a limited band. Perhaps the study of ecological balance is the study of the conditions for maintaining a stable equilibrium, that is, a range protected by some reinforcement mechanisms.[58] For a human body to be healthy where temperature, blood pH, or blood sugar are concerned is not to maintain constant values but to have control mechanisms that keep the values within a certain range; the same is true for ecological indicators.

These two comments have some generally recognized implications as to the most common approach to indicators in this field, the *critical value* approach, the *danger signal.*[59] The *Homo mensura* thesis ("man is the measure of all things") must not be interpreted to mean that "critical" means only "critical to man." Enough is known today of the complex cycles in the man–nature system to locate critical values on variables not only from an anthropocentric viewpoint but also from the view of the total ecosystem, of the total ability of the man-and-nature system to reconstitute itself.

Deeper insight should also lead to insight into deeper-lying variables. Instead of a bundle of pollution/depletion/population variables on which critical limits may be fixed on the basis of how they are related to each other rather than on a one-variable-at-a-time basis, it is necessary to identify and operationalize some variables that come closer to the reconstitution mechanisms themselves. Of the goals previously discussed, "equity" may be said to be a variable of that kind, one that brings much in its wake once it has been conceptualized and to some extent operationalized. Similar variables are needed for ecosystems.

Thus, it would be hoped that the immense research effort in this field will also soon lead to theory-based indicators that reflect a more complex view of

man-and-nature and at the same time are intuitively reasonable and comprehensive. But we are not there yet.

A.4 TOWARD WORLD SOCIAL INDICATORS

Let us now return to the four levels of discourse introduced in section
A.1, to the image of the world as consisting of nature, individuals, and collectivities, with the latter divided into territorial and nonterritorial. The good world is
the world offering the good life to us human beings in our setting; it is not an
abstraction fulfilling some formula. Only at the level of the individual can social
goals be validated. A rich society is not a higher form of social life than a poor
one, nor is a socialist society higher than a capitalist one, unless life is somehow
better for *people*. That does not mean that the good life can only be conceived
of at the level of the individual. Equity is a part of the good life as here defined.
It is an autotelic goal, not a means to obtain something, and it cannot be defined
at the individual level. Nor does our concept mean that efforts to measure how
far a given collectivity has come in providing good quality of life for its citizens
are meaningless—on the contrary, such measurement is even mandatory.

If we now look at the levels defined in section A.1 it is clear that we run
into the "problem of levels" when it comes to conceiving of the good *world*. The
problem appears when one proceeds level by level. Thus, at

Level O   the focus is on *ecological balance;*
Level 1   the focus is on *individual* being (personal growth), *individual*
             having; all the others are meaningless at this level;
Level 2   the focus is on average being and having, on dispersion of being
             and having, on social justice, equity, autonomy, solidarity, parti-
             cipation inside the *collectivity*.

So far there is no problem. Individuals can be viewed in terms of enrichment and
accumulation, what they are and what they have. Collectivities can be viewed as
sums of individual being and having—the latter would also bring in collective
goods—and then there are all the other distribution and structure variables. They
apply to territorial as well as to nonterritorial collectivities, although we are
most accustomed to applying them to the former.

But at the third level we have a choice among three approaches.[60]

First, we can view the world as one big collectivity, with about four billion
inhabitants. In one sense this perspective should be used as often as possible,
since it is the only perspective that clearly sees the human being as the basic
unit. Questions about the world level of fundamental need satisfaction can only
be answered using this perspective which cuts across countries.

Or, we can view the world as a collectivity of collectivities, particularly of
countries. Here there are again two possibilities, depending on the kind of data
used for the countries:

Data derived from the intrasocietal level, where "personal growth" would be average individual personal growth, accumulation would be everything accessible to individuals, equality would be average equality, autonomy average individual autonomy, and so on.

Data derived from the intersocietal level, where "personal growth" would be the "national growth," diversity would be between nations (and not an average of the diversity within nations), equality would be between countries and not an average within them, all the structural variables would be between countries, not average within, and so on.

Actually the first of these two is best served not by calculating sums or averages but simply by the standard procedure of establishing lists, for example, with countries in alphabetical order, giving the social indicators for each country. *But this is not the same as establishing world social indicators;* that purpose is served only by viewing the world as a collectivity (not only a set) of individuals or countries, studying the distributions and structures of this our world, as such. And that is the third approach.

There is no way of combining these three different approaches. They are not mutually reducible, nor is there any reason they should be. They simply express three very different and profound perspectives: the world as a community of persons, the world as a set of countries, the world as a community of countries. All three perspectives are valid, depending on context and purpose.

This concludes my review of indicators. No doubt very much work remains to be done in this field, but it is wrong to assume that the bottleneck lies in the construction of suitable indicators. *The indicators largely exist already; the problem is the willingness to use them.* Out of the total variety of possibilities that I have tried to present here, only some of the indicators of socioeconomic growth, particularly of economic growth, are in widespread use. They are the ones compatible with the actor-oriented view of society, with a capitalistic economy, because they place the most powerful nations high on the indicators, and because they conceal almost completely everything that has to do with politics, that is, with conflicts of goals and interests. Thus, not even simple indicators of how many have fundamental needs satisfied exist today.

For that reason people should demand from all governments statistics that reveal deeper aspects of the societies, particularly those aspects that relate directly to the individual human being, and more particularly to the most deprived—not only to national averages. We should not be fooled into believing that what is often referred to as "social development" or "social indicators" is a substitute for this. More often than not it is merely a subset of the indicators of socioeconomic growth and does not touch personal growth or social structure at all.

Since intergovernmental organizations reflect governmental interests it should not generally be expected that they would take the lead in these matters.[61] On the contrary: it may well be that not only the publication but even the collection of this type of data in a systematic and easily available way would have to be the task of nongovernmental organizations, within and between countries. In this question there is tremendous variation from one country to another and from one organization to another, just as there is from one social scientist to the other. In short, there is much work to be done!

NOTES

References to *Essays* are to Johan Galtung, *Essays in Peace Research*, 5 vols. (Copenhagen: Ejlers, 1975–80) (Atlantic Highlands, N.J.: Humanities Press).

1. It is doubtful whether any major intergovernmental organization, including the UN and all UN specialized agencies and the governments in bigger and richer countries, including many of the specialized ministries, can be found today that does not have some kind of indicators program.

2. In saying so it should also be emphasized that when indicators are developed by bureaucracies, governmental or intergovernmental, there is a tendency to concentrate on means (e.g., enrollment ratios, "schooling") rather than goals (education).

3. Somebody should one day write up the excellent work that must have been done by public relations experts in making this indicator so dominant in the world. There seems to be much to learn!

4. In this way it produces the familiar image of the world today: a small number of countries high on all development indicators, and a vast number of countries low on all or most development indicators. It is high time that indicators are found that can give a more realistic image of the world by introducing other variables.

5. It should be emphasized that for this to happen it is not enough to carry out public opinion polls or informal interviews. These are methods of estimating current public opinion, more or less valid, but no substitute for a real dialogue in society at large about goals. Thus, although the data presented in, for instance, *Images of the World in the Year 2000,* Ornauer, Sicinski, Wiberg, and Galtung, eds. (Mouton, 1974) may be interesting and important, they are only a little step on the road toward some more democratic perspective on indicators.

6. It will be evident that by "political left" is meant something relatively precise: a structure-oriented perspective, as opposed to the actor-oriented perspective more prevalent in the political right and middle.

7. For a theory of units and variables at the various levels, see Galtung, *Theory and Methods of Social Research* (Oslo, London, New York, 1967), part I, chapters 2 and 3.

8. Most important examples have to do with such words as "socialist," "democracy," "developed"—where we now very well know that institutional changes in the sense of collectivization of the means of production with collective planning; free elections in a competitive political system with a presidential or parliamentary democracy; and the introduction of a number of aspects of Western modernization do not necessarily lead to societies in which it is good for people to live.

9. See chapter 3.

10. This is developed as some length in chapter 3.

11. It should be emphasized that this distinction is not so sharp: for instance, *is* a person healthy or does the person *have* health?

12. This is developed in chapter 3. The important thing about work in indicators, however, is that it forces a certain preciseness on the analyst, for good and for bad.

13. Rank disequilibrium is the condition that obtains when *one* actor is high on one dimension and low on the other, for instance well educated but poor.

14. Rank incongruence is the condition that obtains when *two* actors have opposite disequilibrated profiles, so that in addition to the actor mentioned in the preceding note there is also one who is low on education and high on income. For a further development of these concepts, see Galtung, "Rank and Social Integration: A Multi-dimensional Approach," in Berger, Zelditch, Anderson, eds. *Sociological Theories in Progress* (Boston: Houghton Mufflin, 1966); also in *Essays* III, 5.

15. This is developed at some length in Galtung, "On the Relationship between Human Resources and Development: Theory, Methods, Data," in Nancy Baster, ed., *Measuring Development: The Role and Adequacy of Development Indicators* (London: Cass, 1972), pp. 137–54.

16. This is developed in Galtung, *Methodology and Ideology,* (Copenhagen: Ejlers, 1977), chapter 4.

17. See Galtung and Tord Høivik, "Structural and Direct Violence: A Note on Operationalization," *Journal of Peace Research* (1971), pp. 73–76; also in *Essays* I, 5.

18. The only exception that one might like to mention from recent American psychology would be Abraham Maslow, particularly his important book, *Towards a Psychology of Being.*

19. The allocation process is any process whereby people are somehow placed into the various positions in the social structure, whether it is by free choice, by ascribed characteristics, or by achieved characteristics. This is of course a basic aspect of alienation: the lower one is in society, the more substitutable is one. It is mainly at the top of society that one is in a position to create one's own position, so as to be insubstitutable, and thereby in a certain very special sense "immortal."

20. All public opinion studies I know about of work satisfaction and so on tend to show considerable correlation with social position: the lower one is located, the less meaningful and satisfactory most aspects of life. It does not seem to be true, generally speaking, that industrialized societies also have a happy-go-lucky extreme periphery at the bottom.

21. This typology could never have been developed by a Marxist social scientist to whom age categories appear as almost irrelevant. It is characteristic that they stem from a leading anthropologist particularly famous for her studies of the impact of "modern" ideas, artifacts and structures on "traditional" (meaning stable) societies—more or less reversing the entire learning process in society, with parents getting cues from their children as to how to live.

22. The question is of course whether this choice is really free, or manipulated, or even forced upon people. For this reason it should be very strongly emphasized that pluralism is a possibility, an option, not prescribed. It includes the possibility of staying put.

23. This distinction is basic in Galtung "Structural Pluralism and the Future of Human Society," in *Proceedings of the Second International Future Research Conference, Tokyo* (Kodansha, 1971).

24. It can of course be objected that this measure puts too much emphasis on the highest proportion.

25. Thus, in the studies on Japan quoted in note 15, these indicators have been made use of.

26. Thus, it is not even completely clear whether leisure is good or bad. There can be too much of it and too little of it, but what is *quantum satis*?

27. Thus, the ranking position of the United States would differ considerably depending on which indicator one makes use of.

28. Typical examples, so often given, are Liberia, the Republic of Korea, and Iran. Many others could be mentioned, one of them being Brazil.

29. For one effort to formulate the typical aspects of "Japanization," see Galtung, "Social Structure, Education Structure and Life-long Education: The Case of Japan," in *Reviews of National Policies for Education: Japan* (Paris: OECD, 1971), pp. 131–52.

30. To my knowledge nobody has so far worked out a good indicator of this.

31. Thus, in the study *"Educational Growth and Educational Disparity"* by Galtung, Beck, and Jaastad, *Papers,* no. 1, Chair in Conflict and Peace Research, University of Oslo, 1974, indicators like P_{95}-P_{50} and P_{90}-P_{50} were made use of for education, measuring the distance in schooling between the top elite and the bottom masses. Symmetric percentile differences, like the classical P_{75}-P_{25} would not capture social reality so well—although it actually yielded the same general result.

32. Needless to say, this approach to the operationalization of development may put countries high on averages much farther down the list because the approach focuses on what happens at the bottom, not on what happens at the top or to the average. It is also obvious that such indicators will tend to be resented by establishment social scientists from such countries. As once expressed informally in a UNESCO conference on indicators (December 1972): "You see, we are used to an indicator being something that puts the US at the top and Gabon at the bottom."

33. This measure is developed in Galtung, *Theory and Methods of Social Research,* II, 5.

34. The argument is translated into policy in connection with the *harijans* in India, and the experiences gained might be important for similar practices in connection with the fight for increased female participation in politics.

35. By means of such techniques as use of the Gram-Charlier series.

36. Classical Hindu caste societies are usually considered good examples of "law" of this kind: what a person *is* (caste, by birth) determines a very wide range of what he is going to *have*.

37. Historically this will perhaps stand out as a stepping stone in the history of liberalism toward the welfare state: from the conservative idea of an essentially frozen society determined by birth via the social Darwinism of survival of the fittest to a gradually more tamed society, first through equality of opportunity (so that the competition for social position is "fair"), then the welfare state ideas that guarantee a certain minimum level of living. Socialism, however, is still far away; it would include notions of real equality, of

ceilings, not only floors, and of new patterns of division of labor.

38. This is usually required of statistics today, but also has its dangers because the disaggregation can be in less important directions. Thus, disaggregation is usually given in terms of districts (because this is the basis for collecting statistics); much more important is disaggregation on the basis of class, race, sex, so that an image can be made of what role social position is permitted to play in, for instance, mortality and morbidity. Knowing this one might start developing measures of structural violence. See the article by Galtung and Høivik on this in *Journal of Peace Research* (1971), no. 1.

39. See Galtung, "A Structural Theory of Imperialism," *Journal of Peace Research* (1971); also in *Essays* IV, 13.

40. This approach is used by economists in the effort to calculate the costs of pollution. Simply stated, how much would it cost to undo the pollution, or at least the damages it causes?

41. The general approach, hence, is to ask what value is generated internally by the actors in interaction, due to the interaction itself—for instance in terms of experience, learning that otherwise would not take place, and so on. The approach presupposes a clear value perspective and data on positive as well as negative effects along the value dimensions in order to compare the net benefits.

42. See the appendix to the article referred to in note 39. Knut Hongrø contributed important ideas in this connection.

43. This is the approach found in liberal economics.

44. And the most important aspect is the power dimension: some are in a better position to fix prices than others. We cannot use a measure that is determined by the relations of the market to study the market; that only brings us into a *circulus vitiosus.*

45. This is the approach generally found in Marxist economics.

46. For a very good study of this, see Antonin Wagner, *EWG und Dritte Welt* (Fribourg, 1971).

47. A fruitful thought experiment would be to imagine the tariffs reversed, with higher tariffs for unprocessed than for processed goods—virtually discriminating against countries that do not process their raw materials themselves.

48. I am indebted to Karl Deutsch for this suggestion.

49. For this reason the task of future studies is to open the future by exploring more and more options and urging policies that increase the range of future options.

50. One case here seems to be the terrible flood disaster that hit parts of the present Bangladesh (in the Ganges delta), December 1970.

51. This society is defined in terms of the ten value dimensions used here. When it comes to concrete implementation and images they offer enormous scope for variation—as they should.

52. This approach is developed by Nils Petter Gleditsch and Tord Høivik in "Structural Parameters of Graphs: a Theoretical Investigation," *Quality and Quantity,* IV (1970), no. 1, pp. 193–209.

53. This is a standard measure, but there is the problem of how to measure amount of export because of the weakness of any "market"-based measure. If a country exports raw materials in one direction and processed goods in another, and raw materials are consistently undervalued, the measure may become very misleading.

54. See Wagner, *EWG und Dritte Welt.*

55. It will be noted that there is a rather clear value basis in what I am saying: when there is integration at the top it is referred to as marginalization of the bottom; when there is integration at the bottom it is referred to as solidarity. This asymmetry, of course, derives from the tremendous asymmetry in the present world: a "value-neutral" perspective on these matters would, in fact, be value-loaded because it would accept status quo.

56. One thing is certain: we shall not rest content with simple measures of pollution and depletion rates; it has to be referred to something.

57. This is important: it is much too often assumed that nature exists for man's sake and not for and by itself; moreover, it is also assumed that nature when left to itself is harmonious, in balance. I agree that man has not only a right but a duty to intervene and establish or restore balances, even when man is not directly concerned.

58. This points in the direction of a stable equilibrium, but a stable equilibrium that is dynamic, not static.

59. This, of course, presupposes relatively clear ideas about pollution ceilings and depletion floors—the former possibly more easily established than the latter because human physiology is involved; but the latter supported by stronger social forces under private and state capitalism.

60. This is just general methodology; see, for instance, Galtung, *Theory and Methods of Social Research,* I, 3.

61. The tendency to engage in wars, aggressively, could be seen as an example of national maldevelopment, just as the tendency to engage in violence can be seen as a sign of personal maldevelopment—in either case on the assumption that no reasonably justifiable cause can be invoked.

INDEX